Selected Essays of Nigel Harris

Historical Materialism Book Series

The Historical Materialism Book Series is a major publishing initiative of the radical left. The capitalist crisis of the twenty-first century has been met by a resurgence of interest in critical Marxist theory. At the same time, the publishing institutions committed to Marxism have contracted markedly since the high point of the 1970s. The Historical Materialism Book Series is dedicated to addressing this situation by making available important works of Marxist theory. The aim of the series is to publish important theoretical contributions as the basis for vigorous intellectual debate and exchange on the left.

The peer-reviewed series publishes original monographs, translated texts, and reprints of classics across the bounds of academic disciplinary agendas and across the divisions of the left. The series is particularly concerned to encourage the internationalization of Marxist debate and aims to translate significant studies from beyond the English-speaking world.

For a full list of titles in the Historical Materialism Book Series
available in paperback from Haymarket Books, visit:
https://www.haymarketbooks.org/series_collections/1-historical-materialism

Selected Essays of Nigel Harris

From National Liberation to Globalisation

Nigel Harris

Edited by
Ahmed Shawki

H

Haymarket Books
Chicago, IL

First published in 2017 by Brill Academic Publishers, The Netherlands
© 2017 Koninklijke Brill NV, Leiden, The Netherlands

Published in paperback in 2018 by
Haymarket Books
P.O. Box 180165
Chicago, IL 60618
773-583-7884
www.haymarketbooks.org

ISBN: 978-1-60846-010-6

Trade distribution:
In the US, Consortium Book Sales, www.cbsd.com
In Canada, Publishers Group Canada, www.pgcbooks.ca
In the UK, Turnaround Publisher Services, www.turnaround-uk.com
All other countries, Ingram Publisher Services International, ips_intlsales@
ingramcontent.com

Cover design by Jamie Kerry and Ragina Johnson.

This book was published with the generous support of Lannan Foundation
and the Wallace Action Fund.

10 9 8 7 6 5 4 3 2 1

Library of Congress Cataloging-in-Publication data is available.

In memory of our dear friend Duncan Hallas

.•
•

Thanks to Dorian Bon, Randi Jones Hensley and Caitlin Sheehan for their help in getting this volume ready for publication.

∴

Contents

An Interview with Nigel Harris

27 March 2015

AS. How did you become a Marxist – what were the circumstances, the ideological moment?

NH. I came to my teens in the 1950s when the world was dominated by the Cold War – at its height, at its most ferocious. There were supposedly only two options for the world – Washington's capitalism or Russia's supposed socialism. I was of an age to rebel so, in my little way, at school, I sided with Moscow. I started reading the *Daily Worker* (then the Communist Party's daily newspaper).

AS. You said the world was divided between two camps, but you took a third?

NH. Oh, no, I aligned with Moscow, with Stalinism, I suppose I was a crypto-Communist. I stood in the school elections as a Communist when I was sixteen and won. I had no idea what the Communist Party represented – in my little country town, I had never met a Communist. But the school election results hit the local newspaper – 'Communists sweep local grammar school'. And the story followed me round during my two year military service with periodic security checks.

Later on, after the army, I went to Oxford where there was a great upsurge on the Left – an anti-Stalinist Left. A group of Oxford intellectuals founded the *Universities and Left Review*,[1] and a distinguished group of Communist intellectuals[2] began a dissident party journal, *The New Reasoner*. When the two combined, they created *New Left Review* which is still going today. So the Oxford Left, Labour or Communist or neither, was buzzing with discussion. I suppose that's where I became a Marxist.

---

1   Including Charles Taylor (later in life, a distinguished moral philosopher), Stuart Hall (important cultural theorist), Gary Pearson and Ralphael Samuels (later founder of the History Workshops and an important historian of the English working class).

2   Including E.P. Thompson (author of the famous *Making of the English Working Class* [1965]), John Saville (later distinguished economic historian), and Eric Hobsbawm (one of the best known English historians of the second half of the century).

In 1957, the Soviet Communist Party called an immense world youth festival in Moscow, and it was a great chance for us all to go and see the Soviet Union. I embarked with great enthusiasm, like many others, but I don't think that many joined the party as a result.

AS.   Did you ever become a Communist Party member? And if not, why not?

NH.   There was a lot of criticism of the Soviet Union, accusations that could not be easily answered by visiting Moscow. I went to my uncle, John Mahon (a lifelong Communist and at that time, Chairman of the London Communist Party). I asked him – you can see how innocent I was – if he could get me a copy of a book I'd heard about, *The Revolution Betrayed*, by Leon Trotsky. He was pretty brisk, saying 'You could waste an awful lot of time on that sort of rubbish. Here, read this which will give you all you need to know'. And he pressed into my hands *A Short History of the CPSU(B)*, urging me to read especially carefully Chapter 4, which, I learned later, was supposedly written by Joseph Stalin himself. It was almost complete gibberish.

AS.   Did you in fact finally read the *Revolution Betrayed*?

NH.   Of course, but more important at that time was my meeting with a man called Ken Coates, an ex-miner from Nottingham who became an adult student at Nottingham University.[3] We met by chance at the annual conference of the National Association of Labour Student Organisations (a body with a far more prestigious name than it was in reality). And he suggested we take it over from the group of aspirant Labour MPs that ran it and liven it up, which we did. In 1958, we called a conference at a seaside holiday camp in Kessingland in Suffolk. Ken's aim was to seek to unify the three remaining fragments of the Trotskyist Revolutionary Communist Party (of the war years) to see if they could be reunited. It's there that I met Michael Kidron who became the most powerful influence on my thinking at that time.

You must remember, this decade was a time of new beginnings. The second half of the 1950s saw the arrival at university of the first generation of working-class and lower middle-class children, made possible by the 1944 Education

---

3   Ken Coates became Chairman of the Nottingham Labour Party, Member of the European parliament before being driven out of the Party. He founded the Institute for Workers' Control, the Bertrand Russel Peace Foundation and the journal, *The Spokesman*. Unknown to me at that time, he was and remained a lifelong member of the Fourth International.

Act.[4] They were absorbed, resentfully, even rebelliously into the complacent cultural norms of established middle-class life. 'The angry young man' was created ('man', though there were just as many women involved). The intellectual ferment that ensued later supported an angry literary discovery of the working class in novels (*Saturday Night and Sunday Morning*, first published in 1958) and film (*Free Cinema* or the British New Wave). John Osborne's *Look back in anger* (first performed in 1956) became emblematic for a student generation. Later in the early 1960s, a powerful satirical culture, led by the BBC's *That was the week that was*, held the old Establishment up to ridicule.[5]

AS.   Could you say a little more about Michael Kidron's thinking?

NH.   He was of South African origin. His family, who were strong Zionists, migrated to Palestine where Mike completed his education. Mike then came to read for a doctorate at Balliol. His brother-in-law Tony Cliff (Ygael Gluckstein) had come to Britain in the late 1940s and was already established as a writer on Eastern Europe, Russia and, latterly, China. Tony Cliff had been a Trotskyist in Palestine and built a small group in Britain, the *Socialist Review* group.

Michael was intellectually very exciting and unlike many on the far Left, wide ranging, cultured, sophisticated. The years of the Second World War and the Cold War had intellectually shrivelled the Left, turning many of the theories we had inherited into empty jargon. Mike said the most important thing we must do was to rebuild our theoretical grounding, because we no longer understood the world we lived in. Rebuilding that theory was the task of the new journal Mike created, *International Socialism*, launched in 1960.[6] When I moved to London to begin a doctorate at LSE in that year, I immediately began work on the journal.

---

4   And astonishingly by present standards, almost completely funded by local and national educational authorities – getting admission to university almost automatically entitled the child of parents on average incomes to a grant.

5   A second and much more serious student rebellion came in 1968.

6   It was intended to reflect a diversity of revolutionary trends, so the early editorial boards included as well as Michael Kidron and a few others from the Socialist Review Group, Bob Pennington, Ken Coates, Henry Collins, Alasdair McIntyre, Harry McShane, etc. It was also intended to cover culture as well as theory – with poems, short stories and drawings.

AS. Can you say a bit more about what kind of theoretical work was needed?

NH Well there were two immediate issues – first, how to understand the mon-
strous perversion of socialism in the Soviet Russia – that had been accomplished by Tony Cliff's work in the early fifties, culminating in his *Stalinist
Russia: A Marxist Analysis*.[7] Second, how to explain, contrary to the Trotskyist
analysis (loyal to Trotsky's 1938 prediction of world economic collapse following any war), that the world seemed to have entered a phase of sustained high
economic growth. That was the beginning of Mike's work on the permanent
arms economy. There was a third issue starting to emerge – decolonisation,
the end of empire without apparently the economic collapse of the imperial
powers (as the Left had long promised).

AS. And what were you doing at this stage?

NH. I was at LSE doing a PhD. I already knew Ralph Miliband (father of the
two Labour leaders), one of the few academics publicly identified as a Marxist,
and he said that we knew little about the Conservative party. Why not work on
this? So I did.

AS. Ralph Miliband was your supervisor?

NH. No, he was a friend that I consulted. In fact our children went to nurs-
ery school together much later. I set out to write a history of Toryism showing
its enormous flexibility as the structure of British capitalism changed. There
were no permanent Conservative principles as the party pretended, but a tactical opportunism to do whatever was required to protect the ruling class and
advance its interests in a changing world, which is how they ended up – briefly –
as social democrats and believers in planning and public ownership in 1945.
Later on they rediscovered the opposite, what became known as neoliberalism.
The thesis was published as *Competition and the Corporate Society*.[8]

AS. One of your first books was called *Beliefs in Society* which dealt with
the opposite case, communism. Was there a connection between the two
concerns?

---

7 Cliff 1955.
8 Harris 1972; republished by Routledge in 2006.

NH. Oh, yes, that book dealt with the changing nature of Conservatism as the prelude to looking at how communism changed to accommodate a changing material environment – rapidly moving through Marxism-Leninism-Stalinism-Mao Tse tung thought – before becoming at the end a deeply conservative doctrine.

AS. I think you also worked as a freelance writer on India and China for a couple of publications?

NH. The first thing we did after finishing higher education (my wife, Tirril at UCL, me at LSE) was to drive overland to India, a marvelous trip.[9]

At LSE I had become more and more fascinated by processes of economic development – from Britain, to the Soviet Middle East, to Japan (we got to know quite well the leading Japan scholar at LSE, Ron Dore). I would have liked to live in Japan for a while, but it was impossible. Through Tirril's step-father, Thomas Balogh, we met P.C. Mahalanobis, who had set up the Indian Statistical Institute in Calcutta, and he invited us both to come as research fellows for a year. That's how we came to drive to India.

Mahalanobis had fairly strict ideas of what he wanted from our research. He wanted me to prove that Indian wages were too high for its level of development and should be lowered. So I did a comparative study of wages in Russia, Britain and the US at different historical periods to show that wages in India were too low. Tirril was supposed to assess India's family planning programme showing why it was a waste of money.

AS. So she did the exact opposite? Were the fellowships renewed?

NH. Well we were only there for a short time, not in established fellowships. At the same time, I worked as the International Editor of the *Economic and Political Weekly* in Bombay, and started to write for the news weeklies, *The Economist* (in London) and *The Far Eastern Economic Review* (in Hong Kong). After Calcutta we travelled through Southeast Asia, writing for these various papers, and ended teaching for a semester at a Tokyo university. After that, we came back to Hong Kong and caught the train through China, Siberia in the snow, Moscow and on to London.

---

9 With Gavin Macfadyen, a YPSL member from Chicago who was Vietnam War draft dodging in London, at a loose end. Gavin had worked as a mechanic in New York (he kept the vehicle serviced all the way through).

AS. What were your views on national economic development at that time?

NH. The colonial revolution made it an urgent question – what should a newly independent country do? Tirril and I were lucky to be in Delhi at that time, the end of India's second five-year plan – the most statist and anti-foreign plan produced in India. It was supposed to embody the collective wisdom of the Left, from Russia's five-year plans to the wartime experiments in planning, and a diagnosis of why the poor countries were poor (because the rich had robbed them!). So the remedy was to break links with the rich – stop imports, ban foreign capital. It was crazy and led to the exact opposite outcome, economic stagnation. What is fascinating is how economists slipped out of responsibility for the debacle. I once asked Jagdish Bhagwati – doyen of neo-liberal economics now in New York – how he came to change his views from when he was working on the second five-year plan for the Planning Commission in Delhi, and he was dismissive: 'Well, in a few years, it was clear what we had been doing was nonsense and we had to change'. As today, he had no perception of the sociology of social science theory or ideology. The blind remained stubbornly blind.

AS. There was a model for national economic development, exported from Russia to China and the rest. It became the orthodoxy of the Left.

NH. Not just the Left, but also the centre who derived lessons from the author-itarian war economies in Europe during the Second World War, and in the fifties created development economics.
    On the Left, the *Monthly Review* group around Paul Sweezy, Paul Baran and a host of others were the most sophisticated advocates of this quasi-Stalinist approach: total State power, used to tax the rich and divert the money into heavy industry as the fastest way to develop. That's what they were doing in India in the second Plan (inspired, incidentally, by our very own Mahalanobis). The government nationalised or built five giant integrated steel mills in eastern India and a major heavy industry complex as the foundation for rapid all-round development. So the whole of modern India was trapped in stultifying bureau-cracy and denied the means – imports and foreign capital and technology – to escape.

AS. And China?

NH. Was the same, and it seemed to work in the first five-year plan period of recovery from the war and Japanese occupation – rates of growth of 6 or

7 percent. But Russia then pulled out and Mao tried to force a kind of primitive 'communism', driving the peasants into communes and taxing them to the hilt to build heavy industry.

AS This was the period of the Great Leap Forward?

NH. Exactly. Followed by perhaps the most catastrophic famine in the history of the world, as the peasants, locked in their communes, starved. It took many years and much violent political turbulence – the Cultural Revolution, etc. – for China to escape the nonsense package of total State power and heavy industry before everything else.

What none of us envisaged, could not possibly have foreseen,[10] was almost the exact opposite: the prising open of every national economy to a global economy. At that stage, world capitalism takes over the role of the 'national economic development' of both China and India. In China, it had the most spectacular results ever seen.

AS. Current day China?

NH. In the two decades to the turn of the century, China completely transformed itself to become finally the largest or second largest economy in the world. Who could have envisaged that in the 1970s?

AS. To clarify the theoretical implication here – Mike Kidron argues, and I presume you agreed, that this kind of breakthrough was impossible.

NH. Yes, a poor state could never reach the scale of capital concentration to compete with the leading powers, the imperialists. They would always be destroyed by the dominant powers. The view assumes the dominant role of national states in a capitalist world economy, but in a globalised world economy, states, whether advanced or backward, are no longer dominant, markets are. Global capitalism lifted China. Whereas Mao slaughtered or starved thousands to build China's then-little steel industry, global capitalism turned China into the world's largest steel industry in no time at all – and without famine or slaughter.

---

10   Although Mike Kidron hinted at world economic globalization in his *Foreign Investments in India* (Kidron 1965).

The intermediate case – South Korea, Taiwan, Hong Kong and Singapore – showed that state expansion strangled the economy, making it impossible to develop. Once these economies opened up to exporting, they grew with great speed. But the lessons took a long time to percolate. I frequently went to Delhi in those years and was continually having the argument. But it took till 1990 or so for Indian reforms to end the dismal 'Hindu rate of growth' and accelerate growth.

AS. How did that affect your understanding of the state and its role in economic development?

NH. My generation was obsessed with the state and statism, arising from the extraordinary concentration of power in the wartime states, pre-eminently Stalin's Russia and Hitler's Germany.

The colonial revolution was supposed to be about national liberation, but it didn't liberate anyone except new national ruling classes. Each ruling class took over the task of ripping off the population, the 'nation'. Look at Nigeria – billions of dollars ripped off while the population doesn't have electricity.

AS. Or Zaire.

NH. Or Zimbabwe – the Mugabe family is said to have stolen six and a half billion dollars, stashed abroad against the day when they get kicked out. All the hopes we had about the colonial revolution – we spent most of our time agitating for the freedom of Algeria, Cuba, Vietnam, Ghana – just to create new ruling classes robbing their populations.

AS. It seems to me that in your two books *Of Bread and Guns* and *The End of the Third World* you are beginning to push the argument further on.

NH. To push the Kidron argument to try to reconstruct or recreate the theoretical basis for understanding the world system as the basis for universal liberation. But economic globalisation has brought all the old agenda to a close.

AS. How would you describe economic globalisation?

NH. It is the emergence of a single global economy, superseding all the national economic fragments, with a global capitalist class who are operating, not independently of national States, but with relationships to all States. The balance of power has shifted decisively so now states bargain to get in or to stay in the global system. The global system has stripped away sovereignty and any possibility of real representation by populations. Hence, the idea that citizens can, through elections or revolutionary means, take over the state and institute radical change has come to an end – after taking control of the state, exactly the same global forces remain in control of the national fragment.

AS. In a country like Greece, the prescriptions of international organisations bar you from setting your own budget and so forth.

NH. Having a national economic policy assumes you control – or a least, have the power to influence – key economic variables in your local economy. But your little local economy is now revealed to be no more than a conjunction of global flows that start and cease outside not only your control, but possibly even your knowledge. Economic policy only makes sense on the margin. Of course, you can assume, as in sailing, that you do not control the winds, the tides, the weather and what's unseen below the surface, but that a good sailor is better than a bad one. But this is far removed from the old assumptions of national economic policymaking – that the state had the power to direct, that policy mattered, was fundamental and was open to democratic choice.

∴

AS. One of the themes which you have written a lot about is immigration in the context of globalisation. Can you say something about the changes in the structural role of immigration from the 1950s to the present. People talk a lot abut the mobility of capital but not of labour – why this contradictory development?

NH. Yes, capital is mobile, and, in principle, labour should be mobile. But states are immobile and require their citizens to be immobile, so the contradiction is between immobile citizenship and mobile labour in a global economy. There is a constant conflict in a global economy, requiring workforces to migrate to where they are needed, while the state requires unconditional loyalty and some measure of immobility. The tension runs through government – with Cameron here committing himself to holding down immigration as if he had the power to do so. But if you want to be part of the global economy – and the wealth this brings – you give up the power to decide how many people enter or leave. Even with draconian powers – of life and death on the border (as in North Korea or the pre-reform Soviet bloc countries) – migration cannot be determined.

AS. And what about the politics of immigration?

NH. When the system is expanding, migration (legal or illegal) takes place and it is of no great consequence. There might be residual xenophobia, but broadly people accept the benefits to themselves of migration (nowhere more so now than in the medical services for an ageing population). In economic contraction, the state is under threat from domestic discontent, xenophobia becomes an important means to inculcate loyalty and defend the national ruling class with all its costs – the hideous controls, rampant bureaucracy, high financial burdens and a staggering lack of compassion for refugees. At the moment here, amid all the empty blather about British values (or now 'European values') what is Cameron's response to thousands drowning in the Mediterranean? 'We mustn't save them from drowning or it will only encourage more to come'.

Establishing the right of people to move, work and settle freely wherever they wish will finally become the key reformist demand against the divide and rule of a world consisting of national prisons – that will constitute real liberation. The 2006 general strike of immigrants in the states was wonderful in this connection. But it is difficult to see how it can go further without the utter misery of the flow of thousands of refugees through Europe, washing away boundaries (as happened earlier with the reunification of Germany). As far as the Left is concerned, expanding migration ought to be the key demand to force the pace of globalisation. But half the Left has yet to be convinced that the national state has no future and will not embrace globalisation.

AS. It would need both information, propaganda, educational work and practical agitation. That happened in 2006 when there was an understanding that an attack on immigrants was an attack on all.

NH. And there's lots to be done on the practical issues – as when American churches helped smuggle people over the border and offered them shelter. Or when French people financed purchasing boats to rescue boatpeople fleeing Vietnam (just when shipowners were forbidding their captains to rescue the drowning), or others contributed recently to stop drownings in the Mediterranean. And of course, along with vicious xenophobia (symbolised in Hungary's Viktor Orbán), there has been enormous spontaneous humanitarian help to the refugees fleeing Syria along the way in central Europe.

AS. In the US, as you know, something like ten percent of the labour force is undocumented. Most studies show that immigrants are not the cause of job losses among the native-born, but rather fill the jobs the domestic workforce won't take.

NH. Migration is central to the growth of capitalism today. That is why the business federations are the strongest opponents of migration controls. Nor is this about 'highly skilled' workers that everybody talks about. For the population at large, it is about low-skilled and low-paid workers who, for example, sustain the caring services for the ageing population.

AS. I would like to go back to globalisation, because you said half the Left opposes it – because it wipes out the social safety nets that were won in the past and masses of regulatory systems, without which the population is immiserated.

NH. The old social democratic position – that the state can protect its population. I have already tried to suggest why the state has gone – or is going – as an instrument of reform or protection. Half the Left still believes in the old agenda of state reformism. The state's emerging dominant function is to administer the local economy on behalf of the global system, not protect the local population.

The old prospects for revolution seem quite unpromising. The last revolution we had was the overthrow of the Shah of Iran – removing a ruling class but not in the name of liberation, in the name of Islam. We've had other movements – like that against Mubarak in Egypt – but no revolution, and the old ruling class, untouched by rebellion, repaid the rebels with terror and counterrevolution.

It might mean revolution is no longer on the agenda in most countries. Modern armies and weaponry, the enormous secret state (Ministries of the Interior, paramilitary forces, etc.), and the interconnection between the military and business (40 percent of the Egyptian economy is controlled by the military) perhaps make revolution impossible. In fact, that is what Egypt's dictator said – there will be no more revolutions in Egypt without a split in the security force. If revolution is no longer possible, there can be no strategy of the seizure of power in one country at a time (as the Comintern envisaged).

AS. But the mass mobilizations in Tahrir Square were exceptional – and influenced Podemos in Spain and Syriza in Greece. Of course retrenchment has everywhere been very severe.

NH. On the other hand, the undermining of national sovereignty by economic globalisation is leading to a generalised increase in authoritarianism (Egypt, Turkey, Russia). The US and Britain seem to have tossed habeus corpus in the bin just as the signing of the Magna Carta is celebrated – to publicly embrace indefinite detention without charge, trial or sentence, embrace the right of the state to murder or torture whom it pleases and so on. And the numbers imprisoned in the states is staggering, its cost only tolerable because the whole system is privatised.

AS. So established rights appear to be coming to an end – the bourgeois state is in decline.

Are there other questions that we ought to be looking at?

NH. The conditions of universal emancipation in modern times remain. We were under the illusion that revolution, the overthrow of the state, was required to secure the self-liberation of the majority.[11] But in fact, the process of self-liberation has gone grinding on, regardless of political ups and downs. The most extraordinary transformation in my lifetime has been the liberation of women in Europe and North America, but rippling out in different ways to the rest of the world.

---

11   Partly because, in the Marxist account, non-liberation was linked to wage slavery. Until that was abolished, supposedly, the world could not progress. It was just wrong.

PART 1

Imperialism and the World Order

∵

Imperialism Today*

A majority of the world's population has always lived in poverty, but the difference today is not just that the contrast between the rich and the poor, on a world scale, is so much more extreme, but that the productive resources available to the world could in principle conquer poverty. There is no shortage of technique, no shortage of technicians, no shortage of capital. The problem arises because human need and the supply of resources exist in isolation from each other. And those who possess the resources are in the main preserved from experiencing poverty. In Watts, in Parisian bidonvilles, in decaying Durham villages, in the Appalachian mountains or the Brazilian northeast, in Lagos or Manila, Calcutta or Szechwan, the poverty is trapped where the PR men cannot see it, except properly mediated by the photographs of colour supplements. Even where sheer material poverty is hidden behind net curtains, as much spiritual poverty – generated by the emptiness of man's role in the production machine – pervades the life of all but a fortunate few.

Sometimes the poor, for so long staring and wondering in silence, penetrate the hypocrisy. But the occasional riot is more a flash of bared teeth by the hunted than a strategy for changing the world; the violence is that of despair as much as of hope. But the violence does, like lightning at night, suddenly reveal the true landscape. The privileged reach for their guns, for 'law and order'. In the United States the threat of the poor is more tangible, and the powers-that-be more explicit about the dangers:

> unless the Administration and Congress launch a vastly expensive and 'full-scale war on domestic ills, especially urban ills' ... the central cities of the United States will in a few years ... become 'fortresses' in which the wealthy live in 'privately guarded compounds', people will travel on 'high-speed patrolled expressways connecting safe areas'; 'private automobiles, taxi-cabs, and commercial vehicles will be routinely equipped with unbreakable glass and light armour'; 'armed guards will ride shot gun on all forms of public transportation' and protect all public facilities such as schools, libraries, and playgrounds; and 'the ghetto and slum

---

* From: *World Crisis*, edited by John Palmer and Nigel Harris, Harmondsworth: Penguin, 1971.

neighbourhoods will be places of terror with widespread crime, perhaps out of police control during night time'.[1]

This form of repressed civil war in the middle of the 'rule of law' is no more than a microcosm of the coming world. The fortress islands of America and Europe will face a sea of discontents, with tiny colonies of the rich policing the further extremities, linked by the tenuous life-line of air travel. But for the moment even the privilege of being feared is denied the majority of the poor. They live and die far from the eyes of most of the rich. And in Calcutta or Manila or Sao Paulo the local representatives of the world's rich are braver in bearing the offensiveness of poverty. Hearts less stout would crack.

Poverty is sustained by the inability of the world productive machine to employ the human resources available at an adequate wage, and by the unwillingness or inability of our rulers to transform the machine so that it accords with human needs rather than the interests of their own power. The interests of the rulers are fragmented among a multitude of petty local ruling classes, each more concerned to defeat its rivals than answer the central problem. The little principalities of the world, a sort of medieval Germany, squabble, the clerics pursue the higher verities, and the poor wait. The rivalry drives the machine apparently further and further away from the needs of the available population, so that the standard solution to all problems of economic backwardness or oppression – 'economic development' – recedes like a mirage the more we seem to approach it.

In the last half of the nineteenth century the forward thrust of capitalism swept into its wake the rest of the world. But today the enormous expansion of capitalism appears to have fewer and fewer effects on the great mass of poor satellites. Certainly, since 1948, advanced capitalism has been in a frenetic, headlong rush of growth. But the spin-off seems weaker and weaker. In the same way the ripples from the growth of the American economy are more and more sluggish as they approach the black ghettoes. Having dragged the backward countries pell-mell into the market place, having fleeced them, the rich are now fleeing back to their fortresses. They will sit on their heap of treasure, and when there is time from adding more booty to the pile, pity the less fortunate.

---

1   United States National Commission on the Causes and Prevention of Violence, Report (on Violent Crime, Homicide, Assault, Rape and Robbery), November 1969, as reported in *The Guardian*, 25 November 1969.

The problem of world development has to be a *central* concern for any social-ist strategy, not a charitable after-thought if we have something left over. Talk of human emancipation and of freedom is so much parlour prattle, while the experience of the majority of men, women and children is such an appalling picture of hunger and oppression. But to make world development central to any strategy demands that we grasp the nature of modern capitalism and its relationship to the rest of the world. It may be useful to show the hypocrisy of Western governments in concealing the real impact of their societies on the rest of the world, but on its own it is not a strategy. Describing the evil does not necessarily go any way to overcoming it. Indeed, in isolation, it may merely encourage cynicism or apathy. After all, the scale of the problem is so gigantic, what could possibly be done about it? A strategy requires not just the identi-fication of the problem but putting it in context and showing how the problem can be overcome and by whom. What is to be done, how can it be done, and who will do it?

More than fifty years ago it was one of Lenin's remarkable achievements to answer all three questions. The influence of his answers still pervades the Left, so that any new strategy has to start by coming to terms with Lenin. The Left has added remarkably little to *Imperialism, the Highest Stage of Capitalism*. Yet the rate of change of capitalism has, if discontinuously, accelerated over the past half-century. In many respects the backward countries have also been transformed. It would be most unlikely if the relationship between the two had not also been radically changed. Yet the assumption of much of the writing on the Left is that nothing of substance has changed, and that any attempt to identify changes only betrays the cause. We must cling to the symbols, lest innovation betray the substance; lest the baby leave with the dirty water.

But this cowardice nullifies any serious attempt to outline a clear strategy. Myths and phrases become the substitute for serious thought. Fudging the issue is at a premium. And muddled criteria make it impossible to under-stand clearly a whole range of different issues – what happened to the Rus-sian Revolution, and what safeguards are there against the degeneration of any regime which breaks with world capitalism? The muddle confuses Com-munists in trying to detect 'true socialism' in such diverse phenomena as Czechoslovak managerialism, the Yugoslav market economy, in the deadweight of Russian bureaucracy or the rhetoric of China, or even Albania. It dogs the heels of any attempt to understand the Chinese or Cuban revolutions, it subtly blurs attempts to characterise the military regimes of Egypt and Algeria, and the former leaders of Indonesia and Ghana. For the young, it becomes impossible to understand nationalisation in backward countries, and leads them to wonder whether one-party regimes, 'democratic' dictators and all the fraudulent paraphernalia of incipient or full-fledged tyrannies are really symptoms of a higher human emancipation or a deeper freedom. The Left is robbed of its independence, becoming no more than public-relations outriders for one or other official States. For those with no vehicle of their own, fellow travelling becomes a way of life.

The account which follows deals separately with the two central issues of concern: the nature of modern imperialism and some of the means by which imperialism could be overthrown.

The Economics of Imperialism

Lenin and Imperialism

Lenin described imperialism as 'the highest stage of capitalism', the stage preceding the socialist revolution. It was a different stage of capitalism because its characteristics contrasted with the preceding phase of growth. Those new characteristics compelled capitalism now not merely to increase domestic exploitation but to intensify its control of the rest of the world. Internal changes within particular capitalist economies and the external extension of capitalism were part of a single process.

Very crudely, Lenin identified the new characteristics as:

(i) The creation of monopolies and cartels in all the main branches of capitalist production, and an increased concentration of capital. As a result, the price discipline of open-market competition between many small rivals tended to be replaced within each capitalist economy by monopoly-administered pricing, leading to very high profits, made even higher by the control of empire.

(ii) Within each capitalist economy production was increasingly controlled by banks and financial institutions, by the lending capitalist (the *rentier*) rather than the producing one (the *entrepreneur*):

Imperialism, or the rule of finance capital, is that highest stage of capitalism in which this separation (between 'the *rentier*, living entirely on income obtained from money capital, is separated from the *entrepreneur* and from all those directly concerned in the management of capital') reaches vast proportions. The supremacy of finance capital over all other forms of capital means the rule of the *rentier* and of the financial oligarchy; it means the crystallisation of a small number of financially 'powerful' states from among all the rest.[2]

---

2 Lenin 1936a, p. 53.

Financial control, based upon the control of individual firms, now dominated whole capitalist States, and thus the rest of the world.

(iii) But the monopolistic financial control of particular markets did not end competition within capitalism. On the contrary, rivalry now became much fiercer between the leading capitalist States. And as competition tended to be replaced within each economy by administration, so it tended to be replaced internationally by open warfare.

The two limitations on the system which simultaneously drove it outwards internationally and threatened it with disaster were the search for raw materials and for outlets for 'surplus' capital. The rate of expansion of capitalism depended upon an increasing inflow of materials, and the search for materials drove capital out to the rest of the world. In doing so, it created outlets for capital which otherwise would have been able to find no profitable forms of investment within the advanced capitalist economies themselves. Capital was 'surplus' because of the very high rates of profit characteristic of monopoly capitalism, and because the limits of profitable investment had been reached at home: it could not be diverted into improving the conditions of the mass of the population or developing agriculture – 'if capitalism did these things it would not be capitalism; for uneven and wretched conditions of the masses are fundamental and inevitable conditions and premises of this mode of production'.[3]

Hence capital was necessarily driven outwards to the rest of the world, both to seize territory from its capitalist neighbours and to colonise 'new' territory. The rivalry between the capitalist States punctuated economic competition with phases of open warfare: war had become an essential element in the highest stage of capitalism.

The long-term effects of the new system would be to convert the most advanced capitalist countries into financiers for the rest of the world which would, in turn, increasingly take over the functions of commodity production. The financial State, the 'Bondholder State', was increasingly revealed as a purely parasitic element on the production process of the backward countries – 'the world has become divided into a handful of money-lending states on the one side, and a vast majority of debtor states on the other'.[4] Finally, the vast profits made by the rentiers gave them the resources with which to bribe their own working classes, to buy off the proletarian revolution, and this 'sets the seal of

---

3 Lenin 1936a, p. 56.
4 Lenin 1936a, pp. 92–3.

parasitism on the whole country which lives by the exploitation of the labour of several overseas countries and colonies'.[5]

Given that this is inevitably a very crude and oversimplified restatement of Lenin's analysis, how does it stand up today? Clearly, the concentration of capital, the degree of monopoly, has gone much further than it was in Lenin's day, and the conclusions Lenin drew from increasing concentration apply with even greater validity today. Furthermore, the relationship between capital and the State, and between economic rivalry and warfare, has gone even further. In Lenin's day the State was by modern standards ill-prepared for war; today the Western States are in a state of permanent preparation for war. Since the Second World War, in particular, defence expenditure in peacetime takes an unprecedented share of public revenue. In 1937 the *per capita* military expenditure of the Great powers was $25 per year; in 1968 the same figure for the United States – at 1937 prices – was $132.[6]

However, on 'finance capital' Lenin seems less reliable, for the hegemony of the *rentier* did not survive. The power of finance as an independent part of the ruling order depended upon the free flow of funds internationally, on the pre-World War One Gold Standard. But as well as giving finance its international power, it also made it independent of its State of origin abroad. The extension of empire by the State and the free flow of finance internationally were not necessarily matched. Indeed, the figures Lenin used to illustrate the export of capital did not identify the destinations involved, so that we do not know from these figures what proportion of, say, British capital went into the British Empire and what elsewhere. From other sources we know that the dispersion of British capital before the First World War was very wide – to Latin America, Japan, Russia, Eastern Europe, the United States and so on. On the face of it, the demands of finance could only have been a very subordinate interest in the extension of empire. The search for raw materials was probably more important for some parts of empire: for other parts, straight political competition between the advanced capitalist powers seems to have been the main motive. The argument might well have been: seize the territory first, and then try to find some raw materials, rather than locate raw materials and then seize the territory. And seizing the territory was in many cases motivated by the attempt to prevent the French or the Germans or someone else getting in first.

Nor is it clear that empire was related to a high rate of growth for a metropolitan country. If it were so we would have to explain why British capitalism –

---

5   Lenin 1936a, p. 92.

6   See Magdoff 1970, p. 8.

with the largest empire of all – was in relative decline, while German capitalism – with hardly any empire at all – was ascending. Empire was a vital component in the struggle for power between the advanced capitalist countries which culminated in the First World War, but it did not explain the differing rates of growth of different capitalisms.

What transformed capitalism, its relationship to finance and to empire, was Lenin's third characteristic of the 'highest stage': war. Not just the First World War, but the clash of capitalist rivalries embodied in the slump of the middle interwar years, the Second World War and the following phases of localised wars, and the creation within capitalism of a permanent arms economy transformed the system. It made possible the post-1945 growth in real mass consumption (without necessarily changing the proportions of real income accruing to different classes), and a rapid growth in agricultural output, both of which were ruled out by Lenin. The growth in agriculture in Britain was directly the result of the development of economic nationalism, of the attempt to become independent of imports.

Between the First and Second World Wars capitalism underwent a period of long-drawn-out stagnation in which individual States slowly adjusted themselves to the imperatives of military, as much as economic, rivalry. The adjustment shifted the weight of the industrial structure, the flow of resources and the distribution of power. And the wings of finance capital which had permitted it to go where it pleased were effectively clipped in the aftermath of the 1929 slump. The State intervened in all capitalist countries to prevent, curtail or circumscribe the export of capital, except for purposes expressly sanctioned by the State. In Britain, leaving the Gold Standard robbed the City of its independent power, and forced it back into the role of 'national capital'. The State was not acting as an independent force. It pursued the salvation of British capitalism, and to this end sought to force domestic savings into domestic industry rather than permit it to be loaned to foreign competitors. And slowly, over time, it had some success. Between 1928 and 1935 the proportion of available domestic funds going into domestic investment increased from 60 to 89 percent. In the longer term there were major changes in the role of capital exports within the British economy. Capital exports declined from about 8 percent of the gross national product in the period preceding 1914 to about 2 percent now; then capital exports took about 50 percent of domestic savings, now under 10 percent.[7]

---

7   Figures cited in Kidron 1962.

Tariff walls, protection and direct State assistance aided the process of the concentration of capital. And capital concentration with the decline of the *rentier* made the characteristic capital export, not indirect investment by *rentiers*, but direct investment by the largest British companies seeking to escape foreign tariffs on British exports. Protection also made the role of the State vital in the domestic economy. In alliance with corporate capitalism, the State began the process of replacing the *rentier* in order to force up the rate of domestic savings. Neither the State nor the largest companies had any love for the *rentier*. Certainly they did not follow the audacious prescription of Keynes and pursue the 'euthanasia of the rentier',[8] but State assistance to the entrepreneur, even its differential tax rates between 'earned' and 'unearned' income, all had the effect – intentional or otherwise – of reducing *rentier* power. Indeed, the State substituted its own taxes as a means of securing a large part of what formerly went in dividends. Between 1938 and 1956 taxation increased from 14 to 39 percent of net company income; dividend and interest payments fell from 68 to 35 percent. Dividends as a percentage of profits fell from 67 percent in 1912 to 23 percent between 1949 and 1956.[9]

The State intervened to strengthen national production in the economic war on the foreigner. Necessarily it had to destroy the international aspirations of the *rentiers*. That the State was able to undertake such a task demonstrates that it was not simply the creature of the *rentiers*. Of course, the changes introduced only made the *rentier* even more parasitic in appearance, and this had useful political by-products. For the *rentier* could always be held up as a scapegoat for anti-capitalist feeling. Both the Communists and the Labour Party leadership – not to mention Adolf Hitler and the extreme Right (where Jewish finance played the key role) – used the evil *rentier* as a substitute for capitalism itself; the murder of Shylock expiated the guilt of 'healthy' capitalists.

If the thesis of finance capitalism appears incorrect today, so also must Lenin's sociological conclusions. Read in isolation, his account might seem to imply that the world division of labour was being transformed in a way which would culminate in the world's proletariat being concentrated in the backward countries, while the population of the advanced would be entirely concerned either with financial operations or servicing the financiers. In practice and in the rest of his work, Lenin did not frame his strategy around this implication, nor argue that in the future, only a revolt in the backward countries would threaten capitalism. His concern with the 'weak links' of capitalism was the res-

---

8   Keynes 1936, pp. 375–6.

9   Kidron 1962.

ult of a political analysis, rather than designed to deliver simply an economic death blow to the system. In practice he concentrated on the backward countries of Europe where the political implications were strongest, arguing that

> [t]he struggle of the oppressed nations *in Europe*, a struggle capable of going to the lengths of insurrection and street fighting will 'sharpen the revolutionary crisis in Europe' infinitely more than a much more developed rebellion in a remote colony. A blow delivered against the English imperialist bourgeoisie by a rebellion in Ireland is a hundred times more significant politically than a blow of equal weight delivered in Asia or Africa.[10]

Since Lenin's time the division of labour in the world has not led to the backward countries becoming the producing sector, and the advanced simply the lending and consuming sector. The advanced have only increased even further their share of production, as well as consumption and lending.

If finance capital does not accurately identify modern capitalism, we have to formulate a new description so that we can understand why one phase of economic expansion demanded empire, and another, the dissolution of empire. Only then can we begin to understand the present position of the backward countries, and, so, how it can be changed.

Decolonisation

A number of socialists have argued the thesis that the backward countries are vital for the economic survival of advanced metropolitan capitalism. Advocates of this position who are economically sophisticated no longer argue that the backward are vital for the capital exports of the advanced, simply because the available information directly contradicts this, but they do usually imply that it is the raw material needs of capitalism which make it not only dependent upon the backward, but increasingly so. We shall return to this thesis later, but here our only concern is with Left explanations of decolonisation. For if the advanced are increasingly dependent for survival upon raw material imports from the backward, how was it that the imperialist countries could ever bring themselves to grant political independence to their imperial possessions?

---

10   Lenin 1936a, original emphasis.

John Strachey of the British Labour Party argued that British decolonisation occurred as a result of the Labour government of 1945 to 1951 (but not, for some reason, as a result of the two earlier Labour governments). For the first time, he says, the working classes came to power, and immediately began the task of freeing nations ensnared in the British Empire,[11] presumably in ignorance or disregard of the economic dependence of Britain upon its colonies. But the case smacks of wishful thinking, not least because the relationship between working-class wishes and the policies of Labour is tenuous in the extreme. In any case, Strachey's explanation does not help us to understand world decolonisation, only British, nor why economic domination was not ended at the same time as political independence was granted, nor why successive Conservative governments continued the same policy throughout the 1950s. Strachey raises more questions than his explanation answers.

Others, using the opportunity to embellish the image of the Soviet Union much as Strachey wished to embellish that of the British Labour Party, have suggested that it was really the threat of the Soviet Union which compelled war-weary Western Europe to relinquish its imperial holdings. The evidence is even thinner here, for Moscow showed little more than propagandist interest in the colonies of her allies. Indeed, in Vietnam both the Soviet Union and the French Communist Party either supported or acquiesced in France's attempt to re-establish control of Indo-China.[12] In any case, much of the decolonisation took place in the 1950s when Europe was not 'war-weary' but rather in boom. Even after the Second World War unusually large numbers of British and American troops were scattered throughout Asia in just the position to secure the Allied empires. In Saigon British troops, indeed, did just this for the French. War-weary France may have been in 1945 but it did not prevent the French Army waging a bitter and brutal war in Vietnam up to 1954, followed by seven more years of savage warfare to hold Algeria. But the French case – like that of the Dutch in Indonesia, or much later the Belgians in the Congo – was the exception. The overwhelming majority of imperial possessions were granted political independence without anything like this scale of struggle. And the Soviet Union played scarcely any role at all in this.

A different argument states that it was the heroic struggle of the population in the backward countries which forced the end of political control. This is obviously much more plausible, but it is still not enough on its own. For in the majority of cases, there was no popular anti-imperialist struggle at all. Even in

---

11   See Strachey 1959, p. 135.

12   There are numerous accounts of this, but, by way of example, see Hammer 1966.

some of the cases where there was – as in India, for example – independence was conceded without the imperial power really waging an all-out war to retain control. And in some cases the imperialists merely scuttled as quickly as they could.

Certainly American pressure played an important part in the granting of independence. The European imperialist powers were heavily dependent upon the United States, both in waging the Second World War and in coping with the problems of its immediate aftermath. And the interests of American Liberalism in ending imperial tyranny – in advancing the rights of national self-determination – neatly coincided with some of the interests of American business in wanting to prise open protected imperial markets. But, again, the behaviour of France in Vietnam and Algeria, and of Holland in Indonesia, showed how far the European powers could go if they really calculated their colonies were vital for their economic survival. And the United States did not deny assistance to France as a reprisal, since it also needed European support once the Cold War began. On the contrary, Washington in Vietnam demonstrated its willingness to take up part of the White Man's Burden.

In some of the explanations there is obviously much which is valid. It is also true that, as many on the Left have pointed out, political power was conceded to independent regimes without conceding economic power. Backward countries remained subject to the domination, control or influence of foreign capital, foreign finance and foreign commodity markets. But it would be quite wrong to infer from this that nothing at all changed, or that conceding independence was no more than a devious conspiracy to conceal even greater foreign domination. Political independence did make metropolitan capital less secure in the backward countries; very often it permitted the nationalisation in whole or part of foreign interests, even by the most conservative regimes in backward countries. If the metropolitan countries were indeed economically dependent upon the backward, granting independence was a rash gamble.

The gamble paid off. Western capitalism entered a phase of unprecedented growth at the same time as it dismantled its different empires. Any explanation of decolonisation has also to explain this phase of growth. For, on the face of it, it seems that decolonisation was conceded because the metropolitan powers were economically less dependent upon their colonies, not more. The price of retaining empire steadily exceeded the returns on empire. And the possibility of surviving without an empire seemed reasonable. The explanation for the change lies in the mutation of the industrial structure of capitalism. Old-style capitalism contained much more powerful interests, the survival of which depended upon the maintenance of political control of colonies. The more powerful those interests, the more the survival of capitalism itself depended upon empire. But postwar capitalism needed to the same degree neither those domestic interests nor their external extension, empire.

The imperial powers in the postwar period could have made a run for it. The scale of military operations undertaken by them in Korea, for example, as well as the resources sunk in the maintenance of the defensive walls of NATO, CENTO, SEATO and so on – directed not against the 'Third World', but against 'International Communism' (and the two, despite the best efforts of Washington and Moscow, are not the same thing) – show how far the Western powers could go when they felt themselves seriously threatened. The backward countries could not threaten capitalism either economically or politically on this scale. The high growth rate of capitalism sustained its military capability, and the expansion of its military capability had a crucial boosting effect upon its growth rate. A by-product of economic expansion was increased economic domination of the backward countries. But increased economic domination does not necessarily mean increased dependence. It remains true that imperialism does produce wars, but not so much between the advanced and the backward as between the advanced themselves. And this is true even when the backward countries are the scene of the war.

An Alternative Account

Capitalism, Old and New

During this century the centre of equilibrium within each capitalist economy has shifted away from the old core of nineteenth-century industry – the extractive industries (particularly coal, iron and steel) and industries concerned with the relatively primitive processing of raw materials (for example, cotton textile production). It has shifted towards manufacturing proper, and in particular to the most technically advanced sectors of manufacturing, the metal-using, electrical and petro-chemical industries. The change was from more extensive forms of production to more intensive ones, from a process ultimately limited by the supply of raw materials and labour to one limited rather by the technical ingenuity of the production process itself. The intervening stages in the industrial process between raw materials and final output have become longer and longer and increasingly complex.

The changed technology which is sometimes seen as the cause of the transformation was in fact the result of the rivalries bred by 'the highest stage of capitalism'. The struggle for power between the advanced capitalist countries, and, in particular, those characteristic features of imperialism, war and the permanent arms economy, continuously forced the evolution of technology into particular channels. The shift was not a smooth adjustment from one phase to another but a piecemeal, *ad hoc*, twisting and turning, impelled by the fluctuations in the relationships between the rivals, none of them being able to establish sufficient control of their environment to begin to plan deliberately their own self-transformation.

The shift in part transformed capitalist society. The labour force required by the new forms of production had to be much more highly educated, and to sustain the drive to raise its productivity it needed both higher real incomes and an elaborate complex of welfare provisions. The characteristic figure of the old labour movement, the unskilled manual worker, went into slow decline; the new white-collar worker, demanded by the much more highly concentrated and therefore bureaucratised public and private companies, rose to new importance within the labour movement. And politically the old capitalism was not divested of power by the new without a long transitional period and much disturbance to the inherited order. In other countries major crises and new regimes were the backcloth to the shift in political power impelled by the crisis of capitalism.[13] But in Britain it was power in the British Conservative Party which slowly changed hands between the regimes of Bonar Law and Churchill in 1951.[14] The overall shift – misleadingly summarised in the tags 'managerial revolution', the creation of a 'mixed – or Social Democratic – economy', the 'Welfare State', 'People's Capitalism' – seemed to change the appearance of capitalism dramatically. The robber barons and their sweat-shop colleagues gave way to the faceless corporation men.

Appearances overdramatised what had happened. For the system remained driven by forces generated within it – the endemic rivalries of capitalism – and yet beyond its control. The glitter of its achievements still only imperfectly concealed the damage it left in its wake. And nowhere was this more true than in the backward countries. For the shift away from a capitalism heavily dependent upon the relatively primitive processing of raw materials was catastrophic for those historically snared in the role of raw-material suppliers. The earnings which raw-material exports earned had purchased the simple low-priced output of advanced capitalism. But now the exports had declining power to earn, and advanced capitalism produced increasingly complex and high-priced goods, suitable for sale on a large scale only in high-income markets, in mar-

---

13   Although now out of date, the account of R.A. Brady is still one of the best available on
      this subject; see Brady 1943.
14   See Chapter IV of Harris 1968, p. 104.

kets within other advanced capitalist countries. The terms of the exchange –
however unfavourable they were before – now began to break down.

For the interwar slump, the balance of payments difficulties of each capitalism, a whole era of economic nationalism, had compelled each national capital
to conserve its domestic resources, to minimise imported materials. As a result, dramatic economies in the use of raw materials were made;[15] substitutes
for imports were found; and out of the ingenuity and diversity of the petrochemicals industry thousands of synthetic materials were created, at first more
expensively than the raw materials imitated, but finally more cheaply. Quite
accidental factors suddenly released new resources – just as today the anti-air
pollution programme may generate, as one by-product, the retrieval of sulphur
from the smoky atmosphere, and so undercut the raw-material export of every
sulphur exporter. And in some cases the raw materials imported were used in
startlingly new ways that, in the end, could be used as replacements for a different range of imports; British Petroleum is building factories at the moment
to manufacture edible protein as a by-product from oil, at a price which could
undercut the world's fisheries and soya-bean plantations.[16]

Rising real incomes in the advanced capitalist countries provided expanding
markets for the increasingly sophisticated and highly priced output. And it
ensured the profit rates on new investment that continuously sucked in an
increasing proportion of the world's new savings. The trade between advanced
capitalist countries provided the dynamo for an unprecedented expansion
in world trade and output in the period after 1948, and for an even greater
concentration of capital in the hands of the richest countries. What had been
seen by the imperialists as the division of labour in the world between the
manufacturing advanced and the raw material-exporting backward countries
was overtaken by a division between the relatively self-sufficient advanced
enclave and a mass of poor dependents.

In the context of the shift in capitalism one can begin to understand decolonisation. Political power could be conceded precisely because the group of

---

15   As an example of the economies in the use of materials, see for example the decline in
      the average amount of coal burned to produce one kilowatt hour of electrical energy in
      the United States: 1902: 6–4 lb; 1920: 3–4 lb; 1944: 1–3 lb – Statistical Abstract of the United
      States, Washington, 1946, table 531, p. 475. Raw materials are also increasingly re-used after
      extraction from scrap: 'The reclamation and recycling of secondary materials represent
      about 35% of the total UK consumption of copper; 25% of zinc; 55–60% of lead; 30% of
      aluminium; and 5–10% of tin' – T.W. Farthing, *Financial Times* supplement, 19 May 1970.
16   Cf. report, *The Economist*, 6–12 December 1969, p. 104.

metropolitan countries was becoming less dependent upon the commodities produced in the backward countries. The old colonial companies producing raw materials for their metropolitan parents needed political control for the stability and survival of their operations. They had a vested interest in empire. But such companies have been in steady decline since before the First World War. Now the companies operating in backward countries are international ones, whose dependence on any one backward country is slight, whose interest is less in the search for raw materials and more in jumping the tariff barriers to exploit the small internal market of any particular backward country. For political independence permitted new governments to restrict imports from the advanced. Direct investment in the backward country overcomes this obstacle, and though the profits are small in absolute terms, the rates are high. One of the results of this is the outflow from the backward countries not of raw materials, but of profits from foreign marketing operations, and the expansion of imports demanded by the foreign operator. Hence, the balance of payments becomes the main restriction on the expansion of the backward country. This would be partly alleviated if the foreign companies really did bring capital into the country. But in most cases they bring relatively little, relying for their expansion either on abnormally high local profit rates or local borrowing. For example, a Philippines government report on 70 percent of the American companies in the Phillipines estimates that, between 1956 and 1965, 84 percent of the capital used by US companies was borrowed locally.[17]

Even with high profit rates, Western investment flows to the backward countries sluggishly. In general the flow is stable, hardly increasing very much, and heavily concentrated in the areas known to be 'safe', because they are directly accessible to Western political or military power. Latin America has received more than all the other backward regions put together.[18] Wherever it goes, favourable government concessions – in some cases amounting to a quasi-monopoly – keep the profit rates at a level where either the balance of payments is continually strained by the repatriation of funds or the proportion of the local economy under foreign control is continually increased (leading in

---

17   Government of the Philippines, Aspects of US Investment in the Philippines, Memorandum to the Staff Secretariat of the Working Committee on the Laurel-Langley Trade Agreement of the National Economic Council, reported in the *Far Eastern Economic Review*, 26 May 1969, p. 529. Idem Supra.

18   On the distribution, by region and activity, of accumulated direct investment (December 1966, estimate), see Chart 4, p. 100 and Table 13, Annex II, p. 376 Pearson 1969 (are all these from Pearson).

the course of time to an even more massive outflow of funds). Foreign investment, because of its changed purposes, produces few exports (often the affiliate of an international company is forbidden to export lest this compete with the output of the parent company), and tends to increase the volume of imports, and, in time, the outflow of funds. In India, for example, it has been estimated that in 1951 to 1952 foreign companies exported 70 percent more than they imported (the 1952 figure, which more clearly excludes the exceptional effects of the Korean war boom, was 42 percent); by 1956–8 the foreign sector had a net annual *import* surplus of 10 percent; and by 1964–5 to 1966–7 of 330 percent.[19] Because the companies concerned are often international ones, their global interests are less in creating small-scale manufacturing plant in backward countries (although they may do this as the price of keeping up the sale of their parent companies) and more in finding ways to market their home production. Because they are very large they can afford to refuse to invest in a backward country if the terms are not to their liking. And the government of the backward country is very limited in the sanctions which it can take against such a company, short of nationalisation. Behind the international company, those who supply aid, credits, military assistance and so on, Western governments and international agencies, use their power to ensure the 'liberalisation' of the world economy for private – Western – capital. Even if the government of the backward country tries to offset foreign control by developing local manufacturing this may only increase foreign intervention as has happened in Latin America.[20]

The relationship between backward and advanced appears to have changed and to be changing in a way which steadily exacerbates the problems of backwardness. But in the raw material field there are obvious exceptions, of which oil is the pre-eminent one. Of the direct cumulative investment of the advanced capitalist countries in the backward (December 1966), 40 percent was in oil, and only 9 percent in other minerals and in smelting (the rest, 51 percent, was invested in manufacturing, utilities and services). Not all of this investment in oil was in the extraction of resources; a great deal of it went into refining crude oil imported into backward countries with relatively poor local sources of crude. On the other hand, foreign investment certainly does not indicate anything like the raw-material imports of the advanced, even if it gives some indication of the relative profit rates in the eyes of foreign investors.

---

19   As calculated in Kidron 1969, p. 9.
20   See Sunkel 1969.

Decolonisation was certainly a dangerous exercise in countries producing raw materials of importance for Western capitalism, but it was offset in important ways. First, sources of the raw materials were, wherever possible, diversified so widely that it was hardly conceivable that all exporters could combine to pressure Western buyers. Oil is a good example. The seven 'majors' which, by their control of the cheapest sources of crude oil in the Middle East, and of the most extensive marketing outlets, maintain a position of supremacy against both the oil-producing countries and the smaller independent oil companies (as well as the Soviet Union), have led the way in trying to secure a foot-hold in every important oil find. Diversification of oil sources is the trump card in cartel control,[21] for the organisation of oil-exporting countries (OPEC) can never hope to discipline all producers to present a united front. Second, exploration for minerals in the advanced countries has been pushed hard in order to offset dependence on any particular backward country. The mineral strikes in Australia and Canada are particularly important here, and the United States government is quite explicit as to why it is particularly interested in the oil, natural gas, coal, uranium and electricity of Canada – to offset dependence upon sources in 'politically unreliable or unstable', backward countries.[22] Finally, domestic sources of raw materials or energy are sought – whether this is of relatively marginal significance like the reopening of Cornish tin mines, or exploration for North Sea gas, or the development of atomic energy, or the recycling of already used materials.

It is the price of raw-material supplies, and the security and stability of supply, which determine the decision to import from one source rather than another or to find local sources or substitutes. The United States, for example, through the 1960s has steadily increased its import of iron ore (reaching about 44 million tons in 1968). Half of these imports come from Canada and about a quarter from Venezuela. Australia, given the right price, could also be a major producer. The dependence is not upon exclusive sources in backward countries; on the contrary, the availability of supplies round the world makes the backward producer dependent upon the US market. If the price of imports gets too high, new domestic resources will suddenly become economic. Iron

---

21   The point is made explicitly in the portrait of British Petroleum by Barton William-Powlett, *Times Business News*, 5 January 1970. Cf. also Tugendhat, *The Financial Times*, 3 December 1969, and Tanzer, 1970.

22   Cf., for example, the speech by Hollis Dole, Assistant Secretary of the Interior (for mineral resources), US Government, to a conference on natural resources, Oregon State University, 9 March 1970, reported in *The Financial Times*, 10 March 1970.

ore has just been discovered in Nevada (Nevada State says the strike could be up to 1 billion tons), but the US steel companies are reluctant to undertake the investment required to get it out at the present price of ore.[23] An increase in the ore prices demanded by any backward country could prompt a shift to purchases from sources in other countries; and if world prices as a whole rose, the US steel companies would have an incentive to develop home sources.

The manufacturing emphasis of modern capitalism underpins its technological ingenuity. Far from the advanced becoming more and more dependent on the backward for raw materials,[24] the system appears to be becoming more and more flexible, more and more adept at substituting one input for another. No one raw material exporter, any more than any one group of skilled workers, can regard their contribution to production as indispensable. The concentration of technical skill in the advanced countries ensures this flexibility as well as the paramount position of the advanced capitalist countries in the world economy. It is an 'almost impregnable foreign monopoly of advanced technology that comes from concentrating research and development in the world's industrial heartland'.[25]

Indeed, the argument could go in exactly the opposite direction – that the backward countries are increasingly dependent upon the advanced. In so far as the backward industrialise, they become increasingly dependent on the advanced, not just for imported capital equipment and technology but also in part for primary produce and raw materials. The advanced countries export nearly double the volume of food and raw materials that the backward export.[26] The periodic dependence by some backward countries on food grains from the United States, Canada, Australia and France illustrates one element in this relationship. For minerals, many of the backward countries remain dependent upon the world market. For example, in 1969 – a boom year for base metals in world commodity trade – demand for copper, lead, as well as special steels, all at unusually high prices, was significantly affected by the very large purchases made by China. And China, by reason of its size, is one of the richer backward countries in terms of indigenous resources. Indeed, in the case of copper, it was Chinese purchases which prevented a surplus of copper depressing the world price. The same is also true of natural rubber, where the 1969 price was

23   Cf. report, *The Financial Times*, 19 December 1969.
24   As argued, for example, in Jalée 1969, p. 131: 'Imperialism does not pillage the Third World diabolically or for fun, but because of vital necessity, because it could not survive otherwise'.
25   Kidron 1969, p. 13.
26   Colin Clark, Lloyds Bank Review, January 1970.

significantly affected by China's purchases (China is the fourth-largest buyer of natural rubber from the largest producer, Malaya).[27]

Expansive though the demand of industrialising backward countries is, it has still not prevented the deterioration in the different shares of world trade held by advanced and backward, respectively. Between 1953 and 1964 the industrialised countries increased their share of world trade from 37.1 to 45.5 percent. Up to 1967 the share of the backward countries fell from 27 to 19 percent (and if oil is excluded this last figure falls to 12–13 percent). Forty percent of the doubling in world exports between 1958 and 1968 went to West Germany and the United States alone. Even in the best year for the exports of backward countries since 1945 – namely 1968 – they increased their exports by 9 percent (compared to 3 percent in 1967), in comparison to the 11 percent increase in the exports of the advanced countries. The divergence in rates of growth appears to be too consistent to be any 'short-term' factor: the rich are consistently getting richer, the poor poorer.

The flows of capital follow the same paths as those of trade – to other advanced countries. For if direct investment to exploit markets is becoming the characteristic form of private investment abroad, then it is the size of the market, the income level of the population, which determines how large the flow of investment is to be. Nor is it true that cheap labour compensates for the smallness of the market as an inducement to foreign capital. Modern manufacturing requires a highly skilled labour force – for which abundant unskilled labour cannot be substituted – sophisticated manufactured inputs, specialised ancillary services (power, transport, communications) and a stable scale of output beyond the size of most markets in backward countries. Even where unskilled labour can be substituted for skilled the costs may be significantly higher per unit of output.

High profits are made in backward countries, but as often as not, this is the result of domestic protection around the economy. The government concedes or cannot prevent quasi-monopolistic conditions which make for monopoly prices and profits. Without such profits, foreign investment would go elsewhere. The cost of all this cannot be properly estimated. But MacNamara of the World Bank – certainly no disinterested source – has estimated that in 1965 the backward countries spent US $2.1 billion in domestic resources to manufacture automotive products with a world-market value of $800 million. The 'loss' of $1.3 billion is just about the amount in aid advanced by the World

---

27   Cf. John Woodland, *The Times Business News*, 2 January 1970, and report, 'Communist purchases absorbed 1969 copper surplus', *The Financial Times*, 25 February 1970.

Bank in the 23 years of its existence.[28] Of course, 'liberalisation' of the backward economies would merely break down the flimsy barriers at present protecting them, and Western industry would be able to wipe out much of what industry exists in backward countries. But the costs of protection cannot be dismissed.

Why do many of the socialist accounts of modern imperialism argue that the advanced capitalist countries are increasingly dependent upon the raw material exports of the backward countries? It is usually an attempt to explain the exigencies of us foreign policy, to explain the scale of military intervention in, for example, Vietnam. To say 'The United States is just doing it for the money' is part of an old Liberal Populist – muck-raking – tradition. But it appears to be quite false. The truth is somewhat more brutal.[29] On the other hand, many of the accounts of modern imperialism turn out to be descriptions of

---

28   Robert MacNamara, Address to the Annual Meeting of the World Bank and the International Monetary Fund, 29 September 1969, reported in *The Financial Times*, 30 September 1969. On foreign company profits in India, see Kidron 1965, pp. 5 and 6.

29   So far as can be seen, the known resources of the whole of Southeast Asia will hardly compensate the us government for the enormous costs of the war, and the markets concerned are trivial for American capitalism because the income level is so low. What market has developed is the result rather than the cause of us military intervention. What the us government pursued in Vietnam was its global interests – and therefore the location of the war in Vietnam was relatively 'accidental', for it could have been fought anywhere for that purpose. In Vietnam the American ruling class is asserting its Paramount Chieftaincy of the world, at the same time as warning China, the Soviet Union, Cuba, radicals in Latin America, Asia and Africa, and, not least, potential rebels in Europe. Although the war has bred a host of economic interests, each with its fingers in the pork barrel, the American ruling class as a whole is against the war – because of the resulting high taxation, the high commodity prices Defence Department purchases create, at a time when American business is threatened both abroad and domestically by foreign competition. The truth is thus nastier than many of its opponents admit, for at least the pursuit of raw materials presupposes some specific interest, whereas there appears to have been little economic interest at stake at all – so many people were slaughtered as a terrifyingly gratuitous display of barbarity. The history of imperialism has similar examples, although nothing on the scale of the Vietnam War. Take, for example, the Pacifico Incident. In 1850 Lord Palmerston dispatched British warships to blockade the city of Athens. This was a reprisal for the Athenians maltreating a certain David Pacifico, an Athenian moneylender. Pacifico, born in Alexandria, was a British subject, and therefore, Palmerston argued, entitled to the full protection of the British State. This was not a prelude to the seizure of Greece or the Balkans. There were no raw materials or markets involved. The action was no more than forcefully 'showing the flag', or, what is the same thing, 'flashing the knife', not merely for the benefit of the Greeks or even the more important Turks, but for the edification of the whole of Europe.

the domination of the rest of the world by the United States, without simultaneously showing the rivalries between advanced capitalist States. The increasing dependence of the United States on imported raw materials (demonstrated, for example, by Harry Magdoff)[30] does not show an increasing dependence by advanced capitalism on the backward.

The Left Post-independence Alternative

The weakness of the Left position is shown most clearly in what is suggested as the alternative strategy for backward countries. If only the constricting control of the world market can be ended, it is argued, then development can be pushed ahead with great rapidity by the State. Autarky and State enterprise will somehow be able to break through the impasse. Yet hitherto the main forces pushing development have been transmitted by the world market. The demand for raw materials stimulated the opening up and exploitation of whole new areas of the world, creating an exchange system – imposed and regulated, certainly, in the interests of metropolitan capital – between the advanced and the backward. Today the exchange is weakening and foreign capital no longer plays its former role in pushing industrialisation. The advanced drain resources out of the backward without contributing significantly to real industrialisation – in terms of repatriated profits, interest on loans,[31] the net advantage in the exchange between manufactured and primary commodities, and, not least, in the drain of skilled manpower.

Nevertheless, those backward countries with the highest growth rates are all ones which are tightly knit into the world market.[32] The highest *per capita* incomes are in those countries which are major exporters or related directly to an advanced capitalist power. It may be that the country is parasitic upon some large nearby market – as Spain, Greece and Turkey are on the periphery of the European Common Market, Mexico and Jamaica close to the North American market, South Korea and Taiwan to Japan. They may command an important raw material, as do the oil-producing countries, or as Malaya (with tin and

---

30   Magdoff 1969.

31   For example: between 1961 and 1968 the net capital inflow to Latin America was US $11.493 billion; the outflow in income 'from investments remitted abroad' was US $14.749 billion. Latin America lost US $3.256 billion. Cf. Annual Report, Inter-American Development Bank Social Progress Trust Fund, Washington, 1970.

32   'The growth rates of individual developing countries since 1950 correlate better with their export performance than with any other single economic indicator. If the expansion of world trade were to flag, the development effort would undoubtedly be retarded'; Pearson 1969, p. 45.

rubber). Or they may, by the accident of strategic geography, be favoured client
States, with an inflow of foreign capital servicing a defence programme, as is
the case with South Korea, Taiwan and Thailand. And in the case of the last
three the pork barrel of the Vietnam War is important in recent growth.[33]

But 'growth' may not mean 'development'. The statistics may show a rising
national income, even a rising average income per head, at the same time as
unemployment is increasing, there is no change in the distribution of the occupied population between agricultural and non-agricultural employment, and
in the distribution of non-agricultural employment between manufacturing
and other sectors. In human terms nothing very much may have happened,
and things for the majority may even have got worse.

Yet at least there is *some* growth, and that is more than is ordinarily promised
by economic autarky, by cutting the local economy off from the world market.
Even if the economic links can be severed – and they can never be broken
comprehensively and with impunity – military and political threats keep even
the largest backward country snared in the concerns of the powerful. China is
an excellent example of the limits imposed by the system itself. For its entire
development is influenced, indeed governed, by the necessity to maintain a
defence capability, including a missiles programme far in advance of its level
of economic development.

Yet where there is integration into the world economy, what growth takes
place is determined by the demands of the system, the preponderant element of which is advanced capitalism. The backward economy's development
is shaped into that specialisation which ensures its dependence upon the
external market and sustains its backwardness outside the area of its specialisation. The difficulties faced by Cuba in trying to industrialise and diversify its
output are a vivid illustration of the power of the world system in shaping its
constitutuent parts. Cuba could not for a moment make itself self-sufficient.
The only way to pay for the imports of capital equipment and industrial raw
materials was to *increase* Cuba's specialisation in sugar, to make it more of
a mono-cultural economy than it was in the pre-revolutionary period. Cuba
also is governed by the generalisation advanced by those socialists who have
outlined the neo-imperialist or neo-colonialist identification of the modern
world: the present relationships between the advanced and backward countries continue, and indeed, make worse, some of the most oppressive features
of colonialism.

---

33   See Harris 1968b, pp. 7–8.

The Left has excelled in the critique of what happens when a backward economy is bent to fit the world market. It has been less sensitive to the problems arising out of isolation from the world market. As a result, economic nationalism has been used as a substitute for international socialism. Today, the increasing weakness of economic nationalism as a real alternative is becoming clearer, particularly because the model of Soviet development appears increasingly to be a unique case. Soviet economic nationalism was not a matter of choice. It was forced upon Russia by the interwar collapse of the world economy, a collapse which forced all the major capitalist powers into a greater or lesser degree of defensive autarky. To make of this necessity a virtue only obscures discussion. The waste, the terrible cost imposed upon the Russian population,[34] the continuing backwardness of the Russian economy, particularly in its agricultural sector, do little to convince one of its universal desirability. Even more, Russian conditions were the most favourable for autarkic development. Tsarist Russia had the highest rate of economic growth in the whole of Europe in the last two decades of the nineteenth century, and this process created both a stable working class with the required skills, as well as heavy industry and an infrastructure of important services (for example, railways). Russia was certainly backward by the standards of advanced capitalism, but in 1913 it was already well in advance of those countries containing the majority of the population of the backward countries.

There are – sadly – no magic cures for poverty and backwardness. Rhetoric does not wish away the terrible and brutal process of capital accumulation which scarred the capitalist powers and the Soviet Union. Capital accumulation is the aggregation of a surplus. The surplus can come from abroad, on trade, in aid or loans, or from savings out of current consumption by the population at home. In the absence of the first there is only the second. And if the level of current livelihood of the population is low, and the political and administrative machine weak, then any surplus from this source is likely to be small. If the population is simultaneously growing, what surplus there is may only provide a basis for standing still rather than actually improving the situation. On the other hand, only a very powerful army and police force can snatch the surplus for national investment between the peasant's hand and mouth. The obstacles in the way of development constantly grow larger as the advanced countries come to dominate even more the world market from which formerly backward countries could gain some advantage. Implicit in modern efforts at develop-

---

34   On the agrarian costs – and so some of the industrial and development effects – see Lewin 1968, and Harris 1969, p. 37.

ment is a police State, for rational men will not otherwise make the sacrifices asked of them and their families.

In countries where the material problems of survival are great the prospects for development are grim, let alone the prospects for creating a free and equal socialist society. Freedom and equality depend upon the problems of sheer survival having long since been overcome. Those problems could be overcome in the modern world but not without the transformation of world capitalism. One isolated country, sooner or later, is forced backwards by its own poverty into a new stringent division of labour. For the motive force of early capitalism was not human greed but the logic of scarcity, of poverty. It is backwardness itself which reshapes the social relationships men think they have created, leaving the words and phrases intact but giving them a new practical connotation: the reassertion of class rule.

Despite the rhetoric, none of the backward economic autarkies – China, Cuba, North Vietnam and North Korea – has yet been able to demonstrate the superiority of its mode of economic development. And this fact, as much as any other, makes the appeals of Stalinism weaker. Economic independence does not in and of itself overcome the problem of backwardness. An economist, summarising the experience of Latin American countries in pursuing economic independence, recently concluded that 'it must be recognised that economic independence cannot be the magical consequence of an heroic political act. Rather it will be the medium, or long-term result – depending on the case – of the construction of a national economy which is both efficient and flexible, and also capable of generating a large and rapidly increasing surplus of resources for investment'.[35] The conclusion is interestingly in error. For economic development does not, apparently, produce economic independence. No advanced country today has much viable economic independence. All are enmeshed in the world market, and would stagnate or decline without it. It follows that an *independent*, diversified economy is today a Utopian aim, whether to be achieved through autarky or integration into the world market. For the backward countries, in the short-term one or other of these two alternatives – and they are not necessarily open to choice – may ameliorate certain problems, but neither holds out much hope of development, and neither are substitutes for the essential task: transforming the world market itself.

---

35   Sunkel 1969, p. 37.

The Agency of Revolution

Classes and Politics

Lenin's account of imperialism assumed that industrial workers as a class were the people who alone could lead the socialist revolution, the overthrow of imperialism as a world system. Among Marxists of his day it hardly needed saying, since it was so much taken for granted. Indeed, the assumption was central to being a Marxist, rather than some other kind of revolutionary, socialist or anarchist. Without the industrial working class Marxism became *Hamlet* without the Prince.

But although it was taken for granted, it was not a gesture of faith. It was the conclusion of an argument. Capitalism was, Marx had argued, the first system in history which compelled its rulers to accumulate capital as the basis for their very survival, and on an increasing scale. As a result of the accumulation, of the competitive dynamic of the system, for the first time the conquest of all the major problems of material scarcity lay within the grasp of mankind. And as a result of this, the possibility of freedom for all, of socialism, also became possible. It was not that socialism depended simply upon the wishes and intentions of the socialists; it depended upon the solution of a range of problems of material survival, upon a prior accumulation of capital. Without it, the scarcity that had forced upon society a division of labour between rulers and ruled would exercise the same influence as before.

But in creating capitalism, the capitalists also created for the first time a subordinate class which had within its power the transformation of capitalism and the establishment of freedom for all. This class, by its labour, created the accumulation of capital, created and sustained capitalism. Workers were not just exploited – exploitation had existed for thousands of years – but exploited ever more systematically, and the more systematically they were exploited, the more they ensured an even greater rate of exploitation in the future. They were exploited, not in the sense that they were impoverished, but in the sense that a greater and greater share of their increasing productivity was appropriated by the capitalist.

In creating the working class, capitalism had to concentrate it physically in the cities. And the cities were simultaneously the source of the power of the capitalists, and the place where for the first time the collective power of the working class could be expressed. Capitalism had also to educate its labour force in order to operate its industry, to break down the inherited customs of the past and make the workers continuously responsive to the dynamic of an advancing technology. In the great concentrations of the industrial working class, skilled by its daily work in interdependent collective action and the tech-

niques of production, lay the promise of political power, of workers' control
and workers' power. The possibility was created of the self-emancipation of the
working class, rather than its emancipation by sundry enlightened reformers of
other classes.

By contrast, other exploited classes which, in many cases, had existed long
before the creation of capitalism, were kept on the margins of society. The peasants were widely dispersed geographically, trapped in the most backward, non-
collective, forms of production. Nothing in their way of life compelled them to
comprehend society as a whole, as a system, let alone formulate an alternative industrial society. Egalitarian and visionary they might be, but within their
grasp lay neither the vision of, nor the power to achieve, a free expanding interdependent industrial society. Without industry the world returned willy-nilly to
the poverty and barbarism of a pre-capitalist past.[36] Inevitably, scarcity would
restore class society.

Yet if much of the Left today accepts some version of Lenin's account of the
economic relationship between the metropolitan and backward countries, and
of 'finance capital', many socialists reject Lenin's assumptions about the role
of the industrial working class. Analysis and strategy come apart, and there is
apparently no force created within the system capable of transforming it. As a
result many socialist writers concentrate simply upon a critique of capitalism,
rather than framing a serious strategy. In this they retreat from Lenin's account
of imperialism to Hobson's, leaving out any systematic treatment of how the
world is to be changed. The separation of analysis and strategy is not so much
the result of an argument as a reaction to the failure of the industrial working
class in the capitalist countries actually to challenge the system on a political
basis. Facts spoke louder than 'mere theories'.

On the other hand, in the backward countries themselves – where, in many
cases, the industrial working class was very small and rarely of much political
significance – radical opponents of foreign political or economic control found
in Lenin's arguments the most searching available condemnation of imperialism. Less frequently were they aware of Lenin's strategic assumption about
the agency of change, the proletariat. Even more important, Lenin's perception of the class conflict *within* each and every society, backward or advanced,
was scarcely understood at all except as a division between those who opposed
foreign influence (whatever their class), and those who supported it (whatever
their class). Inevitably, the struggle for national independence superseded, and,
indeed, for many nationalists eliminated, the need for the emancipation of the

---

36   For a fuller discussion of these issues, see Harris and Caldwell 1969–70, pp. 18–31.

industrial working class. Internal class divisions were obscured in the search for national unity, and nationalism was rebaptised as socialism.

Leaving out the industrial working class as the agent of the socialist revolution left a vacancy. In some cases it was filled by the conception of the nation, and even by a conglomerate of nations, the 'Third World'. The working class was to lead the revolution because of its position within society. Its substitute, the nation, was now supposed to lead the world. Trotsky once warned against 'that national revolutionary Messianic mood which prompts one to see one's own nation-state as destined to lead mankind to socialism'.[37] The working class was said to have no vested interest in the geographical boundaries of any particular State; it was internationalist. The 'Third World' expressed the – at least aspirant – internationalism of the new candidate for agency of the revolution. An international alliance between the working classes of different countries against their respective ruling classes was replaced by an alliance between backward countries against the capitalist countries. Alliances of States replaced the alliance of workers against all States. And the States in alliance were identified by their level of poverty, of oppression, even though oppression is at least as divisive as it is unifying.

In the alliance of States the language of classes was still used to describe the States. There were 'proletarian States' and 'bourgeois States'. But the bourgeois States included no proletarians. To the workers of the advanced capitalist countries the advocates of this position have nothing to say, except that they are guilty of living off the proceeds of the exploitation of the backward countries, and therefore cannot be considered even as allies in the attack on imperialism. The theory of the bribe – that Western workers have been silenced by higher wages – never carried a great deal of credibility, and certainly cannot be made consistent with Marx's theory of exploitation. But even if we ignore these aspects mutual recrimination is hardly productive. James Connolly, the Irish revolutionary, answered the reproaches of the Irish against English workers in this way:

> We are told that the English people contributed their help to our enslavement. It is true. It is also true that the Irish people contributed soldiers to crush every democratic movement of the English people ... Slaves themselves, the English helped to enslave others; slaves themselves, the Irish helped to enslave others. There is no room for re-crimination.[38]

37   Cited in Deutscher 1954, p. 238.
38   Cited in Sean Matgamma, *Socialist Worker*, December 1969, p. 4.

The Orthodoxy and the Unorthodox

In practice the anti-imperialist struggle has been led by people who were neither from the industrial working class nor identified with its interests. If it is the case, as many socialists today assume, that anti-imperialist struggles, once victorious, have introduced what Marx meant by socialism, then the whole Marxist scheme comes unstuck. Socialism can be, and has been on this account, achieved by forces other than those of the industrial working class.

Those socialists who positively identify with Marxism have been most troubled by this inconsistency. For example, in China the Communist Party tends to call itself 'the leadership of the proletariat', even though industrial workers played scarcely any role at all in the Chinese revolution. By a verbalism the tradition is preserved. Others have argued, more radically, that the industrial working class was only 'the proletariat' – that is, the agency for the socialist revolution – in the peculiar conditions of the nineteenth century. And this was because at that stage the workers were exploited, propertyless, poor, and politically militant, whereas now the class which possesses these characteristics is the peasantry of the backward countries.[39] In fact, the interpretation of Marx and of the nineteenth-century worker is wrong. If being poor and propertyless were the main criteria, much of the peasantry of the nineteenth century were significantly worse off than the industrial workers. On the other hand, there is no real evidence that the differential between peasants as a class and workers as a class in backward countries today is greater than it was in the advanced countries in the nineteenth century. Nor was the nineteenth-century worker notably politically militant. Many socialists have an idealised picture of the Victorian worker as someone who was heroically unselfish, unconcerned with the details of daily life. It is romantic nonsense, as any serious history book will show. Workers then, as now, fought on a daily basis for specific economic gains. Western middle-class opinion today chooses to accept that those battles were justified then, but are *not* justified now. But to accept such an opinion is both to distort the past and identify oneself with one side in the class argument now.

---

39   See the statement of Fanon, for example: 'In colonial countries, the peasants alone are
      revolutionary, for they have nothing to lose and everything to gain. The starving peasant,
      outside the class system, is the first among the exploited to discover that only violence
      pays. For him, there is no compromise, no possible coming to terms' (Fanon 1965, p. 48).
      Paul Sweezy writes: 'The masses in the exploited dependencies constitute a force in the
      global capitalist system which is revolutionary in the same sense that Marx considered the
      proletariat of the early period of modern industrialisation to be revolutionary' (Sweezy
      1968, p. 33).

The relationship between 'high ideals' and immediate concrete issues is not some enormous abyss as those with an adequate income like to think. Grubby selfishness and absurd heroism are necessarily part of the same act, then as now. In the same sense the heroic battles fought in backward countries are about specific issues – not just about freedom, but also about this little bit of land, that foreign bully, this man's hunger and that man's job, about issues of status and standing. The battles are not just about the heroic posturing which the more naive revolutionary posters portray. Particularly when people are far away from the scene of the action they miss the complexities, the wrinkles, the real men struggling under heroic concepts. In doing so they do no justice at all to the real victories which are won.

But are the backward countries more exploited? In the sense of 'impoverished' this is clearly so. But this tells us little about the system involved. For Marx the most exploited are those who produce the most surplus value appropriated by the capitalist. The transformation of capitalism has created a phenomenal increase in labour productivity in the capitalist countries, and has thus permitted an even greater increase in the rate of exploitation. For the poorest are rarely the most exploited: their subsistence takes too high a proportion of their output to permit much 'surplus'. If the basis of the system is the creation of surplus value, embodied in capital accumulation, then clearly the most exploited are the Western working classes, and within those classes, the most productive workers. The Western car worker is among the most exploited of all, and, for the same reason, among the best paid. The Left account concentrates on consumption levels, not on production, so that it is then suggested that low consumption is the index of exploitation. Of course, the relative level of exploitation does not tell us who is likely to be most rebellious. Where the system breaks is not necessarily determined by who is most exploited. The complexities of oppression and discrimination overlay and distort the stratification imposed by relative exploitation.

Those closest to the Marxist tradition have felt most poignantly the inconsistency between what actually happened in the independence movement and the Leninist prognosis. For some Trotskyists the dilemma was resolved by agreeing that, for example, the Chinese Communist Party was composed of people in the main not drawn from the industrial working class, but that the 'proletarian character' of the Party was guaranteed by its adherence to 'proletarian ideology'. Isaac Deutscher adds to this criterion[40] – if I understand his

---

40   See Deutscher, 'Maoism – Its Origins, Background, and Outlook,' in *Socialist Register*, London, 1964, p. 23, *passim*.

argument correctly – two others. Since China is allied to a 'proletarian power', namely the Soviet Union, it is again of proletarian character. And since the Chinese Communist Party is committed to industrialisation it is committed to *creating* a proletariat, and thus again qualifies as a proletarian power.

The curiosities of this argument illustrate the oddities which arise when revisions are only piecemeal. For if any regime which commits itself to industrialisation is thereby 'proletarian' the Victorian bourgeoisie must also qualify for the term. And if an alliance with the Soviet Union (*if* China can seriously be said to be allied with the Soviet Union) has the same effect, then Britain and the United States were presumably 'proletarian' during the Second World War. More to the point, two of the criteria turn entirely upon the 'proletarian' nature of the Soviet Union. Once we hesitate there, the case collapses. In any case, the 'proletarian ideology' in question is the Stalinism of the 1930s[41] and we are to assume that somehow it survived intact independently of any real live workers in China. The ideas have become independent of the men whose ideas they were supposed to be; the smile is independent of the Cheshire Cat.

However, it is more common on the Left today for there to be no illusions about the role of the Soviet Union or its 'proletarian' character. Orthodox Stalinism proved incapable of containing the new revolutionary forces created by the problems of backwardness and foreign domination. Even in the case of China, where, in theory, an orthodox Communist Party led the struggle to free the country from foreign influence and control, it did so only by operating independently of the Soviet Party or the Comintern. Elsewhere there was scarcely even a nod in the direction of Moscow.

Yet if many of the new revolutionaries have rejected the dogmatism of Soviet orthodoxy they have not created a framework of theory to put in its place. Indeed, for some it is a point of principle to reject all 'ideologies', and stress instead spontaneous popular action. Since radical forces have for so long been curbed by Moscow, it is, at least initially, a healthy reaction to demand action rather than debate. But action is self-limiting and can be self-defeating unless it takes place with some sort of strategy. Society is not always and everywhere dry tinder that requires but a spark to set it ablaze. This needs to be established by analysis. The resources of the *status quo* to resist isolated action are much greater than the instant activist allows. In the long haul, theory

---

41   For an attempt to identify some of the main differences between Stalinism and 'Mao Tse-tung's thought', and more extensive discussion of the evolution of Marxism in China, see Harris 1968, pp. 142–228.

and organisation conserve the revolutionary forces and build them, directing them towards the final aim. Without them the rebels become merely society's gadflies, irritants which are tolerated because they are relatively harmless.

For the new revolutionaries, the agency of revolution is less a social class at all than a small body of armed idealists fighting a guerilla war against the status quo. Urban guerilla warfare, in conjunction with the organisation of a working-class mass political party, may or may not be a useful tactic to pursue, but urban guerilla warfare in isolation has few political implications. Societies have been able to support individual terrorism without this having any political implications except to keep the revolutionaries well away from those who actually produce the wealth on which the power of the ruling class is based. And this observation is even more true of rural guerilla warfare. In the Debray scheme the small band of revolutionaries create a rural base from which they begin to demonstrate that the ruling class is not invulnerable. They are protected by their remoteness from the centres of the country, and immunised against infection by the germ of urban corruption.[42] Slowly, they grow, until finally they are in a position to march on the cities and conquer power.

This was not the sequence of events in Cuba, nor in any other known successful guerilla war. Nor, indeed, in the Cuban case did the success of Fidel Castro's forces depend upon his techniques of guerilla warfare (important though they may have been for sheer survival). What was vital in Castro's assumption of power was the collapse of the Batista regime, strongly assisted by the attitude of benevolent neutrality on the part of the mass of the population towards Castro's challenge. The politics, not the military technique or the guerilla strategy, of Castro made him important. And in any imitation of the Cuban events it will be the politics of the existing regime and the attitude

---

42   The 'anti-urbanism' of the new revolutionaries is more powerful than their positive iden-
      tification with the rural population. On the first, see Fidel Castro's opinion that 'The city is
      a cemetery of revolutionaries and resources', and Debray's view: 'The mountain proletari-
      anises the bourgeois and peasant elements, and the city can bourgeoisify the proletarian'
      (note that the first relationship is apparently unconditional). Why the city is so destructive
      is not convincingly explained, although it is the main justification for selecting a rural area
      to wage war in. Not that the peasants, Debray says, can be wholly trusted until the gueril-
      las are strong enough to dominate the villages. The guerillas must always keep themselves
      quite separate from the rural population: 'The guerilla force is completely independent of
      the civilian population, in action as well as in military organisation; consequently it need
      not assume the direct defence of the peasant population'. Citations from Debray 1968,
      pp. 67, 75 and 41.

towards it of the population which will determine the outcome, rather than
merely guerilla activity. In any straight military confrontation Castro's forces
would have been destroyed, as those of Guevara were destroyed in Bolivia.

But to assess the significance of a political challenge returns us to the task
of social analysis and the identification not of where a rural base is to be
established but what popular forces are to play the leading political role. Mere
guerilla warfare is often a matter of pure luck, depending on the existing
regime. For every Cuba there are a dozen contrary examples. To take only one
series of examples: between 1948 and 1950, the Communist parties of Burma,
Malaya, Indonesia and the Philippines all launched armed struggles of guerilla
warfare. In all cases they were disastrous, isolating the Party from the main
centres of population and destroying its political credibility and relevance. In
Indonesia it took ten years for the PKI to live down this abortive episode. In
Burma, the Communists became irrelevant rural fragments, as much bandits
as revolutionaries. In Malaya, the nationalist forces were pushed into the arms
of the British in self-defence, the Left was isolated, and the achievement of
independence postponed. In the Philippines, the Party disappeared into the
Huk revolt and its warring sects contained. Almost nothing of substance was
achieved, except the advance of Western power in protecting the regimes
concerned.

If the only choice were between armed struggle on its own and passively
supporting the *status quo*, then choice of the first would have a clear significance. The role of the Soviet Union in emasculating the revolutionary politics
of Communist Parties has made it seem that only choice of the first alternative
would be revolutionary. And the first puts a premium upon immediate action
rather than building a mass political organisation with a coherent strategy.[43]
But Marxism is irrelevant to success in guerilla warfare. Its words and concepts
may add a decorative embellishment to what would otherwise be more eas-

---

43   Debray is nothing if not cavalier about the political significance of guerilla warfare. He
      says, implying praise: 'During his two years of warfare, Fidel did not hold a single political
      rally in his zone of operations' (Debray 1968, p. 53). In Moscow's account of revolution,
      politics – that is, the creation of a viable Communist Party – is necessarily prior to any
      action. And for other Marxists the definition of purposes in a strategy, with appropriate
      organisation, is similarly prior to action to achieve the purposes concerned. For Debray,
      action – defined simply as guerilla warfare – is prior to finding the purposes or politics:
      'Eventually', he writes, 'the future People's Army will beget the party of which it is to be,
      theoretically, the instrument: essentially, the party is the army' (Debray 1968, p. 104). It
      emerges in his account that 'the party' is in any case not the directing political force at all,
      so much as a public-relations agency for the guerillas among the local population.

ily understood in non-Marxist terms. Marxism as a method of the analysis of society dissolves into pre-Marxist Populist socialism, the closest analogies to which occur in Narodnik thought in Tsarist Russia in the 1860s and 1870s. Narodnik thought is amorphous and fertile. Some of its offspring followed Marx, some Bakunin, some Kropotkin and Tolstoy, and some even returned to the Russian Orthodox Church. But mainstream Narodniks experimented both with trying to spread revolt among the peasantry and with urban terrorism. But many Narodniks were aware of the dilemma facing the dedicated minority: for if the revolution is created by a small minority what justifies that minority in comparison with the old ruling class?[44] Might the elitism of the one seem little improvement on the authoritarianism of the other? Marx's formulation – that the emancipation of the working class can only be the act of that class itself – resolved the dilemma for Marxists. But self-emancipation requires that the revolution be executed by a class which is fully aware of society as a whole and its place within it, which has the power and knowledge to take over society. The most backward sections of the rural population are not in this category, even if their hostility to the *status quo* provides a springboard to catapult a dedicated band of revolutionaries into power.[45] In that case self-emancipation

---

44   Debray's account of Fidel Castro's answer to this question is no more than bland – or naïve – assertion: 'Fidel Castro says simply that there is no revolution without a vanguard; that this vanguard is not necessarily the Marxist-Leninist party [that is, the Communist Party – N.H.]; and that those who want to make the revolution have the right and the duty to constitute themselves a vanguard, independently of those parties' (Debray 1968, p. 96). Debray himself elsewhere argues that a guerilla group is justified in assuming the leadership of the revolution by 'that class alliance which it alone can achieve, the alliance that will take and administer power, the alliance whose interests are those of socialism – the alliance between workers and peasants' (Debray 1968, p. 109), a statement which comes close to perpetuating the error Debray chastises the Trotskyists for: expecting support merely because one declares oneself socialist. If Castro's answer perhaps expresses the perspective of the pre-socialist rebels of the Sierra Maestra, Debray's shows an eagerness to graft this on to the imperatives of the Cuban State's alliance with the Soviet Union.

45   And they are also (a) less able to create a collective organisation without outside leadership: 'The guerilla force unites the peasantry. Unlike the workers, peasants don't have the facilities to organise concerted action; they are scattered, each one on his plot of land or in his village, surrounded by an enemy whose power is embodied in the army and other instrumentalities of repression. The guerilla force, going from village to village, from region to region, is the embodiment of the common struggle and of the common aspirations of the peasants to possess the land. And there is a key fact to be remembered: the guerilleros go with gun in hand' (Gilly 1965); and (b) less critical of the guerillas, 'The peasant possesses a virgin mentality, free from an assortment of influences which poison the

turns into emancipation by proxy, and the heart of Marxism – the struggle for freedom – is extinguished.

The guerillas are guided by their estimate of military tactics, not by the interests of a particular class. They are outside popular control, isolated from the concrete interests of the members of a class (except in so far as they want popular support), and can therefore be as opportunistic as their tactics require. They are under no compunction to fight the daily battles on the factory floor, or on the land, and so they have no need either for a popular party or for a detailed analysis of society. *Elan* and slogans, a stress upon individual morale rather than equally upon objective circumstances, replaces any systematic theoretical framework.

The dissolution of Marxism is common to a very large number of countries, some of which are ruled by Communist Parties, the majority of which are not. The differences between countries where the struggle for independence was led by Communists and those where it was not come to seem relatively unimportant, despite the attempt of some socialists to make the two qualitatively distinct. The relics of Marxist terminology characteristic of one country appear to have little contribution to make to the battle. In Cuba the Communist Party did not support Fidel Castro until he was virtually certain of winning power. And Castro himself, by his own account, was a radical Liberal rather than a socialist or Marxist. The so-called 'proletarian ideology', like the proletariat itself, had no active role to play in the winning of power in Cuba. The similarities and differences between the struggles in India and China are discussed later, but again the qualitative distinction which Communists want to draw seems very doubtful. In the end, rhetoric makes up the credibility gap in the interests of preserving a tradition of orthodoxy. But rhetoric does not win revolutions, and after the revolution it does not wish away the problems of poverty and backwardness.

Workers and Imperialism

The shift in emphasis was achieved by default. Socialists instinctively felt a warm sympathy for those struggling for national independence. New nations, for so long despised, abused, ignored, rose with amazing speed to cry defiance at their European overlords. The White Man's Burden was suddenly and

---

intellects of citizens in the city. The revolution works on these fertile intellects as it works on the soil' (Fidel Castro as cited in Draper 1965).

plainly seen to be no more than the White Man's Jackboot. The sympathy of Western liberals and socialists for the Indian Congress and Indonesian Nationalists, for the Chinese Communist Party and the Vietminh, for the Algerian FLN, for Cuba's David struggling with the American Goliath, and for movements in a host of other countries, had the unintended effect of directing all attention away from the advanced capitalist countries. Many Marxist intellectuals assumed the final victory of Finance Capital in the West: the working class had sold its historic mission to liberate the world for a mess of television sets and washing machines. By contrast, the aspiration for change, the audacity and heroism of the struggle to be free, lived on only in some of the backward countries. The great traditions stretching back to 1789 and beyond to the Diggers and the Levellers, encompassing 1848 and 1871, 1905 and 1917, seemed to receive their only echo in China and India, Indonesia and Ghana, Egypt and Algeria, and in Cuba. And the scale of the movements in some of these countries dwarfed their puny European predecessors.

The fact that it was not the industrial working class which led these struggles, that there was no answering echo from the workers of the capitalist countries, only seemed to reiterate the fact that they had been neutralised by bribes from the 'super-profits of finance capital'. Marxism must remain 'flexible': revolution defined its own character, whatever the inherited theology.

It was true that industrial workers did not lead – and in most cases played no role whatsoever – in the struggle for national independence. But few tried to understand why. In China in 1927, in Cuba in 1935, and in Spain in the Civil War, workers did indeed play a crucial political role, but in each case in the last analysis the interests of the working class were subordinated to those of other classes. The demand for the establishment of workers' power – for the 'dictatorship of the proletariat' – was lost in a welter of other demands, and, in particular, lost in the guiding interests of Soviet foreign policy. 'Betrayal' is too simple an explanation to cover such a diversity of different situations, but nevertheless it played a vital role in diverting worker support into class coalitions.[46]

Most Marxists before the First World War assumed that the role of the bourgeoisie in the bourgeois revolution had been exhausted. For the new bourgeoisies in 'feudal' countries were too weak to break the power of the *ancien regime*, too deeply involved in foreign capital, and too frightened of the rising discontent of their own working classes, infected with the spirit of socialist revolution

---

46   The reasons for the failure of independent political action by the industrial working class in the backward countries is explored in greater detail in Harris 1970.

from the advanced capitalist countries. In Russia Lenin saw the working class as the only force capable of executing the bourgeois revolution, of establishing a republic (and the conditions within which capitalism could grow). If the workers did not play this role, then Tsarism and capitalism would reach an alliance in which the repressive features of both systems would be combined to the immeasurable loss of the developing working-class movement. The militaristic and authoritarian capitalism of the Kaiser's Germany, rather than the democratic republican capitalism of the United States, would result.

What no one seriously entertained was that any other social groups could intervene to execute the bourgeois revolution. Not even Stalin adopted this position. Rather he argued that the working class, alone, in China was too small to lead the struggle against foreign domination. A class coalition – a Four Class Bloc – of all the major classes of China would be the agency to free China. Concretely, this meant an alliance between the Kuomintang, covering the nationalist landlords and capitalists, as well as the Army, and the Communist Party, organised among peasants and workers. In the 1920s the Kuomintang was allowed to grow by borrowing on the popular work of the Communists. Worker and peasant support was delivered to the Kuomintang by the Communist Party. In 1927, when the armies of the Kuomintang swept northwards, when Chiang Kai-shek calculated that his military strength was great enough to dispense with popular support, his followers were permitted to fall upon the Communists and slaughter them. The class coalition came to pieces in Stalin's hands. For the leadership of the coalition had ultimately determined the balance between social and Kuomintang interests which was to be tolerated. And the landlords and capitalists of the Kuomintang had only narrow limits of toleration for the social interests of the Communist workers and peasants.

Trotsky's perspective – that the workers must lead the struggle for independence – seemed triumphantly demonstrated. As the Kuomintang degenerated more and more into a corrupt military oligarchy, compromising with foreign interests to the point where Chiang refused to put up any military opposition to the Japanese invasion, his perspective seemed even more correct. If the workers had preserved their independence, they could have provided the only source of challenge to foreign domination that might have won.

But, contrary to Trotsky's perspective, the force which did finally challenge foreign domination and carry out the revolution was not drawn from the Chinese working class. Nor was it drawn from the bourgeoisie. Its leadership came from miscellaneous sources, from the urban middle class and from the lower stratum of the landlords, from what Marxists had hitherto called the 'petit bourgeoisie'. And this was true not just for the Chinese independence struggle, but around the world. In some exceptional circumstances the movement was led by Communist parties, but in most cases by non-Communist nationalist parties. But in almost all cases, the social composition of the movements was very similar – a middle-class leadership and a coalition following, drawn heavily from sections of the peasantry.

Far from raising the demand for the 'dictatorship of the proletariat', the independence movements all concentrated upon cementing a class coalition, on keeping in tow poor and rich peasants, urban workers and capitalists, and even landlords. In China the Communist leadership devoted its efforts to preventing class conflict surfacing within the coalition, lest some classes be alienated from the central task. Mao himself opposed the demand for radical land reform right up to the revolution lest this alienate landlords and rich peasants: and he assured the capitalists of their right to make a profit in the new China, lest they be frightened off by worker demands for expropriation.[47]

This was not a peculiarly Communist tactic. For, although in very different language, Gandhi in India pursued the 'harmonisation' of interests, assuring both landlords and capitalists that they would have an important role in the new India. Indeed, if anything, Gandhi was more critical of industrialists than Mao, more 'anti-capitalist' than Mao. In both cases issues arising out of the class structure were damped down in order to highlight the anti-imperialist struggle. In both cases peasant hostility to the landlords was diverted into opposition to those landlords who supported the foreigners. The struggle was for the eviction of imperialism rather than the anti-imperialist struggle being part of an attempt to transform the indigenous class structure. For the same reason the struggle was nationalist rather than internationalist.[48] Of course, in

---

47   See, for example, Mao Tse-tung's *On Coalition Government* (1945) – admittedly designed to woo the Kuomintang: the 'task of our New Democratic system is ... to promote the free development of a private capitalist economy that benefits instead of controlling the people's livelihood, and to protect all honestly acquired private property' (in Mao 1955, p. 255).

48   There were also, of course, important differences between the struggle in the two countries. The conditions of China made it necessary and possible to form a private army, and this military component made the Communists distinctively different from Indian Congress. The Communists, as part of their different political tradition, organised a centrally controlled party with an army, and opposition within the party was firmly disciplined. The party was clearly quite separate from its popular support. Congress combined leadership and supporters in a large amorphous crowd in which open public opposition to Gandhi flourished. The military needs of the Communist Party necessitated it be located in a remote area, isolated and far from the main centres of population and power; Congress was the reverse. Gandhi would not have accepted the formation of independent military forces, even if it had been remotely practicable. Indeed, his opposition to Subhas

both cases, promises were made to both peasants and workers to ensure their support, but on the same basis as the promises made to other social classes: not as the representation of interests, as the embodiment of anti-capitalist or anti-landlord interests, but as inducements to either support or benevolent neutrality. Indeed, the welfare promises to workers made by Congress had the even more limited purpose of preventing Communists dominating the trade unions[49] and the threat of Communist control made Congress intervention acceptable to the employers. Thus, 'petit bourgeois' leaderships have filled the

---

Chandra Bhose, who did ultimately favour this, included rejection of such radicalism. But the social base of the two movements was not so clearly different, even though in Congress the small-town petit bourgeoisie was much more important. When the two came to power both tried to reform the distribution of the land, to destroy the hereditary power of the landowners and landlords, to build a large and growing sector of State industry and to plan. Congress did not expropriate all foreign industry, but then the Chinese Communist Party did not have the opportunity to avoid expropriation, given the flight of foreigners. Both aimed at a 'mixed economy' of public and private capital. But in India the aims disintegrated slowly in a resurgence of the old entrenched classes. In China, despite numerous vicissitudes, the process went in the reverse direction, culminating in the collectivisation of land in the mid-1950s, and the slow supersession of private capital (although, for example, interest and dividend payments to private businessmen continued through until at least the beginning of the Cultural Revolution in 1966). It is clear that the degree of political autonomy achieved by the Chinese leadership was always much greater than that achieved by Congress. Congress included many different forces, and floated on top of them. Gandhi was as much victim as master of the movement he led. And the movement was integrally related to Indian society – the peasant members did farm land, the capitalists and workers did operate factories. Thus, the class conflicts of India were transmitted through Congress, and not resolved. By contrast, the Chinese Communist Party was a body of professional organisers, outside Chinese society, and dependent upon its military forces for its independent power. It could therefore inhibit the transmission of the conflicts of Chinese society, and seek, from outside, to resolve or use them. It was only able to do this because of the unique conditions of China, conditions of long-term social collapse over nearly one hundred years. The era of warlords was the seedbed for Communist survival, and the Japanese invasion the precondition for its success in championing the interests of Chinese nationalism. The autonomy of the party, carefully preserved against the infiltration of members who did represent class interests by purges and rectification campaigns, continued into the post-revolutionary period. It was the precondition for sustaining the reforms pursued, for mobilising the peasantry and so giving itself a new legitimacy which it had not created before the revolution. Yet even this independence slowly seeped away, making necessary the grand purge of the Cultural Revolution. See Harris 1964; Harris and Caldwell 1969–70, p. 22; and Harris 1968–9, p. 11.

49   For an account of the origin of the Bombay welfare legislation (Bombay was the leader in labour legislation), see Morris 1965, pp. 178–98.

vacuum left by the failure of the industrial working class to lead the independence movement.[50] But this is not Marx's 'petit bourgeoisie' – small property owners, small-town businessmen and property-owning peasants – so much as the urban lower middle class, employed in white-collar jobs, highly organised by its bureaucratic employment on a collective basis, and, most importantly, property-less. As the ideology of capitalism has decayed in this century, as indeed the class of capitalists as private owners has become weaker by the sheer process of concentration, its appeal has weakened to the point where the bureaucratic lower middle class has very little interest in the extension of private property. Since the State is the biggest single employer of white-collar staff, the lower middle class is more concerned with the extension of the power of the State than of private business. In India the lower middle class was originally created to service the bureaucracy of empire, and it dominated the independence struggle in the cities and was easily able to outbid the Communists for worker support for most of the time. In China elements of the same class made up for its relative weakness (since the bureaucracy of – at least, foreign – empire was insignificant) with independent military power. In both cases, after independence, the interests of this group almost inexorably extended into the public sector unless challenged by other entrenched classes. In India those entrenched classes were much stronger than in China after independence: the capitalists were stronger from the start, and the landlords were not subject to the long-drawn-out war which occurred in China. The difference between the two countries shaped the post-independence regime and its aspirations.

The language of 'socialism' used in both countries – a language inherited from the interests of the European working classes – obscured the social realities. The debate was supposed to be between the proletariat and the bourgeoisie, the two classes dominating capitalism. But in India the debate was rather between the urban lower middle class – pressing for an extension of the State and public employment – and the richer peasantry and small-town businessmen – pressing for the diversion of more resources to agriculture. This is the heart of a struggle between State ownership – identified by the urban lower middle class as 'socialism' – and rural capitalism.

If the extension of the public sector is socialism, the urban lower middle class is the class of socialism par excellence. But it is State socialism, the socialism of order and planning, not of freedom. And it is national socialism, not the

---

50   This is discussed further in Harris, *Perspectives on the Backward Countries*. For an example of a similar process in Africa, see Meillassoux 1970.

international socialism argued by Marxists to be intrinsic to the material conditions of the industrial working class. And the context of backwardness means that even if the lower middle class becomes supreme – as has happened in a number of backward countries – the new State will be compelled to accumulate capital out of the surplus created by the working class. Exploitation must necessarily be increased, and the instruments originally seen as the means to emancipate the working class will be turned into new means to bind it.[51] For example, those instruments of worker interests, the trade unions, in all cases where the lower middle class rules the State, have been converted into instruments to control the workers.[52]

---

51   The present fashionable argument that urban wages – and therefore the trade unions – must be controlled in order to assist the rural population is a good illustration of the kind of attack launched by the new regimes. There is, of course, no assurance that any savings made in this way will go either to the rural population or even to development, rather than to higher salaries for members of the new regime. The arguments used to justify the Labour government's incomes policy had a very similar flavour. As an example of the approach, cf. the speech by Kenneth Kaunda of Zambia, 'Towards Complete Independence' (speech to the UNIP National Council, August 1969): 'If you demand higher wages for the urban workers, the consequent inflation will inevitably hit the majority of our own relatives in the rural areas. We, the urbanites, will in the end have to pay the price, for, in the final analysis our brothers and sisters, our uncles and aunts, will flock to the town to seek assistance to meet the basic necessities of life, the prices of which have become higher. This is why I emphasise that now Government is yours, industries are yours, the whole economy is yours ... to run and manage effectively and successfully ... it is against this background ... that I find it imperative in the interests of the nation as a whole to announce a wages freeze until further notice ... as a corollary, I also want to put an embargo on strikes, whether official or unofficial, as instruments of bargaining for higher wages'.

52   Consult the 'Aims' section of the Constitution of the national trade union federation in any Eastern Bloc country. In China trade unions exist 'to strengthen the unity of the working class, to consolidate the alliance of workers and peasants, to educate workers to observe consciously the laws and decrees of the State, and labour discipline, to strive for the development of production, for the constant increase in labour productivity, for the fulfilment and overfulfilment of the production of the State' (see 'Constitution, 1953', in Labour Laws and Regulations of the People's Republic of China, Peking, 1956, p. 17). In Cuba, the Law of Union Organisation (August 1961) lays it down that Cuban trade unions should 'assist in the fulfilment of the production and development plans of the nation, to promote efficiency, expansion, and utility in social and public services' (cited in O'Connor 1966, p. 19).

The Strategy

Trotsky's theory of permanent revolution outlined most clearly many of the points made here. In particular he was concerned to answer Stalin's argument that socialism could be built in the Soviet Union in isolation from the rest of the world. The revolution, he argued, must be spread until it included a more or less significant section of the advanced capitalist countries. Without this the new regime would inevitably degenerate, overwhelmed by the contradictions of backwardness. As he put it:

> Marxism takes its point of departure from the world economy, not as a sum of national parts but as a mighty and independent reality which has been created by the international division of labour and the world market, and which in our epoch imperiously dominates the national markets ... In respect of the technique of production socialist society must represent a stage higher than capitalism. To aim at building a *nationally isolated* socialist society means, in spite of all passing successes, to pull the productive forces backwards even as compared with capitalism ... means to pursue a reactionary Utopia.[53]

The hope of Liberalism – that securing economic independence was a sufficient condition for economic development – seems no longer valid. The world is one whole, and without the resources accumulated by the advanced capitalist countries by means barbarous and brutal the process of primitive accumulation imposes upon any backward country intolerable strains. The rhetoric may lay claim to traditions of emancipation, but the practice is driven in the opposite direction. Soviet development illustrates what happens even in conditions generally more favourable than those facing most of the backward countries today, when accumulation becomes a vital necessity for the survival of the State. Trotsky had feared the process would lead to the restoration of the bourgeoisie in Russia – up to that time the necessary expression of the division of labour imposed by accumulation. He had hoped that what he saw as the only other alternative, the resumption of power by the Russian working class, would in fact result. But neither change took place. Behind the verbal facade of Marxism a new class regime was created amid the turmoil and terror of industrialisation.

---

53   Trotsky 1962, original emphasis.

But even the Soviet path seems ruled out for most backward countries today. World development has reached an impasse. The bourgeoisie dragged mankind out of pre-capitalist society, but it is now unable to complete the process by developing the whole world. The result is that while the developed countries continue to grow, the rest stagnate. The impasse can be broken not by establishing islands of nationalist autarky – world imperialism is too strong to permit that to be a real threat – but only by breaking the world domination of capitalism, and thereby releasing the accumulated resources of world capitalism for a massive global development programme. Without this, every partial revolt is less a cure than a symptom of the crisis. The social composition of each national regime makes it impossible to unify the 'Third World', and even if unified, a boycott of capitalism by the backward would inflict more damage on the backward than the advanced. And it would not destroy capitalism.

Unless the citadels of capitalism can be challenged from within, the global domination of the capitalist powers remains. The partial successes won in particular backward countries are vital if seen as the springboard to spreading the revolution. But alone, isolated, they inevitably succumb to the logic of backwardness in a world dominated by the rich.

At a whole series of different points in this critique of dominant opinion on the Left we are led back to the original Marxist stress on the role of the industrial working class. It is here that the key to the global system lies. The lack of proletarian leadership in the struggle for national independence shaped that struggle in certain ways, and created post-independence regimes which positively exacerbated both the attempts to internationalise the revolution and to develop the countries concerned. The lack of a response from the proletariat of the West, to an even greater degree, converted the colonial revolution into a basis for new repressive class regimes. Meanwhile, capitalism had grown and transformed its relationship with the backward countries, making the new regimes even more dependent than before.

In the final analysis the beleaguered garrisons of China, of Cuba, of India, can only be relieved by a mutiny in the imperialist forces. Socialists must quite obviously support the struggle for national independence, but without thereby thinking all the problems are wished away. Once independence is secured, then our interest should be focused upon the creation of a proletarian alternative within each backward country, for that is one of the first steps in transforming the perspective. But, even more, the creation of an independent proletarian challenge in the countries of advanced capitalism is the precondition for decis-ive progress. The two together are the beginnings of a new international class alliance. The development impasse, the resulting political and social instability, terrible poverty and hopelessness for the majority of the population of the backward countries: these are the symptoms of the inevitability of barbarism without international socialism.

How Should We Characterise the World Order?
Reflections on Callinicos's *Imperialism and Global Political Economy**

Much of Left has only the archaic term 'imperialism' (and more specifically, US imperialism) to identify the world order. One can sympathise with the wish to condemn the order, but the term has substantial problems, and directs our attention to the wrong targets in the wrong framework: its analytical function is quite misleading.

To start with, the term is contrasted with 'non-imperialism' – national independence – in a world where States, not people, are the dominant actors,[1] and, as argued later, national independence is now so severely limited it hardly offers a realistic ideal for the future. Furthermore, the term 'imperialism' draws our attention backwards historically, not forwards to the future. By implication attention is drawn back to the pre-capitalist Roman, Chinese, and Tsarist empires or the capitalist British, French and other European empires. Such backward gazing tends to wash away the specificity of the current historical moment (its specific causes and outcomes), creating at worst an ahistorical, universal state, a foundation for faith, not science.

Furthermore, are these historical precedents the right models? For the modern cases, the concept draws our attention to the forces that destroyed the last lot of empires, the colonial revolution and the affirmation of the right of national self-determination. In the days of the colonial revolution, it was the

---

*   From: *International Socialism*, 135, Summer 2012.

1   It might seem pernickety to debate terms, but consider the debate in the Bolshevik Party on how to characterise the State achieved in the revolution. It could not be a worker's State where the majority of the population were peasants, nor what the pre-revolutionary Marxists had aspired to, a bourgeois – capitalist – State, since the workers had gone beyond striking to seizing plants. The debate settled on 'State capitalism with bureaucratic deformations', a brutally precise term which simultaneously identified the contradictory present and the problems for future solution. But, such clarity was brief; the sheer force of the new Soviet State overwhelmed such Marxist niceties and nailed 'socialism' to the masthead, for many permanently discrediting the term. Thus, characterisation ought simultaneously to describe accurately the present, current reality and its contradictions, and imply an agenda for changing it in an as-yet unseen future.

natural assumption that attaining national independence freed a people (in fact, it freed a new ruling class) to shape their own destiny. All levers of power – social, economic, political – would be, it was thought, taken by 'the nation'. Was it true? Consider Mugabe or Idi Amin or any of the other horrors. If the world is imperialism – as Mugabe would no doubt agree – are we really fighting to restore him?

The old empires were built on a unilateral territorial extension of the political-administrative power of the imperial capital, even if exercised through some measure of decentralised administration. In some cases, no modern State had existed in those areas before empire. It was not simply military domination of the stronger over the weaker, which had existed for thousands of years. Nineteenth-century empires constituted an attempt to create a multinational political formation, an imperial enclave in the world. As Trotsky[2] noted before the First World War, empire constituted a struggle for a world capitalist system, an aspiration to world government. Today, what we have is not that, multinational empire, but political-military domination, distinguished only by the fact that it is global.

The Left in its heyday developed a grand theory that locked territorial extension into the mutations in the economic centre of the system (and so recognised the historical specificity of the moment – the British empire was not just a repetition of the ancient empires). Combining Hilferding on finance capital with Hobson on the creation of political empire, Lenin in his short popular pamphlet created a spectacular analysis that has been possibly the only one of his works which is still read.

The trouble is that it is wrong. Not only did finance capital not emerge in most of the capitalist powers (Hilferding's example was Germany, not Britain or the US), the link to territorial expansion was obscure; capital did not suffer from a shortage of territory. More to the point the extension of empire did not seem to relate closely to the changing interests of national capital. Indeed, as Kidron showed long ago in his account of India,[3] British political power in India came to protect the more backward sections of British capital. The more advanced sections did not rely on the British State – they hustled and profited beyond its power, in North and South America, in Russia, Eastern and Western Europe. And the more advanced sections of capital in India were not at all unhappy at the British imperial evacuation, managing and prospering in the transition to independence. Indeed, this lack of close association between British capital

2 Trotsky 1971.
3 Kidron 1965.

and the British State undermined the classical account, raising the question, if the State was the 'executive committee of the bourgeoisie', what was it doing in India, incurring unnecessary military costs? Of course, the State might find raw materials, markets, loot, manpower for its armies, some of which might benefit British capital, but these were not normally the initiating motives. Imperial expansion was driven, first and foremost, not by the aims of business, but by the rivalry of States – to prevent other States getting an advantage. This is at its clearest in the late nineteenth century carve up of Africa.

Some of these motives remain important today, but are much weaker (*pace* the US, oil and the Gulf) simply because world markets now force all resources into sale, without the need to bear the costs of expropriating them by force. Thus, each historical phase of the system is different and must be characterised by its specific context. Today, one might infer that the world's oil companies (including those called 'American') would have a powerful interest in opposing wars in the oil-producing areas because it is so damaging to oil production (the wells and refineries), and the companies know any oil-producing States are obliged to sell their oil to those who control the downstream market outlets. Of course, none of this may influence the dominant States whose power is vested in violence – and their competition with other States may impel them to grab what they can to exclude competing States, whether or not this wrecks the oil wells. Such armed intervention would only make economic sense if, for example, Washington had a coherent bloc of US companies that it intended to supply on a privileged basis with its captured oil. But that is a fantasy. In the real world, the US State cannot pre-empt the oil supply to 'its' companies, and Washington knows that Iraq is obliged to sell its oil to survive.

More to the point, important segments of what used to be called US companies have gone global, adopting whatever nationality suits their commercial interests and their global supply chains (crossing many countries). Such a case should not be exaggerated – after all, one of the largest territorial concentrations of capital in the world is the 'military-industrial complex', supporting the US military forces, and of necessity that is tied closely to Washington. However, this also should not be exaggerated – while the US military budget (and the US taxpayer) remain important for this complex, companies here are also being driven to globalise – to supply global arms markets and depend on global supply networks and global sources of technical innovation. Thus, even in this, the most extreme form of national capitalism, globalisation is, despite the best efforts of Washington to frustrate the process, undermining the national hold. In much of the rest of 'US capitalism', the denationalisation of capital is sufficiently advanced to suggest it cannot be renationalised without insupportable economic damage.

The current economic crisis has shown us, however, that despite the deep-rooted trends, the State has been required to finance its threatened segments of business, primarily in banking and automobiles. This has undoubtedly recon-solidated the power of the State over what is left of national capital. And the joy of some national politicians – Sarkozy, Berlusconi – at this reaffirmation of State power against economic globalisation is apparent. But they are fools if they think they can restore the *ancien regime*. 'French business' cannot survive without global markets – certainly not on the basis of the little French market.

The globalisation of capital – shown most vividly in the extraordinary speed with which companies from some developing countries have embraced the trends – has sharply underlined that the agenda of States is not at all the same as that of business. Lenin's phrase to describe the State – 'the executive committee of the bourgeoisie' – was rarely true historically. Now it is rarely ever true.

Thus, to return to the discussion of imperialism, national self-determination does not give power to a national State to shape or create its economic destiny, the basis for the material welfare of its inhabitants. That requires an accom-modation between the new State and global capital. National self-determi-nation has become a utopian aspiration. Nor is this simply a matter of eco-nomic issues. The State system predetermines the context within which each State acts, determines the choices to be made, and this is the most powerful component in State activity, rather than the wishes or interests of the national population.

To describe the world as US imperialism implies that liberation lies in nat-ional self-determination, an aim that has become simultaneously utopian and reactionary. It conceals the reality – a global capitalist economy (determined by global markets), and a fractured political order of competing States, incapable at the same time of unified political action or of creating a global government.

Capital itself appears incapable of filling the vacuum, of creating a global political order that corresponds to a global economic system. In such a context, Washington's power of violence is the nearest there is to world government, except that it is too puny to govern the world – that would require an order that drew on the voluntary support of the world's inhabitants, not the deals of the national mafias.

Mike Kidron, half a century ago,[4] deployed the case as to why the term imperialism should be consigned in the main to the historic past where it could retain some precision. In its place he put 'international capitalism' – he

---

4   Kidron 1974b, pp. 124–42. See also Kidron 1974c, pp. 143–67.

was writing long before globalisation was dreamed of, but, with remarkable prescience, I think he was already sensing our world.

What are the political implications? The Left has remained enslaved to the nationalism of oppressed nations for far too long – it is time that it rediscovered people, rather than nations, States or proposed States. In this process, States – and their monopoly of violence – rather than capital (and its exploitation of labour) are the central target, the central obstacle to human progress. Globalisation is profoundly weakening the State, but the process is very slow and must be speeded if we are to reach a world of people.

Can the West Survive?*

This article discusses the now universal process of macro-economic reform or structural adjustment, and its implications for the growing importance of developing countries for the economic growth of the developed countries. However, a negative by-product of this growing integration of the two is seen in the decline in incomes of the lowest stratum of the workforce in developed countries and the increasingly unequal distribution of income, attributed to labour-intensive imports from developing countries. The Stolper-Samuelson theoretical explanation for this is discussed and assessed, along with the now substantial economic literature on the description and explanation of the declining incomes of the low-skilled. The article then discusses the signific- ance of the growing role of services in the developed economies, arguing that developing countries are likely to be increasingly competitive in a growing range of labour-intensive services, without which technically more advanced activity cannot take place. Furthermore, the ageing of the developed countries' population is likely to increase the demand for services, particularly labour- intensive ones, and hence increase the dependence upon the youthful labour forces of developing countries. In sum, these trends seem likely to make the maintenance of the standard of living of the developed countries increasingly dependent upon the labour forces of the developing countries, making the old patterns of political domination impossible to sustain.

Introduction

Over the past two decades, the world has undergone an extraordinary process of structural change, a process far from complete even now. After at least a century and a half of State-domination of the economy in the developed coun- tries (and a shorter period in the developing countries), almost all governments are instituting programmes of reform both to reduce and reorganise the State domestically and open their economies to world markets. While the package of reforms is varied in detail and timing, in essence it has a remarkably similar form, regardless of the income level or stage of development of the country concerned.

---

* From: *Competition and Change*, 1995, I, pp. 111–22.

The package has also been implemented apparently independently of the political commitment of the governments concerned. It is best known as part of the agenda of the liberal Right (as opposed to the corporatist Right) in Britain and the United States under the respective administrations of Mrs Thatcher and President Reagan in the 1980s. But there were earlier examples of comparable policy shifts following the military coup against Sukarno's regime in Indonesia (1965) and against Allende in Chile (1973). Those were on the supposed political 'Right'. But the dramatic changes of policy in China after 1978 were initiated and sustained by a Communist regime, supposedly of the 'Left'. Even Cuba has made some gestures to the same trend, and Vietnam has been among the more radical in adopting the liberalisation programme since 1989. In Chile and Indonesia, authoritarian regimes following a military coup, spearheaded the reforms. In South Korea, Taiwan and Eastern Europe, democratising regimes followed suit. In Argentina (with the Peronist President, Menem) and Mexico (under the PRI Presidents de la Madrid and Salinas), corporatist-populist regimes with a strong earlier commitment to import-substitution industrialisation strategies, have completely reversed long-standing policies of economic nationalism. In Australia, New Zealand, Spain and Portugal, Labour or Social Democratic governments have been the reformers.

Such a universal process suggests governments are reacting not so much to changed domestic conditions (although this is how reforms are most frequently justified), so much as a changed world economy. The reforms are attempts to adjust and readjust the domestic economy and public administration to changed external conditions. The timing is different as governments are pushed into reforms of growing radicalism by short-term crises (in the external or budgetary balances), but the trend appears universal. The changes in the world which impel these adjustments are not under the control of governments, so they have the appearance in each country of being inexorable, outside the power of choice: governments appear to be faced with the stark options of reform or collapse. The shift disorients all politics based upon the assumption that government controls the destiny of the country concerned rather than simply managing an element of a world system. It is especially disorienting for the socialists since historically they vested in the idea of the State virtually unlimited power to determine the domestic economy.

The elements of the changed world economy of greatest importance are now well-known: the international integration of manufacturing systems and commodity trade, of capital and financial markets, and to a much more limited extent, of labour markets. A by-product of the process is the beginnings of a shift – or a diversification – in the geographical location of the world economy with important implications in terms of the distribution of political power. On the World Bank's Purchasing Power Parity values (with the Bank's projections), the developing countries will overtake the developed in terms of share of world output by 1996; and by the year 2020 the share held by the developed will have declined to not much over one third.

The developed are for the first time in the modern period becoming increasingly dependent upon trade with the developing countries. The developing will account for possibly two thirds of the world's imports over the next quarter century. Even now, the developing take 42 percent of the exports of the United States, 47 percent of the extra-European trade of the European Union, and 48 percent of Japan's exports.

Furthermore, the growth of the countries of the Asia Pacific Rim in the period since 1987 has, for the first time, become partially decoupled from the growth of the United States and Europe so that growth in East and South-East Asia was not depressed by the downturn on the other side of the Pacific. At least for the moment, these countries have come to constitute an alternative centre of growth in the system.

The speed of change in East and South-East Asia is likely to exaggerate the relocation of trade flows and industrial capacity. OECD calculates that with only a 6 percent rate of annual growth in the three major economies, China, India and Indonesia, by the year 2010, they will have created a market for Developed Country exports of 700 million people (with an average income equivalent to that of Spain today, and roughly the same size as the markets of Europe, North America and Japan today).[1]

Capital flows from the developed countries are, despite short-term countertrends, beginning to reflect the emergence of these high growth 'emerging' markets. International banks are seeking to tap the new incomes generated in the Asia Pacific rim, and a clutch of new transnational corporations have emerged there. International companies generally are suddenly willing to risk their name and a little of their capital in positioning themselves in these new areas of growth.

Changes in technology interacting with the opening up of markets are tending to produce a long-term decline in manufacturing in many developed countries, and the disproportionate growth of services. There are, of course, severe conceptual problems in measuring services, but it does appear that a decreasing proportion of the workforce in developed countries are engaged in the direct production of tangible goods.

---

1   *The Economist* 1994, pp. 13–14.

Furthermore, manufacturing output in the developed countries is already increasingly dependent upon manufactured imports, a growing share of which derives from developing countries. The supposedly autonomous national basis for production (upon which government policy seeks to act) is tending to decline, and governments are increasingly required simply to react in clear well-known and unequivocal ways to external signals. The term 'countries' becomes analytically a problem since it is unclear how far there is either a clearcut entity or, if there is, a coincidence of interest between government, the inhabitants of a given geographical area and a discrete share of the world's capital, leading Robert Reich to ask, 'Can we any longer be a society if we are no longer an economy?'

Global integration does not take place on terms of equality, nor are its effects on different countries the same. There are few guides as to what kinds of effects can be expected. One of the few theoretical positions available deduces that 'factor prices' will be equalised, an alarming proposition for many in the developed countries. This theme provides the entry point to a discussion of the possible future of the relationship between developed and developing countries.

Wages and Employment

The growth of the world economy has in the past continually produced a redistribution of capacity, output and income – in contrast to the common belief that 'centres' always remain central, 'peripheries' peripheral. This is illustrated in the clear shift of economic and political importance from Britain to the United States, Germany and the rest of Western Europe, and then to Japan – without this lowering the incomes of the former leading powers. Nonetheless, redistribution of activity can be an alarming element in the normal restructuring of economies, appearing to change the balance of political power in the world and encouraging popular fears. Everyone knows what they once worked at, but no one can see in advance what future jobs will be available – who could have foreseen the growth of computer programming alongside the decline in coal mining (especially given that different people were involved)?

In terms of academic economics, the fears that Europe and North America will be denuded of employment have revived an interest in a theoretical proposition originally advanced in 1941 and known as the Stolper-Samuelson theorem. This argues, under a given set of assumptions, that with increasing free trade, rewards to the factor of production employed most intensively in imports will decline (and rewards to the factor of production employed most intensively in exports will increase). Later refinements produced the more general theorem that, with free trade (and under very restrictive assumptions), factor prices would tend to equalise between the trading countries.[2]

Put in contemporary terms, this would imply that insofar as the developed countries import goods which employ intensively unskilled labour, the pay of unskilled workers in those countries would fall, and insofar as they export goods which use intensively skilled labour, the pay of skilled workers would increase (correlatively, the pay of unskilled workers in the countries from which the imports come, say developing countries, would rise and that of skilled workers decline). Thus, as a result of freer trade, the developed countries would experience increased inequality of income from work in the external trade sector, and the developing countries, decreased inequality of income. This would constitute the mechanism by which the equalisation of factor prices between the trading partners would occur.

The theory might have seemed relevant to the United States during the long postwar boom in the world economy. In 1950, German wages were 13 percent of those in the United States, and British wages, 17 percent (Mexican wages today are about 12 percent of US levels).[3] In the following two decades, the United States lowered its trade barriers and expanded its trade with low income Europe. However, contrary to the theory, real wages in the United States rose steadily and the differential between the skilled and unskilled actually declined.

In the 1980s, however, this trend changed. For over a century, productivity had doubled every 32 years and hourly output per worker increased by over two percent per year. Each generation came to take for granted a doubling in the standard of living between parents and children. In the two decades from 1973, however, average real compensation increased in total by something of the order of 5.5 percent (whereas, if the past projections had been borne out, it should have increased by over 50 percent). Furthermore, the negative effects increased, the lower the level of skill – in the 1980s, the real wage of men with 12 or less years schooling declined by 20 percent. Household incomes could only be improved – as they were – while productivity stagnated through increased employment (increased numbers working and increased hours worked) and, for the country as a whole, through borrowing abroad.

In Europe, where real wages grew annually by some 1 to 2 percent, institutional constraints are credited with preventing a decline in wages for the

---

2   Samuelson 1948 and 1949.
3   Lawrence 1994.

unskilled – but at the cost of rising levels of long-term unemployment (in 1991, whereas 6.3 percent of the unemployed in the United States had been out of work for 12 months or longer, in Germany, France, Britain and Italy, the share was closer to 40 percent).[4]

Whether it is the intellectual stimulus of the Stolper-Samuelson thesis or the objective social problem, the issue has provoked an avalanche of economic analysis. Both in popular opinion and in some academic contributions,[5] imports from low-income countries have frequently been identified as the source of the problem. It is not necessary to stress the grave political dangers involved in the argument – no sooner have some developing countries achieved some success in exporting manufactured goods (as Western governments have been urging for several decades) than popular opinion seeks to terminate the opportunity.

Forty years ago the creation of development economics was in part founded on the Prebisch proposition[6] that trade between more and less developed countries, 'centres' and 'peripheries' in Prebisch's terms, would inexorably lead to the underdevelopment of the weaker partner – trade was the source of underdevelopment, created and sustained it. It is ironic that now an opposite proposition should be attaining equal popularity – trade leads to the decline of the developed countries, and in particular, the deterioration in the position of the poor in the rich countries. Parts of the centres are becoming peripheries.

Economists do not agree about the source of the declining real wages of the unskilled. On the face of it, the share in apparent consumption of the developed countries of manufactured imports from developing countries (4.5 percent for the US, 3 percent for the European Union, 2 percent for Japan) would seem far too small to influence the domestic labour market or the distribution of income. However, Wood argues that the impact of these imports on the sectors which in the past employed unskilled workers is very much greater than allowed for in the aggregate figures on shares of consumption – hence the increase in poverty.[7]

There are stronger objections to the thesis than simply the size of current imports of labour-intensive goods. Stolper-Samuelson is built upon highly restrictive assumptions, and the factor price equalisation thesis indicates no time period of adjustment nor in which direction adjustment takes place (in

4   OECD 1994, p. 47.

5   See, for example, Reich 1991; Murphy and Welch 1993; Learner 1994; Wood 1994.

6   See ECLA 1950 and 1951; Emmanuel 1972; Amin 1974; Frank 1979.

7   See Wood 1994.

the case of the United States and Mexico, there are grounds for believing Mexican wages will be raised rather then those of the United States lowered). More importantly, matching elements – including the price behaviour of labour-intensive goods[8] and the failure of skilled wages in developing countries to decline – encourage scepticism that imports can explain in large part the changes in incomes in the developed countries. On the other hand, increasing inequality of income is reported from developing countries (whereas, on the theory, it ought to be declining if trade were so important). Furthermore, in the United States, the income changes seem to affect all sectors, not just those directly involved in foreign trade, an outcome which would seem to suggest new technology affecting all sectors was the primary source of an increasing demand for skilled workers and a decline for unskilled workers (at the going wage) rather than increased imports from developing countries.

The absolute decline in the position of the poorest workers in the United States has raised an old issue in Marxist literature – that of 'immiserisation'. Indeed, it led Bhagwati and Deheja to subtitle their solidly orthodox contribution, 'Is Marx striking again?'. However, the issue is not the general pauperisation of the working class as a whole, but the impoverishment of the very lowest stratum of workers alongside increased income inequality. Between 1964 and 1988, income from work in the top decile of the United States earners increased 40 percent but in the bottom decile, declined by five percent. In the European case, a similar widening of differentials seems to have occurred in most countries, although not in Denmark, Finland, Italy and Norway; and in Germany, incomes of the bottom decile increased relative to the top. The OECD attributes these deviations from what seem to be a common feature of developed countries in the 1980s to 'institutional constraints' on the operation of the labour market.[9]

However, each national labour market need not be directly influenced by external factors (as embodied in imports) while a minority of workers are – global integration may have created a world market for a small minority of the more scarce skills. The defence of a disportionate recent salary increase for the Chief Executive of British Gas borrowed from this argument – in an international market, scarce skills had to be rewarded at international rates. Leaving aside the blatantly self-interested character of the argument in this particular case, it is possible that top pay rates are being pulled up to those prevailing in the highest paying centres, while the national pay earnings structure remains

---

8   Bhagwati and Deheja 1994.

9   OECD 1993.

determined by local productivity levels, producing an increased dispersal in the distribution of national incomes. However, the number of people concerned is very small, so small it would seem the phenomenon would not be capable of influencing general levels of income inequality.

Nonetheless, popular perceptions of increasing poverty and inequality (the two are not necessarily related) feed growing anxieties which can – on the ancient conservative principle of always blaming the foreigner for anything which goes wrong – attribute both problems to growing internationalisation. This is particularly so when the increasing influence of external markets appears to oblige governments to reassess prices in the non-traded sectors, particularly social and medical provision. Part of the population, exposed for whatever reasons to declining incomes or increased unemployment, are thus faced with a withdrawal or dilution of social support at just the time when it is most needed. A reaction to internationalisation would then appear to be an attempt to return to the golden age, combining high employment and accept-able wages for the unskilled, the protections of a welfare State, and powerful, apparently autonomous national governments. The case for a revival of eco-nomic – and hence political – nationalism would have been established.

However, serious analysis suggests, as mentioned earlier, that if 'factor price equalisation' is at work through labour-intensive imports, the effect can only be a small one. This is not to say such forces will not exercise a more powerful influence in the future, particularly as some very large countries – China, India, Indonesia, Bangladesh – come fully on stream in terms of manufactured exports. However, if the overall rate of world growth is high, even those changes can be absorbed without major rupture – as powerful structural changes in Europe and North America were absorbed in the high growth years of the 1950s and 1960s.

Dependency

While the share of the markets of developed countries taken by manufactured imports from developing countries still remains small, their rate of growth, magnified in particular sectors, is still high enough to suggest a sustained shift in manufacturing capacity is taking place. The manufactured output of each of the developed countries seems set to become increasingly dependent upon imports – and thus the workforce – from the developing countries. Fur-thermore, the manufactured exports of the developed countries seem likely to become increasingly dependent upon the purchasing power of markets in developing countries (a trend apparent in the vehicle industry).

However, the world's obsession with manufactured goods is misplaced. Services are growing more swiftly, and the international trade in services is becoming increasingly important. Contrary to many views, the shift to services in the developed world is unlikely to reduce the dependence upon inputs from developing countries – on the contrary, as we argue below, this dependence is likely to increase.

The issues concerning international trade in services emerged but remained unresolved during the Uruguay GATT round of negotiations. Initially, the US representatives pressed leading developing countries to permit the entry of US providers of services (banking, insurance, shipping, etc.), to which the developing country representatives countered with the demand to ease the entry to developed countries of their providers of temporary labour-intensive services (for example, in hotels and restaurants, domestic service, cleaning, construction, hospital work, etc.). In both cases, liberalisation of the trade required increased international movement of the service-providers, the workers, directly affecting national immigration controls. The discussion stopped although after the Round, US trade representatives continued to press governments in the larger developing countries to admit American service exports (as in the case of US insurance services, pressed on India during the visit of the US Trade Secretary in January 1995).

However, the arms-length exchange of separate services is less important than the division of labour emerging in the world production of the same services. Earlier manufacturing was unbundled, with labour-intensive inputs being outsourced to developing countries. Now the same thing seems to be happening in services – for example, in data-loading and processing, accountancy, software programming. The evidence is anecdotal – Swiss Air moving its accountancy services to Bombay, India emerging as a software programming centre for Silicon Valley, British police records being loaded in the Philippines, Canadian medical records and US airline ticketing being processed in the Caribbean, Japanese real estate transactions being handled in China, etc. – but the trend fits what seems intuitively to be the case in terms of factor endowments.

However, important service provisions in the developed countries cannot be relocated nor easily unbundled. As W.R. Bohning once put it, 'if dustbins need emptying in Munich, the workers for the job must be found on the spot'.[10] Furthermore, the unskilled labour inputs involved here are often vital in making possible the work of skilled workers (most starkly in the relationship between

---

10   Bohning 1972.

the provision of creches or home-help and the employment of highly skilled parents – most commonly, skilled women). Despite high levels of unemployment in Europe, there are serious labour scarcities in many of these unskilled activities – at the wage on offer, there is an insufficient supply. This suggests that, for whatever reason, the average expected wage in developed countries prices out the provision of key services, which in turn jeopardises the possibility of skilled workers attaining full productivity.

However, in the world at large, labour at the wages on offer in a developed country for labour-intensive services is not a scarce factor. Indeed, at those rates of pay, the supply is virtually unlimited. The possible future liberalisation of world trade in services thus implies a relaxation in the current immigration regulations governing entry to the developed countries in order to allow the mobile service-providers to move to the immobile service-consumers. Internationalising the competitive tendering for public contracts raises both the possibility of firms in developed countries raising workforces, even if temporarily, in developing countries (as already happens in construction for projects in third countries, in the merchant marine, in some sectors of agriculture, etc.), or firms from developing countries tendering for contracts directly – in a mass of activities, from cleaning, staffing hospitals and restaurants, domestic and personal services to construction. If liberalising trade in services weakened migration controls, then one of the last protectionist bastions of the old national economic order of the world would have started to crumble.

Ageing

The problem of labour supply in the developed countries is scheduled to get worse. The developed countries, closely followed by the East Asian Newly Industrialising Countries, face a demographic conjuncture of declining fertility (and thus, in due course, a declining number of new entrants to the labour force) and increasing longevity. Consider some of the projections. In the 1990s, the world's labour force is projected to increase by 800 million, 93 percent of this increase occurring in developing countries. Between 1985 and the year 2000, the developed countries are expected to increase their total population by 14 percent (and the developing by 103 percent); their working population, aged 15 to 65, by 6 percent (developing countries, 130 percent); their young labour force, aged 20 to 40, will actually decline by 10 percent (but in the developing countries it will increase by 108 percent).

Even this overstates the position since simultaneously increasing numbers in the working population of the developed countries are not working. Education takes a growing proportion of working life, workers are taking retirement increasingly early, and the working week and year have for a long period tended to contract. With rising levels of skills in the workforce, the shortages will occur particularly in the army of unskilled support workers.

Is it conceivable that automation could fully make up for this shortfall at an acceptable cost? There are clearly areas where this would be feasible, so that labour demand need not increase in the developed countries as fast as the decline in the labour hours on offer would imply. But there are at least two issues here where qualification is needed. The first concerns the relationship between household incomes of the mass of the population and the cost of substituting capital – for labour-intensive services. Automation may be economically feasible for richer households, but can it resolve the problem for the mass? Second, much of the increased labour demand as the population ages is in the 'caring professions', personal services, and these are least susceptible to automation – or at least, even where capital substitution can take place, it will not relieve the dependence on human inputs.

Leaving aside the fiscal problems in the provision of pensions for a growing number of the aged, drawn from a declining workforce (the subject which has received most attention), the implications of ageing are much wider and affect both the distribution of economic activity and labour force, and the balance of political power. Suffice it to note that countries most affected face a decline in the size of population – for example, Germany is projected to decline from 76 to 65 million between 1986 and 2010. The supply of young workers will fall even more drastically, and the cost of employing them is likely to rise significantly. An observer of the US relationship to Mexico, Charles Crowder, addressing a Congressional hearing, anticipating the shortage of labour, saw Mexico's supply of young workers saving its northern neighbour:

> As our population becomes older, the problem will not be to find jobs for people, but people for jobs. For many years, Mexico with its relatively young and expanding population will complement and balance our own as well as provide a formidable defence to the attack on our position in world markets.[11]

Indeed, the heart of the power of the State, its armed forces, depend directly on the supply of young men (and now women). Can we envisage a time when the supply of recruits will be insufficient to execute US policy? Will it be possible for

---

11   US Congress 1990, p. 309.

modern governments to return to the old policy of hiring young mercenaries – from developing countries? It would fit the modern rage for privatisation, putting out the US Marines contract for global tendering, but it would also strike a profound blow at the idea of the nation-State and its citizen-army. On the other hand, the Great Powers would no longer have to be concerned with the domestic political implications of high casualty rates.

In sum, for the developed countries as a whole, the shortage of labour-time on offer at the going wage, particularly in unskilled occupations, coincides with ageing, and as a consequence, a major increase in the demand for labour-intensive services.

The processes are already underway, and as a result are producing a relocation of some labour-intensive services. For example, medical services are disportionately developed on the Mexican side of the southern border of the United States. They have been created to cater for the aged Americans who spend the winter there (as well as the Hispanic population of the southern States; the unrestricted availability of drugs legally controlled in the north is also a factor). Other Americans are choosing to move to where the labour force is, migrating southwards to Mexico and Central America. The RV parks dot the Pacific coast of Mexico far to the south. Already the development of settlements in developing countries designed for the aged (the better-off ones) from the developed countries is a growth area for property speculation.

However, on present prospects, it seems unlikely that enough of the aged will migrate to the developing countries (which may, in any case, be ill-prepared to accept the newcomers), or that the aged will be able to commute to services (as is possible with health provision on the US-Mexican border). It will be the poorer majority who will be the least mobile, the least able to meet the costs of moving to labour-intensive services. If the welfare of the populations of the developed countries is to be protected, there will have to be a relaxation of immigration controls for unskilled workers.

Conclusion

In sum, the next half century is likely to see a more remarkable change in the distribution of economic activity and political power than has been seen before. This will involve the continued relative decline of 'the West', that is, the domination of the world by a small group of very powerful States in America, Europe and East Asia. The developed countries are set to become increasingly dependent upon the developing, in terms of markets for their output and capital and a workforce to sustain their economies. Part of that dependence seems likely to force a lowering of the last great barriers dividing both humanity and the world economy, migration controls.

It is, however, part of a broader process, the relative decline of the State. The State, for so long the incubator of national capital, is losing this role to global markets. The West, the group of dominant States, initiated world capitalism, contributed mightily to its expansion and technical transformation. But it also has responsibility for the savageries of empire, for two World Wars, the Great Depression, the long years of Cold War punctuated by the growing barbarities of sporadic hot wars. Such achievements dwarf our contemporary problems.

Thus, the West is being superseded by a global system with much more diversified sources of wealth and power, much of it outside official supervision. This does not mean the material decline of the inhabitants of what was the West (any more than the relative decline of 'Britain' over the past century and a half entails the decline in the living standards of the British). The comparative advantages of the workforce of the developed countries remain powerful even if the capacity of their governments to bully the rest of the world declines. The density of skills and the mastery of technical innovation remain strong. The leading developing countries will rapidly catch up on present standards, but by then the workers of the developed countries will have moved on to new fields. Furthermore, the diversification of sources of economic growth may give much greater stability to the world system than was possible when the major part of modern economic activity was focused simply upon the Atlantic area.

Thus there are no grounds for particular pessimism in the decline of the West; indeed, it could be seen as a matter for rejoicing, particularly if it reduces the possibility of world war. The decline does not, of course, remedy the endemic problems of the world. Entrenched poverty in sub-Saharan Africa and South Asia, inequalities and oppression, localised savage wars remain – and in some cases, may get worse. But, hopefully, classical imperialism can at last be declared at an end.

On Economic Globalisation, Neo-liberalism and the Nature of the Period[*]

For long, the term 'imperialism' was popular to denote a world political order embodying systemic relations of domination with Washington at the centre. That thesis is no longer considered valid. Washington itself is victim to a global capitalist order and is mired in an apparently insoluble economic crisis. Here are some notes for discussion on an alternative approach to characterising the world order.

The charge of 'imperialism' has served the Left for a very long time as a supreme accusation against the political order of the world. The term implies not that strong states invariably try to bully weaker ones, nor that 'imperialism' is just a fancy name for Washington, but that there is a world political order embodying systemic relations of domination. However, while once there might have been relatively robust theoretical underpinnings to this approach (in Lenin's popularisation of the combination of Hobson and Hilferding),[1] the thesis has long since been shown to be doubtful.[2] On the other hand, imperialism's opposite, 'national self-determination', seems equally of doubtful validity in conditions of economic globalisation. Indeed, these theoretical difficulties become even sharper when it is recognised that Washington, the supposed global hegemon, is itself trapped in an apparently insoluble crisis in the global economic order – the political agenda comes apart from the economic. What follows are some notes for discussion on an alternative approach to characterising the world order.

(1) Since about 1980, the world economy and its constituent national parts, has been dominated by the transition to a single global economy, 'economic globalisation'. This imposes on the world a changing pattern of territorial specialisation and interdependence, organised by global markets, not – as hitherto rightly or wrongly believed – by national states. The economic integration of

---

[*] From: *Economic & Political Weekly*, 47/22, 2012.

[1] The literature is now so historic, it hardly seems worth enumerating but see Lenin 1936a, p. 53; Hobson 1902; Hilferding 1981.

[2] The literature here is enormous, but by way of example, see Kidron 1974b, pp. 123–39 and Harris 1974, pp. 155–205.

the separate political territories (former 'national economies') into a single economic system has been achieved by states (at different times and stages) relinquishing control of external trade, of capital movement and finally, albeit partially, of labour. Indeed, by now it is doubtful in the core of the system whether 'national economies' – discrete territorial areas of autonomous economic activity, defined by political boundaries – any longer exist as objects of effective government policy. States here at best seek to manage global economic flows that begin and end beyond both their authority and even knowledge. The free flow of the global factors of production is creating a single integrated economy outside the control of any one national political authority[3] (as in the original creation of national economies free movement within carved out a national economic entity from what had been often a regional economy – witness, for example, the formation of Germany or the partition of India). The destruction of the old Soviet Union and the former eastern bloc, of apartheid in South Africa, as well as the coming transformations of others (North Korea, Myanmar, Cuba, etc.) can be seen as only the more extreme examples of this apparently inexorable process of economic globalisation.

(2) The first phase of the current transition has been characterised both by extraordinary levels of prosperity in the heartlands of the system (the Atlantic economy and Japan) and an unprecedented geographical spread of economic growth (to China, East and Southeast Asia, Eastern Europe to Latin America, and latterly to India). This in turn may now draw into the process sub-Saharan Africa. In the first phase, opinion rejoiced that apparently the world had mastered the secret of sustained and spreading economic growth; in the second, marred at the end by severe economic crisis in the heartlands, there were growing fears that globalisation had robbed the world of political governance, the state, and imposed a global territorial division of labour which made it impossible to employ the mass of the labour force, implying long-term mass unemployment. There seemed to be simultaneously an existential political crisis of the state and an economic crisis of material survival.[4]

---

3 The topic is difficult to discuss, in part because the data and policy discussion are defined by the current distribution of political power. Statistics and concern are defined by national states and their interests. The subject of a global economy is thus mystified through the perspective of competing states. Indeed, some see the story of the world economy as little more than the competition for shares of output of different states, rather than states being, as it were, corks on the waves of global economic churning.

4 In an overheated political context, the fears were wildly exaggerated, muddling the relative position of one state with the condition of populations. The concentration of skilled labour, research facilities and infrastructure, not to mention the role of the heartlands in providing

(3) Historically, the current transition is the second[5] great surge towards economic globalisation. The first, between say 1870 and 1914,[6] ended with two world wars and the Great Slump in which states not only clawed back powers they had conceded to global markets, but immensely enhanced and centralised political control over their respective national economies to an unprecedented degree, epitomised in the extraordinary concentration of state power in Nazi Germany and Soviet Russia. More generally, the period established an uncritical faith in the potential of state planning and dominant public sectors, nowhere more so than in Nehru's India. Everywhere governments mimicked the imperatives of the war economy, even in peacetime. It took nearly another half century after the end of the Second World War to resume the drive to economic globalisation, now with much enhanced vigour and comprehensiveness, and encompassing the whole world, not just the Atlantic economy.

(4) Indeed, never before in the history of capitalism, it seems, has the ethic of competitive markets and 'neo-liberalism' penetrated so deeply into the domestic operations of the state, into virtually every cell of the social order. 'Neo-liberalism' has established an extraordinary intellectual hegemony, founded not upon an excess of greed (that was always there), nor an intellectual error among economists, but rather as the ideological expression of an order of global capital – the neo-liberals are the product of the process, not its source. We are now within sight of the reversal of many of the major historical efforts to limit the power of markets – from the New Deal and Great Society legislation in the US (even including the right to collective bargaining) to the welfare state and social services in Europe. In the period from the 1950s to the present, there has been an almost complete reversal of the dominant statist narrative. In that time, in the developing countries, accelerated economic growth was seen as exclusively attainable through economic isolation, closure to the world; now it is seen as exclusively attainable through 'opening up'.

---

safe refuges for the global rich, should give the heartlands an indispensable global role far into the future, even if the relative pecking order of states changes.

5   A still earlier 'surge' might be seen – following Kautsky – in the period of colonial empires. See also Tirthankar 2012, pp. 98–105.

6   Summed up presciently (if prematurely) in 1914 by Leon Trotsky: 'The natural tendency of our economic system is to seek to break through the state boundaries. The whole globe, the land and the sea, the surface as well as the interior, has become one economic workshop, the different parts of which are inseparably connected with each other ... The present War (World War I [NH]) is at bottom the revolt of the forces of production against the political form of nation and state. It means the political collapse of the national state as an independent economic unit' – Trotsky 1971.

(5) 'Opening up' the national economy (and undertaking all the domestic reforms for this to work) involves allowing the integration of national and global economies, allowing domestic economic activity to be decided by global markets rather than by the state – or electoral – priorities. By implication, the state relinquishes any ambition to shape the domestic economy in any particular direction, restricting itself to managing efficiently and facilitating the accommodation of global forces.

(6) However, the emergence of a national 'global state' (that is, a state, the function of which is to manage the local economy and society in conformity with global, not local, imperatives) profoundly weakens the political position of the State, compared to the past. The state is obliged to relinquish much of what used to be a national political agenda which involves the management of external trade, capital movements and, in principle, labour flows. It relinquishes power to bribe the electorate and to secure its political perpetuation, to reward patrons, etc. To put it simplistically, it faces contradictory options – to secure economic growth (through integration in the world economy) but with weakened state control over its political environment; or to enhance its political dominance at home with economic stagnation. Of course, depending on specific circumstances of a particular state (and the cumulative effect of past policies), opening up to the world may not lead to economic growth, in which case the state has no recourse except to rule by violence. In an existential crisis (such as, for example, faces the Assad regime in Syria), the state will be obliged to sacrifice present and future economic growth – and indeed, the inhabitants – to hold on to power.

(7) The threat to state power is political in a different way – through undermining the domestic social solidarity that is supposedly a precondition for stable government. No population is likely to remain indefinitely loyal to a state seen as working exclusively for foreigners (the 'world system'). Nowhere is this more apparent in developed countries than in the field of immigration. The mobility of labour internationally seems now to be a precondition for economic growth. No advanced economy is now self-sufficient in labour (including here the changing diversity of skills required to cope with changes in the economy imposed by changing global demand). However, the solidarity underpinning the old state required levels of xenophobia, and sometimes racism which are incompatible with continued immigration, required to sustain the 'churning' of the labour force to sustain economic growth (especially where there are high levels of native unemployment). Everywhere today, certainly in the heartlands, there are increasing restrictions on immigration and mobility, despite the damage this does to economic growth (not to speak of the welfare of an ageing native-born population). States are again caught in a

contradiction – the conditions of growth undermine the elements of national closure (zero net migration) supposedly required to make state power secure (seen most vividly in North Korea and the old Stalinist states).

(8) It is perhaps this contradictory position which today inhibits states from copying the reactions to the interwar Great Depression which ended the first surge of globalisation – economic closure and domestic authoritarianism. The reaction now is fragmentary and contradictory – moves to authoritarianism,[7] along with continued neo-liberal reform, attempts to cut immigration, to demonise 'illegal immigrants' (and Muslims) but without systematic protectionism. Of course, the longer the crisis persists, the more it may become an existential issue for the state, especially if marked by popular revolt against economic austerity. The greater the danger, the more states will seek to recover their lost powers, and reverse economic globalisation, sacrificing the welfare of their own – and the world inhabitants – to their own political survival. The issue of a world slump was only settled last time around by resort to a world war and a terrible orgy of self-destruction. At the moment, world war seems unlikely but one should not underestimate the potential for auto-destruction when one or other state's existence appears threatened, producing the 'common ruin of the contending nations/classes'.

(9) These trends – if 'trends' they are – go with attempts to disenfranchise the citizenry, to isolate government from 'politics', to protect the global system (and states) from popular demands and pressures, and install technical or expert administration (the World Bank and International Monetary Fund play a key role here in training a global cadre of experts to direct the financial administration of states). Independent central banks – and independent national statistical agencies – are required to reassure 'global investors' that mere governments – or 'politics' – cannot be allowed to interfere with either monetary policy or basic data. In the special case of Europe, experts have been parachuted in to run Greece and Italy, and binding clauses inserted in respective constitutions to enshrine conditions of national management. Some of the language betrays the displacement of the sovereign people – 'citizens' become 'clients' or customers for state services, where the criterion of judgement becomes efficiency and cost of provision, not the exercise of popular sovereignty. Undermining popular representation further erodes the legitimacy of the state.

---

7   In the US, the moves to end habeas corpus, institutionalise state use of torture, etc. are well known – and see the 2011 National Defence Authorisation Act to allow indefinite detention without charge or trial (in the UK there are comparable steps to allow indefinite detention without trial). Meanwhile, the US has one of the largest prison populations – over 7 million; China does not publish figures, but the number may be larger.

(10) In crisis, the limits imposed on national sovereignty by the new order are slowly becoming clearer. On the economic front, the global economic nexus and global market, severely discipline national policy, and those constraints are reinforced by the political order of states, the so-called 'international community'. The state begins to behave as an agent for an economic and political world order, enforcing global imperatives on the domestic population, rather than representing it to the world at large (let alone defending it against external threats). If state sovereignty is no longer practicable, will the world's fascination with 'national liberation' be undermined? Not while aspirant ruling classes are willing to fight for a place at the top table and there are no alternative options for popular self-emancipation. Winning national independence and a new state allows privileged access to loot the new country – and then deposit the proceeds in Vermont or Kent or Provence (as with the Gaddafis or the Bhuttos).

(11) The conjuncture exposes the separation of what we might call two ruling classes: a territorial national ruling class, whose very existence depends on holding a national territory (composed of the state administration, armed forces and security services, crony capital, owners of land and infrastructure, etc.), and a global ruling class which directs the companies and corporations which constitute the global economy, the mobile global rich, the staff of international agencies and non-governmental organisations (NGOs), etc. That is, a global social stratum for whom nationality is a mere contingency, not a matter of defining identity and loyalty. In practice, the two classes are not at all clearly distinguishable, and members pass freely between the two. What is distinguishable is a political interest (for example, between neo-liberalism and economic nationalism), and a role (national versus international).[8]

(12) Thus, we may be entering a period which combines both the extraordinary potential for an end of world poverty,[9] and an existential crisis of the fractured political order of the world. The danger is that the territorial ruling classes may use their overwhelming control of the powers of physical coercion to restore national dominance of the global economy, resulting in domestic

---

8   It might be said that the global ruling class cannot be said to exist as 'a class for itself' without identifiable institutions of self-realisation, of global governance. The issue is important but it would carry this account far off course to pursue here.

9   The reduction in world poverty since 1980 – the period of economic globalisation – is staggering, and seems to have persisted through the onset of world economic crisis; although subject to much dispute, partial World Bank summary estimates for 2010 suggest that global poverty has been halved since 1990, a reduction replicated in all regions of the world (see 'A Fall to Cheer', *The Economist*, 3 March 2012, p. 75).

authoritarianism with economic stagnation (with possible perpetual warfare on the borderlands to enforce social discipline, a combination so brilliantly imagined in George Orwell's *1984*). In practice – and hopefully – global economic integration is by now so advanced that it cannot be comprehensively reversed, even if components can be qualified (for example, free movement of labour), and states will continue to try to cheat on the rules. States have an interest in the developed countries, in inflating the popular fear that the new international division of labour will render redundant larger sections of the labour force, to support populist authoritarianism that could damage economic globalisation – and hence global welfare. Elements of possible national capitalisms already might be seen to exist in the marriage between national militaries and crony capitalism in some important states (Russia, China, Pakistan, Iran, etc.).

(13) As we have noted, many states have already been making adjustments to the new circumstances. One of the more curious – if not risible – by-products of this has been the ubiquitous spread of debates on what it is to be a native, the 'values' supposed to unite the natives, often under the pretext of the need to 'integrate' non-natives (immigrants, refugees, etc.). The discussion is obscure since what united, say, the British, was never shared values but common subordination to the British state. But it is embarrassing to admit that there is nothing else in common. As so often, out of its peculiar circumstances (including immense cultural diversity), Israel appears as a pioneer making these adjustments, combining militarised ethno-nationalism, religious orthodoxy and authoritarianism, employing the Arab Israelis and Palestinians as an anvil on which to forge unity out of immigrant diversity, with perpetual war in the occupied territories as a source of popular fear. However, the combination in the medium term could be suicidal for an economy as globalised as that of Israel.

(14) Left to itself, the global system appears incapable of resisting self-destruction. Markets and the competitive drive to profit seem incapable of establishing the self-discipline to escape crash. The global capitalist class shows little potential for political self-government. For that, they are dependent on the existing political order. Yet the fragmented political order appears incapable of overcoming its ferocious rivalries to achieve unified action. The core problem, in sum, is an integrated world economy, driven by global markets (the outcome of which can be neither determined nor predicted) and which faces a fractured political order of competing states, each undermined by global capital. Capital for a very long period was able to hide behind one or other state, but now in the final phases of the completion of a global bourgeois revolution, it is obliged to step into the limelight, unprotected by political power.

Meanwhile, the opposition to global capital – from the scattered occupations, the Arab Spring, the trade union fight against austerity in Europe, to the hundreds of peasant agitations and strikes in China – remains trapped within each national context, each assuming a state which can change their environment for the better. The creativity of these movements is not in doubt, yet we cannot even begin to visualise a realistic road map to one world, a world without war, with a unified drive to end world poverty, secure a livelihood for all with security, in a safe and sustainable environment. Revolutions in one country can no longer achieve 'national liberation' (that requires breaking the global order), and though revolutions may spread (as we have seen in the Arab Spring), the outcome only reiterates the same order of competing states, itself at the core of the underlying problem.

(15) These notes began with an implied criticism of the Left insofar as it identified the contemporary world as 'imperialist'. The charge put Washington at the centre of a world system of domination, implying that achieving self-determination by overthrowing Washington would achieve the liberation of the world. However, Washington itself is victim to a global capitalist order. Not only is it mired in an apparently insoluble economic crisis, it has lost its economy (and its capital, now global), now a junction in global flows. Its spectacular armaments in no way resolve the economic problem. Washington's extension into the world is not 'imperialism' but an attempt to create a substitute for the missing world government, not in the interests of the people of the world so much as the tiny minority that directs the US.

PART 2

The State and Economic Development

The 'Scissors Crisis' in India and China*

I

Economic growth in a country where a majority of the labour force is engaged in low-productivity agriculture is conditioned by two interrelated relationships – that between the urban and rural sectors, and between the urban sector and other countries. Historically, it seems that external trade – part of the second relationship – has been the most important stimulus to the domestic transformation of economics, changing the first relationship and thereby creating a geographical specialisation which raises general levels of productivity.[1] By implication, the lack of a spatial division of labour, an economic order consisting of relatively self-sufficient communities of producers, is associated with economic backwardness: for economic development, localised low-productivity independence needs to be replaced by high-productivity interdependence.

In a trade-based growth pattern, the size, income level and general character of the intermediary element between the two relationships, the urban sector, are determined by the interdependent exchanges, domestic and external. Planned economic development introduces a different element since it is directed at the control or manipulation of the external relationship to produce a disproportionate growth in the industrial-urban sector. The core of the process is to increase domestic savings, whether from current consumption, a reorganisation of the domestic economy, or from external assistance in order to sustain a high rate of investment in key modern sectors. By these means, it is hoped to increase the utilisation of the labour force and raise the proportion engaged in high-productivity activities, located in or economically associated with the urban sector.

If external assistance is limited in relationship to the tasks, domestic savings from current consumption or stocks must bear the main burden of accumulation. Given that the majority of the population is engaged in agriculture, it is

---

* From: Development Planning Unit Working Paper, 1977.
1 Marx rated this factor particularly highly: 'The foundation of every division of labour that is well developed and brought about by the exchange of commodities is the demarcation between town and country. It may be said that the whole economic history of society is summed up in the movement of this antithesis' (Marx 1930, pp. 371–2).

this sector which has been required to bear a major part of the savings effort, sustaining a net transfer of resources from rural to urban sectors until such time as a majority of the labourers are engaged in urban, or at least, non-agricultural, activities. In contemporary conditions, the threshold for undertaking the general social transformation associated with economic development appears to be very much higher than in the past. If this is so, the scale of the required transfer has also to be higher and sustained over a longer period of time before the returns become apparent, assuming the scale is still in principle attainable at all.[2]

In the early years of the Soviet Union, the phrase 'the scissors crisis' was used to describe a series of grave obstacles to the net transfer of resources between rural and urban sectors. Peasant agriculture was the 'accursed problem' for the new Soviet regime. The alternative policies expressed within the Soviet Communist Party are of some interest in the light of the experience of economic development – and the strategies pursued – in India and China today. Given the length of the paper, the treatment must be tentative and guilty of statistical rashness, but the exercise does assist us in appraising the two countries concerned. Part 2 rehearses the two main Soviet arguments. Part 3 examines relevant elements of Indian experience, and Part 4, Chinese.

II   The Soviet Industrialisation Debate

The period of War Communism, of foreign intervention and civil war, was brought by necessity to a close in 1920–1, and the Soviet regime introduced its New Economic Policy. This partially re-established a private trading system/market in consumer goods. It released private peasant production from the onerous State appropriations policy. The economy was in severe disarray. In 1920 agricultural output was some 60 percent of the 1913 level (the Soviet territory had lost some of the most productive agricultural areas of the Tsarist Empire), and industrial output not much more than 20 percent. The urban sector had disastrously contracted. The transport system was in chaos, there were severe shortages of fuel and industrial raw materials; as a result, stocks of industrial goods were drastically reduced.

---

2   The topic of the threshold for economic development is discussed in Kidron 1974, pp. 95–153; some of its settlement implications are explored in United Nations, Effects of economic conditions on human settlements, Centre for Housing, Building and Planning, paper for the UN Habitat Congress, Vancouver, May 1976.

However, in 1922, a bumper harvest flooded the market, driving down grain prices at the same time as industrial goods remained in very short supply. As a result, the ratio between agricultural and industrial prices widened dramatically. The Party leadership inferred from the 'opening of the scissors'[3] that there was grave threat, not only to the 'division of labour' and the future of the economy, but also to the political alliance, the *smychka* of workers and peasants, said to be the current political basis of the Soviet regime. At the point of greatest divergence (October 1923), industrial prices were said to be three times higher than the comparable ratio of agricultural prices to the aggregate price index. The Party leadership feared that the peasants, affronted at the scale of transfer from rural to urban represented in declining grain and rising industrial prices, would withdraw from the exchange altogether.

In Bukharin's colourful phrase:

> The economy of the society decomposes into two autonomous spheres – the hungry city and the open country, which, despite the partial destruction of productive powers, disposes of fairly large stores of 'surpluses' for which the market is not available.[4]

There were severe methodological problems in measuring the crisis;[5] and the picture was by no means uniform for all crops. The prices quoted did not necessarily indicate what was inferred. Nevertheless, it was argued that the land redistribution of 1917, the destruction of the large estates and of landlordism (large estates had been the source of the marketable grain surplus in Tsarist Russia), as well as the appropriation policies of the period of War Communism, had had disastrous effects on the marketable foodstuffs supply, whether for export (pre-revolutionary Russia had been a significant grain exporter) or domestic urban consumption. By implication, rural consumption now absorbed what was left of the former marketed surplus, thereby robbing the regime of both its means to feed the city dwellers and of domestic savings. On the other hand, the destruction of industrial capacity – and the severe

---

3 The diagram of the opening gap between industrial and agricultural prices, used by Trotsky to dramatise the problem at the 12th Congress of the Communist Party of the Soviet Union, appeared as it does on the following page.

4 See Bukharin's *Economics of the Transformation Period* (with critical comments by Lenin 1971, p. 88).

5 These are discussed by Corinne Ann Guntzel, *Soviet agricultural pricing policy and the scissors crisis of 1922–23*, unpublished PhD thesis, University of Illinois (Urbana-Champaign), 1972.

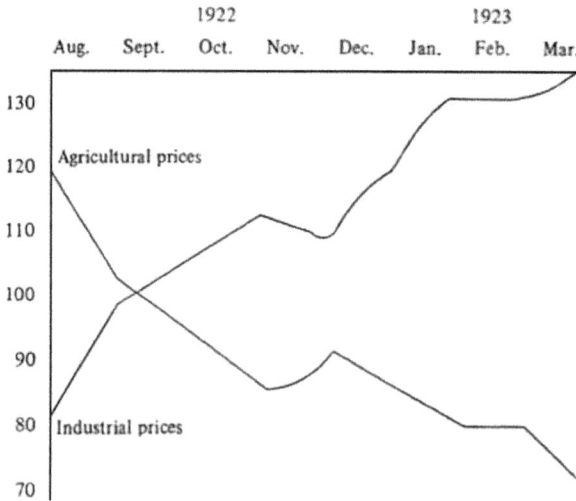

FIGURE 2.1 *The 'scissors crisis': movement of industrial and*
agricultural prices (retail), Aug. 1922 to Mar. 1923
(presented by L.D. Trotsky to the 12th Congress,
Communist Party of the Soviet Union, April 1923).
DVENADTSATYI S'EZD ROSSISKOI
KOMMUNISTICHESKOI PARTII
(BOLSHEVIKOV), MOSCOW, IZDATEL'STVO
POLITICHESKOI LITERATURY 1968, P. 321.

deprecation of what remained – severely limited the supply of industrial consumer goods for rural markets, reducing the peasant incentive to sell grain, and
making the regime even more dependent upon savings from the rural sector.
Thus, the sources of industrial investment – from returns on domestic and foreign grain sales – and of industrial raw materials and urban foodstuffs were all
curtailed.

In 1927–8, when the crisis returned with an aggravated 6 percent drop in
grain prices, the State procurements of grain were 630 million pounds, compared to 1913's marketed volume of grain of 1.3 billion pounds; in 1913, eleven
and a half million tons of grain were exported, but in 1928, grain was imported. The grain supply now seemed inadequate to support industrialisation at
a grain price which would permit the requisite volume of savings. The hope of
external assistance which had been the justification for the privations of the
period of War Communism – was by then no longer in prospect.

There were a number of policy responses to the problem in the mid-1920s of
which two are outlined here. The first, associated with Nikolai Bukharin, was
embodied in government policy up to 1928. Bukharin diagnosed the problem
as essentially one of peasant incentives, not of economic development. All

government efforts must be bent to increasing the incentive to grow and sell grain; no 'plan' should be permitted to complicate this major task (Bukharin and his associates mocked what they saw as the naive faith of their opponents in State planning). The government must guarantee a good price for marketed grain, reduce or abolish taxation on agriculture, monetise what tax obligations remained, expand the provision of rural credit, and reshape industrial output to meet peasant demand.

Adapting Turgot's injunction, Bukharin in June 1925 proclaimed: 'We have to tell the whole peasantry, all its strata: Get rich, accumulate, develop your economy!'

A severe obstacle to this process, however, was, in Bukharin's view, the monopoly structure of State industry. Monopoly pricing brought a disproportionate share of savings to the public sector, encouraging a rate of growth of industry substantially higher than the increase in peasant consumption. As a result the exchange was constantly tending to become imbalanced, the scissors to open once more. The 1927–8 grain crisis was, he argued,[6] the result of three years of 'over-expansion' of industry, and particularly heavy industry which not only provided no goods for the rural market but also tended to have long investment maturation periods. The warning of crisis was less the urban-rural exchange than the increase in the volume of transactions within the State industrial sector. The *smychka* would be severely jeopardised unless industrial expansion could be restrained to the rate of increase in peasant purchases and related directly to peasant demand. Economic development through 'balanced growth', Bukharin acknowledged with what in retrospect was dangerous naivety – would be very slow: 'We shall move ahead by tiny tiny steps, pulling behind us our large peasant cart' and 'We shall move at a snail's pace ... but we shall be building socialism'.

The Left Opposition (led by Leon Trotsky, and, on this particular question, by E. Preobrazhensky) regarded the views of Bukharin and his chief ally, Joseph Stalin, as extraordinarily dangerous. The New Economic Policy, they argued, created increasing differences in the countryside between the rich peasants (kulaks) with a marketable surplus and the mass of rural producers. Policies favouring those with a marketable margin might stimulate output but at the potential cost of tilting the political balance in the Soviet Union. In the absence of external help from a successful revolution in Western Europe, the kulaks would ultimately overwhelm the Soviet State and the political aims of the Octo-

---

6 'Notes of an economist, at the beginning of the economic year', *Pravda*, 30 September 1928, cited in Carr and Davies 1969; cf. also Lewin 1968; Erlich 1960, and Cohen 1971.

ber Revolution. Indeed, they saw Bukharin in the Party as the expression of this very danger. The sole method of offsetting this preponderant rich peasant influence was to create an industrial sector large enough to be relatively independent of the peasantry. For this purpose, a State plan was vital as the formal guide to unbalanced growth, an expansion of industry consistently faster than that of agriculture.

Preobrazhensky argued that capitalism's initial phase of 'primitive accumulation' had been at the expense of non-capitalist small-scale production at home and in colonies abroad. The Soviet Union had no colonies (in an unguarded moment, however, he referred to the Russian peasantry as an 'internal colony'), nor did it have easy access to external markets. There was only one real source for industrial accumulation, the Russian peasantry. Industry was too small to provide an adequate source of savings from its own activity. It was inefficient and required protection from foreign competition, as well as a monopoly position in the domestic market for the period of accelerated accumulation – until such time as the scale was great enough to reduce Russian industrial prices to the level of its foreign rivals. He formulated his views in a general law:

> The more backward economically, petty bourgeois, peasant, a particular country is which has gone over to the socialist organisation of production, and the smaller the inheritance received by the socialist accumulation fund of the proletariat, of this country when the socialist revolution takes place, by so much the more, in proportion, will socialist accumulation be obliged to rely on alienating part of the surplus product of presocialist forms of economy and the smaller will be the relative weight of accumulation on its own productive base, that is, the less will it be nourished by the surplus product of the workers in socialist industry.[7]

At the risk of some distortion, we could reformulate this as: the more backward an economy, the smaller the contribution to savings generated by the existing industrial sector, the larger the contribution from the agricultural sector.

Preobrazhensky denied any intention to 'plunder' the countryside but urged systematic manipulation of the urban-rural relationship to the advantage of industry. Controlled pricing, taxation, appropriations should discriminate in favour of industry, all 'within the limits of what is economically possible, technically feasible and rational'.[8] In two decades, he estimated (that is by 1947), the process would be complete and the Soviet Union industrialised.

---

7   Preobrazhensky 1965, p. 124.
8   Preobrazhensky 1965, p. 87.

But to follow a balanced path 'would mean jeopardising the very existence of the socialist economy, or prolonging endlessly the period of preliminary accumulation'. To subsidise agriculture would mean 'we shall have a steady decomposition of large scale socialist production and a gradual selling off of its products below cost'.

Neither Bukharin nor Preobrazhensky envisaged interfering in the ownership of land; both assumed the indefinite survival of private agriculture, although Preobrazhensky – and towards the end, Bukharin as well – proposed the formation of State farms with the collaboration of poor peasants and substantial State investment so that the urban sector would have a grain reserve. If Bukharin did not face squarely the long-term implications of his proposals, Preobrazhensky was less than realistic about the short-term grain supply problem. It was the latter which, in 1929–31, prompted Stalin to cut the Gordian knot. By then the need for grain had been partly overtaken by the need for expanded defence supplies, and thus, a substantial heavy industrial sector. Stalin produced, less from a strategy than as summary of what he had done, a third alternative: collectivisation, the 'plunder' of the countryside.[9] The performance of Soviet agriculture today perhaps bears melancholy witness to some of Bukharin's fears of what the results of such policies might be.

Our concern is not with the detail nor the elaboration of the two cases, but rather with the components of the diagnosis:

1. the difficulty of Russia's agriculture expanding fast enough to support the required rate of growth of industry;
2. the difficulty of industry expanding fast enough from its own resources without discrimination against agriculture;
3. the impossibility of external assistance expanding fast enough to support either agricultural or industrial growth (or some combination of both);
4. the reshaping of social and political institutions to fit the imperatives of stagnation, this in its turn exacerbating the first two problems.

III   India

In 1947, India was far poorer than the Soviet Union in 1917. Partition, it is claimed, removed a fifth of the population of British India but a quarter of the

---

9   Between 1913 and 1932, the grain harvest was reduced from 82 to 63 million tons, but the 'surplus' (marketed in the first year, procured in the second) declined only from 21 to 20 million tons.

total food supply.[10] Levels of agricultural productivity were among the lowest in the world and the man-land ratio was much more unfavourable than in Russia. Indeed, the 'agrarian question' was not centrally one of the existence of large landed estates, but of complex tenurial systems and a great scarcity of cultivable acreage. The rural inheritance was much poorer, and the urban not much better; if Preobrazhensky's generalisation is correct, the dependence upon rural savings for the industrialisation effort would be that much greater (without considering the possibility that the 'threshold' had also risen in the intervening years).[11]

In British India, the mechanisms by which resources[12] were transferred from rural to urban sectors took, put crudely, three basic forms: through commodities (urban-rural trade favoured the urban sector), cash (taxation and other monetised obligations paid by the peasantry; the urban expenditure of absentee landlords and traders), and manpower (the rural immigrant share of the urban labour force was raised at the cost of the rural areas).

The peasantry, or an important part of it, was constrained by the need to meet monetised obligations (taxes, rents, interest on loans and the purchase of urban products) to sell part of its output. The landlord either directly or in his role as moneylender or merchant played a key role in this transfer (the picture is of course much more varied than this account suggests, clearest where the Zamindari or other quasi-landlord system operated). At the extreme, the landlord supplied credit in the off-season at high interest rates, foreclosed at harvest time when prices were lowest and held the grain until prices were high, as well as securing free services on his own land. In sum, the land tenure system provided 'a set of unprecedented mechanisms for drawing away from the peasants everything but a bare minimum to keep cultivation going'.[13] The benefits accrued in part to the urban sector and in part to the metropolitan power.

---

10   Cited by Prem Shankar Jha, unpublished manuscript from M.S. Randhawa, *Out of the Ashes*.

11   Cf. note 2.

12   This account has eschewed the concept 'surplus' except in relationship to the volume of grain actually marketed or procured at a given price. Soma of the problems in the use of the concept are reviewed in Currie, Murphy and Schmitz 1971. Riskin applies the idea of an 'excess product above some specified measure of the subsistence needs of a population' to pre-Communist China in 'Surplus and Stagnation in Modern China' (1975, pp. 49–84).

13   Thorner 1955, p. 126.

The years following Independence coincided or produced important changes in this structure. The more important changes can be summarised as follows:

(a) land reforms placed a ceiling on the size of individual holdings and encouraged a resumption of cultivation by absentee owners; tax changes and the consolidation of holdings subsequently discouraged the former function of absentee landlords in the rural-urban transfer;

(b) land taxation was virtually eliminated, and the balance of political power at the level of State assembly has consistently impeded efforts to tax the rural population.

(c) the foreign demand for the products of Indian agriculture has not expanded at a rate commensurate with the needs of economic growth, and the import of manufactured consumer goods was largely ended in pursuit of an import-substitution industrialisation programme.

(d) industrialisation raised the demand for imported industrial equipment and raw materials, and the urban demand for foodstuffs. In neither case was the agricultural performance able to support this expansion.

The national planning strategy reflected these changes. Initially, there was much optimism that ending the external 'drain' to Britain would provide a stream of savings adequate for a sustained rise in output and employment. The experience of the first plan encouraged the high ambitions of the second (1955–6 to 1960–1) which concentrated resources on a major effort to expand public sector heavy industry. The plan was much closer to Preobrazhensky's proposals than Stalin's – there was no provision for a decisive element in the first Soviet plan period, collectivisation. However, unlike the Preobrazhensky proposals, the Indian plan made no serious provisions for raising a major share of resources from the agricultural sector. It was industrialisation by stealth in the hope that, in due course, public sector industry would generate a stream of savings adequate for future growth without the necessity of controlling the consumption of the richer peasantry.

The second plan collided, first with external constraints – the balance of payments – and then with the sluggish performance of agriculture. In the third plan period, much of the industrial investment of the second plan years came on stream, sustaining relatively high rates of industrial growth, but the plan itself reoriented attention on the tasks of raising agricultural output. The measures taken earlier to improve crop production were considerably fortified and more resources were devoted to raising output. Even so, the balance of payments became an increasing constraint upon growth, particularly when (from 1962–3), defence expenditure began to absorb an increased volume of domestic savings. The only room to manoeuvre for Delhi appears to have been the high level of foreign food imports – at its peak in 1966, when imports were equivalent to 14 percent of the total net availability of food grains or double the level of government procurements.[14]

Since the Third Plan, the government has moved steadily closer to a Bukharinite strategy (without terminating the institutional structure of planning which would be required to be consistent). However, curbing the growth of industrial output and a package of policies to raise peasant incentives (subsidies, incentive prices, controlled water supplies, increased fertiliser and pesticide supplies, high-yielding varieties of seeds, etc.) has had – apart from the brief period of the 'Green Revolution' at the end of the 1960s – undramatic results in the output of foodstuffs. Continued food scarcities, exacerbated by hoarding and speculation (fuelled by the movement of 'black money'), as well as the close control of the prices of industrial output, have produced a 'scissors crisis' which is the reverse of that experienced in 1922–3 in the Soviet Union – rising food prices relative to industrial prices. On an index base year of 1962–3's 100, official food prices reached 321.7 by 1973–4 (foodgrains 336.1) and manufactured goods as a group, 205.6 (transport equipment and machinery, 234.2).[15] In Preobrazhensky's terms, this gap represents a net drain out of the urban-industrial sector into the rural; in Bukharin's, perhaps it reflects no more than the necessary readjustments involved in re-establishing the balance.

Fragmentary evidence tends to suggest that income differentiation on the countryside has increased (as Preobrazhensky suggests would occur), both between strata of the cultivating population and between different geographical areas (particularly between irrigated and non-irrigated areas). If we can assume a common statistical basis for the National Sample Survey (16th and 17th rounds, 1961–2) and the recent agricultural census, the number of operational holdings has increased from 50 to 71 million; the share of holdings of under 1 hectare in size has increased from 39 to 51 percent; holdings of ten hectares or more covered just under a quarter of the cultivated acreage in 1961–2, and nearly 31 percent in 1970–1.[16] The proportion of the rural population that

---

14   Cf. Share of imports in total net availability of foodgrains, Table 1.9, Government of India 1975, p. 69.

15   Reserve Bank of India 1975, Bulletin, March, no. 38, cited by Ashok Mitra, forthcoming, pp. 222–3 (manuscript). Relative prices of manufactured and agricultural commodities, 1955–6 to 1968–9, is contained in Government of India 1969, Table 14.

16   The agricultural census volume is reported in the *Far Eastern Economic Review*, 23 April 1976, p. 136.

is without land has also possibly increased; the volume of rural indebtedness has grown, and possibly the incidence of bonded labour. It is not clear that rural employment has been significantly stimulated by the rising incomes of the richer farmers. Rural wages do not appear to have shown any increase, and the stagnation in the output of those food crops most important for mass consumption – pulses and coarse grains[17] – would imply a deterioration in the nutritional standards of low income households.

The stimulation to urban industry arising from a growth in income of the richer farmers has been restricted to a relatively small section: consumer durables (a 50 percent increase in output through the years of general industrial stagnation, 1966 to 1972) and tubewells (a four and a half fold increase in the number of tubewells installed between 1965 and 1974). The public sector savings, which, it was hoped, would fuel the next phase of growth, have proved illusory; indeed, public sector heavy industrial projects have tended to absorb part of the savings of the rest of the economy rather than giving the industrial sector some autonomy. Stagnation with a rising cost of imports and cumulative debts has exacerbated the external balance so that it is now an even more severe constraint upon expansion.[18]

The institutional structure has slowly changed to reflect the changed balance of interests. The entrenched position of the richer farmers at the State level and their strong influence at the national level,[19] has consistently tended to preserve their relatively secure position – preventing tax measures that affect their income, measures of redistribution, effective institutional reforms, raising procurement prices regardless of the level of procurements or the size of the harvest, and making ineffective the government's appropriation of the wholesale wheat trade in 1973.

In an inevitably superficial treatment, certain points seem to stand out clearly, confirming much of Preobrazhensky's critique of Bukharin. Of course, it could be argued that the basic poverty in India renders anything other than a Bukharinite approach utopian. The size of the surplus[20] makes possible only a relatively small industrial enclave rather than the complete transformation of

17   Cf. Growth of selected crops, 1949–50 to 1959–60 and 1959–60 to 1969–70, Government of India, *Draft Fifth Five Year Plan*, Planning Commission, II, 1, Annexure III, p. 48, cited by Prem S. Jha, op cit.

18   According to Chishti and Bhattacharya, the 1974–5 deficit on external trade was larger than total external aid in the preceding five years; cf. Chishti and Bhattacharya 1976, p. 429.

19   The particular influence over procurement prices is explored by the former Chairman of the Agricultural Prices Commission, Ashok Mitra, in the work cited, cf. note 12.

20   Cf. note. 12.

the society. This is not the place to argue this wider case, but, if it is true, it raises the question as to whether what has historically been known as economic development is at all feasible in current conditions in India.

IV   China

As in the Soviet Union in 1921, China's economy was in severe disarray in 1949 when the new regime came to power (following the years of Japanese occupation, world war and civil war). The government was almost immediately faced with severe external problems – the Korean War, and to a lesser extent, the war in Vietnam – which required a high defence capability. Nevertheless the optimism of the party leadership[21] was partly confirmed by the early results – between 1949 and 1952, industrial employment is said to have increased by nearly a fifth each year, and industrial output by a spectacular 27 percent each year.[22]

The government moved from the beginning towards a carefully controlled transformation of ownership relations in agriculture, in marked contrast to the popular land seizures of Russia in 1917–18. Reforms were staggered over a number of years while the administrative structure was being constructed, and organisational forms were not allowed to become secure before the next wave of changes began (land redistribution moved, in different areas at different times, into Mutual Aid Teams and then *hsien* co-operatives). Through co-operatives, the government aimed to secure economies of scale, the consolidation of holdings, improved water control, utilisation of labour and double cropping, without major investments in the land. Through the administered nature of the changes, the government retained the function of 'improved landlordism' in its own hands so that the transfer of rural resources into industrialisation could be sustained.

---

21   For example, in 1945 Mao Tse-tung seemed quite confident about the perspective: 'The peasants are the future industrial workers of China and tens of millions of them will go into the cities and enter factories. For if China wants to construct large scale indigenous industry and to build a great number of large modern cities, then she will have to undergo a long process of transformation in which the rural population becomes residents of the cities' ('On Coalition Government', Seventh Party Congress, 24 April 1945. The version published in Mao 1965, p. 300, has slightly different words, but the sense is the same).

22   Between 1929 and 1932, the Russian industrial labour force increased from 3.1 million to 8 million.

Agricultural output did not increase fast enough, and already by 1953 there was evidence of a widening gap between agricultural and industrial prices.[23] Nonetheless, the government persisted in the basic task of the first five-year plan, the building of heavy industry, while recognising the difficulties.[24] To this end, urban and rural consumption was controlled through administered prices, foodstuffs were procured on a compulsory basis at relatively low prices, indirect taxation assisted the maintenance of high levels of savings, and mass low-waged labour schemes were instituted for large scale projects.

By 1955–6, industrial output was increasingly hampered by severe shortages of consumer goods and raw materials, producing inflationary pressure and exacerbated by poor harvests. Agricultural output could not keep pace with the demands of the expanding industrial sector, and Soviet assistance was not on a sufficient scale to compensate. In some cases, agricultural reorganisation further jeopardised the output of the farms[25] as it had done in the years of collectivisation in the Soviet Union. Unrest among both peasants and urban workers were danger signals for the government. Further efforts to secure external relief so that industrial growth could be sustained (Mao himself visited Moscow in November 1956) were apparently unsuccessful, and in 1957 the government was compelled to retrench.[26]

This was the occasion, one must presume, for a fundamental review not of the aims of economic development but rather of the methods hitherto pursued. One key problem was the poor performance of agriculture and the con-

---

23   The government promised 'the gradual reduction of the scissors differences in prices for industrial and agricultural goods' (*People's Daily*, 26 March 1953, cited by Gluckstein 1957, p. 103).

24   For example, Chou En-lai argued that: 'heavy industry needs more capital, takes longer to build and yield profit, and ... most of its products are not for direct consumption by the people. Consequently, in the period when the State concentrates its efforts on developing heavy industry, the people have to bear some temporary hardships and inconveniences, notwithstanding the corresponding development of light industry and agriculture' (1st session, *1st National People's Congress*, 23 September 1954, Peking, p. 3).

25   One source claims that pig stocks dropped from 102 million in July 1954 to 84 million in July 1956; (cf. Chen Yun, NCNA, Peking, 10 March 1957; let's say 100 million to 80 million) in June of the same year, the National People's Congress, third session, recorded complaints of the excessive pressure on peasants; subsequently the pricing system was altered, and pig stocks are said to have reached 146 million by the end of 1957. See Hsinhua B, 1, 1957, pp. 88–90, cited by Hsia 1972, pp. 116–18.

26   Howe estimates that 35.8 percent of Shanghai's population was employed in 1957, a decline on 1926–7's 45.2 percent (Howe 1971, p. 228).

tinuing underutilisation of the rural labour force.[27] The government's response was the beginning of sustained efforts to limit the growth of the urban population and of urban consumption.

Limiting the growth of the urban population took two forms, through (a) the use of ration, residence and movement controls; and (b) periodic attempts to encourage or enforce urban outmigration – the *hsia-fang* movement is said to have relocated some 20 million urban residents between 1961 and 1963,[28] and 8 million between 1969 and 1973[29] (the volume of return migration is not available).[30] Curbing urban consumption took the form of (a) food rationing (introduced in 1956); (b) tighter controls over wage increases after the 1956 national wage reform;[31] (c) closer bank supervision and financial control of enterprises to curb the hiring of labour (in 1957, 1961 and 1965, managers were temporarily forbidden to hire rural labour for industry);[32] (d) periodic thinning of 'non-productive' labour (clerical and staff grades); and (e) the dilution of the settled and relatively high-cost urban labour force by low-cost temporary and contract labour.[33] In addition, the regime dispersed some labour intensive activities outside urban areas (commercial and storage departments, for example) thus escaping the relatively high costs obligatory in the urban areas.

The emphasis on raising urban labour productively complemented these measures. In the first plan, modified forms of Soviet incentive payment systems were adopted – the use of wage premiums bonuses, piece rates, etc. – as well as campaigns. Perhaps some of these were modified in subsequent years, but the main emphasis upon raising labour productivity rather than increasing the urban labour force remains, assisted by the encouragement of mechanisation.[34]

---

27   In January 1956, Chou En-lai claimed that the current agricultural output of China required 30 billion eight-hour labour days, whereas there was on offer from the country's 120 million rural households, 45 billion (cited by Snow 1970 p. 426).

28   Table 1, Aird 1967, Vol. 2, Pt. 3, p. 353.

29   The last figure is from an interview of Po I-po, Chairman of the State Planning Council, by Strong 1964. The problems of dealing with Chinese population statistics, and the peculiar status of UN figures, are reviewed by Orleans 1975, pp. 69–80.

30   Prybyla and Hsia-fang 1975.

31   For details, see Hoffman 1974 and Howe 1973.

32   Donnithorne 1967, pp. 184–7.

33   Lewis claims that there were some 12 million temporary workers by 1958, not necessarily in urban employment; cf. footnote 31, Lewis (ed.) 1975, p. 404. On temporary and contract labour, cf. Hoffman 1968, and sources cited there.

34   The degree of mechanisation in urban industry is, by general report, high. One corres-

Finally, the government endeavoured to narrow the urban-rural wage differential – in 1958, the two lowest industrial wage rates were reduced to this end – and stimulate rural employment and new rural activities both to absorb excess labour and increase the intensity of utilising the existing labour force. It also acknowledged that rural incomes were too low, and took steps to stabilise and later increase rural incomes.[35]

The Great Leap Forward of 1958 brought together many of these measures in a sustained national campaign to break through the supply bottlenecks. On the one hand the growth of urban output was accelerated; on the other, major efforts were made to expand agricultural output and develop some rural industrial production (but without increasing the call on central investment resources). Institutional changes – the creation of communes – permitted mass mobilisations for major irrigation, land reclamation and flood control works.

It was a brief phase, supported by an excellent harvest. The poor harvest of 1959 and two years of subsequent agricultural disasters (as well as the withdrawal of external assistance) compounded the disorganisation of the economy and did nothing to offset slump.[36] The lack of supporting capital and skills in the efforts to accelerate agricultural and rural industrial activities placed a severe brake on growth; scarce resources were wasted,[37] and indeed the future of the economy jeopardised. War Communism in the Soviet Union, impelled by an overwhelming threat to the regime, persisted for a much longer period, perhaps reflecting the much higher per capita income available in Russia at that time.

The government was compelled into a New Economic Policy, restoring the incentives removed in 1958 and permitting an increase in consumption for those in a position to secure it. Presumably, the urban-rural differential was permitted to expand.[38]

---

pondent claims that over half of Shanghai's 1,600 horizontal knitting looms are now electronically controlled and a major part of the woollen knitwear mills are automated; cf. *Far Eastern Economic Review*, December 1974.

35   The 8th Party Congress noted in 1958 'the need to increase consumption for otherwise there would be a serious contradiction between the party and the masses which would lead to unforgivable errors' (cited by Deleyne 1973, pp. 185–6).

36   Eckstein argues that the downturn after the Great Leap Forward 'may have cost a decade of economic growth, for the gross national product in 1965 does not seem to have been above the 1958 level' (Eckstein, Galenson and Ta-chung Liu (eds.) 1968, p. 7).

37   The *People's Daily*, 27 August 1959, suggested that some 3 million tons of the iron output of 'backyard furnaces' was too poor to be refined: other estimates have been higher.

38   Hoffman cites the *People's Daily*, 3 May 1962, as estimating for 1960 the average value of output of an industrial worker as ¥10,000 and his average income, ¥560; the comparable figures for an agricultural worker were ¥900 and ¥140 (Hoffman 1967, p. 13).

In the countryside, the retreat of 1960–6 led to the restoration of the incentives operating before the Great Leap Forward, including private plots and free rural markets. As before, this apparently accrued to the benefit of the better-off cultivators which in turn affected the social foundations of the rural party. Although private plots were supposedly limited to 7 percent of the cultivated acreage, some observers report a much higher proportion under private cultivation (in 1962, some 50 percent of Yunnan's cultivated acreage is said to have been under private cultivation).[39] There is also considerable evidence of the corruption of rural party cadres; with surprising speed the 'rich peasant economy' reasserted itself.[40]

The 'rich peasant economy' had been a recurrent theme of the party leadership in the years before the Great Leap Forward,[41] a phenomenon which had similarly occurred during the Russian New Economic Policy.[42] Corruption (the chief complaints of the press were speculation, embezzling, misuse of State property, black marketeering, petty trading) and increased income differentials affected not only the political standing of the regime but also diverted potential savings from accumulation in the hands of the state to consumption or accumulation in the hands of private households. The Socialist Education Campaign and the ensuing Cultural Revolution can thus be seen not simply as methods of changing the awareness of Party cadres or those outside the Party, but as elements in the struggle for survival by the regime, attempts to ward off the relative decay in the social foundations of the regime's power.

The Cultural Revolution at some stages seemed to be moving towards another phase of 'War Communism', whether by design or simply as events unfolded. However, its economic effects were not at all on the scale of the Great

---

39   Wheelwright and McFarlane 1973, p. 70.

40   On corruption in the party, cf. for example, the collection of documents edited by Chen 1969, and the evidence presented by Baum 1975.

41   In 1951–2, during the rectification of the rural party, Kao Kang warned: 'If no active steps are taken ... to lead the peasants towards the path of co-operative economy rather than to the rich peasant economy, then rural village government is sure to deteriorate into a rich peasant regime. If the Communist party members all hire labour and give loans at usurious rates, then the party will become a rich peasant party' ('Overcome the corrosion of bourgeois ideology; oppose the Rightist trend in the Party', *People's Daily*, 24 January 1952, cited in *Current Background* Num. 163, 5 March 1952). In 1955, Mao complained of 'new rich peasants springing up everywhere and many well-to-do middle peasants striving to become rich peasants', alongside 'many poor peasants still living in poverty for lack of sufficient means of production with some in debt and others selling or renting their land' (Mao 1966, pp. 18–19).

42   Lewin 1968, p. 121, *passim*.

Leap Forward. It ended apparently in stalemate,[43] checked by the occurrence of urgent external threats (the border clash with the Soviet Union in 1969). Once more, the regime permitted a relaxation, a restoration – or at least, the public acknowledgement – of private cultivation, perhaps as the basis for an increased defence effort. Industrial output rose rapidly. For the first time since the first plan period, the expansion was supported by a remarkable increase in imports (particularly fertiliser, plants, special steels and technically advanced equipment). The onset of generalised world recession in conditions of inflation checked the expansion; Chinese export revenue (derived in the main from exports of agricultural origin), one presumes, stagnated while industrial import prices rose, producing the first balance of payments difficulties in the autumn of 1974.

In agriculture, the relaxation phase policies of raising peasant real incomes continued. In the second half of 1971, there were substantial prices adjustments[44] to increase the incomes of the rural sector (presumably the effects of this were differentially distributed, richer households in richer communes reaping the maximum benefit). However, after quite a brief period, the press resumed its campaigns against corruption,[45] and intensified efforts to lower urban consumption (through the removal of premium payments, overtime pay, etc.).

Chinese policy thus has the appearance of considerable 'zigzags', the time between each turn apparently declining. At the risk of oversimplification, we can describe the process in the following form: the administration attempts to accelerate the pace of accumulation by direct control, curbing consumption and emphasising administrative direction of the economy, up to the point when this approach seems liable to reduce the growth of output by affecting incentives, at which point the 'rich peasant economy' is permitted to reassert itself. Income differentiation then increases as output rises, the social basis of the party is affected, which then in turn produces a period of radical 'pruning'. Over time, however, the terms of this process change, each 'pruning' phase has

---

43 This is not the place to argue this point, but cf. Chapter 4, 'The Chinese Cultural Revolution', in Harris 1974, pp. 107–20.

44 The prices of fertilisers, insecticides, kerosene, diesel oil and farm equipment are said to have been reduced by between 19 and 21 percent. Some State purchase prices were raised (for example, there was a 15 percent increase in the purchase price for sugar, 17 percent for oil seeds).

45 The references here are too copious to be listed, but see, for example, *People's Daily*, 28 March 1975 and 22 April 1975; or Harbin, *Survey of World Broadcasts*, 3.FE/4856, BII/5, and Peking, ibid, BII/11.

perhaps less effect unless it is intensified to the point where other forces are released which exacerbate political stability; the Cultural Revolution is just such a case. The thread which gives consistency to the whole process is the continuing preoccupation with the building of heavy industry, even if the stress on this component varies slightly at different times.[46]

The 'relaxation' phases seem to correspond to the Bukharinite strategy, and produce the social results suggested by Preobrazhensky. The 'pruning', now detached from the complementary expansion of output which took place in the Great Leap Forward, do not correspond apparently either to the Preobrazhensky or the Stalin strategies. For – and the evidence is less than certain in this respect – the systematic manipulation of urban-rural relationships to the benefit of the urban sector has not taken place, nor the 'plunder' of the countryside. On the contrary, it seems rural incomes have been stabilised and in certain conditions permitted to rise. If this is correct, the burden of industrial accumulation must have been borne by industry itself to a greater extent than was envisaged in the Soviet Union (a possibility Preobrazhensky specifically denied). The much enhanced productivity of industry today in comparison to the 1920s perhaps makes this possible; but it also in part explains why Chinese industrial performance has not been as dramatically expansive as might have been expected (although considerably better than many countries with a similar economic starting point). To rely on enhanced labour productivity in this way requires strict urban-rural controls, and produces not a transformation of the society as a whole but the development of industrial enclaves: a 'production dualism' if not a 'consumption dualism'.

v   The 'Scissors Crisis' and Development in India and China

India and China started contemporary efforts to develop from different base points. On the one hand, the Chinese economy was severely disorganised when the People's Republic was established, and some basic agricultural inputs had been neglected for many decades. On the other hand, Chinese agriculture has

---

46   In 1969, an article in *Red Flag* reaffirmed this aim, citing Mao in support: 'It must be affirmed that heavy industry is the core of China's economic construction. At the same time, full attention must be paid to the development of agriculture and light industry' (*On the Correct Handling of Contradictions Among the People*). This is interpreted as 'heavy industry enjoying priority development' (cf. *The Road to China's Socialist Industrialisation*, by the Writing Group of Peking Municipal Revolutionary Committee, *Red Flag*, no. 10, 30 September 1969, p. 11, in *Survey of China Mainland Magazines*, no. 666, 31 October 1969).

been consistently more productive than Indian for a very long historical period, and, as a result, there has been a consistently higher availability of food-grains per head of the population in the modern period.[47] However, both economies were much poorer than that of the Soviet Union in the 1920s – the Soviet Union in 1928 is estimated to have had a per capita income three or four times higher than that of China in 1952, China's per capita availability of cereals is said to have been 46 percent of the 1928 and 38 percent of the 1913 Russian level. Neither India nor China had much margin to offset fluctuations in activity. Nor did external markets provide much stimulus.

The decade of highest growth rates in both countries was apparently achieved by a once-and-for-all mobilisation of savings in the hands of the State, fuelled by an import-substitution boom. In both cases, although to different degrees, the two central relationships mentioned in the introduction, the external and the urban-rural, checked the growth process. In both cases, one must surmise, defence expenditure has been an important constraint on growth in the 1960s[48] in China, running at possibly US $10 billion per year (or $12 per capita), in India about $2.7 billion (or $4 per capita).[49]

Over the quarter of a century since the first two regimes came to power, the overall rates of growth do not apparently differ qualitatively.[50] In agricultural production, while there are disagreements in detail, the range of estimates for both countries is remarkably small – between 2 and 2.5 percent per annum, or scarcely much more than the rate of growth of population.[51] For the indus-

---

47   D.H. Perkins's contribution to Ping-ti Ho and Tang Tsou (eds.) 1968, I, 1, p. 200.
48   A study of Indian defence expenditure up to 1966–7 (when it was still relatively modest) concludes that it 'slowed down the average growth of the civilian economy by as much as 0.4 percent a year – which is about one eighth of its actual recorded growth' (Benoit 1973, p. 195).
49   Cf. Table, *Far Eastern Economic Review*, 7 May 1976, p. 28.
50   There are a number of studies in this area: cf. for example Kuan-I Chen and J.S. Uppal (eds.) 1971, or Swamy 1973; for a survey of some of this material, cf. Harris 1974, pp. 273–96.
51   Growth of husked foodgrains, million metric tons, 1952–7 compared to 1968–73.

	India	China	% superiority of China
Average first 5 years	69.2	134.4	94
Average last 5 years	101.2	195.0	92.7
Percentage increase	46.2	45.1	

(For original sources and alternative estimates, cf. Harris 1973a).

trial sector, China seems to have experienced a higher long-term growth rate (between 9 and 11 percent per year)[52] than India (between 6 and 7 percent). China's industrial growth rate has been thus not so much more than its rate of growth in the pre-Communist period of peace (8–9 percent).[53] Both countries appear to have experienced declining rates of growth between the two decades (1950s and 1960s), and China's has experienced considerable fluctuations of output (without which, no doubt its performance would have been more sharply contrasted with that of India).

In both cases, the employment effect of – by historical standards – relatively high rates of industrial growth, has been poor, and possibly in most striking contrast with the experience of the Soviet Union. Eckstein argues, for example, that between 1952 and 1972 the source of China's gross product shifted radically: in 1952, 28 percent came from industry, and 1972, 37 percent; agriculture's contribution declined in the same years from 45 to 21. However, 75 percent of the active population remains engaged in agriculture. By the employment criterion, China is still in the very preliminary stages of economic development. The same generalisation would apply to India.

Preobrazhensky's critique of Bukharin's strategy seems broadly borne out in both India and China. Agriculture has so far proved unable to support the transfer of resources required to support rapid industrialisation (that is, growth of industrial output, let alone the growth in industrial employment). Industry's own savings permit quite high rates of growth of output, but so far not sufficient to spread industry very widely, particularly when both defence and consumption pressures reduce the resources available for investment. India has received considerably more external assistance than China and this has proved important at various stages, but again insufficient to change the overall course of growth. Finally, the institutional changes which Preobrazhensky predicted would flow from a Bukharinite strategy seem borne out both in the Indian Congress and what have been called the 'relaxation' phases of the Chinese Communist Party. How long the periodic 'pruning' phases can be sustained in China in the face of such severe problems is not clear. The income level in both India and China would seem to be too low to support either a Preobrazhensky or a Stalinist strategy, and it could be that, in similar fashion, social stability will demand an end to even the Chinese attempts to curb the 'rich peasant economy'.

---

52   There are sharper disagreements here, but cf. Field 1975; Rawski 1973, p. 3 ff.

53   Chang 1969 constructs an index of industrial production showing a rate of increase, 1912–36, of 9.4 percent per year (and 1912–49 of 5.6 percent per year).

CHAPTER 2.2

Agriculture, Peasants and Accumulation*

Marxism takes its point of departure from the world economy, not as a sum of national parts but as a mighty and independent reality which has been created by the international division of labour and the world market, and which in our epoch imperiously dominates the national markets ... In respect of the technique of production, socialist society must represent a stage higher than capitalism. To aim at building a *nationally isolated* socialist society means, in spite of all passing successes, to pull the productive forces backwards even as compared with capitalism ... means to pursue a reactionary Utopia. If the heralds and supporters of this theory nevertheless participate in the international revolutionary struggle (with what success is a quite different question), it is because, as hopeless eclectics, they mechanically combine abstract internationalism with reactionary Utopian national socialism.[1]

Thus Trotsky on Socialism in One Country. But while the comment is correct in relationship to socialists who pursue an isolated revolution, it tells us little concretely about the processes which would transform the Soviet Union from the first workers' State to a State capitalist regime. Trotsky certainly identified some of the contradictions which would force Stalin in directions inimical to socialism. To develop the Soviet economy, in isolation from the world market, capital must be accumulated out of the surplus value generated by the mass of the population. More exploitation, not less, was the sole remaining avenue for progress until the European revolution arrived to relieve the beleagured proletarian garrison.

One element in Stalin's response to the central problem was his treatment of the majority of the population, the peasantry. His response is important, not just for understanding the evolution of the Soviet Union, but also for analysing the powerful pressures on any regime in any backward country today. M. Lewin's remarkable book, *Russian Peasants and Soviet Power*,[2] begins the account of the factors precipitating collectivisation in the Soviet Union, 1928–

---

* From: *International Socialism* (1st series), No. 40, October/November 1969, pp. 37–9.
1 Trotsky 1962.
2 Lewin 1968.

30, and lays out in full detail the central contradiction facing Stalin's regime. To redistribute the land, to break up the great estates of the Russian nobility, was the vital element for the Russian peasantry in its acceptance of the leadership of urban workers in the Russian Revolution. But the Bolsheviks were aware that this element was a noose they put round their own necks if they accepted the demand.[3] They had no option if they were to keep the peasantry from joining the bourgeoisie in opposition to Soviet power. Land redistribution simultaneously created a new class of private owners of land – or strengthened the position of the existing class of owners – in Lenin's terms, a 'petty-bourgeoisie', committed to the defence of private property in agriculture. It also deprived urban industry of a significant part of the agricultural surplus. The new regime lost its capacity to export grain (an export important in the growth of the Tsarist economy), and a flow of resources to build industry.

Politically, the regime had to try and retain the neutrality – if not the support – of the peasantry lest it, the majority Russian class, became the seedbed for counter-revolution. Yet to do so was to accept development only at the pace at which the peasantry voluntarily expanded its output – the peasant would control the generation of the agricultural surplus, and thus the pace of urban capital accumulation. Yet to accept this was to accept that the Soviet regime would be inherently weak, continually subject to the possibility of foreign intervention or pressure. And even this slow pace depended upon urban industry producing a flow of goods at prices acceptable to the peasantry so that an urban-rural exchange could operate at all.

Nor would the situation remain stable, given the slow pace of change. The administrative machinery – in this case, the Party in the rural areas – was itself changing. As in China, in the Kiangsi Republic,[4] or just after 1948,[5] the richer peasants constantly encroached on the Party, became Party members and manipulated the local Party to their own advantage. In a similar manner, in India's Panchayeti Raj, the richer peasants constantly overshadowed the 'representative institutions' and took the lion's share of development funds. But it was not a one-way process. For, as Lewin shows, the rural Party cadres in Russia were also able to use their position to become richer peasants. Thus, in the absence of counter-pressures, the Party – an urban beachhead in the countryside – would tend to become an instrument of the richer peasants. If it did, then there would be no way of preserving the class character of the Party

---

3   See the citations in Cliff 1964–5, p. 4.
4   See Isaacs 1961, p. 344 and *passim*.
5   See Walker 1966; and Bernstein 1968.

and its political aims, let alone having available a means to siphon off resources from agriculture to industry.

During NEP, the balance of economic power tilted away from the cities. Urban industry, shattered by Civil War and the destruction of the Russian working class, did not produce a sufficient flow of goods to induce the peasants to expand their exports to the towns. The first 'scissors' crisis – a 'goods famine', a contraction of the rural market – occurred in 1923. In the mid-20s, agricultural output was still far below its 1913 level. The grain the peasants were prepared to market never resumed its pre-war level, although the population had increased substantially in the interim.

The State procurements for 1928–9 were 630 million poods; before the war, 1.3 billion poods had been marketed annually. Before the war, Russia exported 11.4 million tons of grain annually; in 1928, Russia was compelled to import grain to feed both the towns and sections of the poorer peasantry.[6] The population, both urban and rural, had increased; the demands of the cities had increased; the land redistribution, the destruction of the larger estates, had radically cut back the surplus.

Intrinsically, the situation was most alarming. In the last two months of 1927, a sudden fall in State procurements threatened the towns – or, at least, some of the urban population – with starvation. It was this jolt to the unstable system which precipitated a process of State intervention to seize the grain by force, a return to some of the elements of War Communism. Yet to intervene in this way was to prompt the peasants to cut back their output to their own needs: they had no incentive to produce what could be simply looted by force. The peasants' reaction then further forced the State to increase its efforts to seize the foodgrains that the peasants would otherwise have consumed. The moves developed 'pragmatically', but in sum they constituted Stalin's Final Solution to the Russian agrarian problem: to destroy the peasantry completely as a class, and leave the land as a place to be looted at will for the needs of urban capital accumulation. The periodic bread queues in Russia today, the poor productivity of Russian rural workers, show one of the results.

Lewin's book is one of the most important works to appear on the agrarian question. At no stage is he content with a shallow explanation of events in terms of the particular personality of Stalin (although this gave some differential emphasis to particular elements in his policies). With a superb wealth of concrete detail, he shows the nature of the problem, of the crisis, and the impossibility of the decisions.

---

6 See Lewin 1968d, p. 177.

But the Right (whose most articulate spokesman was Bukharin) and the Left (under Preobrazhensky and Trotsky) understood the nature of the dilemma, and accepted that private farming would remain the dominant element in Russian agriculture in the foreseeable future (that is, neither considered collectivisation as a serious possibility). Bukharin chose to accept the situation, to seek by all means available to preserve the goodwill of the peasant producers (which effectively meant the richer peasants). The State should assist the poorer peasants and help them to work in co-operatives. Gradually, the co-operatives would come to dominate the countryside, would move into collective farms, and then the richer peasants would see it was in their interests to join the richer and more powerful collectives. Socialism would have triumphed in the countryside by gradualist means. Yet, this meant that urban industry must produce in the short-term the goods the peasants wanted to buy, even though it could not expand at a rate faster than the peasantry would permit. Had the situation been 'normal', industry already satisfied peasant needs such that an expanding flow of grain reached the cities, the strategy might have made more sense. But it did not, and the towns led a precarious existence in terms of grain supply. On the other hand, the poorer peasants were not just weak vis-à-vis the richer, they were also economically a poor risk in terms of production. To divert State funds into this sector was possibly – although not at all inevitably – to improve peasant welfare, but not to create an area capable of supporting the towns, let alone capable of expanding industry to employ the surplus rural population. Long before the co-operatives became even self-supporting, the richer peasants would have achieved an absolute stranglehold on the market.

Was the Left any more realistic? Was there a visible alternative to Stalinism? Preobrazhensky and Trotsky acknowledged that the terms of the urban-rural exchange operated to the disadvantage of the towns because industry was backward and weak after the long period of economic dislocation in Russia. Industry must be expanded rapidly if the terms of the exchange were to be corrected, and if the Soviet regime was to survive. But where was the surplus for accumulation in expanding industry to come from? In 1926, Preobrazhensky was arguing that agricultural taxation for industrial development must be increased, but that the main source for capital accumulation must come from the industrial working class itself. As Trotsky put it, at the 12th Party Congress: 'there may be times when the State fails to pay you a full wage, or only pays half, and you, the workers, will give your State credit, out of your own pockets'.[7]

---

7   Cited in Carr 1954, p. 25 and Lewin 1968, p. 146.

But the workers were already very poor; indeed, their poverty was a key factor in the low productivity of Russian industry. To strike at them in this way was to strike at whatever basis the regime had in Russian society.

A temporary sacrifice for a short-term emergency might have been defensible, but to base a long-term policy of capital accumulation on workers' living standards would negate all the achievements of the revolution. In any case, the workers were few and already poor, so that to raise the rate of their exploitation would not realise a sufficient surplus for rapid accumulation. The peasantry, however, was enormous. Preobrazhensky moved on. The main source of capital accumulation should be from the petty bourgeoisie, and in particular, the peasantry. Through taxation, through profits on the State monopoly of external trade, through the State use of credits and loans, and, above all, through the manipulation of the exchange between agricultural and manufactured goods, accumulation for urban industry would take place. There was no *intention* that this would be a ruthless process of looting; a substantial surplus must remain in the hands of the peasants, and the poorer peasants should both be protected by tax exemption and encouraged into State-assisted co-operatives. State collectives should be created to meet an increasing proportion of urban consumption needs.

But where was the process to begin, and how long was it to last? If this was no more than a temporary holding operation until the socialist revolution overtook at least one advanced capitalist country, it might have been possible. But without that revolution, it was likely the policy would diverge either towards Bukharin's position, or more likely, towards Stalin's. To start the process in any case demanded some immediate surplus, not automatically generated by the urban-rural exchange. To lay hands on the surplus in the countryside would have begun exactly the process Stalin became trapped in. The situation had its own logic in the absence of the revolution in the West, a logic which perhaps permitted differences of emphasis but not of the basic process.

It is this logic which Lewin superbly demonstrates. Once the process began, Stalin – or, indeed anyone else – had little option but to move towards collectivisation to avoid even greater disasters. The myths Stalin invented to justify his policies, the paranoia about the kulak plot, the insanity of the class classification of the rural population, all these were only tenuously related to the real problem; but the problem remains when the myths are despatched. Although Lewin himself suggests there were alternatives to Stalin's policies – in the Opposition Platform, in the First Five-Year Plan[8] (the Plan was abandoned by

---

8   Lewin 1968, p. 358.

Stalin in practice before it was even ratified), both of which strategies eschewed collectivisation – the weight of his evidence suggests that by 1928 there were no alternatives. Even a run of bumper harvests, which would have removed perhaps the immediate crisis, would only have been a temporary relief. In the absence of outside assistance, the peasantry remained the only source of accumulation.

Again, had the Party remained a politically conscious organisation of Bolshevik workers – instead of, in its rural units, a collection of richer peasants and bureaucrats, manipulating the poorer peasants to ratify decisions – the process might have been modified. But the Left Opposition could not have recreated the Party from their offices in Moscow. Stalin purged the Party of richer peasants, and then used his crude 'apolitical' rural instruments as a blunderbuss. The cadres were reproved for the excesses which the leadership made inevitable, and thus Stalin exonerated himself in the eyes of the peasants. He recreated the Tsar, the Little Father, who protected his people from his evil satraps.[9] An identical process in China promoted the same 'cult of personality' in which the peasants found an illusory saviour in Mao and the cadres were adjudged not on their politics, but on their absolute obedience to the Leader. Pressure from the top within the Party led to the same 'spontaneous' zeal by the cadres, the same abandonment of political persuasion among the peasantry for the use of crude force. The same cult of 'bigness' led to the creation of vast administratively impossible units in the countryside. In Russia, the brutality of the process stands out with sharp clarity. Perhaps as many as ten million peasants were deported, and many of them perished on the way.[10] The incredible history of misery and oppression of the Russian *muzhik* reached its climax in his destruction. Prison socialism, a barbaric despotism filled the gap created by the failure of the socialist revolution in the advanced capitalist countries.

Collectivisation – and Lewin is to publish a volume on the years of collectivisation proper – destroyed the problem of accumulation by force. With profound irrationality, it also radically lowered the potential rate of accumulation itself. One set of problems was overcome, but another was thereby created. Russian development became immediately much more difficult and strangled, and Russian agriculture an almost unrelieved tale of disaster. But the regime survived intact. It did so by making it impossible to contain within itself genuine socialists. For the Bolsheviks, the peasantry might have been a 'petty bourgeoisie', but this was not an argument for their destruction as a class by force.

---

9   Lewin 1968, p. 452.
10   Lewin 1968, p. 50.

Collectivisation gave supreme power to the mindless bureaucrat prepared to savage anyone in the name of the Party, and robbed the political cadres of any organisation. Henceforth, the hectic priorities of Stalinism overruled any scruples at all. Thus the embryonic ruling class of Russia received its first baptism in peasant blood.

Lewin's book is a magnificent and sombre account of this process. For obvious reasons, his account lacks the authentic reply of the peasant, a reply still secreted in rural Party archives and in the memory of untold injustices by those still in exile. But given the material available, Lewin has written a superb synthesis and analysis. We are all in his debt.

The Revolutionary Role of the Peasantry*

The sheer diversity and immensity of the rural population in the world's backward countries makes general discussion of 'the peasantry' very difficult. However, certain important generalisations can be made, but it must be borne in mind that such generalisations may have different implications for groups as different as owner-occupier peasants, subsistence tenants, share croppers, landless labourers – for the serfs of Latin American *haciendas*, for the depressed small tenants of South Asia, or for the tribal farming groups of sub-Saharan Africa.

But, on the other hand, the sheer size of the peasantry in the world suggests something of its possible political importance. The nature of that political importance, however, is the subject of considerable disagreement. In particular, this article is concerned with the debate between those socialists who identify the industrial proletariat as the *sole* agency for the achievement of socialism (the Marxists), and those who identify other groups or classes – including the peasantry – as capable of achieving socialism. The debate is an old one. Its themes are an important element in Marx's disagreements with Bakunin and the anarchists, in the critique by the Russian Marxists (in particular, Plekhanov and Lenin) both of the Narodniks (Russian Populists) and the Social Revolutionaries. And they recur again in the debates within the Comintern in its early years. The themes are certainly important today – even if in a distorted way – in the Sino-Soviet dispute, in the repressed disagreements between Moscow and Havana; and, much more generally, between the 'Third World' socialists and others.

However, in the past the Marxist position has been reasonably clear. Supporters of 'peasant socialism' have, quite rightly, seen the Marxists as critics, and, in some circumstances, as opponents. Today, so great is the muddle about Marxism after its systematic perversion in the Soviet Union and China, that Marx (and Lenin) has been called in as both supporter and critic of peasant socialism. It is ironic that the Maoists and their sympathisers call themselves 'Marxist-Leninist', with so little knowledge of how sharply Marx – and even more so, Lenin – condemned some of the most favoured positions held by the

---

* From: *Debate*, International Socialism (1st series), No. 41, December 1969/January 1970, pp. 18–24.

Great Helmsman. Thus, it is important to restate – even if crudely – what the Marxist view of the peasantry has been,[1] and why the proletariat – that is, the industrial working class – was identified as the *sole* agency for the achievement of socialism.

Marx on the Peasants

In analysing the perspective for socialists in France and Germany, Marx noted that in countries where the peasantry constituted a majority of the population, the peasants held the power to decide whether or not the proletariat could win and keep power. Where the peasants were solidly conservative, then the proletariat would not be able to hold power indefinitely. But in Germany, the peasants were fighting the feudal aristocracy on their own account, to establish freehold land rights and rid agriculture of feudal restrictions. Thus, the peasantry were waging the bourgeois revolution. The proletariat accordingly must win the support of the peasantry in the proletarian struggle against capitalism by supporting the peasant struggle against feudalism. The two battles must be synchronised for either ally to win its aims.

But clearly a common struggle would include contradictory elements, and socialism could not be won unless the proletariat was clearly the leader of the struggle. The leadership of the proletariat was essential because the nature of the peasantry made it impossible for it to lead, and in any case, the peasants were aiming at ends not necessarily consistent with the achievement of proletarian aims. What was this 'nature of the peasantry'? Perhaps Marx's best known outline of an answer to this question – in relation to the small French peasantry – occurs in *The Eighteenth Brumaire of Louis Napoleon*, and it is worth quoting at some length:

> The small peasants form a vast mass, the members of which live in similar conditions but without entering into manifold relations with one another. Their mode of production isolates them from one another, instead of bringing them into mutual intercourse. The isolation is increased by France's bad means of communication and by the poverty of the peasants. Their field of production, the small-holding, admits of no division of labour in its cultivation, no application of science, and, therefore, no multiplicity of development, no diversity of talent, no wealth of social rela-

---

1   This is dealt with in detail by Tony Cliff 1964–5.

tionships. Each individual peasant family is almost self-sufficient; it itself directly produces the major part of its consumption and thus acquires its means of life more through exchange with nature than its intercourse with society ... Insofar as millions of families live under economic conditions of existence that divide their mode of life, their interests and their culture from those of other classes, and put them in hostile contrast to the latter, they form a class. Insofar as there is merely a local interconnection among these small peasants, and the identity of their interests begets no unity, no national union, and no political organisation, they do not form a class. They are consequently incapable of enforcing their class interest in their own names, whether through a parliament or through a convention. They cannot represent themselves, they must be represented.[2]

It is true that we cannot jump directly from this description of the small French peasantry in the middle of the nineteenth century – a peasantry with half a century's experience of relatively unfettered private ownership of land – to the rest of the world's rural population at all times and places. But certain key aspects of the conditions of material existence of virtually all peasants are outlined in this quotation, and it is these aspects which underlie the Marxist position.

The Nature of Peasant Life

Thus, the peasants are isolated from the national society, isolated physically in villages which have little consistent need for continuous communications both with each other and with the cities. At most, the peasant is likely to be aware of his district, within which members of his own family meet or secure marriage partners, and of the local district town, perhaps the source of the merchants who buy his crop, the market place, the site of the police station and so on. Second, the peasant is dependent almost entirely upon himself and his family for his way of life. He is not part of – or at least, is not aware of – a complex interdependent national division of labour. Since there is little division of labour outside the family, there is little specialisation, and as a result, production is primitive, the peasant is poor, the cultural and technical resources of the village are most backward.

---

2 Marx 1969–70a, p. 414.

The peasant's important relationships are not to a wider economy of which he sees himself as a constituent part, but rather to nature, to the rhythms, to the arbitrariness of soil, weather and season. The production unit is the family, and personal relationships are thus also production relationships. Family relationships, rather than competence and technical specialisation, determine the primitive division of labour within the family (the relationship between man and wife, between man and his eldest son, his youngest son, his aged father, and so on), and the production relationships exaggerate and intensify the family relationships. The desperate family feuds within the village exhibit the intensity generated within what is simultaneously the basic personal, production and property unit. The rural family embodies all the exploitative relationships of the wider society, and it is the peasant household father who is of necessity the agent for the worst forms of exploitation of the members of his own family; the agent which sustains all that is worst in pre-capitalist society in terms of personal relationships. The violence locked up in the family is matched by the violence between families, the violence intrinsic in the gross subordination of the peasantry as a whole.

Thus, if achieving a socialist revolution were merely a function of the savagery of exploitation, then undoubtedly the peasantry would always have pre-eminently qualified for the role of agency of the revolution. But revolution requires also collective organisation, a mass division of labour, a concentration of advanced technical and political abilities. And it is these which the peasantry – by the nature of its way of life – cannot produce. It cannot, as a class, produce the abilities required to operate a society with a collective division of labour. It can only duplicate the ideal of its own members, the small peasant holding. The aim of peasant rebels thus becomes, not the advance of society as a whole, but no more than a just sharing of a common poverty. This is certainly egalitarianism, but it is the egalitarianism of communalists, of independent identical participants, not the egalitarianism of collectivists, of interdependent people organised in a social division of labour. The peasantry cannot, as a class, constitute itself the ruling class in order to realise the full economic potentialities of society. On the contrary, it can, on its own, only drag society backwards into the poverty of the past.

Peasant Opposition

It is for these reasons that the revolt of the peasant is so often a purely localised occurrence, restricted to the district he knows. His enemy is the local landlord or landowner, the local money-lender, policeman or merchant, not a national ruling class of which he is inevitably only very dimly aware. But without destroying the national ruling class, the local peasant's cause is lost. The destruction of only the local minions of the ruling class will invoke massive reprisals on a scale with which the local peasant cannot cope. Indeed, so muddled may be the peasant's view of the world outside his district, he may completely exonerate the ruling class for responsibility for the crimes of its local officials. In Tsarist Russia, the peasants often certainly hated their local noblemen, but they worshipped the Tsar as the 'Little Father', explaining that the Tsar did not know the crimes committed in his name by his noblemen. For them, there was no 'system' within which Tsar and noblemen fitted as complementary elements within a common exploitative class. Thus when the Narodniks assassinated Tsar Alexander in 1881 with the expectation that this would precipitate a peasant revolt against the regime, the peasants were appalled, and blamed yet again the evil nobles for depriving them of their only defender. Lewin suggests that Stalin was similarly exonerated by the Russian peasantry for the Communist rape of the countryside during collectivisation.[3]

Thus, historically, the peasant is a figure of the utmost tragedy. He is grotesquely exploited, forced into self-subjection, forced into preserving all that is most backward and reactionary. And yet he makes his own straitjacket. He cannot, by his way of life, conceive of a real alternative. He cannot emancipate himself, and self-emancipation is one of the preconditions for socialism. His opposition to his own exploitation, when he is solely dependent upon his own resources, is thus either purely negative, or marginal to the system – that is, the opposition does not challenge the existence of the system so much as check certain practices within it. The most common form of this opposition – and the least effective in revolutionary terms – is social banditry. Small bands of armed men prey on the forces of authority, acting as Robin Hoods to take from the rich and give, at least in principle, to the poor. The small size of such groups, their great mobility, and the willingness of the dispersed peasant families to protect and supply the rebels as a sort of 'counter police' force, make them almost invulnerable to counter-attack by the authorities. Hobsbawm has described the features of such forces in parts of southern Europe,[4] and perhaps these features are shared with the Indian *dacoits* and similar bands which operated in China. Hobsbawm also notes the similarities between social banditry and guerilla warfare, and how the second sometimes absorbs the first (thus, no one should be shocked to find that the guerilla forces of the Chinese Com-

---

3   Lewin 1968, p. 452.
4   Hobsbawm 1959.

munist Party incorporated erstwhile bandits).[5] Banditry is the most primitive form of taking sanctions against the system, where self-interested criminality is scarcely distinguishable from socially conscious rebellion, and where the sanction is no more than a marginal irritant to the system.

The sporadic riot in densely populated agricultural areas has more possibilities. Here, rural Luddites directly attack the symbols of immediate oppression – the merchant hoarding grain, the big farmer cutting his labour force or the wages he pays, the state reducing the price it regulates for wine. If such riots are a response to a general condition on the land, the riot may spread. And if it coincides with movements in the towns, it may provide a contributory element in a movement for radical change. But it is only one tributary to the river. Alone it can do little. When Wat Tyler's rebels took London, as when Zapata's warriors reached Mexico City, they did not know what to do with it. Finally they could only retire back to the world they knew, to the village and the dispersed land holding. They left the real power of the ruling class, chastened perhaps, but not destroyed. Of course, if the status quo is already under threat from other sources, the possibility may exist for a temporary enclave of peasant power. Makhno and the Green armies in Russia relied on the Civil War raging around them to defend their islands of power. And in China, the decay of the Manchu dynasty under the corrosive forces of imperialism permitted the Taiping rebels similarly to establish their own domain along the Yangtze. But once the wider issue is settled or moderated, the national ruling class can react with a force capable of destroying the enclave.

More effectively and more characteristically, the peasantry can in certain conditions control much more massive sanctions of a purely negative kind. They can refuse to obey the law, and if this spreads far enough, the ruling class has insufficient power to garrison the whole countryside. But the organisation capable of co-ordinating such a strike usually can only be found in the cities. The intellectual formulation of this tactic is clearest in the doctrine of passive disobedience as advanced by Tolstoy in Russia and Gandhi in India.[6] But what is to be done when the countryside is paralysed? It is at this point that again the strategy breaks down, for the peasants have no positive alternative to present. The same applies to a similar tactic: withholding the food on which the survival of the cities depends. This is unlikely to occur normally, since the peasants also depend on the cities for certain goods, and many need to sell their crop

---

5 Some cadres also moved into banditry, cf. Isaacs 1961, pp. 328–9 and 348.
6 This point is made by Teodor Shanin, along with much else of interest, in Shanin 1966, pp. 5–27.

quickly to meet their debts. But in Russia between 1927 and 1929 when the cities could not supply the goods the peasants wanted, there was something of a strike which produced a major crisis in the society as a whole. The strike was *not* an organised act, one of collective solidarity and depending on political consciousness. It was a simultaneous reaction to a market situation. And the peasants had no defence when Stalin launched his counter-attack and set about destroying the Russian peasantry once and for all.

Rural Strata

What is lacking in all of these examples is the role of a national class for itself. In the citation from Marx, he makes this point explicitly. The peasantry as a class of men certainly exists. But by the nature of its way of life, it cannot become aware of itself as a class, a body of men sharing a common class interest which extends throughout society. In the sense of recognising a common interest, peasants are normally only a class in one district. And the peasants of one district may regard those of another with as much hostility as representatives of the ruling class. In some cases, the hostility is greater, for at least they know their own rulers in the district, and the known generates fewer fears than the unknown.

Some Marxists have tried to apply a class analysis to the countryside to overcome some of these problems. They have identified poor, middle and rich peasant strata (with other, more complex, patterns as well), landlords and landowners, and argued on the basis of the conflict of interest between these strata, for identification with the poor peasantry. In a feudal land distribution system, socialist identification with the peasantry as a whole against the large landowners is reasonably straightforward. Again, in certain circumstances, and in some localities, a proletarian alliance with the poorer peasantry may embody a real class struggle. Indeed, on some occasions, the poor peasantry has attacked its rich brethren, as seems to have been the case in the Telengana revolt in India in 1947 (to the horror of the Maoist sympathisers in the Indian Communist Party who wanted an alliance of all peasant strata). But these cases are not necessarily the standard ones, particularly where the land distribution system is a complex one. For some peasants may also be landlords, and the social mobility (up and down) of peasant families may be high. Thus, a rich peasant father with many sons may divide his land among them all, making all his descendants poor peasants. There may be constant interchange between strata – the landless move into and out of cultivation; the small peasants into labouring, or, if their families are small for a couple of generations and there are no outside crises, into the ranks of the middle or richer peasantry. And one peasant family may fit into several strata – it farms some land, it rents another small piece, it works as labourer on someone else's land, at different times of the year. With such complexity, it makes little political sense to identify the 'natural allies' of the proletariat in *general*.

The peasant situation itself can also make nonsense of such identifications. The poor peasants, like the landless labourers, are the most depressed group – less analogous with the proletariat than with the lumpenproletariat. And the poor peasant's natural sense of identification is more usually upwards, to the richer peasant strata the poor peasant aspires to join, rather than outwards to poor peasants in other – unknown – districts. The rural society is bounded by the district boundaries, and it is within these boundaries that the strata can be identified most accurately. Outside the district one usually has only statistics, not a political strategy. The instability of the lower strata has prompted socialists and Communists more frequently to rely on the middle and richer peasants for radical organisation, for they are the village leaders and, as such, most likely to be more aware of the outside society. In times of relative peace, a 'poor peasant movement' is likely to be a myth of urban politics. For identical reasons, radical attempts to set up all-India alliances of the lowest castes have always proved abortive. The natural identification of village Untouchables is, sadly, with the dominant peasant castes of the village (even when they murder some of them) rather than with the millions of Untouchables in other districts. To know of the existence of those other Untouchables, to recognise a common interest, is already to be part of another – urban, and so national – world.

Thus, the peasant revolt needs the intervention of parts of other – national – classes to take it beyond its prescribed role. It is not accidental that the peasantry has always been more oppressed than any other class, has a history of revolt, and yet has so few successes. Success comes when other ambitions are allied to peasant grievances. In classical China, peasant revolt was successful when members of the nobility came to lead it, came to use it in order to establish a new dynasty. On rare occasions, peasants themselves became members of the new ruling order, but only on terms which negated any real revolutionary transformation of Chinese society. In the bourgeois revolution, the struggle of the bourgeoisie to establish its own political power borrows heavily from the peasant struggle to destroy the great feudal estates, and is the precondition for the success of the peasants.

The Crude Materialist Case

Socialists who have seen the peasantry as an agency for the achievement of socialism – leaving aside what could be meant by 'socialism' in this context – have usually been impressed by the violence of peasant struggle,[7] by the complete alienation of the peasant from the forms of urban (or 'bourgeois') life. But the violence is a function of the backwardness of the peasantry and its relative weakness, the lack of political means to change other than violence, rather than revolutionary fervour or vision.

Such socialists also often utilise a particularly crude materialistic explanation of political militancy. This materialism does not, however, rule out a simultaneous romantic idealism about the possibilities of human action whatever the material circumstances. The case runs something like this: revolution is a function of exploitation; so that those who are most exploited will be the most revolutionary; those who are the most exploited are the poorest; thus, the poorest peasantry, the most backward tribal groups (in some countries), the lumpenproletariat, are all candidates for the agency of revolution.

There are obvious surface similarities to a Marxist case, but a major difference lies in the obscure word 'exploitation'. In this case, 'exploitation' means impoverishment. In the Marxist case, 'exploitation' means 'the degree to which surplus value is produced'. Thus, for the Marxist, sheer poverty is not a necessary index of 'exploitation', nor is it a guide as to the agency of revolution. If Marx had believed that poverty of itself was the source of revolution, then it is a signal failure on his part not to have identified the nineteenth-century peasantry (or the lumpenproletariat) as the agency of socialist revolution: the peasants were undoubtedly poorer than the proletariat. Again, within the proletariat, the poorest strata would obviously be more revolutionary than the richer, the unskilled more than the skilled. In fact, for Marx as well as historically, revolutionary political consciousness tended to develop in exactly the reverse order. More to the point, Marx actually allowed for an increase in the real consumption of the working class, a decline in its absolute poverty, without this affecting his case. He writes, for example:

---

7 Consider, for example, Frantz Fanon's comment: 'In colonial countries, the peasants alone are revolutionary, for they have nothing to lose and everything to gain. The starving peasant, outside the class system, is the first among the exploited to discover that only violence pays. For him, there is no compromise, no possible coming to terms ...' (Fanon 1965, p. 48).

If, therefore, the income of the worker increases with the rapid growth of capital, the social gulf that separates the worker from the capitalist, increases at the same time, the power of capital over labour, the dependence of labour on capital, increases at the same time ... Even the *most favourable* situation for the working class, the *most rapid possible growth* of capital, however much it may improve the material existence of the worker, does not remove the antagonism between his interests and the bourgeois interests, those of the capitalist.[8]

The dimension missing in the crude materialist case is power. Skilled labour is not only more 'exploited' than unskilled, the proletariat than the peasantry, but it is clearer to skilled labour how much capitalism depends upon it, just as it is clearer to the proletariat how much the whole of society is sustained by its efforts. There is thus a real, daily, contradiction between the economic power of the proletariat, and its political impotence – the proletariat *is* the economy, but it does not run the economy. Thus, it is exploitation in the Marxist sense, not in the sense of 'impoverishment', and the contradiction of power and impotence rather than depressed consumption, which are the driving forces for the revolutionary mission of the proletariat in the Marxist scheme.

The Proletariat

One can take the case further than this. For on all the criteria mentioned earlier in relationship to the peasantry, the proletariat is contrasted. It is heavily concentrated in great cities, and within those cities, in particular districts; not dispersed over an enormous area, and isolated in small units. Daily, the workers operate the most advanced sectors of the economy, where innovation and change are constant dynamic elements destroying the inherited customs of the past. They have forced upon them, as part of their very daily existence, a mass division of labour which includes high specialisation, including the most advanced technical knowledge, and elaborate interdependence. Of necessity, the workers are a collective, covering the whole of the most important parts of the economy, not a community of independent producers. By their daily work and daily struggle, they are aware that society as a whole is the arena, not one district, nor even just one factory. The employer is part of an employing class, standing in a certain relationship to the state and its agencies.

---

8 Marx 1969–70b, p. 273. Marx's emphasis.

Of course, in practice, many different levels of perception exist among workers and make for many variations from this rather abstract pattern. However, the difference between the proletariat and the peasantry is that, in principle, workers can comprehend society as a whole, and given the Marxist perspective for the development of capitalism, will be driven to do so. The peasantry, in principle, cannot comprehend society as a whole, and are not driven to do so by the nature of their way of life. On the contrary, the peasant who acquires a knowledge of society as a whole is an anomaly, someone who has to fight against the intrinsic conditions of his way of life rather than being led necessarily by those conditions in that direction.

Where the proletariat is a majority, its own emancipation is within its own power, and its self-emancipation is the emancipation of society as a whole, including the peasantry. Thus, the role of the proletariat is not an optional element in Marxism. Without it, Marxism becomes nonsense, and we have to start from scratch all over again. Whatever form of 'socialism' could be formulated on different grounds could not, validly, borrow from Marxism except by changing the essential meaning of the words involved (as we have seen is the case with the term 'exploitation').

The Worker-Peasant Alliance

In countries where peasants are a majority of the population, Marxists have had to formulate what should be the relationship between the proletarian struggle and the peasantry. Marx himself always supported the small peasant struggle against large feudal owners – a constituent element of the bourgeois revolution – but he opposed the struggle of small property owners against large capitalist concerns – a counter-revolution.[9] Large-scale capitalist enterprise had to be preserved for collective ownership, for it was the source from which the wealth of socialist society would come. When the proletariat begins its battle against capitalism, making socialism for the first time possible, large-scale production was not to be broken up among the producers. In the 1850 programme for the Communist League in Germany, Marx proposed that the royal and large feudal estates should *not* be distributed to the peasants, but preserved under state ownership.[10] Similarly the Bolshevik programme in Tsarist Russia demanded the nationalisation of commercially important landed estates, *not* their

---

9   For further discussion of this, cf. Cliff 1964–5.
10   Marx 1969–70c.

redistribution among the peasants. In this, the Bolsheviks went flatly against the demand both of the peasants and their main political champions, the Social Revolutionaries.

In the event, the Bolshevik programme was irrelevant, since the peasants just seized the land, and the Bolsheviks could do little about it except ratify the seizure. But in seizing the land, the peasantry created a new class of owners of private property. It was an albatross around the neck of the Soviet regime. The regime only freed itself by Stalin's Final Solution of the peasant question, the complete destruction of the peasantry in collectivisation.

Implicit in both Marx and Lenin's writings is a stress upon the inconsistent aims of peasant and proletarian, their *different* targets. Many Populist socialists have refused to accept this sharp distinction, even though the distinction is a crucial line between libertarian socialism and the autocratic state socialisms which occur when outsiders ride the back of the 'People' into power. Since the peasants are not a national class for themselves, they cannot control their own leaders, they must be represented (cf. the quotation from Marx above). When these leaders are intent on ends other than those of the peasants – ends such as industrialisation, national unity, and so on – the populists can be the worst dictators of all.

Thus, the distinction between peasant and proletarian is not a pedantic aside, a piece of irrelevant sectarianism. It defines different roads to *different things*. Lenin was particularly emphatic in stressing the difference, in refusing to muddle all the issues in the 'People'. He constantly criticised the Social Revolutionaries for doing just this. For example, in 1909, he wrote of the Social Revolutionary programme:

> The fundamental idea of their programme is not at all that 'an alliance of the proletariat and the peasantry is necessary', but that there is no class abyss between the former and the latter, and that there is no need to draw a line of class demarcation between them, and that the (Marxist) idea of the petty-bourgeois nature of the peasantry that distinguishes it from the proletariat is fundamentally false.

The peasant movement was indeed fighting, but not capitalist relationships so much as pre-capitalist relationships. The complete victory of the peasant movement 'will not abolish capitalism: on the contrary, it will create a broader foundation for its development'.

This does not mean that peasants will not play an important role in the battle for socialism, but that role is only possible under leadership from the proletariat. Without that leadership, the peasant struggle leads to other things.

Of course, like Lenin, we must 'support the peasant movement to the end, but we must remember that it is a movement of another class, not the one that can or will accomplish socialism'.[11]

China and the Peasantry

If the foregoing case is broadly true, then it becomes important to explain a number of modern revolutions which have been claimed as 'peasant revolutions'. What follows mainly concerns China, although elements of the analysis could also be applied to other countries, for example, Cuba. The leadership of the Chinese Communist Party was drawn in the main from urban classes, particularly from the urban intelligentsia. It utilised different segments of the population in its advance to power, but undoubtedly the bulk of its support was drawn from the peasantry. The struggle for power was, for various reasons which cannot be cited here, not a *class* struggle in the Marxist sense. It was not primarily a struggle taking place between elements of the contending classes within the same production unit. Rather the struggle was a military-territorial battle, while the social struggle – which certainly occurred – was no more than a supporting element for the military operation. Of course, the final phases of any revolutionary movement may be a military-territorial struggle – the Civil War in Russia was just such a struggle. But in China, the essence of the movement was military-territorial, and the direct class struggle marginal from 1928 through to 1948.

The party used different demands in different localities to build up its support, demands designed to build not a class force so much as a national force, drawing on different sections of the population. Nationally, the party restricted itself to demands for relatively mild reforms in order to carry the whole coalition against the main target. Thus, the party opposed the demand for land reform up to 1945 in order not to frighten the larger land holders, and its only

---

11   Useful comparisons can be drawn between current socialist attitudes to the struggle in the backward countries, and, for example, views expressed by Marx on Bolivar in the struggle for the freedom of Latin America, and by Lenin on Sun Yat-sen in China. For Marx on Bolivar, cf. Draper 1968, pp. 64–77. Lenin on Sun Yat-sen is contained in Lenin 1936b, p. 305. Lenin writes: 'They (viz. the Chinese nationalists) are subjectively socialists because they are opposed to the oppression and exploitation of the masses. But the objective conditions of China, of a backward, agricultural, semi-feudal country, place on the order of the day, in the lives of a nation numbering nearly half a billion, only one definite historically peculiar form of this oppression and exploitation, namely feudalism' (Lenin 1936b, p. 308).

concession to its poor peasant supporters was the reduction of rent and interest to be paid to landlords. Even after 1945, it appears now that it was the discredited Liu Shao-chi who championed land reform in the face of the opposition of Mao Tse-tung, who resisted such 'sectional' demands in the interest of national unity. All that Mao would concede was that 'excess land' should be compulsorily purchased.

Thus, the Chinese Communist Party cannot be seen as the agent of the Chinese peasantry, and indeed, cannot be seen as the agent of any class. It sought to operate *outside* the peasant social structure, drawing support from all rural strata. It was not responsible to any particular segment of the population, nor yet to the peasantry as a whole. No section of the peasantry controlled the party. Rather did the party and the People's Liberation Army control sections of the peasantry.

If the party had not operated outside the peasant social structure, it would have been infiltrated by the richer peasants and subordinated to their interests, a change which would have led to the disintegration of the party between different districts. At times the party was threatened with this. For example, Mao complained in 1933 that 80 percent of the central district of the Hunan-Kiangsi Soviet was controlled by the landlords and rich peasants.[12] Again, in the early 1950s, when peasant communists returned from military service to their homes, the rural party threatened once more to become no more than a rich peasant organisation.[13] The peasant cadres expected to be rewarded for their services, and to be left alone to till their new land after the sacrifices of war. The

---

12   Lenin 1936c, p. 150. Compare Marx 1969–70c, p. 160: 'The relation of the revolutionary workers' party to the petty-bourgeois democracy* is this: it marches together with it against the section which it aims at overthrowing, it opposes the petty-bourgeoisie in everything by which they desire to establish themselves'.

     * This 'comprises not only the great majority of the bourgeois inhabitants of the towns, the small industrial businessmen and guild masters, it numbers among its following the peasants and the rural proletariat'.

13   Isaacs writes: 'Mao Tse-tung, president of the "Soviet Republic" wrote: "Many landlords and rich peasants put on a revolutionary colouration. They say they are for the revolution and for the division of land ... They are very active and rely on their historical advantages – 'they can speak well and write well' – and consequently in the first period they steal the fruits of the agrarian revolution. Facts from innumerable places prove that they have usurped the provisional power, filtered into the armed forces, controlled the revolutionary organisations, and received more and better land than the poor peasants". Mao estimated that this was the case in "80 per cent of the area of the central district, affecting a population of more than 2,000,000" (Mao 1933, 'Re-examination of Land Distribution in the Soviet Districts is the Central Task', *Red Flag*, 31 August)' (Isaacs 1961, p. 344).

rural party was used to make cadres rich peasants, and rich peasants became cadres as a means of advancing their position. Kao Kang in 1952 castigated cadres who had become exploiters, lending money and hiring labour:

> 'If no active steps are taken', he argued, 'to lead the peasants towards the path of co-operative economy rather than to the rich peasant economy, then rural village government is sure to deteriorate into a rich peasant regime. If the Communist Party members all hire labour and give loans at usurious rates, then the Party will become a rich peasant party'.[14]

The same phenomenon occurred in the Soviet Union during the New Economic Policy, rendering the rural party useless as an agency for change.[15] It is a striking demonstration that the Chinese Communist Party is *not* a peasant party – that it did not degenerate in the way Kao Kang feared. It was possible for the party to purge its rural organisation and to whip errant cadres into line simply because it was *not* a peasant party.

Thus, the Chinese Communist Party was not a 'peasant party' in the sense in which we might speak of a 'proletarian party', or, indeed, a 'bourgeois party'. Certainly people of peasant origin provided the bulk of the party rank and file, but even then, such recruits had usually long since left the land to become professional cadres or soldiers. The party's ability to transform China depended upon it being independent of peasant interests, and in this respect, it was largely successful. Rather was it the case that a section of the urban intelligentsia organised peasant discontent. And even then, success depended heavily upon the occurrence of the Japanese invasion and the Japanese policy of ransacking and burning villages in the wake of their advance. By and large, peasants do not seem susceptible to nationalist demands – unlike the urban middle class, and for fairly obvious material reasons – unless such demands are closely linked to demands of immediate concern for peasants, demands over land, or, in this case, sheer survival. It is open to doubt whether the sections of the Chinese peasantry which did respond to communist appeals would have done so if the party had not provided the only real opposition to the Japanese, whose actions directly affected the existence of some of the peasants. In India, certainly, tying the demand for independence to the demand that those who supported the British, the landowners, should be expropriated, and their land

---

14   Kao Kang, 'Overcome the Corrosion of Bourgeois Ideology: Oppose the Rightist Trend in the Party', *People's Daily*, 24 January 1952, cited in *Current Background* 163, 5 March 1952.

15   Lewin 1968, p. 121, *passim*.

redistributed among the peasants, was a vital factor in eliciting peasant support. And in Vietnam, without the Vietminh and National Liberation Front's land reform programme, it is unlikely the war against the American army could have been waged.

Because the leadership of the Communist Party in China was not securely tied to the interests of any class, it was able to act as an elitist force, and its politics have striking similarities with the elitist flavour of much populism (and, including in this, some brands of anarchism). Populism can be roughly defined as a passionate belief in the spontaneous energies of the 'People', and a powerful elitist belief in one's own necessary role in bringing enlightenment to the 'People'.[16] But rejecting identification with any particular class is rejecting responsibility to any class. It leaves the leadership free to pursue whatever ends suit its tactics. In Maoism, populism includes a powerful nationalist element, a belief that anything and everything is possible within one's own national boundaries, that nationalism encompasses socialism. Everything is possible because there is no given objective society – if hearts and minds can be changed. Thus the target becomes souls rather than a definite ruling class, and no objective laws of capitalism or anything else can, it is said, defeat this infinite voluntarism. There are certainly aspects of Marxism which lend themselves, in isolation, to a populist revision,[17] even though such a revision also directly contradicts Marxism.

Backwardness and Socialism

None of this bears directly on the kind of problems which face Marxists in backward countries. Thus: is the thesis of permanent revolution, and in particular, the role of the proletariat, still relevant in backward countries today? If it is not, then what should be the role of Marxists in backward countries? These are major questions which demand separate answers at length, and cannot properly be discussed here.[18] Suffice it to say that even if the proletariat can no longer be seen as the agency of revolution in backward countries today, this does not change the validity of the points made here. It means only that proletarian socialism cannot be achieved in the backward countries on their own

---

16   This definition is taken from Meisner's biography of an important Chinese populist, Li Tachao, one of the two founders of the Chinese Communist Party. Cf. Meisner 1967, p. 251.

17   On this, cf. the extended discussion in Harris 1968, Chapter 6, pp. 185–227.

18   For an attempt at this, see Cliff 1963. An American author has also attempted some comparisons – cf. Halperin 1967.

today. But then it never could. Socialism is not possible in one country or one region, particularly when these are the most backward. Certainly, imperialism can be defeated at various points in backward countries – but not destroyed in the world as a whole. Certainly, important and progressive changes can be made in backward countries – but these changes do not constitute socialism. No amount of rhetorical *élan* can convert poverty into wealth, can give men in a backward society the basic conditions of life already secured in an advanced one. Indeed, the rhetoric alone should make us suspicious. Where objective conditions permit little rapid improvement of material circumstances, governments have often seen the next best thing to real progress as trying to persuade people that there is really progress anyway, that the things of the spirit are so much more important than the next bowl of rice.

What one must not do is bend one's estimate of objective reality to accommodate short-term tactical considerations. Thus, the progressiveness of the revolution in China leads on to arguing that the Chinese 'model' is the sole means to achieve socialism, and all things Chinese are, by definition, progressive. The left intellectuals of the 1930s played the same game with the Soviet Union, and ended being taken for a ride. Moscow came to equal socialism, and all criteria for judging Moscow on a socialist basis thus disappeared. The sympathisers ended as apologists for the Russian state (of course, it is also true that the Chinese Revolution has not played nearly so important a role in the political awareness of non-Chinese socialists as did the Russian Revolution, nor has Mao achieved anything like the international significance of Stalin).

Progressive steps are important, even if they are not the final step. But in present conditions, whatever happens in China – or anywhere else – is continuously threatened by the continued existence of the imperialist powers. In Vietnam, the American forces may be defeated, but this will not end the existence of Washington. The existence of the advanced capitalist powers, private and state, makes the prospects for any sustained economic development in the backward countries grim. Thus, the future of the backward countries, like the future of the peasantry, depends not on one defeat of one element of imperialism, but on its global destruction. And it cannot be destroyed globally in Vietnam, nor can it be destroyed by the world's peasantry. It can only be destroyed in the advanced countries themselves, and only by the proletariat. Thus the issue – peasant or proletarian – is not about who can achieve 'socialism' in one country, but about the emancipation of mankind as a whole.

China: Decentralisation and Development*

The face which the People's Republic of China presents to the world is truly an astonishing one. At one moment, China is rotten with resurgent capitalism, the decay reaching as high as the top leadership of the Communist Party and some of its most trusted members. A short time later, the capitalists turn out to be the tiniest group of people, easily excised to reveal once again the picture of happy China, a sort of continuous Methodist Sunday School (no wage pressure, no strikes, no riots, so appealing to the visiting representatives of foreign ruling classes). At one moment, continuous political discussion is the only way of saving China; all remnants of private enterprise must be rooted out; Red Rebels in the factories must revolt against all who seek to impose 'capitalist' norms. At another, the *People's Daily* – without so much as the hint of a blush – calls for an end to time-wasting meetings and discussions (23 October 1972), praises the peasants' private plots (22 October 1972), and demands punishment for those who resist managerial authority and discipline in the factories (30 May 1972). It must be a strain for even the most agile cadre to know what is correct.

Suddenly all the old slogans have become 'ultra-Left'. And the fears as well – the creeping shadow of Japanese imperialism across east and southeast Asia which a short time ago seemed so worrying for Prime Minister Chou En-lai – have suddenly disappeared. Once Japan's Prime Minister had been able to exchange a few diplomatic words with Chou on his visit in September 1972, it was all cleared up. They signed a treaty, of which Chou – without batting an eyelid – said: 'The new relationship is not directed against third parties. Neither of us are seeking hegemony in the Pacific region, and both are opposed to those who are'. Imperialisms pop up and fall down simply on the nod of the Chinese Prime Minister, it seems.

Yet there are casualties in this zigzag policy which moves so rapidly from 'ultra-Left' to the most conservative orthodoxies. Prominent leaders of the party turn out to be insufficiently 'flexible'. There are now only two effective members surviving from the 1969 five-man Standing Committee of the Politbureau (Mao and Chou). A third of the Politbureau itself seems to have been purged in the past 18 months, and of the remaining 14, only eight are active (that is, neither very aged nor ill).

---

* From: India–China: Underdevelopment and Revolution, Delhi, Vikas, 1974, pp. 107–20.

Then there are those foreign Maoists and pro-China liberals who bravely defended all things Chinese through the difficult years of the Cultural Revolution. Now they find much of what they defended was 'ultra-Left', and some of those whom they praised now purged. Even that little Red Book, bravely waved by so many millions, now turns out to have been part of the wicked plot of Lin Biao to embroil his modest master in the cult of personality. If those supporters were right then, they must be wrong now, or vice versa. And if they are right now, but mistaken in the past, how can we be sure that next year they will not decide they were wrong now? One must be a little shameless to act merely as an unpaid public relations agent, regardless of all twists and turns.

Between the leadership and their foreign acolytes are many millions of young Chinese who believed Mao's promises, but have now been betrayed. They did not inherit power. They have been whipped back to school or exiled to remote rural areas. A small minority of them – perhaps 20,000 – last year defied death to break through the Chinese border controls and swim to Hong Kong. The rate of illegal immigration to the city is now higher than in any year since the famine exodus of 1962. Half the swimmers are young people banished to rural areas, and a quarter are regular young farm workers.

The key factor in the period since the end of the Cultural Revolution that has produced this great swing to the Right has been the behaviour of the Soviet Union. In 1968 Russia invaded Czechoslovakia. In 1969 it launched border attacks on China in the north,[1] and for a time it looked as though it might push matters to war. At that stage, the Chinese army was ensnared in administering China, since efforts to restore the administrative capacity of the Communist Party had not been successful.[2] The first priority for the government was therefore to restore the army – or a significant part of it – to its military functions, and rapidly improve and develop its weaponry, equipment and transport. To do these things, the party had quickly to be restored to administration, trade expanded (to import materials for stockpiling and defence production), and State civil expenditure radically reduced to make room for an expanded defence budget. All these things, as well as the Soviet border threat itself, required most urgently a return to domestic peace, an end to factional warring and real attempts to soothe the feelings of the mass of the population, to give people something worth defending.

---

1   See Harris 1969–70.
2   For the development of this point, see Chapter 4.

The Economy

To make room for an expanded defence programme, the government has radically cut its financial obligations and made extensive changes in economic policy. There has been a general campaign for economy in the Central Government bureaucracy. Edgar Snow reports from his interview with Chou that the employment of cadres in the Central Government had been cut from 60,000 before the Cultural Revolution to 10,000 by December 1970, and this shrinking has continued. Those sacked have been bundled off to rural areas rather than being allowed to join the urban unemployed; the communes have to support the redundant bureaucrats, although admittedly at much lower rates of pay and without the obligation to provide the welfare provisions customary for urban workers. The Red Guards were similarly broken up and dispatched to the countryside – some 10 to 20 million of them. All the young people who got back into the city will now have been expelled again. Wuhan, for example, a city of three million people, claims to have sent 220,000 of its young people to the countryside over the past years. To encourage the communes to accept these unlooked-for mouths, some public authorities are said to be offering subsidies of Y200 to Y240 per head.

Second, the State has drastically cut its expenditure on education, health and culture (a quarter of the central budget in the 1950s). The length of compulsory schooling has been cut from ten to seven years; all pupils must simultaneously work in a factory or on the land, and their education is subordinate to the demands of their work. More important, education must now be financed and supervised by the production team in the villages (production teams vary in size, but roughly correspond to a small village) and factories in the cities (formerly, it was financed by the Ministry of Education). The same is true for health, culture and administrative services. Whatever this saves the central budget, it will inevitably produce an increase in inequality between districts. The most backward areas will have the most backward services for they will be deprived of the subsidies which formerly came from the richer areas through the central budget. In education and health, the general decline in standards in much of the country could be dramatic. On the other hand, the richer areas – like the city of Shanghai – will improve their services and in the longer term, their relative superiority. In higher education, no one can now go straight from school to university without a few years' work in between; in the physical sciences, this could also produce a radical lowering of standards. Introducing social criteria for selection and putting selection in the hands of the local authorities also means anybody who tends to raise awkward questions in the locality is unlikely to get higher education.

Third, the communes and factories have been told to be increasingly self-sufficient. Communes should use any surpluses they have to manufacture simple light industrial and consumer goods to meet their own needs (producing such goods on the communes will be much cheaper in wage terms since the peasants will not be paid urban industrial wages nor be granted urban welfare standards). The constant theme reiterated in the national press in connection with 'self-reliance' is that it is absolutely wrong to ask for financial assistance from the State, which again fits 'decentralisation' into a general economy drive. The government claims that 'local industry' (that is, on the communes) is now a major component in the economy – producing 60 percent of the national output of chemical fertiliser, 40 percent of cement, a third of steel.

Industrial decentralisation was originally justified on strategic grounds – dispersed industry would be protected from Soviet attack. But the policy was also perhaps recognition of the existing state of affairs after the Cultural Revolution and of Peking's inability to recentralise the economy. For the middle – provincial – levels of the party had been destroyed, leaving the local cadres very much to get on as they might. Local self-sufficiency is one way of trying to insulate one's bit of territory from the fluctuations beyond its borders. Decentralisation is also a means of inducing the support of the commune leadership – or, in Indian terms, the rich peasants. It is a common mood in almost all developing countries, particularly in backward regions that feel neglected by the development process. Breaking up industry and distributing it round the country seems to be a logical and desirable process to the leaders of backward areas.

In China's case, decentralisation saves the State a lot of money, might tap commune savings that would otherwise not be available, forces the use of raw materials and labour that would otherwise not be employed, and produces goods that are a net addition to the stream of commodities produced in the Chinese economy. But it can have other effects as well. Where raw materials are scarce, the policy can – as in the Great Leap Forward – be very wasteful, and deprive efficient national industry of its inputs in order to supply inefficient local industry. Shanghai, which grows no cotton, can be deprived of its supply of raw cotton so that primitive mills can produce at much higher cost inferior goods in the cotton tracts. Furthermore, where raw materials are scarce, communes are likely to stock up with raw materials far in excess of their immediate needs so that production will not be interrupted later; the same goes for producer goods, transport and so on. The result of that is a lot of unutilised capacity going to waste in conditions where everything that can be used should be used. The central justification of central planning is just to avoid such waste, to avoid the duplication which is inevitable with a mass of small competitive firms.

The same points apply to investment. If the savings would not otherwise have been used, local industry is an excellent way of tapping resources. But it is more likely that, of the available supply of investment, communes will now be diverting a larger proportion of it into relatively uneconomic – because small – and badly run plants (badly run because there are few on the communes with the appropriate industrial skills). The commune leadership is likely to use its power within its own territory to ensure its own goods are sold, and competing goods from outside the commune kept out, which simultaneously robs national industry of its market and forces inferior goods onto the commune's captive market. The commune leadership can set its own prices so that it may well try to maximise its profits on the goods it manufactures so that more savings will be available for further investment. The last stage in this process is when the commune leadership tries to produce more than the commune can take, and exports the surplus at much lower prices than the prices of national industry's output (it could not otherwise sell the goods outside its own borders).

At this point, each commune is behaving like a small country, increasing its exports and trying to reduce its imports. Each country pursues an import substitution policy, even though it is clearly cheaper and more efficient to produce some things elsewhere in the national economy, to specialise, to develop a division of labour. Of course, 'dumping' – selling cheaply abroad, dear at home – would be modified by the development of a black market. With each commune behaving like a separate country – or, at least, a separate private firm – the whole national economy suffers. If each factory has to grow its own rice, both its rice growing and its factory production will be relatively more inefficient than if it specialised while someone else grew the rice. All the advantages that come with development, which make possible the enormous productivity of an advanced economy – an elaborate division of labour, specialisation, concentration, planning – are deliberately abandoned. The loss grows more serious the more developed and complex the economy becomes.

'Decentralisation' is reactionary in the strict sense of the term (as opposed to the emotive sense): it tries to drive the economy backwards into a sort of feudalism, it disperses the resources that need concentrating if development is to take place. It makes it impossible for there to be effective planning, for the power to plan is now vested in the mini-countries. No economy can remain without coordination if it is to survive, and if a national plan does not coordinate the units, the revival of a market most certainly will. The trading relationships become the method of coordinating the economy. In the long run, that would mean a very slow-moving capitalist economy whose dynamic would be competition between the communes and other districts, in contrast to the State capitalist economy of the Soviet Union which operates, very roughly, as one coordinated conglomerate.

Marx and the Marxists have always been great centralisers. For without centralisation, mankind could never escape backwardness, never put together the enormous power at its disposal. Always, the dispersal of resources and power would make all equally weak. The same would be true after a socialist revolution: the only possibility of democratic control is if power can clearly be located at one place and subjected to popular check; if power is dispersed, there is no power with which to do anything. Mao is not checked by the thought that his scheme is associated with the name of Proudhon and the conservative anarchists who wanted not that power should be used in the interests of all, but that power should be abolished altogether. Localised self-sufficiency has always been the ideal of the petit bourgeois, the peasant with his small patch of land or the small capitalist or craftsman with his little workshop. In economic ruin, the search for 'independence' has often become a frenzy for such people so that they run away to build a utopia in new lands, or turn to unmitigated violence as the expression of how little dependent they are upon society.[3]

All this is far from China and the Chinese leadership. Mao is less interested in the ideological aspects of the turn to the Right than the economies to the State in trying circumstances. If he were interested in the ideas, he would not have remarked to Edgar Snow in his last interview that 'China must learn from the way America developed, by decentralising and spreading responsibility and wealth among 50 states'. This is such compounded nonsense as a comment on US capitalism and imperialism that it can only indicate an almost complete indifference to the political issues of importance to revolutionaries.

There is some evidence that already the leadership has begun to check 'excessive' decentralisation, perhaps as part of the drive to economise on raw materials and prevent the loss to the State of local investment resources. For Peking tried initially to alleviate some of the financial strain on local bodies of setting up industrial units and taking over educational, health and administrative services by leaving more of the tax revenue in the hands of rural communes and raising public revenue almost entirely from urban areas. This has been a trend for a long time – certainly since 1958 – and places the main burden of financing the State on the exploitation of urban factory labour rather than peasants. It has a paradoxical resemblance to other regimes – for example, India – that do not tax the conservative rich peasantry in order to assure its political support. The Chinese Finance Ministry recently claimed that whereas

---

3 See Kolpinsky 1972, and Harris 1973b.

in the early 1950s, the Central Government took 13.2 percent of farm incomes, now it takes around six percent. Of course, that only gives the figure for the Central Government – not the Provincial Government, *hsien* (country) or commune administration. And it concerns only direct taxes, not the surpluses taken from the communes in compulsory State grain purchases, indirect taxes, etc. In the past, a sizable part of government revenue has come from profits and taxes on the processing and sale of agricultural products. The relaxation of control during the Cultural Revolution may well have changed the terms of bargaining between commune and government. Audrey Donnithorne[4] argued recently that it was no longer practicable nor politic for the Sate to compel the peasants to deliver up enough grain under the compulsory sales system to meet the needs of the State, despite good harvests; this was why Peking continued to have to import significant quantities of grain. The government, as always, makes a virtue of necessity; it has claimed that it is deliberate policy to change the terms of rural-urban trade to favour the peasantry; farm produce prices have been increased while industrial prices were lowered over recent years.

Leaving more in the hands of the communes, restoring material incentives for work, allowing the peasants to cultivate private plots and sell the produce for profit, all help to soothe the commune leadership after the 'ultra-Left' excesses of the Cultural Revolution. Perhaps this is also the reason why – despite continued calls for austerity, discipline and increased savings – there seems to be more colour in the cities, a modest revival in music and the opera, and the end of some of the sillier slogans (see the Red Guard cry: 'Making Love is a Mental Disease Which Wastes Time and Energy').

Strengthening the peasant market forms the vital part of a Bukharinite economic strategy which is said to be embodied in the unpublished fourth Five-Year Plan (said to have begun on 1 January 1971). Bukharin[5] was one of the main protagonists in the great debate on economic strategy in the Soviet Union between 1924 and 1928. He argued that industrial development should be geared to the expansion of agriculture, to the rate of growth of the rural market and of the supply of agricultural commodities. Everything should be done to encourage the peasant to expand his output. Nothing should be done which smacked of draining resources from the countryside into industry. The opposition to Bukharin's argument, particularly in the work of Preobrazhensky,[6] said that it would lead to the strengthening of the rich peasantry to the point where

---

4 Donnithorne 1972.

5 On the application of Bukharin's case to China, see Cliff 1967; on Bukharin's case, see Erlich 1960, and Lewin 1968.

6 See Preobrazhensky 1965.

it could precipitate counter-revolution. Rather must the State use all means – without alienating the peasantry – to accumulate capital in its own hands, to build an industrialised economy which would no longer be dependent upon peasant goodwill survival and could begin to build socialism.

The debate in China has scarcely challenged the basic Bukharinite orientation that has dominated Chinese policy since the Great Leap Forward. Admittedly there seems to have been some dispute about the place of defence expenditure (i.e. men and munitions or technically sophisticated weapons, missiles, etc.). But the discussion on the main direction of the economy has not been between supporters of heavy industry and of peasant agriculture, but rather between those who see agricultural mechanisation as the first task, and those stressing the development of local light industry. The press by and large did not argue so much as assume Bukharin's case (for example, see *Red Flag* through July 1971): only agricultural prosperity could make possible industrial advance; light industry serving agriculture should be the key link transmitting peasant demand into the growth of heavy industry. However, unlike Bukharin, no one pointed out that such a strategy made rapid economic development impossible; for industrial growth would be determined by the speed of increase of peasant consumption, the slowest expanding element in the national economy and the one least susceptible to rapid expansion. As Bukharin put it with characteristic but foolhardy – so far as the later Stalinist strategy was concerned – honesty: 'We shall move at a snail's pace, but ... we shall be building socialism'.

The main aim of the leadership in the Cultural Revolution – to restore central control of the provincial surpluses so that accumulation could be geared to a new high level – was defeated. Now, accumulation – economic development – is to be sacrificed, on the one hand to defence, and on the other to standing still at a politically tolerable level. But even the latter depends upon the good grace of the weather. The harvests in 1970 and 1971 were good, but the 1972 output was severely affected by droughts and floods. With the population increasing by nearly 15 million each year, a quirk of the weather can spell disaster. Even in good years, the increase in grain is hardly a hair's breadth ahead of the increase in population. The room to move is very small.

The Soviet intervention of 1969 drew a very clear line for Peking between the need for a domestic purge and the costs of instability. Unlike the US war in Vietnam, China could not ignore the Soviet attack and just continue with its home concerns. The defence budget and the weather have become the two central factors, which determine the operation of the modern Chinese economy. Neither is likely to do much for economic development.

Foreign Policy

The 1969 attack made the Soviet Union China's 'Number One Enemy', and revealed to Peking how far its diplomatic isolation had gone during the Cultural Revolution. The regime set out to find friends, anywhere and everywhere, but especially wherever the Russians were. This sudden flurry of activity coincided with US efforts to escape from the Vietnamese war. These two could therefore collaborate to mutual advantage (as Foreign Minister Chen Yi declared in 1965, 'Peaceful coexistence with US imperialism which is pushing ahead its policies of aggression and war is out of the question'). As a result, all other cold war relationships changed – China entered the UN, the Foreign Ministers of France, West Germany, Britain and many others searching for markets dutifully followed Nixon to Peking. Finally, Japan mended its fences with the People's Republic.

In 1964–5, the Chinese leadership had already tried to build an alliance in the 'intermediate zone' – that is, all countries between itself and the United States. As Mao put it to a startled French parliamentary delegation in 1965: 'France itself, Germany, Italy, Great Britain – provided the latter stops being courtier of the United States – Japan and we ourselves: there you have the third world'. By 1973, the US is no longer the main enemy, and the revived intermediate zone is now directed against Russia and Russian influence. To this end, Chou En-lai offers public support to the European Common Market (and British entry, regardless of the stand of British labour) as a counterweight to Soviet influence, and opposes the security talks between the European powers and the Soviet Union lest they reach agreement. He even went so far as to modestly approve the five-power Commonwealth security arrangements policing southeast Asia and the US military presence in Asia (excluding Vietnam) as a means of keeping out Russian influence – and its notorious Asian security pact.

The same principle has guided Chinese foreign policy round the globe. The cases of Pakistan and Ceylon (Sri Lanka) have already been mentioned. Chou is currently wooing Iran – the Shah's sister and wife have both made recent state visits to Peking – even though the Iranian secret police, SAVAK, has only recently carried out a massive purge of all opposition including the summary execution of rural guerillas. China's long-standing association with the notorious Emperor Hailie Selassie of Ethiopia is not troubled by the Eritrean National Liberation Front fighting him. Chinese aid assists the stability of the Ethiopian regime, assists the maintenance of its capacity to root out armed opposition. Former association with the United States is no obstacle to Chinese friendship – after all, Pakistan was a member of both CENTO and SEATO during the years of association with China, and Iran is still a pillar of CENTO. Thailand is currently being wooed by China, partly to prevent Soviet influence, as also is the Philippines. So is Malaysia, and Peking (Beijing) has even made soothing noises to Taiwan since the Soviet Union sent an unofficial emissary there. Nor is this just a matter of polite diplomacy. When the pro-Soviet group in the Sudanese government made a bid to oust President Numairy, it was the Chinese-Sudan Friendship Society which organised demonstrations in Peking in support of Numairy – following this up with the offer of $45 million aid.

So far Peking has – largely for public effect – refused to consider Western aid, but this is not a point of principle despite appearances to the contrary (see Chou En-lai's coat-trailing statement to the 1956 National People's Congress: 'We have no objections to economic aid by Western countries to economically underdeveloped countries'). The stockpiling of 1969 certainly seems to have produced a deficit in China's balance of trade, and all the Western countries are now vying with each other to offer attractive terms for their wares. It has always been clear to the Chinese leadership that a quick increase in the capital stock of the country was possible by borrowing on the right terms; China's current needs are on such a large scale that the terms could be relatively favourable, certainly much more favourable than Ford offered Lenin when he explored the possibility of US investment in the Soviet Union. China is currently buying a great deal abroad – grain, Tridents, Concordes, petro-chemical and vehicle plants – and giving a lot of aid to win political favour with other backward countries (much more than is currently offered by the Soviet Union; China committed itself to long-term aid of $700 million in 1970, over three times the Russian commitment), so that it seems likely that sooner or later Peking might well bite the bait.

The Party

Successes abroad do not do much to console people inside China for the continuing political vacuum. Despite massive efforts, the new provincial administration is still dominated by the army. It is supported by rehabilitated party leaders, but almost always in second place. Real newcomers among the Red Rebels of the Cultural Revolution seem to have no role in administration.

At the centre, the situation is little short of disastrous. It is astonishing enough that the second-in-command of the regime, Head of State and respected party leaders of many years standing, Liu Shao-ch'i, and the General Secretary of the Chinese Communist Party, should be found secretly scheming to restore capitalism in China. Yet no sooner had a success been found, a man notorious for his slavish devotion to Mao, then he too turns out to be rotten.

Yet Lin Biao's name was enshrined in the 1969 constitution as the sole legitimate heir to Mao. Now what is left of the Politbureau has to summon another Party Congress to ratify the destruction of Lin. No replacements have been appointed to the posts of those purged – Head of State, Party Secretary, Minister of Defence, Chief of the General Staff (Huang Yung-sheng), Commander of the Air Force (Wu Fa-tsien), Political Commissar of the Navy (Li Tsa-pang), and many other senior officials and officers. If it is true that Lin's group, along with Politbureau member Mrs. Lin, was in the plane which crashed in Outer Mongolia in September 1971, it is a staggering commentary on the stability and integrity of the Chinese regime that the top leadership of the armed forces had been induced to flee to the Soviet Union. Chen Po-ta, for 35 years Mao's private secretary and appointed by him as Chairman of the Cultural Revolution Group that directed the Cultural Revolution, fourth in precedence in the leadership, has also apparently been purged.

In contrast to Stalin in the 1930s, Mao has been able to rid himself of his rivals, but not to appoint successors, nor ratify the changes under the existing State and party procedure. Only a quarter of the ministers and vice-ministers of 1966 are said to have survived through to 1969. Yet the present leadership still cannot summon the fourth National People's Congress (scheduled originally for 1969) to ratify the changes and replacements. Even the leadership line-up on Tien-an-Min Gate has too many embarrassing gaps – so the traditional national parades (May Day, 1 July anniversary of the foundation of the party, 1 October National Day) have had to be abandoned. All the leading bodies of the party appear still to be in disarray, and despite the border clash, only the army is the thin line between the ruling class and chaos.

Economically the country is standing still; politically it is still in stalemate. This is in vivid contrast to the picture presented by Western journalists recently on visits to China. Many write as if they were twentieth-century Columbuses just discovering America (and finding it strangely not populated by unbelievable monsters). The gap between the domestic reality and the external image of the country has probably never been greater, although it has always been very great in the case of China.

It is the domestic stalemate which will determine future reactions by China's leadership. That will make necessary further campaigns against both 'revisionists' who are apparently after all the events of the past eight years still operating within the party, and the 'ultra-Left' that continues to resist the army-old party carve-up. For the moment, the leadership is forced to tolerate the recreation of some form of market economy and a kind of kulak class, the cadres who run the communes. This positively encourages people to seek private solutions – speculation, embezzling, profiteering, black marketeering, all current targets for press attack. Having raised so many hopes of a new deal in the Cultural Revolution, it will now prove most difficult to hammer out people's ambitions. For the mass of people there are few private solutions – whether it is profiteering, private plots or flight to Hong Kong. Cynicism and bitterness are the likely responses of the majority.

The retreat forced on the leadership by the collapse of the party and the Russian attack leave unsettled all the outstanding issues. Indeed, the retreat makes matters worse. The more Peking restores the old party bosses and relies on them, the less is the flexibility and the possibility of a real mobilisation of resources for development. That is the reason why Mao or whoever it is who runs China will be forced to make the present pause temporary. Then the attack will have to begin again. Watch the Western liberal sympathisers, then jump yet again on the new swing of the roundabout, just as their predecessors jumped every time Stalin changed line in the 1930s. The real target for their attention ought to be world imperialism that subordinates the struggle of the Chinese people to the needs of the Soviet Union, the United States and all the rest. But that would mean opposing their own ruling class here and now instead of myth making about dreamlands.

CHAPTER 2.5

New Bourgeoisies?*

Indonesia: The Rise of Capital. By Richard Robison. Sydney: Allen & Unwin, 1986.

Government and Private Sector in Contemporary Mexico. Edited by Sylvia Max-field and Ricardo Anzaldua Montoya. San Diego: Center for US-Mexican Stud-ies, University of California, Monograph Series 20. 1987.

The African Bourgeoisie: Capitalist Development in Nigeria, Kenya, and the Ivory Coast. Edited by Paul M. Lubeck. Boulder, CO: Lynne Rienner, UK distributor Eurospan, 1987.

Entrepreneurship, Equity and Economic Development. By E. Wayne Nafziger. Greenwich, CT: JAI Press, UK distributor Eurospan, 1987.

As these lines are being written, the period of maximum collision between riot police and demonstrators in downtown Seoul appears to be over, after major concessions by President Chun. The reportage of these events has noted the significant participation not just of the educated middle class, but of busi-nessmen, young brokers and bankers of the city's downtown area. During the occupation of Myongdong cathedral, the *Financial Times'* Maggie Ford noted the executives at their office windows cheering the demonstrators; the business centres seemed closed, for senior managers appeared to have given permission for their departmental heads to leave their desks to participate. In a country where car ownership is very restricted to the rich, at one stage motorists were persuaded to blow their horns for 20 minutes in protest at government repres-sion. Furthermore, the demands of the movement seemed to embody many of the frustrations of businessmen – doctored elections, arbitrary and corrupt government, politically dominated tax collecting and judiciary systems, cen-sored information. It seemed as if sections of the business class had grown so tired of sacrificing their commercial judgements to government imperatives, of tolerating public extravagance, that they were willing to risk violence by oppos-ing the President.

---

* From: *The Journal of Development Studies*, Volume 24, Issue 2 (1988), pp. 237–49.

The evidence is anecdotal, but at least on first acquaintance, it sounds like some of the issues of 1848, the demands of a bourgeois revolution. Nor in the Korean case is the restlessness of business related in any simple way to slump. The economy has grown with remarkable speed since the last violent downturn of 1979–80. Industrial production has nearly doubled since then, and in the first quarter of 1987, national output was nearly 16 percent above that of a year earlier.

The rebelliousness of a significant part of the business class is in striking contrast to what happened in the quarter of a century of very rapid growth after 1955. Most observers then noted the remarkably subordinate position of business relative to the State, particularly in the years of General Park's regime.[1] Not only was business dominated by the State, the State owned and directed a major part of the economy. One commentator regarded the public ownership of the banking system as decisive – 'No State outside the socialist bloc ever came near this measure of control over the economy's investible resources'.[2] The 1979 murder of Park and the ensuing disorders of 1980 perhaps crystallised some of the discontents of business that had been developing through the 1970s – a growing opposition to the State's appropriation of a large share of national investment for its heavy industry programme (related to the State's preoccupation with military defence), starving key export industries (like textiles and garments) of adequate funding, fuelling resentment at the apparently arbitrary discrimination of government officials, at the prodigious waste and corruption of the State. The Fifth Plan (1982–6) made some official recognition of these charges – it acknowledged that the slump of 1979–80 was due to 'Excessive Government intervention in the private sector ... [discouraging] private initiative and efficiency of investment which are vital to growth in a market economy'. A Minister subsequently summarised one of the elements in the government's diagnosis of what went wrong in 1979–80: 'The economy is already too big to be managed in the old way by heavy-handed Government bureaucrats'.[3]

The new government of President Chun offered reforms – controlled liberalisation of imports, denationalisation of the banks, other measures of privatisation and deregulation, mergers and rationalisation in the public sector, etc. A World Bank Structural Adjustment Loan was on hand to soften the impact. But it was not enough. Companies strongly resisted – on an unprecedented

1   See, for example, Jones and Sakong 1980, p. 296.
2   Datta-Chaudhuri 1981, p. 56.
3   Economic Bulletin 1984, p. 21.

scale – measures of rationalisation in the private sector and attempts by the government to make them release land hoards to increase company liquidity. A widening gap between the opinion of private capital and the government seemed to be developing.

If the South Korean business class has reached a new stage in its social, economic and political development such that its relationship to the State must be changed, it may be the result of 30 years of very rapid growth. If this is so, other Newly Industrialising Countries might be developing similar phenomena, depending in part on the past role and nature of the State. There is some evidence from Taiwan, another fast growing economy, of moves towards democratisation that are stronger than in the past, although there has been nothing as dramatic as the Korean events. However, there is a different type of evidence from Latin America. At roughly the same time as the 1987 Korean events, the Chamber of Commerce in Panama organised a one-day closure in protest at the rule of General Noriega, and again, the better-off organised car hooting sessions. In this case, the popular movement was receiving some moral support from Washington (engaged in a different game, trying to prevent nationalisation of the Canal) which led the Sandinista leader, President Daniel Ortega, to make a visit from Nicaragua to offer his support for the beleaguered dictator. In the return to civilian government and representative rule in Uruguay, Argentina and Brazil, the role of the business classes is said to have been decisive. In Brazil now, the business class appears to be sharply divided between those who favour the old public sector-dominated protectionist form of development and those who urge on liberalisation. The key to this debate is not external forces – multinational corporations, foreign governments, banks, the International Monetary Fund or the World Bank – but the domestic relationship between different segments of business which, on the economic nationalist side, unite the more backward and vulnerable companies and the Left. The issue of public sector corruption is no less important than in Korea, particularly since the press discovered the 'Maharajas', public officials receiving extraordinarily high salaries (in the key case for the campaign, a Sao Paulo traffic police officer is said to be paid $203,755 per year, the leader of a group of 19 top earners in official posts).

Can something similar concerning the 'maturity' of private capital be said of South Africa? Merle Lipton's excellent *Capitalism and Apartheid* (1985) provided a vivid insight into the changing economic interests of different sections of capital – agrarian, mining, manufacturing – culminating in an almost united opposition to apartheid. Perhaps the jagged edges of South African society permit a privileged perception of the social structure which is denied those living in less tense environments. The visit of the group of leading South African businessmen to Lusaka for discussions with the African National Congress leadership was presumably made public deliberately to symbolise the alienation of manufacturers from current government policy.

The 'maturity of capital' thesis may have several different explanations, not simply the relative size of capital after an extended period of high growth. It may also relate to the composition of output, which in turn relates to the potential for export as opposed to simply supplying the home market (so affecting the State's pursuit of particular strategies and the possibility of a viable public sector). An economy dominated by the production of crude raw materials is susceptible to an interventionist State's direction in a way that is not so in an economy producing a diverse and complex manufactured output. The more sophisticated the output, the less the capacity of a single national agency to direct its growth and change, to foster innovation and the destruction and creation that follows from innovation, to be sensitive to the appropriate imports required to sustain a changing output, to ensure a pattern of skills constantly readjusted to changing demand for labour in an innovating economy. In fact, this hypothesis, turning upon the nature of the output, is only half true, for historical time needs to be introduced – production of raw materials has been transformed in technology to become also 'sophisticated'. Merle Lipton shows how the increasing capital intensity of South African farming makes necessary an increased use of advanced and diverse skills in the labour force, workers who must be settled with their families in reasonable living conditions if they are to reach appropriate levels of productivity. The white farmers, for so long dependent upon a mass of unskilled labourers, come to demand village schools and housing schemes for their now much smaller and skilled workforce. Furthermore, as their exports expand, they increasingly demand the right to import as they wish and as cheaply as possible in order to ensure exports remain competitive.

The local factors that might determine the 'maturity of capital' are not easily separated from the evolution of the world economy, particularly the onset of a period of slump and stagnation. Increasing competition for declining or stagnating markets inevitably reduces business toleration of the iniquities of government. One need only recall the 1980 attack of Sir Terence Beckett as Director General of the Confederation of British Industry on Mrs Thatcher's government's policies to see how much irritability slump generates without this being a maturation of capital. Slump, however, in present conditions coincides with an unprecedented degree of world economic integration and, for the Newly Industrialising Countries, unprecedented opportunities to export manufactured goods in certain sectors. But the precondition for exploiting the opportunities is a supportive government, not one with a will and direction of its own. Being supportive now includes maintaining an external value of the currency which makes exports possible, making available the assets of the public sector (and not mopping up the lion's share of investment), allowing the market to select the directions of growth rather than imposing other – and prodigiously expensive – priorities, and so on. It is not at all a programme of *laissez-faire*, but rather an external market-oriented opportunism which does not at all exclude important elements of protection.

This second group of factors relating to the external market perhaps goes a little way to explaining why the 'business revolt', if such it be, does not fit closely any 'stages of development' framework. For many governments are now well advanced in orienting policy towards external markets and reorganising the domestic economy to make possible high exports. The Philippines is not at all as advanced as South Korea, yet Mrs. Aquino's defeat of President Marcos seems to have been powerfully supported by the majority of Filipino businessmen, outside the charmed circle of the Marcos cronies. And in terms of liberalisation of economic policy, some of the leading countries include China and the Soviet Union, as well as on a lesser scale, India, a sample that cuts right across any 'maturity of capital thesis'.

The idea of a 'maturation of capital' in a number of developing countries does contradict many of the assumptions about economic development that were made in the past. It was generally assumed that private domestic capital would not play a significant role in the economic development of developing countries; on the contrary, it would be an obstacle to development. Colonialism in particular was seen as a system which frustrated any repetition of what was supposed to have happened in Europe. Consider, as a possibly representative view of this perspective, the judgement of Bassam Tibi:

> Marx assumed that after the enforced disintegration of their social structures under colonial rule, the colonial countries would develop in a capitalist, that is, historically more progressive direction. Hence he justified colonisation with world historical arguments ... This thesis has proved untenable. Capitalism in the colonies has not taken a strictly capitalist character, but has become an exploitative mechanism which has preserved the local feudal structures in a modern form [the author sees modern ex-colonial developing countries as much the same as the colonised].[4]

---

4 Tibi 1981, p. 192, note 1.

In fact the view – on the exhaustion of the historical role of capital – is much older than contemporary development studies. There are what might be construed as hints in Engels, particularly his view that a Bonapartist dictatorship is the appropriate form of capitalism after the early heroic days. The first Manifesto of the Russian Social Democrats in 1898 attributed the frustration of the bourgeois revolution historically to capital's fears of the new threat of a worker rebellion:

> The farther east one goes in Europe, the weaker, meaner and more cowardly in the political sense becomes the bourgeoisie, and the greater the cultural and political tasks which fall to the lot of the proletariat. On its strong shoulders, the Russian working class must and will carry the work of conquering political liberty.[5]

In fact, the Social Democrats, both Menshevik and Bolshevik, were wrong in the early phases of the 1905 revolution. Then, at least some important employers in St. Petersburg paid their workers to join the anti-Tsarist demonstrations. But in the chaos of 1917, they were right – business was far too fearful of the Bolsheviks to oppose restoration, or at least a Kornilov dictatorship. The *smychka* was required to implement the bourgeois revolution.

Communists remained committed to the proposition that the bourgeoisie would not undertake its historic role, now in the backward and colonial countries (as they are called). Just as Russia's capitalists were seen as wedded to the Tsar by their fear of worker rebellion, so those in the colonies were wedded to the colonisers, the imperial State. There might be some symbolic but shadowy role for a 'national bourgeoisie', but they could not be decisive; capital was 'compradore' in essence. National liberation, a kind of surrogate bourgeois revolution, would have to be constituted from non-bourgeois forces, workers and peasants, and in practice led by members of the Western-educated intelligentsia or technical cadres (such as army officers). It followed that the post-revolutionary order would not build a private capitalist or market economy.

Paradoxically, a not dissimilar evolution occurred in the heartlands of world capitalism, Europe and North America. The Great Depression seemed to demonstrate the impossibility of an ordered and progressive private market economy. The 1930s were an era of fashionable State capitalism, founded upon a supposed corporatist federation of State, capital and labour, in which the State, by reason of its monopoly of the legitimate use of physical force, its control of

---

5   Carr 1950, p. 4.

the economic frontiers and its privileged access to the surplus generated in the economy, was overwhelmingly the dominant partner. In the expansion of Germany's war machine, business was bullied, badgered and bribed, and in the event of determined opposition, expropriated and its directors liquidated – an oppression even more extreme than that which occurred in Park's South Korea.

Roosevelt's New Deal was less dictatorial. And in Britain, successive Conservative governments had more limited autonomy than in Germany. But the Conservatives did seek to create an alliance between the State and the largest monopolistic or oligopolistic businesses that would establish an ordered, not a competitive or market, economy, the heart of an economically protected empire and controlled currency zone. In 1938, Keynes, an enthusiastic supporter of this corporatist ideal, could speak with approval of the euthanasia of the rentier, and Harold Macmillan, a rising backbencher, of the nationalisation of all basic and food industries as the condition for the survival of capitalism.[6] In 1945, the Westminster Conservative Association produced a paperback edition of Macmillan's *The Middle Way* to prove Labour had stolen its programme from the Conservatives (in fact, Labour's aims were less radical than Macmillan's).

The world system appeared to consist of a set of warring empires, at the heart of each of which was an overwhelmingly dominant State, fused with a subordinate and discrete segment of capital: the world as national capitalism, within Sterling, Franc, Dollar, Reichsmark and Yen spheres of influence. Bukharin's vision of 1917 seemed entirely vindicated. The Second World War seemed only to confirm the picture, for the State now formally assumed the role of a board of directors of a single national conglomerate, a war-making machine, that superseded most private rights. And even after the war, with the blander breezes of prosperity, the theorists of modern capitalism still accorded the decisive economic role to the State, not the market.[7]

It was hardly surprising that this experience was inherited by those preoccupied with the problems of economic development, particularly given the far weaker role of private business in the newly independent countries. Private capital, it was said, had no drive to expand production or accumulate capital. Its interests were far too closely interwoven with foreign capital (the compradors) or with 'feudal' forces, land, or short-term commercial speculation, to undertake the great process of economic development. In any case, economic reality militated against any such role – the income level and so the size of market

---

6   See Macmillan 1938 and Harris 1972.
7   See Shonfield 1965 and Galbraith 1967.

made efficient production impossible; technology and skills were too primitive; and cultures, religions, ideologies and psychologies militated against the
energetic pursuit of profits. Private capital had become parasitic, a consumer
and squanderer of scarce resources, not a producer, much less a Promethean
force of historical change.

In its day, it was a powerful case. The stark alternatives seemed to be stagnation or domination by foreign capital or State capitalism. The third alternative
appeared to be the only one that carried some chance of swiftly improving popular welfare at the same time as building a secure base for national economic
independence. The State could eliminate duplication, the waste of competition, curb the extravagances of the rich, direct investment at key sectors so that
development rather than profits would be maximised, and all independently
of the vagaries of a world market. There might be disagreements on how far
it was necessary to eliminate the old ruling orders, but the emphasis upon the
role of the State was universal, regardless of political differences. For many, the
direction seemed symbolised by the Indian second Five Year Plan, where the
role of businessmen was a very marginal question. The high officers of State
in Delhi had no reason to regard businessmen as other than vaguely immoral,
a vulgar and barely tolerated minority whose survival often depended entirely
on decisions of the government.

It took a remarkably long time for some of these assumptions to be ques-
tioned. Indeed, some of them may need the teargas of Seoul's downtown district to dissipate. The opening of the markets of North America and Europe
in the 1960s and 1970s changed the reality fundamentally for the new manufacturers of the Newly Industrialising Countries, as did the two rounds of oil
price increase in the 1970s for larger oil producers. A surprisingly large number of countries were persuaded to embark on heavy industry programmes
in the 1970s, ventures which were State initiated, financed and directed (for
example, South Korea, Taiwan, Singapore, Mexico, Brazil and Indonesia). The
debt incurred to support this type of programme was often an important element in the debt crisis of the 1980s. Then, numerous forces conspired to beat
back the public sector and to liberalise, forces that also engaged in a debate
not just about national economic policy but about the distribution of political power in society and curbing the autonomy of the State. In a number of
countries, local capital had become less concerned to defend its home patch
against the foreigners, although that still needed to be done, and more concerned to invade the world at large. The debt mechanism added a painful edge
to the argument of the liberalisers. This is perhaps the index of 'maturity'; when
national capital is obliged to become international. Indeed, Engels long ago
foresaw that the bourgeoisie cannot rule at home unless it is international. 'The

industrial bourgeoisie can govern', he wrote, 'in a country only whose manufacturing commands for its produce the universal market: the limits of the home
market are too narrow for its development'.[8]

Only with the benefit of hindsight can we see how the changing objective
situation was forcing a reconsideration of the theoretical inheritance. Bill Warren[9] was among the first to doubt some of the orthodoxy in his critique of what
he identified as Leninism, a critique recently elaborated in an application to
Africa by John Sender and Sheila Smith.[10] But the case remained very much
at the level of a world order, stronger in statistical refutation than in what was
happening in particular countries, linking economic performance, social structure and political power.

It is the integration of these three elements that is the great strength of
Richard Robison's analysis of Indonesian capital. From his opening sentence –
'The most important revolutionary force at work in the Third World today is
not communism or socialism but capitalism'[11] – to his final conclusion that,
in the 1980s, major private business groups are able to stand free of the State
in Indonesia (even if they still need monopoly privileges, contracts and concessions), he offers a superbly detailed account of the creation of a capitalist
class. Part I outlines the historical background up to the spectacular coup of
1965. Part II covers the period since then; Part III identifies some of the complex nature of capital, linking the State, military-business groups, and Chinese
and non-Chinese indigenous capital; and Part IV offers some perspectives on
the future.

Indonesia is probably not at the stage discussed earlier relative to South
Korea. But nonetheless the general critique of the orthodox position on a
private capitalist class applies. Dr Robison shows how premature were many
of the judgements made about a weak or comprador bourgeoisie in Indonesia.
The process of class formation was slower than expected, although by the
standards of Europe exceedingly fast. Observers were misled by the apparent
domination of the State, a ruling order without the expected division of labour
between public administration and capitalist, the apparent autonomy of the
political order in the 1950s and 1970s, the domination of the military, and the
lack of an explicitly bourgeois party (although they are often rare birds, and in
the Indonesian case affected by the Chinese or quasi-foreign character of the
largest business groups).

---

8   Engels 1978, p. 361.
9   See Warren 1980.
10   See Sender and Smith 1986.
11   Robison 1986, p. vii.

Dr Robison shows how the military expropriation of Dutch assets, starting in late 1957 (and covering 90 percent of plantation output, 60 percent of foreign trade and 246 manufacturing enterprises, banks, shipping and service companies) created an instant Indonesian 'bureaucratic capitalist' class. Military commands assumed direction of the nationalised companies, creating the nuclei of broader business groups which included other military business initiatives (both official and unofficial, if such a distinction made much sense at the time), other private Chinese business, government ministries, the business enterprises of political parties, foreign companies, etc. This kind of baronial economy survived the liberalisation of the immediate post-Sukarno period (1965–74), and was then strategically placed to gain maximum advantage from the second phase of import substitution industrialisation – with a major public sector infrastructure and heavy industry investment programme, undertaken by the State and fuelled by the oil receipts following on two rounds of price increases. Oil prices, as it were, briefly restored the autonomy of the State, permitting State-directed forced accumulation to create a more advanced economic structure than would have been possible if the preceding liberal phase had been continued. The oil price declines of the 1980s then pushed back the State and public sector, forcing a new phase of liberalisation, but now one in which there existed substantial groups of private capital.

Pertamina was among the more spectacular of these groups. There is a whole area of fascinating analysis to be undertaken concerning the role of national public sector oil corporations – Pertamina, ENI, Petrobras, Pemex, etc. – as instruments for leadership in national industrialisation and spectacular vehicles of personal ambition. Until the heroic scandal of 1975 and his disgrace, Ibnu Sutowo, Pertamina's chief, created a philosophy of national development and a gigantic empire, covering not merely oil but also steel, petrochemicals, metal fabrication, engineering, telecommunications, property, air services, shipping and so on, a modern diversified economy in one group.

Each phase of the history of Indonesian capital was distinguished not just by policy, but by the different groups, people and alliances involved. Thus, Robison portrays well the role of Japanese companies and government in supporting the import substitution phase, while American companies and government were strong influences in the liberal phases. The economic nationalists attributed the anti-Japanese riots of 1974 – the occasion of the visit of Prime Minister Tanaka – to United States interests. More detail would have enriched the book here, for the role of foreign capital, an even more complicated bundle of contradictions than domestic capital, is rarely detailed. Indeed, to speak of *the* role is a mistake. Companies from the same country can hardly be expected to be necessarily aligned on the same goals, let alone being at one with their respective home governments (where policy again is often changing). The explicit interests of companies may or may not reflect the pressures of export markets (or import prices) or the purchasing practices of foreign buyers (and it is here that we get closest to the forces creating a 'new international division of labour', rather than in the activities of multinational corporations). Nor can we assume that the more important collisions are between local and foreign interests – that is an unwarranted political simplification of the complicated competition of economic interests. Similarly, pressures to liberalise Indonesian government policy are not necessarily from external sources; important Indonesian business groups may now be at the stage where they need controlled liberalisation to expand their position, not the heavy fortifications of economic nationalism.

We owe a considerable debt to Dr Robison for this excellent account of the creation and the maturation of a new capitalist class. The story is by no means over – the Chinese domination of business makes it, as in Malaysia, highly vulnerable to political attack. The strains of uneven development can still wreck the New Order, just as external events wrecked the booming Newly Industrialising Country of Lebanon. The end of the patronage of President Suharto and his family, associates and clients, can threaten those who have made most. Nonetheless, it is most valuable to have this vivid and well researched account, worth a ton of phrase mongering about 'dependent capitalism on the periphery'. Let us hope it inspires others to develop similar portraits of the rising classes.

Mexico is very different from Indonesia. Private capital has been important there since the 1930s, and in the past 40 years the national economy has grown by six to seven percent annually, producing a world class manufacturing sector (Mexico is now the tenth largest industrial power in the world, excluding the Eastern bloc). However, there are similarities in two respects – the size of the public sector (and, at different phases, the relative autonomy of the State) and the massive growth of oil revenues in the 1970s that fuelled a major State-led boom up to 1982.

Through the years of high growth, Mexico's private businessmen were apparently content that a monopoly of power should be exercised by the Party of Institutionalised Revolution (PRI), a quasi-corporatist federation of three elements, the official trade unions, the official peasant associations and 'popular forces' (mainly, the intelligentsia and middle classes). Some businesses favoured constituting a fourth component. Raymond Vernon[12] noted that government kept business, at least officially, at arm's length since it was held in dis-

---

12   Vernon 1963, p. 158.

repute by many; in particular, the intelligentsia held business to be ruthless and greedy, so government treated businessmen with reserve, protecting an image of being Left-wing. Business in turn seems to have felt a mild paranoia, summarised in the retiring speech of one of the business federations' presidents in 1978: 'Mexico's businessmen will never again be second-class citizens, as they were in recent years, maliciously excluded from the national political arena'.[13]

However, in the 1970s, one group of businessmen in the north, known as the Monterrey Group, became well known as sharp critics of the government from a position of economic liberalism. They were forceful opponents in the closing years of Echeverna's presidency (1975–6).

Since 1982, the economy has experienced some sharp contractions under the heavy weight of the cumulative external debt, high interest rates and, for a time, a disastrous decline in oil prices. If the official figures are to be believed, unemployment (in officially registered terms) has more than doubled (to 18 percent) as the total labour force has been increasing by 3.8 percent annually; real wages may have fallen by up to a half, and the government has radically cut subsidies on staple foods and transport.

However, the political opposition to the current government has come not from the trade unions, community organisations or the Left. It has come, on an unprecedented scale, from sections of business, operating through an old, but now radically refashioned, conservative nationalist party, the National Action Party (PAN). The literature on Mexico's business classes is much more extensive than that on Indonesia's, but the shift in business opinion (or some parts of it) – and the extremism of some of the public pronouncements – has taken observers by surprise. Sylvia Maxfield and Ricardo Anzaldua present a set of seven essays (prepared originally for a workshop at the San Diego Centre in the spring of 1986) that seek to analyse the issues at stake.

There is much of interest in the volume, but it is very mixed and rarely touches on the broader theoretical issues – for example, on whether the social weight of private capital has now grown to the point where its relationship to the State must be radically changed. There is also a tendency to be merely descriptive, rather than analytical, and to be 'over-politicised' – for example, the argument that 'loss of political confidence' produces capital flight, which produces economic crisis, rather than the reverse. By and large, businessmen are more sensitive to changes in profit expectation than to the nature of the political order, and it is usually changes in the first which produce criticisms of the second. Merle Lipton's work, referred to earlier, is excellent in this respect,

---

13   Cited in Maxfield and Anzaldua 1987, p. 98.

for she grounds the political attitudes of sections of South African business in their changing estimate of what is in their best economic interest.

The weaknesses are a pity because Mexico is an important case, and we need to understand how and why a section of business moved from support for import substitution economic nationalism to straight economic liberalism. That shift produced a transformation in the PAN, from its former emphasis upon Christian Democratic corporatism, to *neopanismo* with a complete trust in freed markets. The same transformation can be seen in the French Gaullists or, for that matter, the British Conservatives (from what Mrs Thatcher describes as corporatism). Furthermore, in the Mexican case, the businessmen felt so strongly about this issue they risked the displeasure of a very powerful State by publicly campaigning for an opposition party, standing as candidates against the PRI, and financing subsidiary campaigns (for example, on the need for Church schools). In at least one case, the PRI forced the resignation of a leading businessman from the board of directors of a major business group because of his public support for the PAN.

However, in the detail of the book, we can guess some of the answers (and there is much of value in the historical essay on the changing relationships and leaderships of the leading business associations by Ricardo Carrillo Arronte). In the 1970s (1972 to 1981), public investment increased by 20 percent annually, the pace accelerating after 1977 with the oil revenue based boom. At different stages in this process, there were important acts of nationalisation, and even in the mid-1970s, officially encouraged land seizures of the great irrigated farms of the northwest. The process of growth culminated in the spectacular collapse of 1982, and the nationalisation of the banks (a measure designed to support private banking debts with the authority of a sovereign borrower, rather than to fight the class war). This measure brought into the public sector a mass of manufacturing companies that were owned in part or whole by banks. This brought to a head a mass of simmering discontents that had been perhaps soothed in the rapid growth of the late 1970s, but now broke out with great fury. When the new President, Miguel de la Madrid, in the first flush of power, promised that the government would respect opposition election victories, many northern businessmen threw themselves into the PAN campaign – and made considerable progress until the PRI organisers, from 1985, began to fix the elections.

There was much business talk of the PRI's uncontrollable drive to State capitalism, to totalitarianism, of its capture by an international socialist conspiracy, and so on. The mildly conservative politics of the PRI seem quite remote from this fantasy. The critique is especially unkind, given the considerable favours shown to business over many years, as well as the public sympathy of President de la Madrid. The President has promised (and in part implemented) the privatisation of nearly three quarters of the companies in the public sector in 1982. In his 1985 *Informe*, indeed, he indicated a more fundamental criticism of an expanding public sector – 'excessive proliferation of public enterprise has weakened the State by upsetting its financial balance and by limiting its ability to adequately fulfil its primary responsibilities'.

Mexico is already a mature capitalism by most of the kind of measures that might be formulated to indicate this. Yet it retains a political structure appropriate to an earlier phase. Of course, as the PRI never tires of saying, Mexican business has a peculiar position because of the proximity of the country to the United States, which makes possible the involvement of North American interests. The PRI alleges the Republican Party controls, directs or patronises PAN, and the cross-border contacts are very extensive. Nonetheless, if the maturation of capital thesis makes much sense in terms of impelling elements of the bourgeois revolution, Mexico is where it ought to be occurring.

Lubeck's *The African Bourgeoisie* indicates some sharp contrasts (as one would expect), but also similarities (Nigeria, like Indonesia and Mexico, shared in the great industrialisation boom of the 1970s, fuelled by oil revenue). However, while this is a rich and interesting collection of 12 essays (the product of a 1980 Dakar conference), it is only distantly related to the issues of the 1970s. There is a sensible and well-worked essay by Kitching on some of the theoretical issues, but many of the contributions have an imperfect grounding in the economic histories of the countries concerned, the changing composition of output and the different types of capitalist. Indeed, relatively little of the book is concerned with the present bourgeoisies – there are five essays on the historical origins of business, two on the role of the State and two on industry (with two introductory pieces, and a very brief closing note). As a result, we often have little sense of the different sectors, groups, companies, geographical areas, and the sheer dynamic changes in relationships as economies expand. Too often, writers are saddled with the debilitating simplification of 'internal' and 'external' forces. However, exception must be made of Tom Forrest's account of Nigerian development, and there are a few, regrettably brief, portraits of Kenyan companies in Langdon's contribution. The writers, in general, question some of the orthodoxies of dependency theory, but uneasily and without rigour.

Professor Nafziger presents a series of his own essays. They are of very uneven quality and only very loosely related. Much of the material is long out of date and repetitive. His two empirical contributions – on Vizakapatnam in India (from 1970) and somewhere in Nigeria (1964–5) – are not located in the economic histories or geographies of the countries concerned, and seem preoccupied with somewhat pedestrian issues. We will not find the rise of the bourgeoisie here. The book is well produced, but its point is unclear.

The works have sharp differences of method. Robison has a strong perception of mixed groups, business clusters that straddle many sectors, and this phenomenon is much more important in late developing countries than in Europe and North America (witness the clusters of Japan). It has much to recommend it in comparison to a division which relies solely on sectoral distinctions (textile manufacturers versus engineering, etc.). The contributors to the volume by Maxfield and Anzaldua refer in the main to differences between large and small to medium enterprises, a division possibly even more obscure than that so familiar in peasant studies, between rich, middle and poor. The contributors do sketch many specific collisions of interest, but without it being clear why these took place. The division provided by Merle Lipton offers more powerful insights (agrarian, mining, manufacturing), although these would be strengthened by showing the divisions within each group. Capital is, it must also be remembered, opportunistic rather than ideological, so that circumstances are constantly reshaping perceptions and behaviour (even when the slogans seem to suggest a stability of view). One of the contributors to the Mexico volume notes what happened to the powerful businessman critic of the government when he was elected as a PRI deputy to the assembly: he became very peaceful.

Can we then identify the long drawn out events in South Korea (the present phase beginning in 1979), in Mexico and perhaps other countries, as stages in the process of the 'bourgeois revolution'? I think we can. We can also see, with the benefit of hindsight, that the development of national capitalism, a system by which accumulation can be sustained, usually requires a preliminary phase of State domination and initiatives, whether this is described as economic nationalism or socialism. Import substitution organises a transfer of resources from consumer to selected monopoly accumulators, a system of unequal exchange, vital for forced development in a highly competitive world system. In countries where the State cannot achieve sufficient autonomy to institute such a process (as, for example, under colonialism), the full potential for accumulation is frustrated.

However, when the State establishes a system for forced accumulation, this is not simply a set of arrangements that can be changed at will. It constitutes a social order, with a weight of inertia constituted by vested interests, the immediate beneficiaries, that inhibits the creation of any other order. What was set up to speed development becomes an inhibition to growth as capital develops, as output diversifies, as businessmen are increasingly drawn to participate in the world economy, and as the need for the psychological participation of a skilled labour force supersedes the dependence upon masses of unskilled labour: capitalism 'matures'. The old State must be reformed or overthrown, to establish the common conditions for all capital: a rule of law, accountability of public officials and expenditure, a competitive labour market and, above all, measures to ensure the common interests of capital can shape the important policies of the State.

Thus, the enemy of capitalism as it matures is not feudalism, but the State, whether this is the corrupt particularist State, State capitalism, or, as is more often the case, a combination of these. 1832 in Britain was not about the squires so much as it was about the refashioning of the State to support the interests of manufacturing capital.

The reshaping of the State may or may not involve establishing represent-ative democracy. Where businessmen – or their political representatives – are unable to subvert the State, they may be obliged to collaborate with a mass movement, involving many other interests and programmes. That breadth of interest is more likely to lead to the establishment of a more universal suffrage than peaceful reforms. The resistance of the State – as in Mexico and Korea – makes it increasingly difficult to avoid a violent confrontation. That resistance, however, has an economic basis, for the autonomy of the State depends upon the surplus it can extract from society unless it can find sources outside society (through aid, borrowing, or expanded oil revenue). It is at that point, that busi-ness can apply pressure, just as John Hampden challenged Charles I on what became later the issue of 'no taxation without representation'.

Of course, there is no mechanical or invariable process at work here. For, an opposite state of affairs can develop where the State, supported by popu-lar forces, increasingly restricts business, and a coup is required to allow ele-mentary accumulation to take place, or simply to protect the existing position. Robison's account of the 1965 coup in Indonesia identifies Sukarno pushing to the limit the autonomy of the State in his struggle to balance the Commun-ist Party and the military. Indonesian capital can scarcely be thought to have exercised any particular role at that time; none the less, the appalling events of the year following the September seizure of power by the military were vital in securing the survival of business. 1965 was, in one sense, a rehearsal for Chile 1973, when a much more advanced capitalist class played a much more import-ant role in the overthrow of Allende. Neither event can be separated from changes in the world economy – both herald a turn that we find Mrs Thatcher claiming as her own in 1979.

The earlier-mentioned scepticism of Marxists about the role of the bour-geoisie has not been invalidated. For the Bolsheviks assumed, like most social-ists at that time, that there would always exist an independent and politically organised working class which would challenge the right of the bourgeoisie to seize the State. In the postwar world, workers have played important roles in many collisions – for example, in South Korea in 1980, in Iran in the rise of Khomeini, and especially, in South Africa today. Furthermore, the largest concentrations of the world's industrial working class are now probably in developing countries – in Sao Paulo, Mexico City, Shanghai, Calcutta or Seoul. But workers have not played an *independent* role; they have been supporting forces, loyal to whatever interests dominate the movement (as they were in 1832). So an important factor in the return of the bourgeois revolution, if such it be, is the disappearance of an independent workers' movement.

The prospect for the continued expansion of the Newly Industrialising Countries is not at all as gloomy as that for the world economy (or Europe and the United States). The role of the NICs is still not large enough to affect decisively the wider picture. If growth continues, then we can presumably expect further collisions as business classes seek to throw off the inhibitions of the Protectionist State. There are no reliable ways to measure the growth of a capitalist class in the Less Developed Countries, but we might take as an imperfect surrogate index the recently produced estimates of the World Bank's International Finance Corporation of the value of assets traded on the equity markets of the 33 leading LDCs. This is expected to increase five or six times over by the year 2000, reaching a combined total value of between 500 and 800 billion dollars (by way of comparison, the current value of the assets traded on Europe's combined stock exchanges is put at 500 billion dollars). That surely indicates some kind of bourgeoisie.

It is now possible to see, with the benefit of hindsight, how curious the case was that national capitalist classes could no longer play their supposed historical role. Between the millstones of the domestic working class and foreign capital, it seemed there was no room to grow. That vindicated a role for the State, precisely what was required to create a private capitalist class. The problems of the case were compounded by a mythological view of European history that failed to note how late in capitalist development was the emergence of the bourgeois republic, how corrupt and protectionist, and how dominant, the State was, and what a diversity of cases there were – from Britain's eighteenth century war economy to the Kaiser's Germany.

The theories will have to be reconstructed. Let us hope we have many more studies like that of Dr Robison's to show us how the world actually works.

Nationalism and Development[*]

Much social science theory is made and remade relative to the great events of the moment. In August 1991, one such event was the rather astonishing climacteric in the Soviet Union, of which the implications for the national state and national economic development will take quite some time to absorb. Hitherto, the state system, which directs the political administration of the world, has enforced a fair degree of unity on each of the constituent national parts, making it most difficult to divide old or create new territorial states. The instincts of the Great Powers have been to retain the forms and resist territorial change, even when governments are violently overthrown. But in the case of the Soviet Union, as also Yugoslavia, the disciplines have not worked. Indeed, the new states are scarcely formed before being threatened by further subdivisions, as in the case of the Russian Federation, Azerbaijan, Georgia, and so on. If the disciplines have weakened, the system – for so long held in place by the rivalries of the Great Powers, particularly since 1945, in the competition between Moscow and Washington – may no longer be able to enforce territorial integrity.

If that is the case, is there a government that can afford to be complacent on the issue of national unity? The implications affect most directly the large powers – India, now with almost a continual civil war in one part of the country or another; China, with growing tensions between the economically advancing south, and to a lesser extent, the maritime provinces generally, and the more backward inland areas; Indonesia, Brazil, Nigeria. There is even talk of the Pacific and Atlantic economies pulling apart the United States somewhere in the Midwest.[1] Smaller powers are not immune, as the persistence of Quebecois, Catalan, Basque, Breton, Scottish and Welsh nationalisms or the rise of German secessionism in northern Italy suggest. A redistribution of power in unified Europe is encouraging the currently fashionable talk of a *Europe des regions*. Do these straws in the wind augur a new phase in the history of the territorial State, or are they no more than a passing impulse, the indulgence of a legion of fantasy Ruri-tanias?

---

[*] From: *Market Forces and World Development*, edited by Renee Prendergast and Francis Stewart, London, St. Martin's Press, 1994, pp. 1–14.

1   Democratic Staff of the Joint Economic Committee of the Congress of the United States 1986.

Apart from the settlement of the two world wars, only decolonisation permitted a general reorganisation of the state system, and in all three cases, the process was one ordered and executed by the dominant powers. Now however, the disintegration of the Eastern Bloc, the disappearance of Soviet nationalism into 15 Republican nationalisms – without revolution or a clear alternative programme – was accomplished in the face of the opposition of the Great Powers.

However, we should note that this political fragmentation has been accompanied by the openly expressed wish of the resulting new governments for greater economic integration, whether in the world at large or in the European Community. Indeed, some commentators have detected part of the impulse for national independence in the different degrees to which parts of countries have already been economically integrated in the European Community – for example, Slovenia and Croatia, as compared to Serbia.[2] In some sense, political nationalism seems to be the companion of an explicit economic internationalism (even when a new country's nearest neighbours are rejected for economic collaboration, as the Ukraine has rejected Russia). Thus, the programme for political national self-determination appears to have become entirely detached from any aim of economic self-determination: politics are national, economics global.

Definitions and Assumptions

There are some underlying assumptions in this account which should perhaps be specified at the outset. First, nationalism is seen not as primarily embodied in, or a product of, an affection for a locality, community, people, culture or language; on the contrary, these affections are the result of a nationalist commitment rather than its source. Nationalism is defined as loyalty to, or the aspiration to create, a modern national state. It is thus interwoven with the institutional structure by which the world is administered and subjected to the disciplines of a competitive state system. Nationalism is thus fundamental to the organisation of the world polity, so much so that it is almost impossible for us to detach ourselves from its operation. A quiet and even resentful obedience to the State and its laws is rather more the norm of nationalism than the aggressive forms of national liberation.

---

2 In the spring of 1990, *The Economist* observed that 'Slovenia's economic survival depended on how quickly it cut itself free from the Yugoslav disaster' (14 April 1990).

Secondly, 'national economic development' is seen as a process designed to create, or leading to the creation of, a fully diversified modern national economy, in principle a microcosm of the world economy, with the full range of sectors of production of goods and services and only a marginal dependence on external trade, foreign capital and technology. In its early formulations, it is supposedly driven by domestic demand; the economy was fully self-reliant if not necessarily entirely self-sufficient. The process is marked, as is well known, by radical changes in the composition of a growing output – the expansion of heavy and capital goods industries, the capacity to 'make the machines which make machines'. The sectoral and geographical redistribution of the labour force, increased intensity of work and in the participation rate, sustained increases in the capital and skill level per worker, and in final productivity, supposedly followed on from the central drive to transform national output. In its economic formulation – and in historical practice – the process was compatible with many different forms of political order, social and income inequalities and moral codes. But it is decisively defined by its national form.

The alternative model made the centrepiece of national growth external markets. There was no question of creating a 'balanced' or fully diversified economy, only of participating in a much wider pattern of specialisations which were far beyond local control and even knowledge. Indeed, attempts to create a fully diversified economy, regardless of any comparative advantage, would, in this account, waste resources and so reduce the level of world output and welfare below the optimal. The nearest contemporary equivalent to such a model would be Hong Kong.

Thirdly, the chapter assumes – in highly simplified fashion – that there are two parallel and interacting systems, each with comparable but different attributes. The first is a world economy, consisting of competing companies that produce an output of goods and services, the main short-term determinant of which, 'other things being equal', is relative prices. The second is a system of competing states, defined territorially. Within each country, the State normally holds a monopoly of the legitimate use of physical force and 'moral domination' within its territory. States are driven to compete in order to secure, defend or extend the prerogatives of national independence, sovereignty over a share of the world's territory, people, production and capital.

States and Economies

This last distinction – between a state system and a world economy – allows us to consider relationships between capital and the state which otherwise tend to become lost in 'the nation', as if loyalties were generally self-evident (as governments would like them to be).

In the early years of the growth of European capitalism, the political scene was dominated by the permanent rivalries of states in the form of princes and dynasties. War was of the essence of this competition, and its scale and duration were often limited only by the capacity of the rulers to raise funds and troops to fight. It would take this account too far afield to discuss the different phases of this history and the ways in which competitive rivalries shaped each state.[3] However, the issues concerned dominated the methods of rule, the modes and scale of state financing and the forms of public bureaucracy. The obsession with war was a powerful motive for governments to take an interest in the economy, the source of funds with which to fight (an interest which ultimately became rationalised in the creation of economics) and, much later, in the concept of national economic development. The state system imposed a particular form on economic development that was most commonly guided by or rationalised in mercantilism. Indeed, mercantilism – economics formulated almost exclusively in the interests of state power (disregarding whether it is presented as being governed by the interests of the 'nation') – seems everywhere to be the instinctive theory of a developing state, particularly where it is in competition with more powerful states. Import substitution industrialisation strategies are thus only the modern variant of an old tradition of mercantilist practice and theories.

The underlying governmental motive for national economic development is the pursuit of the means to enhance the capacity of the state to compete in the state system. An interest in the welfare by-products of development for the mass of the population would then be only an incidental spin off, albeit a useful one if this induced greater loyalty, greater willingness and capacity of the citizens to pay and to fight for the state.

The effect of the competition of states upon economic development can be illustrated from the history of many countries. In the British case, an extreme one since it is one of the earliest, industrialisation appears almost as an accidental by-product of state rivalries, as embodied in war-making. During the most important period of the transition from mercantile to industrial capit-

---

3 The basic issues are discussed with great illumination in Tilly 1990.

alism, the maintenance of the armed forces was the main rationale of first the English, and then the British State. From 1695 to 1820, between 78 and 95 percent of public spending was devoted either to military – particularly naval – matters, or to servicing debts incurred to finance past wars (in real terms, the volume of public spending increased five times over).[4] In the 127 years from 1688 to 1815, the country was engaged in major wars for roughly 70 years. In the last years, during the Napoleonic Wars, some 350,000 men were under arms (1801), a total that had risen to half a million – or nearly 10 percent of the domestic labour force – by 1811. Many more civilians were engaged in supplying the armed forces. By 1801, gross public expenditure to cover this phenomenal operation may have been equal to over half national expenditure. Indeed, in the half century after 1780, government consumption was larger than the value of exports, suggesting the process of British economic development was led by government spending on war rather than the stimulus of production for export.[5]

In summary, the government's reaction to systemic rivalries produced a sustained rise in national output, transformed its composition (with disproportionate growth in the metallurgical, textile and coal industries), and flattened the output fluctuations which a market-led pattern of growth might have been expected to produce. The curtailment of imports from Europe during the Blockade period of the conflict with France not only did not precipitate the slump for which Napoleon had designed the policy of depriving English producers of continental markets, it accelerated growth by introducing an element of protection, increasing the intensity of the use of the factors of production and further diversifying national output. The burden of this process appears to have been borne by a familiar redistribution (implicit in most import substitution strategies) from popular consumption to public revenue and profits. To oversimplify, British industrialisation in this period appears to be a by-product of the ancient rivalries of states rather than the 'spontaneous' expansion of commercial markets.

One might usefully explore other cases of the sequence: state rivalries to increasing military spending to industrialisation. The case of Tsarist Russia in the 1890s or of Mehmet Ali in early nineteenth-century Egypt would be relevant. So also would be Japan, despite the very different industrial and military context. Between 1874 and 1945, Japan was engaged in ten major wars,

---

4   The basic data are derived from Mitchell and Deane 1962 and Mitchell and Jones 1971. See also Mann 1980.

5   See Deane 1975.

two of them world wars. From 1886, military spending was on average equal to 10 percent of gross national product, and 12 percent in the three decades to 1945. Starting from a very low base point in terms of modern military capacity, by the 1920s, Japan had become the third largest naval and fifth largest military power. In the 1930s, the demands of war were the source of both the giant zaibatsu, subcontractors to government demand, and the prodigious growth of key industries – heavy and chemicals, electrical and transport equipment, and so on. From the experience of the 1930s, Morishima draws the conclusion that:

> Economic growth was certainly not achieved through using the mechanism of the free operation of the economy; it was the result of the government or the military, with their loyal following of capitalists, manipulating and influencing the economy in order to realize national aims ... [T]he price mechanism scarcely played an important role, and the questions of importance were how to raise capital and to meet the government's demand and the nature of the demand generated from the enterprises at the receiving end of a government demand.[6]

Finally, in the postwar period, systemic rivalries were powerful forces motivating the drive of South Korea (scene of an extraordinarily destructive war) and Taiwan (the government of which was driven from the mainland by war to become an active participant in the Cold War) to industrialise in the 1960s and 1970s. One of the differences with the earlier cases was that the process of national economic development, driven by military insecurity, came to depend – through, on the one hand, a series of accidents affecting the States concerned, and on the other, a structural change in the world economy[7] – on exporting manufactured goods. However, the process still depended on continuing State initiative and import substituting policies, now married to export promotion. Of course, military rivalries do not invariably produce the same effects. Circumstances determine all. The world rivalries shaping the British government in the late nineteenth century may have led London to use India as, in Lord Salisbury's words (1882), 'a barracks on the Oriental seas from which we may draw any number of troops without paying for them',[8] and without the need for Parliamentary approval, but the resulting drive to national economic development was very weak. It might have been that nearly half Indian gov-

---

6   See Morishima 1982, pp. 96–7.

7   These issues are explored in more detail in Chapter 2 of Harris 1986.

8   Cited by Johnson 1990, p. 238.

ernment revenues were spent directly on the maintenance of the army, and its interests lay behind most infrastructural development policies,[9] but the benefits in terms of industrialisation were to the Empire and to London.

We can see also that the peculiar form of national economic development in the Soviet Union was perhaps more the result of the state insecurities of the interwar period than the imperatives of an inherited ideology. Born in world war and civil war, maturing in the Great Depression, and precipitated yet again into a second world war, the Soviet Union was created in a period of unprecedented state rivalries (and savageries). The USSR entered the system with two peculiar features. First, a post-revolutionary social structure where the normal patterns of established interests did not exist to constrain State action and the bureaucracy had almost unlimited power over society. Second, Moscow, governing a vast but poor society, chose to enter the system as a Great Power, competing in conditions of the most intense rivalry. The combination led, as is well known, to a no less unprecedented degree of social, economic and administrative centralisation, a semi-militarised society, governed by a continuing paranoia. National economic development, seeking to create a completely independent economy, reached its most extreme form in the Soviet case with little distinction tolerated between state and civil society, between systemic imperatives and domestic accumulation, between civilian and soldier. The extremity of the case was only heightened by the employment of the language of liberation to describe it.

States and Capital

The Soviet case highlights the historical specificity of the relationship of capital accumulation (normally the activity of companies) and systemic state rivalries, particularly in relationship to what seems to be a rather different relationship between the two in our own times. Indeed, with a touch of heroic oversimplification we might identify a series of historical phases, exaggerating the differences to highlight this relativity.

(i)   In the early phases of historical accumulation, capital was promiscuous – in the main, operating almost independently of the interests of states[10]

---

9   Washbrook 1990, p. 42.

10 In Braudel's world, the merchants operate apparently with only distant relationships to rules, often little better than territorial tax collectors.

although always with a minority of companies exploiting corrupt relationships to different aspects of state power, using state authority for
private advantage (not unlike 'cronyism' in the Philippines), to eliminate
rivals and so on. On the other hand, the state tolerated capital as a kind
of necessary parasite in the pursuit of its main purposes, its justification
being that it provided most superior and swift sources of funding, material and transport for war-making.

(ii) Such a system led in the nineteenth century to the creation of what
Charles Jones (1987) calls a 'cosmopolitan bourgeoisie'. Taking advantage
of the areas of peace laid out by empires, but not at all constrained by the
interests of the imperial power, businessmen seem to have interacted as
rivals without, in general, close alignments to states.[11] Empires were useful
areas of operation, but by no means defined the destinations of capital.[12]
States were also increasingly concerned to draw sharp lines between their
own interests and operations and those of private companies. Global
markets provided the basis for a classical economics in which the state
had strictly only a passive economic role if there was to be the optimal
employment of the world's factors of production.

(iii) These earlier features stand out in striking contrast to the subsequent 'age
of imperialism' (as opposed to the operation of empires), roughly after
1870. Now the interests of states increasingly began to divide a cosmopolitan bourgeoisie into constituent national (and racial) entities, even
where the 'national' included empire. The state now came to take a much
closer and continuing interest in the 'economy', that is, the affairs of companies, even to the point, in time of war, of partial fusion. State capitalism and corporatism were growing responses to a period of extraordinary systematic rivalries in the twentieth century's wars and slump, most
extreme, as we have seen, in the case of the Soviet Union, but leaving no
Great Power untouched. The patriotism of capital may never have been
as great as it seemed, but the heyday of national capital involved a marriage between business and the state. Virtually all governments returned
to strong traditions of mercantilism, now embodied rather misleadingly

---

11   Compare a comment on the relationship between companies in eighteenth-century Brit-
      ish India:
          'in their [unorientalised] world categorical oppositions, [they] did not separate the
      "Indian" and "European". Alliances formed and opposed one another for reasons that
      made sense in that world; and they fought for the fruits of merchant capital' (Ludden
      1990, p. 164).
12   Discussed with much illumination in O'Brien 1988.

in something called 'Keynesianism' (and east of the Elbe, 'socialism').[13] As always, the perception of how peculiar the system was came only late in the day; even as Andrew Shonfield was completing *Modern Capitalism*[14] (an account of a set of national economies, each in principle fully controlled by state policy), the world economy was beginning to be transformed once again.

(iv) From the early 1960s, a single integrated world economy appears to be emerging, superseding the old form of a set of interacting but relatively autonomous national economies. Of course, the process still has far to go to be fully realised and still only covers part of the world. But it has already created a pool of global capital and patterns of integrated manufacture which make it most difficulty to identify what the economic interests of any particular state are (and therefore what a positive national economic policy ought to be). Even the most powerful state, the United States, is decreasingly able to manage its domestic economic affairs without global collaboration. On the other hand, global capital, embodied in transnational enterprises, appears to recreate, if not a single cosmopolitan bourgeoisie, at least a set of global baronies that operate with limited contingent relationships to many states. Indeed, governments appear now less as representing a people to the world at large and rather more as representing a world system to a people. Liberalisation, privatisation, structural adjustment, affecting all states and companies, establish consistency between domestic and external prices, and the predominant influence of world markets on domestic economies. Of course, the process assumes a dramatic transformation in technology, providing the technical basis for almost instantaneous global operations. Finally, the transition from Keynesianism to neoclassical economics offers a theoretical counterpoint to the re-emergence on a much grander scale (without the old scaffolding of empire) of an integrated world economy.

---

13   The theoretical parallels are not chronologically exact. Classical economics and its neoclassical, marginalist descendants did not cease with the onset of 'imperialism' from the 1870s, but continued to exercise predominant influence to the 1920s, at least in the country with the most persistent adherence to free trade, Britain.

14   'The state controls so large a part of the economy that a planner can, by intelligent manipulation of the levers of public power, guide the remainder of the economy firmly towards any objective that the government chooses' (Shonfield 1965, p. 231). Compare Galbraith 1967, p. 296 – 'In notable respects, the corporation is an arm of the state' and later on, 'the state, in important respects, [is] an instrument of the industrial system.'

In an open world economy the system seems, for any individual competitor, to be much more unpredictable (a feature perhaps reflected in the present disatisfaction with macroeconomic forecasting). Major changes can occur with extraordinary speed – as when the United States moved within three years from being the world's largest creditor to the world's largest debtor. There is a resulting premium on organisational flexibility, affecting not only the old command economies but also the old form of centralised transnational corporation. Enhanced risks lead to the increased spinning off of ancillary corporation activities and the rise of hosts of subcontractors and consultants who absorb the risk in their sheer multiplicity. Markets come to appear as the sole means available to manage such dynamic complexity. Without timely change, whole sections of the system are threatened with economic decline – forcing, for example, the implosion in the Soviet Union and Eastern Europe.

There is, as we noted earlier, still far to go in the process.[15] Stagnation and recession in the system conjure up the ghosts of the past, not necessarily in the form of the old territorial State (although there are also resistances to economic integration) but rather in the semi-internationalised form, not now of empire, but of regional federation: Europe, North America and the Asia Pacific Rim.[16] The concept of these regions concerns primarily trade since no one is yet raising the question of the reimposition of controls on capital movements and the free international movement of labour has in general never been liberalised, although Europe is now moving towards this aim within its boundaries. Yet even with trade, the prospects for regionalism are limited, since, to different degrees, the United States, Europe and Japan are pre-eminently global economic powers, not regional. For them to be restricted to their respective regions would be an economic catastrophe for them. Intra-regional trade provided just over a third of the trade total for the proposed East Asian Economic Group, and about 44 percent if China and Australia were included. North American trade accounts for around 40 percent of US trade. Europe's intra-regional trade supplies two thirds of its total. The situation can change but it would seem that the chances of political authorities being able to coax an increasingly large share of intra-regional trade from each region to the point where a significant

---

15   Perceptions – if not behaviour – by the managers of international companies still lag
      behind what seems to be the structure of the global economy (see Kanter 1991, pp. 151–
      64).
16   With an appropriate reconsideration of free trade and industrial policy, see Thurow 1989,
      Dornbusch et al. 1988 and Dornbush et al. 1989.

degree of economic and thus political autonomy came to exist are very limited. When 55 percent of US exports go to Europe and Asia, it seems hardly
credible that Latin America – let alone Canada and Mexico – could take over
that share. In economic terms, regions make little sense; but as part of the
bargaining weaponry of the leading powers to combat each others' protectionism, particularly in the context of a floundering Uruguay Round and the
possible threat of Europe's political integration, they may make much more
sense.

On the other hand, the Great Powers are now, despite their disagreements
about their particular positions, more united in their view of what should be
the economic and political behaviour of governments than at any time since
the First World War; the 'new world order' mimics the heyday of empire. The
Great Powers now as then make and change the rules governing activity, and
seek to do so in their own collective and individual interests. The orthodoxy of
today, embodied in an explicit agenda making democratisation, privatisation,
liberalisation, etc. mandatory, has become the condition for borrowing. In the
past, such conditionality would have been denounced as political interference
in the sovereignty of the borrowing power (as an example of the shift, compare the articles of the World Bank with those of the new European regional
development bank). However, seeing the change of policy stance in developing countries as simply imposed – whether directly through bilateral aid programmes or through the loan conditions of the International Monetary Fund
and the World Bank – is to underestimate the profundity of the change in
the system. The Great Powers have been no less obliged to conform to the
agenda, and the developing countries have, in many cases, embraced parts of
the programme less because they were imposed conditions, more because they
seemed 'to make sense', that is, they had become sensible as the result of radical
changes in the world economy.

The consensus must be temporary. Too many conflicting interests are imprisoned in the orthodoxy to give it long-term viability. But whatever the new
heterodoxies, they will be forced to start from a global economy. The structures
now seem so well established, it is difficult to see how they could in general be
reversed.

Conclusions

National economic development, as defined here, appears now as a historical phenomenon, part of the last period of imperialism and state capitalism,
marked by two world wars and the Great Depression. Nationalism embodied a

drive to create a fully diversified independent national economy. For developing countries, the programme of political national self-determination included as an intrinsic part the aim of economic self-determination, covering trade, technology, the ownership of capital. Each state strove to act as the exclusive agent or dominant partner in national capital accumulation.

That system is now in an advanced state of decay, robbing both the old political Right (the corporatists) and the Left of their inherited programmes. For the Left, the State – supposedly the neutral agency to transform the material conditions of the mass of the population – can apparently no longer be employed successfully for reform, except on conditions laid down externally. The old national economies become increasingly specialised contributors to a global output, drawing on a global stock of capital. Indeed, it becomes increasingly difficult to identify economically what is national and what foreign.[17] Only for those managing the national balance of payments does the distinction matter, and even then it is by no means self-evident what policies should be pursued in the interests of the state (in the British case, consider the slightly comic public disputes over who should be allowed to take over Westland helicopters, Cadbury's chocolate, etc.). The national economy becomes less a fixed location for the manufacture of a finished good, a starting or finishing point in manufacture, and more a junction in flows of goods, finance, people (although here mobility is still the most limited) and information. The source of domestic change lies beyond the power – and often, even the knowledge – of government.

In closing, we might indulge ourselves in some little fantasies. It seems that what has happened in the Soviet Union is affecting the most long-lasting expression of the state system, military power. For most of this century, disarmament talks have been a permanent career for those involved in them; one could be confident that there would never be serious disarmament. Now however, there is a significant trend to disarm which, if sustained, is powerful evidence of a fundamental change in the state system so far as the Great Powers are concerned. The new conditionalities of World Bank lending now include an insistence on shifting defence to social spending. Despite some aspiration to be the world's policeman, even the United States, driven by the destabilising effect of its budget deficit on the American and world economies, is obliged to undertake some radical trimming of its military might. Sadly, the trend among

---

17   *The Economist* noted some examples recently: a $55,000 John Deere excavator purchased in the United States was assembled in Japan, and its 'Japanese' rival, a $40,000 Komatsu, was made in Illinois. Of seven US car models – made by Pontiac, Chevrolet, Mercury, Honda, Dodge and Plymouth – only one was built in the United States, the Honda.

the leading powers is yet to affect the developing countries – the highest rates of increase in military spending are now in the Middle East and East and South East Asia. War will be with us for a long time yet, and at its worst, among some of the poorest people. But if the power of the state weakens, it is possible that nationalism then may cease to have its ferocious military-economic focus of the past period, dominated by the centralised and authoritarian state, and become more an innocent affection for localities and cultures. Political fission may become a permanent fashion, quite tolerable while accompanied by economic fusion.

If the state is relatively weakening, is power rising to a regional and global level (transnational corporations and international agencies), and sinking to a local level? The fashion for decentralising governments and initiating city economic strategies is another part of the new orthodoxy. It is too early and uncertain to hazard many guesses about the trend. The rivalries of the State system still remain a powerful element in corseting the old state form, and deterring any dispersal of power.

However, if that change is coming about, another Utopian aim perhaps begins to enter the realm of practicality: world government. In one sense, it is already here, not as a single institution but as a complex of regulatory agencies located in many different parts of the world and subject to greater or lesser degrees to the influence of the dominant powers. With time, these institutions may grow into effective governance, but it will require the weakening of the states to achieve it.

If the old programme of national economic development is now past, the economic future of the developing countries depends upon the relationships they establish with the world economy, the patterns of changing specialisation that they can capture. Many governments in developing countries have, willingly or not, acknowledged the changed context; some at least have become champions of free trade, opposing the incipient protectionism of some of the developed.

The decline of war and the state is a daydream, far from reality at the moment. The horror of Sarajevo, the appalling slaughter of Iranians and Iraqis, the terrifying exhibition of United States military power in the Gulf, the growing numbers of those driven out of their countries, all indicate the samurai are far from being pensioned off to doze in Cheltenham. Famine, poverty in village and city slum, the exploitation of child labour, all the horrors remain. Yet amid the bleakness of a world still so dominated by poverty and the sacrifice of hopes, the trends may be a little more promising on at least one part of the programme of progress after August 1991. Charles Tilly observes at the end of his analysis of states in Europe over a thousand years: 'States may be following

NATIONALISM AND DEVELOPMENT   173

the old routine by which an institution falls into ruin just as it becomes complete. In the meantime, nevertheless, States remain so dominant that anyone
who dreams of a stateless world seems a heedless visionary'.[18]

----

18   Tilly 1990, p. 4.

The War-Making State and Privatisation*

Nigel Harris and David Lockwood

States, created with the central purpose of defending national independence, res-ist the process of macroeconomic reform since it appears to limit their power to pursue this aim. The states of the former Centrally Planned Economies were marked out by their extreme subordination to the military drive, so the resistance to reshaping the 'war-making state' into a 'market-facilitating state' is consider-able. The transition tends to be halted where the old structures of central control are ended without markets supplying alternative imperatives – a 'rent-seeking state' is created. These themes are examined in relationship to privatisation of state owned enterprises in four countries: Russia, China, Vietnam and the Ukraine.

Macro-economic reform has become a global fashion, and each national pro-gramme has tended to converge on an agenda of surprising uniformity – sum-marised in part in John Williamson's 'Washington Consensus'.[1] It has also come to govern the policy-making of the majority of governments, providing the tar-get for what Bergstein and Williamson call 'a global stampede in the last quarter of the twentieth century'.[2]

Countries of every geographical region, income level and ideology have joined the rush. Asians, Europeans, Latin Americans and Africans; countries once among the richest in the world (such as Argentina, Australia and New Zealand) and countries near the bottom; capitalists, socialists and those in between.

The political range is indeed remarkable – from Communist (China, 1978; Vietnam, 1989; Laos, 1990; not to mention the longer-run efforts in the then Soviet Union and Eastern Europe), through Social Democratic (Australia, New Zealand, Spain, Portugal), to Liberal Conservative (United States, Britain), and Leftish-populist regimes (Menem's Peronists in Argentina, Salinas's PRI in Mex-ico). Structural adjustment – wrongly – has a reputation of requiring an author-itarian initiative, but only a handful of countries have experienced a military

---

* From: *Journal of Development Studies*, 33/5, Jun. 1997, pp. 597–634.

1   See Williamson 1990.
2   Williamson 1994, p. 3.

coup in advance of reform – Suharto in Indonesia, Pinochet in Chile, Turkey in 1980, Ghana in 1983 and South Korea in 1980 (as opposed to the many more military coups without reform). On the other hand, the emergence of a global economy may in future years be credited with ending authoritarian regimes, from the old Soviet Union to apartheid in South Africa.

In some cases, political leaders have come to power on one platform and been rapidly converted to the other, as occurred to Menem in Argentina, to India's Finance Minister Manmohan Singh,[3] to Mitterrand in France, or to Ghana's Kwesi Botchwey. Furthermore, where the reform regime has been overthrown or replaced by its rivals, in most cases there has been no attempt to return to the *status quo ante*, but rather the reforms have been continued – this is even true where the reform regime originally came to power through violence (as with the successors to the military dictators – Aylwin in Chile, Turgot Ozal in Turkey, Roh Tae Woo in South Korea).

The advent of macroeconomic reform has also destroyed the traditional political alternatives. The old corporatist conservative Right with its emphasis on the decisive importance of a powerful state, has gone, surviving only where its proponents have transmogrified themselves into what was formerly the enemy: advocates of free markets in all practicable spheres. The Left which for so long fashioned its political alternatives on the basis of a *dirigiste* state, in part or whole absorbing civil society, found its chosen vehicle an increasingly weak instrument for its purposes; it shrank and turned to adopt the softer focus of 'community' rather than class.

The universality of the change, the diversity of sources apparently converging on a uniform agenda, suggests a common force at work. Each local peculiarity is being shaped by reactions to the emergence of a single world economy, enforcing common disciplines on all regardless of local peculiarities. The shift is far more dramatic and universal than the earlier one, the move against free trade in the interwar years.

For the developed countries, the process of unwinding the mercantilist structures put in place in the 1930s and 1940s (in response to slump and war) was spread over a long period of time, but even so the two world recessions of the 1970s (roughly 1973–5 and 1979–81) forced radical reform in the 1980s at just the time when the processes of global integration had moved on from trade to capital. For the developing countries, many of the mercantilist structures were only put in place in the 1960s and 1970s (for the former colon-

---

3   With a reputation for great caution, but once in office, acting 'with unprecedented boldness and speed' (Little et al. 1993, p. 127).

ies, part of the mercantilism was something they inherited from the colonial period). Latin America, however, followed the European model, except that the phase of mercantilism persisted much later – until the early 1980s for Mexico, Brazil and Argentina, when financial crisis forced reform in the most painful circumstances. In sub-Saharan Africa, elements of economic autarky were put in place in the 1960s when overall growth was sustained by buoyant demand for Africa's raw material exports; the decline in raw material prices was offset by borrowing in the 1970s, but terminated in severe recession with the second global downturn and the round of oil price increases in the late 1970s.

East and Southeast Asia were engaged in a headlong process of growth, led by the export of manufactured goods, and this growth itself, as well as the pressure of trading partners to open domestic markets, impelled reform – but without pain. Even so, the last of the old sort of heavy industrial drives – in South Korea and Taiwan in the 1970s – severely destabilised those countries with the onset of the second round of oil price increases and world recession. The murder of the Korean President in 1979 interwove a major political crisis with slump. Nonetheless, high growth economies based upon manufactured exports seem to possess a greater degree of flexibility: the macroeconomic performance returned to high growth with extraordinary speed (and also absorbed without strain the upsurge of worker and democratic militancy in 1987, leading to major increases in wages).

However, while dismantling structures which have been in place for a long time is one thread in the story, the behaviour of developing country governments in the short-term – in the 1970s – is a key element in undermining older structures in the 1980s. Many governments endeavoured to accelerate out of the slump (and the increase in oil prices)[4] of the early 1970s. They did so through increased external borrowing (gaining access to the now easily-available recycled petrodollars), and – like the governments in Europe and north America in the 1930s – a major expansion in state investment. On the then current prognostications for world growth, it made sense, and many governments felt vindicated by an acceleration in growth. The second round of oil price increases and a world recession brought this to a sharp close with a rapid end to the possibility of borrowing and a major debt crisis – which this time round, forced structural reform.

---

4   In 1974, 'probably the largest quarterly economic shock the world economy has ever experienced', redirecting in three months some 10 percent of the world's trade payments (Little et al. 1993, p. 17).

The short-term crisis was embodied in two insupportable deficits – on external payments (trade and capital) and the government budget, often in conditions of high inflation (in Bolivia, 25,000 percent; in Poland in late 1989, 3,000 percent) as the result of a high government deficit. But the long-term problem was a degree of rigidity in the economy which prevented governments responding to unanticipated economic shocks with adequate flexibility.[5]

Not all reform programmes were precipitated by this scale of crisis, where the damage of severe slump cannot be distinguished clearly from that of the reactions to slump. China, the former Czechoslovakia, India, Australia and Spain had much less extreme introductions, and therefore less need of emergency measures, 'shock treatment'. For Australia, a classic import-substituting economy for much of this century, tight protection of domestic activity and a large public sector were perfectly consistent with high growth and high employment up to the late 1960s.[6] From then, a deterioration in the external balance, economic instability and rising unemployment, a product of world recession, forced a reappraisal. A new Labour government, with the strong support of the trade unions,[7] began liberalisation.

Within the context of global macroeconomic reform, we examine these issues in a selection of what used to be known as the 'Centrally Planned Economies'. The central preoccupation is in assessing the movement from a *dirigiste* state order to one where governments manage a market economy, concentrating on the issue of the privatisation of state enterprises. The next section examines the onset of the reform programme in Eastern Europe and the former Soviet Union. Section III endeavours to locate this discussion in a simplified typology of states – war-making, market-facilitating and rent-seeking. The fourth part then examines the impact of war preparations in the 1980s in precipitating the breakdown which forced reforms. The fifth section looks in greater detail at the process of privatisation in Russia, China, Vietnam, and the Ukraine, with some final conclusions and perspectives in the last part.

---

5 Caneri seeks to illustrate the increase in Turkish government flexibility as a result of reform as follows: 'it took six years for the government to react to the first oil price increase, over six months to the major financial crisis of 1983, six weeks to the exchange crisis of 1987, six days to the 1990 Gulf War, and now six hours to major external changes' (in Williamson 1994).
6 Garnaut 1994.
7 With a price: 'a substantial reduction in real wages and real unit labour costs that was probably unique in Australia's twentieth century history' (Garnaut 1994, p. 68).

Eastern Europe and Russia

Are there any parallels between the world process and what occurred in the former centrally planned economies? There are some, particularly in the similarities within the East Asian group. But reform in economies with strong elements of private ownership and domestic markets was inevitably different. Bus writes:

> Instead of transferring individual enterprises (largely commercialized) from a public into an existing private-dominated domain with operating market institutions long habituated to such operations by the society, the process of transformation in post-communist countries consists of privatization of the entire economy accompanied by its marketisation.[8]

This involved a major institutional transformation, a radical change in social behaviour, often taking place in conditions of severe economic instability. They were economies of peculiar rigidity, characterised by predominant political direction, without mechanisms of self-adjustment, and with, by modern standards, a high degree of inward orientation.

The rigidities were painfully demonstrated in the relative decline in output experienced in Eastern Europe: –12.5 and –9 percent in Poland (1990 and 1991); –10.2 and –26.0 in Bulgaria; –3.5 and –16.4 in Czechoslovakia; and despite a much longer reform period, –6.5 and –7.8 in Hungary.[9] In three years, the Ukraine experienced a 40 percent decline.[10] The data are unsound – compared to inflated estimates before reform, biased towards heavy industry, and underrecording the new private and servicing activities – yet a decline there almost certainly was.

The declines in output seemed greater and more drawn out than many of those experienced in reforming economies elsewhere. Chile had a one year fall in output of 18 percent (but output fell only for one year), while in Argentina the output fall was only 12 percent. By way of comparison, during the Great Depression of the interwar period, US output fell by 30 percent, Germany's by 23.5, and France's by 16.7 in different years in the first half of the 1930s. In the conversion of European war economies to peacetime production in 1945 there were comparable falls, and the break up of the Austro-Hungarian Empire after

---

8   UNCTAD 1994, p. 49.

9   See Solimano 1992.

10   See McCarthy et al. 1994.

the First World War also led to a sharp fall in the output of the constituent countries (and a halving in the volume of trade between them).[11]

The declines in output in the Soviet bloc, however, were more the result of a series of extraordinary shocks which, in part, preceded reform and made for emergency responses – 'more a generalized recession than a shake out of the economy associated with structural reforms'.[12] What were the shocks?

First, the collapse of the central planning system unwound the linkages of the economies with alarming speed, without there existing either market or monetary mechanisms to establish alternative means to distribute the output.

Second, this disaster was associated with the reaction of the Soviet Union to what was seen as the failure of the Eastern Europeans to meet their trade obligations in CMEA,[13] leading to the reduction or suspension of Soviet supplies, and thus the disintegration of the network, particularly important for trade in capital and military goods, for material-intensive products.[14] The collapse of the CMEA hit particularly hard Czechoslovakia and Bulgaria; 60 percent of Czech exports to CMEA were machinery and equipment (particularly from what was to become Slovakia), much of it technically tied to specific patterns of consumption in the CMEA group and not saleable elsewhere. In the first quarter of 1990, Romania's exports to non-convertible currency areas declined by 62 percent.

Third, of particular importance to CMEA buyers of Soviet exports was the supply of oil. Very cheap oil (by world standards) had created an industrial

---

11   Havrylyshyn 1994b, p. 174.

12   Commander et al. 1991, p. 8.

13   The trading association set up in 1949 and including the Soviet Union, the European 'Six', Mongolia, Cuba, Vietnam and formerly Albania; Yugoslavia was an associate.

14   The scale of dependence on CMEA trade can be seen below.

Shares of CMEA in exports, 1985 and 1989
(Including, for 1985, the share of the member's exports taken by the Soviet Union)

	1985	1989		1985	1989
Bulgaria	83 (79)	63	Hungary	39 (62)	45
Czechoslovakia	54 (57)	51	Poland	35 (60)	44
East Germany	42 (57)	–	Romania	40 (58)	25
Soviet Union	46				

SOURCE: SHRENK 1991; HAVRYLYSHYN AND TARR 1991: BALCEROWITZ 1994

structure in the Soviet Union and Eastern Europe which was heavily dependent upon continued supply – the Soviet steel industry, for example, utilised 50 percent more energy per tonne than the Japanese. And the capacity could not easily or swiftly be converted either to economise or to utilise other forms of energy. For example, oil prices for wholesale industrial consumers were 26.3 percent of world market prices in 1989, and 19.4 percent in 1990 (while gas prices were 32.7 and 21.4 percent respectively).[15] The problems particularly affected the Urals, the Ukraine, Slovakia and other components of the CMEA heavy industry network.

Fourth, the break up of the Soviet Union was even more destructive economically for the constituent parts of the USSR, completed by the disintegration of the Rouble zone in 1993. Political and military instability compounded the disasters, leading to some of the most severe output declines: Armenia –52.0 and –28.0 (1992 and 1993); Azerbaijan –26.8 and –14.4; Georgia –20.6 (1991), –45.6 and –30.0; Tajikistan –30.0 and –30.0.[16]

Fifth, with the break up of both CMEA and the Soviet Union, Russia endeavoured to move export prices for oil towards world market levels and to demand hard currency payments – thus Ukrainian imports (from Russia and Turkmenistan) were 19 percent of world market prices in 1992, but 37 percent in the first quarter of 1993. If Russian prices had reached world levels, the Ukraine would have been obliged to transfer to Russia revenue equal to 30 percent of its gross domestic product.[17] As the Ukraine's hard currency exports fell by two thirds (1992–3), import costs soared, and the government was able to meet only half the cost of its daily energy imports of, at the then current exchange rate, US$15 million. The Ukrainian problem was vastly exaggerated since the government endeavoured to hold the domestic price of oil well below the world market level.

Sixth, if the heart of the crisis of output was heavy and military industry within both CMEA and the Soviet Union, the problems were exacerbated by changing government policy priorities. The cutting of state purchases of output and the decline in investment was crucial here, as was the attempt by the Russian government to cut military procurement by 80 percent in 1992.

Seventh, furthermore, conversion of exports to hard currency markets was made much more difficult by the onset of recession in the OECD group, as well as the muddled protectionism which so often characterised Western trade policy.

---

15   IMF et al. 1990.

16   See Havrylyshyn 1994b.

17   See Dabrowski 1994.

Eighth, there were also the familiar symptoms of crisis – high inflation, high debt service problems, debts spreading through the economy and covered only by soft banking credits, capital flight and severe problems of basic supply. They made suddenly much more severe the long-term issues of an overproduction of unsaleable heavy industrial goods that went to stocks along with a gross shortage of consumer goods and an excess supply of money.

Ninth, and finally, there were the shocks specific to particular countries and moments – for example, the Gulf War severely affected Romanian oil imports and hence its export of refined products; the embargo on trade with Serbia affected Hungary, Bulgaria and Romania; the peasant seizure of lands in Romania led to a break up of common services to agriculture, and a disastrous decline in irrigation and fertiliser inputs, and hence of agricultural output; a couple of years drought exaggerated the problems.

It could hardly have been a worse time to undertake structural reforms. The emergency character of the shocks as well as the political crisis severely limited government options. Yet it gave a rare popular mandate for radical change, a moment of opportunity, a phase of 'extraordinary politics'.[18] However, it also fell upon a political and economic order that was demoralised and without direction, one that had in some cases pursued reform for a decade or more without success. The failure of an epoch was at stake, symbolised in the appalling decline in Russia of the male average life expectancy figures;[19] in the knowledge that Czech per capita income, ten percent below Austria's in 1938, was 80 percent below half a century later; that whereas Spain and Poland were roughly similar in standard of living in 1950, in the late 1980s, Spanish per capita income was between four and seven times that of Poland.[20]

Yet three years later, there were some signs of recovery from the Great Depression of Eastern Europe. Poland in 1995 experienced its second year of good growth (including the grey economy, possibly between 5.5 and 6.5 percent), and Eastern Europe as a whole achieved just under four percent, the first aggregate increase since 1989.[21] Hungary was still stationary, and the output of Russia falling (–15 percent in 1994, with worse performances in other members of the Commonwealth of Independent States). However, some detected signs of revival even in Russia.[22] Everywhere – except in the Czech

---

18   See Balcerowicz and Gelb 1994.

19   Easterly and Fischer 1994, p. 30. See also Shapiro, 1994.

20   See Solimano 1991.

21   See UNECE 1995.

22   Vasilev 1994, p. 127.

Republic, Russia and the Ukraine – official unemployment rates remained very high and the average period of unemployment seemed to be extending. In Russia, the crisis of the state loomed as large as that of the economy.

How are we to understand this extraordinary process of violent implosion, and the sharp differences between countries in the process of regearing their economies? For this we need some conception of the role of the state historically and its relationship to a radically changing global economic order. This the next section seeks to provide.

Types of States

Why, in the past two decades, have governments moved so decisively but not with equal consistency to open up their economies to a technical integration in a global pattern of specialisation? On the face of it, it would seem an unlikely evolution that those directing the state should relinquish in any respect those powers of patronage and influence which in part secure the political means to perpetuate their position in office. However, perhaps the point of departure is to turn the question round: why did governments seek to close their economies, to – implicitly or explicitly – defy a global division of labour?

Part of the answer relates to the central historical rationale for the existence of states: to defend a share of the world's population and territory, and if needed, extend that share and strip one's neighbours' territories of assets. In Tilly's crisp aphorism: 'War made the State, and the State made war'.[23]

The preparation and periodic waging of war can be seen as the predominant motif in the history of the states. Furthermore, economic development on one account can be seen as a by-product of the state's pursuit of war – from Britain in the eighteenth century to Japan in the twentieth (and South Korea and Taiwan in the 1960s and 1970s).[24] Between wars, the struggle of princes to pay for their preparations for the next war and the cumulative costs of past wars dominates public finance and the political relationships between government, taxpayers and the mass of those who generated society's income. The struggle of Phillip II with the Spanish Cortes and the Burghers of the Netherlands provides a vivid illustration of the theme; the one seeking to persuade the nation to pay for the defence the King thought appropriate, when the other

---

23   Tilly 1975, p. 42. See also Tilly 1990.

24   Harris 1992, pp. 27–9.

suspected that all that was at stake were the imperialist fantasies of the King and the rent-seeking propensities of his courtiers and friends.[25]

War preparation also provides the rationale for a public interest in the performance of the economy – and the development of a formal discipline, economics, to inform policy-making – and for public intervention. It provides the reason for extending the perimeter of the 'nation' to include all (or most) of the inhabitants of the territory the state holds, to seek to create a secure social foundation for war-making – and as a by-product, the basis for populist politics. In the welfare state, the material survival of the population – the basis for the quality of the citizen-army – is lifted from its fluctuating fortunes in the labour market. Market demand can no longer be permitted to determine the size and quality of the labour force, and thereby the strength of the army. Of course, in some cases, the central rationale disappears – the drive to sustain a 'socialised nation' became remote from the original purpose of a war-making state.

In some of the best-known cases – Frederick's Prussia was famous in its time – the war-making state entirely absorbs civil society. Civilians become auxiliaries to the army, the 'administrative tail'. Soviet War Communism and China's Great Leap Forward were even more extreme cases. The workforce was entirely subject to direction of labour, to orders, housed in barracks and fed in communal cookhouses on a rationed diet determined by what the planners considered sufficient for material survival. This essentially military regime became identified – even in the minds of Lenin and Mao – as the prototype of socialism, of collective self-sacrifice for common ends. All sectors now became subordinate to supplying war: agriculture was no longer an economic activity, but a matter of providing the war-making state with resources and a means to keep the population alive to supply the army, the fuel for a military machine.

In the war-making state, the government has a paramount interest in not being dependent on supplies from the domains – or dependent on the goodwill – of any other government. It needs therefore, first and foremost, to develop under its direct control the means to meet its needs for weaponry and equipment. For more than a century this has meant, for those powers which could afford it, developing their own capacity to make steel, heavy capital goods and the final products, weaponry. In the relevant theory of economic development, heavy industry was to advance in order that the supposed historical development, from light industry, could be bypassed, moving straight to the growth of the capacity to 'make the machines that make the machines' –

25   Ibid.

despite the punishing sacrifices this capital-intensive development imposed on capital-scarce economies. The argument in terms of economic development warrants scepticism, and the debate of the 1920s within the Soviet Communist Party between Bukharin and Preobrazhensky was slightly beside the point. The proper rationale for the disproportionate growth of heavy industry in the Soviet Five Year Plans was provided not by the theoreticians, but by the practice of Stalin – and his estimation of the urgent and overriding priority for the Soviet Union to be as militarily prepared as its nearest rivals.

The heavy industrial bias – combined with labour-intensive activity in low-priority sectors – was bequeathed not only to all centrally planned economies, but to all other autarkic or mercantilist developing countries (the same approach had governed West European policy in the 1930s and 1940s). It became again identified as peculiarly socialist.[26] The same was true of the general tendency to identify economic development as a quasi-military campaign, a war on backwardness, replete with assaults, attacks and seizure of the 'commanding heights' of the economy – along with the idea of 'strategic industries', 'a concept that is so elusive', according to Little et al. 'as to be of doubtful validity'.[27]

The phenomenal social stresses and strains of industrialisation in a militarily competitive context have required closure against the spiritual pollution of foreigners, most starkly in the case of Stalin's Russia, Eastern Europe in the 1950s, Mao's China, North Korea and North Vietnam. In the case of Albania, the price of isolationism, of 'ultra-Stalinism', was an extraordinary degree of economic backwardness, leaving in the early 1990s 'a grim picture of economic decline and poverty not seen in Europe this century'.[28] The speedy collapse of some of the closed societies – once they began to open up – vindicates the fears of their former rulers.

---

26 Three Chinese authors note a related point: 'In the literature, many authors equate this distorted policy environment and the administrative controls as socialism. However ... we find that the rationale for the existence of these policies and controls was not "socialism". Rather, the distorted macro-policy environment and plan allocation system arose because of the adoption of a heavy industry oriented strategy in a capital-scarce economy. The socialist economies had similar policy environments and administrative controls because they all adopted the same development strategy, probably under the influence of Stalin. Even some non-socialist developing economies, such as India, imposed similar policies and controls because they also pursued the same development strategies, grounded in accelerated industrialisation' (Lin et al. 1994, p. 11, note 7).

27 Little et al. 1993, p. 311.

28 World Bank 1994c, p. 6.

A military drive to expand production has historically had some striking successes – not least in the performance of the German and Japanese economies in the 1930s. But the expansion by military order tends to be effective only extensively, for an output of fairly crude quality: coal output is, for a short period, easier to expand than computers, let alone computer software. The more sophisticated the quality of output, the less subject to sheer *blitzkrieg* (even if backed by ferocious punishments), are the targets of the national plan. It becomes necessary to engage psychological incentives, the willingly volunteered skills of the worker in sustaining and improving quality.

In the century after 1870 – the year of the onset of the nineteenth century's long-drawn-out Great Depression – the world order was dominated by the global rivalries of the Great Powers. These culminated in two world wars of unprecedented destructiveness, and the Great Depression of the interwar years which inaugurated in policy the most extreme scale of economic nationalism and economic warfare – what we have identified here as mercantilism and economic autarky. The ferocity of the rivalries reshaped all significant political forces and options, forcing the complete alignment of business and the national state (thus destroying the basis of a cosmopolitan business class, associated with the boom of 1840 to 1870),[29] and creating centralised all-powerful states, dominating society and economy, founded often on large public sectors and, a necessary adjunct of this, directed by means of central planning.

The process was long drawn out, and not exclusively related to the immediate occurrence of war. The creation of predominant public sectors and a panoply of welfare protection came after the Second World War in Europe, not so much to prepare for the third world war, but to guard against the social instability which was thought would be the result of the likely postwar slump. But through all the vicissitudes, the continuing centralisation on the state and expansion of the public domain had an apparently inexorable character. Open collisions or a sudden increase in the fear of war increased public expenditure, but after the end of hostilities or the fears, there was no complete return to the *status quo ante*, that is, until the 1980s. It seemed as if public spending was on a ratchet which constantly encouraged upward movement, never downward.

The fateful decision of the Soviet state around 1923 to resume Tsarist Russia's role in the contest between the dominant states and to do so as a Great Power, albeit an economically backward one, transformed the options facing Soviet

---

29   See Jones 1987.

society. Without the significant role of entrenched interests – wiped out by the 1917 Revolution and the Civil War – it was possible for the Soviet state to reshape society in a much more purified manner than that aspired to in other Great Powers (where, at most, a softer corporatism ran parallel with the Soviet military society). The precepts of Fordism, of the Taylorist organisation of large-scale assembly manufacturing – so welcomed by Lenin and so parallel to the organisation of the large field army – intensified the drive to turn society into one gigantic military factory. The residue of a socialist discourse – the 'self-emancipation of the working class' – was hijacked to offer an opaque screen for this extraordinary tyranny.

The drive to arm has important implications for the rest of the economy. The economic impact of military spending varies with the scale of spending, the character of military technology, the economy concerned, the world trade context, and so on. It can serve as a vital means to precipitate and sustain economic growth, or as a means of 'capital consumption', partially destroying the civil economy. As will be argued later, the economic crisis of the Soviet Union in the 1980s flowed from the excesses of a war-making state. Landau[30] estimates for a sample of countries that military spending below a level equivalent to nine percent of gross domestic product has economically beneficial, and above that level destructive, effects; but this generalisation must turn on how far armaments draw on local production as opposed to imports, and the capacity of the state concerned. Levels up to 20 percent (of gross domestic product) – as in Saudi Arabia in 1988 – can be tolerated for periods of time in some places; in others, it can break the state.

The ending of the cold war has thus important implications for the civil economy. The decline in spending is less important than the removal of the lynchpin of the old world order, the ending of almost a century of world struggle for domination and generalised insecurity (the general decline is still consistent with a multiplicity of extremely destructive local wars). The case for sustaining military expenditure becomes politically much weaker.

Simultaneously, the logic of global economic integration is rendering increasingly expensive the maintenance of the old self-sufficient economy, capable of meeting all defence needs from within national boundaries. The fate of the steel industry in Europe and North America is a commentary on this change. Thus, the market encroaches upon the old Military Industrial Complex (MIC), redirecting the state's needs for defence supplies to the global market. The same may become true of the military labour force, and lead to the end

---

30   See Landau 1993.

of the citizen-army. The market equivalent of a professional citizen-army is an army of mercenaries, recruited from wherever they are available and paid the rate for the job.[31] The 'market distortions' of military conscription and reserved monopoly suppliers, whether within or without the public domain, are also under threat in a globally integrated economy.

There are no smooth transitions. Institutions do not gently fade from one mode of operation to another. The interests in the employment of the old state, its armed forces and the MIC, do not quietly accept their liquidation as the war-making state moves into being a 'market-facilitating' state. With enough political leverage these interests can indeed halt this evolution at an intermediate stage, the rent-seeking state.

However, the discussion has been unrealistically simplified to three types of states, as if each excluded the others. In practice, rent-seeking occurs in the other two, so does war-making, and in some cases, market-facilitating. Furthermore, on the basis of these three functions, many other roles are acquired which immensely confuse the picture. However, it is useful to retain a set of exclusive categories to highlight the changes taking place.

Against this background, structural adjustment takes on a different significance. All important states in the last period were obliged, as a condition of defending their survival, to seek to create an independent war-making capacity. These structures now impede the growth of the world economy, and macroeconomic reform is the means to ease the transition from war-making to market-facilitation. In this context, the countries formerly identified as 'centrally planned', were no more than the most extreme versions of war-making states, a model governing to different degrees both East and West. However, that extremity has created a structure with great political power to frustrate the transition, to trap society in the intermediate phase of a rent-seeking state.

The Military Character of the Centrally Planned Economies

Socialist industrialisation and particularly very rapid industrialisation which was necessary in the first socialist countries, particularly in the Soviet Union, as a political requirement of national defence ... requires

---

31 The possibility is of more than simply theoretical interest, given the demographic decline in the numbers of young men and women in the developed countries (see Harris 1995).

centralized disposal of resources ... essentially it can bedescribed as a *sui generis* war economy.[32]

If we are to capture faithfully the aims of the Soviet ... elite, then we must accord first place to military defence, and derivatively to heavy industry, as the aim of economic development ... the military and heavy industrial attainments of the advanced capitalist countries are the principal goal towards which development has been directed.[33]

The war economy in Europe and North America reached its apogee in the Second World War, with a second peak in the 1950s with the Korean War and the most intense period of the cold war. But unwinding the structures installed in the period of most intense rivalry (which includes, economically, the 1930s) took an immense time. Now, half a century later, the process is still not complete. The developed countries, despite all the moves to liberalisation, retain powerful components of political direction in the defence field (as they do also in agriculture). Protection – encouragement of monopolies and cartels, price fixing, state subsidies, severely restricted markets for procurement – remains the norm for European defence production.[34] Many governments may have relinquished control of the steel or capital goods industries, but when it comes to aircraft, tanks, artillery and capital ships, they still tend to be directed by the state. Even Britain, with supposedly the most privatised and open system of public procurement, purchases 90 percent of its defence needs from domestic firms.

The size of the Soviet MIC, the heart simultaneously of the Warsaw Pact and the CMEA, is difficult to estimate. Brown et al.[35] calculate the direct military employment at 9.3 million, and the associated civilian workforce at 13.8 million. Winiecki estimates another four million were employed here but not acknowledged in official figures.[36] He also argues that 80 percent of national spending on research and development was for military or military-related purposes.

Defence spending in the old Soviet Union, according to Easterly and Fischer,[37] rose from some two percent of gross domestic product in 1928 to between

32   See Lange 1957, pp. 15–16.
33   Berliner 1988, p. 162.
34   The rhetoric of liberalisation in the non-defence sectors is often stronger than the practice – private monopolies, 'national champions', are allowed to replace state corporations.
35   Brown et al. 1994.
36   Winiecki 1992.
37   Easterly and Fischer 1994.

15 and 16 percent in the late 1980s (in the 1980s, they calculate, spending rose from 12 to 16 percent). A defender of the old order argued that Western estimates of Soviet expenditure could not be true since they would involve economic collapse; at rates of spending at 15 percent or more of gross domestic product:

> a modern State is not able to secure economic growth, is compelled to eat away at the accumulation of national wealth or to live at the expense of the credits of other countries. Fortunately, we are not yet observing Such a picture in the USSR.[38]

It now seems the author was wrong in estimating the scale of Soviet spending, but correct in his inference of the likely consequences.

The ramifications of the scale of expenditure were wider still. The MIC had priority in the distribution of scarce resources, the most scarce skilled labour, domestic inputs, foreign exchange and imports. Virtually all sectors of the economy were involved in some way. Lopatin writes:

> In practice, the economy has been militarised to such an extent that perhaps you do not find branches of the national economy which would not work for military needs. Even enterprises which are producing equipment for civilian needs, do it with regard to military utilisation.[39]

Indeed, the MIC also produced an important share of output for the civil economy. In 1980, Soviet military industries produced 30 percent of bicycles for the civilian market, 60 percent of trams, 10 percent of passenger cars, all motor scooters, television sets, radios and cameras.[40] By mid-1990, they produced 83 percent of medical, 92 percent of light industrial and 76 percent of agricultural processing equipment.[41]

However, the problems of improving productivity were steadily increasing. Poland, Hungary and Yugoslavia, facing comparable problems, had tried to employ in the 1970s the importation of foreign technology to improve productivity. However, external debts increased faster than the stream of exports from the new capacity. The Soviet Union attempted something similar, paying for the imports with expanded exports of oil and other raw materials. Weakening oil prices, however, obliged the regime to promote manufactured exports,

38   Iudin 1989, p. 50.
39   Lopatin 1990, 'Est'li vykhod iz krizisa', *Voprosy ekonomiki*, 4 April.
40   Hewett 1988, p. 174.
41   Gonchov 1991.

but again, attaining the quality required for sale in open markets required domestic reform. In any case, such a tactic could affect only a small part of the giant Soviet economy, and only then if the matching inputs – and the relations of production[42] – were available to exploit the innovations. The remedy also flouted the central rationale of the Soviet system, self-sufficiency.

By the 1980s, Moscow was finding it increasingly difficult to sustain military spending to match the scale and quality of the defence output of the United States and its allies without radical improvement in the civil economy, a general increase in productivity. The composition of output was changing and no longer driven by the old imperatives of the command economy. The rate of growth of the world economy provided a less hospitable environment for Soviet exports, and domestic demand for oil constantly threatened exports. The regime was moved slowly to accepting that self-sufficiency must be qualified, but the movement was not fast enough to offset the emerging social crisis, the rebellion against a poor and deteriorating quality of life.

Furthermore, the quality of even military output was beginning to decline,[43] To make up, the military increased its demand for resources, and there were no policy mechanisms to control this; as Brezhnev once put it, 'As much will be spent on defence as is necessary'.[44] It seemed the MIC had slipped out of control. Simultaneously, Reagan's Strategic Defence Initiative – 'Star Wars' – opened up an entirely new and economically impossible scale of military competition. The Afghan War sucked in the Soviet army to a military debacle as demoralising as that of the US army in Vietnam, and much more devastating for the Soviet economy. The structure appeared to be immobile, its leadership paralysed by the structures they were supposed to direct. It was the role of Gorbachev to recognise that domestic paralysis was held in place by the external military threat – détente became the precondition of economic reform.

If the MIC was the great burden during the years of development, if in the end it precipitated the collapse of the economy – and with it CMEA and the Soviet Union – it was only appropriate that it should be the MIC which was most devastated by the crisis. The effect was magnified in much smaller economies where the specific gravity of military and heavy industrial production was greater. Over half the industrial assets of the Ukraine were designed to produce

---

42   A point made in Kagarlitsky 1990, p. 241: 'The worst of it was that even when new technology had been successfully acquired, it did not have the necessary effect because the appropriate relations of production did not exist'.

43   Kagarlitsky 1990, p. 342.

44   Cited in Iudin 1989.

heavy and military equipment. With the end of the networks of which it was a part and the decline in military procurement (among many other factors), the Ukraine experienced a 40 percent decline in its official output between 1991 and 1994.[45] At this stage, in Russia, the civil output which military factories had produced became a saviour,[46] especially since they were still underpinned by public support.

The loss of direction of the regime was even more destructive. The great federal Ministries which directed from Moscow vast centralised industrial baronies across the constituent territories of the Soviet Union, collapsed with as much speed as the centralised network of the Communist Party. The military itself shared in this disintegration as it lost both its forward defence line in Eastern Europe, and its inner defence line in the Soviet Union. The decay was symbolised by the disintegration of the military conscription system – in 1994, 84 percent of those eligible for the draft evaded it (against 48 percent in 1989); the rate for 1995 was put at 80 percent (and 90 percent in Moscow). Efforts to restore the role of the military within the CIS and in Chechnya; the role of the Ministry of Defence in protecting or seeking to reclaim from privatisation its erstwhile industries; efforts to expand the military budget (taking, on press accounts, a third of current spending); all suggest that the restoration of the role of the armed forces remains a decisive component of the attempts of the current leadership to restore the state.

China was protected by backwardness from achieving the consistency of the Soviet alignment between the MIC and the rest of the economy. The regime adopted the same principles: between 1953 and 1985, 45 percent of state investment was devoted to heavy industry, as was much of the 'other' category in government expenditure (worker housing, infrastructure, and so on); at its peak, heavy industry took 54 percent of state investment. But relatively, it was a much smaller share of the total economy. Agriculture, on which three-quarters of the population depended, received ten percent of state investment (this share peaking in the years following famine, 1963–5, at 17.6 percent). Essentially, agriculture was a servicing sector to supply cheap food for the industrial labour force and, as in the Soviet Union in the 1930s, to contribute to exports (if we include processed agricultural goods, the sector supplied 60 percent of China's exports in the 1950s). But China's backwardness, and the resulting incapacity of the state to absorb the major part of the economy, saved it from the

45   McCarthy et al. 1994.
46   Vasiliev 1994.

Soviet debacle. In the late 1970s, the state opted to concentrate on what it held and give free rein to the rural majority and rural industrialisation.

Vietnam offers a striking case at both extremities of the equation – it was more militarised than Russia and more backward than China. There can rarely have been a more completely militarised society than the former North Vietnam. For nearly four decades, the regime was engaged in real war, as opposed to war preparation, leading to the complete absorption of civil society in the war effort. Yet it was also continuous war which made impossible the creation of anything remotely comparable to the MIC which dominated the Soviet Union and China's state sector. There were very few large plants and none of the great industrial baronies of Moscow's Ministries. In the mid-1980s, the share of gross domestic product of Vietnam's State Owned Enterprises (SOEs) was just over a fifth – much the same as in supposedly free-enterprise Malaysia – compared to 80 to 90 percent in the Soviet Union, Poland, Czechoslovakia, and the German Democratic Republic. North Vietnam was a client-state; its people did the fighting, but the industrial capacity was located in the Soviet Union and Eastern Europe. Thus, once reform began, economic growth in the most militarised of the former Centrally Planned Economies (CPEs) took off as fast as it had done in China.[47]

In the former CPEs, the weakening of central control while political discretion remained important, even predominant, opened up enormous opportunities for corruption. They were always present to some degree in the old order, but they have flourished now in the hiatus between plan and market. Rent-seeking of a significant kind is limited to the old elites, but those much larger sections of the population which were beneficiaries of public largesse can constitute a major obstacle to market reform. They can force the suspension of the process of change, leading to what Olsen sees as the tendency of society to sclerosis.[48] The transition from war-making to market-facilitating halts on the way at rent-seeking.

However, the dichotomy between war-making and market-facilitating is too primitive to capture the differentia of the intermediate phase. There, market competitiveness is finely interwoven with political discretion and favour; each is exploited to strengthen the other. This appears to be particularly true in certain armed forces as reductions in military spending occur or extraordinary opportunities arise. With the ending of civil wars in Central America, military pension funds in Honduras and Guatemala have been used to take over a

---

47   World Bank 1993.
48   Olsen 1982.

range of manufacturing, banking and media enterprises. The rise of 'khaki cap-italists' has been noted in Pakistan.[49] There, a series of military welfare funds have become the nuclei of rapidly expanding commercial groups. In Indonesia, Robison has shown the emergence of commercial baronies, combining dif-ferent sections of the armed forces, of government Ministries, and of private business, each with a different set of relationships to foreign goverments and business.[50]

A comparable translation has occurred in former CPES. For example, dif-ferent sections of the Chinese People's Liberation Army created among the largest and fastest growing business groups in the country – the Poly Group (under the General Staff Department), Norinco (under the Commission for Sci-ence, Technology and Industry for National Defence), Xingxing Corporation (under the General Logistics Department), and a host of others (China Elec-tronic Industrial Corporation, China Shipbuilding Trading Corporation, Great Wall Industries, China National Aero-Technical Import-Export Corporation, Huitong, Sanju or the 999 Group).[51] Hardly any modern sectors of the civil eco-nomy were unaffected by this very powerful group of enterprises with a foot in both the old and the new camps – and with perhaps a strong interest in preventing both a return to central diktat and a full transition to pure market operations (where they would lose political patronage). Public control of the armed forces is weakened in so far as they have access to funds beyond budget-ary supervision – the expenditure of the People's Liberation Army is, on some estimates, two to three times larger than its officially budgeted revenue.

State Owned Enterprises (SOEs)

Thrust into a market environment, bureaucrats tend to behave, not like capit-alists, but like black marketeers.[52]

State property is the last defensive line for the opponents of reform. The branch Ministries are eager to control the process of privatization and to get a control package of shares or to create huge industrial-financial corporations in order to restore the traditional forms of management.[53]

---

49   *Financial Times*, 7 April 1995.
50   See Robison 1986.
51   *Financial Times*, 29 November 1994.
52   Prybyla 1990.
53   Yevstignevev and Voinov 1994, p. 6.

Four cases of privatisation are briefly examined here – Russia, China, Vietnam, and the Ukraine – not because any of them are prototypical, but because each illustrates one or other theme in the resistance of the old state to relinquishing its entrenched position.

Russia

The SOEs of Russia, the heart of a social system of much greater longevity than the other CPEs, were always likely to be most resistant to being launched on open markets. Yet it was Russia, with the Czech Republic and Slovakia, which made the most rapid progress in privatisation and where there was 'probably the largest sale of assets ever conducted'.[54] By 1995, there were 2,500 private licensed commercial banks, 600 investment funds, 15,779 medium and large private corporations that had been SOEs, and 40 million shareholders (out of 140 million voucher holders). An estimated 62 percent of the economy – and 86 percent of the industrial labour force – were private, a transition achieved in little over 18 months. The editor of a World Bank volume on Russian privatisation found the achievements 'border on the miraculous';[55] however, as with so many miracles, the closer the examination, the less miraculous they become.

First, the Russian SOEs secured their survival – and continued to do so after privatisation – through not repaying bank credits, not paying suppliers, not meeting tax obligations, and sometimes not paying their workers. At their peak, intercorporate arrears equalled 40 to 45 percent of the gross domestic product (a mechanism in which the inefficient destroyed the efficient).

Second, three-quarters of the privatisation in the first tranche of sales constituted 'closed subscriptions' in which managers and workers, the Enterprise Councils of Labour Collectives (STKs) purchased 51 percent of the shares. The Privatization Commission of each SOE was appointed by the Chief Executive of the SOE, and this body set the value of the SOE. The book value of the assets was accepted in July 1992 for sale purposes, which in conditions of high inflation constituted 'a huge transfer of wealth from the State to insiders'.[56] On the basis of voucher auctions made by June 1993, Lieberman and Rahuja estimate the value of all Russia's industry at $5 billion, or roughly the same as one of the Fortune 500 companies of the United States. For the open subscription, privileged access was given to existing managers; they could employ company

---

54 Lieberman and Rahuja 1994, p. 10.
55 Lieberman and Nellis 1994, p. 1.
56 Lieberman and Rahuja 1994, p. 13.

welfare funds to buy shares, and special arrangements for them to obtain finance meant that very little of the personal funds of managers was employed.

A survey cited in the same source suggests that, at the end, about 70 percent of the equity of the former SOEs was in the hands of 'insiders', 16 percent with local authorities, and the rest in various forms of outside investment, with 9.5 percent falling to large shareholders. Other survey evidence suggests that it is management, not the workforce, which have been the beneficiaries. As Schleifer and Boycko note:

> Most enterprises continue to be run unchallenged by the old management teams ... [T]heir management is principally dedicated to preserving traditional product lines, which may have no markets, as their core activity. In many cases, enterprise managers have consolidated control by buying shares in the aftermarket and are simply killing time, hoping for a miracle (and credits).[57]

The procedure followed is justified as a bribe to existing stake-holders to accept the new deal: 'to ensure speedy privatization ... breaking the ownership position of the branch Ministries was the overwhelming priority if the irreversibility of the transition was to be ensured ... [T]he speed deemed necessary could not be attained without "bribing the insiders"'.[58]

It might be expected that, sooner or later, companies would have to turn to capital markets for loans, and borrowing might only be possible with changes of ownership and management. However, the cheap credits of the Central Bank or house banks offset this need. It seems still to be true that a 'management team's most valuable asset may turn out to be its lobbying connections and power'.[59] In sum, the process of privatisation has made it extremely difficult for outside interests to change the operation of most of the companies.

Third, the end of the control of central Ministries and the empowerment of local authorities – oblast or municipalities – to be the main representative of the state in privatisation has enormously increased the speed of the transition; but it has also encouraged the emergence of local ruling groups, administration and former SOEs, to defend their interests against outsiders. A study by Alexandra Vacroux of Primorsky Krai vividly describes the emergence of a group of the largest former SOEs, PAKT (Primosky Manufacturing

---

57   Schleifer and Boycko 1994, p. 75.

58   Sutela 1994, p. 418.

59   Lieberman and Rahuja 1994, p. 31.

Shareholders Corporation) as a cartel to defend their interests. Four of the leading members took over the regional administration (as Governor and three deputy Governors), using this position in order – ultimately unsuccessfully – to block bids by investors from outside so that managers could retain control. Vacroux concludes that 'Widespread voucher privatisation may actually inhibit progress towards a competitive, decentralised Russian market by empowering large enterprises to recentralise the economy along geographical rather than industrial lines'.[60]

Finally, the MIC was in general exempt from the transition, although informally some companies have been privatised. Indeed, this sector of industry is explicitly excluded from the process, and firms are not even to be turned into joint stock companies. They remain executive arms of the Ministry concerned, funded entirely by the Central Bank. The exact numbers are not known, but they could be equal to the large and medium SOEs privatised – 12,000–14,000 in all. Thus, the important sectoral lobbies – energy, defence, heavy industry, agriculture – remained protected and privileged within the public sphere.

It could be that a major part of the MIC is, as some observers believe, unsaleable – there was too little to be salvaged in companies too big to be reformed (on the other hand, sheer size provides immense political strength in pressurising public authorities). In many cases, the net value added at world market prices may be negative, particularly where existing managers – the so-called 'kleptocrats' – have stripped the assets and/or diverted profits to their own private or co-operative enterprises. 'For the director of such an enterprise', Burtin comments, 'full ownership would mean rapid and inevitable bankruptcy. Why would he start digging his own grave?'[61]

Russia's 'managerial revolution' defied the former diagnosis – that the SOEs needed reorganisation and new entrepreneurial management.[62] The old bureaucratic officials of the SOEs, essentially civil servants, drilled through a lifetime of routine operations in obedience to their Ministerial directors, had none of the characteristics required of capitalists: risk-taking rather than rule or order obeying, and innovation rather than routines. So far, few of Russia's successful businessmen and women have been drawn from the ranks of the

---

60   Vacroux 1994, p. 43.

61   Burtin 1994.

62   The government was aware of this – see the comment of Deputy Prime Minister Brosi Federov in Åslund and Layard 1993: 'many people do not seem to understand that real privatization is not over as soon as a mechanical transfer of title has been made ... [T]he new entities must be restructured to run more efficiently, and enjoy the benefits of corporate governance'.

senior echelons of the nomenklatura,[63] and few SOEs seem to become successful without a wholesale change of management (as, for example, with the
much-lauded case of Uralmash – where, incidentally, the workforce shrank
from 45,000 to 19,000). Indeed, privatisation of the SOEs has immensely fortified the position of the old industrial nomenklatura against easy challenge.

Nor did the privatisation of banks introduce more rigorous criteria governing credit. Frequently, large industrial groups set up 'house banks' to act as a
pipeline for Central Bank credit to companies in the group. Observers noted
that many of the new banks, owned by their managers, were simply uncritical
suppliers of credit to their shareholders and customers, rather than independent auditors assessing relative risk.

The real private sector was the mass of small competitive firms that had
been started from scratch in those sectors of the economy formerly shunned
by the larger SOEs: retail and wholesale trade, hotels and restaurants, and
other services. Within the ranks of the 215,000 'co-operatives' there were some
of these, although others were no more than means for SOEs to hide profits
through transfer pricing.[64] Beyond these two, the grey economy was said to
encompass unrecorded activity equal to a quarter or more of the gross domestic
product.

The Russian economy, whatever its legal structure, remained sociologic-
ally in the hands of the old order. It was still a state-dominated economy
(whether this was federal, republican, regional or local government). Despite
price decontrol, different levels of government still set prices of a wide range
of goods – from bread, in some regions, to oil (still sold domestically at 40
percent of the world market level). The state continued to act as owner, reg-
ulator, partner and policeman. Even the privatised SOEs remained dependent
upon public credits and contacts. The discretionary character of a politically
directed economy remained strong. Most notorious was the case of Prime Minister Viktor Chernomyrdin, creator of the giant energy corporation, Gazprom,
allegedly one of its largest shareholders and the last Soviet Minister of Energy,
who played the key role in ensuring the energy industry was taxed at only one
third of the level in comparable countries (as a percentage of gross domestic
product).

Privatisation has not created a market economy, nor made it possible with
any ease for Russian corporations to become competitive – without subsidies –

---

63   As Sergei Grachev, marketing director of the new airline, Transaero, put it: 'We refuse to
      hire anyone who has ever had more than five minutes work experience with Aeroflot'
      (cited in Galuszka et al. 1994, p. 40).

64   Shatalov 1991.

in world markets. Indeed, the reforms generally have had only one substantial achievement so far as the world economy is concerned: it has frustrated the efforts of the Russian government to make the country a major exporter of manufactured goods. The export of oil, metals and diamonds made up 58 percent of Russia's exports in 1990, and 72 percent in 1993; if we add other raw materials, this increases the figures to 70 and 86 percent (when the total value of exports declined by 40 percent).

China

The differences between Russia and China are immense, most strikingly in the low per capita income of China but also in China's record of extraordinary growth through the 1980s. Real per capita gross national product increased 7.2 percent per year between 1978 and 1990, with average annual economic growth at over ten percent; in the 15 years to 1994, exports increased by 16 percent per year. Furthermore, the institutional structure has for long been quite different. Chinese central Ministries never concentrated the degree of power seen in the Soviet Union.[65] The break up of the Moscow Ministries has led to a high degree of decentralisation, but this is very recent; national industries tend to overshadow the local authority where they are located. In China decentralisation to the provinces is very much older and the provinces are very much more powerful *vis-à-vis* the centre (and the 80 percent of SOEs for which provincial authorities are responsible are much more dependent on them).

The reform programme had initially no clear agenda: it proceeded by adjustment or 'muddling through'.[66] The SOEs were never scheduled for privatisation, although there has been discussion of the sale of a minority of shares. Officially the regime has not revised its original conception; in the words of the director of the State Council research office: 'Privatization is not a model for us … [SOEs] still represent our country's general economic power and are the chief source of the State's budget and the main force for economic stability'.[67]

The growth of the Chinese economy has come disproportionately from enterprises outside the ranks of the SOEs, the Town and Village Enterprises (TVEs) – under local authority direction – and the small private and foreign (or Joint Venture) sectors. However, a number of SOEs have also exploited the opportunities of a high growth economy to transform themselves, if not into

65   White 1993, p. 22.
66   McMillan and Naughton 1992, p. 131.
67   *Economist* Survey, 18 March 1995.

private corporations, into entrepreneurial and expansionist firms (keeping a foot in both profitable markets and political patronage).

However, for many other SOEs, the growth of the new sectors and of imports – as well as the development of provincial protectionism, interrupting interprovincial trade flows – has imposed new burdens. Of the 108,000 SOEs (employing 108 million workers, three in four of the urban labour force), between a half and two thirds are said to be losing money. In 1994, intercorporate arrears reached 600 billion yuan (equivalent at the then exchange rate to US$70 billion), or equal to 30 percent of the value of industrial output. Bank credit finances 80 to 90 percent of SOE current operations, and the SOEs take the bulk of bank credit (for example, 68 percent of fixed investment funds last year), although their share of industrial output is now down to 43 percent (compared to 81 percent in 1978).

The picture of SOE cumulative debt is as misleading in China as it is in Russia, since the framework of incentives guiding Chinese managers encourages allowing debt to increase in order to pursue other options. Gang Fan and Woo, on the basis of a survey of 300 SOEs between 1984 and 1988, argue that decentralising responsibility for SOEs to the provincial and local level has allowed managers to realise their 'innate tendencies to over-consume and over-invest'.[68] Bank credit is seen as virtually a free public good, so the demand for it is infinite whatever the official price. Furthermore, local banks have a strong incentive to lend to important borrowers, and then seek to force the Central Bank to cover the resulting deficit. Local authorities which are administratively responsible for local banks also have an incentive to press the banks to finance their own industries. So far, the Central Bank has proved reluctant to risk bankrupting the borrower or offending the provincial leadership.

The resulting credit – at least in the mid-1980s – may then flow into improving the incomes of workers (factory cadres of the party have an incentive to maintain their popularity, one of the elements in possible promotion); managerial perquisites; or investment in other enterprises or in Hong Kong (for speculative purposes, or for reentry to China now as 'private foreign investment' to exploit the tax advantages for foreign investors). Simultaneously, tax payments and profit remittances decline. Between 1978 – when SOEs profits and taxes supplied over 83 percent of government revenue – and 1992, SOE profit rates declined from 15.5 to 2.7 percent. The redistribution from public bank credit to private gain is summarised in the saying 'The losses of SOEs are socialised, but the profits are privatised'.

---

68   Gang Fan and Woo 1993.

SOE borrowing helps to expand the government deficit to possibly three or four times what is officially recorded, and is thus a powerful factor in promoting inflation. Furthermore, at low interest rates, SOEs have a strong incentive to on-lend funds to the non-SOE sectors. If SOEs can borrow at 11 percent, they can sometimes on-lend at 40 percent; Gang Fan estimates that this diversion of credit covers some 30 percent of state lending to SOEs.[69] It is, as Lin et al. put it, 'rampant rent-seeking', and they put the total leakage of funds as high as a fifth of the national income.[70] The Central Bank appears captive to the process. In 1993, in an effort to curb the excessively high rate of growth, the bank ordered the return of a 220 billion yuan credit which had not been authorised; officially, only a third was returned.[71]

It follows that much of the banking system is technically insolvent. At least 30 percent of the loan portfolios of three of the top four banks are credit extensions to SOEs, and are said to be equal to 70 percent of the working capital of the banks. If interest rates were to be employed seriously, then not only would a major part of the SOEs founder, whether directly or through the mechanism of intercorporate arrears, but also the banks themselves. Officially, there might be agreement with the Chairman of the Bank of China: 'We can't continue to behave like the People's Bank, throwing meat to dogs which can't be recovered'.[72] But if the alternative is the death of the dogs, the government cannot face an abrupt end to meat supplies.

While there are giant corporations operating nationally in China, the majority are closely related to provincial or local government, something which may in time also develop in Russia. In China, the richer provinces can afford to offer their SOEs soft loans or reduce their tax burden if they are large employers. On the other hand, some SOEs complain that they are heavily burdened by tax payments to local authorities – losing, some claim, up to 90 percent of their net income. Since SOEs are probably simultaneously indebted, the tax flow may represent only a means of transferring funds from the Central Bank to the local government.

Local authority finance is divided into budgetary and extra-budgetary, the first being shared with the Centre, the second not. SOE after-tax profits are one component in local authority extra-budgetary funds. These increased as a proportion of budgetary funds between 1978 and 1990 from 66 to 84 percent, suggesting that local authorities are partly escaping from the financial tutelage

---

69   Gang Fan 1994, p. 110, note 4.

70   Lin et al. 1994, p. 28.

71   Blaho 1994.

72   *Financial Times*, 1 December 1994.

of the centre. Simultaneously, local government gained de facto control of budgetary tax rates and tax bases, leading to an increased diversion of revenues away from the centre (and a tendency for local government to hide funds through reclassification). Between 1978 and 1992, total government revenue as a proportion of gross national product declined from 34 to 17 percent, and the share of central government in total budgeted revenue declined from 57 to 41 percent.[73]

The result has been seen as a clear shift in the balance of power between the centre and the provinces, producing a framework where, as the World Bank notes, 'individual provinces are tending to behave like independent countries, with an increase in external (overseas) trade and a relative decline in trade flows with each other'.[74] The SOEs play a crucial role here in forming the basis for independent local economic development, and provincial authorities have a strong incentive to protect and advance the economic role of 'their' SOEs.

The central government makes persistent efforts to reverse these trends, both in terms of the indebtedness of the SOEs and the growing power of local government. In late 1993, a plan to restructure the SOEs, selling off some and allowing others to be liquidated, was shelved in the interests of macroeconomic and political stability. The 1994 local government fiscal reforms are designed to reverse the take of the centre from shared taxes, but it would be rash to suppose that the provinces will permit this to occur or that the centre has the power – short of a major conflict – to override them.

China's MIC is a mixed bag. As we have seen, some military industries have diversified successfully into commercial operations (albeit underpinned by public privilege and funding). But where a concentration of MIC activity occurs tends to be the place most resistant to reform. This is true in the northeast, particularly in Heilungjiang, with its high concentration of very large-scale heavy industry. Reform has been slow and the cumulative SOE debt is high. One by-product of attempts to enforce greater financial discipline in 1994 was a failure to pay part of the workforce – the miners for four months, the lumber workers for six.[75]

The most remarkable feature of Chinese local government and the source of much of national economic growth, are the TVEs. They have grown from a 22 percent share of gross industrial output in 1978 (with the SOE share at 78 percent), to, in 1990, 35.6 percent, with an annual rate of growth (1979–90) of

73   Ma 1995; Fan Gang 1994, p. 117.

74   World Bank 1994b, p. xiii.

75   *Far Eastern Economic Review*, 7 October 1994.

18.2 percent.[76] From 1981 to 1991, the average annual increase in the number of TVEs, the numbers employed and the value of output were respectively 26.6, 11.2 and 29.6.[77] By contrast, the private sector share in 1990 was put at 5.4 percent, and 'other' (mainly Joint Ventures with foreign partners) at 4.4 percent.

Some argue that the TVEs are essentially market-oriented, and perhaps in comparison to many of the SOEs, they are. They have certainly been set up in response to market demand, unlike many of the SOEs (which are a response to government demand). But they are also public sector operations. Local government obliges local banks to allocate investment funds by criteria other than profitability.[78] Political and administrative criteria shape TVE behaviour through local government control of finance, labour, management, land, material inputs and much of the marketing of the output. The constraints here may be tighter at a local level than those governing SOEs since municipalities have less access to resources than provinces, but TVEs are still instruments of public policy. In terms of private ownership, less than ten percent of the industrial sector of China is involved.

China is a market economy. Domestic economic activity is in the main determined by domestic and foreign market demand. Many of the SOEs have exploited the growth of the economy and become highly commercialised. The TVEs are similarly primarily focused upon markets. Given the high rate of growth of the economy, the MIC must be economically of declining significance. But China is not a private economy, and the process of growth has led to a redistribution of activity between two parts of the public sector, SOEs and TVEs. The private sector proper remains relatively small, although of great significance for exports. High economic growth has made this less problematic than in Russia and Eastern Europe – deficits in public finance and local favours to state industry are more tolerable with a buoyant income. The radical structural change is rather the creation of local-government-led competitive conglomerates in which SOEs and TVEs are arms of local government development strategies, operating in open markets. This is, at the level of the province, rather more like the South Korean and Taiwanese national development strategies than a simple free market model – that is, industries, backed by cheap state finance, whether public or private are focused firmly on external markets rather than supplying state or domestic demand.

---

76   White 1993, p. 127.

77   Lin et al. 1994.

78   Wong 1993.

Vietnam

Vietnam provides a striking contrast to both Russia and China. On the official figures, it is one of the poorest countries in the world (with a per capita gross national product below us$200 per year), devastated by decades of war and the economic imperatives of survival imposed upon a war-making state. It absorbed the shocks of both the end of Soviet and East European aid (equal to nine percent of gross domestic product in 1989) and the collapse of CMEA (supplying 57 percent of imports in 1988, five percent in 1991). Yet Vietnam's gross domestic product registered the shocks only in a decline in the rate of growth to five percent in 1990 and six percent in 1991 (before rebounding to 8.3 percent in 1993). Total investment and imports did not vary, although industrial output declined by four percent in 1989. Furthermore, for much of this period, the country operated under a US trade embargo and without external assistance.

The reform programme of 1989, *Dong moi* (the first reforms date from 1986), returned agriculture to family farming, decontrolled prices, introduced positive interest rates, devalued the currency, introduced fiscal reform and cut the armed forces by half a million men. The country's good fortune arising from the coincidence of oil exports coming on stream at the same time as the reforms, made for an extraordinary increase in agricultural output – rice exports, zero in 1988, were two million tonnes in 1992. The broader reforms stimulated raw-material- and labour-intensive manufactured exports, so that by now, under half of exports are provided by oil and rice.

Vietnam combined the chronic deprivation of an extreme war-making state, with the status, in terms of the supply of war equipment, of a client-state.[79] As a result, the government did not create what would have become a heavy burden in the present phase, a significant, self-sufficient and politically directed heavy and military industry.

There were some 12,000 SOEs in total in 1988, employing about 2.7 million workers or seven percent of the labour force (and 40 percent of the industrial labour force), to produce 44 percent of the official gross domestic product. A third of them were said to be making losses in 1990, the rate of return was below the rate of inflation, and the cumulative SOE debt was put at the dong equivalent of us$800 million.

In 1989, direct subsidies to the SOEs were cut, the supply of imports at below cost ended in 1991, and subsidised credit ended in 1992 (some low-interest loans continued). Since 1990, 2,000 SOEs have been closed and 3,000 merged (with

79   World Bank 1993.

a reduction of employment of 1.7 million), leaving 7,000 operative. Of these, 5,000 are small. Of the rest, about 35 percent were directly administered by the central government, most of them through the Ministries of Defence and of Agriculture. They include the largest and most capital intensive factories. However, the state remained dependent upon the SOEs as a whole for current revenue (the 1994 taxes on sales and profit remittances made up about 60 percent of government income).

The reform programme – including changes to strengthen the position of managers – has produced some familiar reactions: asset stripping and the diversion of public resources to the private companies of SOE managers or to Joint Ventures with foreign firms. As in China, SOEs have disposed illegally of some of their extensive land-holdings, turning them to other uses, and have converted company assets to commercial purposes – as in the guesthouses of Ministries and other public agencies that have been converted to unofficial tourist hotels. But intercorporate arrears and debts to the banking system have not loomed large – under five percent of the gross domestic product (compared to 100 percent in Russia in 1992, or 80 percent in Romania in late 1991). Nor have the claims of workers on the social security funds of SOEs been an obstacle to changing jobs. Unlike Russia and China, there seem to be few welfare privileges attached to SOE employment in general, and with a buoyant demand for labour in the economy at large, lay-offs have been relatively easy to accomplish. Furthermore, an important share of worker income is linked to bonuses based upon profitability; in prosperous firms, the bonus can provide an addition to income equal to half a year's basic pay. Indebted firms cannot pay bonuses, so workers have a strong interest in forcing their employers to avoid debt (whereas in both Russia and China, increasing bank credits have sometimes provided the basis for wage increases).

The government has not proposed privatisation. In 1992, an experiment was initiated to issue shares in 21 smaller SOEs, with the state retaining a 30 percent holding. By 1995, ten of the firms had been withdrawn from the scheme because, it was said, the workforce opposed it. Three had been sold, but to the employees using government loans and factory funds.

By 1995, two thirds of the Vietnamese gross domestic product was derived from the private sector. But this had not been achieved by privatising industry so much as by permitting, in effect, private agriculture and the creation of new private firms. The figure is an heroic guess since so much of the economy is now below the threshold of statistical detection. Smuggling is a major activity, importing scarce inputs to labour-intensive exports. Illegal imports have been estimated at possibly US\$ half a billion annually, or close to a fifth of official imports.

The dynamism of the Vietnamese economy is as great as that of China, although the economy starts from a much lower base point. The country is very much smaller and therefore more susceptible to central control. The government – perhaps continuing to exercise the power of a war-making state – seems to have had greater success in making hard budgets stick and minimising rent-seeking in the SOEs, at the same time as exercising very little control over the new private sector, legal and illegal. It seems possible that the combination of quasi-military discipline over the public sector with benign neglect of the private, may allow high growth without significant privatisation – or that privatisation can be postponed until, as the result of differential rates of growth, the SOEs are too small a proportion of the economy to be politically problematic. If this is so, Vietnam stands one of the better chances of making the transition to a market-facilitating state without getting caught en route in rent-seeking.

Ukraine

In important respects, the Ukraine is at the opposite end of the spectrum and overburdened with the MIC. By 1995, the new republic had become mired in a self-paralysing condition of rent-seeking activity.

With some 10,000 large and medium SOEs, the economy has been dominated by an all-Soviet Union and all-CMEA Military Industrial Complex. Heavy industry supplied between 60 and 70 percent of total output in 1991, and the direct military component of this was put at 10–15 percent of industrial output. Furthermore, the structure of output was peculiarly energy-intensive (and energy-wasteful), so the continuation of a supply of cheap energy was a condition of survival.

The series of shocks sustained in the early 1990s and enumerated earlier, paralysed the political order of the new state up to late 1994, so there were few reforms. On the contrary, the government tried to react to the crises with intensified controls – the old formula of the directed economy.

Government deficit and bank credits were the primary mechanisms for keeping the economy afloat, reaching in value up to one third of the official gross domestic product. They were also powerful factors in generating possibly the highest rate of inflation in the world for a peacetime economy. In 1992, for example, off-budget subsidies and capital transfers constituted 16 percent of gross domestic product when there was a 62 percent shortfall in planned Value-added Tax VAT collections (producing a budget deficit equal to 28 percent of GDP).

Increased administrative regulation was the other arm of government policy. However, without the support of a regime of institutionalised terror to induce obedience, increased regulation produces perverse results, increased unofficial activity: 'beyond a certain point', writes Kaufman, 'there appears to be an *inverse* relationship between the degree of central administrative controls and intervention over the official economy ... and the degree of administrative control by the State over the *overall* economy'.[80]

The unofficial economy has boomed, offsetting some of the disastrous implications of the official decline. This arises from both 'spontaneous privatisation' of the SOEs – asset stripping and decapitalisation in favour of private operations – and the growth of new activities. A survey of 200 companies, cited by Kaufman, implies 55 percent of activity was unofficial; other estimates range from 25 to 75 percent of the official economy.[81]

The persistence of the old economic system had one merit. While output officially declined by 40 percent, unemployment remained officially low, although possibly a third of the labour force was said to be on short time or unpaid leave.[82] However, the SOE managers are said to be broadly opposed to any effective stabilisation measures lest these reduce the credits sustaining industry and agriculture, the rents available from trading in export licences (introduced to stop the outflow of raw materials to Russia), or access to heavily-subsidised oil imports which SOEs can re-export to foreign markets or sell on the domestic black market.

The Ukraine – like the Urals, Slovakia, Manchuria and other areas – has an extreme form of the MIC syndrome. Collapse did not lead to an open private market but to generalised rent-seeking. However, both the Urals and Manchuria are part of much larger economies, so more complex social forces are available to press for continued reform. In the Ukraine, the alliance of government and SOEs exercises far too great a role to permit easy reforms that might affect the position of the SOEs. Only the unofficial economy has – expensively, wastefully and messily – achieved part of the reform programme.

Conclusions: Disarming the State

Each case of privatisation considered in this article is in important respects unique. Key differences turn upon the endowment of the economy (both in terms of the size and composition of output, and the involvement of the MIC),

---

80   Kaufman 1994, p. 63, original emphasis.

81   See McCarthy et al. 1994, and *Financial Times*, 28 November 1994.

82   McCarthy et al. 1994.

on the political order, and on the intensity of economic shocks experienced, etc.[83] But there were also features in common.

First, as soon as central direction weakened, debt, intercompany arrears, failure to pay taxes and 'spontaneous privatisation' were used to evade reorganisation or decline, and to enrich the managers. In Albania, by the end of 1992, gross arrears, including unpaid tax, reached 180 percent of outstanding bank credit.[84] Everywhere governments, willingly or not, tolerated this effort to defeat their declared purposes and secure the survival of the old discredited economic order. In Bulgaria, the head of the national bank noted publicly this lack of government commitment to its reform programme which 'paved the way for the uncontrolled plunder of the country's financial resources'.[85]

Second, the preservation or enhancement of the position of the old managers can also be seen in the mode of privatisation, especially in the popularity of management or worker-management buy-outs, co-operatives, and the voucher system employed in Russia (although the voucher system in the Czech Republic vested power in the state-controlled banks). On the face of it, the most popular forms of privatisation made speedy reorganisation and reform more difficult and postponed indefinitely creating structures which would lead to increased productivity.

Third, the state very often retained a predominant role even in the most successful cases of reform. The figures of the proportion of the economy that had become private were misleading if they were supposed to indicate the degree to which state and political dominance had declined and a market economy had been introduced.

Finally, the resistance to privatisation – even in its most managerially privileged form – was strong and grew, the longer the process of reform took. Sometimes it was involved in fears of a foreign takeover – as expressed by Poland's former Prime Minister, Waldemar Powlak: 'if the foreign presence is not controlled or is too large, then it could lead to our own companies being dominated or even closed down before they even begin to learn how to deal with competition. The country would become a "white semi-colony"'.[86]

Sometimes the resistance was the result of effective challenges to the entrenched position of the existing managers. In Slovakia, the government changed the rules to limit the role of Investment Privatisation Funds (IPFS) on

---

83   For a factual survey of the privatisation progress in Eastern Europe and the countries of the Commonwealth of Independent States, see Havrylyshyn et al. 1994, p. 373 ff.

84   World Bank 1994c.

85   *Financial Times*, 25 October 1994.

86   Cited in Commander et al. 1994.

the grounds that this would ensure 'no one shareholder would dominate, and to increase the role of small shareholders'. In reality, it seemed it was a response to the alarm of existing managers that IPFs might be able to build up shareholding positions which would allow them to overturn existing managers.[87]

The countries now said to be 'in transition' were the most extreme and thoroughgoing in creating war-making states, embodied in the case of Eastern Europe and the Soviet Union in a giant international MIC. The system proved incapable of the incremental self-reform that had proved possible in Western economies through the operation of the market. As a result, reform could come only through an extraordinary crisis, a political implosion and disintegration. In China and Vietnam, their very backwardness permitted incremental reform and high growth made it relatively painless. But the structure of power, both in the SOEs and the political order, remained much less reformed than in eastern Europe and the Soviet Union.

With the benefit of hindsight, we can see that the old structures were much more resistant to change than first prognoses suggested. Macro-economic reform was relatively easily accomplished (even if with some violent social changes), and also allowed the extraordinary growth of new private sectors, legal and illegal. But on the reform of the old institutions, real privatisation to secure the separation of the units of capital from the state and their subordination to market competition, 'progress made to date remains frustratingly modest'.[88]

The MIC was able to keep a powerful hold on its entrenched positions; the social relations of the old order were not abolished by edict. The old war-making state was pulverised, part of it destroyed, part retained on sufferance, and part converted to new commercial tasks; but the bulk of it has not been transformed. It waited for a return to its old dominance – and in Russia at least, the prospects of such a return were not unpromising.

Hopes for rapid fundamental change were often based on a Utopian assessment of the power of markets. Against this, the experience of the transitional economies might better be seen as providing a test-case supporting the Brenner thesis[89] – put crudely, that social relations predetermine the impact of markets. The reformers and their Western supporters saw the triumph of the market as automatic and the transition period as brief. In much the same way, the IMF and the World Bank saw the role of structural adjustment lending in Africa as

---

87   *Financial Times*, 5 April 1995.

88   Brabant 1994, p. 80.

89   Ashton and Philips 1985.

essentially short-term – 'sound' policies to accommodate markets would swiftly allow the resumption of growth. The combined wisdom of the IMF, the World Bank, the OECD and the EBRD found in the Soviet Union in 1990 that: 'A recovery from the reduced level of output should be able to get underway within two years or so ... Further, strong growth of output and rising living standards could be expected for the remainder of the decade and beyond'.[90]

The old Soviet leadership vested a similar faith for a time in the impact of imported technology.[91] It was to be a quick-fix which did not require structural changes to create the social and production relations without which the technology could not be exploited. The great Fordist factories, like the Stalinist/Le Corbusier cities, were not wished away overnight. The danger was that the structure of social relations would not dissolve but would impel collapse.

At the heart of the rigidity of the structure was the MIC and the set of purposes which it embodied – the political will of the state to secure its survival regardless of the operations of the market. While that structure existed – and was sustained by the power of the state to tax, to borrow or to print money, and to make the rules, backed by a monopoly of the use of legitimate force – it was reasonable to question, as Gang Fan and Woo do, 'whether any State where the predominant mode of ownership is public can have the political will to enforce tight budgetary constraints on SOEs'.[92] The evidence from many different types of economy encouraged little confidence. In market economies, privatisation could be employed to secure this end. However, in transitional economies, it appeared not to be so – painting the signboard of the firm a different colour did not change the managers or the social networks within the bureaucracy of which they remained a part.

Part of the over-confident optimism in the West derived from orthodox economics. The ethical vindication of this system of thought lies in the idea that popular welfare is to be optimised. But the central purpose of the state is quite different (although it might choose to express that purpose in terms of the nation's welfare). It is to maximise its power to deter invaders and, if required, extend its power against its rivals. The criterion of its achievements is thus not the extension of welfare, or conformity to commercial criteria of efficiency, but success in pursuing its political purposes. The criterion of success of a war-making state is its capacity to wage war. In this context, both state planning

---

90   IMF et al. 1990, pp. 18–19.

91   A contemporary commentator noted with disgust: 'this policy of transfer (of technology) involves as well a silent capitulation before the more and more pronounced parasitic character of the development of those [Western] societies' (Markus 1981, p. 256).

92   Gang Fan and Woo 1993, p. 27.

and the role of the SOEs have a quite different significance from that envisaged in orthodox economics. And there is less disagreement than might be imagined here between East and West. The European governments in the Second World War also employed central planning and a public sector that encompassed the entire civil economy to wage war. Thus, the 'mistake' that the old Centrally Planned Economies were alleged to have made was the same one which in practice guided all the Great Powers in the period of world war.

The economic rationale of the state's endeavour is better expressed theoretically in mercantilism, in the corporatism of the 1930s and its descendants in the doctrines of radical economic nationalism (mystifyingly identified as something to do with Marx). The theory was a response to a world dominated by the competition of the Great Powers, not what came later, the domination of world markets (and with it, the restoration of neoclassical economics). Today, orthodox economics confuses the war-making with the rent-seeking state. Yet paradoxically, reform supposedly to reach a 'market-facilitating state' is exactly what is pushing the transitional economies into creating a rent-seeking state.

If the SOEs, even when privatised, do not turn into market-governed competitive firms, perhaps the macroeconomic reforms have created a framework which will ultimately lead to their breakup and the severance of their links to the state. The old Bolshevik leadership in the early 1920s saw the New Economic Policy as just such a threat: it would allow an alliance between NEP men and kulaks which would conquer the state. China's experience may prove these fears correct. In a less highly politicised context, some observers believe the reform programmes will have the same effect: 'Once a crack is opened in the monolith that is the Centrally Planned Economy, cumulative forces take over and prise the crack open ever more widely'.[93]

Or does the old guard regroup to neutralise the challenge? The comment is on China and there the non-state sector (the TVEs, etc.) has been allowed to overtake the SOEs in output, if not in access to capital. Yet the growth of the non-state sector may be providing part of the resources to secure the survival of the SOEs, so the evidence here is not clear-cut. High growth has so far permitted the Chinese regime to have its cake and eat it.

Left simply to the forces of domestic reform, it seems unlikely that the state and its public sector, even if privatised, will wither away. There will have to be a sharp destructive break – writing off a major part of the capital stock, breaking up the giant corporations, and redistributing the labour force. In essence, the state will be contradicting its central rationale. It is in slump

---

93   McMillan and Naughton 1992.

that ordinary capitalist economies achieve these therapeutic transformations, renewing capital through its destruction. Presumably therefore, if the newly privatised economies keep open their economic frontiers, the world at large will through slump achieve similar if painful effects. But that requires the state to keep open the borders, and to be willing to sacrifice major units of capital to renew the economy. We return, not to the independently operating market, but to the political discretion of the state. There is little to encourage optimism there. It seems that, faced with the test of slump, the transitional economies will wish and will be able to retreat, to shore up the old structures.

Western economies are now so closely integrated, it seems almost impossible for them to restore the old forms of economic nationalism. We have seen, however, that in the defence sector and other elements of the modern economy, the instincts of governments remain centrally protectionist. The same is true on a much broader basis where national economies are not as integrated in the global system, India, for example, with 1,000 or so SOEs (producing about a quarter of the non-farm GDP) is resistant to privatisation.

Thus, the 'revolution' may prove to be rather like China's Cultural Revolution. Despite all the damage and the destruction of particular people, when the dust subsided – and the Chairman was safely embalmed – much of the old Establishment was found to be still in place, blinking perhaps with surprise in the unfamiliar sunlight. The Communist parties of Eastern Europe and the Soviet Union may have disappeared, but the original nucleus of power – government, banks, heavy and military industry, the army and the police – still has some life left in it.

The Rise and Fall of the Concept of 'National Economic Development'*

How long will the system last? ... The state system the Europeans fashioned has not always existed. It will not endure forever ... Its obituary will be hard to write. Destroy the State and create Lebanon. Fortify it, and create Korea. Until other forms displace the national state, neither alternative will do ... The only real answer is to turn the immense power of national states away from war and toward the creation of justice, personal security and democracy ...[1]

Introduction: Foundations of the National Economy: A Reinterpretation

1. Historically, in Europe, the State was institutionally a necessary (if far from sufficient) condition for the rapid accumulation of capital on a national (i.e. politically defined and therefore territorially limited) basis. In forcing this process, the State created something strikingly new, a *national economy*, with economic activity focused on a politically delimited territorial unit (even if the reach of agents based in this territory extended far beyond its boundaries). The State gave priority to activity within the territory as opposed to the ancient forms of unbounded cosmopolitan capitalism beyond the territorial limits of any particular government.

2. As part of this process, the State forced the creation of appropriate social agencies, a class of national capitalists, directly responsible for capital accumulation, and a national workforce. The process – essentially one employing physical force and bribery – invented and imposed a national culture (and often a single religion or religious cult, subordinate to the ruler) through a common language and an invented history and ethnicity (including the complementary identification, persecution and even expulsion of 'minorities'). In time, this process also created the idea of a common national character or psychology

---

* From: Paper, Autonomous Metropolitan University, Xochimilco, Mexico City, May 2008.
1 Tilly 1990.

and a nationally defined community as the supposedly now voluntary component of the national State (bound together by 'values' and choice rather than
obedience, fear or the ancient obligations of formal fealty).

3. There were many different purposes involved in this long historical creation of a 'nation-State', but, to simplify, the central imperative was not to
expand the gross domestic product or national income (much less enhance
the welfare of the inhabitants), but to create the resources and material means
to enhance the capacity of the State to defend or extend its territory against
the threats of rival States, to cover the costs of past wars and pay for present or
future wars.[2] The interest of the State was thus not directly to help the capitalists make profits (the crude populist or Marxoid[3] account) so much as raise
resources for war and create the physical means to wage it. The appropriate
measure of national progress in this context is, therefore, not the accumulation of capital nor the growth of GDP, but the accumulation of weaponry, naval
ships, etc., compared to the comparable accumulation of rival States.

4. Part of this State-military endeavour was to achieve the highest practicable
degree of economic self-sufficiency – minimising imports, the inflow of 'foreign' capital, and dependence on 'foreign' technology (inverted commas stress
the peculiarity of the use of this adjective since none of these concepts possesses inherent nationality). In essence, the capitalist class, far from leading –
much less directing – the process, was the instrument of State purposes, at most
a compliant intermediary between current economic activity and the State's
war-making capacity. In practice, capital was always drawn to exploiting opportunities wherever they occurred, not just where the State required them to be
exploited, and only great efforts by States (and a continuing suspicion of, or
active hostility, towards capitalist activity) enforced a continuing national discipline.[4]

5. Once one State undertook in part or whole the economic reforms required
to create and sustain a single economic policy, designed to accelerate national

---

2 The literature is immense – particularly pre-eminently in the work of Charles Tilly. But see
   also Winter 1975 or Mann 1988.

3 By contrast, Marx, in his historical writings, at no stage underestimated the direct role of the
   State: 'The different momenta of primitive accumulation distribute themselves now, more or
   less in chronological order, particularly over Spain, Portugal, Holland, France and England.
   In England, at the end of the seventeenth century, they arrive as a systematical combination,
   embracing the colonies, the national debt, the modern mode of taxation and the protectionist
   system. These methods depend in part on brute force, e.g. the colonial system. But they all
   employ the power of the State ...' (Marx and Engels 1996, p. 739).

4 This is documented in more detail in Harris 2003b.

capital accumulation, all rival States were obliged, insofar as they could, to copy the process or risk defeat. In sum, the States of Europe (recognising that in reality they were of very different sizes and substance) came to constitute a system of competing agencies, not unlike a market of competing companies, each obliging all to emulate each other as the condition of retaining their position, thus creating national economies, and national societies out of the heterogeneous peoples and tribes inhabiting the continent.

6. Competition between European States in the nineteenth century expanded their respective national economies and, more importantly, both the stock of weaponry and its destructive capacity, culminating in the cataclysm of the First World War. In the postwar period, an unprecedented slump in the Atlantic economy, however, demonstrated the limitations of private capitalism in sustaining the European arms economy. The State was required, to a greater or lesser degree, to organise capitalism directly if its military objectives were to be realised. This resulted in the two most heavily militarised modern States ever seen, the Soviet Union and Nazi Germany. Here the historic partnership between the State and capital was entirely superseded by State ownership and/or direction. The Second World War between heavily Statised economies (true even in the US although not to the same degree as the Europeans) was the outcome of this competition.[5]

National Economic Development

7. This historical experience of 'national economic development' powerfully informed the postwar world, both in Latin America and the newly independent countries of, first, Asia, and then Africa. The State was from the beginning everywhere given the decisive role. The measure of its success was the achievement of national economic self-sufficiency (as driven in part by strategies of import-substitution industrialisation) and the creation of a national capital-goods or heavy industry (that is, the sector capable of producing heavy weaponry without imports, although that was not the theoretical rationale). The agenda was to be achieved through a new technology of national planning. Both in developing and developed countries, economists acquired a quite extraordinary confidence that economists knew the way to develop national economies and that State power had mastered markets, national and global.[6]

---

5   See Harris 2003b.

6   Consider Shonfield 1965, in its time an authoritative work, expressing a common opinion

8. In practice, with the exception of some short episodes, the general experi-ence of autarkic State-driven economic development was not impressive. Each spurt of growth tended to lapse into long-term stagnation or even decline (often exaggerated by the corruption of the State bureaucracy once it was equipped with the extraordinary discretionary powers required to plan). With-out markets – competitive capitals, domestic and external – national eco-nomies seemed ultimately to fail. Contrary to the experience of the Second World War, autarkic economic development was not the route to rapid eco-nomic growth, nor to the structural transformation implied by the concept of national economic development, and therefore not to sustainable national mil-itary independence.

9. However, a group of countries in east Asia – Japan and the 'four little dragons' (South Korea, Taiwan, Singapore, Hong Kong) – achieved unpreced-entedly high rates of national economic growth. This was secured, certainly with strong directing States, but not through any drive to national economic self-sufficiency but rather through the exploitation of external markets, that is greater economic 'dependency'.[7] In subsequent years, this became the uni-versal recipe for 'national economic growth' (omitting now the idea of isolated national economic development) – and hence the route to an adequate mil-itary capacity. By now, even originally such arch-defenders of the idea of self-sufficient national economic development as China and India (in the 1950s) have abandoned the project; in sub-Saharan Africa, the heroic 1960s aspira-tions of African socialism ended in almost universal failure, if not economic catastrophe.

10. In practice the definition of 'national economic development' was smudged into, to cite a recent UNDP formulation, 'creating an enabling envir-onment for people to enjoy long, healthy and creative lives'. Thus, the historic aim of the process of national economic development, to create a strong State, capable of defeating its rivals and extending its possessions, was displaced by welfare criteria – to enhance the welfare of the inhabitants, reduce poverty, etc. The only concession to the old agenda and its proposed structural transforma-tion of the national economy was that these welfare objectives should be on a

---

among economists: 'The State controls so large a part of the economy that a planner can, by intelligent manipulation of the levers of public power, guide the remainder of the economy firmly towards any objective the government chooses' (p. 231). Or Paul Samuelson's assurance that the business cycle had now been mastered (Zarnowitz 1972, p. 167), a point reiterated by Arthur Okun (former chairman of the President's Council of Economic Advisers), saying that recessions were now, like airplane crashes, 'preventable' (Okun 1970, p. 33).

7   These issue are explored in more detail in Harris 1986.

'sustainable' basis: that is, the national economy should have been restructured to be capable of sustaining these objectives.[8] What used to be called 'national economic development' had been superseded now by economic growth, implicitly an intrinsic component of *world*, rather than national, growth.[9]

Globalisation

11. The experience of national growth/development in East Asia was only the prelude to a much more radical and sustained change – globalisation or the opening up to external trade, capital movements and technological and cultural influences of almost all national economies and societies, in sum their integration and thus refashioning to create a single world economy, governed by the economics of global markets rather than by the politics of national States. Thus, a global pattern of interdependent territorial specialisations threatened to undermine one defined by politically identified territories.

12. Indeed, the reform of public sectors to ensure they became fully 'competitive' (now emerging as the key operational criterion of economic performance) and therefore efficient has ensured that global market imperatives seem to penetrate even the most obscure corners of each national economy. Indeed, the difference between public and private sectors disappears. Thus, even when private or voluntary agencies do not assume responsibility for formerly public services, the public services remaining are expected to conform to commercial standards, that is to operate in conformity with prices ultimately determined in global markets. Of course, this issue is not simply a technical one – the original nationalisations often had the covert agenda of rewarding friends of the government with public positions; similarly privatisation has also had a covert agenda of rewarding other friends with access to former public assets (particularly acutely where public monopolies were converted into private ones, statutory power employed to fortify market domination).

13. We are still engaged in this transition but already the results, in terms of the significant redistribution of world economic activity in favour of developing countries has been dramatic, even if we are still conceptually trapped

---

8   The current state of wisdom on economic growth in developing countries has usefully been summarised in the Commission on Growth and Development: *The Growth Report: Strategies for sustained and inclusive development*, 2008 (see http://www.growthcommission.org).

9   Intellectual concern with 'world economic development', an alternative paradigm, is still dominated by the interests of national governments, and hence, in practice, a somewhat sickly child, a contextual rather than operational concept.

in identifying these changes in terms of the political interests of competing national States (the 'rise of China', the 'decline of the United States', etc.). This political mystification of the emerging world economy in terms of competing political/territorial interests rather than global non-territorial markets is an increasingly severe obstacle to understanding.

14. In a parallel sense, it becomes difficult to decide the operational sense of, for example, something as apparently elementary as the 'British economy'. At most, this is a territorial conjuncture of a set of global economic networks (by no means separable from each other nor from other global networks), quite outside the control, direction or even knowledge of the government of the British Isles (and certainly not acting in pursuit of its interests, whatever these might be). The British administration claims to be directing a British economy and presents itself in this guise both to the British electorate and the world at large. But it is becoming a responsibility without adequate power, a ceremonial or decorative function which relies on sustaining a now possibly outdated conception concerning the territorial coincidence of political authority and bounded economic activity.

15. On the other hand, the opening up of national economies cannot be separated from radical changes in the conditions of world security and the *relative* decline in inter-State warfare. Initially, this was achieved through the exercise of us military domination and the military stalemate with the Soviet Union (in the Cold War period and subsequently) and perhaps this allowed the relaxation of the drive to national self-sufficiency, permitting the reduction, first, in barriers to trade, and then to restrictions on capital movements. By now, none of the developed countries retains any serious measure of economic self-sufficiency, whether in trade, capital, or now, labour. Despite the level of political noise, the developed core of the world economy constitutes a single interdependent economic system, but without common effective management which might supersede the territorially limited authority of the constituent States.

16. The initial phase in the security context, us military domination, appears to have been followed in our own times by a growing inability of military capacity, even of the most advanced kind, to be politically decisive, even as the destructive power of modern weaponry achieves unprecedented levels. Both features are perhaps exemplified in the current wars in Iraq and Afghanistan.[10]

---

10   Without mentioning a growing succession of 'failed' States, Congo, Somalia, Haiti, etc.; or Israel's clash with Hezbollah in Lebanon and military inability to pacify Gaza. There are success stories but they seem to grow fewer as military strength increases. For an

The coalition forces appear simultaneously unable to achieve a decisive victory – much less rehabilitate the societies and polities concerned – but also are unable to avoid inflicting such extraordinary destruction on the societies involved, they will remain failed States, dependent on the goodwill of the 'international community' long into the future. Whoever 'wins', all lose. If this is a correct judgement, an important rationale for the existence of States as 'communities of security' is considerably weakened. Thus, simultaneously the State's capacity to manage its economy and its security seem to weaken in tandem.

17. With the benefit of hindsight, we can see that allowing capital mobility in essence broke – or profoundly weakened – the link between capital and the State, or at least made it, from the viewpoint of corporations, one of contingent calculation rather than unquestioned predetermination. New investments become, to quote the investment strategy of the chairman of an 'Indian' multinational group, 'geographically neutral' (and therefore, by implication, 'politically neutral').[11] It is as if, to employ Marx's categories, there has been a global 'bourgeois revolution' in the economic base without a transfer of political power (since no institutions equivalent to the national State exist at the global level). In the great conflict between capitalism and socialism, capitalism won but not at all *national* capitalism. It was the State which lost.

18. Of course, 'global capital' is a misleading concept. The North American and European markets are still the geographical location of by far the largest components in the world economy, implying that all capital, whatever its national origin is obliged to seek a strong position there. Nor are States simply administrative units. In the larger advanced countries, they are also the central component in major economic groupings, most famously in the US, in the 'military-industrial complex'. Here, capital is obliged to be patriotic – and immobile (which does not exclude outsourcing) to preserve its relationship to its paymaster. However, the US defence corporation is not at all the prototype for capitalism as a whole, and there, it seems, patriotism is no more than a tactical convenience to minimise taxation.

19. On the other hand, the still imperfectly realised emergence of global labour markets – and a transnational migrant workforce – is perhaps beginning to undermine the social foundations of the national State in the developed world. The demographic trend in the developed countries towards shrinking

---

interesting discussion of the issues, see Polk 2007. For discussion of the end of the Clausewitzian/Napoleonic conception of warfare, see Smith 2005.

11   Compare the recent comment by Edward Greene, General Counsel for Citigroup, that 'we are absolutely agnostic as to where we do business' (*Financial Times*, 10 May 2007, p. 11).

labour forces, interacting with disjunctures in the local training systems, has ended self-sufficiency in national labour supplies (as earlier it was ended in consumption, capital and technology). Governments are slowly – and painfully – coming to confront the need for a permanent worker – and student – recruitment approach to world labour supply, and doing so in conditions of intensified competition for labour among most developed States. On the other hand, the emergence of significant diasporas of citizens living abroad confuses the old clarity of sovereign States and citizens.

20. However, the historic bonds of solidarity supporting the national community and the State have already been subject to drastic pruning through many reforms, including the allowance of religious diversity, the overthrow of male, white and ethnic/class supremacy, etc. The end of universal military conscription, a function of a changed military ethic, has, in an immediate sense, weakened the institutional basis for inculcating national social solidarity. Mixing populations of different nationality through migration – symbolised in the right to keep multiple passports[12] – goes much further in allowing the transnational to begin to challenge national identities, in weakening the instinctive xenophobia which underpins national identity (now, hopefully, more restricted to sporting events). One could imagine – for the sake of argument – a situation in which a majority of the inhabitants of a country are 'foreigners' and a majority of the native born are resident abroad. The emphasis on the 'integration' of immigrants in all developed countries[13] illustrates the possibly futile attempt to reconstruct the old nation out of the new mixture.[14] Appadurai comments on the emergence of global 'diasporic pluralism' in the United States: 'neither popular nor academic thought in this country has come to terms with the difference between being a land of immigrants and being one node in a post-national network of diasporas'.[15]

21. The discussion of the implications of this for 'national communities' (insofar as, in reality, they ever existed) and for their collective constitution as

---

12   See the earlier position, as expressed by prominent US diplomat, George Bancroft, to Lord Palmerston, British Prime Minister: states should 'as soon tolerate a man with two wives as a man with two countries, as soon bear with polygamy as that state of double allegiance which common sense so repudiates that it has not even coined a word to express it' (cited in Spiro 2008).

13   With accompanying risible rituals supposed to symbolise this 'naturalisation' – that is, the return from being 'unnatural', a foreigner, not connected to his natural lord, to being in accord with nature, a native with an exclusive fealty to one State.

14   This is discussed most interestingly in Spiro 2008.

15   Appadurai 1996, p. 171.

the popular foundation for the democratic exercise of sovereignty is important but would take this account too far from its primary focus. Suffice it to note that Europe, the historic source of a world of warring States, has found it possible to merge its national identities and powers, even if in qualified form, in a European Union. After centuries of guarding and fortifying the immense number of national frontiers that crisscrossed the continent (at its most extreme along the old 'Iron Curtain'), the dismantling of borders within the Schengen Group has taken place with extraordinary indifference by the populations concerned.

22. Of course, some of this speculation is to push trends well beyond the existing tendencies, let alone the available evidence. Uneven development (if we can assume a unitary direction) is therefore more striking than uniform change. For example, an important – but declining – difference between developed and developing countries is that capital is more obviously still national in the second, so the paradigm of national, as opposed to global, development may have greater purchase. However, as we see in the capital exports of major Chinese, Indian and other developing country corporations, this is changing rapidly.

23. The unevenness of economic progress also means old political agendas overlap with new ones – some peoples have not yet achieved national self-determination,[16] let alone any recognisable level of economic development; some national entities have not yet achieved a coherent effective State (Congo, Somalia); some have not achieved elementary levels of the social incorporation of their inhabitants ('democracy').[17] Yet in some of the developed countries, the State, its social foundations and its embodiment in democracy (as measured by participation in elections, membership in political parties, etc.) may be weakening. Although it may be exaggerated, there is occasional talk in some developed countries of a 'crisis of State power'.

Concluding Remarks

24. The burden of this paper has been to suggest the slow weakening of the national area of economic management as it was understood in the past, transforming not only the technical role of that management, but also the

---

16   Thus, for example, Chechens, Kurds, Palestinians, Thai Muslims, Tibetans, Taiwanese, Basques, etc.

17   For example, Myanmar, Zimbabwe, North Korea, etc.

nature of politics and democratic representation. The change in the security role of the State (from the externally oriented military role to an internal policing/intelligence function) perhaps further weakens the old rationale for the existence of State power.

25. However, states do exist and are quite unlikely simply to 'wither away' because part of their original *raison d'être* has weakened. Furthermore, the State remains an immensely powerful economic agent in its own right, with privileged access – through its monopoly of legitimate violence, of fashioning the law and control of the institutions of legal implementation – to the economic surplus generated in the territories under its control. That control is, however, now by no means secure. With globalisation, the local generation of surplus can no longer be easily or equitably distinguished from the global. Richer inhabitants and companies can escape the demands of the State by relocating abroad, and, as yet, no global agencies exist to trace or ensure payment by those in flight. Indeed, perversely, while transnational corporations may frequently manage the location of their activities to minimise national taxation, the taxpayer who cannot escape abroad may now be required to pay to attract and hold global capital and, in a downturn, save companies threatened with collapse, a negative redistribution of income.

26. The old national State had, in theory, a clearly identifiable share of the world's territory, population and capital. The world at large, other States, recognised that it possessed absolute rights to dispose of those assets as it decided. The territory remains (even if its boundaries have become increasingly porous), but the other assets – population and capital – have become much less stable, less immobile. The management of domestic economic affairs remains important if local incomes (including that of the State itself) are to be sustained through effective links to global economic growth, but, in the new order, local power is dependent on the world economic environment to deliver its electoral promises. The old messianic hopes vested in the national State and its liberation, the substance of radical politics, fades into the mundane technicalities of management, 'citizens' become 'clients' or customers.

27. The argument of this paper has been that the most important function of the State, the mobilisation and employment of physical violence, was the original source of the drive to national economic development, and it was this primarily military purpose which set the agenda of priorities. However, the resulting outcome, a world of national economies and societies has been overtaken by the beginnings of economic globalisation, a system where the growth in each national economy depends on its relationship to the world. The old idea that State stimulation of domestic markets could sustain indefinite growth now appears a species of Utopian thought.

28. The possible decay in the regulatory functions of the State has many immensely dangerous potential hazards. One of these is that the State may employ its monopoly of physical power to protect its political position against the processes of economic integration. This would be economically damaging to both the power concerned and the world economy. It is also possible that the more powerful States may employ the threat of war – and actual warfare – to stabilise the government's political position at home against the erosion of power implicit in globalisation. While armies and defence programmes persist, war is never completely off the agenda. An only slightly lesser danger may lie in the reversal of democratisation as States sacrifice constitutional and democratic rights to fortify their domestic political authority and their covert global reach.

29. Perhaps an even more dangerous possible trend lies in the emergence of a globalised illicit economy, linking diverse territorial criminal networks and presided over by a variety of corrupt secret official agencies, linked in a set of parasitic States, 'stationery bandits' or rent-seeking public authorities, with access to the State's instruments of physical violence and intelligence to enforce their wishes. We know that the effect of globalisation and privatisation on the old Soviet Union and its allies was to liberate various secret services (notably the KGB and the Bulgarian secret services) to operate both at home and abroad in clandestine trades to the benefit of both Russian oligarchs and State officials.[18] Here the discretionary power of the State was decisive in the growth of illicit activities. In a not dissimilar but much weaker form, the discretionary power of Washington[19] in banning narcotic consumption sustains an immense illicit trafficking trade, corrupting many State agencies or officers from the US border southwards to Colombia and to Bolivia[20] (as with the heroin networks from Afghanistan and formerly Myanmar). Other territorial networks – for example, the exploitation of scarce minerals and diamonds in the Congo – corrupt the surrounding States along routes to markets (and freeze political regimes, members of which fear that political change may expose them to prosecution). The networks cover an immense range of illegal transfers – of weapons, minerals and gems, narcotics, stolen goods and trafficked labour. In extreme cases, it seems State power becomes no more than a thin facade for

---

18   The story is excellently told in Glenny 2008.

19   As occurred in the Prohibition period in US history and the significant development of the Chicago mafia.

20   William Blum seeks to document CIA involvement in illicit or mafia activities, on a lesser scale than the KGB but in not dissimilar form (see Blum 1995).

the operation of clandestine criminal networks, facades that quickly disinteg-rate in the face of warring militia fighting to capture the trades concerned, leaving a 'failed State' until a militia can reinvent one. Even in less extreme cases, corruption often seeps deep into official structures, protecting a hidden global economy that makes doubtful the reliability of our statistical picture of the world and national economies, let alone our interpretation of government behaviour.

30. However, on the other side of the equation, the truly remarkable growth in NGOs and voluntary organisations, taking over functions performed by the State (or not performed at all) offer some hope that civil society may be robust enough to substitute a world founded on social consensus and co-operation for one founded on violence. Civil society has proved remarkably successful in interventions to seek to compensate for official failures and creative in new initiatives. Many new innovations await us and it would be wrong to take the State's past claims of indispensability as a guide to what might be needed in the future.

31. Disprivileging the State, implicit in our discussion here, makes it possible to begin to think about a world of people, rather than national States (or even classes of States, 'developing countries', etc.), to think about sources of change other than public policy and to allow people to emerge from beneath the long shadow of national governments – to ask, as Pritchett does: 'How long must *only* Bolivia figure on the international agenda, and *not* Bolivians?'[21]

---

21   Lant 2003. See also Collins and Graham 2006.

PART 3

Issues in Political Economy

∴

Food, Development and Crisis*

> If the rate of food production cannot be significantly increased, we must be prepared for the Four Horsemen of the Apocalypse.
>
> B.R. SEN, Director General, UN Food and Agriculture Organisation, October 1966

> In our own country, we believe that the opportunity to gain increasing returns from the market will result in substantially larger production in the year ahead ... The incentive is there in the form of market opportunity – the opportunity to profit.
>
> EARL BUTZ, US Secretary of Agriculture, November 1974

There are eight years between the pessimism of Mr. Sen and the optimism of Mr. Butz. They are eight years which include famines in Eastern India and in Africa as well as the 'Green Revolution' in India. Despite Mr. Butz's confidence, the prospect of increasingly frequent famines has grown more, rather than less, likely. But despite the spasm of anxiety this autumn, there are no crises so severe that they cannot be translated into platitudes or forgotten. Now that the autumn harvests in India and Bangladesh have pushed prices down, world political leaders and newspapermen have moved on to other interests. The plight of the hungry fades away once more. A pragmatic and sober observer of the world scene might assume that in the face of all the warnings this indifference ought to evoke despair as the only moderate response. Perhaps this is what moved the former German foreign minister earlier this year to cry: 'Things cannot go on like this. No one with a clear head and a feeling heart should still be able to sleep calmly ... We are stumbling in the dark'.

Let us assume – purely for the sake of idle argument – that it is a good thing that people should not be allowed to die of starvation or associated ailments, and that this is a matter of overriding priority. How has the world order measured up to this standard in the last few months? The answer does not concern one isolated problem, the hungry and the poor. The problem of feeding people is a microcosm of the world's problems. If we could feed everybody, there are very few other problems that could not be overcome. For the physical

---

* From: *Contemporary Review*, 226/1310, Mar. 1975.

shortage of food is quite small (last year's output was probably 2.5 percent down on the year before). But the maldistribution of both food and, even more, the means to grow it is wildly unequal. It is in the inequality of distribution that the problem lies. The maldistribution is not solely between areas – the more and the less industrialised regions – nor between countries. Within each country, within each district, town and village, the maldistribution exists, and is chained together in one whole, one world economy. Examining a few key links in the chain illustrates this.

Rangpur

Rangpur is the province of Bangladesh worst afflicted by starvation in the 'lean' season before the autumn harvest was available. *The Times* correspondent there compared conditions with Belsen (4 November); the estimated number of deaths rose to staggering heights. At the same time, a United Nations FAO official in Dacca, the capital, alleged that there was little physical scarcity of foodgrains in the country. The problem was hoarding and smuggling grain (up to one million tons) out of the country to neighbouring India.

There were other factors at work. Rice prices had increased far beyond the capacity to buy of nearly two-thirds of the population. It is ironic that, during the 1970 election campaign, the present Prime Minister, Mujibur Rahman, promised to get the rice price lowered from Takas 40 (about US$3.20) per maund (about 40 kilograms) to 20. Yet by August, the price was over Takas 200, and in some cases ultimately went as high as 400. Meanwhile, the capacity to buy had declined. It is reckoned that the proportion of cultivators without land increased from 18 percent in 1961 to 40 percent in 1973. Real wages went down by nearly a third.

However, not everybody loses in a famine. Some people make fortunes. Great families were founded in the terrible 1943–4 Bengal famine (when three and a half million people died). The same has been true on this occasion. Lawrence Lifschultz noted the stages of rural decay which raised the fortunes of the rich peasantry.[1] In mid-August, the poorer peasants and the landless labourers fled from the villages to the district towns in search of food. In the first week of September, the price of beef and bullocks dropped precipitately by 50 percent, showing that now the middle peasants were affected and driven to panic sales of their draught bullocks. Next season, they will have no animals for ploughing,

---

1   *Far Eastern Economic Review*, 15 November 1974, p. 16.

and will – if they can – be compelled to hire them from those to whom they sold them. The future crop, still standing in the fields, was sold at a third of its real market value; the buyers will now scoop the high profits of high rice prices when they sell, and those who sold will be unable to repay their debts. Finally, in early October, there was a rush of land sales. In one district town, the local officials estimated that not since records were begun (in 1918) had so much land changed hands, and at half the normal price. Yet the cruel rice prices continued to rise. Those that could sold the rest of their belongings, blankets and clothes; with the onset of cold weather, pneumonia was added to cholera and dysentery, the jackals that follow famine. In Bangladesh as a whole, perhaps as many as 150,000 died.

South Asia

A lot of money, land, animals and belongings changed hands. As the flood level of the rice price subsided, it reveals a changed landscape. There are many more permanently destitute who, even if they have survived this catastrophe, will be destroyed by the next. But the people who rule Bangladesh – the local politicians, rich farmers, merchants, traders, moneylenders, and their gangster supporters, organised loosely in the country's governing party, the Awami League – have made fortunes both out of smuggling and hoarding, then out of the resulting inflation in prices. Many of them must find it an intolerable strain to avoid rejoicing. Some of them give in to temptation; in mid-November, as the starving limped into Dacca, a most lavish wedding reception was held for 3,000 guests (including government ministers) in the fashionable Dacca Club, at an estimated cost of US$18,750. But for those that might find this juxtaposition distasteful, we need only remember that even more expensive banquets were being held in Rome for Dr. Kissinger and other distinguished visitors to the UN World Food Conference at roughly the same time.

The same picture is repeated wherever disaster afflicted south Asia (that is, for our purposes, Bangladesh, India and Pakistan). It was Mrs. Gandhi, India's Prime Minister, who argued not long ago that 'what food we have in this country is not far short of what we need, provided hoarded stocks are unearthed'. But the Indian administration, like its Bangladesh counterpart, is part and parcel of a rich peasant society. It cannot be directed to attacking the interests of its kinsmen which include its own interests. Indeed, it has pursued as a matter of policy the opposite course. For more than a decade, the government has attempted to provide massive support to the rich farmers as the primary method of raising farm output. Food output in fact soared under this policy (the 'Green Revolution'), but it was never at a price the mass of rural folk could afford. Furthermore, the food output that did meet the buying capacity of the mass suffered by the redistribution of resources towards the rich farmers. A third of the population is without land and, as in Bangladesh, real wages are declining. A year ago, daily rural wages in West Bengal were said to be Rs.3.00, but now they are Rs.1.50. At the height of the famine, the unemployed offered themselves for Rs.1.35, but there were few takers (simultaneously, the rice price was around Rs.3.30 per kilo). To conserve their grain stocks for higher prices, the rich farmers converted their former payments in grain to labourers to cash, with the result that the labourers could no longer afford to buy.

The rich farmers have the whiphand. A year ago, they destroyed the government's half-hearted attempt to nationalise the wheat trade in order to curb prices by withholding supplies to the market. They have stifled every attempt at radical land reform, at lowering the guaranteed government wheat price, even at introducing some modest measure of rural taxation. Now they complain that grain prices are too low to compensate them for the increased prices of fertiliser, oil and pesticides. To add point to their complaints, they withheld supplies to the market until prices rose to a level agreeable to them. The famine was an incidental. The rich farmers have been buoyed by a flood of illegally made money that has flowed into agriculture to reap some of the rich rewards. A West Bengal Minister estimated recently that US$ 111 million of what Indians call 'black money' has flowed into grain speculation.

The World Grain Market

The rich farmers of south Asia are only, however, the little men. They measure their rewards in land and in thousands of Rupees. Yet their relationship to the poor of south Asia is identical to the relationship of the rich grain dealers abroad to the subcontinent. If the landless labourers are driven to mortgage their future just to survive, the poor countries of south Asia are driven to an identical course of action vis-à-vis the world. The world scarcity of foodstuffs is slight, much less proportionately than it is inside India. But in both cases, it is the price which puts food beyond the reach of the poor buyers. The grain market of the world, like that of Bangladesh, feeds well those with the right income.

The poor have been driven to market. Bangladesh's growing hunger – and its exchange rate – has led many farmers to convert their acreage from jute, the country's main export crop, to rice. Output of jute last year may be down by nearly a third. Foreign buyers are prompted to change permanently from jute as a packing material to synthetic fibres because of the scarcity, a loss to Bangladesh's future earnings. The country's present export earnings are radically reduced, and so is its capacity to pay higher prices for food imports.

The goods imported by the backward countries are tending to increase in price rapidly, while the value of their main exports declines (the increase in oil prices is only the last straw). Two years ago, for the first time for a long while, the price of the exports of backward countries increased rapidly. The poor countries' share in the value of world exports which had declined from 30 percent in 1950 to 17 percent in 1970, rose to 27 percent. Of course, within those averages, there were very different performances – the average increases in value of exports was 40 percent, but the richest reached 55 percent, and the mass of the poorest countries, only 18 percent. But in the past year, only oil, foodstuffs and fertilisers among the primary commodity exports have continued to rise. The value of exports of base metals, rubber, cotton and fibres has halved in value in the last six months. Copper, for example (the key export of Chile, Zaire, Peru and Zambia), is now 60 percent cheaper than it was in April. As a result, it takes far more exports to buy the same level of imports, particularly where prices of imported industrialised goods have continued to rise. To buy foodstuffs exacerbates the whole imbalance. Again, as in Rangpur, it is the poorest who suffer most.

If we add to the effects of this, the fact that the servicing of past borrowing has now reached the level where, in many cases, a sizeable share of export earnings are immediately the property of foreign lenders, we can see that the room for anything approaching the import of goods for economic development is disappearing. And then there are the effects of increased oil prices.

The Western world likes to blame inflation and sundry other evils on the increase in oil prices. But the trends were well established long before the oil producers set out to restore the decline in the real value of their exports. As the Minister of Economic Affairs and Finance of Iran pointed out not long ago, between 1947 and 1970, the posted price per barrel of Persian Gulf oil was 'manipulated' down from $2.17 to $1.30, while other commodity prices increased several times over. 'This', he said, 'was conveniently labelled the law of supply and demand, the principle of free trade, and no one in the industrialised world then spoke of price rigging'. Once the oil producers attempted to loosen the cartel control of oil by using the principle of supply and demand, they have been held responsible for all the sins of mankind. Iran, the Minister said, tried to force the oil companies to lower their profit per barrel from an average of $2 to 50 cents. But without success. The Western governments decided to treat the profit margins of the oil companies in exactly the same way as Mrs. Gandhi or

Sheikh Mujib treat the profits of Indian and Bangladeshi rich farmers. In both cases, it is the poorest consumer who is made the sacrificial victim.

However, important as oil is, the increase in its price is not the cause of inflation, but the result. In the last boom in the world economy, commodities were sucked into the industrialised countries. With currency instability and scarcity, commodity prices soared. The demand for better quality foodstuffs in the industrialised countries – because of the boom – shifted the balance of consumption. Increasing beef and mutton prices prompted farmers and governments to expand livestock herds. In Britain, for example, 2.7 million cattle and 2 million sheep were added (an increase of 25 percent in the size of the herd). But there was little increase in the pasturage, so the new mouths were fed from stocks. Fodder stocks dropped from over 1 million tons in June 1973 to 162,000 tons a year later.

The United States is one of the main exporters of animal fodder, but it had also expanded its herds. As a result, it was reluctant to expand its exports. Indeed, when the maize and soyabean crops were less than expected this year, for a time it banned exports. The US government argued that this was necessary to keep down American prices. But it had the other effect of prompting European farmers to buy, among other things, American wheat with which to feed their cattle. The wheat price accordingly soared at the same time as, with the onset of economic decline, the demand for beef and mutton was falling. The Bangladesh poor were now crucified by the attempt to feed the extra cattle of Europe and the United States which no one would buy. There were other effects. As the FAO Director-General, Mr. A.H. Boerma, noted recently, Western governments are currently subsidising the use of 1.5 million tons of skim milk powder to feed livestock – that is, three times the annual import of skim milk to the backward countries as a whole.

In every aspect, the situation is the same. Take, for example, fertilisers, the necessary condition of high food output. It has been estimated that the application of one ton of extra fertiliser on good soil in an economically backward country will yield an increase of ten tons of foodgrains, but in an industrialised country, only three tons (because the land is already heavily fertilised). That would seem a strong case for redistributing fertilisers to where they would yield the maximum returns. Except that the price does not allow it. To build a fertiliser industry requires very substantial capital investment, energy supplies and technical knowledge. It is therefore not surprising that 90 percent of world fertiliser output is manufactured in the industrialised countries. The poor countries, with 70 percent of the world's population, produce only seven and a half percent – and consume 15 percent – of world output. Like other commodities, fertiliser experienced a rapid price increase from 1972. Because of the high demand for food, the increase in fertiliser prices continued when other commodity prices collapsed. Now all the major industrialised countries complain of a shortage, which has pushed prices even higher. Even on present operations – that is, without increasing the use of fertilisers – the poor countries need an extra one and a half million tons, but meanwhile the United States persists in using about two million tons each year for non-agricultural purposes (lawns, cemeteries, golf courses, etc.). In July, the United Nations' FAO appealed to the industrialised powers for fertiliser aid. The British Labour government, administering a country where 100,000 tons of fertiliser is used annually for non-agricultural purposes, made the princely offer of 5,000 tons at world market prices (which were three times higher than domestic British prices). The rich farmers of Europe and the United States were not prepared to allow their respective governments to jeopardise their profit margins for the sake of preventing starvation any more than the rich farmers of Bangladesh and India.

However, the heart of the problem is not simply the rich farmer, but the system of which he is a characteristic representative. The American government is not the creature of its farmers. It was deliberate policy by the American government to take out of wheat production one hectare in every five during the 1960s (land that, it is estimated, would have produced between 50 and 80 million tons of food) to prevent the income of farmers declining if food prices dropped. It was a policy that required high stocks to offset possible high prices, and as a by-product of this, the US government helped to stabilise world prices. The policy was to prevent 'surpluses', but on a world scale, there has never been in the history of mankind a real surplus, only a surplus that could not be sold at current income levels. When world prices increased, the American government saw the opportunity for much larger profits if output could be increased. So, again as an act of deliberate policy, it 'freed' the domestic producers to grow as much as they liked and ran down stocks. Without the stocks, any quite small variation in the world's production can produce staggering increases in prices, and vice versa. The old wild boom-slump pattern was re-established.

The same exercise is now under way for American rice. At the moment, the United States grows about 2 percent of the world's rice, but provides nearly a quarter of the world's exports. The growers are protected from domestic price decline by limits on their output under a quota system, fortified by high stocks. But world prices are high and rising while the profits are restricted to the rice farmers of Texas, Louisiana and California. Other farmers are eager to break into what the US Agriculture Secretary calls 'vicious little monopolies'. A bill is now before Congress to 'free the market'. If it succeeds, then the same sequence of events that has happened in wheat will follow in rice.

Control of such a large share of world foodstuff exports confers great power. As Mr. Butz put it, food 'is a tool in the kit of American diplomacy'. The current crisis provides the United States, as the *Financial Times* noted, with 'an opportunity to reassert its influence' in the world.[2] At the Rome World Food Conference, the US government was anxious to reassure the gathering that 'With no acreage or marketing controls, and *with strong price incentives*, we fully expect that 1975 will bring a renewed upward curve in our breadgrains, feedgrains and soyabeans'.[3] But if the 'price incentives' are strong, then the price of the output will not affect the problem; American farmers can double their output and still the Bengalis or the Ethiopians will starve. The US government firmly resisted any infringement of the right of its farmers to exploit the scarcity, but urged that everyone else should pay, buying the grain at the going price and then giving it away to the hungry. In particular the US was anxious that the so-called 'new rich', the oil producers, should pay the lion's share, thus in one move recapturing what the oil consumers had lost (and indeed, thereby securing a share of the oil revenues paid by those most affected, the European powers). The plight of the dying became no more than the decorative pretext to 'recycle' the oil revenues and so reconquer the rebellious oil powers. The rebels were to be corralled into financing what one delegate called 'a wonderful guaranteed market for US farmers'. More succinctly, the Conference newspaper described the American proposals as: 'we'll play, you pay'.

Few other governments emerged with much more credit. Protecting the German or the French or the British farmers took priority over feeding the starving. Mr. Peart, on behalf of the British Labour government, suddenly discovered that: 'I believe a lot of people in Britain are not eating enough. I do not want malnutrition to appear in Britain'.

Britain, therefore, could not quickly reduce its herds to release the grain to feed Bengalis. Of course, he is right and there are people suffering in Britain. But neither he nor his government will do anything about that. The argument is strictly for the consumption of the Romans, not the English.

---

2 *Financial Times*, 6 November 1974.

3 US Agriculture Secretary, 4 November, Brussels, my emphasis.

The Alternative Responses

Much ingenuity has been exercised to explain the famine without referring to the price of food and the income of the buyers. We are entering, it seems, a second Ice Age. There has been peculiarly poor weather. Raw materials are running out. The people of the West are universally greedy. There are too many of us, and so on. The problem is smaller and larger. Food is only one thread in the single cloth of the world economy. There are not too many people. Nor is there too little food. There is only too many people without the right income to buy the food. But that is a classical condition of the system within which we live. The inadequate income is itself the product of the world economy and the maldistribution of power. The world system, despite its unprecedented wealth, is incapable of employing its entire labour force at wages above subsistence. Redistribution could achieve that end, but is utopian within the present political order.

Meanwhile, history does not stop. The price of Malaya's rubber exports has collapsed, and there are riots in Kuala Lumpur. Zambia's copper price has fallen, and Mr. Kaunda is driven into the unlikely embrace of Mr. Smith of Rhodesia and Mr. Vorster of South Africa. There are food riots in India, and the government dutifully increases its police and military expenditure – if it cannot feed its people, at least it can kill them swiftly. Indian expenditure on its central police has increased 52 times over in the past 24 years, and State (or provincial) police spending doubles every ten years. Meanwhile, the rate of economic growth, starved of resources, stagnates or declines. In Pakistan, police expenditure is said to have increased 28 times over since Mr. Bhutto came to power. With more policemen, there must be more prisoners. As Amnesty recently reported, there are possibly 25,000 political prisoners held in the prisons of one State, West Bengal, most of them without charge or trial. Meanwhile, the government of India continues to increase its military expenditure – it has increased five times over since the early 1960s (at an average rate of 17 percent per year). This provides further means to maintain civil order and the capacity of the rich farmers to profit undisturbed by the hungry, as well as the occasional circus stunts of nuclear explosions and a satellite launching next year.

But the reaction of the South Asian powers is again only copying their more powerful brethren. The Western powers are so heavily armed already, they do not need to expand their weaponry with quite the same alacrity. They hold the lion's share of annual world military expenditure which is running at over £83 billion at 1970 prices (or £24 per head of the world's population). The British, a fairly minor warlord, spend five and a half percent of their Gross National Product on the means to kill (or £70 per head of the population). A tiny fraction of this enormous expenditure could have meant that those who died in the famine were still alive today.

The four largest arms traders – the United States, Soviet Union, Britain and France – have a flock of salesmen eager to demonstrate the means by which the government, if not the people, of India can be saved from disaster. The moral issues are tricky, but as Mr. Healey for the Labour government in 1966 showed, a skillful man can thread his way through the rocks:

> While the Government attaches the highest importance to making pro-gress in the field of arms control and disarmament, we must also take what practical steps we can to ensure that this country does not fail to secure its rightful [sic] share of this valuable commercial market.

Britain's sales of £500 million is of some significance when one reflects on its need to buy grain to feed its cattle. Indeed, since arms sales to economically backward countries are now the growth area of the arms trade, they are possibly subsidising Western food consumption.

However, the hypocrisy of Western political leaders is of no great signific-ance beside the scale of the crisis. There was little enough hope of economic development before, but now that the world is moving to – at best – stagna-tion, there is no hope at all. The influenza which London is supposed to catch when Wall Street contracts a cold, becomes double pneumonia for the cities of the backward countries. Ensuring the survival of the local government and its friends takes priority over all other considerations, including mere hunger or unemployment.

Yet there is no technical problem. It is technically feasible for India to double its food output. It is technically feasible for Bangladesh to control its water courses so that there is no flooding as there was last year, or typhoon disasters as in 1970. It is technically feasible to release from the tsetse fly a cultivable acreage in Africa larger than that in North America. It is technically feasible to create a vast cultivated acreage in Latin America. The oil and climatic conditions of the Amazon Valley are not so dissimilar to those of Bangladesh, but the Bengalis are not there to cultivate the rice. There are hosts of technically feasible schemes. But they are not profitable for those who make decisions on such questions. The capital is therefore not available. The ingenuity of the planners must then be exercised solely on those few schemes that can produce a profit for those who control the capital. *The Sunday Times* comment on the Rome Conference applies here also: 'When the widely predicted emergency comes, and because there are no adequate stocks in reserve, tens of millions of people starve to death, one trusts they will understand why'.

No mechanism exists whereby the technical suggestions can be executed, or the genuine compassion that exists can be translated into action. Indeed, in both cases, any action would be defeated if it looked like affecting the problem significantly since it would inevitably affect profit margins. The provision of free grain ultimately affects the price of traded grain.[4]

The power to profit links the rich peasants of Rangpur, the Chicago grain merchants, the East Anglian farmers, and their respective governments. Each of them is not in sole command, so that in some unexpected swing of the market, one of them can also be affected. But they are part of a structure, the product of which is, in the coming circumstances of the world economy, sporadic famine. It is a problem of power, and the basis of the power depends upon keeping isolated from each other the poor of Rangpur, of New York City, of the bidonvilles of Paris or the slums of Birmingham. The law keeps them separate, and increasingly so as the economies of the world weaken – immigration controls are being universally strengthened in the industrialised countries. In the past, the illusion of some common 'national interest' was sustained by the fact that more people in the industrialised countries benefited. But now the mists are clearing once more to show the same embattled classes as before. In the last great crisis of the system before the war, the poor failed to break through. This time they must if the starving are to be helped. Then we can talk of freeing people instead of freeing markets.

---

4   *The Sunday Times*, 10 November 1974.

Deindustrialisation[*]

A spectre is haunting the treasuries of the advanced capitalist countries. It is not yet, regrettably, the spectre of proletarian revolution, but of the obsolescence of capitalism itself, or rather of its great productive engine, industry. In Britain, the trend is known as 'deindustrialisation'. Elsewhere, less alarmed commentators speak glibly of the advent of 'post-industrial society'; but the scale of the problem is revealed in some of the recent figures:

Percentage change of labour force employed in industry

	(1961)	1974	1978
Belgium		41.2	36.7
Holland		35.6	32.5
France		39.6	37.1
Britain	(47.5)	42.3	39.7
West Germany		47.3	45.1
Italy		39.4	38.3

In West Germany's case, the full decline in these four years is concealed by the fact that the total German labour force was simultaneously declining – by 600,000 – so that the absolute loss of jobs in industry is a full 913,000 larger than any other Common Market country. In sum, the European Economic Community has lost 2.5 million jobs in industry, and gained 3 million in services (since the labour force has been increasing faster than the small increase in jobs in most of these countries, there has been a simultaneous increase in unemployment).

Changes taking place in four years of world slump would not necessarily indicate a structural decline in industry. For that, we would need a longer period of time. Comparing the past record for the major capitalist powers with 1975–6, what is the picture?

---

[*] From: *International Socialism*, no. 7, Second Series, 1979.

Three countries expanded the size of the manufacturing labour force:

Japan. Manufacturing workers in Japan reached a total of 8.5 million in 1957 (or roughly the same as the peak in Britain, 8.6 million in 1961), 10.1 million in 1961 and 13.5 million in 1975. As a proportion of the Japanese labour force, these three years recorded: 19.8%; 22.5%; and 25.8% (that is, still below the British proportion of 1976: 30%).

West Germany reached 8.4 million in 1958, 9 million in 1961, and then declined very slightly to 8.9 million in 1975. As a proportion of the German labour force in these three years, the figures are: 33.4%; 34.7%; and 35.9% (these figures are for manufacturing employment; earlier ones were for industrial employment, so the two are not comparable).

Italy, a late starter in the advanced capitalist league, increased its manufacturing labour force from 5.5 million in 1961 to 6.1 million in 1975; the proportions were respectively, 27.7 and 32.6%.

Of the rest of the advanced capitalist countries, most experienced decline:

Belgium's peak manufacturing employment – 1.2 million – came in 1965, and from there it declined slightly to 1.1 million in 1975. The proportion declined more sharply, from 33.9 to 30.1%.

France peaked at 5.9 million in 1974, and then began a slow decline; as a proportion, from 28.1 to 27.9%.

Holland reached its largest manufacturing employment in 1965, at 1.2 million, and then declined slightly to 1.1 million in 1975; from 28.2 to 24%.

Sweden's highpoint, 1.2 million, came in 1965, followed by a slight decline to 1975, 1.1 million; from 32.4 to 28%.

In the *United States* manufacturing jobs increased from 22 million in 1961 to 26.7 million in 1973, thereafter tending to decline – from 32.5% to 31.6%, and in 1975, 29%.

On the latest figures, it seems that West Germany and Italy have also joined the downward trend.

Rising labour productivity, however, can ensure that while manufacturing employment declines both absolutely and relatively, the value of manufacturing output is frequently increasing. For example, the value of manufacturing output as a proportion of Gross Domestic Product increased in Belgium from 31.4% (1965) to 34.5% (1975); in Holland in the same period, from 39.1 to 41.8%. In the United Sates, by contrast, the proportion fell from between 27 and 29% in much of the 1960s to 26% in 1975.

What are the reasons for the decline? It is difficult to separate the effects of at least four processes taking place: changes in the relationship between 'productive' and ancillary labour; the effects of world slump from 1973–4, with particularly severe effects on heavy industry (steel, coal, shipbuilding, heavy engineering, etc.); the relative obsolescence of existing core industries, and the relocation of manufacturing areas geographically; the increasing centralisation of the system. Let us take these elements in turn.

The relative decline of productive employment – while labour productivity increases – has massive implications for agitational work against the system, but none for the system as a whole in economic terms. Much of what is called 'unproductive labour' is vital in making possible 'productive labour', and much of productive labour produces waste. The relationship between the two fluctuates constantly, and a relative decline throughout the world system in and of itself has no particular significance; it constitutes a redistribution of activities within the working class, part of efforts to increase the rate of exploitation, and, for us, a hint of the promise of the mastery of labour in the system.

The world slump has had the most dramatic effects on old industry. Increased competition for a stagnating market has threatened all marginal producers, kept alive where they have survived by protection and subsidies from the local State on a purely temporary basis. The devastation of the Western steel industry is well known, from the closures in Alsace Lorraine, the threats in Benelux, Sweden, in Britain and the Indiana-Ohio area of the States; the same is also familiar in the massive destruction of shipbuilding. The job losses in 'manufacturing' have been most marked in this area. The key geographical regions present a similar picture. Take for example the old heartland of German capitalism, the Ruhr. Since 1966, 400,000 jobs have lost been in the region, 330,000 people have left the region, and still the regional unemployment rate is double the national average.

Capitalism is a system that, in its process of change, effects areas very differently. Thus, the transition from the industrial core of the late nineteenth century (textiles, iron and steel, coal, shipbuilding, etc.) to that of the period after the Second World War (vehicles, light engineering, petrochemicals) was also a shift in location. In Britain, it involved a shift from the old industrial centres in the North East, the North West, Scotland and Northern Ireland, to the West Midlands and the South East. The system follows the same principle as that involved in open cast mining or a plague of locusts – the devastation of an area takes place for a given period, then industry moves on. Now, it is said, the postwar core of industry is increasingly obsolete. Those areas dependent upon this set of industries will increasingly decline: this is

the death sentence for the old West Midlands, based on vehicles and engineering. The process in Britain is complicated by the decline of light manufacturing in the urban areas, producing another phenomenon, the 'inner city
crisis'.

New areas, it is proposed, will generate the next core of industries to push
the system forward. In the United States, the decline in the North East (and
now also the North) is contrasted to the developments in California in the West,
and the explosive growth in the South, Texas and Georgia among others. The
core industries proposed are already well-known, electronic products, petro-
chemical products, marine biology products, etc. It is not usually mentioned in
this connection that the last major transition of the system, from 1914 to 1945,
involved mass unemployment, Nazism in Germany, two World Wars and various other 'transitional factors'.

Most of the last three factors are presented frequently by commentators
on the question. There is, however, another element that gives meaning to all
three, the differential effects of slump and structural change on the leading
competitors. The different degrees of 'deindustrialisation' on different countries reflects the savagery with which the world competitive struggle is now
being fought. Implicit in deindustrialisation is an increased centralisation of
the system, increased dominance and control by a smaller and smaller group of
powers. The hysteria arises not from some common process, but rather because
of the unequal distribution of the process between countries, so that some
advanced capitalist countries are being shoved out of the competition.

Changes in the share of exports of the 12 leading manufacturing exporters –
not the most accurate guide – gives us some crude index of this centralisation
process. Three countries – the United States, Japan and West Germany – had
a combined share of these exports of about 38% in 1952; by 1970, they held
50%, and on average, 52% between 1972 and 1977. The United States is one
of the countries in relative decline in manufacturing terms, and this is partly
reflected in the export figures. West Germany's share of the exports of the 12
leading manufacturing countries increased from 15% in the early 1960s to over
20% in the mid-1970s. Japan expanded from 9% to over 15%, while the United
States declined from 22 to 16% (Britain, incidentally, with a share very close to
the United States in 1950, 26%, declined to 16% in 1960 and between 8 and 9%
in the mid-70s). While there is much talk of some backward countries securing
the part of world manufacturing, in this, the top league, there is no room for
them to compete except on the margins.

∴

Before looking at Britain in greater detail, it is useful to note in passing not only the common decline in manufacturing employment, but also the general rise in the size of the labour force and in the service sector. The most important factor in the increase has been the entry of married women to the labour force. In Britain, the female labour force increased from 2.7 million in 1951, to 5 million in 1966, 5.8 million in 1971 and 6.7 million in 1976. Between 1971 and 1976, years registering the impact of major crisis in the world system, the British male labour force declined by 123,000 while the female labour force increased by 786,000.

Figures for the main advanced capitalist countries show a general increase in women's employment, and particularly for the employment of married women (with the notable exception of Japan):

Percentage of workforce participation rates for married women

United States	(1960) 30.5	(1973) 42.2
West Germany	(1962) 33.5	(1975) 39.1
Britain	(1963) 34.4	(1972) 40.1
Japan	(1963) 50.1	(1973) 47.1
Sweden	(1963) 47.0	(1975) 66.2

The trend is also marked in the participation rate of women in the main reproductive years. The participation rate for married women in their twenties is between 50 and 60% in the main industrialised countries (for Britain, the figures in the mid-70s were 59–60% for the 20–24 years of age group, and 49% for the 25–29 years of age group).[1]

The reasons for this remarkable expansion are not at all self-evident, but the increased supply of women workers accounts for a major part of the expansion of the labour force and its redistribution. Possibly, the adult male wage has been steadily declining relative to the rising family costs of the reproduction of fewer children at competitively higher standards, and this may have been a powerful factor in expelling an increasing proportion of married women from household work. The ending of immigration and the decline of hours

---

1   The increase in the employment of married women has pushed up the figures for women's participation (as a percentage of the labour force) to a high of 46.8 percent in Finland and a low of 27.5 percent in Greece (among the countries of the OECD) Britain and the US have a common range of 38–9 percent.

worked – in Britain, from an actual average of 46.3 hours in 1951 to 43.2 in 1971 and 42.6 in 1976 would have meant that, even without changes in productivity or fluctuation in activity, an increased number of workers would be required to produced the same output. The impact of slump, from 1973–4, seems to have increased the number of married women entering work as if to try and keep up household income at a time when stagnating or declining real male wages, unemployment and an increasing tax 'bite' from gross pay were affecting incomes.

Married women were also induced to work by a remarkable expansion in traditional 'female jobs' at, of course, lower rates of pay – in community, social and personal services (employing around 41% of all employed women); in wholesale and retail trades, hotels and restaurants (21% of all employed women).[2] The work is frequently part-time – part-time work increased in, for example, Britain to reach about 17% of all jobs in 1975 (in terms of employed women, some 40.1% work in part-time jobs). In all cases, the pay is frequently so low, that relatively high rates of unemployment coincide with high rates of unfilled vacancies, as we can see at the moment in the dispute over the lack of catering staff to provide midday meals in schools. Considerable scarcities of labour exist in skilled or semi-skilled sectors of 'female employment' – nurses, typists, sewing machinists, catering staff, etc. In some of these cases, pay is so low it does not induce a supply of workers of the required skills; the pay is low in part from a general narrowing of skilled pay differentials, the effects of incomes policy in holding down skill differentials and the weak organisational power of the workers concerned.

Put crudely then, the expansion of 'welfare' sectors – services – has partly compensated for the decline in manufacturing employment and has constituted a shift between male and female employment (but since the increase in the supply of women workers has been higher than the creation of jobs, female unemployment rates are often still above male rates). The change is so widespread in the advanced capitalist countries, it implies a common structural shift and a change in both the role of women and the significance of the family – independently of whatever brand of political rhetoric governs the local State.

Britain shows a much more exaggerated form of the general trend of deindustrialisation, and it is this which underlies the sporadic hysteria of the British

---

2   The expansion by sector can also be seen in the occupational distribution – the expansion of traditional women's occupations – clerks, typists, nurses, healthcare workers, teachers, childcare workers, social workers, cleaning and household service workers, sales clerks, etc.

ruling class – the relative decline in the capacity to compete of this bit of the world system. In this sense, the terrors of deindustrialisation are not at all new, but link to the growing obsession with survival that has dominated the British ruling class since the mid-1950s. For much of this period, the immediate preoccupation has been with the balance of payments, but for essentially the same reasons.

British manufacturing employment fell from 8.6 million in 1961 (36 % of total employment) to 7.4 million in 1976 (or 30.1%). Manufacturing was not at all the sole loser. If we compare average employment figures between 1961 and 1966 (to eliminate short-term variations) with those for 1976, the break down of declining job sectors was as follows:

Job losses (1961–6 compared to 1976)

1.	Agriculture, forestry, fishing	384,000	(or 40 %)
2.	Mining and quarrying	327,000	(or 48.4 %)
3.	Manufacturing	1,199,000	(or 14 %)
4.	Construction	5,000	(or 0.3 %)
5.	Gas, electricity, water	51,000	(or 12.7 %)
6.	Transport and communications	164,000	(or 9.6 %)
7.	Distributive trades	202,000	(or 6.0 %)

Total loss: 2,332,000 (of which manufacturing provided 51.4 %).

Thus, while the proportionate decline in manufacturing was not at all the worst – that position is held by the mines, followed by agriculture – its absolute size is more than half of the total job loss. At the same time, other sectors generated a larger number of jobs:

Job gains

8.	Insurance, banking, finance	403,000	(or 51.8 %);
9.	Professional and scientific	1,377,000	(or 55.8 %);
10.	Miscellaneous services	381,000	(or 17 %);
11.	Public administration and defence	275,000	(or 20 %);

Total gain: 2,436,000 (of which professional and scientific provided 56.5 %).

The net addition of jobs was 104,000, far too small to take up the expansion of the labour force, even if we could assume that sixty-year-old miners or toolmakers could convert to being Social Security clerical staff.

Simplifying the figures, we can see a net shift between manufacturing and professional and scientific; between 1961 and 1976, the first declined by 1.3 million, the second increased by 1.5 million; between 1971 and 1976, to put it another way, 'production industries' lost just over half a million jobs, and 'other industries' put on just under a million. The changes reflect an overall tendency for British capitalism to become converted to a servicing centre in the world system. Given British capitalism's consistently higher orientation to foreign financial activities, it could be argued that at long last Lenin's Bondholder State is emerging.

What are the reasons for the industrial decline? Since at least the mid-1950s, British capitalism has apparently had a consistent tendency for profit rates in domestic industry to be low relative to its nearest rivals.[3] Immediately after the Second World War, only British and US industry remained intact, and profit rates were high in supplying the devastated rivals in Europe and, for the US, Japan. The returns to British capitalism were not used to renovate the old depreciated stock, or at least not on the scale adequate to compete with the leading overseas rivals. Some went abroad, some into services, and an important chunk into the very substantial military spending programme. Defence spending was – when added to the much larger US programme – vital for the stabilisation of world capitalism, and served the external purposes of British imperialism, but its effect on British manufacturing was disastrous.

The cumulative effect of a sustained failure to invest is at the heart of the growing crisis of British capitalism. By now, the British workforce is, relative to the workforce in other advanced capitalist countries, required to work increasingly hard, for longer hours for lower pay, and, because of the relatively low capital per worker, at disastrously low levels of productivity: at some 40% below the levels of Germany and France in manufacturing in the mid-1970s.

Low profit rates induce poor investment performances. Since the early 1950s, both British and US capitalism have had the lowest rates of investment of the advanced capitalist countries. The US level hovered around 17 to 18% (investment as a proportion of Gross Domestic Production) in the 1960s, declining to 15% in 1975. Britain's 15% rate in the 1960s rose very slightly to 18% in 1975. Most

---

3 Gross rates of return (gross property income as a proportion of total or tangible assets or 'gross capital stock') have been consistently low in Britain, as also in recent years in Sweden and Italy. In the 1970s, British rates declined from 3.6 to 2 percent (1975), Sweden's hovered around 5 percent, and Italy's sank from 4.9 to 3 percent.

recently, Italy's former rates of around 22% have declined to 18%. Compare these proportions to West Germany's 25 to 27% (although by the mid-1970s, the German rate had declined to 23%) or the spectacular performance of Japan, rising from 24% in 1960 to 37% (1973), and still hovering around 32%.

British employers have annually created the lowest level of gross fixed capital per head of the population (but Britain has been overtaken over the past decade by Italy). Gross fixed capital formation per worker in manufacturing has run at about a quarter of the US figures and a third of its other nearest rivals.

All elements of the central strategy of British capitalism have become subordinated to this question, which in its turn flows from the past structure of British imperialism. Thus, the programme of scientific and technology research has been wilfully twisted to defence questions, producing far fewer innovations for civil industry to develop. Government finance, the major part of research and development spending, has been directed to improve aircraft, particular military prototypes, to aerospace and military electronics; that is, the British ruling class has endeavoured to compete with the leading rivals in the system, the US and the Soviet Union, but with nothing like the industrial base to support such activities. By contrast, the much lower levels of Research and Development spending in West Germany have been devoted heavily to civil industry; as a result, the value per ton weight of German machinery exports is about double that of Britain. Expenditure on training workers has followed the same direction, so that now Britain has one of the lowest rates of participation in full-time education in the 16 to 18 years old group. The numbers completing engineering apprenticeships fell by one third in the 1970s.

But the most dramatic and recurring demonstration of the incapacity of British industrial capitalism to compete with its rivals is the external balance of trade. When British capitalism expands, imports rise much more sharply than exports – that is, British industrial capacity cannot meet home demand, nor can it export enough to cover the cost of imports. This produced throughout the 1950s and 1960s the familiar lurching of 'Stop-Go', a mild expansion, followed by a payments crisis and the braking of expansion. The payments problem is just as severe now in trade terms but masked by the arrival of oil exports.

Take four key sectors of manufacturing, at the heart of the engineering industry. By 1976, imports took – of the domestic market – 53% in instrument engineering, 32% of electrical engineering, 42% of shipbuilding and marine engineering, and 31% of vehicle production. In the case of vehicles, the downward trend has been very long in the making and very rapid in its final results. 4.5% of the domestic market was taken by imports in 1963, 11.5% in 1970, and now – nearly 60%. In fact, exports now are limited in the main to a narrow range of luxury cars and the internal transactions of multinationals (General

Motors, Ford, Chrysler-Citroen). Only a couple of years ago, car component manufacturers consoled themselves that, for every £1 of assembled car imports, there were £2 of car component exports. In the first half of 1979, however, for the first time, the exports of cars and components failed to cover the deficit on the import of vehicles (£210 million).

The high value of sterling acted as the final straw. In textiles, the trade deficit has nearly doubled in the past year. Chemicals, which recorded massive export surpluses in the 1960s, is now threatened with massive imports. Finally, services themselves have begun to show signs of weakness as well.

The balance between imports and exports is not the most accurate index of the performance of British capitalism. The structure of informal State controls, domestic monopolies, public subsidies (whether direct or through tax concessions, credit terms, etc.) changes any simple reading of the meaning of the trade balance. To a greater or lesser extent, all advanced capitalist countries cheat the spirit of the formal rules of international trade to push up exports, robbing the domestic population to subsidise foreign buyers. So that as imports have 'invaded' Britain, so British manufacturing sold abroad has risen from 15% in 1966 to 19% in 1971 and 22% in 1974. In the case of the four engineering sectors mentioned earlier, they are also the sectors with highest share of output going to exports – 55% for instrument engineering, 37% for electrical engineering, 34% for shipbuilding and marine engineering, and 44% for vehicle production. In addition, 45% of mechanical engineering output is exported. But the total value of exports does not rise as rapidly as the value of imports nonetheless.

The 'deindustrialisation' thesis is thus indeed a cause for hysteria, particularly for that segment of capitalism operating in Britain that is stuck with Britain as a source of its profits. For the world system, however, there is not going to be any sort of self-liquidation of capitalism by slow decline.

The hysteria is under careful control in *Deindustrialization*,[4] a set of conference papers published by the National Institute of Economic and Social Research. Some of the country's leading economists take a cool look at the process, providing a wealth of most valuable information.[5] However, while some of the authors are effectively able to demolish some of the arguments about what the causes of the process are, there is no general diagnosis, no analysis showing what the government should or can do. It is understandable. Many of the authors have been advisers to successive governments, and no doubt have the

---

4   Blackaby 1978.
5   Particularly in Brown and Sheriff 1978.

bruises to show for it: the problem is far more intractable than can be tackled by governments anxious to survive politically.

Evidence is available in the book to indicate that Mrs. Thatcher's simple assault on 'public expenditure' is largely irrelevant to the core problem, whatever it may do to stiffen the social power of the State. Between 1960 and 1975, public sector employment increased 5.5%, most of the increase being expanded local authority jobs, particularly in health and education. If we combine the figures for employment in housing, education, National Health Service and Social Security, the increase in the proportion of public sector jobs in these sectors rose from 16.4% (1960) to 22.4% (1970) and 27% (1975) – that is, the most rapid increase came during the Heath government. But the absolute figures involved are relatively small, and even smaller if compared to employment in comparable sectors in Britain's leading rivals. In practice, Mrs. Thatcher will not do much to lower public spending, but rather to redistribute it towards police and defence and lower real wages to finance what is left. The central aim is political rather than tackling the problems of British capitalism's survival.

The hysteria that periodically infects the ruling class has its most useful effects for the nationalist Left of the Labour and Communist parties. The argument that British capitalists have failed British capitalism could evoke considerable response in the coming period, and the data in this book, as also in the work of the Cambridge economists who are here represented, would seem to back it up. If only the Left can be permitted to run this bit of the system, British capitalism can be made to work. The argument has credibility only so long as one does not probe the figures too deeply. Once one does, then the scale of obsolescence can be seen to be so gigantic that much more than a reformist government will be required to change it. The Cambridge CEPG estimates that restoring British capitalism to a competitive position would require a 50% increase in manufacturing investment over the past trend rate, sustained for at least ten years. That would require the complete destruction of the trade union movement (or, the same thing, its complete incorporation into the State), the radical reduction of the welfare-education segments of the State, and still a sharp cut in real wages. For that, the nationalist Left would need a police State.

For us, the figures show the scale of the mess, the necessarily bitter and harsh struggles ahead, and how the issues of reform disappear for the ruling class into the question of its very survival. Britain, like Italy, is in a relatively unique position. It is one of the big capitalist economies, yet it is necessarily being strangled by the world crisis. Because of the crisis, its nearest rivals can afford little in the way of help, even though the decline of such large bits of the system jeopardises the position of the whole ruling order of the world. We are among the 'weak links' in the chain. Our task is not to concentrate on the single link, but to see the British crisis as the crisis of capitalism itself: the only solutions lie in the destruction of the world system.

CHAPTER 3.3

The Road from 1910*

Hilferding, Rudolf (1981), *Finance Capital, A study of the latest phase of capitalist development*, edited with an introduction by Tom Bottomore (from translations of the original (1910), *Das Finanzkapital: Eine Studie über die jüngste Entwicklung des Kapitalismus*, by Morris Watnick and Sam Gordon), Routledge & Kegan Paul.

Hilferding's *Finanzkapital* is a classic of Marxist scholarship, one of the most outstanding products of the leading school of Marxist thought in the period before the First World War, the Austro Marxists. It has been influential among such diverse writers as Schumpeter, Bukharin, Lenin, and, in our own times, Sweezy. However, for some 70 years, access to the work in its complete form has been denied those without a grasp of German. So we owe a particular debt to Professor Bottomore for initiating the publication of this translation, for his scrupulous and scholarly editing, and for the preparation of a bibliography and introduction (with an account of Hilferding's life).[1] The translation is excellent, clear and sober (with the exception of the use of that dreadful word 'valorisation').

It is still, in 1982, a remarkable work, instructive, full of novel ideas, and unified by considerable intellectual audacity. Many of its preoccupations remain with us to the present – for example, the 'rise of the white collar worker', discussions of different national patterns of the development of capitalism, and so on. A central concern, the changing patterns of the centralisation of business

---

* From: *Economy and Society*, 11/3, Aug. 1982, 347–62.

1 Rudolf Hilferding (1877–1941), an active militant and leading theoretician in both the Austrian and German Social Democratic Parties, was a close associate of Karl Kautsky. After the split in the German party, he was active in the Independent Social Democratic Party (USPD, created in April 1917). He opposed USPD affiliation to the Third International, and participated in the founding of the 'Second-and-a-half International' in 1921. After the 1922 reunification of the SPD and USPD, he became a member of the Reichstag in 1924 (member of the Reich Economic Council from 1920); twice briefly Minister of Finance (in the Stresemann Coalition, 1923, and the Hermann Müller administration, 1928–9). He fled to exile, February 1933, to Switzerland, and then Paris (1938), then Vichy on the fall of France. Arrested in 1941, he was handed to the German Occupation Forces, and presumed executed in Paris.

power, would fit well in current discussions of what, in the early 1960s, Sargent Florence described as the 'triple distillation' of corporate control.[2] Hilferding would immediately have understood the issues in dispute within postwar Social Democracy, British Labour's debates over public ownership, the separation of ownership and control, and the Labour leadership's earlier hostility to the rentier but great favour to professional managers.

Hilferding's work is part of a tradition of thought, aspiring to identify the essence of the world system as a whole – or rather, its central causal dynamic. The tradition is regrettably sporadic. It is partly a function of the degree of objective stability in the system itself, of the changing possibility of asking fundamental questions. In many ways, little has been added to the Marxist perception of the system as a whole since the most creative period of thought, ending in the early 1920s.[3] In the post Second World War period, the tradition has tended to narrow on particular subsidiary relationships – from the structure of business power or the operation of particular national units, to the relationship between more and less advanced national components of world capitalism, to multinational corporations, and so on.[4] But putting all the bits together in a single consistent whole so that we understand the relationship of the parts remains to be done. In the interim, socialists rely on rather antiquated concepts. However, the onset of sustained crisis within the system – from 1974 – is the material precondition for taking up the issues once again, for pushing forward the boundaries of self-consciousness, now on a much more well-founded basis since not only is the system much more integrated, much more of a similar character, but also the statistical resources are far greater than ever before. The republication of Hilferding's contribution is then doubly welcome, both as a work in itself and as a contribution to the exploration we now require in the 1980s.

Hilferding's purpose is to restate Marx's theory of money and credit in order to identify the new structure of capitalism in his time. From the initial steps, he derives an account of the circulation of capital, the changing institutional forms and the relative balance of power within the system, before discussing

---

2   Florence 1961, p. 29. The New Left rediscovered comparable phenomena in the debate over
    public ownership in the Labour Party, associated with the 1957 Policy Statement, Industry and
    Society – ULR (1957) and on the nationalised industries, Jenkins 1958.
3   The most notable works, apart from Hilferding's, include Luxemburg 1913 and 1915, Bukharin
    1915 and 1921, Lenin 1917.
4   The relevant works will be familiar. They include Sweezy 1942, Strachey 1956, Baran 1957,
    Baran and Sweezy 1966, Kidron 1968, Emmanuel 1969, Amin 1970–4, Mandel 1975 and 1977,
    Frobel et al. 1976, Gunder Frank 1980, Warren 1980.

the relationship of this to crises in the system and the implications for policies of imperial expansion by the dominant powers.

In general, it was not the first part of the exercise that excited attention – it is a conservative restatement involving important errors noted by his critics – although there is a good critique of the subjective basis of the orthodox theory of value and a restatement of Marx's objective and social account of value. In practice, the earlier part is not a precondition for understanding what follows.

The work becomes much more interesting as Hilferding begins to identify the significance of the separation of the capitalist from any specific forms of production (the separation of ownership from control) through the creation of a 'pool of social capital' (not Hilferding's phrase) operating collectively through the diversity of separate enterprises. The first step in this process is the creation of the corporation. For the individual capitalist this represents the liberation of the industrial capitalist from his function as industrial entrepreneur. As a result of this change, the capital invested in a corporation becomes pure money capital so far as the capitalist is concerned. The money capitalist as creditor has nothing to do with the use of his capital in production, despite the fact that this utilisation is a necessary condition of the loan relationship.[5]

So far as the enterprise is concerned, 'the corporation does not have recourse to the relatively small stratum of working capitalists who must combine ownership with the entrepreneurial function. From the beginning and throughout its life, the corporation is quite independent of these personal qualities. Death, inheritance, etc., among its owners, have absolutely no effect upon it ... the corporations, especially the most important, profitable and pioneering ones, are governed by an oligarchy, or by a single big capitalist (or bank) who are, in reality, vitally interested in their operations and quite independent of the mass of small shareholders'.[6]

Furthermore, through institutional shareholdings, the exchange of directors and so on, power becomes even more concentrated in the hands of a very small group.

Through the corporation's capacity to borrow, its expansion does not depend upon its own accumulation out of earnings, but can take place directly through an increase of its capital. The limitation which the amount of profit produced by the enterprise places upon the growth of the privately owned firm is thus removed, giving the corporation a much greater capacity for growth. The cor-

5   Hilferding 1981, p. 107.
6   Hilferding 1981, p. 121.

poration can draw upon the whole supply of free money capital.[7] The corporation breaks through the 'personal limits of property … [to] the aggregate social
capital'.[8]

The corporation thus, we might infer, becomes analogous to the State, an
agency based upon the class of capital rather than the individual capitalist, on
a collective controlling interest rather than individual ownership rights. The
process reduces all except the largest shareholders to the position of simply
privileged claimants to the surplus value produced, without any function in the
enterprise, reduces them to parasitism. In our own day, even the mass of shareholders can be removed altogether; for example, Pension Funds, 'owned' by
no-one, become owners of enterprises, even of those companies, the employees of which provide the contributions to the Pension Fund concerned.

Thus, accumulation becomes to some degree independent of short-term
market and profitability considerations. The corporation acquires the possibility of charging prices below the costs of production and still distributing
dividends. It is not obliged – at least, in the short-term – to realise the average
rate of profit. This consideration, Hilferding notes, makes possible long-term
planning by the professional managers of the corporation, which in turn means
the corporation can begin to span a wider range of specialised functions:

> The social division of labour – the division into diverse spheres of pro-
> duction which were only integrated as parts of the whole social organism
> through exchange – is constantly diminished, while on the other hand,
> the technical division of labour within the combined enterprise contin-
> ues to advance.[9]

However, the vast enlargement of the power of the corporations over the system is circumscribed, according to Hilferding, by another feature, the growth
of finance (that is, in the growth of the technical division of labour within the
corporation, finance is not included; Hilferding does not explain why this is so).
The mobilisation of such large volumes of money capital gives the banks and
other financial institutions a much enhanced role. To their capacity to aggregate the money capital of the capitalist class, to build upon this a credit structure,
is added the 'promoter's profit' – that is, the banks appropriate the difference
between the yield on capital invested in the given firm and the yield on shares

---

7   Hilferding 1981, p. 122.
8   Hilferding 1981, p. 123.
9   Hilferding 1981, p. 235.

of enterprises of comparable risk. With time, the bankers come to command the industrial economy, and, among the banks, the largest control a disproportionate share of the whole economy, so that, in Hilferding's words, 'taking possession of six large Berlin banks would mean taking possession of the most important spheres of large scale industry and would greatly facilitate the initial phases of socialist policy during the transition phase'.[10]

The expropriation of industrial capital by finance, Hilferding says, is an inevitable stage in the evolution of the system:

> At the outset of capitalist production, money capital, in the form of usurers' and merchants' capital plays a significant role in the accumulation of capital as well as in the transformation of handicraft production into capitalism. But there then arises a resistance of 'productive capital', i.e. of the profit-earning capitalists – that is, of commerce and industry – against the interest-bearing capitalists. Usurers' capital becomes subordinate to industrial capital. As money-dealing capital, it performs the functions of money which industry and commerce would otherwise have had to carry out themselves in the process of transformation of their commodities. As bank capital, it arranges credit operations among the productive capitalists. The mobilization of capital and the continued expansion of credit gradually brings about a complete change in the position of money capitalists. The power of the banks increases and they become founders and eventually rulers of industry, whose profits they seize for themselves as finance capital, just as formerly the old usurer seized, in the form of 'interest', the produce of the peasants and the ground rent of the lord of the manor.[11]

In sum, 'the specific character of capital is obliterated in finance capital. Capital now appears as a unitary power which exercises sovereign sway over the life processes of society'.[12]

Finally, corporations and banks, as a result of their domination of particular markets and their necessarily close relationship to the State, are able to combine to control competition. Through trusts, cartels and the institution of economic controls over the national borders (in particular, tariffs), the oligarchy both protects itself and increases its share of the aggregate social profit.

---

10   Hilferding 1981, p. 368.
11   Hilferding 1981, p. 226.
12   Hilferding 1981, p. 235.

The final step – the establishment of external protection to defend domestic monopoly – is only the prelude to an attack on the markets of the rest of the world:

> From being a means of defence against the conquest of domestic markets by foreign industries, it (the tariff) becomes a means for the conquest of foreign markets by domestic industry. What was once a defensive weapon for the weak has become an offensive weapon in the hands of the powerful.[13]

> There is a problem, however. For Cartelization brings exceptionally large extra profits ... these extra profits are capitalized and then flow into the banks as concentrated sums of capital. But at the same time, cartels tend to slow down capital investment; both in the cartelized industries, because the first concern of a cartel is to restrict production, and in the non-cartelized industries because the decline in the rate of profit discourages further capital investment. Consequently while the volume of capital intended for accumulation increases rapidly, investment opportunities contract. This contradiction demands a solution, which it finds in the export of capital.[14]

Thus, in pursuit of overseas markets and outlets for capital, the State is required to extend its external economic frontier, to build empire. In time, the globe becomes divided into the dependencies of the advanced powers as each national capital seeks to extend its dominion over the largest possible territory (both for its own sake and in order to pre-empt the same tendencies in competing national capitals).

Whereas, on one side, the generalisation of the protective tariff tends increasingly to divide the world into distinct economic territories of nation States, on the other side, the development towards finance capital enhances the importance of the size of the economic territory.[15]

The ideology of the Liberal State, founded upon an open competitive market, gives way to the aggressive nationalism of monopoly capitalism, denying the right of national self-determination to all except the imperialist power.

---

13   Hilferding 1981, p. 310.
14   Hilferding 1981, p. 305.
15   Hilferding 1981, p. 311.

In sum, the policy of finance capital has three objectives:

(1) to establish the largest possible economic territory;
(2) to close the territory to foreign competition by a wall of protective tariffs, and consequently;
(3) to reserve it as an area of exploitation for the national monopolistic combinations.[16]

War is one of the possible outcomes of the increasingly fierce international competition between the different States and their associated national finance capitals.

This, in essence, is Hilferding's case. There is a wealth of other discussions on the political and social implications of this process, but the thread of the argument is clear. The importance of the work at the time when it was written covers both a number of specific topics (his analysis of the 'promoter's profit', his path-breaking account of the significance of tariffs, etc.), and, for the first time, identifying a new structure of capitalism and its link to imperialism. If many of these ideas are, to us, familiar, it is a mark of the originality of the work and its considerable influence (not least on Lenin's popularisation of some of the ideas).

What comments are appropriate on Hilferding's account? It is important to comment, not in the spirit of picking holes in his argument nor complaining that he did not more accurately foresee the future, but rather in order to draw some lessons about our own times by measuring the appearance of our world against his picture of his. The system is in constant flux, and it is most difficult to identify its essential character at one moment. Hilferding identified what he saw as 'the latest phase', but elsewhere, he, like Lenin, called it 'the last phase'.[17] The phase turned out to be only one more transition – that is, there were resources within the system not identified by Hilferding but which permitted not only its survival but yet another transformation. The temporary trips our view of the permanent. For example, a review of this book in the 1960s might well have come to quite different conclusions to one written in the early 1980s. Then, it seemed, finance was entirely subordinate to industrial capitalism, and some of us, somewhat prematurely, were willing to declare the end of 'finance capital'[18] (as well as doubt its exist-

---

16   Hilferding 1981, p. 326.
17   The system of protective tariffs 'ushers in the final phase of capitalism' (Hilferding 1902–3).
18   In discussing Lenin 1917a, see Kidron 1962 and Harris 1971.

ence in Hilferding's time). Now, with the melancholy financial condition of Poland, Brazil, New York City, Chrysler, British Leyland, and sundry other agencies before us, the role of the banking sector must be treated with more caution.[19]

One of the problems in Hilferding's account concerns methodology, the tyranny of concepts. In examining the empirical reality of capitalism, we have available concepts of sectors of production (steel, textiles, shipbuilding, etc.), of great departments (industry, commerce, finance), of national units, and of companies. In the history of the system, it has been fruitful to analyse conflicts of interest within the ruling order by means of some or all of these concepts.[20] But in the final analysis, only the centres of power, companies and States, have a significance spanning the entire history of the system. At any moment of time, it has to be proved, not assumed, that 'fractions' of the bourgeoisie are a useful means to explain events, that subgroups have a systematic and continuing relationship to what happens. In our own times, the integration of the system is much more impressive than the permanent existence of sectoral or departmental divisions.

Quite often, the divisions have a function other than that of analysis – to vindicate particular political tactics, and, at an extreme, to separate what are alleged to be the bad bits of the system from the less bad or even the good bits. Thus, British Labour – like Keynes – laid much stress on the parasitic rentier, as opposed to the productive manager; even today, the City of London is always an easy target. Paradoxically, the fascists used a similar division between the cosmopolitan Money Power (Jewish) and honest native productive capital, a perspective that in some respects comes perilously close to the contemporary division between the evil multinationals and, again, the honest 'national bourgeoisie' (the first identified as anti-democratic, in league with fascism, and the second as democratic and patriotic).

---

19   No one is safeguarded from mistaking one moment for the essence. Professor Bottomore's introduction sometimes seems to mistake the 1960s for the 1980s also: 'the competition among capitalist States has been very highly and largely successfully regulated since the end of the Second World War; and the threat of armed conflict among the capitalist States is one of the least of the dangers which humanity now faces' (Hilferding 1981, p. 10). The competition is highly unregulated; wars between capitalist States occur; and we have poor grounds for identifying the Soviet Union as 'non-capitalist', so the US-Soviet contest accords with the original perception. Professor Bottomore distinguishes States on ideological grounds – 'States which claim to be socialist and to be guided by Marxist doctrine'.

20   There are many examples; for one, see Harris 1972.

Such divisions may help understanding and thus effective political action, but their validity must be proved, not assumed. For the divisions detract from the unity of the system, a unity forged by the market, by exchange. They also provide the entry point for reformism – if one part is reformed or appropriated (for example, the banks), the whole becomes tolerable. Furthermore, the divisions contradict the dynamic character of the system, the continuing drive to centralisation and unification. These observations have a particular bearing on Hilferding's account of the role of finance. Thus, it is instructive to note that in the newer areas of capitalism – for example, Japan, South Korea, Brazil, Mexico, etc. – it is the business group rather than the single corporation which is the characteristic form of accumulation, a group whose member companies often include all the main sectors of industry (heavy and light), a giant trading company, and banks. That is, sectors and departments are incorporated in the same agency (in Hilferding's terms, the technical division of labour within the corporation includes both commerce and finance). Something very similar has happened in the giant companies of Europe and the United States.[21] Thus, in institutional terms, the diversification of the corporation's activities, the search to maximise and stabilise long-term profits globally, has eliminated the divisions of interest between companies operating in particular sectors or departments.

It is the market – and, in this case, the growth of the global market – which dissolves the temporary divisions. It may be that today, the financial bits of the 'corporation', its banks, may be earning disproportionately large profits – and this may give a particular character to our times – but this does not prove the existence of a separate Finance Capital any more than there is a separate Industrial Capital (if by those terms, we mean to identify – as Hilferding did – different sets of actors). It was similarly the market and its

---

21   Take, for example, the 1980 percentage distribution of sales (with percent of total profit earned in brackets) for International Telephone and Telegraph (ITT):

Telecommunications	30.0 (31.0)	Hotels	5.1 (9.2)
Industrial products	12.9 (8.8)	Forest products	4.4 (6.5)
Motor components	7.3 (6.6)	Energy	1.3 (2.1)
Electronic components	5.8 (6.2)	Insurance	19.4 (26.4)
Food products	7.6 (1.5)	Finance	2.8 (6.1)
Consumer appliances	3.2 (−1.4)		

– calculated from *Financial Times*, 6 January 1982.

growth which dissolved what Hilferding saw as a fundamental and permanent change, cartelisation.

The issue of cartels and of monopoly throws into relief a much more damaging weakness in Hilferding's work, his account of the State. For cartels and monopolies are more closely related to the activities of the State than he assumes. Outside the economic territory of the State, there can be no long-term monopolies, nor permanent cartels, nor even the much weaker, permanent 'commodity agreements'. For unregulated competition with free entry to new operators constantly erodes any market controls or agreements.[22] Even in the case of the international cartel in crude oil, a case Hilferding notes – the contemporary Seven Sisters – their control of raw materials was still only a temporary phenomenon, ultimately infringed by the development of national oil companies, the demands of the OPEC group of States, and the feverish search to open up new crude sources outside the control of the dominant companies. International cartels are possible in a boom when the expansion of the market makes them unnecessary, and impossible to sustain in contraction, particularly today when the sheer number of competing agencies has become so great. No single framework can meet the diversity of interests simultaneously. By contrast, within a country (or, as in the case of the Common Market, with some common administrative centre), the power of the State can police market agreements and defend the domestic market from foreign competition.

Hilferding's weak account of the State similarly misleads him in understanding the historically temporary role of the banks. The later in time a State undertook the process of sustained accumulation, the more urgent became the need to create novel arrangements to mobilise increasingly large volumes of finance. What the market could slowly achieve over a long period of time in Britain, the banks were required to achieve much more speedily in Germany and the United States. For later entrants, however, even the banks were insufficient. It

---

22   Hilferding's formulation is as follows: 'There is no doubt that the exclusion of foreign competition gives an exceptional impetus to the formation of cartels' (Hilferding 1981, p. 305). In fact, long-term cartels are only possible with the backing of the State to control imports, sanction – inflict penalties on recalcitrants – market sharing, price fixing, etc. Hilferding recognises the relative weakness of international cartels – they represent a kind of truce rather than an enduring community of interest, since every change in the tariff defences, every variation in the market relations between States alters the basis of the agreement and makes necessary the conclusion of new contracts. More solid structures can only emerge when either free trade more or less eliminates the national barriers, or the basis of the cartel is not the protective tariff but primarily a natural monopoly, as in the case of petroleum (Hilferding 1981, p. 313).

required the State itself – whether Tsarist or Soviet – to mobilise the finance for investment.[23] As finance became incorporated in the later capitalisms within the business group, so also the business group became – at least, initially – heavily dependent on the initiatives and funding of the State (and in the Soviet case, the 'business group' included the whole economy). Nor was this simply a factor in the newer capitalisms. In the interwar period, the intense competition between the dominant States saw a vast increase in State intervention in the heartlands of the system, a retrospective vindication of Bukharin's perception of a world dominated by competing State Capitalism.[24] In some cases, the State effectively replaced the rentier,[25] and moved towards directing the peacetime economy as if it were a War Economy. Finance Capital could not be said to control a system, to dominate it, if the State could with such relative ease displace it.

Hilferding's weakness on the State is consistent. The ruthlessness with which he appraises the corporation mellows in the face of the State. Implicitly, he does not follow the Marxist account.[26] Take, for example, his borrowing from his Austro-Marxist co-thinker, Otto Bauer, on the origins of the State: 'The modern state arose as a realization of the aspiration of nations for unity'.[27] That is, in the beginning were nations which created States as instruments of self-government; nationalism is therefore in origin the embodiment of a genuine communal spirit, not the ideological instrument whereby the State, the necessarily oppressive product of 'insoluble contradictions' in Marx's terms, imposes uniformity on a given population, inventing the concept of 'the nation' for that purpose. In Marx's terms, Hilferding, like Bauer, had turned history on its head.

The weakness underlies another assumption that might be derived from Hilferding's account, namely that the extension of the territorial control of the State (colonialism) is a precondition for the expansion of capitalism. In Hilferding's own times, the extension of imperial control was a function of the adequacy of the local State and the contest between the dominant States. In Latin America, the British State eschewed the direct appropriation of territory since it was more profitable to operate through the existing client States. Thailand survived as a buffer between British Burma and French Indo-China. The purpose of the point is not so much concerned with Hilferding's work, but rather in understanding how decolonisation after 1945 does not necessarily

23   This is a gross oversimplification of a thesis advanced by Gershenkron 1952.
24   Bukharin 1915.
25   See Kidron 1962.
26   As outlined in Engels 1884 and the other references summarised in Lenin 1917b.
27   Hilferding 1981, p. 335.

contradict the spirit of his account of imperialism. Decolonisation was possible when local independent States could assume responsibility for guaranteeing the conditions for the expansion of international capital (of course, to turn the possible into the actual required independence movements).

With the benefit of hindsight, we can see that Hilferding's poor recognition of the role of the State was not accidental. In 1910, revolutionaries and those who were to become reformists could still share some common tradition. Only later did it become clear that the reformists needed the State as the agency of change, as a replacement for the unruly proletariat. The State became not the 'capitalist State', but an agency in principle independent of capitalism, an instrument by means of which the Social Democrats could reform capitalism. The divisions – between finance and industrial capital – are now matched by a divide between capitalism and the State.

In the 1920s, for Hilferding, cartelisation and industrial planning came to be the necessary means to make effective a State plan, the core of 'organised capitalism'. The Weimar Republic was no longer 'bourgeois democracy', but a 'democratic State', subject to the direction of popular interests. The 'popular interests' were expressed by the Social Democrats themselves. Analysis bent under the weight of political tactics and class labels faded. In our own times, there are numerous socialist States that have nothing at all to do with working-class interests – and the doctrines of 'socialism' appear to be no more than the ideology of State power.[28]

Within Finance Capital, there was a deeper theoretical assumption that legitimised a reformist perspective. For Hilferding followed the non-Marxist economist, Michael Tugan-Baranowski, who argued that crises in capitalism flow from disproportionalities between production and consumption (in crude terms, an 'underconsumptionist' thesis).[29] If the Social Democrats commanded the State, they could ensure through a national plan that the disproportions would not occur. In what later became Keynesianism, the control of net investment along with variations in public revenue raising and spending could compensate for the deficiencies of the market. The 'historic mission of

---

28   See the interesting discussion by Kalecki 1967. See also Harris 1964 and 1974.

29   Formally, Hilferding accepted the thesis of the long-term tendency for the rate of profit to decline, but it plays no part in his basic account. He seems to accept Tugan-Baranowski's view that 'If social production were organized in accordance with a plan, if the directors of production had complete knowledge of demand and the power to direct labour and capital from one branch of production to another, then however low social consumption might be, the supply of commodities could never outstrip the demand' (cited in Sweezy 1942, p. 166).

the proletariat' thus became not the conquest of the State (let alone its destruction), or of existing society, but the development of the capacity of the working class to participate in existing institutions. As Hilferding put it to the Congress of the Social Democratic Party (of Germany) in 1927:

> We have always been of the opinion that the overthrow of the capitalist system is not to be fatalistically awaited, nor will it come about through the workings of the inner laws of the system, but it must be the conscious act of the proletariat.[30]

The Marxist account has lost the sharp edge of necessity, the drive to collapse or, at least, stagnation, which was to have impelled the working class to become the ruling class. As a result, the Austro-Marxists were left with the problem of finding a moral justification for revolution. Rosa Luxemburg's comment is apposite:

> If we assume, with the 'experts', the economic infinity of capitalist accumulation, then the vital foundation on which socialism rests will disappear. We then take refuge in the mist of pre-Marxist systems and schools which attempted to deduce socialism solely on the basis of the injustice and evils of today's world and the revolutionary determination of the working classes.[31]

The sharp boundaries of the concepts blur. What were before necessities, now became manageable, subject to manipulation. In the case of Finance Capital, this is most evident in Hilferding's discussion of the implications of the new economic order. For imperialism is not, for Hilferding, an intrinsic product of the new organisation of capitalism, but only 'a policy', a policy which could be changed, presumably without changing the system itself. In 1931, we find him attributing the relative stabilisation of imperial rivalries to the pressure of the working classes,[32] not the exhaustion and temporary stalemate of the contending States. By contrast, Bukharin had a better grasp of Hilferding's logic in affirming the identity of imperialism and the nature of the system: 'finance capital cannot pursue any policy other than an imperialist one ...

---

30   Cited from Grossman by Sweezy 1942, p. 208.

31   Luxemburg 1915, p. 76.

32   'It is the stronger control over foreign policy in the democratic countries which limits to an extraordinary degree finance capital's disposal over State power' (cited in Sweezy 1942, p. 332).

imperialism is not only a system most intimately connected with modern capitalism, it is also the most essential element of the latter'.[33] After him, as is well-known, Lenin took the term 'imperialism' to identify the new form of world capitalism.

In a comparable manner, Hilferding saw war as not necessarily the outcome of imperialist rivalries. It could be prevented by popular pressure. Perhaps such an assumption was understandable in the days of 1910 when the apparently invulnerable, growing and international legions of Social Democracy stood guard. It was impossible after 1914 when the first whiff of grapeshot converted the worker legions into imperial armies. And two World Wars later, the Bolsheviks seem much more accurate in their assessment that war was intrinsic to the new nature of the system.

There is another major area of weakness in Hilferding's work, but one much more understandable in the context of 1910. Hilferding accepted that

> the development of capitalism has created an ever closer international interdependence of economic processes, such that when a crisis occurs in one country, all the features specific to the stage of technical and organizational development which it has reached have repercussions on the crises in other countries.[34]

But, in practice, it is the national market which dominates his perception – external activities are, as it were, grafted upon a system basically determined within the national unit. The scale of production perhaps in some respects still roughly corresponded to national markets, and it was therefore much more plausible then to conceive of the State supervising a discrete, autonomous national economy.

In our own day, the assumption – despite its continued popularity – is much less credible. There appears to be, in essentials, only one economy, a world system, and one world capital operating in many different countries. Furthermore, some of world capital's most important activities operate outside the supervision of any official agency – for example, the Eurocurrency market (with a value of assets now larger than the combined reserves of the OECD group of countries). There are offshore markets, free trade zones, offshore production, and so on. The unregulated segment of world capitalism in the international sphere (leaving aside the black economies) is more powerful

---

33   Bukharin 1915, pp. 140–2.
34   Hilferding 1981, p. 288.

than any individual State.[35] Indeed, its operation has sapped the foundations of just that nationally 'organised capitalism' that Hilferding wanted to plan. In the 1970s, the national 'managed economy' in the industrialised countries had steadily declined, each national part being increasingly incorporated in an integrated global production and financial system.[36]

A global system provided just the context to escape many of the structural necessities identified by Hilferding. It permitted a different kind of decline in specificity (Hilferding portrays thus only one kind of 'despecification' – that between the capitalist and a particular form of production). First, the firm was able to diversify over a wide range of different sectors and departments (which does not exclude the possibility of increased specialisation within each sector and department in which the firm operates), and second, part and parcel of the first process, to diversify between countries. Indeed, the identity assumed by Hilferding and most later writers between capital and particular States has weakened as a global capital emerges.

Hilferding's 'last stage' of capitalism – whether his Finance Capital or Stalin's later State Capitalism – was thus only part of the final phase of national capitalism. His conclusion, 'Finance capital in its maturity is the highest stage of the concentration of economic and political power in the hands of the capitalist oligarchy. It is the climax of the dictatorship of the magnates of capital',[37] is accordingly incorrect. The magnates of today make those of Hilferding's time seem puny by comparison.

This review has, in the main, ignored the great strengths of Hilferding's work, his breadth of vision and diversity of preoccupations, as well as the smaller – and inevitable – errors of judgement, in order to concentrate on a few major issues. This was not intended to devalue the work, but to take it seriously, to see how far Hilferding's perception illuminates the capitalism of today, how far Finance Capital can be used as a building block in the reconstruction of a theory of the system appropriate to our times. Hilferding was wrong in identifying the system he saw as Finance Capital, just as – *pace* Sweezy – the term Monopoly Capital is not accurate today. However, in the process of his

---

35   This is explored in Harris 1982.

36   The concepts – and therefore the statistical data – constantly drag us back into old theories. For example, 'global' or 'world' are among the few concepts that do not trap us in the notion that the world is simply the relationships between States – as in 'international', 'multinational', 'transnational', etc. The global system is certainly influenced by States (if they all go in the same direction), but if it were determined by them, 'capitalism' would no longer exist.

37   Hilferding 1981, p. 370.

argument, he raised issues of fundamental importance from which we can learn much today. Indeed, there is more to be learned from his errors since where he was right, much of what he had to say has been absorbed into the mainstream of Left-wing thought (regrettably this is not true of his appraisal of tariffs and import controls under capitalism; proponents of the Alternative Economic Strategy could usefully consult Hilferding on why they are wrong).

To repeat: we are in considerable debt to Professor Bottomore for making this important work available.

Trade in Early India: Themes in Indian History[*]

Books reviewed:

Trade in Early India: Themes in Indian History
Edited by Ranabir Chakravarti, Oxford University Press: New Delhi, 2001.

Origins of the European Economy: Communications and Commerce, AD 300–900
Michael McCormick, Cambridge University Press: Cambridge, 2001.

Professor Chakravarti has collected here some of the most significant articles of the past half century on trade in Indian history – Shereen Ratnagar (1994) and Maurizio Tosi (1991) on Harappan trade; Romila Thapar (1976) on Dana and Dakshina as exchanges; Ivo Fiser (1954) on Setthi in Buddhist Jatakas; B.N. Mukherjee (1996) on pre-Gupta Vanya and Kalinga; Lionel Casson (1990) on maritime loans; D.D. Kosambi (1959) on feudal trade charters; Chakravarti (1990) on northern Konkan (AD 900–1053); Brajadulal Chattopadhyaya (1985) on early medieval Rajasthan; Jean Deloche (1983) on ancient seaports; R. Champakalakshmi (n.d.) on South-Indian guilds; V.K. Jain (1989) on merchant corporations; R.S. Sharma (1983) on usury in early medieval times; John S. Deyell (1990) on the Gurjara-Pratiharas; and S.D. Goitein (1980) on trans-Arabian Sea trade. The editor provides a masterly long overview of the field in the introduction and a most useful annotated bibliography at the end. The book – nearly five hundred pages – is excellent, consistently stimulating, judicious and throughout most scholarly. The detail and the detective work are impressive.

Professor McCormick's book is both narrower (in time period) and, given its great length (1,101 pages), much denser. His is a grand attempt to put together from many different sources a picture of the emergence of the European economy in what used to be the Dark Ages. He uses a great diversity of sources most creatively: documents (including those from the Baghdad Caliphate), coin hoards, the provenance of holy relics, etymology, early medieval monastic medical recipes, archaeological sites (the location and residues of toll posts, industrial waste sites, sunken ship contents, as well as the remains and sources of cargo). It is, of course, difficult to identify what is commercial trade in all

---

* From: *Historical Materialism*, 12, no. 4, 2004, pp. 455–62.

these sources, but he is adept at rigorous inferences from limited data. As he notes, those who wrote the records disdained trade and merchants in favour of kings, officials and prelates, so trade is least documented. Nonetheless, he has identified a wealth of evidence to contradict earlier notions that Europe in these times had very little trade.

He begins with an attempt to assess what of the late Roman imperial economy survived as the polity disintegrated, concentrating on the persistence or change in routes of communication (of pilgrims, prelates, diplomats and rulers as well as traders) from the beginning of the revival in the seventh century. He plots the creation of new clusters of economic activity, urbanisation, in the Mediterranean, the Frankish and Carolingian Empires, as well as the peripheral areas (Britain, Eastern Europe and the far north). Out of this, he identifies – in response to the major expansion of the richer and more advanced Islamic world (up to the tenth century) – the remarkable rise of Venice and the north Italian cities, the revival of river trade and development of new trade points. It is an impressive and fascinating compilation, a masterly summing up of the point we have reached in the enquiry, a bench mark for further explorations.

What is the justification for putting together these two works? It is to consider the essence of historical research, revisionism. The perception of the past is continually changing and must do so as evidence accumulates and new sources become available. Yet revisionism is, in principle, always a challenge for governments and the intelligentsia, for settled ways of considering the past and thus our present. What makes history important outside the ranks of historians is thus its impact on the present, how we see ourselves and our times. Historians, whether they know it or not, are thus continually undermining the present, subverting our comfortable assumptions that we know who we are. It is not just more immediate questions – as with the work of Israel's revisionist historians,[1] to the violent protests of the government, showing that the official account of the foundation of the State in 1948, is remote from the 'truth' and this bears directly upon the appalling conflicts in the Occupied Territories at the moment (no less, the myth of the lands of the ancient Israelites is a powerful – if in principle absurd – moral element in present Israeli claims). The revision of Irish history[2] has less painful relevance but is no less upsetting for the ruling order. A recent London satire on the performance of British generals in 1914 produced strong protests from the Conservative backbenches, and one need not mention an obscure mosque at Ayodhya in a similar connection.

---

1   Morris 1987, Silberstein 1999.
2   George and O'Day 1996.

However, surely ancient or medieval history cannot have any such importance? Yet, even here, the cultures within which we grow up do indeed equip
us in certain ways that can be challenged. Both Chakravarti and McCormick
present arguments that our views of the past are seriously wrong. One of the
most powerful reasons for this, in my view, is that history as a formal study is
an intellectual by-product of the rise of the modern state over the past three
hundred years or so, and these origins easily turn it into a glorification of the
present and a reorganisation of the past to show the steps by which the glories
came about. Hegel's extraordinary history of the world as the saga of the self-
realisation of the spirit of Reason, culminating in the pinnacle of achievement
in the Prussian monarchy of 1818 is, thus, not an unlikely model for histories
written in the nineteenth century and after. Chakravarti sees the myth of the
brutish past as imposed by British imperialism, a myth contrasting the 'eternal,
immutable, static and stagnant India ... stuck to its rural agrarian inertia' with
the 'vibrant, innovative, adventurous, progressive and dominant West'.[3] But
McCormick shows that the British also invented a world of 'static subsistence
villages', 'feudalism', in their own past, this time to enhance the glories of the
present. After his immense work, he concludes that it is no longer possible to
defend the idea of a Europe as the 'impoverished, inward-looking and economically stagnant place many of us learned about in our student days'.[4] Indeed,
the word 'feudalism' does not occur in his index (though footnote 28, p. 734,
gives a short non-committal reference). In other sources, the 'industrial revolution' has disappeared or rather there are many industrial revolutions, not all
equally well-documented, at different points of time in the last three millennia.
Angus Maddison, in his recent statistical account of the last thousand years of
the world economy,[5] similarly has no use for 'feudalism', 'the industrial revolution' or a transitional phase of 'merchant capitalism'. Capitalism, in his view,
rises unevenly in Europe from 1000 AD up to 1820, when it finally emerges fully-
fledged.

   The reason why this is emerging now, I would like to suggest, is as a by-
product of 'globalisation'. The slow, contradictory and uneven emergence of a
single global economy is exposing how far history in the past has been presented as the story of a separate, self-realising, autonomous 'country' or 'society'
(for which, read the population governed by one independent sovereign state).
The national defined the universe of concern, whether a polity, a society, an

---

3 Chakravarti 2001, p. 2.

4 McCormick 2001, p. 797.

5 Maddison 2001.

economy or a culture (at the same time, often imposing a quite implausible homogeneity on the domestic). Globalisation thus exposes not only the Euro-centric (or Anglocentric) character of the past history of the rise of capitalism and its industrial revolution, it exposes the idea of an autonomous national history in the premodern state period in favour of a history of the world and its communities.

One element in the old history is the idea that capitalism arises only in north-western Europe (and Britain specifically) at a particular moment. Part of that is to deny the significance of trade in the past, or – as in the case of both Rome and China – to say that what appears as large-scale 'trade' (in grain, for example) is only the movement of state appropriations. Thus, for example, in ancient Greece – now emerging as the first prototype for free enterprise – de Ste Croix[6] finds the merchant class 'a wholly imaginary' concept since significant com-mercial trade did not occur in Greece and Rome. A capitalist class is reserved for, say, the Netherlands in the seventeenth century, England in the eighteenth century, and so forth. The insignificance of trade earlier partly fits the ancient European prejudice against the trader (usually a foreigner) by peasant and lord, both natural mercantilists. Such trade as there was, it is said, concerned only the supply of luxuries to a small class of the wealthy, a phenomenon entirely marginal to the isolated subsistence economy of the village. Yet, as Chakrav-arti notes, what are luxuries at the point of consumption may not be luxuries at the point of production (he mentions black pepper from the Coromandel coast), so that trade may indeed not be at all marginal but compel the reorgan-isation of production. More important, the basic proposition is false as shown in both these works. Thus, only modern conceptions of 'international trade' induce us to separate long- and short-distance trade, 'external' and 'domestic' or 'internal' (implying the modern separate national economies). But, if we look at both, then it is abundantly clear that necessities were always traded and gen-erally in bulk. Even long-distance trade occasionally handled necessities – salt, grain, industrial, building or war raw materials, and so on. Some of the large estates that McCormick cites – and that earlier writers might have identified as prototypical feudal domains – were important producers of marketed goods, agricultural and craft manufactures, for long distance shipment. In some cases (the evidence includes 2,500 industrial waste dumps and iron pits at different sites throughout Western Europe), the great estates were important sources of exported metal manufactures. By implication, a pure exchange economy was already important and sufficiently so to induce the reorganisation of produc-

---

6   de Ste Croix 1981, p. 4.

tion so that producers were dependent upon exchange. Furthermore, even if we accept the idea of trade being significant in the past, the conception of a merchant class separate from production looks increasingly doubtful – as both volumes show, often merchants were landowners, mine owners and organisers of manufacturing.

The economic geography of this economy was, however, quite unlike modern 'political-economic geography', where development occurs almost independently of natural endowment. It is a world of cities along water courses, trading clusters, not political enclaves, with often only contingent relationships to territorial rulers. International trade – trade between 'nations' – exists only in the sense that inhabitants of different cities are called 'nations' – Venetians, Florentines, Goans, Malaccans, and so forth.

McCormick stresses the important role of the more advanced and wealthy Islamic world in stimulating clusters of activity in backward Europe between the seventh and tenth centuries, and perhaps the same may have some bearing on the growth of Indian cities in the same period. The Abbasid Caliphate in Baghdad (750–870) established some measure of economic interaction within its sphere from the Atlantic to what became Iraq, with linkages through the Gulf to littoral India and Southeast Asia, and through Andalus to the rest of Europe, particularly to the great trade fair of St. Denis near Paris. Neither book is, understandably, concerned to explain the emergence of this engine of growth; McCormick suggests some possible factors: the economic effects of territorial integration and some measure of security of communication, a green revolution in some agricultural areas, a propitious political and religious context, an urban civilisation as the result of conquest, and so on – but its effects in Europe seem substantial. McCormick records the appearance of Arab coins in hoards in the Italian cities, in Frankish and Carolingian Europe, and records of some Arab traders and, more important, Jewish traders from the Muslim world. Europe imported luxuries (with some industrial raw materials) but still, he estimates, ran an export surplus, arising, he suggests, from the export of slaves. Slaves were drawn from the Mediterranean littoral, but then from further inland and finally from the periphery (Britain, Eastern Europe – whence the word 'slave' derived from Slav). He estimates that the export was a response to the demographic disasters in the eighth century Islamic world following on the ravages of bubonic plague (the first recorded slave ship was in 748 from Venice). Slaves were, he says, also drawn from Africa and Asia. But the European 'Dark Ages' are only one fragment in a story that, in Chakravarti's volume, suggests the importance of trade throughout earlier periods, indeed, for much of recorded history. The subsistence village, that stalwart character in so much of social science, can hardly ever have existed. Of course, the trade in some ages may have been largely state appropriations (especially of raw materials for war – for example, tin for bronze), pillage or purchase by territorial rulers, but the movement of goods on whatever account seems to be as old as any other economic activity, and often on a scale that must have depended upon a reorganisation of production, creating a class of producers dependent upon exchange. This is not necessarily the same as the creation of private merchant capital, although that also seems to have been crucial at particular historical moments. Of course, there have been great fluctuations in the importance of this trade economy. Europe in the sixth century appears to be one of those troughs in activity, particularly marked (as also its reversal) in the Mediterranean. The obverse to the troughs are great surges of growth that in particular areas were sustained for quite long periods before being curtailed by, one speculates, natural disasters, foreign invasion and widespread destruction particularly of communications, the apparently infinite depredations of territorial rulers, the collapse of markets elsewhere, and so forth. But the surges take place on a long-term rising – albeit slowly – plane of productivity, population and innovation.

Many of our notions of the historical periods in the rise of capitalism owe much to Marx. He performed a brilliant service in seeking to capture the essence of a system, 'capitalism', and the historical logic which preceded it and defined its peculiarities. Given the exiguous basis of the knowledge available to him, a tiny fragment of what we have now, it was heroic. But his scheme bears the marks of the time of its origin, already into the period of domination of the modern state and its sociological shadow, the 'nation'. His is an account of national capitalism in which the rise of manufacturing is seen as the core distinctive feature, and the resulting conflict of national classes sets the whole in political and social movement. The national stress perhaps explains why he devoted so little attention to the earliest phases of post-Roman European commercial and manufacturing growth in the north Italian cities. He could not have seen the earlier phases of growth outside Europe – from those clusters in ancient India, Mesopotamia and China. He would, no doubt, have been astonished to learn of the extraordinary growth of manufacturing under China's T'ang dynasty or, even more, the southern Sung (960–1279), with a coal-fired metallurgical output not matched in Europe until the late eighteenth century.

If globalisation undermines the old forms of national history, the collective self-glorification of the state, the postindustrial age undermines the notion that manufacturing is the peculiarity of capitalism. An age witnessing a decline in manufacturing in the developed countries either suggests a postcapitalist system, or that capitalism is not so defined and the predominance of manufacturing was no more than a phase. The second would seem more plausible and more consistent with the core of Marx's thought. But, if capitalism is defined as a system of competitive production for private profit and accumulation, an exchange system focussed on market-establishing prices which, in turn, determine the conditions of production and territorial divisions of labour, then this has been a thread in the economic story for perhaps thousands of years in one form or another, one locality or another. In some cases – for example, southern Sung China or even the time of Greek city-states – it appears to have been economically dominant. It did not always include free labour and if that – the existence of a free labour force – is made a defining element, it narrows drastically the number of cases (but this still does not restore the primacy of Europe or the modern period).

Only in the past couple of centuries has capitalism begun to have a dominance over the world capable of surviving the disasters that afflicted it in the past. But, even then, the system still has far to go to achieve an unchallenged position – and far to go in many fields to establish a set of world markets and prices, with the corresponding division of labour of a single global economy. Meillassoux[7] – according to Shereen Ratnagar in Chakravarti's collection – argues that any suggestion that capitalism is as old as recorded society is to suggest it is 'natural' to human beings and therefore cannot be changed. But this does seem a weak objection – as weak as to suggest that agriculture or handicrafts are equally 'natural'. An exchange economy has been part of the agrarian, mining and handicraft economy for thousands of years without any suggestion that these need to last for ever.

If we disallow Marx's account of capitalism as founded on the recent phenomenon of national economies, as Eurocentric (and more narrowly, Anglocentric), it does not mean he did not detect something genuinely new in the European case. But that was, I think, not capitalism *per se*, but a state-directed capitalism, emerging out of the war-driven rivalries of the European powers. Of course, warring rulers are as old as anything else in recorded history, but not rulers who, in the interests of waging war directly, shape or facilitate the accumulation of capital in the interests of territorial purposes. Marx himself put his finger on the question in the famous citation:

> The different moments of primitive accumulation can be assigned in particular to Spain, Portugal, Holland, France and England, in more or less chronological order. These different moments are systematically combined together at the end of the seventeenth century in England; the combination embraces the colonies, the national debt, the modern tax

---

7   Meillassoux 1972.

system and the system of protection. These methods depend in part on brute force, for instance, the colonial system. But they all employ the power of the State ...[8]

This is, incidentally, a good example of the omission of the Italian cities – since they did not constitute a valid historical character, a country or national state. Nor was this process one of 'primitive accumulation'; that had occurred many times before. But the decisive role of the state was, I suggest, very new, dedicated to forcing the creation of a national 'political economy', rather than exploiting an existing cosmopolitan economic geography of trading cities. This peculiar conjuncture – of the State and its obsession with warfare forcing private capital and trade into an exclusive national framework – may be Europe's peculiarity.[9]

∴

This has been a rather long excursus from these two excellent volumes. But both have some importance in undermining our inherited conceptions both of the economic system that exists now and of the past, of the relationship between trade and the production economy in the past (and indeed, on the doubtful distinction between merchant, agrarian and industrial capital). Above all, they suggest that what is peculiar historically is not the return to a 'globalisation', which was the norm historically, but the intervening period of state capitalism. Once we are able to displace Europe (or Britain) as the exclusive source of 'capitalism', we can begin to see many other false starts on the road to modern capitalism in many parts of the world, and ask questions about why they did not succeed. In the end, both volumes are powerful contributions to defining the present.

---

8 Marx 1930, Chapter 31.
9 This is explored in much more detail in Harris 2003.

PART 4

Migration

∵

The New Untouchables: The International Migration of Labour*

The rise of imperialism is also the rise of the modern State. The manifestation of the power of the State is in the first instance its tight control of one patch of very clearly defined territory and the population trapped within its boundaries. The imposition of this pattern on humanity by the first group of modern States, those of Europe, produced a defensive reaction by the ruling classes of the rest of the world. They in turn were obliged to establish the same type of tight control over whatever territories could be appropriated. The pattern which emerged is reminiscent of the enclosure movement in Britain: the appropriation of common lands by private owners to the point where all territory within Britain was officially parcelled up among a category of 'owners'. The process both within the territory of any given State and internationally eliminated all 'free lands' and all free men and women: all who do not officially belong to one or other local ruling class (and can, in principle, acquire a valid passport to prove that they actually exist).

By now almost all inhabitable territory in the world has been demarcated, and humanity corralled within licensed national pens. Indeed, the division is so all-embracing, its sheer novelty is no longer apparent; most people cannot conceive of a world not divided into national patches, not dominated by baronial fiefs.

The development of the internal control of States over their respective territories and populations – the increased 'nationalisation' of the globe – is the other side of the coin to increased 'internationalisation'. For what is meant by internationalisation is increased interaction between increasingly defined national patches. The growth of the one necessarily presupposes the increase in the other.

Now, each national patch is almost equally related in economic terms to every other one – a condition in sharp contrast to the imperatives of political or military interaction where geographical proximity is of primary significance. This interaction ensures increased synchronisation of the world system, or rather, its increased subordination to the dominant centres of world power.

---

*   From: *International Socialism*, 8 (new series), Spring 1980: 37–63.

Yet such subordination should not conceal the necessary parallel process of 'internal colonisation', the attempt by particular States to subordinate all areas within their control to a single centre, usually the capital city.

Thus, the obverse of increased nationalisation of the areas of the world is increased interdependence of the national patches. It is a contradictory process, for the interests of individual States are in collision with the imperatives of a world economy, with capital accumulation on a world scale.

The State's primary interest is in retaining and extending its territorial control, not assisting the development of an international economic order outside its control. In slump, the contradiction emerges so sharply, the accumulation is sacrificed to the maintenance of the power of the State, of the local ruling class, over its inhabitants.

The 'internationalisation' of labour is one element in these processes. Throughout the history of capitalism, workers have moved in search of work, or been driven to work, in areas other than those where they were raised. This common phenomenon, however, becomes remarkable only when national boundaries are laid down and become of sufficient importance to impede, block or shape the international movement of workers. That is, political controls are imposed in the attempt to break a movement impelled by the operation of a world labour market. To put it in another way, growth in the world system prompts the ruling classes of growing and dominant economies to despatch raiding parties to capture part of the labour force, belonging to a weaker ruling class. Then the passport and visa, with the whole complex of subsidiary controls, become an instrument for the control and direction of the marginal labour force.[1]

---

1 Compare the contemporary tolerance of the passport as a means of labour control to Marx's comment on internal labour passports: 'The excess of despotism reached in France will be apparent to the following regulations as to working men. Every working man is supplied with a book by the police – the first page of which contains his name, age, birthplace, trade or calling, and a description of his person. He is therein obliged to enter the name of the master for whom he works, and the reasons why he leaves him. But this is not all: the book is placed in the master's hands and deposited by him in the bureau of the police with the character of the man by the master. When a workman leaves his employment, he must go and fetch this book from the police officer; and is not allowed to obtain another situation without producing it. Thus the workman's bread is utterly dependent on the police. But this again is not all: this book serves the purpose of a passport. If he is obnoxious, the police write "bon pour retourner chez lui" ["valid for return home"] in it, and the workman is obliged to return to his parish! ... No serfdom of the feudal ages – no pariahdom of India has its parallel' (Marx and Engels 1978, p. 578).

Whether the system is expanding or contracting determines the precise form of the contradiction between the interests of the State and those of the world economy. In expansion, the world labour market acts like acid upon territorial controls, other things being equal; either ruling classes are obliged to dismantle trade, finance and labour movement controls, or black markets in each area threaten the structures of control: 'liberalisation' is the product, rather than – as is frequently claimed – the cause of expansion. Nonetheless, although in the 1950s and 1960s many labour importing countries liberalised entry procedures, the essential formal controls were retained, and with the onset of contraction, strengthened. Protectionism in trade was matched by a protectionism in labour, and both exaggerate the severity of contraction.

The unprecedented expansion in the world economy after 1948 was a highly uneven process, producing disproportionate growth at certain key points in the advanced capitalist countries as well as in particular regions in the backward countries. This disproportionate growth was reflected in an increased concentration of the demand for labour. The two most important centres of the world system, the core zones of the American and European economies, attracted a sustained inflow of workers from abroad. But many other smaller centres, at various times, also attracted inflows – in the 1970s, the Middle Eastern oil producing States; South Africa, Ghana, Nigeria, Ivory Coast, Venezuela, Singapore, etc. The legal movement was accompanied to a greater or lesser extent, depending upon the restrictions in force and the powers of the local State to enforce them, by both a black market in labour, illegal migration, and the 'unscheduled' movements of refugees – for example, the large scale movements in Africa, the flight of Cubans, Argentinians, Cambodians, Vietnamese, Bengalis, and now Afghanis.

The concept of a crude undifferentiated 'labour' is quite inadequate to understand the process of official worker movement. Those who move tend to be in the most active age groups, 18 to 35 years of age, and in terms of ability and skills, to be above the average for the sending area. The jobs they move to are restricted, although they range across the spectrum from temporary seasonal work to permanent highly skilled jobs (for example, doctors). Each stratum of occupations has a separate dynamic.

For relatively unskilled workers, the areas of recruitment have often been geographically close – Eire for Britain, the Mediterranean countries for Germany and France, Mexico and Central America for the United States. But it is also true that European labour demand stretches far into West Africa, to Turkey and Iran, British demand to India, Malaysia and the Philippines, and American to Korea, Taiwan and the Philippines on the opposite side of the Pacific. Territorially, each national labour market expands and contracts geographically with the rhythms of growth. There are also countries now which supply unskilled or semi skilled labour globally; for example, the Philippines. As the level of skill in demand rises, so the extent of the catchment area expands, until a world labour market operates, as for example with doctors.

Where labour exporting countries are geographically close to the place where labour demand is increasing rapidly and the controls on movement are weak, the emigration of workers can be proportionally very large. North Yemen, adjacent to Saudi Arabia, has some 44 percent of its adult labour force working abroad. Lesotho supplies to South Africa some 21 percent of its domestic labour force; Algeria and Tunisia at one time had between 11 and 12 percent of their workers abroad. In the heyday of movement, emigration amounted to 70 percent of the increase in Portugal's labour force, and, before 1962, to over 100 percent of Eire's.

Since emigrants are not drawn uniformly from a country as a whole but from particular districts, these national figures conceal the much greater effect on particular sending districts. For example, Indian migration to Britain is drawn from one medium sized state State, Gujerat, and a small State, Punjab, and within Punjab, largely from one district, Jullundur; Indian migration to the Gulf is drawn mainly from another small State, Kerala, while the largest State in India, Uttar Pradesh (with a population of around 100 million) provides few emigrants.

The movement is not just one way. Most countries export and import labour at the same time. Greece, with over two million workers abroad, imports workers from Egypt and Pakistan. Jordan, a major supplier of Palestinian labour to the oil producing countries, uses labour also from Egypt and Pakistan. Sicilians move to North Italy and Germany, leaving their harvests to be collected by Senegalese. Mexicans move north for the harvest in the United States, while Guatemalans enter southern Mexico for the harvest there. The United States and Britain supply highly skilled labour to the Middle East. The movement of labour is thus an exchange of skills, a continual redistribution of a margin of each national labour force in response to changes in the geography of capital accumulation.

The Price of Labour Power

The orthodox explanations of worker movement usually turn on the 'over-production' of labour in some countries (the backward) and a 'scarcity' of labour in others.[2] But there is never a 'scarcity' of labour, only a scarcity of workers willing to sell their labour at a given price. In so-called 'population surplus' countries, there is rarely a real surplus; for example, in both India and China, a good harvest produces full employment, a 'labour scarcity' and rising agricultural day labourers' wages. The problem is employing people at an adequate wage all the year round; but so far as the system is concerned, the existing labour force is only the 'right size' for producing the existing output.

In the advanced capitalist countries, a number of factors have reduced the physical availability of labour power, the number of labour hours on offer per year, in the postwar period: a decline in the birth rate (reflected 15 years later in the new entrants to the labour force); a decrease in the number of hours worked per week; an increase in the holidays per year; an increase in the number of years of full-time education, or the conversion of apprenticeships

---

2   This phenomenon is usually related to apparently accidental changes in the birth rate, reflec-ted later in changes in the size of labour force. In fact, there is often no correlation with birth rates – for example, Greece, Spain, Portugal and Yugoslavia have the same sort of birthrates as those countries to which their nationals have migrated. 'Surplus workers' is the obverse of 'lack of the means to employ' (or 'capital deficit'), just as 'scarcity of labour' means 'excess of the means to employ' (implying an excess demand for goods or services, 'capital surplus'). But differences of this kind have existed for a very long time, so they can hardly account for particular movements of workers at particular times. There are many areas, in any case, with a 'capital deficit' but hardly any emigration. Furthermore, the argu-ment implies that it is the 'surplus' workers, the unemployed, who move, when frequently it is not. 'Scarcity' implies a general spread of unfilled vacancies in labour importing coun-tries, when such a situation never exists, only particular scarcities in particular trades. The argument also assumes that the existing labour force in destination countries is 'fully util-ised' when it never is nor could be outside the realm of theory. There are always sections of the population which could be employed if the wage and conditions offered were good enough – women working at home, people under the age of 15, the sick, invalided and retired. If the price of labour, the wage, were to rise high enough, it would induce a move-ment of workers out of low into higher paid jobs (as happened in Germany, France and the United States with agricultural workers in the 1950s and 1960s). Alternatively, jobs can be exported or subcontracted abroad, as today when the Lancashire millowners are trying to subcontract garment making to the Mediterranean countries (the 'outward processing' system). Thus, the occurrence of 'scarcity' or 'surplus' does not explain the movement of workers; on the contrary, it is the movement which alone gives rise to the invention of these terms.

to part-time education; earlier retirement, and, perhaps, the continued process of the decasualisation of the labour force.[3] On the other hand, there are factors working in the opposite direction – the end of the National Service in Britain or the draft in the United States, the remarkable increase in the number of women entering paid employment, immigration and temporary workers entering work from abroad; at certain times, the considerable increase in part-time work by the pensioned (offsetting the earlier retirement); the expansion in second and third jobs ('moonlighting'). How are we to explain these different changes, and the creation of specific 'labour scarcities'?

The price of labour power is determined by what Marx calls the socially necessary cost of maintaining and reproducing labour power; by 'reproduction', we mean not the biological creation of a baby, but the process of creating an adult worker from the age of 0 to, say, between 12 and 15 years of age. Marx's statement is applicable collectively, not necessarily individually – that is, the return to the working class for its labour power is determined by the costs of maintaining the working class and reproducing it. What is determined here is the value of labour power; actual collective wages may, to a greater or lesser degree, diverge from value, but will ultimately remain in some definite relationship to value.

---

3   In Britain, the numbers in higher education have roughly doubled every 25 years in this century. Between 1950 and 1970, numbers were doubling every eight years. On comparative expenditure and enrolments, see:

Increases in higher education (average annual growth rates)

	Years	Expenditure	Enrolments
France	1958–68	13.3%	9.8%
West Germany	1957–66	16.3%	5.0%
Italy	1950–65	15.0%	3.9%
Japan	1950–65	11.1%	6.9%
UK (England & Wales)	1950–66	9.6%	5.1%
US	1955–67	11.4%	7.5%

OECD OBSERVER, NO. 50, FEBRUARY 1971, P. 15

Decasualisation reduces the labour hours available if we assume that casual workers formerly took several jobs, and after being decasualised, remained in one job without working the same number of hours as they previously worked in more than one job.

What determines the 'socially necessary costs'? There are obviously many factors, but one of the most important for modern capitalism is the need to attain a given level of productivity by the labour force. Defining what is 'necessary' is obviously difficult, for the productivity of labour is a function not simply of the more obvious training and educational inputs, the quality of diet ensuring consistent concentration and discipline, the quality of housing ensuring the worker does not spend much of his or her attention worrying or seeking a roof, the condition of the worker's family, parents and children, so that he or she is 'free' to work fully, etc. There are factors relating to the possible exhausting or psychologically debilitating results of work – and an adequate level of recreation and leisure, and the facilities to pursue these, etc. Which of these elements are necessary, which optional extras?

In some backward countries, levels of productivity in particular plants can be pushed up to roughly the same level as those pertaining in an advanced economy, even though the labour force in the plant does not receive wages remotely comparable to similar workers in an advanced country, nor does he or she have access to anything matching the services available there. Does this mean the wages received and services available in advanced capitalism are not necessary? It does not. For while particular plants may emulate the same level of productivity, the society as a whole cannot; it can utilise a particular range of technical innovations, but it cannot generalise them, nor itself innovate.

Average labour productivity in the advanced capitalist countries has increased enormously over the past century. There has been a substantial but much smaller increase in the absolute level of real wages required to sustain the worker at these rising levels of average productivity. If we took the return to labour as a whole which, today, is much more than simply the wage, we could divide it into two elements: (i) the cost of maintaining the workers at a given level of productivity; and (ii) the cost of reproducing the workers' children so that, when they enter the labour force, they can attain a given level of productivity. While the first element has increased considerably over the past century, the increase is dwarfed by the growth in the second element. Leaving aside the family cost of rearing, the growth in the public sector inputs – through the expansion in educational, housing, welfare and medical services – has been very considerable, particularly in the postwar period (in practice, of course, it is exceedingly difficult to separate 'maintenance' and 'reproduction' in looking at the public sector services, and to separate these elements from the costs of the control and supervision of the population).

To deal with the average for a class is misleading. For much of the history of capitalism, the bottom third of the workforce has not been paid enough to meet the costs of reproduction at the average level of productivity then prevailing.

Some sections of the workforce have not been paid sufficient to meet the bare minimum costs of reproduction (the infant mortality rate, like the rate of deaths to women in childbirth, is a partial index of this). And at certain times, the wages of the lowest categories of labour have been insufficient even to maintain the worker, a factor producing increasing levels of malnutrition and, during epidemics, a very high death rate.

So far as the world labour force is concerned, this situation has not changed very much. For example, a recent study of Calcutta small firms shows that, if we assume the going day labourer's wage rate is the minimum subsistence and reproduction price of labour power, then both small capitalists and the family labour employed in their firms receive returns which are some 41 percent below what they should be – they are, as it were, 'committing suicide' by working.[4]

Thus, the labour force is a highly differentiated object. If we could imagine a national capitalism as an unchanging entity – output and employment, both absolutely and relatively, remaining constant – then the hierarchy of skill grades would persist indefinitely. Reproduction would consist in replacing a set number of workers of given skill by exactly the same number with the same skills. If reproduction costs were entirely born by the wage paid out to the worker through the family, then household incomes would form a hierarchy exactly corresponding to the hierarchy of skills and the hierarchy of productivities. Each skill stratum of workers would reproduce its successors in the stratum at the average costs of reproduction of labour at the level of productivity appropriate to the stratum. Of course, instability would arise at the base of the hierarchy if the price of labour power there was too low to ensure the reproduction of the numbers required. Nonetheless the main idea of a stable pyramid in which maintenance and reproduction expenditures are

---

4 The 1971 survey of 47,000 industrial units, employing between one and four workers, and covering 116,000 workers in all, showed:

1.	Value Added	Rs. 104 million
2.	Hired labour costs (at Rs.1,375 per year)	Rs. 66 million
3.	Imputed wage for employers and family labour	Rs. 93 million
4.	Profits	Rs. 55 million
5.	Actual return to employers and family labour	Rs. 38 million (or R8.559 per person).

(See Bose 1978).

proportional to the size and productivity of each stratum is the important element. In practice, there are no stable strata; the essence of capitalism is change, the continuous transformation of relationships and productivities so that the literacy of today is the illiteracy of tomorrow.

The Public Sector

The only purpose of the abstract exercise at the end of the last section is to allow us to identify more clearly what happens when the State intervenes to meet a major part of reproduction costs directly. Then the link between the wage received by the worker, the productivity on which we assume the wage is based, and the outlays incurred by the worker's family to meet reproduction costs is broken. Variations in productivity and wages are no longer directly reflected in variations in family expenditure on reproduction.

By necessity, the State must now set some average minimum standard for the provision of its services to ensure the proper reproduction of the labour force. Leaving aside social and political factors, it can only do so in relationship to some notional average level of productivity for the labour force as a whole. Even if it endeavoured to tailor its services to a more complex structure of productivities, since there is no guarantee that a given worker would work at the trade for which he or she had been raised – and in conditions of rapid change, the trade itself may have disappeared altogether by the time the child enters the labour force – setting an average minimum standard is the sole method available. Alternatively, the State could identify a special category of people for high productivity jobs and concentrate reproduction expenditure here. To a greater or lesser extent, in reality this does happen in particular services (for example, education), but there are political constraints on how far such a discriminatory system can be generalised.

The State assumes this role for a variety of reasons, one of which is that the speed of change and the nature of the skills required mean that the skills can only be transferred collectively, on a standardised basis; as capitalism develops, parents become increasingly poor instruments for transferring skills required in the future.

A powerful factor in determining what average the State chooses is competition. States compete with each other – indeed, the State is the single most important agency of competition in the world system. A factor identified as important in the State's ability to compete is the quality of its labour force. Public welfare programmes in Britain began with an official report on the quality of troops recruited for the Boer War – that is, the ability of the British State to compete in military terms with its nearest rivals was jeopardised by the poor physical quality of its young men.[5] In modern times, the output of graduates or toolmakers in the United States or the Soviet Union, as proportions of the labour force of those countries, become standards for all lesser powers. The argument was explicit in the British Labour Party's propaganda for the 1964 general election, and provided the justification for the Wilson government's programme to expand higher education rapidly. Thus, the level of labour productivity on the basis of which a programme for higher educational expansion was based was not the actual level of 1964, but an aspired level – the level thought to be necessary to keep up with or overtake the leading industrial powers of the world. Of course, the *intention* of the State is not the same thing as the actual performance; the British new universities may have been intended to produce engineering graduates, but in fact produced many more sociologists! Nor does the fact that the State had the intention mean that what it proposed is correct; it can and does make major errors of judgement.

The potential for mistakes when the State endeavours to establish a minimum requirement for reproduction costs is enormous. Such errors are compounded by the conflicts and rivalries rife within the public sector itself, by the competition for funds. For example, educational standards are not simply the product of a cool appraisal of what is required to meet certain levels of productivity (that is difficult enough); they are weapons by which, for example, the Ministry of Education endeavours to capture a larger share of finance and defeat rival agencies. There are pressure groups pressing on all sides: building contractors for hospital construction, universities for expanding higher education, MPs seeking favour for their constituencies, for their brothers and mates. Bribes and threats bend decisions to paradoxical conclusions. And beyond the narrow circle of power, from time to time, the class struggle itself reshapes government priorities.

In periods of growth and relative optimism, the State gambles by setting standards at high levels, even though, on strict calculations, this is not justified relative to the needs of the system at that time. In fact, the decisions may be errors even though expansion continues. In a number of backward countries, decisions to expand higher education in order to expand economic growth have merely produced an excess of graduates and the problem of educated unemployment.

---

5   The Report of the Inspector General of Recruiting, following the Boer War, noted 'the gradual deterioration of the physique of the working classes from whom the bulk of recruits must always be drawn' (cited in Titmuss 1958).

But there are other problems which arise. First, State intervention in this field imposes a rigidity upon the system which renders it much more inflexible when expansion changes into contraction. Expenditure on reproduction could, when the family was the primary spender, be varied with fluctuations in economic activity – wage cuts were reflected in a decline in family nutrition, for example. But public expenditure is an issue of public debate and public employment, issues discussed in conditions for a competitive political party system where, for example, demands for more housing are weapons in the battle to win elections. Large changes in public expenditure to stabilise the profit rate under the pressures of slump cannot be secured speedily without economic disaster, nor without political challenge. There are other rigidities in particular sectors; for example, workers hang on to their houses even when local unemployment rises, even though jobs are available in other areas where housing is not.

Second, the State's assumption of an *average* standard for the whole labour force is, from the viewpoint of the interests of the system, enormously wasteful. Advanced capitalist economies exhibit great unevenness of development. Parts of the economy operate at levels of labour productivity far below the average. It follows that the bottom strata of the workforce are 'over-educated' or physically 'over-maintained' for their role in the economy. This contradiction receives subjective expression in the unwillingness of workers, trained to work at an approximation to the average level of productivity, to work for wages well below the average. The price of labour power in the sectors where there are vacancies is below the rate of return which is appropriate to the costs of reproduction of the unemployed. For the unemployed to work at such a price would permanently jeopardise the chances of them ever working at the appropriate price. Thus, in the Greater London Council area in 1979, with the unemployment total standing at 130,000, there were severe labour shortages on London Transport, in the clothing, timber, metal goods, and electrical engineering trades, not to mention in the case of school canteen supervisors.

Third, the State institutes regulations to prevent the employment of minors, in part to protect the quality of the subsequently available adult labour force. This in turn reduces the contribution of child labour to household income, thus weakening the economic incentive to families to have children. The introduction of pensions for the aged removes another element in that incentive – that is, reduces the need to have a sufficient number of children to support the worker's old age. The results of this, in conjunction with the introduction of birth control techniques, have been a decline in average family size – and, in due course, a decline in the number of new entrants to the labour force (this decline has been partly compensated by an increase in the survival rate of children, a decline in infant mortality). There is a further factor, however, in the decline in family size. The intervention of the State produces not only standardisation of the publicly borne reproduction costs. The costs have been further increased by the transformation of household activity since the Second World War. The capital intensity of household activity has been advanced very rapidly, enormously boosting the productivity of household labour at the same time as considerably increasing the costs of the family unit. It appears that adult male wages have not increased commensurately with this process, so that today, the adult wage male wage cannot, as it was supposed to do in the nineteenth century, cover the costs of a wife and two children. Two adult wages now appear to be necessary to meet family based reproduction and maintenance costs. One result of this process has been the expulsion of housewives from the home to pursue paid – albeit, very low paid – employment. It should be noted in passing that the family can be no wiser than the State in assessing what is a socially necessary level of costs; parents perforce must, like the State, gamble. 'Keeping up with the Joneses' is thus not an eccentricity, but a primary mechanism of capitalist competition relative to the household.

In practice, the system heavily qualifies its commitment to an average standard for all. The labour supply to low paid worker sectors is identified by using special social criteria, by instituting a kind of 'caste identified' labour supply – certain occupations are reserved as temporary, for 'amateur workers' – the aged, school students (for example, newspaper delivery, Saturday morning shop assistants, etc.), students on vacation or looking for work, housewives. As is well-known, there are whole strata of 'women's jobs'. In the United States, a special category exists of 'native immigrants', that is, those who are by all ordinary legal criteria fully natives, but are treated as if they were not: blacks, Puerto Ricans, Chicanos, etc. However, the more sustained the process is to reproduce the whole population to a particular average level of competence, the more such groups resist the typecast employment, preferring to remain unemployed rather than jeopardise their long-term job prospects. Nor is this preference simply a function of the availability of social security support for the unemployed. Educated unemployment in Calcutta illustrates that people will fight to the bitter end to prevent their occupational downgrading, preferring starvation to indignity.

Sectors of 'Labour Scarcity'

What types of employment are affected by a general upgrading of the labour force? The factors at stake are not simply questions of the price of labour power if by that we mean the take home pay. It is rather the price of labour power relative to the intensity and conditions of work (which includes the danger, the physical hardship, the cleanliness, the noise, the tedium of work, the provision for paid holidays, the hours and shifts, the health and safety conditions, the quality of local facilities – housing, medical services, schools, creches, etc. – and so on). Industries with old plants and poor conditions exist everywhere, and survive because the overall costs of upgrading (as opposed to simply investing in a new machine) are higher than the expected rate of profit. Parts of the textile industry and plants in the old areas of engineering exemplify some of these factors.

There are other activities where price competition is severe and the workers poorly organised because of the structural conditions at work. Take, for example, catering, hotels and restaurants. If we assume for the sake of argument that in 1979 Britain, the Supplementary Benefit rate of £55.90 per week for a couple with two children represented a benchmark for the 'maintenance and reproduction' costs, a worker would have to earn £61.75 in gross earnings to reach this level. The lowest grade of non-service hotel workers received a weekly minimum rate of £40.40, rising to £42.80 (with, for London workers, an allowance of £2.40). Younger workers, employed on a seasonal basis, could expect £36 for a six day, 40 hour week in London (out of London young cleaners might expect £27.30). There are between half and three quarters of a million workers in this activity, 63 percent of them full-time, with average gross earnings in 1978 of £59.60 per week (or 8.5 percent below the 'socially necessary' level).

In construction and agriculture, seasonal work produces short-term demands for labour which cannot be met if the workforce is being simultaneously upgraded. In construction, as in the coalmines in Belgium and West Germany, the key factor is less the price of labour power alone, and more its relationship to the danger and hardship of the work.

At its base, the labour market fades away into outworkers; people, usually housewives, working at home at rates where there is no pretence at all to meet even the lowest maintenance wages, let alone an element for family reproduction. There are estimated to be a quarter of a million home workers in Britain. In Nelson in Lancashire, some 6,000 mainly Asian women sew ribbons and bows for the textile trades at rates equivalent to 10p per hour. Garment workers on a rate of 9 to 35p per garment can expect weekly pay of £20 to £25. Nineteenth-century conditions continue to flourish in modern capitalism.

Migration

When the system grew rapidly, masses of native workers were drawn into sectors where the price of labour power was relatively higher, sectors we have identified – somewhat oversimply – as those of higher productivity. Thus, agricultural workers in France, Germany, the United States and Japan moved in the 1950s and 1960s into urban industrial and service jobs. In the sectors vacated, equipment was substituted for labour on a considerable scale but without this eliminating labour scarcities. It is here that labour demand was created for workers from abroad.

Immigrant labour has been reproduced at costs below the average for the destination country. It was therefore subjectively willing, at least initially, to work for wages well below the average, or work at average wages in conditions inferior to the average. The picture is more complicated than this because in many cases, the immigrant worker was drawn from that minority in the backward country which had been reproduced at costs well above the local average. The wages on offer to the worker in his or her home country were fixed relative to the local average level of productivity, but were below those appropriate for his or her costs of reproduction, as assessed by the open world market. Thus, the excesses of the rivalries between States – the underproduction of 'low productivity labour' in the advanced, and the overproduction of 'high productivity labour' in the backward – receive some partial equilibration by the international movement of workers.

There are also important socio-psychological factors at work. Workers who grow up in a particular social environment, tend to absorb the defensive ethics developed by preceding generations to protect themselves from the ravages of capital. There are jobs they will not do, paces or hours or conditions of work they will not accept, moves from one locality to another that they will not make for the sort of wages and terms on offer. A worker torn out of this environment is much more appropriate to the needs of capital, much more ruthlessly driven to earn, whatever the wages on offer. Such a worker is less able to support himself or herself during unemployment by borrowing from local networks of relatives and friends, and less likely to have reserves on which to fall back in hard times, less likely to have possessions that can be sold or pawned. Such workers are likely to be much more responsive to differences in wages – regardless of conditions – and, lacking local social ties, much more geographically mobile in response to changes in the labour market. This – as well as overt discrimination – is a factor in the general picture of immigrants working longer hours, working more night shifts, doing more piece-work, with a higher rate of job changing and of geographical mobility than native workers.

It is also a factor in explaining what seems to be a more extreme mismatch between the qualifications of immigrant workers and the jobs they actually do. If the natives refuse to be downgraded even if this means the misery of long-term unemployment, the immigrants start in grades well below what the natives, with the same qualifications, would accept (of course, it is also true that at least at first foreign workers are more uninformed about what is locally considered reasonable, what alternatives exist, etc.; they may also be consoled by the fact that a poor job in an advanced country often offers better returns and conditions than a good job in a backward country). Some employers recognise this factor: migrants make the best workers; and they always try to recruit new immigrants since those who have lived for some time in the country are likely to have become 'spoiled', i.e. conform to local working-class standards.

Moveable Jobs

The import of labour is necessary where the price of labour power is too low to induce a sufficient number of workers to work in 'immoveable' jobs: that is, jobs which cannot, at least in the short-term, be relocated abroad. For example, local coal mines cannot be mined abroad, nor can local dustbins be emptied, local houses built, and local soils cultivated abroad, although in almost all cases, alternative supplies from abroad can be found. There is, however, no permanently fixed boundary between moveable and immoveable jobs; changes in comparative wage costs, in technology, and so on, can radically shift the boundaries.

Capital can gain access to labour power at prices well below those govern-ing in its home territory where jobs are moveable. Parts of manufacturing (for example, in the recent past, labour intensive parts in textiles, electronic com-ponents, television sets, etc.), some agricultural tasks, tourism, conform to this. States, recognising the dangers implicit in the dispersion of activity, sometimes impose regulations to prevent jobs moving; the US government, for example, does not permit US aircraft manufacture to move (but does permit imports). Export processing zones in South Korea, Malaysia, Brazil, the Caribbean, etc. have attracted industrial activities from the advanced countries, at the same time as these countries have exported labour. On Mexico's northern border In-Bond plants have been permitted, set up by United States companies to manu-facture consumer goods with raw materials and equipment imported from the States and Mexican labour; all the output is exported back to the United States. The In-Bond plant areas have thus been expropriated by the US labour market. At the same time, US nationals have started horticultural farms in northern Mexico to produce foodstuffs for the United States market. Finally, Mexico is a major exporter of labour to the States for farmwork and employment in textiles and services.

There are other examples of this kind, although not on such a large scale. Thus, India exports labour to the Gulf States, and Saudi Arabia finances vegetable farming in the Indian State of Andhra Pradesh, the produce being flown to Riyadh.

Firms with equipment and productivity standards derived from the advanced capitalist countries are able to transplant activities as isolated colonies to backward countries, providing the political context is right. Capital in the backward countries can then emulate the activity. But while productivity in the plants can be sustained at high levels, the general social average remains low. The workers in such plants are, as it were, 'home based emigrants'.

The Theoretical Significance

Access to foreign workers makes possible the continued growth of certain national capitals for three main reasons. Firstly, it allows more workers to be utilised by a given capital stock: the small farmer in the Punjab produces much more surplus value when he is imported to work in a foundry in Wolverhampton, and in doing so he is benefitting the capitalist class as a whole.

Secondly, the costs of reproduction of such labour are, as we have seen, less than those of the average labour in the advanced countries. Utilising it enables the capitalist to increase the proportion of the working day that goes in surplus to him rather than in the maintenance of the worker. Ideally then, from the point of view of profit maximisation, the native workers would be expelled to permit the lower cost immigrants to take the jobs. The absurdity of this idea illustrates clearly why the State cannot, in slump, pursue directly the accumulation of capital; on the contrary, it must sacrifice accumulation to social stability. The State consists of people, linked by social bonds to the rest of the population. Attempts to expel the natives would involve the State in political self-destruction. On the contary, the State must do the opposite, stressing the inviolable rights of the natives in order to direct blame at the foreigners.

Finally, apart from the effect of the import of labour on the long run decline in the profit rate, it constitutes a net subsidy from one national capital to another. The sending country bears the cost of reproduction of the worker from its domestic product; the destination country receives adult labour power without the costs that would be needed to raise and train the worker. The higher the skill level, the greater the subsidy involved in the transfer. The subsidy is between national capitals (it could also be called 'theft'), between countries. It does not necessarily benefit any individual employer who may employ the immigrant worker at the same rates as native labour. How far the destination country in fact is able to realise the full value of the subsidy varies, in particular with the terms of entry. Immigrants who settle and establish families, who draw on local public 'maintenance' services (including ultimately old age pensions) will, in time, reduce the net subsidy. The subsidy is maximised for single adult workers on temporary contracts without any right to participate in local reproduction and maintenance services.

Russia and Japan

The framework presented here does not have the same application to all movements of workers internationally. For example, in the oil producing States of the Middle East, some of the relationships are reversed. Backward Saudi Arabia imports labour from more advanced Egypt, as well as from Europe and the United States (but it also imports labour from more backward North Yemen). Reproduction costs for an important part of the Egyptian labour force were certainly much higher than those in Saudi Arabia at the beginning of the migratory movement. The 'raiding operation' is much more extreme – the loss to Egypt is the same as it would be in emigration to an advanced country, but the gain to Saudi Arabia is much greater.

The Soviet Union has a very highly educated labour force but poor levels of labour productivity. Does this refute the general argument presented here? First, a high level of reproduction costs is a necessary but not a sufficient condition for attaining high levels of productivity. There are many other factors at stake in productivity, including the volume and quality of equipment available to the workforce, the organisation of the capitalists (in this case, the State bureaucracy), and so on. Second, as the earlier discussion noted, the components of the conditions required for sustaining high productivity are very varied and cannot simply be reduced to education; they include adequate and easily available housing conditions, recreational facilities, and perhaps a given measure of 'social freedom', all elements notoriously poor in the Soviet Union. High educational levels alone would not make up for the generalised poor quality of existence for the average Russian worker.

The case of Japan is an interesting one. First, its public services are much inferior to other advanced capitalist countries, but the levels of productivity attained in its leading industries are well in advance of its nearest rivals. Second, its rates of economic growth have been spectacularly high without this generating the sort of specific demands for labour which impel immigration. There is virtually no immigration to Japan, although there is a significant minority of Korean immigrants in the country (left over from the Second World War and the partition of Korea, formerly a Japanese imperial possession).

Japan has reached the position of an advanced capitalist country very recently. Far from exhibiting labour scarcities, as recently as the early 1960s, the government was endeavouring to increase Japanese emigration by subsidising migrants to leave. In the mid-1950s, some 15,000 emigrated each year under agreements between the Japanese government and those of Brazil, Bolivia, Paraguay and Argentina, as well as those who moved to the United States (much as the Netherlands government encouraged emigration up to the mid-1950s in the belief that the country had too many workers). In the last half of the 1950s, 75,000 departed; in the first half of the sixties, 43,000; in the second half, 25,000 (there are said to be now 630,000 people 'of Japanese origin' in the States, 760,000 in Brazil). Second, the reserves of agricultural labour in Japan have remained intact until relatively recently as can be seen in this comparative table:

Percentage of the labour force in the primary sector

	1960	1970	1975
Japan	33	20	12.5
United States	–	4	3.8
France	22	14	10.8
West Germany	–	8	6.6
USSR	42	26	–
United Kingdom	–	3	2.5

(– = not available)

Thirdly, Japan is alone among the advanced capitalist countries in having a decrease in female participation rates as income has risen (from 50.1% in 1963 to 47.1% in 1973). This suggests that Japan has not exhausted its domestic labour reserves to the point where women's employment begins to increase. The poor level of public services also tends to keep a higher proportion of women at home; home based reproduction services must replace those of the State. Even today, in many companies women are still expected to retire at the age of 40, or, in some cases, on marriage, indicating that employers are not under pressure to keep women at work.

There are other indications of 'relative labour abundance'. Most workers still retire at 55 (although pensions are not payable until the age of 60). There is still a low rate of turnover in the large scale sector – employers are not bidding against each other for scarce skills. To some extent, the decline in labour hours available has not matched the other advanced capitalist countries – between 1960 and 1974, West German hours worked per week in manufacturing declined by 20% (from 48.8 to 39.1), Japan's by 5% (from 45.7 to 43.3 hours).

Japan's economy is, in comparison to its rivals, a fractured one – between a bloc of very high productivity modern industries of enormous scale, and a fluctuating mass of small enterprises, many of them subcontractors to the large firms, with relatively low productivity, low pay, little security of work and poor conditions. The high growth of the leading companies is purchased at the cost of the small enterprises.

In general, Japanese growth is achieved by a high concentration on certain key sectors, not by attempting to generalise performance on all fronts. The increase in reproduction costs required to support the advanced sector is not spread through society and there is much heavier reliance on the family (but not, of course, in education). The low level of public intervention in the provision of maintenance and reproduction services is thus much more characteristic of a backward economy than an advanced. There is no supplementary benefits system, unemployment pay is very low. Hospital and medical services are notoriously bad for the majority. There are few homes for the invalided or elderly. Housing is very poor and extraordinarily expensive; a 1978 survey showed that a quarter of households lived in tiny one room flats; a quarter of households had no bathroom; ten percent no running water; and two thirds were not connected to the sewerage system. Parks are rare (London has 22.8 square metres of park per head of the population; Tokyo has 2), as are libraries and museums.

In sum then, Japan is still arriving at the state where the State is obliged to seek to guarantee a minimum reproduction standard for the whole labour force. The obligation is also affected by the political context; the class struggle in Japan has never reached the point of forcing standardisation as happened in, for example, Britain immediately after the Second World War. The State in Japan has also no doubt delayed embarking upon this transformation as it observes the gambles undertaken in other advanced capitalist countries and their effect on gross investment[6] and thus the overall rate of economic growth.

Low public expenditure in Japan becomes another factor of competition in conditions of slump. The other advanced capitalist countries on the one hand press Japan to raise its public spending; on the other, they are tempted to try to sacrifice reproduction expenditure and lower their own rates of spending to the Japanese level. Meanwhile, South Korea and Taiwan seek to emulate the Japanese trajectory of growth, to Tokyo's alarm.

There is a final factor worth noting in connection with 'moveable' jobs. Japan's investment abroad – unlike other advanced capitalist countries – is mainly in backward countries. In particular, Japanese companies have invested heavily in certain sectors of production in South Korea, Taiwan, Singapore, Malaysia, etc. (in textiles, electronics, etc.). To some extent it may have widened its low priced labour pool to a greater extent than its rivals.

There is an enormous number of unanswered questions in examining the relationship between reproduction costs, labour productivity and immigration. But at least on a superficial level, Japan does not seem to defeat the main argument.

The Functions of Immigration in Primarily Destination Countries

When world capitalism expanded, migration to the core zones of the system made possible the performance of low productivity jobs important for the national economies concerned. Perhaps, without the remaining structures of protection, many of those jobs would have been 'exported', or reshuffling of

---

6 Distribution of the Gross Domestic Product, 1976:

	GNP per capita, 1976 ($US)	Public consumption	Private consumption	Gross investment
Japan	4910	9	57	33
US	7890	17	64	16
France	6550	13	62	23
West Germany	7380	18	55	24
USSR	2760	–	–	–
UK	4020	19	60	17

occupations would have made possible high growth without immigration. Be that as it may, the degree to which immigration was necessary depended upon the size of existing labour reserves (in agriculture, in home labour, etc.) and the rate and pattern of growth of the particular national economy concerned.

Native labour moved upwards to jobs, the return to which more closely related to the appropriate return to average levels of productivity. Once immigrant workers had been drawn in, they were able to follow native labour, depending upon how freely they were permitted to change jobs and sectors – out of construction, agriculture, mining, to former native strongholds, metal manufacturing and assembly. This in turn created new vacancies where they had formerly worked, necessitating new immigration. By now, the foreign born are roughly 6 to 7 percent of the population in most West European countries (the remarkably low figure for Britain – 3.3 percent – is a mark of the poor growth rate here); and possibly 9 to 10 percent of the local labour force (but 18.4 percent of the Swiss population). Between a fifth and a third of the labour force in the metal trades in Switzerland, Holland and Germany are immigrant workers.[7]

The situation in the United States is more complicated since it has the largest minority of 'native immigrants' (black people, Puerto Ricans, Chicanos, etc.). In the case of black people, there has been a sustained movement over a long period out of southern agriculture to metal manufacturing and steel production in the old industrial centres of the north and north east. Later, the expanding new industries of the west coast, and now the south (aircraft, electronics, science based industries, etc.) have attracted white skilled workers from the north and north east. Currently, the expansion of southern industry is for the first time since the Civil War attracting net black immigration. The possibility of immigrant labour moving up the hierarchy cannot be separated from the movement of 'native immigrants'.

Seasonal migration by agricultural workers is important in parts of Europe – for example, the movement of casual labour from southern Spain to southern France.[8] It is also important in the United States. The only contract labour

---

7   One estimate of the net subsidy from immigrant homelands to West Germany puts the figure for workers who have moved between 1957 and 1966, and 1968 and 1973 (there was a net outflow of foreign workers in 1967) at US$33 billion (1962 prices). Remittances returned to the homelands in the same period were US$8.8 billion. There are no estimates of the immigrant net contribution to West Germany's gross domestic product. Another estimate, solely for highly skilled and professional immigrants to Britain, Canada and the United States, 1961 to 1972, puts the subsidy at US$46 billion.

8   This migration increases shortages for casual labour during the harvesting in parts of Spain which encourages the larger farmers to buy labour saving equipment, which in turn increases

system for foreign workers still remaining there brings Caribbean workers to Florida's apple orchards each year. Elsewhere, illegal seasonal workers from Mexico plug the gaps left by the upgrading of the American labour force. In this case, not only does the farmer not meet annual reproduction costs since the work is paid only in the season of employment, he does not pay annual maintenance costs. In the case of illegal migrants, the farmer can pay wages below the legal minimum by using the threat, if the worker does not accept this, of denouncing him or her to the police and immigration service. Real returns to the workers can scarcely be much above what he or she might expect to earn in Mexican agriculture – if jobs were available. It is hardly surprising that there are too few native Americans willing to work for such pay even when there are high rates of official unemployment in the district concerned. Texan farmers, in trying to strengthen their case to the government against the imposition of fines on employers taking on illegal migrants, advertised 4,000 farm-hand jobs at the minimum legal hourly rate (then $2.20 per hour). They received only 300 applications from workers with legal status.

In Europe, it has often been argued that, in the absence of strict border controls, the flow of immigrants varies with the level of unemployment in the destination country – as unemployment rises, immigration falls. But this affects only legal movement. There are no useful figures on illegal movement. In the United States, it is argued that illegal migration has increased during the current phase of stagnation since 1974. This could represent a substitution of cheap labour for more expensive native workers. Or it could reflect changes in the structure of the labour market – a sharp contraction in the core metal using industries, without an equivalent decline in labour intensive agriculture, and possibly even an expansion in catering and restaurants (which could result from a big increase in tourism, for example). The same could be happening in Europe in the illegal sectors.

This illustrates that the demand for cheap labour power does not disappear in slump. On the contrary, it can increase. The British government has pursued policies of deliberate discrimination against black people in the name of its immigration policies, in defiance of the needs of the British economy, but it has made consistent concessions to permit the entry of European workers on work permits. Some 120,000 permits were issued in 1978. Any increase in foreign tourism increases the pressure of the restaurants and catering trades on the government to permit the import of labour. Nonetheless, last November the

emigration: 'to their paternalist relationship with the big landlords, has been added a further dependence on the European trade cycle' (Kayser 1971, p. 196).

government tightened the regulations to reduce work permits as part of its attempts to bludgeon native workers into accepting low paid jobs.[9]

The French government has recently cut residence permits for foreign workers from ten to three years, and now to one, affecting between half and one million north and West African workers. This was supposedly done to increase the job opportunities for the native unemployed. Yet a recent official report calculates that for every 150,000 foreign workers sacked, only 13,000 jobs become available for native workers. Indeed, we could go further and infer that, since French workers will not accept the wages on offer for most of these 13,000 jobs, important tasks in the economy will not be performed and one possible result will be an increase in native unemployment in other sectors dependent upon the performance of these tasks. The government's policy has little at all to do with unemployment – it is designed to incite racialism on the one hand, and lower public expenditure by reducing the cost of maintaining the unemployed by expelling them from the country on the other.

Immigrants provide a target in slump, a measure of flexibility made necessary precisely because of the rigidity of structure of modern capitalism. The expulsion of immigrants is a substitute for increasing the level of unemployment more dramatically,[10] even though it is deleterious to the economy. Between 1974 and 1977, the number of foreign workers in West Germany fell by 19%, and in France by 16%. Or take the example of the British merchant fleet between 1976 and 1979. Carrying capacity fell by 20%; the number of British officers fell by 5%, and of British ratings, hardly at all. The number of non-British ratings fell by 20%. Given the difference in wages between British and non-British ratings, this change must have raised labour costs per unit of freight carried – thus, the employers purchased the loyalty of British ratings at the cost of a decline in their capacity to compete internationally.

The function of immigrant labour depends on an accepted level of social discrimination; the exclusion of immigrants from the same rights as the natives is accepted by the natives without protest. It is this which makes possible

---

9   In a study of Cologne in Germany, a writer notes: 'the throng of foreign workers does not form a simple quantitative supplement, elastic by definition: on the contrary, it is for the most part an essential force in the economy because of the sectors of which it is in possession. For the main feature of immigrant manpower on the labour market is its practically irreversible specialisation: it seems out of the question that, even in a period of crisis, nationals should demand again for themselves jobs which have become considered inferior and abandoned to the foreigners' (Kayser 1971, p. 175).

10   It is for this reason that Böhning describes immigrant labour as a 'conjunctural shock absorber' (Böhning and Maillat 1974, p. 18).

the harassment of foreign workers by the State. Whether it is the obscene persecution at Heathrow airport, the manhunts in Texas or the border States, or the French police checking everyone with dark skins on the Metro, the aim is the same – to keep open the division between native and foreigner.

In the Middle East, these mechanisms are often more advanced. In Saudi Arabia, the regulations governing the mass of immigrant workers include a ban on strikes; employers are, in theory at least, fined for employing illegal immigrants; immigrants have no right to change their jobs without a passport check (drivers on intercity buses are supposed to check passenger passports). To add terror to the regulations, there are periodic mass expulsions – for example, 30,000 people called by the government 'Pakistanis' were expelled from the country en masse in March 1978. In the United Arab Emirates, under the July 1977 regulations, the government assumed the right to deport any foreign worker who disobeyed the orders of his or her employer, tried to organise a work stoppage, damaged production, assaulted an employer or representative, or committed any other serious misdemeanour. The aim of such regulations appears to be to force the solidarity of the native population by the continual demonstration of the 'disprivilege' of the foreigner. Such demonstrations are particularly required when economic contraction is continually reminding the poorest natives of their own misfortunes. Thus the panoply of intimidatory controls has nothing to do with the specific characteristics of the foreign worker concerned, but rather is related to the need to secure the loyalty of the natives. The argument that immigrants are the cause of the native response is of the same logic as blaming the poor for their poverty, the unemployed for being jobless, and so on.

Controls can work in a slump provided there is sufficient police power. But they do so with paradoxical results. First, they have negative effects for native employment (tending to raise native unemployment rates, and force natives into poorer paid work) and for the economy as a whole, leaving aside the waste involved in employing a bureaucracy and police force to implement the regulations. But secondly, regulations drastically reduce just that flexibility which is one of the main advantages of immigrant labour to capitalism. For example, in West Germany in the 1960s, 60 percent of Italian workers stayed for under two years, returning to Italy after that time. If tight border controls are introduced, foreign workers will not return to Italy for fear of not regaining re-entry to Germany – they are forced into permanent settlement, exile. And it then becomes politically difficult to expel them. Similarly, if the United States succeeded in controlling the Rio Grande border with Mexico, it would no doubt curb seasonal migration but increase the numbers permanently resident in the United States.

Singapore, being a very small territory with a powerful State, has apparently succeeded in operating tight controls. The city is an industrialised economy, based upon a mass of cheap labour (but the State maintains possibly the most advanced system of publicly provided reproduction and maintenance services in Asia, restricted to natives). Every expansion in the economy produces a shortage of labour in certain sectors – construction, ship repair (for men), textiles and electronics (for women). Immigrant labour fills the gaps, but under tight control – employers are permitted to recruit abroad, but remain responsible for their labour force. The State, with the close collaboration of the trade unions, ensures control to hold immigrant wages down, to prevent the labour market operating. Immigrants are used as the lever to keep down wages in general in the city for the mass of workers. Foreign workers are permitted to enter in the first instance for six months in construction; others, many of them young women, may not change jobs for three years, hold trade union office, marry or have children; they have no right to public housing, medical services or schools; those that ultimately secure permission to marry do so only on condition of signing a bond to accept sterilisation after the birth of their second child. The penalty for disobeying the rules is expulsion.

These regulations apply to those entering the city on work vouchers (granted to those earning below 750 Singapore dollars per month). They do not apply to the highly skilled, professional or business classes who are granted employment vouchers (for those earning 750 Singapore dollars or more). In 1979, the government announced a new policy to reduce or eliminate the island's dependence on immigrant labour, by trying to force an increase in the capital-intensity of production (that is, substituting equipment for labour by changing the industrial mix of the city's output). Companies utilising a great deal of labour are expected to leave the island, locating in the countries from which immigrants are drawn (the Singapore government is also trying to locate labour intensive industry on the Indonesian island of Batam). To achieve this aim, the government has proposed increasing wages for three years by 7 percent, plus 32 Singapore dollars. In fact this is a very small increase to achieve such a change; the Singapore Manufacturers' Association estimates the wage bill for its members at between 8 and 15 percent of total costs, so the increase will add only between 1.6 and 3 percent to costs. Of course, consistent with its record, even this small increase is not to be paid to the workers (lest 'they get used to high wages') but paid into the government Provident Fund. The payments can be stopped if the Singapore leadership decides the policy is in fact jeopardising the city economy.

In other countries which are expanding, the controls are much weaker. In the Middle East, governments have moved from accepting general immigration to, at least officially, tolerating only temporary project-related entries (and the employer in the project is required to remove the labour force from the country at the end of the project). But the labour market continues to operate. Workers escape from the project or take second jobs. In mid-1978, 5,000 Indians working for Engineering Projects of India went on strike when the company, under government pressure, tried to prevent moonlighting. EPI asked the Ministry of the Interior to deport 250 of its workers, and made a small pay increase to the rest.

In summary then, foreign workers are necessary when the system grows to compensate for the deficiencies of national planning (whether the planning is declared or not), to straddle the contradiction between the development of the State and the growth of capital. In slump, they are also necessary, but this economic function is subsidiary to their social role: they are the anvil upon which the loyalty of the natives to the existing State can be forged.

The Effects of Emigration on Primarily Sending Countries

If a State exports workers, labour power, on a significant scale in competition with other States, then the world labour market would begin to exercise an influence over the domestic production of labour, as the world market guides the domestic production of any other commodity. The more developed the export of labour, the more an exporting State would seek to control the lease or sale of labour power (to become a labour contractor or supervisory agent for labour contractors), to standardise its quality and tailor it to the specific vacancies abroad. To maximise its profits, it would need to minimise the costs of reproduction, ultimately to convert the economy to a manufacturing plant for breeding and raising workers. This might be done directly, or through the medium of the family, with State incentives and services being directed to induce the family to produce and train the numbers required (the family would then become, as it were, a private firm under the supervision of the State). It follows that such a State would have relinquished any ambition to create a diversified national economy in favour of filling one specialised niche in the world system.

At the moment, States 'pillage' their domestic labour forces – or permit them to be pillaged by other States – without paying attention to sustaining future supplies, much as capitalism ransacked pre-capitalist sectors in the early phases of its growth. But exporting States do seek to control emigration, to ensure certain levels of pay and remittances, and to supervise their nationals abroad to prevent conflicts which might jeopardise their competitive position. In particular, in east and south Asia, prices are partly set in relationship to competing States in the provision of labour to multinational employers for construction work in the Middle East or merchant seamen's jobs.

What are some of the immediate crude effects of large scale emigration for work? Some of them can be listed as follows: firstly emigration is drawn from particular districts, so that an important first effect is localised depopulation – as in parts of Eire, northern Portugal, Algeria, Lesotho, North Yemen, etc. Those leaving are workers in the most active age groups, so the effect of departures is magnified in the age group 15 to 35, and often, among the most skilled. Thus, the domestic labour force is stripped of its most decisive elements. Sometimes, emigration draws heavily on one sex, producing a sex imbalance, which has maximum effects on those in the reproductive age groups, reflected in a decline in the marriage and birth rates. Thus, not only is the present generation stripped, the next generation is jeopardised.

Secondly, the resulting shortage of skills can produce considerable labour scarcities in particular trades, and wage inflation. It is reported, for example, that the daily wage rate for masons in Pakistan used to be 15 rupees, but by 1979, under the impact of emigration of building craftsmen to the Middle East as well as a local house building boom financed from the remittances of workers abroad, the daily rate was 40 rupees. In North Yemen, large scale emigration has generated such wage inflation that now child labour can work as drivers at high wages. While this is good for low paid workers, it is catastrophic for local ruling classes with any ambition to speed capital accumulation. More generally it indicates a tendency for emigration to draw wages in the sending country up towards the level in the destination country, to create a single price in an international labour market.

A sequence of events in South Korea also illustrates this. In March 1977, Korean workers were involved in a three day riot at a Hyundai project in Saudi Arabia. President Park of South Korea intervened to raise the minimum pay level to (US)$240 per month. This in turn almost certainly encouraged more workers, particularly drivers, to opt for work in the Middle East. In May 1978, Park was obliged to raise the pay of Pusan bus drivers by 70% to discourage emigration, but without success since shortly afterwards he imposed a temporary ban on the recruitment of drivers for work abroad.

Thirdly, for some exporting countries, remittances from their nationals working abroad have become very important as sources of foreign earnings. Take three countries importing labour to Europe:

Remittances as a percentage of export earnings

	1970	1973	1974
Greece	54%	58%	35%
Portugal	55%	62%	50%
Turkey	46%	90%	94%

These cases are not as extreme as North Yemen which is said to be able to import one hundred times more than it exports.

Having workers abroad firmly yokes the growth of local incomes to growth in the centres of world production abroad. Contraction in the world system similarly has reverse effects. For example, the virtual end of European recruitment of Turkish workers – as well as a flourishing black market in remittance payments to Turkey – was a powerful element in the severity of the crisis in Turkey. Official remittances peaked at (US)$1.42 billion in 1974, and fell to $0.98 billion in 1978 (unofficial payments, 1973 to 1978, are put at just over $2 billion). The pressure of the Turkish government to be admitted to the Common Market and the EEC provisions for the free movement of labour are a measure of the despair of the Turkish ruling class – only by leasing its labour for exploitation by foreign capital can it retain its hold on Turkey.

Fourthly, while in theory remittances make possible industrial imports to accelerate domestic growth; in practice States have to offer incentives to persuade their nationals to return part of their earnings through the official markets. That means that the exchange rate must either give special advantages to those wishing to return remittances or permit the currency to float so that any advantage in operating on the black market is removed. Such measures make it extremely difficult to control national finance in the interests of capital accumulation. Furthermore, since workers abroad can buy foreign consumer goods, they will do so abroad unless they can buy such goods at home at the same price – thus, incentives to repatriate earnings include the 'liberalisation' of the import of consumer goods. This further reduces the chances of building national industry on an import substitution basis.

Finally, in general, emigrants regard home as merely home, not a place where they can use their foreign earnings to set themselves up as small capitalists (an illusory aim, given the relatively small earnings they individually make). Thus, remittances converted into local currency are used to buy land for house-building, to build houses and buy consumer goods. One result is, as noted

earlier, inflation in the construction industries. In sum, the districts of emigration become dormitory suburbs or country cottages of workplaces abroad,
places where foreign earnings are consumed not where productive activities
are improved.

These elements indicate some of the pressures on world labour demand
that restructure labour exporting countries, making even more difficult any
independent strategy for national economic development. In practice, States
react empirically, adjusting policy step by step without being conscious of the
overall drift until it is too late to reverse the process. Their preoccupations are
more directed at supervising the return of remittances.

The power of the State over nationals outside its frontiers is limited. At most,
it can withold the renewal of passports, seize property left behind or punish relatives. But abroad, no international policy yet exists to trace recalcitrants in the
way, at least in principle, stolen goods can be traced. Usually, documentation
is its sole power, which explains in part efforts made to enforce the necessity
to travel with documents, to eliminate the possibility of undocumented movement.

Other measures are taken to strengthen control. Where local companies
employ local labour on contracts abroad – as happens with Korean, Turkish
or Greek construction companies in the Middle East, or Mexican construction
companies in Venezuela – controls can be tight. The State can penalise the
company. In turn the company handles the transport (and keeps the return
ticket until the worker is instructed to return), housing, feeding and supervision
of the worker. The South Koreans stiffen this control by appointing, in charge
of each gang of workers, a volunteer craftsman demobilised from the army for
the purpose of supervision.

Such controls require local capital to be developed enough to act as employer. For the Philippines, this is not usually the case. The government has
therefore moved towards leasing labour in groups to foreign employers. Hirers
of labour are required to sign a contract with the government guaranteeing
certain conditions and accepting an obligation to return a certain proportion of
foreign earnings to the Manila agent directly (that is, not through the worker).

Regulations on remittances vary widely, as does the power to enforce them.
South Korea demands remission of 80% of foreign earnings. India requires, in
theory, 10%. Filipino workers abroad are required to return 40% of earnings,
and 70% if they are seamen. Pakistan demands that 20% of the earnings of
professional and technical staff be paid to the State as tax, but it has little or no
power to enforce this.

The People's Republic of China has recently entered the market by permitting provincial governments to offer Chinese labour to foreign employers for

work abroad. Guangdong province has recently published details of its proposals in Hong Kong. It offers 'unlimited numbers' of workers, aged 18 to 35, to work a 48 hour week, with three days holiday per year. The government promises that its workers will be 'diligent and obedient to the employers' reasonable instructions and work assignments'. Workers will receive free board and travel; they will be given 10% of their total earnings (which should be between £69 and £104 weekly) as pocket money while abroad, and 10% on the termination of the contract, the rest presumably accruing to the Guangdong or Chinese governments.

Perhaps the Chinese are copying the Philippines government which has developed a marketing strategy for what is known as 'the export of warm bodies'. The Overseas Development Board of the Ministry of Labour circulates glossy brochures to multinational companies proclaiming the superior character (and very low cost) of this 'prized living export', 'the best bargain in the world labour market'. The government lays out its terms and promises, on signature of the contract, to 'package and deliver workers to various worksites round the world'.

In conclusion, then, the national organisation of the sale of labour power is, at the government level, already well organised. Private labour contractors tout their wares round the globe and have done so for much of the history of capitalism, but State organisation – with a close eye on the balance of payments – is relatively new. If the process were to persist, sooner or later States would have to intervene in the reproduction process to ensure continued supplies and proper maintenance.

Conclusion

International migrants are a particular stratum of the world working class, embodying the contradiction between a world economy and its national political and social organisation. Relative to the national ideologies which dominate the world, they should not exist at all. Endeavouring to eliminate them, regardless of the damage thereby inflicted upon the world economic system, is part of the self-destructive drive of capitalism in crisis: the growth of world production is sacrificed to the maintenance of class rule.

The legal migrant is still a person. Although frequently oppressed, immigrants are still in an infinitely superior position to those who dare to move without a licence: the illegal migrant and the mass of refugees. Since these people belong to no ruling class, any barbarity may be inflicted upon them. They can be treated as cruelly as those lost peoples encompassed by the expanding modem national State: the Red Indians, the aborigines, the no-mads.[11]

The ruling classes of the destination countries seek to stabilise their national power at the cost of the world system, at the same time as borrowing or stealing the labour forces of more backward ruling classes. There is a strikingly vivid model for a different method of achieving similar results. South Africa reclassified the majority of its natives as foreigners, nationals of a set of hastily run up independent States, the Bantustans. To do this, the distinction between 'labourer' and 'labour power' was vital, as the Minister of Mining explained in 1965: 'They [black workers] are only supplying a commodity, the commodity of labour ... [I]t is labour we are importing and not labourers'.[12] Apartheid, insofar as its aims in the field of labour were actually achieved, secured the purpose of offloading the costs of the reproduction of black labour to the Bantustans while retaining access to the labour power of adult workers. It also prevented black workers seeking to emulate the reproduction costs of white South Africa. Its viability depended upon being able to maintain a divided economy, between a majority low productivity sector and a minority high productivity sector. It has analogies with Japan. Insofar as this structural condition is superseded, apartheid comes to act as a powerful constraint on the growth of South African capitalism.

No issue today so sharply differentiates revolutionary internationalists and national reformists as that of the international migration of workers. The issue at stake is a challenge to the very existence of the national State and its prerogatives in the control of a territory and the inhabitants. Much of the politics of the Left is concerned with gaining control of the State and accelerating the growth of its power over its inhabitants, not with abolishing the State. Deploring the ill treatment of immigrants is seen not as an attack on the powers

---

11   Compare Victor Serge's observation on the exiled: 'I have witnessed the birth of the enormous category of "stateless persons", that is, of those men to whom tyrants refuse even a nationality. As far as the right to live is concerned, the plight of these men without a country ... can be compared only to that of the "unacknowledged man" of the Middle Ages who, since he had no lord or sovereign, had no rights and no protection either, and whose very name became a kind of insult' (Serge 1963, p. 373).

12   And once their labour power was exhausted, they must carry their bodies off, out of the territory of the State. General Circular no. 25 of 1967 stipulated that: 'as soon as they become, for some reason or another, no longer fit to work or superfluous in the labour market, they are expected to return to their country of origin or the territory of their national unit where they fit in ethnically (even) if they were not born and bred in the "Homeland"' (cited in Andrews 1979).

of the State, but as an argument for ending all immigration. Demands for a 'humane immigration policy' rival the fantasies of 'send capital to the countries from which the immigrants come, not immigrants to the countries where capital exists'. If the Left had power to direct capital to new locations, it has the power to abolish capital. In the United States, it is part of the Left which stresses that illegal immigrants menace only the oppressed but native groups – blacks, Puerto Ricans, women – and that, to protect these groups, illegals should be expelled. Yet to permit the expulsion of illegal immigrants is to take one step nearer to the expulsion of immigrants, which in turn is a step closer to the expulsion of selected sections of natives. That way madness lies. Accepting the right of the State to control immigration is accepting its right to exist, the right of the ruling class to exist as a ruling class, the right to exploit, the 'right' to a world of barbarism.

In South Africa, the white trade unions allied with the State for immediate gains to a minority of workers at the expense of the majority. It is the AFL-CIO which campaigns more consistently for the rounding up and expulsion of illegal Mexican workers; they 'permit' US business to locate across the southern border to use cheap Mexican labour, but refuse to follow them to recruit Mexican workers and establish parity of wages on both sides of the frontier (a demand which would of course bring them into direct collision with the interests not only of US business but also the Mexican ruling class, also dependent upon cheap labour). It is the British TUC which continually presses for an end to the issue of work permits, an aim which, if achieved, would rob the TUC leadership of the opportunity of banquets in expensive London hotels. While it is the labour movement which leads the attack on foreign workers, employers may sleep quietly in their beds: whatever the secondary quarrels, the unions accept 'the national interest', the employers' interest, that this is the best of all possible worlds.

The Economics and Politics of the Free Movement of People*

The development of modern industrial capitalism has always involved large-scale migration at various times. Where the population was historically settled – especially in the great river basins of Asia – was not where the modern economy, including its agricultural dependencies, developed. At least 10 million slave workers were moved from Africa to the Americas between the seventeenth and nineteenth centuries,[1] and when that transfer was ended, indentured labour systems moved Indians and Chinese to Africa, to Malaya, Ceylon, Australia, North America and the Caribbean. Much of this movement was developed to initiate and expand the supply of the raw materials, mining and plantation output (or to build the means to transport this output) required to feed the voracious appetites of the new industrial machines of the developed countries. In the same way, workers were moved within colonial territories for the same purpose – from central to southern Africa for the mines, from Eastern India to the tea estates of the northeast and the coal and iron mines of Bihar and Orissa – as within North America they moved relentlessly westward to open the prairies to cattle and grain.

Meanwhile, masses of Europeans were freely moving to the Americas, to Australia and to South Africa, Rhodesia and Kenya. Late nineteenth-century European expansion could not be sustained without people moving from the periphery – Poland, Italy, Spain, Ireland – to Europe's heartlands of Germany, France, Belgium and Britain.

It was not a smooth process. The fluctuations in the demand for workers followed the surges of growth and contraction in the new world economy. But if anyone had suggested in, say, 1910 that migration was an unusual phenomenon, they would have been regarded by any knowledgeable person with astonishment.

---

* From: Antoine Pecoud and Paul de Guchteneire: *Migration without borders*, UNESCO/Berghahn, Geneva, 2007, pp. 33–50.
1 There have been debates surrounding the exact figures. The number of slave workers is often estimated to have been somewhere between 10 and 15 million, although other sources speak of 25 million.

What interrupted the process of long-term growth, which required insistently that a margin of the world's labour force move, was the Great Depression, the years of stagnation between the two World Wars, and the bitter wars fought between the Great Powers, disciplining each national population to a loyalty that could only embed an institutionalised and popular xenophobia. There were still movements in the rest of the world, local booms, but the overall picture in the heartlands of the system was stagnation. In North America, as unemployment rose in the US, the Mexican flow to the north dried up: failing labour demand accomplished far more effectively what xenophobic legislation by Congress to ban immigration had failed to achieve.

However, after the Second World War, economic growth resumed on an unprecedented scale and with an unprecedented geographical spread. Large-scale worker movements became inevitable. Part of this continued the former process of opening up sources of raw materials, as with the expansion of oil centres from the 1970s leading to migration to the Gulf and Iran, and to Libya, Nigeria and Venezuela, along with continued migration to South Africa and to Malaya/Malaysia (with its rubber and palm-oil estates). But there was also another movement, with a much wider recruitment area: to the old industrial centres of the world in Europe and North America. This migration enabled the native-born to upgrade out of, for example, agricultural labour, construction, transport and then manufacturing. Later, following the first major postwar recession (1973–5), when governments in Europe endeavoured to close this supply, rapid industrialisation in the 1980s and 1990s in a number of developing countries in Asia again stimulated new movements – of Javanese to Malaysia, of Burmese to Thailand and Thais to Singapore and Taiwan (and, for other reasons, to Israel), of Korean Chinese to the Republic of Korea, and of Filipinos to Taiwan and elsewhere. As its economy restructured towards services, Japan (which, during the days of its most rapid postwar growth, could rely on substantial reserves of native-born workers in agriculture) attracted increasing flows of low-skilled Chinese and highly skilled Taiwanese (among many others). At the same time, Japanese companies spread their manufacturing plants through South-East Asia. South Koreans were doing something similar – importing workers and exporting manufacturing plants. So ingenious are the labour brokers handling this business, like termites boring channels through migration control barriers, and so unpredictable are the patterns of growth, the observer is always a few steps behind.

However, demography's picture of migration – even if the data were reliable, which they cannot be – conceals the immense and all-important changes in the composition of flows in terms of skills, age, gender, etc. The Middle East is interesting here, because in a fairly short time span we can see a shift from the immigration of relatively low-skilled (but literate) men working in construction, agriculture and basic industry to those with a higher level of skills (and who bring their families) working in processing industries, management (including government) and maintenance, and to service workers, particularly maids (so the labour flow is feminised). It seems clear that the specific nature of labour demand, as managed by labour brokers and facilitated or obstructed by governments, determines who is selected to migrate; it is not at all a blind process. It follows that the scale and composition of migration will continue to change as the world economy continues to restructure (since innovation is now built into the very core of the system) and the location of its key points of activity changes.

As one would expect in a world economy characterised by local specialisation, the emergence of a world labour market is encouraging some countries to specialise in providing particular types of worker (as well as particular types of goods and services). The Philippines is an advanced example, supplying the world with maids (facilitated by the competence of Filipinas in English), nurses and merchant navy personnel. India and a number of other countries are beginning to specialise in the supply of medical doctors, engineers and information technologists. Of course, this is not new – 150 years ago, a great number of the engineers working the steamships and ports round the world were Scotsmen (just as laundries in the US were run by Chinese, ice-cream making and selling by Italians, etc.).

However, the present resumption of migration flows to the developed countries is not simply a recurrence of past surges in the redistribution of the world's workforce (and in any case, relative to the world's population, the margin redistributed is still very small – under 3 percent or 150–200 million). Today, the surface of the world has been cut up into national territories, each part fenced to include some and exclude others, all in the name of the defence or affirmation of sovereignty and its psychic reflection, national identity. Thus, migration – of foreigners – becomes a major *political* issue: it affects the pretensions of sovereignty and national identity. Yet it does so when we are already well set on the process of globalisation – the opening of national economies to flows of trade, capital and people, and the results of this in the restructuring of national economies to accord with new global patterns of economic specialisation. In migration, we are in the midst of a process of transition from closed or semi-closed labour markets to a world labour market, with continual contradictions between the changing nature of domestic labour demand (itself reshaped by new specialisations) and a world supply of workers, facilitated by the growth of a literate labour force in developing countries, a radical decline in transport costs and no less radical reforms in developing countries releasing large numbers of workers for domestic migration.[2] China offers a vivid illustration of this.

In the old order of national economies, the political boundary was assumed to coincide with the economic, and the economy was, as we have noted, relatively self-sufficient – neither imports, foreign capital nor immigrants were, supposedly, of decisive importance. However, in the newly emerging order, national output is the product of world interactions and no government can aspire to self-sufficiency in either the production of goods and services or capital; rather each government is concerned with managing flows that start and end beyond its authority and often its knowledge. Such a system requires growing mobility – of business people, students, tourists, consultants – within which it is almost impossible to identify those who wish (or might come to wish) to work without permission. In the field of labour, the instincts of the old national workforce planning and self-sufficiency in local supply collide with the imperative for economic growth.

Immigration policy has historically dealt with actual or potential settlers rather than transient workers. In important senses, it forced transients into exile from their home country if they wished to protect their access to work. Today, insofar as policy deals with migrant workers (and for many countries, family reunification still provides the bulk of immigration, although this is changing), it is a form of workforce planning – estimating future demand by skill level and setting quotas on the numbers of workers to be admitted in a given period for a set time. Such a policy approach has all the negative aspects of central planning. The unexpected fluctuations of a dynamic economy cannot be accommodated (as was shown so painfully in the misestimation of required information technology specialists just before the collapse of the 'dot.com' boom); the delays and costs of bureaucratic processing are notorious.

The political demand that we rely on a self-sufficient national economy is constantly being revived, most recently in support of an educational and training policy that will make skilled immigration unnecessary. It is a significant aspect of this argument that it presents the options as alternatives – either educate the native-born or encourage immigration – rather than as being complementary. To make such an approach effective, it was proposed that Californian software companies should be required to pay a significant fee to employ an immigrant worker; the proceeds, it was said, would be used to finance US-born students to train in the same fields. In fact, as the employers noted, there

---

2   Martin et al. 2000, pp. 149–52.

was no evidence that labour shortages in the US were the result of a lack of funds to finance US-born students; their preferences for particular disciplines was not determined by available finance. Thus, the fee was better regarded as an economically unjustified tax on employing foreigners. In fact, the preparation for large-scale immigration of highly skilled workers into the US proved quite unnecessary – the collapse of the dot.com boom showed that had American students been successfully induced to study software programming, there would now be a much higher rate of unemployment. Two lessons seem appropriate here. Employers should be allowed to recruit directly, bearing the costs and risks of their activity. Second, education and training policies cannot be governed by short-term fluctuations in the employment market without grave errors of policy. The reason for doing so is simply the desire not to use the world labour supply to ease the flexibility of the domestic labour market, which, in current circumstances, must lead to negative effects on domestic employment.

Workforce planning requires a closed or semi-closed economy. In an open economy, compensatory movements across borders are constantly nullifying domestic policy changes or leading to perverse outcomes. Thus, the attempt to make planning of the labour force effective requires the control of irregular movement. On the one hand, this would entail considerably greater internal police controls to check those who work while on a visa that does not allow this or has expired (in fact, it seems governments are unwilling to risk popular hostility to enforce this). On the other hand, borders would become militarised, brutalised and criminalised, and the asylum system would be effectively wrecked in pursuit of 'economic migrants'. In Europe and North America, we are within sight of restoring the border fortifications – backed by state terrorism – that divided East and West Germany in the Cold War: now between Poland and the Ukraine, Hungary and the Ukraine, Spain and Morocco (and, on occasions, between France and Britain), and between Mexico and the US. The fortified borders represent a permanent war against the compensatory imperatives of the labour market and its attempt to meet the demand for low-skilled workers – with the same discouraging results as the US war on the narcotics that Americans so insistently demand to consume.

Temporary migration – already a major force in irregular movement might seem to be some remedy here if there were not such a prejudice against it. The negative model is seen as the German guest-worker programme of the 1950s and 1960s, where large numbers of supposedly temporary workers were invited but proved impossible to remove at the end of their contracts – their human rights prevented expulsion. Yet this is far from what happened. The majority of workers, in fact, did leave Germany (emigration data do not allow us to say how many returned to their homes). Of those that did not, they stayed not simply because of their preferences or the moral constraints of the German authorities, but because of the wish of employers to retain workers (particularly experienced ones) when it was clear no more immigrants were to be available, and the agreement of the government to this. Thus, immigration controls were themselves crucial in forcing immobility – exile – on guest workers. Of course, moral constraints exercised a role – and the negative political appearance of enforcing expulsion – but these were of lesser significance than the economic interests of the participants.

In the 1990s, there was a rapid growth in immigration through family reunification and asylum seeking. In policy terms, however, the crucial factor in the late 1990s was that the developed countries decided they could not compete in information technology without expanding their skilled workforce – they entered a competition to persuade IT workers to come to them. It was a startling reversal of the policy that had been entrenched in Europe for two and a half decades: a ban on new primary immigration, and a change in the emphasis on family reunification as the primary criterion for immigration (Canada and Australia, however, had long sought recruits by skill). However, the partial relaxation in the US only underscored the inequality of the migration regime. As in South Africa's apartheid system, the skilled 'whites' have the right to migrate, while the low-skilled remain, supposedly, tied to the soil of their birth, denied the opportunity to escape poverty.

A Little Theory

The theory of international trade turns upon the proposition that where there are differences of factor endowment (raw materials, labour, capital, entrepreneurship, etc.) between countries or localities, disproportionate economic gains will result from exchanging factors. This is well-known in trade and is the rationale for the liberalisation of the world trading economy – it allows us to understand the high growth rates in activities in Special Economic Zones, border regions, off-shore, etc. But is the same proposition true of migration?

It would seem intuitively that it is and that, accordingly – to turn the proposition round – great losses are incurred by the world by sustaining barriers to labour mobility. A number of studies have endeavoured to put some figures on these losses, or – the other side of the coin – the gains from decontrol. Hamilton and Whalley in a pioneering study using 1977 data suggested, on set assumptions, that gains to the gross world product (then US$7.8 trillion) from lifting migration controls could range from US$4.7 trillion to US$16 trillion.[3] Recent reworking of more up-to-date figures confirms these outcomes.[4] UNDP presents a different calculation of more limited changes.[5] Walmsley and Winters offer a model in which worker migration to employment in services in developed countries equal to 3 percent of the developed countries' labour force would yield benefits of US$156 billion, shared between developed and developing countries, compared to the estimated US$104 billion generated by a successful outcome to the Doha trade round (and the roughly US$70 billion granted in aid to developing countries by the OECD group).[6]

The direction of change – and its size – is important, even if the precise figures turn upon the assumptions that have been made. But workers are not commodities in a very important sense. They may be abstract 'labour' within an economy, but they are also part of society (citizens) and of a polity (electors, the embodiment of national sovereignty), apart from the detail of being human beings as well! Economics gives us a valuable perspective on some matters from one restricted angle, but it does not tell us how people will behave in general. The migration of foreigners can provoke astonishing fears. It may be demonstrable that the economic dislocation caused by immigration is far smaller than that caused by changes in trade patterns or capital movements, or by domestic changes in the supply of labour (for example, the entry of the postwar 'baby boom' generation to work, or the large numbers of women who entered employment in the postwar period), but the fact that migrants are foreigners, speak strangely, are of different physical appearance, etc., may prompt people to oppose them: regardless of any real losses to their welfare.

The social issues are well-known and are not the subject of this chapter. However, the problems of adjusting to higher levels of mobility need to be acknowledged – in particular, we must consider the rights attached to citizenship (voting rights, the right to participate in the exercise of sovereignty, etc.), the different degrees of 'temporariness' of temporary workers and the rights attached to their status, and the transition between these two. Issues of accommodation and services raise similar questions. In the past, migrant workers have often been housed by employers – and often in very bad conditions (for example, the hostels for single men in apartheid South Africa) that undermine the standards of housing of the poor in general. In principle, the problems are no different from those of maintaining minimum standards for the native-

---

3   See Hamilton and Whalley 1984.
4   Iregui 2005; Moses and Letnes 2004.
5   UNDP 1992, pp. 57–8.
6   Walmsley and Winters 2005.

born (given, in some cases, different cultural practices), but the foreignness of workers can complicate any resolution. In an open housing market, poor immigrants tend to concentrate in areas of deprivation and then, quite unreasonably, become blamed for the deprivation. Again, in principle, the issues are no different for the native-born poor, but xenophobia – and the quality of political leadership – can turn such issues into intractable political issues, rather than questions of the quality of housing.

However, xenophobia or not, the emerging problems of labour supply are going to force some confrontation between the different dimensions of perception and discussion. Take Europe as an example.

Europe's Labour Market: The Supply of Workers

There are a number of self-reinforcing factors of relevance here:

1. The size of the European labour force over the next half century is set to decline – in 2005, over a third of Europe's regions face a declining size of workforce. The process of contraction will be exaggerated as the generation of the postwar 'baby boom' enters retirement.
2. However, within this projection there are other indications that show a more dramatic contraction in the available working time on offer:
    (i)   An increasing proportion of working life (defined as the years between the ages of 15 and 60/5) is being devoted to education and training – thus simultaneously reducing the available work time and radically reducing the number of people available for jobs requiring less than a university education.
    (ii) An important part of the existing labour force is not engaged in paid or recorded work, but has retired early, lives on disability pensions, or in other ways has withdrawn from work. The size of this underutilised workforce ranges from between 18 and 22 percent of the labour force in Sweden to 40 percent in Italy. This is not necessarily unemployment. The mark of an increasingly wealthy society is that people can afford to work less. On the other hand, such workers may be working in the black economy or other statistically unrecorded sectors, or may work unpaid in caring for the elderly, for the young, for the disabled, etc.
    (iii) A changing mismatch between the output of domestic training systems and the demands of a rapidly restructuring national economy is made worse by the aggravated lags in reshaping training systems.

(iv) The working life, year, week or day are all tending to contract with growing wealth.

These trends coincide, in some cases, with high levels of unemployment (and especially of long-term unemployment), a sign of a mismatch between labour demand and supply (or also a lack of complementary low-skilled workers). Within the European Union, this allows areas of high labour scarcity to coexist with those of high unemployment (or non-employment). Nor do Europeans seem willing, or not in sufficient numbers, at least, to move from one European country to another. Figures for the proportion of internal migrants to population in 1999 put it no higher than 0.2 percent.

The result of this combination is peculiarly damaging – growing labour deficits with a significant under-utilisation of the existing workforce. Assessing labour shortages is difficult, but we have some estimates for 2000–3 in the OECD *SOPEMI* report of 2003.[7] It is interesting to note that, contrary to government assessments of what shortages they should respond to, it is the shortage of low-skilled workers that is most often mentioned. In many of the activities with high vacancy rates, the rising average age of the workforce, promising high rates of retirement in the short-term, indicates a failure to recruit adequate numbers of new entrants despite rising relative wage levels.

In the short-term, the deficits are already affecting the performance of the European economy and the capacity of governments to meet current objectives, thus affecting electoral prospects.

In the medium term, the picture is very much worse. Ageing, apart from the other factors cited, will increase the reduction in the size of the working population at the same time as the demand for age-related labour-intensive services increases.

Government Responses

Despite the dangers of a negative political reaction, governments have made some attempts in terms of raising the discussion of increasing the retirement age, reducing the disincentives to work (encouraging housebound women to enter work, encourage those who have withdrawn to return) and raising the costs of leaving work, increasing training facilities to meet the requirement of

---

7 OECD 2003, pp. 124–5.

mid-level occupations, and increasing productivity. In the Lisbon Agenda, the target is set of raising European participation rates to 70 percent by the year 2010.

However, while the deficits are urgent and immediate, the remedies take much longer. Thus, alongside these measures there have been changes to ease the issue of temporary work permits, and not just for the highly skilled. There are schemes covering seasonal agricultural workers, working holidaymakers, work-experience schemes, contract workers and cross-border commuters. More importantly, the principle that migrant workers can be employed again has been established in practice even if political leaders have yet to set about convincing their electorates.[8]

The changes being introduced will, however, be insufficient to cope with future scarcities, particularly given the intensified competition for some types of workers – for example, nurses from the Philippines, Bangladesh and the Caribbean.

Nor is the search for labour necessarily consistent with other government priorities. The British 'working holidaymakers' scheme, originally directed at the old British Commonwealth dominions but now expanded, collides with British aid policy's promise not to recruit scarce middle-level skilled people from, for example, South Africa. In addition, occupationally specific quotas do not allow for the inclusion of non-specific, self-employed activities. Immigrants are over-represented in self-employment,[9] and have famously saved from extinction retail outlets, corner shops, newsagents and cafes, in poor city neighbourhoods and in provincial towns, and seem now to be doing the same in rural localities (Greece is reported as a prime example of this last phenomenon). Such workers are not included in the current quotas.

Europe and North America are aspiring to be providers of highly skilled services and innovative technology to the rest of the world. However, as noted earlier, even if low-skill tradable sectors are relocated to developing countries, the high-skill economy will require a cluster of low-skill and non-tradable support services to be effective – from cleaners to retail trades, construction, transport, and domestic and caring services. The task, even in this extreme

---

8 As Papademetriou writes: 'one of the issue's unfolding (and fascinating) paradoxes is watching how mainstream political leaders who have sought to accommodate the minority appeal of xenophobic impulses by adopting restrictionist rhetoric and policies will deal with the emerging realisation that immigrants are fast becoming demographically and economically indispensable' (2003, p. 9).

9 OECD 2002, p. 65.

case, is to make such services affordable to the mass of the population without requiring high levels of taxation that, even if politically possible, stimulate the emigration of both the highly skilled and of business. In practice, the outcome is likely to be less sharp than this since irregular migration will meet the deficits with whatever incidental costs this incurs.

Migration and the Poor

It is a persistent theme in much of the economic literature on migration that employers and the better-off (who can afford maids, etc.) gain from the immigration of the lower-skilled, and that it is the lower-paid native workers who are disadvantaged. However, on reflection, this cannot be so. We can make two pertinent observations:

1. A large number of studies using data from the US have found that increased immigration has no impact or an insignificant impact on native wage and employment levels.[10] Where there are small negative effects, they tend to affect earlier cohorts of immigrants rather than the historical poor of the US. This could be because migrants move to labour-scarce areas where wages are rising in any case, so that their effect is masked in the general movement. There is, however, much evidence that unskilled immigrants do the jobs that the natives, even if unemployed, are unwilling to do; rather than compete with the native population, new low-skilled immigrants compete with earlier low-skilled immigrants. Immigrants then fill places not because they are cheaper – in general, they seem not to be but because they are the only workers available (as happens with seasonal migrant workers in some sections of European agriculture).

On the other hand, few studies have tracked the impact of immigration on raising employment for complementary native workers – how the availability of foreign-born unskilled production workers increases the demand for native-born supervisors and managers, skilled workers and technical staff, truck drivers, etc. Fewer still estimate the multiplier effects of immigrant expenditure – on demand for accommodation, furnishings, foodstuffs, transport, and so on.

Borjas, along with others, has changed the nature of this discussion by suggesting that native unskilled workers often take anticipatory action to avoid

10   See, for example, Greenwood et al. 1997.

competition – by leaving sectors of the economy or geographical areas where such competition is likely to occur (great play is made of the changing balance between domestic and foreign migration of the low-skilled into California in this respect).[11] Borjas argues that local studies of the impact of increased immigration greatly underestimate its effects, which can only be assessed at a national level. The argument is ingenious and well presented, and it may have some validity, but the deficiencies of the empirical evidence do not yet allow a decisive conclusion and, as a result, the case is as yet far from being a consensus among migration specialists.[12]

2. However, if we broaden the focus from work to consumption and prices, it seems intuitively that the case must be false. For example, immigrant workers in agriculture ensure fewer imports and the survival of small farmers and the rural economy, as well as lower food prices. The primary beneficiaries of this are the poor (who spend a larger share of their income on foodstuffs). Immigrant workers in manufacturing, construction, public transport, and so on, have similar effects. Women are able to undertake paid work outside the home if childcare and cleaning services are available, and often these are only available at affordable prices through immigrant carers. In certain regions, immigrants have saved the small corner shop in the poorer areas of big cities and provincial towns, as mentioned earlier, and they are beginning to do so also in rural areas. And the immigrant labour force is crucial in public healthcare services – particularly in the poorer districts of our larger cities. Indeed, the 'disadvantaged' may be the primary beneficiaries of the immigration of un- and semi-skilled workers, and would suffer most if the supply were curtailed. The better-off can afford to manage without the services provided by immigrant labour. Of course, it might be argued that wages should be paid that would induce native-born workers to do these jobs, and that this could be done without increasing taxation to an electorally suicidal level, or raising prices to a level that would make services prohibitive for the poor. That case, however, has to be demonstrated.

---

11   Borjas 1999.
12   See Anderson 2000 and Bhagwati 1999.

Migration and Developing Countries

It is well-known – but worth repeating – that continued protectionism in world trade reduces the employment potential in developing countries, and that this may affect the propensity to migrate to work elsewhere. Nowhere does this appear to be more true than in agriculture, where, in the most notorious case, the Common Agricultural Policy not only deprives developing-country exporters of markets in Europe, it also deprives them of other markets by subsidising exports to Third World countries (and this is achieved through higher European food prices, affecting most severely the poorest consumers).

To the employment losses incurred through protectionism can be added those experienced through worker emigration. This is greatest with the highly skilled and magnified where such workers leave permanently or for the bulk of their working lives, depriving the developing country of skilled inputs (and the productivity of the average worker is strongly related to the average skill level of the labour force as a whole), of complementary employment of lesser skill, and of tax payments that the emigrant would otherwise have made. If the emigrant's skills were acquired with public subsidies, these also are lost.[13]

Worker remittances returned to countries of origin are some compensation here. But a much greater benefit would accrue if migrant workers could return with enhanced skills. Low-skilled workers who travel without families have always tended to return; they work abroad primarily to strengthen their position at home. This tendency is much reduced the tighter the controls on migration: the higher the costs of accessing work, the greater the tendency to settle in order to secure continued access to work.[14] On the other hand, anecdotal evidence suggests some increase in the propensity of highly skilled workers to return to Asia if not to Africa. Domestic reform and stabilisation are obviously crucial here. However, given relatively abundant labour supplies in developing countries, standards of living for the highly skilled at much lower levels of pay than are available in developed countries (even if much closer in Purchasing Power Parity terms) can be much higher. The development of high-level research facilities in developing countries supports tendencies to return (or indeed, not to set out in the first place). Numerous national and interna-

---

13   On the Indian case, see Desai et al. 2003.

14   This is shown in US data following the tightening of southern border controls after 1986 (Massey et al. 2002; Cornelius 2001). The return of Greek guest-workers from Germany, once Greece joined the European Union and Greeks thus secured the right to return to work abroad, suggests the same conclusion (Constant and Massey 2002, p. 6).

tional schemes exist to support the process of return,[15] but more can be done to remove existing anomalies which force migrants to settle as a condition of work, and which weaken the 'social embeddedness' of migrants in their country of origin. Aid programmes can be of assistance here in financing training for migrants in preparation for their return and in employing returning migrants as agents of development, applying their funds to strengthen the creation of new businesses. Migration might then come to be seen by most migrants as an important part of their education, enriching their skills and work experience rather than being simply an opportunity to earn money.[16]

The issue of migration to the developed countries may prove temporary. Present demographic projections suggest that over the next half century, the bulk of the world's labour force will become concentrated in developing countries. It may be expected that the bulk of the world's tradable sectors will follow, led by those most sensitive to labour costs. It cannot be conceived that migration flows between developed and developing countries, even if completely free, would be on a scale sufficient to change this significantly. Furthermore, the developed countries' concentration on research and education, and on quality of life, may be expected to complement the concentration of the world's manufacturing and service production in developing countries. It could be that over the next half century, as a fully integrated world economy emerges, migration flows may come to decline or even shift to the reverse direction.

Remedies

The most obvious remedy to the problems of the present system is to accept the inevitable integration of the developed countries in a world labour market and move towards free migration and open borders. Employers would then recruit abroad as they do at home and bear the risks – the costs – of any errors made in assessing their future labour needs. The role of government would be restricted to extending its present responsibilities for the regulation of employment of native-born workers to the foreign-born. At the moment, private brokers and agents organise the regular and irregular recruitment and movement of workers, so the basic social infrastructure exists for such a change. Such a system would eliminate irregular migration and the bulk of asylum seekers who

---

15   See *International Migration*'s special issue on 'The Migration-Development Nexus' (*International Migration*, 40, no. 5).

16   German medieval craft apprentices were required to migrate between different localities or even countries to learn additional skills as the final qualification for craft accreditation.

could take work immediately and not be obliged to call on public support (this would not be true of asylum seekers without the capacity to work, but that would be a much smaller problem than the current one).

Would direct recruitment by employers threaten the maintenance of acceptable levels of pay and standards of working conditions, as employers competed to lower costs? In principle, the problems are no more severe than those experienced with the native-born low-skilled workers. Indeed, they may be fewer insofar as migrant workers ought to be recruited on a standard – and government-approved – contract for a given period. Such standard contracts should be vetted and policed by both source and destination governments, by relevant trade unions and by NGOs. Of course, no system is foolproof – for native-born as much for foreign-born – but making such employment fully explicit offers some basis for regulation, whereas at present, with irregular migration, there is no such possibility.

However, the immediate needs of developing countries for the return of their migrant workers, combined with the fear that a significant sector of the European electorate has of being 'swamped' by foreigners, suggest that, while the aim should remain intact, we need a second-best transitional arrangement that allows governments to retreat if required. It is not the task here to design such transitional arrangements – and there are now increasing numbers of schemes on offer.[17] However, a number of points might be made concerning revisions to the present system:

1. The first issue of importance here is that, in principle, all migration should be temporary, even if some migrants apply to stay longer. The overwhelming bulk of evidence is that populations are relatively immobile, but that a small margin seek migration as, in the first instance, a means to broaden their experience and earn on a sufficient scale to improve their position at home. Of course, negative conditions at home can tilt the balance as a migrant becomes accustomed to life at the destination, but, even then, it is surprising how durable the loyalties remain and the hope of return. It has already been argued that immigration regulations (and the rising cost of getting past borders) and the pressure governments can place on migrant settlement can change this, forcing migrants into exile. The stress placed on assimilation, whether forced or voluntary, follows from a preoccupation with settlement; but if migrants were free to come and go, enforced assimilation would be a serious threat to the human rights of the migrant who does not wish to join in the host society at all, merely to work

---

17   For examples, see Veenkamp et al. 2003; Harris 2003 (Appendix); Ghosh 2000.

in order to return with enhanced skills and savings (from the migrant's point of view, assimilation could become an additional cost). Of course, access to social security can also tip the balance here, but arrangements can be made to reduce the impact of this (migrants could, for example, be exempt from all but the minimum social security contributions and benefits, or benefits could be accumulated and repaid in the home country at the end of the work period, etc.). There will always remain unresolved cases, but these should not be allowed to deflect the principle issue.

Temporary worker status would be one element in restoring equality of treatment between high-and low-skilled workers. While it is assumed that most migrants will want to return home provided there is a reasonable possibility of future opportunities to work abroad, nothing should be done to weaken their commitment to return and to do so without any forms of compulsion. In some present schemes there are additional incentives paying part of the wage in a cumulative sum in the home currency on their return (or possibly adding a bonus and/or refunded social security funds). I have mentioned the possibility of aid programmes financing training and offering business start-up funds on return. Given a well-managed pattern of circulatory migration, applications to stay longer for whatever reasons can be treated with generosity.

2. Irregular migration is first and foremost a response to a demand for workers (even if it may be precipitated by push factors), so that generally migrants move to previously identified jobs (or to agents controlling such work) and have very high rates of participation and low rates of unemployment. Accordingly, the expansion of the work-permit system should be designed to eliminate irregular migration. However, this cannot be done through government controls on recruitment on the basis of estimates of future labour demand. Not only must such estimates be erroneous in a dynamic economy, they cannot easily accommodate predictions for the type of demand that irregular migrants meet. Any system that is going to meet economic requirements has to end the idea of set annual quotas of workers and invest in the initiative of employers to recruit at their own expense in such numbers as they require, albeit within a framework of government supervision to ensure that the basic conditions of work and pay do not undercut alternative local supplies of workers and are clear to migrant workers before they leave home, and that robust provisions are made for the proper return of workers and for their social security during the period of their visit.

3. This chapter has not dealt with the family reunification category of immigrants, which raises a quite different agenda of policy issues. In general, with

globalisation, one would expect increasing mobility and growing crossovers between the citizens of a country – who live in that country or who live abroad (the present 'polity') – and those who work in that country or contribute to its output from locations abroad (the 'economy'). If this is so, then the family reunification category of movement will inevitably grow and, if the welfare of the country is to be assured, must be facilitated.

4. The ban on asylum seekers working – whether for six months or, as in some countries, until their claims are sanctioned or rejected – is one of the most obvious sources of social tension. The combined accusation of having entered a country irregularly (given there is, in many cases, no other way for them to obtain entry) and then 'living off social security' (as work is forbidden) seems almost deliberately designed to provoke the greatest xenophobia. With an expanded work-permit system to eliminate irregular migration, able-bodied asylum seekers can, if circumstances permit, apply for work before they arrive; if this cannot be done, then they can be granted temporary leave to remain while they seek work. Part of the funds at present devoted to supporting asylum seekers can then be directed to providing short-term support for those who cannot work.

Would increased temporary migration of low-skilled workers from the South to the North exaggerate the polarisation between the two? In the larger picture, the capacity of developing countries to raise their incomes through the temporary emigration of workers will reduce this polarisation, a change enhanced if workers return with upgraded skills and increased savings to expand their home economy. If this process is part of a reordering of the world economy, marked by the relocation of a major part of the world's tradable manufacturing and service sectors to developing countries, then present arrangements may be seen only as transitional, part of a process of moving to a much more equalised world order. On the other hand, the contrary policy of preventing the poor from escaping from poverty through migration – even if it could be achieved (which is doubtful) – would vastly exaggerate the inequalities of the world.

Conclusion

The present system for all except the skilled is opaque and costly relative to its returns. A world labour market is in operation, but without any of the transparency required to put the right worker in the right job. Governments operate as large monopsonist buyers, while private agencies recruit and distribute irregular migrants without being subject to the open competition that reveals the marginal cost/value of the work proposed. Criminalisation is inevitable in such circumstances. A global labour market requires a global exchange in which real scarcities in many different localities can be matched against the immense diversity of those offering work, and where wage levels reflect those scarcities.

If the developed countries are unable to establish an acceptable order in the field of migration, the danger is that their political leaders will continue to seek to exploit the issue for xenophobic purposes, that they will impede the development of developing countries (regardless of what aid programmes are employed), that they will lock out the poor, at whatever cost to the civil rights of their own citizens and the growing numbers of irregular migrants (growing because the labour shortages for low-skilled workers will worsen), and that they will damage the welfare of their poorest citizens. Protectionism here is, as elsewhere, directed to trying fruitlessly to capture benefits for a minority at the cost of the world at large – and particularly of the world's poor.

Immigration and State Power*

For the past thirty years or so, the study of economic migration has been almost exclusively preoccupied with the social and economic impact of immigration on labour-receiving countries (as opposed to, for example, the impact of emigration on labour-sending countries). But now, in the new century, it seems that the key issues concern not the economic but rather the political implications of immigration for State sovereignty, for the viability of nation-States. The processes associated with economic globalisation make the questions at stake much more urgent than before, progressively raising immigration as an issue in the policy agenda of almost all developed countries.

Globalisation, as understood here, is the beginning of a process that creates a single global economy, by implication superseding the old world of separate and politically defined national economies. Such an economic order implies the increasing mobility of capital, goods and labour, just as the earlier creation of national economies required the increasing mobility of the factors of production within national borders. However, whereas the creation of national economies usually enjoyed the supervision of one governing authority, the political State, economic globalisation has no such single supervisor. On the contrary, the world remains politically governed almost exclusively by a mass of separate States, each in principle limited to a geographically defined fragment of the whole, and each therefore immobile in a world of growing mobility. To put it in a simplistic form, the economics of the new system collide directly with the politics of the old.

This question is briefly explored here in three parts, relative to internal migration, to international migration, and finally to the 'integration' of immigrants.

---

* This article is the revised version of a lecture given to the Society for International Development at the Institute of Social Studies at the Hague in May 2009, subsequently reproduced on the ISS web site (http://www.iss.nl/DevISSues) and in the *Economic and Political Weekly*, Mumbai, 30 January–5 February, 2010, pp. 8–10.

Internal Migration

A central concern of the State, one of the underpinnings of its capacity to rule, is control of the country's population. One component of this historically has entailed attempts to regulate or prevent movement, at an extreme, to enforce on the inhabitants, a measure of immobility. Efforts vary over time and in impact, limited always by the administrative capacity of the State relative to its many other objectives.

Some of the more extreme historical cases occur in authoritarian regimes, requiring the inhabitants to carry internal passports (the identity card is perhaps the relic of this order), permits or visas to move, domestic and inter-provincial check points, and in some cases direct prohibition on movement between provinces, districts, parishes, between villages and cities. There are many examples here but some of the best known might include medieval France, Tsarist Russia, seventeenth- and eighteenth-century Prussia, and, outside Europe, Tokugawa Japan. More generally, serfdom in European feudalism – tying the worker to the soil – illustrates an extreme form of legal immobilisation, the subordination of the labour force to the will of the lord.

In the twentieth century, comparable regulatory regimes existed in, for example, the former Soviet Union and its allies. Tying the population to its place of registration or birth survives in the identity card or *propiska*. Such an immobilisation of the workforce is economically tolerable only when married to forced labour or worker conscription, directing workers to move to places where they are required (to, for example, the large construction projects, dams, power stations, etc., undertaken in the 1930s in the Soviet Union). In essence, the difference between the soldier and the civilian is eliminated; the workforce is reduced to being an army, subject to State orders, with severe penalties for those who move without permission.

There are more homely examples of the difficulties arising under such regimes. In the late 1980s, Boris Yeltsin, then Mayor of Moscow, grumbled publicly at the difficulties of keeping Moscow clean; he was then importing young workers from the provinces on temporary work permits to do jobs Muscovites refused, only to find them disappear (becoming thereafter illegal migrants, working in the black economy).

In a number of newly independent developing countries, governments assumed they knew where the population should be best located, and proceeded to try to employ police power to enforce this – as with *transmigrasi* policy in Indonesia, Malaysia's FELDA programme to populate the Western provinces; policies to prevent urbanisation in many countries (for example, the Philippines); *ujaama* in Tanzania, etc.

More brutally, the apartheid regime in South Africa endeavoured to control the black population by classifying them as foreigners (citizens of the *bantustans*), and enforcing exclusion from white areas through the notorious pass system and extensive internal police checks. A comparable system is enforced in the occupied Palestinian territories (the West Bank and Gaza), again through identity cards, numerous checkpoints, controlled routes and other obstructions to movement.

While there may be different local justifications for internal migration control, in all cases the mobility required for rapid economic development – the creation of a national labour force with the ability to move to wherever work is created – is sacrificed to the need for political control.

One of the more interesting cases in this connection is the evolution of migration policy in China. On the eve of assuming power, Mao laid out the Party's programme in *On Coalition Government*. It is clear there that the new Republic took for granted that tens of thousands of rural dwellers would move to the cities in the normal process accompanying industrialisation; by implication, freedom of movement was assumed. A decade later, following the extraordinary growth of the first Five Year Plan period (and the major effort required by the Korean war), the government's nerve seems to have failed in the face of a major surge of urbanisation (a panic replicated in many other developing countries at that time). Freedom of movement was ended. The urban population was registered, and registration entitled the legal urban-dweller to *hukou*, (social security, pensions on retirement, to housing, education and medical care) rights denied to those registered as rural inhabitants (as it were, classified as foreigners). Elaborate controls were introduced to prevent transfer from rural to urban residence – non-transferable food ration cards; requirements for permission to leave the rural commune, to travel, to enter urban areas, to reside and work there. Police raids at railway and bus terminals and in poor city areas were designed to enforce this regime and expel the illegal migrants to their place of origin or registration.

As in the Soviet case, mentioned earlier, such an order could work only with forced labour to direct workers to the places where the State required them (for example, for oil or other resource exploitation in underpopulated areas, to settle areas with low population density – for example, Inner Mongolia, Tibet, etc.). During the Cultural Revolution, there were also, for political reasons, mass expulsions of the urban population to temporary exile in rural areas. However, accelerated economic growth also raised the demand for unskilled work in existing cities in jobs the urban dwellers refused (as in the Moscow case cited). The regime allowed cities to import rural labour on temporary contract (and without access to *hukou*), what the regime called a 'worker-peasant system', supposedly a revolutionary attempt to overcome the ancient contradiction between town and country. The scale of resentment among the *gastarbeiters* concerned exploded in the Shanghai general strike of 1966 during the early phases of the Cultural Revolution.

The controls on mobility were completely incompatible with accelerated and sustained economic growth, and while, following the Deng reforms of the late 1970s, they were not formally removed (and *hukou* was not ended), they were allowed to lapse, or applied only selectively. The sheer pace of economic growth washed away the politics of mobility control.

The cumulative costs of immobilisation must have been considerable, not just in terms of foregone economic growth, but in losses to the rural population in earnings from migration. Consider the 2003 Ministry of Agriculture rural household survey. This suggested that the 192 million Chinese working outside their province of domicile (that is, an underestimate of China's migrant population since it excludes people who migrate within their home province) contributed in remittances close to 60 percent of rural household income. The costs of State policies to restrict or prevent migration were born by the poorest segment of the Chinese population, the rural inhabitants.

In sum, the State's efforts to control, curb or prevent internal migration provide suggestions on the issues at stake in international migration – and the sacrifice of the immense potential to reduce world poverty to the maintenance of the world political order. It is thus not entirely fanciful to identify rising immigration and free world mobility as an existential threat to the inherited forms of the State.

International Migration

The creation of national economies and the forced expansion in economic activity within now sharply defined political boundaries, forced radical change to an inherited hitherto borderless economic geography. It forced also an increase in the mobility of the factors of production, capital and labour, within national boundaries, severing linkage that had hitherto extended beyond the borders. It also created new patterns of domestic interdependent economic specialisation at the expense of what had now become external transactions. This experience provides us with some suggestions as to the results of globalisation, the creation of a single global economy.

However, some aspects of economic globalisation featured even as national economies were being created, particularly when much of the world was dominated by European empires. Thus, large-scale movements of forced and free labour took place in the modern period – of slave labour from Africa to the Americas, and following the end of slavery, of indentured labour. Furthermore, in the first great surge of economic globalisation in the second half of the nineteenth century, there were unprecedented flows of migrant workers from Europe, to the Americas, the Antipodes, and to Africa. The second surge, in the second half of the twentieth century, led to some 150 million living outside their country of birth (the UN figure is an underestimate since it excludes returnees, whereas gross figures must be very much larger). Again, these are figures that cover only countries, excluding the very much larger numbers who migrate within countries (as we have seen in the Chinese example mentioned earlier).

The present phase of steady growth in global migration is, so far as the developed countries are concerned, much exaggerated by two special features:

1. The demography of the developed countries (and China), leading to a decline in the active population. This is threatening the end of self-sufficiency in the national labour forces of the developed countries and, other things being equal, a growing incapacity to sustain current output with existing levels of technology and capital-output ratios. Indeed, to sustain current output requires the developed countries either to locate activity to areas where workers are available ('outsourcing' or 'offshoring') or create mechanisms for the permanent recruitment of additional workers from abroad, whether as permanent or temporary residents.

2. However, there is an additional complication here. The long-term emphasis in the developed countries on raising the skill-intensity of their respective national outputs is producing almost perpetual scarcities of workers with the appropriate skills (even in conditions of recession). Furthermore, the continual enhancement of the skills of the native-born workforce is exaggerating the scarcity of workers willing to undertake unskilled work, or at least undertake it at the wages on offer. This has produced a growing dependence by developed countries on foreign-born skilled workers, a growing competition for the world's stock of skilled (to the relative impoverishment of many developing countries), and the establishment of mechanisms for permanent recruitment (now affecting the recruitment of foreign students to higher education in developed countries). The dependence is most pronounced for the most highly skilled, as US figures suggest – the US Census records that in the year 2,000 nearly 47 percent of the US stock of scientists and engineers with doctoral qualifications were foreign-born (as were two thirds of the net addition

of such workers to the labour force in the last half of the decade of the 1990s). It seems that the foreign-born contribute disproportionately, and increasingly so, to innovation in the United States (where in 2006, the foreign-born were included on a quarter of applications for patents, up from 7.6 percent in 1998).

Within a global economy, one would expect patterns of territorial special-isation to emerge to contribute to a global output. The same phenomenon might emerge relative to skilled labour, whether as the result of deliberate government policy or a global market organising the distribution of training facilities. A striking, if limited, example of government initiative here is the Filipino supply of two categories of workers (albeit not necessarily counting as 'skilled') – nurses and merchant mariners, both produced by Filipino train-ing institutions in numbers far in excess of the domestic requirements. In the future, given current investment in higher education, possibly China and India will come to provide the world's main supply of engineers and medical doc-tors.

However, we should note in passing that we are still employing the 'archaic' concept of countries, politically defined units, to identify what are often bor-derless economic transactions. Outsourcing now covers global networks of interdependent collaborative activities in many countries where the States concerned may be entirely unaware of the economic logic involved. What has happened in advanced manufacturing and services may now be affecting what were formerly identified as 'non-tradeables' – for example, medical services (where patients are treated in different locations internationally, according to local specialisations) or higher education (where students travel between dif-ferent campuses for different special fields of a global university). Such devel-opments might well reduce the need for workers to travel to different countries.

Will the present economic conjuncture affect these trends, restoring the old national economies?

There is certainly evidence that governments have reached for economic nationalism to offset the slump – from trade protection measures to national financing of banking. However, I believe, governments have left it far too late to restore the old order. The attempt itself would be economically – and therefore politically – devastating. Whenever the world resumes growth, as it certainly will, it will start from where it left off which suggests that while economic glob-alisation (and its relationship to national States) may be changed in important ways, it will be a process in substance resumed.

In sum, whatever the current position, the developed countries will be obliged to establish mechanisms for the permanent recruitment of workers (if

not settlers) if governments are going to be able to meet the welfare expectations of their inhabitants and thus secure political survival.

The Integration of Immigrants

If mobility of the factors of production remains a fundamental feature of the
new global economy, States remain preoccupied with their own immobility –
not with facilitating circulation in the interests of the welfare of the world
and their own populations, but with migrants as settlers, new members of
the national political club. The economic question of facilitating mobility is
subordinate to the political issue – migrants as new citizens or as invaders. Such
an approach almost completely dismisses the economic benefits of migration
for the native-born to concentrate on the fears of losing political power. It is
this context which in the developed countries leads to a preoccupation with
the 'integration' of immigrants, turning them, whether they wish it or not, into
citizens.

However, as many people have discovered it is almost impossible to say what
constitutes a native, a rightful member of the national club. Most of us have
no choice – we are born into the club and spend our lives within it whether
we approve of it or not. It is an existential condition, not a free choice. Some
of us, in random swings of the political pendulum are violently excluded – as
were the German Jews under the Nazis, and with a terrible shock bludgeoned
into being foreigners. Fortunately most of us never have to face this crisis
(unless you live in the Balkans or Rwanda, etc.). But the occasional violence of
exclusion justifies the earlier point that immigration constitutes an existential
threat to the nation-State.

There are various approaches to trying to define what constitutes a true
member of the club and a loyal citizen (even though the majority of the native-
born are not required to adhere to the club or declare their loyalty). Let us
restrict ourselves to two extremes:

1. The nation is defined by a common culture, adherence to a common set of
    values. However, in practice it is impossible to make explicit this common
    culture, or to specify what values all or a majority of the inhabitants
    share. Either the specification is impossibly vague (and does not exclude
    things shared by many non-natives), or it is subject to the prejudice or
    vanity of the person concerned – we are all kindly and truthful. More
    to the point, the native-born are not obliged to accept either the culture
    or the principles. Governments retreat to the archaic – all newcomers to

Britain are expected to swear loyalty to the monarch although there are no explanations as to why republicans are excluded from British nationality (and natives are not).

2.   The second approach lays down no such conditions for acceptance; the newcomer has to do no more than accept the rules until changed.

The first approach illustrates, in my view, a dangerous authoritarianism, an illiberalism, implicit in the procedure, and its dependence on hypocrisy about the status quo. By contrast, liberal principles might suggest as long-terms objectives:

- In general, people should be free to travel, to work and settle where they choose, and to be able to do so with their rights protected by the State in whatever country they reside. In essence, the conditions of international migration should be the same as those for domestic migration;
- People should have freedom of thought, and not be obliged to abandon their existing beliefs or adopt other beliefs because these are locally fashionable;
- All residents should be treated equally – nothing should be required of the foreign-born which is not required of the native-born.

Implicitly, joining the national club means accepting the club rules, paying club dues, etc., without necessarily sharing the same opinions or customs as existing members. These were broadly the conditions that pertained in parts of Europe in the past.

In current conditions, such principles are completely Utopian. In Europe, the legacy of xenophobia and hundreds of years of internecine war makes foreigners potential or actual enemies. Furthermore, human rights are currently secured only by States, and those without citizenship may be severely disprivileged.

However, the attempt by many governments now to make the conditions of entry to citizenship both onerous and expensive, is liable to considerably increase the disincentives to try. Even now passports are no longer sacred badges of identity so much as simple conveniences for travel.

Given what has been said before about increasing mobility in the world, the disincentives to seek citizenship might suggest increasing numbers of inhabitants will choose not to naturalise where they live and work. In addition, the growing bureaucracy seeking in vain to match labour demand and supply will give great incentives to move illegally or move legally and work illegally. Such workers will accordingly slip out of whatever control the State retains until such time as governments recognise reality and assume responsibility for all who live within their domains, regardless of origins. But there may be many who are severely damaged before such a state of affairs comes to prevail.

The Freedom to Move*

In 1944, Karl Polanyi wrote that the history of capitalism from the late eighteenth century to the third quarter of the nineteenth century was a long drawn-out struggle to subordinate society to a completely self-regulating market. In his view, the simultaneously absurd and oppressive character of this endeavour was embodied in the attempt to make land and labour simply marketable commodities. However, from the depression of the years 1873 to 1886, he saw a sustained and successful campaign to reverse this process and establish national (or State) regulation of land and labour as well as of finance and trade. In the case of labour, this process was embodied in the creation of strong trade unions that sought to regulate labour markets and, in alliance with the government, to regulate hours and conditions of work, and create measures of popular welfare, education and health.

From the vantage point of 1944, the achievements seemed impressive. The trade unions had moved from barely tolerated marginal organisations to one of the great institutions of state. With the settlement of the Second World War, many governments established more comprehensive systems of welfare than ever before, in effect guaranteeing a minimum level of livelihood for all.

Yet half a century later, what then seemed permanent accomplishments now appear as temporary victories, and those victories were only part of a larger process in which the Great Powers settled their domestic class struggles in order the better to fight each other. The other side of the coin to Polanyi's triumphs of 1944 was total war. What we have called elsewhere[1] the fully 'socialised state' in which the mass of inhabitants became citizens and, in return for complete loyalty to the state, were accorded both consultative and welfare rights – a kind of social contract – now appears as a temporary phase in the evolution of the system. It is as if world capitalism needed a period of national incubation, and that for nearly a century up to about 1970, this was indeed what occurred with all the attendant horrors of war implied by the unification of capital and the state within a system of competitive Great Powers.

The creation of the modern national State, however, opened a gulf between those who were legitimate citizens – members of the 'social homogeneity' –

---

* From: Gareth Dale and Mike Cole (eds.), *The European Union and Migrant Labour*, Oxford: Berg, 1999.

1 Harris 1995.

and the rest of the world, the vast majority of people. Access to full participation became a precious privilege, a route to what was presented as participation in the exercise of national sovereignty. It was not that national loyalty or sentiment was created by the change – they had existed to some degree and for various classes for a long time – but the sentiment was now armed with specific legal privileges and material benefits.

The project of building a national state of self-governing citizens in which all have rights and duties is now part of the past. It implied a strict control of the economic and political boundaries of the state, consistently discriminating between native and foreigner both in trade, in capital movements as well as in terms of people. The process of rapid postwar economic growth has forced the governments of the developed countries – and latterly those of the developing countries – to decontrol if they are to enjoy the benefits of growth; for the best part of thirty years, the developed States have been dismantling the regulation of trade and currencies, capital and finance, and more recently, of domestic labour markets, conditions of work and the structure of social support (welfare, health and education). Thus, the profound difference between citizen and foreigners, upon which the socialised state was founded, is being progressively blurred. Indeed, so great is the complexity of the system, no one can any longer be sure where a commodity is made or to what country a unit of capital belongs or even if the question any longer makes any sense (although the newspapers and popular discussion still assume it does).

In periods of sustained growth the developed countries have always experienced serious labour scarcities – that is, their economies have rapidly exceeded the potential of the domestic labour market and spilled over to other countries. That has been an even more extreme phenomenon in the postwar period – labour demand in the developed countries has not only invaded areas of formerly non-labour (housewives, for example), not only drawn in new legions of immigrants, but also swept into production the labour forces of a mass of developing countries, particularly in east and southeast Asia. Indeed, the process started by the labour demand of the developed countries has by now assumed an autonomous drive, leading to the creation of a single integrated global economy (albeit still far from full accomplishment). We can already envisage what has long existed for the higher professions (such as doctors, engineers, airline pilots), a range of world labour markets, setting the prevailing pay rates in each national economy. The full emergence of that process is still blocked by more-or-less elaborate immigration controls, some of the few systematic barriers remaining to obstruct the mobility of a 'factor of production' and a form of protectionism still accepted by liberals and non-liberals alike.

Thus, as governments have been driven – admittedly to different degrees – to end the old social contract with their citizens, to dismantle the socialised state, so also the emergence of global labour markets makes for continuously increasing rates of worker mobility whether this means settlers, internal company movements, temporary migrants or whatever. Indeed, the operation of global markets is imposing a crisis on the state system, at its most dramatic in the old Soviet Union, but no less severe wherever the state structure is vulnerable – as in sub-saharan Africa, the Balkans, the Caucasus and former Soviet Central Asia, parts of the Middle East, and so on. Now, the same violent process has been inflicted on those hitherto thought to be most invulnerable, in East and South-East Asia. The migration of finance between countries is one of the more obvious sources of instability, but the movement of unprecedented numbers of refugees across international borders is an even more painful index of that crisis.

In developing countries, the old project of national economic development – usually founded upon some aspiration to create a socialised State – has also come to an end. Growth now implies increased integration and specialisation, not increased economic independence. The collapse of the vigorous movements of economic nationalism of the 1950s is one sign of the change – and the rise of alternative ideologies, pre-eminently religious fundamentalism, which try, at least initially, to reject the 'Western' aim of economic development along with secularism.

For the unskilled workers of the developed countries, the prospect is alarming. On the one hand, the old social contract has been unilaterally scrapped by what was supposed to be their own patron and protector, the state. On the other, the material foundations of their existence are radically contracting, represented by high levels of unemployment in Europe, and declining relative incomes in North America. The jobs on offer do not provide anything like an adequate subsistence, by the standards of society at large – and ill accord with the expectations of those raised to envisage quite reasonably that their earnings shall accord with the social norms and average levels of productivity. However, for those workers, immigrants, whose expectations are governed by a society of origin with far lower levels of productivity, such pay can be, by means of prodigious effort and abstemiousness, the means to attain some prosperity (and for their children, entry to upward mobility to the professional classes), and in some cases, the basis for a medium-sized business.

The prospects appear worse still: the entry into production for the rest of the world, in an open world economy, of – say – China and India seems capable of not only transforming world technology (by profoundly changing the factor endowment of the world economy) but also of making possible pay levels that will marginalise sections of the world's workforce far more drastically than any-thing Polanyi envisaged (after all, he was discussing market imperatives only in a relatively isolated national economy). Indeed, some observers think this process – equalising wages between developed and developing countries – has already begun and that this accounts for the decline in the relative position of the unskilled worker in the developed countries.[2] The evidence is not clearcut, and the time period still short to draw such drastic conclusions.

The old working class, after the appalling experience of the nineteenth century, rejoiced at the new security offered by the state in a turbulent and dangerous world. The decline in this sense of security induces both periodic panic and continuing resentment at the harsh regime that has replaced it. At the other extreme, for the new cosmopolitan worker, nationality is no longer a sacred honour, but a garment to be donned or shed according to convenience; income and class also divide the cosmopolitan and the local. The freedom to move for one individual is the threatening insecurity of the other. Immigration controls are thus equivocal – as *The Economist* put it: 'universal immigration controls keeping people out are tantamount to a Berlin Wall shutting them in. It is time to recognize that the right to freedom of movement implies a duty to permit immigration.'[3]

The ideas that people of necessity are permanently located in one national entity, that the distribution of the world's population is complete forever, and only temporary anomalies now occur are also being challenged. It would be a curious outcome if the size and composition of the labour force of each coun-try was exactly optimal, requiring no exchanges. In practice, world economic integration continually increases rates of mobility, so that in future it is going to be as difficult internationally to give an unequivocal answer to the question 'where are you from?' as it already is in developed countries. Native places are in decline and often the complexity of an individual's origin is well beyond the conventional mythology. The marks of identity may remain individual, ances-tral, tribal, occupational – and even religious – rather than national.

The fears of the competition of workers from developing countries are misplaced, even though Western politicians are adept at reinventing this threat as a means to secure their power. The scale of trade is still relatively small for it to have had profound effects.[4] In any case, the differences in the productivity of workers are so great, mere differences in wages tell us little either about where

2   Wood 1994.
3   *The Economist*, 18 April 1987.
4   See Lawrence and Slaughter 1993; Bhagwalti and Kosters 1994.

production should be located or the tactics of bargaining. There is no inevitable downward auction in wages, and the record for unskilled workers in Europe and North America is affected not only by labour-intensive imports but also by the choices of employers in terms of technology and management. In any case, the figures do not make allowance for the change in numbers – the growth in the class of better paid and the shrinkage in those on low pay. In a well-ordered world, the pet prescription of economists would apply – as the incomes of the majority have increased, unskilled workers have a powerful claim for full compensation if they alone are bearing the costs of that adjustment that is benefiting everyone else; in the real world, the transfer rarely occurs.

The Structure of the World's Labour Force

The need for increased movement of workers as the world economy grows is exaggerated by the changing demography of the world's labour force. As noted earlier, the world's young workers are becoming increasingly concentrated in developing countries. This is shown in the distribution of those who enter the labour force – for example, for the developed countries (the OECD group), there are 13 under the age of 15 for every 10 over the age of 65, whereas in sub-Saharan Africa, the region with the fastest growth of population, there are 156 under the age of 15 for every 10 over the age of 65.

If the distribution of workers is changing, it is also true of the highly educated. In the late 1980s, Asia produced annually some nine million graduates compared to three-and-a-half million in the developed countries. Or to look at the issue from a different angle, between 1970 and 1985, the developed country share of particular categories of the world's educated people declined as follows:

1. For high school enrolments, from 44 to 30 percent;
2. For College students, from 77 to 51 percent.[5]

If we compare the 1986 output of the highest qualified workers in the United States (the world's largest producer) with six major developing countries (Brazil, China, the Philippines, Korea, Mexico and Egypt), then the gap is narrow or exceeded (and if we include others – India, Indonesia, Bangladesh, Pakistan – then the gap is reversed):

---

5   Johnston 1991, p. 121.

	Total college	Scientists	Engineers	PhD graduates
United States	979.5	180.7	77.1	394.3
'The six'	1,053.1	153.8	172.6	66.2
	(in thousands)			

UNESCO 1988, TABLE 3-10, PP. 3-306

Indeed, developing countries appear to be becoming major world suppliers of engineers and medical doctors to the developed countries, or rather, to the world. Students and staff from developing countries also tend to be predominant in these faculties in universities of the developed countries. In 1987, in US universities, 51 percent of doctorates in engineering were awarded to students from developing countries (compared with 48 percent in mathematics, 32 percent in business studies, and 29 percent in physical sciences).[6] Coincidentally, these two faculties – medicine and engineering – are the strongholds of Muslim Brothers in Cairo University, as if simultaneously, these traditional spearheads of secular modernity are being globalised and localised.

The emergence of national specialisations in the higher skills is already advanced, and this parallels specialisation in the provision of unskilled labour. It could be that in the future all engineers working in developed countries will be recruited from developing countries, that consumers of medical services will go primarily to developing countries to receive treatment, and so on. Thus, developing countries will not be simply suppliers of unskilled labour to the world, nor will the developed countries be able to monopolise the higher skills. Nor are the flows simply of workers travelling from developing to developed – consumers will increasingly travel in the opposite direction. This is what a single world economy means.

Morality and Migration

The overwhelming majority of the world's population are foreigners, and all of us are part of that great majority for most people. Even for someone from China. 79 percent of the world's people are foreign, and 84 percent for that other population giant, India. For a small country like Britain, 99 percent of

---

6 Johnston 1991, p. 124.

the world's people are foreigners. The figures put in some perspective the awful egotism of nations who see themselves as the centre of the known universe.

The morality of discussions on immigration does not start from the interests of the world, the universal, but from the minority. There is no political lobby for the majority, no agency to press for internationalism. Yet in the shift from semi-closed national economies to an open world economy, the principles by which issues should be judged are also under revision – especially so in the field of labour where moralising is most developed. Of course, this does not mean abandoning the specific interest of a people, regardless of how big or small it is, but rather placing that interest in a universal context. This is no more than following the standard practice in morality or the law – few try to justify murder on the simple grounds of egotism, but rather acknowledge that it is universally wrong to murder, even though in this case some exception is asked.

Yet all discussions of immigration policy start from the monopoly position of government, without even a nod at a universal interest. Public debate assumes a level of state egotism and particularism that would never be tolerated in an individual. No government is required to justify its immigration policy in terms of the interests of the world; no properly constituted tribunal is empowered to judge the state. Not even a forum like GATT or the World Trade Organization exists to apply common principles or adjudicate disputes. It seems that, for governments, people are very much less important than traded commodities – or else too important to allow foreigners to be involved in deciding their fate.

Yet the need for common policies is inexorably emerging. At the moment, virtually all governments cheat on the agreed rules for accepting refugees, and do so with impunity. Those who by geographical or other accident find themselves receiving a disproportionate number of those in flight – as Germany did in the early 1990s – complain and demand a sharing of the burdens. So far this has not led to any common position, and governments continue to subordinate issues of international compassion to often the most trivial questions of local parochialism. Yet sooner or later, common policies will be required to protect any individual power, at which stage the possibility of both developing some higher set of principles and bringing practice into some relationship with those principles may arise. Then building higher walls round the country – and the most shameless cheating – to avoid lending help to those in flight might give way to collective mechanisms either to make flight no longer necessary or help to accommodate all who wish to flee (on the reasonable assumption that no one embarks on such an intrinsically dangerous option without reasonable fears of disaster). Indeed, it seems that most people do not want to move, and if they are obliged to do so, do it with great reluctance and, if at all possible, return as soon as feasible. Only in the absurd fantasies of paranoid governments are foreigners assumed to be guilty until they can prove their innocence, assumed to be desperate at any cost to break in to the destination country.

A world economy cries out for a world morality and a world system of law, but the rise of the modern state subverted that universalism – in Christianity, the duty to love thy neighbour was displaced by one's duty to kill him if the state so willed. The military chaplain became the symbol of this subversion.

The Future

The regulation of immigration assumes that the norm is either a citizen or a foreigner, and the distinction is clear cut. The citizen has rights, normally lives at home and is relatively immobile; the foreigner has no rights (other than those agreed under bilateral agreements between governments), is mobile and temporarily in the country concerned. The transition from foreigner to citizen is difficult, but if made, then the former foreigner is presumed to become immobile with the acquisition of rights.

However, the norm is coming to include mobile workers for whom nationality is no more than a means to facilitate travel although these are still a very small minority. The rights of citizens are no longer needed, only the right to work. In Germany, with its rather more strict distinction between the two, the concept of *gastarbeiter* was the intermediate form. Those intermediate forms are now multiplying as the national economy needs to import a growing number of workers, even if only for a day or a week. The provisions must be rendered increasingly elastic to allow in those who are wanted but exclude those who are not, and immigration law becomes both opaque and hypocritical (at least Singapore is honest in its sharp distinction between a class of desired professional migrants and a class of resisted manual workers). Lionel Castillo, President Carter's Commissioner of the INS, noted this paradox in US immigration regulations: 'The actual policy of the US government is quite different from its stated policy, which is the strict control of the border and strict restriction of entry. The de facto policy is to keep the door half open'.

The half-open door allows the recruitment of foreign workers for particular jobs – New York hospitals advertise for nurses in the Irish or Philippine press. British hospitals send recruitment officers to the Caribbean. It allows a growing mass of workers to come frequently for short visits, like a type of international commuter. It allows the recruitment of seasonal unskilled workers – Caribbean workers to the apple orchards of Florida or the farms of Western Ontario, Polish workers to Germany. It obliges all governments from time to time to acknowledge the failure of their controls by legalising illegal immigrants.

Most of the legal exceptions are for the highly skilled. The unskilled – those who make possible the work of the skilled – must rely on illegality to help the output of the developed countries grow, and therefore, potentially, undergo the most pernicious regimes of oppression. In some cases – but sadly too few – trade unions have wisely campaigned to protect illegal immigrants since the toleration of bad conditions undermines the position of both legal immigrants and native-born workers.

In the present political climate, particularly in Europe, it is difficult to believe the numbers of unskilled foreign workers admitted could be expanded without public outcry – or rather, political challenge from the extreme right – even though the economic arguments for doing so are strong. Furthermore, the numbers of immigrants required to make up for the decline in the size of the labour force and, particularly, the decline in the younger age groups, would have to be large. Zlotnik estimates that over one million immigrants would be required in Europe annually for the first half of the next century to compensate for the declining rate of natural increase.[7]

However, once we separate the question of citizenship from that of workers, and accept that in increasingly flexible economies, temporary workers are likely to be the most rapidly expanding sectors, the issue is no longer one of large permanent transfers. Indeed, if the immigration controls were less draconian, fewer immigrant workers would be obliged to seek citizenship. For the unskilled, the right of settlement is little more than a route to security and easing the crossing of borders. The form of immigration rules itself produces a high demand for the right to settle and secure citizenship (in the same way, state regulation forces the creation of an unregulated economy, the informal or black activity). For some, settlement also carries the right to bring in close relatives, but this may also not arise if there are rights to come and go at will. If there were less of a difference between resident alien and citizen – as in the United States – fewer would bother to move permanently. Furthermore, once a worker is obliged to settle in order to work, he or she then has a powerful interest in bringing in a spouse and children, and then the worst fears of the bigots are realised – the controls have forced a net increase in the foreign-born population.

Reforming the law and easing movement would make for a considerable increase in temporary migration without settlement or acquiring the rights of a citizen. In the future, this might allow foreign workers to tender for, for example, city or hospital cleaning services, for computer programming or data

---

loading, coming for set periods per month while remaining resident at home. Agricultural subcontracts might be run in the same way. Construction companies might similarly be able to recruit foreign work teams (and foreign construction companies bid for contracts) on a project basis. Already entertainers, singers, dancers, and so on, are hired on a seasonal basis on international circuits. Thus, the cheapness of foreign travel might make it possible for a variety of jobs to be turned into temporary subcontracts, legal – and legally regulated – tasks that allow people to remain living at home.

For jobs which cannot be defined in discrete time periods pre-eminently, domestic service, staffing in hospitals, hotels and restaurants, longer term but still temporary contracts might be feasible (but 'temporary' does not mean without normal rights, or access to benefits such as pensions). Again, this might be organised by companies that bid to supply labour for set periods (as Korean companies did on Middle Eastern construction contracts) and organise the turnover and replacements. Having a company responsible for this means that, in principle, it can be legally obliged to operate according to the local standards of pay and working conditions and can be sued if it does not adhere to these standards. Government authorities have too little power to check individual workers, and the immigrant home country governments are even less well equipped to ensure tolerable conditions. Of course, the horrors of indentured and contract labour are notorious, but even those horrors are superior to unemployed hunger (and very superior to working conditions taken for granted in many developing – and some developed – countries) and they can be improved provided workers have the same rights to act against their employers as the natives do and trade unions make it their business to facilitate this.

A company-organised system of immigration (whether organised by governments, voluntary organisations or private companies) would make normal immigration controls unnecessary. The market demand for workers as shown in the contract would determine the numbers. There would be no need for arbitrary quotas or limits, since in conditions of local economic contraction, no new arrangements would be created. It would also serve to undercut the constant need to reassure the citizens that whatever privileges supposedly attached to their nationality were not being arbitrarily ignored or diluted.

With no legal restrictions on migration, the second phase would involve proper – and fair – procedures to allow that minority which might wish to translate from temporary contract worker to resident (with a right to change jobs) and so to citizen, to apply to do this. Again, there is no reason to believe that, if immigration regulations are eased, the numbers moving would be large; but no doubt some would wish to marry locally or make some longer term commitment. The issue of continuing migration for work, while staying resident at home, would have become separated from the issue of nationality.

With increased movement, there needs to be an international forum where governments can negotiate mutual concessions on the restrictions to movement, as they do on trade in the World Trade Organization (WTO) – a general agreement on migration and refugee policy. Such a forum would also be a clear focus to reprimand governments that sought to use resident foreigners as scapegoats for domestic discontents or catspaws in foreign policy concerns. Such a body could seek to secure standard rights to protect foreign workers, procedures for entry and exit, standardised taxation rules, rules or the transfer of remittances and goods, pension transfer procedures, and so forth.[8]

More jobs for developed countries will be done abroad. Together, through flexible working practices and eased migration controls, it may be possible, first, to avoid the disasters that seem implicit in the declining size of labour force and ageing in the developed countries, and second, to give growing access to workers in developing countries to earn and to learn in the developed countries. Both have a mutual advantage in such arrangements. Furthermore, the overall expansion of the economies of the developed countries as a result of expanded immigration might produce a general expansion of labour demand to the benefit of unskilled native-born individuals, allowing an upgrading of their position (as happened in the case of the Los Angeles garment industry).[9]

It is a second best remedy, compromising on the essential underlying principle that the inhabitants of the world ought to be free to come and to go in the world as they please – and that they can be as trusted to do so sensibly in this field as in any other activity beloved of advocates of freeing the market. The compromise is to seek a means which reconciles the fears and interests of the citizens, settled in one territory, and the need for the income and output of the world to be expanded and for workers to get work.

Such arrangements do nothing for the issue of refugee flows. Here different procedures are required to establish funds to offset the financial implications of sudden large-scale movements of those in flight, to mobilise the power to protect those who are persecuted and strengthen the volunteer agencies that currently are the most effective in reacting to emergency. Treating refugees as illegal immigrants, which is what many governments are coming to do, is full of absurdities – it denies the person seeking refugee status the right to work; the numbers applying go well beyond the existing bureaucratic capacity of gov-

---

8   See *The Economist*, 16 March 1991; Straubhaar 1992, p. 478.

9   See McCarthy and Valdez 1986.

ernments (so those in flight are kept in limbo for long periods of time) and is of very high cost because to prevent the refugees working, they are interned. Seeking compassion, they are imprisoned for longer or shorter periods. Allowing those in flight to work would simultaneously relieve the public purse (and so the supposed resentments of the natives), allow the refugee to restore some self-respect, and meet genuine labour needs.

Sooner or later the world's governments are going to be obliged to place a tax on themselves to establish a global fund to cover the transitional costs of refugee flight, funds available to bribe governments into a greater measure of compassion than is currently allowed. With an international agency responsible for refugees, it might become possible to link refugee skills with acknowledged labour deficits so that temporary work permits for those in flight become available in places that need the workers. So important could this become, governments might compete to gain access to refugee workers rather than currently turning all away. Would making it easier to flee encourage illegal immigrants? It might, but is that issue of such moment that it should allow the ending of the supposed compassion of governments – and the current brutal hypocrisy?

For worker migrants, the suggestions here imply an increasing separation of place of work and of residence, of 'home', a dissociation long established for long-distance commuting. Internationally, it is already common, with workers moving between countries on a regular basis. It is even more common in border areas, with daily commuters travelling between the US and Mexico, Poland and Germany, France and Germany, Hong Kong and China (although officially the latter two are now one country, border controls still operate). As transport grows faster and cheaper, geographical distance is becoming increasingly less of an obstacle to such movement, and in the future, we may expect people who live in Mumbai to work in New York, or residents of San Francisco to go to an office in Shanghai.

Some countries might come to employ more foreigners than natives. At an extreme, the entire labour force might live outside the country, while the natives work abroad. Domestically this has long been the case – central business districts in important cities employ a labour force, most of whom commute from outside the employment area. In such cases, the idea of democracy – residents or citizens having the exclusive right to vote – has to be amended to give some rights of participation to those who also work there. At an extreme we can imagine a country that is no more than a junction in flows, where no one 'belongs', where there is neither polity nor electorate corresponding to the national economy. It would be a perverse embodiment of Marx's principle of a communist administration – simply the administration of things, a transport terminal, not people. However, unlike communism, this would be market driven, not subject to an egalitarian democracy. The sanction against its survival would not be an adverse vote by the citizens for there are none; but travellers would fail to use it. In less extreme cases, there will be many different types of ad hoc and messy arrangements to establish a democracy of users, whether resident or not, and there are many precedents already existing for such forms.

Prediction is hazardous, as the 1950s judgement of Brinley Thomas illustrates: 'migration is ceasing to be a major factor in the rise of per capita incomes, not because of legal barriers to movement but because of its reduced economic significance'.[10]

The argument here has been the exact opposite. Global integration is making the movement of commodities and of finance greater and greater – movement increases far faster than output. The world economy, it seems, has by now passed the point of no return and we are set upon the road to the creation of a single integrated global economy, regardless of the wishes of government or citizens. Indeed, any efforts to reverse the process spell catastrophe – and particularly for the central project, the employment at tolerable incomes of all those in the world who wish to work.

By whatever route, workers will come to secure the same 'liberation'. The costs are already apparent – as always, the poor and insecure suffer the depredations. However, that was always true within the illusory security of one national state. One needs only the most cursory acquaintance with nineteenth-century Europe to see that. The promise now is a scale of growth that will allow all to get work. This will not touch the great historic inequalities of the world, let alone achieve universal justice; that is a different political agenda, but those with work gain the confidence to pursue these other issues. The promise is also for the ending of the record of devastating war, which is the product of the heyday of national egotisms. Fierce nationalisms have reappeared even as economic integration proceeds – indeed, economic fusion seems to be making possible a greater degree of political fission and a downsizing in the scale of political management, but the disjuncture of political and economic power makes for a decreasing scale of war, and that is some advance on the epoch of world wars.

In the new world economic order, global markets are tending to swamp national politics. Governments have decreasing power to determine what happens in their domestic economies, so that the key focus of politics in the old

---

10   Thomas 1958.

order is declining. The old left became almost completely submerged in the issues of state power, so that the decline in public power robs them of the supposed means to change their world. But it is not the end of politics. Younger generations take for granted that issues of State power are only one element; there are a bewildering array of other issues, from the defence of the new rapidly growing working classes of the developing countries, to issues of human rights and the future of the world. There is no programme, as there was for the old left, linking diagnosis of current disorder, who is to blame, the means to transform matters, and a comprehensive programme to change the world. The means to change, the old state, is weakening before global markets, producing a sense of helplessness in those who used to work for change. It will be a long time before any similarly comprehensive programme becomes possible. However, it will be reconstructed, as the struggle for the freedom of the majority – including that freedom to decide collectively the material means of existence, rather than just what is left over after markets have settled all the important questions – is a stubborn theme of all human history. The transition to a global politics involves the painful destruction of the old national politics of right and left, of corporatism and state socialism. There remains an intellectual vacuum within which the old left shrivels, shell-shocked by the completeness of its reversals. Trade unions in the developed countries are grateful to be still alive, preoccupied with individual grievances rather than collective action, with few aspirations beyond immediate interests. The bold promises of universal freedom on their banners mock the humdrum reality. The outcome of the long confrontation between capitalist nationalism and socialist internationalism sliced the wrong way, leaving confident capitalist internationalism and defensive socialist *étatisme*. Thus the world made mock of the dreams.

If the world economy in its new guise seems to be restoring elements of the economic order of the nineteenth century (particularly that surge of cosmopolitan growth between 1840 and 1870), the world polity seems to be emulating the order of fifteenth-century Europe, a mass of principalities and city-states, based upon many different principles of foundation.

History does not repeat itself; it offers us only paradoxical echoes. The world today has no earlier parallels simply because of both the extraordinary wealth of the system and the even greater potential to overcome the severe material constraints on the lot of the majority of people. All endeavours to change that state of affairs are fraught with dangers, but the dangers are still less than those offered by the past. If it is true that 40 million people died in the Soviet Union in the Second World War, that 12 million perished in the concentration camps, there is a long way to go before those triumphs of European civilisation are superseded in the new world order.

An antiquated national political order is being dragged along by a world economy. There are many cruelties and injustices involved in that process. But within this, world interest and a universal morality are likewise struggling to be reborn after the long dark night of nationalism and the god-like state that incubated world capitalism. There are grounds for cautious optimism.

PART 5

Journalism and Shorter Pieces

∴

Japan: From the Other Side of the Hill[*]

Japan, which seemed to have mastered the magic of rapid growth, is now super-developed but stagnating, the old sinews of nationalism decaying. This is not merely a matter of a pendulum swing. Japan is qualitatively changing and profoundly so. Even with reform and a restoration of growth, it is going to be very difficult to manage the process – requiring a much expanded immigration of young workers and emigration of an increasing part of what in the current Japanese economy is moveable (like manufacturing). In sum, not just the restoration of growth, but the completion of the stalled process of Japanese globalisation.

It is 36 years, a generation and a half, since my wife and I lived for a few months in Japan, so to return now is, as it were, to view the country through historical spectacles – and from the other side of the hill. Then, the Japanese economy was becoming a matter of great excitement among economists – it had, it seemed, mastered the magic of rapid growth – and was just about to enter its fastest, indeed, spectacular, period of expansion. It was doing so when all the marks of the past were still present, the legacies of the Second World War and ultra-nationalism, and of underdevelopment, still hinting at a land of peasants and lords. Now it is super-developed but stagnating, the old sinews of nationalism decaying; and there are barely any traces of the past (except as provided for the tourists) – it seems it is hardly the same country or people.

'Modernisation' seems to have flooded to the very edges of the country, dissolving the past in a frenzy of rebuilding. You might travel in Vermont or Bavaria, even in Arizona, and be aware of the architectural past, but it is possible to miss these fragments in Japan. This is a world almost completely of commuter trains and early morning joggers, giant traffic jams and Barbie dolls, coffee and breakfast cereals, of walking dogs in the misty dawn and 7-to-11. The once distinctive cultural features – sushi, karaoke, Pokemon and the rest – are now as global as Coke, so they no longer seem distinctive.

It is a fond illusion in Japan that the country is more culturally distinctive than other developed countries, the homogenised 'West'. Thirty-six years ago it seemed a plausible point. Now it seems the opposite – Japan is a model of modernity, as squeaky clean and neat as Switzerland and more efficient than

---

[*]   From: *EPW*, xxxv/37, 9 Sept. 2000.

any of the others. The Shinkansen, the high speed bullet train, initiated the last time we were here, has, they say, never had a serious accident, and it runs on some lines every quarter of an hour. It is quite appropriate therefore that in this, a model of modernism, people should live longest in the world – 84 for women, 77 for men.

Of course, we exaggerate. On occasions, one glimpses in a neglected corner a cottage of wood and rice paper, a shrine, but they are marginalised, either monuments, isolated from daily life, or a last bit of the past awaiting the developers. The calm simplicity, the austerity, of old Japan, the minimalism and quiet elegance, have been swamped by modern clutter and endless movement. Only rarely is one reminded of a now fictional past – a silent heron standing amid the reeds, a line of flying ducks above the perils of the motorway, mists veiling the woods and peaks.

∴

Yet, in stark contrast to the success of modernism, the economy rolls like a rudderless hulk in open seas, a derelict ship without direction or momentum. The crew have not abandoned it, but scuttle from side to side, like cartoon characters in a comedy of impotent activism, bailing this leak or that, but without an idea of where to go or what to do.

You would not know it without the figures. The shops and cafes are full, the tills would ring if there were now any left. Compared to many of the cities of Europe or North America, there is precious little evidence of the poor or the unemployed. A few homeless live in card boxes on the river bank (some with neat gardens attached), but nothing like the secret shanty towns beneath the bridges of New York or the doorway sleepers of London. And what there is of poverty seems swamped by the hordes of shoppers, by the continual festival of consumption for the young where the only authentic Levi jeans (the original looms are now in Japan) are selling at over Rs 7,000 per pair. The clothes and music shops are packed, the shoppers in the latest designer clothes, fashionable bags on their shoulders, and that ubiquitous piece of youth jewellery, the tiny cellphone.

It is the young who are the most striking contrast to 1964. First, they are so large, much the same as the average in North America or Europe, but towering like giants over their grandparents. And they walk, tall, proud and free, unlike the nervous scuttle of the *sararaman* of old, besuited, exhausted, almost cringing before the awful majesty of the Japanese State. The growth between generations means that much of the infrastructure is too small – hotel rooms, bathrooms, airport trollies, seats on trains.

Especially among young women, liberation seems to have arrived. There are seven million women workers in their teens and twenties, well-educated, well-travelled and adventurous, a mighty consumer market and, in principle, a demanding electorate. They marry late (fertility is now down to 1.4 per woman), and spend more riches than women in old puritan Japan could ever dream of. And the hair! Both for boys and girls, from brown to auburn to blonde, and on the wilder shores flaunting blue and green and orange. Some of the girls try to walk on ludicrously tall platform heels, with tiny slit skirts, tottering as fragile and delicate as any geisha in the old world – except that their faces are alive with merriment and mischief.

Perhaps the preoccupation with lifestyle rather than career is part of the explanation for why so many of the young opt for only part-time work. The Japanese level is the fourth highest in the OECD group. The labour ministry thinks it represents a terrible collapse in the incentive to work rather than a failure to find full-time jobs, but then it would. In the broader context, it may be only a part of the remarkable trend in all developed economies towards a contraction in the active full-time labour force – with early retirement and later starts, increasing years of education and time off, shorter working days, weeks and years. It would be good to think the trend was, at least in part, a revolt against the age-old tyranny of work, made possible by unprecedentedly high levels of income.

The unashamed and open preoccupation with lifestyle offends the hard-working adults – 'they have no ideals, no aims or purposes beyond fashion and themselves'. It is an ancient complaint of every generation – from the Romans onwards, and the first Tokugawas would no doubt have sympathised. However, in the sum of things, a preoccupation with style is an infinite improvement on the obsessions of the grandfathers and great grandfathers of young Japanese – with killing the enemies of the Emperor (and the same applies to the young of North America and Europe). But the adults tend to notice the handful of cases of murders of parents or the physical abuse of teachers by class bullies. The new minister of education urges two years 'mandatory voluntary activities' (what a delightful contradiction) for the young: to divert them from the 'recent heinous crimes ... beyond our imagination'. Yet, despite some bizarre appearances, the young in general seem to have kept the remarkable courtesy of their parents. Even the 17-year-old who recently killed his mum, did so, he says, so 'she should not be troubled' by his beating up of four members of his school baseball team for teasing him over his refusal to shave his hair off.

.•.

Yet still the second largest economy in the world flounders, stagnates, and has done so for a decade, trapped in the very structures which once propelled spectacular growth but now, in the new world economy, have so far made it impossible for Gulliver to get off his knees. In the 1950s and 1960s, it seemed easy. The government – through the ministry of international trade and industry (MITI) – decided the direction and scale of investment, the composition of future output, and made available to selected client corporations the cheap loans (pre-eminently through the ministry of finance's fiscal investment and loan programme, fuelled by the post office's access to household and other savings) that removed the risk of investment. Shareholders – like workers – were kept sedated on the sidelines. This allowed investment without much attention to rate of return or risk, let alone comparative costs or advantages – that is, to consistent overinvestment to capture market share. In the 1950s, the government supplied 40 percent of the investment in its chosen industries – steel, coal, electricity, petroleum, cement, shipping. In addition, the government controlled credit to keep interest rates low and block foreign penetration of the local capital markets. Finally, the government facilitated the creation of the *keiretsu*, the restoration of the pre-war business groups, the *zaibatsu* (supposedly liquidated by the US occupation as part of postwar reforms). These families of corporations, operating in all major fields and in banking, were united by interlocking shareholdings and directorships (to prevent takeovers), with preferential prices on internal trade and lending – that is, the group as a whole carried its weaker members, regardless of the rate of return. With high growth, next year's profits would always wipe out this year's cumulative borrowings.

It was a marvellous mechanism for growth, producing in the 1950s, a 10 percent rate of annual expansion of gross national product (17 percent in manufacturing, 33 percent in investment), and 14 percent in the 1960s (16 percent manufacturing, 21 percent investment). It succeeded in the transformation of Japan, the substantive achievement whatever happened afterwards. But it did rely on the continuation of growth – and on a world system where both Japan was still small enough not to count and the Great Powers were, for whatever reasons, tolerant of Japan flouting the spirit, if not the letter, of an open world economy. Through the 1970s and 1980s, the global regulation of Japan's economy steadily increased, forcing the government to conform to the general rules of any open economy – if its companies were to be allowed to continue to enjoy a free run of the world.

At the end of the 'bubble' in 1990, growth failed – and the mechanism of growth became a no less powerful instrument to ensure stagnation. The sudden swift accumulation of debt, the sheer number of failing enterprises, swamped both government and *keiretsu*, and carrying this load of 'sick' industries (Indira Gandhi's concept fits like a glove) made it impossible to restore the profit rate and thus resume investment and growth. Worse than that, the mechanism to finance national growth now became a means to finance the government's cronies – in the banks, in the construction industry (which finances the governing Liberal Democratic Party), in the retail and wholesale trade (which sustains employment) and in farming (which delivers the rural vote).

Thus, Japan's government, proud to have presided over the creation of a group of global corporations dominating world markets, was now required to reform the domestic economy so that it too became open to global operations – without a hidden agenda or hidden debts. All the former strengths – a high rate of savings, low interest rates, government finance, the *keiretsu* 'family' system of absorbing losses to sustain growth, became disastrous weaknesses. Each attempt to escape, to reform, was ultimately knocked back – most dramatically by the 1997–8 crisis in east and southeast Asia (and the 1998 Russian default). By now, much of the old economy is sustained only by public finance on preferential terms (and a refusal to call in the debts) – a life-support system without any sign that the patient has the capacity to recover, a 'pensioned capitalism'. The government has the largest public debt in the OECD group, equal in the spring of 1998 to 129 percent of gross domestic product (without counting other obligations in the fields of pensions, and banking and credit guarantee systems). Two of the largest banks are effectively nationalised, and the rest dependent on injections of public funds – the final debt here is likely to be well in excess of what the government authorised in 1998, 7 trillion yen.

Debt finance has forced some reforms, and some of these are exposing the hidden debts. But there is still far to go – to include insurance, the regional banks and co-operative credit unions. A large part of the financial economy has still to be discovered – and opening the cupboard door on the army of skeletons within is something the government is most reluctant to do.

The central paralysis is political, embodied in the incapacity of the ruling Liberal Democratic Party (LDP) to abandon its friends and financiers by reforming the structure of the economy so it is capable of competing in the new world economy – but in doing so, risking the unwinding of the status quo that has governed Japan since the Second World War and thus jeopardising the very existence of the LDP. Take some of the key sectors in this political economy:

(1) *Agriculture.* Despite the decline in the agricultural population (a third of households included someone engaged in farming when we were last here; now it is a twentieth), rural constituencies still have three times the weight of the urban in the electoral system. Rice is no longer the exclusive

staple of the population, yet still the government offers the rice fanners massive support – producers support is equal to 63 percent of the value of production (much of it maintained to dissuade farmers from growing rice). This is only possible while watertight protection-tariffs are kept at three times the American price of rice. In sum, the Japanese consumer pays eight times what the American does for rice (five times for beef and processed food) – a result with particularly deleterious effects on the poor (who, despite official disclaimers, do exist). All efforts at reform have foundered here – the government kept at bay the demands of the Uruguay Round, and its recent Basic Law on Food, Agriculture and Rural Areas reaffirms the central aim in agricultural policy as food security and sustaining the 'multi-functionality' of agriculture regardless of the cost to the majority of non-farming Japanese consumers. Of course, the security of the rural seats of LDP members of the assembly was not mentioned.

(2)   *Retail and wholesale trade.* Under a hammering from Washington, the government made sufficient reforms in the 1990s to produce a sharp contraction in the number of small grocers – and to jet in to the domestic market foreign grocery chains (7–11, Lawson Station, Circle K, etc). But when reforms started threatening to affect the government's friends or the banks which had loaned them money, there was an attempt to reverse direction. Most recently, Sogo, a giant retailer (employing, it is said, 10,000, and buying from 10,000 suppliers), was faced with closure on the basis of 1.87 trillion yen debts (the largest non-financial failure to date). Sogo's banker was recently sold off to try to master its debt problems, but the bank's new foreign owners, refused to absorb the loss and passed it to the government. Despite the government's staggering level of existing debt, it announced it would inject new funds into the company, provoking not only dissent in the three-party coalition but public outrage that the foolhardy should thus be saved from the punishments of excessive risk-taking – and foreigners should be the indirect beneficiaries. The government beat a hasty retreat (although it did offer cheap credit, ¥180 billion – or US$1.66 billion – to help Sogo's suppliers). The chairman of the Federation of Economic Organisations noted politely, but perhaps regretfully that 'caring about the public reaction is becoming more important for companies'. The shareholders have awoken, and so has public opinion, making it very difficult to keep the old alliances – and their secret financing – intact. Yet how far does the wave of bankruptcies have to go to restore the profit rate of those who survive? A second large collapse, of Seiyo, a property company, has just been announced – when the banks refused their customary reflex of rolling over bad debts. The nightmare

of the government is that the revolt of the workforce against the expected mass layoffs flowing from bankruptcy will checkmate any attempt to
prune the system enough to make it work.

(3) *Construction*. The building industry – employing some six million workers – is a major financier of the LDP, and the government has been in this
decade a major financier of the building industry through the gigantic
public infrastructure programmes which are supposed to restore economic growth (the current programme is said to be worth some ¥110 trillion, or US$1 trillion or so). The macroeconomic effects of this pump prim-
ing have been extraordinarily limited, but they have littered the country
with a plethora of bridges, spanning impossible distances, flyovers, tunnels, highways, railways, and a new Tokyo on reclaimed land (with its own
gigantic 'Rainbow' bridge). Yet despite all this generosity, the level of debt
of the construction industry (¥9,000 billion or so) has barely changed,
and still many companies are kept alive only by being able to ignore
debts (or hide them). Nonetheless, the relationships are embarrassing –
recently, a former construction minister, Eichi Nakao (who lost his seat
in the 25 June election after sitting continuously since 1967) was arrested,
accused of taking bribes of ¥30 million in 1996 from Wakakchiku Construction to steer public contracts in their direction. As the case has unfolded, it seems the enterprising company had also made regular donations
to the election funds of the Defence Agency Chief (¥3,60,000 in 1996, half
a million in 1997), the policy chief of the LDP, another ex-construction
Minister, three ex-transport ministers, the LDP chief, a former trade minister, education minister and agricultural minister, and so on. The case is
still pending, but it is fuelling public fury – and increased popularity for
the opposition.

The intermediary to these three politically important sectors is the banking
system, itself heavily burdened, as we have seen, with debt, declared and still
hidden. The variety of means by which the public sector keeps the head of
banking above water is not always clear, but more of it is becoming clear, especially as more rebels to the political status quo are created. Take, for example,
interest rate policy in the Bank of Japan, now in theory (and law) independent
of the government. The bank has, since February of last year, operated to keep
its main interest rate close to zero. This shamelessly robs Japan's savers (and
pensioners) to secure the debts of the indebted (particularly, as we have seen,
in construction and real estate). The bank has hesitantly publicised the issue of
raising the rate since holding it down has done nothing to force the reorganisation of the indebted to restore growth and penalises the successful. Despite the

bank's supposed independence, the prime minister has protested, along with the governing party, the finance minister and some larger companies – it seems this is not the time to try to force reform.

∴

The stalemate in policy, the paralysis of reform, encourages a mood of pessimism if not despair. The old order has been halted, the new has not yet broken the surface. Pay has been cut in many sectors and total incomes stagnate; lifetime employment in the big corporations is now heavily qualified – up to one million have been laid off since 1997, and there are more to come. Unemployment may be close to 7 percent, low by European standards but catastrophic on the Japanese record, with one in five of the young out of work. Suicides have increased 53 percent since 1991, and are now concentrated among men in their 50s (rather than teenagers as in the past). Violent crime has increased, and also well-publicised cases of schoolgirl prostitution and classroom violence. After a series of scandals – including the discovery of falsified evidence, ignoring serious complaints, etc – the police are said to have lost public trust and require purging and reform.

People feel globalisation has arrived with a vengeance, robbing them of the old safe national capital project and the secure society that went with it. When recently a leading supplier of dairy products, Snow, was accused of selling polluted milk to general horror, it touched a much broader fear – 'After all', one senior government officer observed, 'we Japanese invented quality control – this would not have happened 20 years ago'.

The new coalition government that resumed office on 4 July inspires few hopes. The three collaborating parties (dominated by the 233 seats of the LDP) lost a total of 60 seats between them in the election, so it was hardly a vote of confidence. The new lot include many of the old guard that have a decade-long history of failure, and there is little confidence that any lessons have been learned.

But is the gloom justified? The violent crime rate – like the evidence of police failures – is small stuff by American standards (and the Americans are here, as in so many fields, among the world's leaders). And it is not at all clear how the complaints link to globalisation, the current scapegoat for anything negative that happens. A lack of confidence in the government is hardly new – and again one is reminded of the long years of Clinton discredit. Moods have been powerfully wrong before – witness the US 15 or so years ago when the intelligentsia, astonishingly so by present standards, saw the country as doomed, forever trailing behind those champions of manufacturing, Japan and Germany, and set upon a course of inexorable decline that would turn the US into a developing country in no time. Those were the days when Robert Lawrence wrote his *Can America Compete?* – an extraordinary question now.[1]

Japan remains the second largest economy in the world and, though burdened by the great weight of the old economy, it still has one of the largest cadres of computer engineers. Some see this as already exhibiting dramatic and dynamic growth that will ultimately transform the economy once it can clear the old sectors out of the way. Pessimists argue that Japan is far behind in digital technology, and without competence in English, it is impossible to compete. India is quoted as the superstar; even Malaysia and Singapore are said to be ahead by the standards of e-commerce. Gloom is fashionable and sometimes seems vindicated by some of the evidence – the optimism of the will has still to make its appearance. But in 15 years' time, we may well look back on the present with equal astonishment – with the Japanese now absurdly chortling once again at how clever they are, and the Americans once more in gloom. Or else by then we shall have stopped such silly nationalist games and will just rejoice at progress which benefits us all regardless of where it is initiated.

However, these are not simply matters of pendulum swings because Japan is qualitatively changing, and profoundly so. In 1960, 30 percent of the population were under the age of 15, 5.7 percent 65 or more. In 1997, the equivalent figures were 15 and 15.7 percent. That is, the country is already set upon a demographic transition which will radically reduce the size of the labour force and expand the number of aged dependents (leaving aside the pension problem – possibly 80 trillion yen of uncovered obligations to be found). Even with reform and a restoration of growth, it is going to be very difficult to manage the process – and will probably require a much expanded immigration of young workers (an issue just beginning to be discussed), the emigration of some of the elderly and an increasing part of what in the current Japanese economy is moveable (like manufacturing). In sum, this should not only restore growth but also lead to the completion of the stalled process of Japanese globalisation.

Before we left this time, we retraced our steps to Mitaka, the Tokyo suburb where we had lived in 1964. We tried to find our little wooden house under the trees. We could recognise almost nothing in the cement structures that, we presumed, had replaced it. Tokyo had spread and engulfed the rice fields we remembered – but, whatever the losses, the Japanese were more splendid and vigorous than ever. There were no grounds for gloom.

---

1 Lawrence 1984.

Nicaragua 1979[*]

It began at Mexico airport. A youth and a girl in black berets and T-shirts emblazoned, 'Free Nicaragua', were playing tapes of revolutionary songs on a boogie box. All through the flight it continued.

The plane was packed with exiles, chattering, bowed down with luggage. They had not thought they would ever return; or if they could, not to a land free of the tyrant, Somoza.

The excitement rose in waves, with singing and cries of the Sandinista slogan, 'Free country or death!' The air hostess, tearful with excitement, began to announce to 'Señores y señoras: we are about to land at Sandino Airport, Managua, in Free Nicaragua'. Her words were drowned in the shouts and cheers and clapping.

And there they were, the compañeros. In jungle green, unshaven young men, and girls, with machine guns, slouching around the terminal building, grinning as we streamed out of the aircraft to the sounds of the hymns of the revolution. Everyone was hugging and weeping and kissing and cheering: 'Long live free Nicaragua!'

So it was throughout the time. For now is the fiesta of the Nicaraguan revolution.

Not that the savageries of the Somoza regime are not all about. There are lines of little crosses along the road. A pathetic red and black bandanna hangs limply from a lamp post to mark where a compañero fell. The gutted shells of factories, the houses splattered with thousands of bullet holes, mark the passing of the old order. The walls of a cottage enclose only a rain filled bomb crater. The great silver body of a crushed aircraft lies marooned in the field where it fell.

Each day the newspapers are filled with photographs of those still missing, with appeals from parents for any news of them. Most of them are in their early teens, bright innocent faces. The news columns record the discovery of unmarked graves and unidentified corpses. Somoza marked his rule and his passing most cruelly.

But the irrepressible excitement of victory hides the tragedies. 'It was hard, Señor', says the old market woman, fanning her meagre stock of bananas. 'It was hard – but now we have hope, and then we did not'.

---

[*] From: unpublished Mss, 1979.

The compañeros are everywhere, shy teenagers in jungle green or tattered cast-offs, in US Marine T-shirts and 'Kiss me, baby' hats. But all with automatics over their shoulders and pistols in their belts. They grin and giggle, and demand to have their photographs taken, for now what they do is history and must be recorded. One day, their grandchildren will see them, as they saw Sandino, in funny clothes, a legend.

'We are going to build a new world', an older man observes gravely, 'and lift ourselves out of the ruins'.

The new world needs discipline. When the FSLN marched into Managua in July, they forbade those aged under ten to carry arms. They counted and signed up the many thousands who had fought outside the ranks of the FSLN. Most are very young. They know how to fight, and not to drink when carrying arms. But for the rest, they are boys and girls. A 17-year-old, searching bags at a ministry, has silver painted fingernails. She finds it difficult to listen to top of the pops on her transistor while balancing the heavy automatic on her knees. She is one of those who patrol the night, when the hot silence is occasionally broken by the sound of firing, the boom of a grenade.

A teenage mother of two, dressed in khaki, says with a cheery smile:

'If Sandinismo works, we'll stay. If it doesn't, we'll have to go back to school again'.

∴

The main hotel, the Intercontinental is still two thirds owned by a United States company. It is packed with senior compañeros. Security is lax in the excitement and good fellowship. Members of the government flow through, using food coupons for lunch. Ministers, members of the junta, in T-shirts and jeans, stop to joke in the lobby. Serious men and women, in jungle green and heavily-armed, pack the dining room to eat, cheek by jowl with seedy arms dealers, the CIA men, the KGB men, a party of lively Cubans, some dour East Germans, the bristly little man from *Pravda* and the well-washed girl from the *Wall Street Journal*. Here is a melancholy businessman, trying to resume imports of wicker from Taiwan to make chairs for Miami. Here is a gypsy from Bordeaux, cadging Gitanes from the Greek *Le Monde* man from Paris. The gypsy has a single earring and a straggly beard. He fought on the southern front and is now a bodyguard to the junta. He is an anarchist, passionate and simple; he says Marxism in Europe is all bourgeois nonsense, but not here.

There is an Ethiopian in a bush hat. He speaks very slowly and carefully, tip-toeing through the barbed wire of these alien words. He came to Nicaragua 'to fight for the liberation of mankind'. A Bolivian architect fought on the southern front with a Mexican filmmaker in khaki. There are hosts of Chileans, Miristas, of Peruvians and Colombians; some Canadians, a couple of Germans, an Australian and an Englishman; half passionate idealists, half soldiers of fortune, now all their diversities rendered incognito in jungle green.

Outside, small boys beg. Middle-aged women tout round the giant American cars for US dollars.

The Intercontinental is far from the barrios, the dispersed working-class villages of Managua. There, the local committees work to repair the destruction. Money is scarce. Along the road, boys with automatics politely stop the few passing cars with collecting tins – 'for the paper for the commandante of the barrio'.

The shacks are festooned with the red and black flags of the FSLN. Between the bullet holes on the walls, there are generations of slogans. Some are poems or cartoons. A sudden radio booms out: 'This is radio Sandino, broadcasting from Free Nicaragua', the folk songs they play in the streets have been rewritten:

> Who are the men in jungle green,
> the men with clear eyes?

On the road to Esteli in the north, a man ploughs a field with bullocks. At a small town, a man sprays the wheels of passing trucks with insecticide; he did it all through the war. Women wash clothes in the brown river. In a broken down shack, a grubby infant crawls across the dirt floor with chickens and empty Coke bottles. His frightened mother in tatters, clutching a naked baby says: 'Yes, the revolution is a good thing. I hope now things will be better'. Two giant Mack trucks rumble by outside, loaded with soft drinks.

In Esteli, the committee commandante sits in a bombed out department store. Rain drips through the open roof. He adds up the losses: between six and eight thousand killed or wounded; 70 to 75 percent of the buildings damaged.

> For 22 days we were out of touch with Managua. They bombed the hospital to pieces, and the town is ruined. We had no food. People were very patient – they had been promised much, but got very little.
>
> But everybody came together. We went to the peasants and farmers to beg and borrow. We made soap to barter for food. We sent our people out to do jobs for the farmers. Now we are planting maize and beans on Somoza's old land. Students came over the border from Honduras to help. A medical team from Spain set up an emergency unit in the wreck of the hospital.

Outside, cheeky boys beg. And a grave young man on crutches watches the world impassively.

In Monimbo in the south, where the first revolt started spontaneously in February of last year, the great covered market was completely destroyed except for the outside walls. Now the market has spilled down the side streets. Hundreds of stalls sell small quantities of the same thing to very few buyers.

'Because so many have no jobs, they go to the country, get a few bananas, and then set up a stall to sell them', a market woman tells us. A boy with a megaphone goes round the stalls collecting money to rebuild the local school. In a main street, the traffic is cordoned off to make space for 12 wooden crosses, laid under an awning on the tarmac. Passers-by bring flowers.

· ·
·

The paradoxes persist. 'Welcome to the City of Managua. Another city where you can use your Diners' Club card'. A giant neon sign winks in the night sky to remind you of the existence of Coca Cola; another offers you panty hose. 'The Bank of London and South America as usual offers you its excellent services'. As does Fiat and Toyota and the rest. In the Intercontinental, the staid gentlemen in suits hold a meeting of the Managua Rotary Club. And in one of the main dailies, La Prensa, the American Chamber of Commerce appeals to its members to help in national reconstruction.

In Matagalpa in the north, there is a meeting of coffee farmers. Most are small and brown as trees, skins wrinkled by countless days in the sun. They wear battered sombreros, patched pants and broken down shoes. But at the back are the great farmers, white and plump, dressed like golfers from Miami. They listen politely to Jaime Wheelock, a young man in jungle green, Minister of Agrarian Reform, and a member of the junta. The compañeros stand around them, guns at the ready. Wheelock is there to appeal to the farmers to get in the crop so that it can be exported to the United States; otherwise, they cannot import, not even the pharmaceuticals to keep alive the infants. There is a cheer when the local farmers' leader at the front says bluntly, 'We want the truth, not beautiful words'. The nationalised banks won't give credit; there is talk of nationalising the coffee farms; the Sandinistas have put rural wages too high. The farmers grumble and Wheelock concedes. The meeting is in the local cinema; after the revolutionary leadership, they will be showing David Niven and Lee McKern in 'Candleshoe'.

Granada, far to the south, is a handsome Spanish colonial city, the oldest, they say, in all the Americas. It is on the edge of a great lake where there are freshwater shark. Grumpily a volcano steams in the distance. More small boys demand to polish shoes; they beg or steal food from the diners in the open-air restaurant in the main square. A seven-year-old is selling lottery tickets. 'The reason you don't win the lottery', he tells me gravely, 'is because you don't buy from me'.

Granada is the ancestral home of the old ruling families of Nicaragua. There are revolutionary slogans on the walls, and men in jungle green have set up a local committee. A black girl, a nanny all in starched white with a little white bonnet, shepherds two white toddlers along the pavement. In Granada, not much has changed, although the friends of Somoza had fled to Miami. Their houses and cars have been expropriated for the revolution.

Granada supplied some of the revolutionary leaders. For the leadership is part of the educated upper classes of Nicaragua. In the garage under a rich farmer's house where they built a hide hole for the local FSLN commander before the revolution, a brand new Volvo 244 stands, a line of bullet holes tattooed neatly across its windscreen.

Each day, the editorials of *La Prensa* argue that the revolution belongs to everyone. 'There is too much loose talk about "the bourgeoisie" and "exploitation". We should say firmly that some of the bourgeoisie exploit, some do not, and some of the bourgeoisie are exploited'.

Some eight hundred of Somoza's National Guard, with their families, are camping in the grounds of the Guatemalan Embassy. At the wire gates, a stream of people hand over to those inside baskets of food and vacuum flasks. Inside, a square heavy man with scowls stares at a world suddenly hostile. But the spirit is not unfriendly. The young compañeros guarding the gate outside help an old woman lift her heavy sack of food over the fence. A tall National Guard thug buys cigarettes through the mesh. A girl outside asks him for someone inside, her uncle. He tells her to get lost. She flushes, 'You bunch of fucking traitors, you swine!' For a moment, there is a flash of reality. But the tall man turns away indifferently.

A young boy in rubber shoes leans on a broom outside a small motel on a country road.

'I buried them all. There were a lot of National Guard fleeing this way with lorries full of heavy army gear. They killed 65 people on the road, men and women and children. But they were stopped at the bridge. A lot of them were killed, and Sandinistas too. I buried them all. It was sad. After all, they were all Nicaraguans'.

••

The plane from Managua is half empty, and silent.

Vietnam: Old Men Remember*

Vietnam has not just forgotten the war; it has positively rejected what it was supposedly defending.

You would think it must be a land of ghosts, forever mourning that the bravest, the cleverest and the most beautiful are dead: all that was finest has been lost. There was one press photograph that summarised the horror of the Vietnam war – a shockingly naked girl of eight or nine, running down a track, with arms held high, eyes blazing with terror (like that Munch painting) at the napalm streaming through the firmament. Where is she now? Did she escape?

For the generation young in the 60s, the very names – Danang, Hue, Dalat, Bien Hoa, the DMZ and 17th Parallel, the Tet Offensive – are wounds of one of the most cruel and unjust wars of our times (a time not noted for wars which are kindly and just). In those days, we harried ministers here in Britain with the latest data from International Control Commission Reports, reproached their indifference, their hypocrisy, their slavish subordination to the fantasies of Washington. 100,000 or more continually and frustratedly expressed their fury to the hooded windows of the US embassy in Grosvenor Square. These were only tiny tributaries in the great tide that finally led to the collapse of the US armed forces in Vietnam – and the appalling indignity of all those choppers lifting off in panic from the US embassy in Saigon (you can still see the same grubby building there now, with the same hooded windows).

It was the finest hour of the American people. Any fool could fight, could rejoice in what is now politely called 'collateral damage'. Any fool, including an American president, needs to 'live down Vietnam' by slaughtering a 100,000 fleeing young Iraqi conscripts. But to have *stopped* a war, to have halted the juggernaut in its tracks, is something again. Let them put that proudly on the banners of the US Marines alongside Guadalcanal and Iwo Jima.

Now, two decades later, we foreigners are the ghost ridden, trapped in our time warp, as we wander through the lush paddy fields and the streets of the decaying cities. The children are gay and sparkling. The shadow that lay across the lives of their parents and grandparents, 35 years of cruel war against Japanese, French and Americans, has left no apparent trace. After all, a majority

---

* From: *Economic and Political Weekly*, 26 September 1992.

of the Vietnamese may have been born since 1975 when the Americans fled. One must be thankful for that collective amnesia, for the past has such horrors that, if remembered, it would reduce the present to a nightmare.

In the ministry of health, the official gravely reminds us that teenage heroin addiction is far more worrying than any residual war traumas. And indeed, in the shade of the trees in a Hanoi park, the old men sit at peace, all passion spent. But further south, each village has its obelisk and the serried ranks of war graves, the men and women as regimented in death as they were in life, a ghostly army to guard an emperor. And there are still bomb craters and bridges broken like toys. But most signs have disappeared. They say the birds sing and butterflies flit amid the foliage now on Bikini Atoll: green is the tree of life.

There must surely be a better way of ordering our affairs than this periodic mass sacrifice of young men and boys. Killing the first born male to appease the gods is a very ancient practice, and the world still clings to the ritual long after it has abandoned so many other cruel traditions. Even now, Bosnia bleeds.

Think of all those Iranians and Iraqis, Somalis and Liberians, Afghans and Koreans, and the mighty army of grieving mothers and widows in black. Does the soil really need so much blood?

Vietnam's amnesia – if such it is – is more extreme than a simple loss of memory. The Vietnam war was the centrepiece of a whole world order, an imperialist and capitalist assault on the third world. On the other side stood the forces of progress and reason, of justice and equality, embodied in a civilisation shaped by the altruism of public service and the state, founded upon collective – not private – action and on planning. Yet winning the war lost precisely that peace. Vietnam has not just forgotten the war; it has positively rejected what it was supposedly defending.

Within four years of the end of the war, the government began to dismantle collectivism in agriculture, the co-operatives. From 1981, peasant households were allocated land for their exclusive cultivation, albeit with set procurements to be delivered to the state. From 1988, cultivating families were able to contract land and water for 15 to 20 years without any state instructions on what should be grown.

For the two-thirds of the population engaged in agriculture; the effects have been electric. Peasants in the famous conical straw hats are stooped low over the paddy almost every day, weeding the lush carpet of brilliant green rice, scooping irrigation water by hand-held bags into minor channels, grazing livestock. The country ended its reputation as an area of endemic famine, withstood the ending of subsidised food supplies from the Soviet Union, achieved self-sufficiency in foodstuffs both through expanded total output and area yields, diversified cultivation (more rapidly expanding, for example, coffee, rubber and sugar output) and became a significant exporter of rice (1.5 million metric tons in 1990) and other crops.

The countryside sizzles with activity – new houses are everywhere being built, the roads congested with new bicycles, scooters, motor bikes, small tractors and trucks. There seems to be no end to the vast rural markets where apparently everyone is selling something on the side of the road (but it is not clear who is buying). Government officers may speak gravely of the future problems involved in a planned transition to a market economy, but for the overwhelming mass of the population, markets are, with a vengeance, already here.

Six years ago, what had happened to agriculture was begun in the economy at large. What is known elsewhere in the world as 'structural adjustment' is *doi moi* in Vietnam. The private sector was given its head; foreign investment was welcomed; and external economic and monetary controls relaxed. As in China, with an older reform programme, the effects have been dramatic. The cities are bustling with new businesses (now said to number 80,000 in the capital alone). New buildings are going up everywhere – the Hanoi government claims that 200,000 square metres of new private housing were built in 1990, compared to a peak level of 150,000 when the state was solely responsible. And even more than in the countryside, markets sprawl all over the pavements. The ending of migration controls has led to a rapid expansion in the cities – Ho Chih Minh City (our old Saigon) has now over 4 million people and is growing swiftly.

What is to be done, however, with the old state-owned enterprises? In what has now become a standard formulation, the Central Institute for Economic Management argues that state corporations employ three-quarters of the country's fixed capital (and 86 percent of the official volume of credit) and 30 percent of the workforce (but almost all the technical and professional cadre) to produce 26 percent of the gross social product. As in China, the corporations are slowly sinking deeper into debt and are a major drain on public resources. Tightening the costing system has led to some layoffs – additions to the visible urban unemployment – and stagnating public pay levels (so that public employees are forced to take second and third jobs in the private sector). Since at the same time the government is trying to halve the armed forces (numbering one million men in 1989), this further increases the numbers searching for work. The government has now launched its first pilot scheme to sell shares in state corporations (the first dozen companies have been nominated). The logic of the market is almost complete.

The surface appearance is of considerable prosperity, symbolised in all those new little palaces, aggressively modernist and pseudo Beverly Hills or Monte Carlo, visible – unashamed – signs of the emergence of a new private bourgeoisie. But the problems are horrendous. The country is still very poor, with

a per capita income of barely $200. There is much poverty to be seen down
the sidelanes and in the legion of beggars. Housing in the older areas of the
old cities is appalling, narrow corridors with sleeping places at the side, drip-
ping in the rain with open drains. Old buildings look as though they have not
been touched since the French left and since when the population has vastly
increased (Hanoi, 200,000 at the time of the French evacuation, is now nearly
three million). Inflation, running at something of the order of 75 percent per
year, continually depreciates the currency, making vital imports for agriculture
(for example, fertilisers, formerly imported at heavily subsidised prices from
the Soviet Union) and industry prohibitively expensive.

The bottlenecks in infrastructure are especially severe, symbolised in the
fact that only one very poor 2-lane road and one single track railway line
connects the capital and Ho Chih Minh City. Power is a continual problem.

Apart from dealings connected with oil exploration, foreign investment
has been sluggish despite increasingly favourable terms. It will continue to
be so while Washington maintains its current economic embargo (Honda,
fearing the imposition of penalties in the US market, pulled out of its Vietnamese motor cycle project). The embargo blocks most bilateral and multilat-
eral aid programmes as well as foreign bank loans. What foreign investment has
occurred has tended to be by small and medium sized companies from Taiwan,
Hong Kong, Korea and Japan (in fish and food processing, timber and textiles).

But there is great promise, despite the problems, and those who see Vietnam
as capable of repeating the experience of Guangdong in China are not hopeless
utopians. Yet the transition is bizarre. The slim and graceful young women
whose mothers split their nails and cut their hands to haul artillery pieces
through the paddy or down the Ho Chih Minh Trail through Cambodia or
through the labyrinth of tiny tunnels approaching Saigon, now wear long gloves
against the sun as they ride their scooters in the Saigon streets. The conical hats
are still everywhere and the green topees, ubiquitous symbols of that ragged
army of heroes. But the preoccupation is now with the fast buck. Coca Cola is
everywhere. The present is everything. The past can be postponed.

What will happen to the politics? The great decentralisation of power in
Vietnam – as in China – suggests a competitive pursuit of economic expansion which makes the political penetration of the market much greater. It is
symbolised in Guangdong by radical debureaucratisation. There is far to go in
Vietnam. The country is still festooned with cobwebs of tedious and useless
regulations – police permission is needed to move between provinces, police
registration required on arrival, entry and exit visas required. And each regulation requires the appropriate rent of dollar fees and photographs (one host
suggested the whole racket was a carve up between the immigration depart-

ment and private photographers; when I told him Spain had over 40 million tourists a year, his eyes sparkled at the photography profits to be made).

The upsurge of prosperity – and especially the radical improvement in food supplies – has silenced much complaint. But the government treads warily, withdrawing when substantial opposition is promised. This year, the harvests look good and food prices should decline to the advantage of the vulnerable. There has also been some relaxation in the terms of inner party debate for its two million members, and some liberalisation of the press.

But police power continues as successive Amnesty Reports show. The government knows that if it opened the borders as it did once before (and as Cuba did), hundreds of thousands would take a chance on becoming Boat People rather than risk staying. Nearly one million fled last time. A whole quarter of Hanoi emptied. A giant Chinese Buddhist pagoda still stands there, once no doubt an object of great pride to the dignified Chinese Vietnamese burgers who built it. It is now a kindergarten for those who moved into the empty houses. For all the world, it reminds one of synagogues in old Berlin.

A girl stands at dawn, waist high in the paddy, holding a snub-nosed black buffalo, watching our train steam by on its way to a different world. Her life will be even more transformed than those of her parents. Perhaps when she is old, she will need to remember the war she did not experience, or rather to invent it, to create the fiction of history out of the gravestones that remain. Her good fortune will be that she and her fellows will have made a land prosperous enough to nurture the fictions of history, to escape the cruel immediacy of war and poverty.

CHAPTER 5.4

Teheran Diary*

In the Eye of the Storm

Friday, December 1
It is the eve of Muharram, the great Shi'ite Muslim month of mourning for the death of Hussein.

It is a bright clear day. The sun glistens on the mountain snow high above Teheran. From there, you could see the whole sprawling city spread out, the bare brown hills churned to make way for a metro, for blocks of flats, highways and luxury hotels for foreign consultants.

The city holds its breath. It has vowed to destroy the 35 year old tyranny of the Shah during Muharram. The Shah sits in his gigantic palace to the north, cold as an icicle, while a dozen white telephones ring at his elbow, an endless stream of messengers bring documents to sign arid advisers to worry, all to befuddle the moment of crisis.

In the barracks, the young soldiers polish their automatics, worrying: what will happen if they ask me to shoot my brother or my sister tomorrow? In the bazaar, the fortress of revolution, they are busy scribbling the illegal wall newspapers that will later be photocopied illegally on the Shah's machines, and are now the only source of news. And in numberless living rooms the argument rages: what will the Shah do? The talk, replenished by a new arrival with a new fund of rumours, is broken only on the hour to listen, with gasps of disgust, to the official news broadcasts, or in the afternoons, to crouch, straining to hear the crackling BBC. It is wartime Europe again.

Already the general strike has begun. The oilworkers whom the new military government promised to whip back to work remain defiant. An engineer, just back from Abadan, says no oil is moving; he counted 42 giant tankers anchored off Kharg Island, the terminal, waiting in vain for some nourishment.

The telephone workers are out. A girl reports the army has taken over the television studios, to break a strike of the workers; the world service of Iran broadcasting is paralysed; quick, find a television set to see what fools the generals make of themselves. The one newspaper still appearing after the military crackdown (the government's own paper) has been killed by a strike of the printers.

---

* From: *Economic and Political Weekly*, 16 December 1978.

The universities and schools are closed. Teheran University is occupied by troops to prevent the students gathering. Almost all shops have boards up; but breadshops collect enormous queues, and a mile or more of cars wait at petrol stations.

But still the city waits. On street corners, women in black veils wait, like sentinels or witnesses. Boys fill the time with a football. A solitary lad on a skateboard skims down a hill, between the banks of golden leaves that fall from the trees.

The foreigners flee. The hotels are empty, staff loafing without customers. Every flight from the airport is crammed, whole families scrambling with mountains of luggage to escape. 50,000 dollars a day leaves with them; Central Bank staff have just released unofficially a list of government officials who have taken out of the country sums of over 10 million dollars each. The customs are on strike, so no raw materials or equipment leave the wharves for the factories. At the airport, it is another hurdle to free a single case. In one corner, I notice a container of US mails, Los Angeles to Frankfurt, stranded by mistake.

The city waits, but the army prepares. Three Chieftain tanks, belching smoke and swaying dangerously, get caught in a traffic jam at the crossroads. Young men on the pavement jeer and lob a brick; the stranded soldiers in fury fire a volley. But not too low lest it hit a general in a trapped car. The tanks are impotent, like beached whales, while the young torment them. One miracle of modern technology is neutralised by another, the humble car.

One hour after the curfew (at 9.00pm), the first greeting for Muharram begins. From every area – it seems from every house – the shout rises: Allah-o Akbar. Surely there cannot be so many loudhailers or Tannoy systems? First the deep shreik of men, answered by a shrill chorus of women, growing louder with confidence. Then from all around, the roar of crowds, followed by the chatter of automatic fire. The power workers pull the switches, and the city is plunged in darkness, lit only by the sporadic flash of the shooting. Helicopters, clattering hawks, plunge to launch a volley at those on the ground. And a squadron of Phantoms rip across the night sky to try to terrify us.

But shoot as they may – officially five were killed, unofficially a couple of hundred (but Reuters rashly says 1,000) – they cannot silence the endless chorus, the macabre chant of a city in darkness. Only exhaustion does that, as the cries grow hoarse and faint around 2.00am.

Saturday, December 2

It is the first day of Muharram. You must wear black. It is appropriate that it is raining, and the mountains have disappeared in cloud. The rainwater swirls the ground free of its red stains.

The strike is now complete, but it does not stop Teheran's blessed cars flocking the roads.

Soldiers are now everywhere, young men in steel helmets, unshaven and scowling to keep up their courage. They guard every piece of waste ground lest the phantom demonstrators leap from the cracks in the buildings. Truckloads of troops and armoured cars sit on the roads opposite the bazaar. Soldiers sit in rows on benches, with automatics between their knees, breathing into the barrels. Some grin sheepishly at passers-by. Someone asks one whether he will shoot more people today, and he flushes; he shoots no one, he protests hotly; it is the others.

There is an English leaflet from somewhere, for Americans. 'The Shah shoots us from US helicopters. You help the Shah. Please, now, go home, and you may return when we have destroyed the Shah'.

No one knows what is happening. There is almost a total news blackout. Rumours blossom like jungle flowers. The Shah has sacked the new military government, and installed the most compromising leader of the old opposition groups; but no one believes it, for the Shah's backbone is too stiff to bend so far. Half a million have marched on the Shah's palace. Thousands are coming from Isfahan, Qom and Meshed, to fight the Shah. Who knows any longer what is fact and what is fiction?

Again, at a fourway junction, an armoured car is trapped in a gigantic traffic jam in all directions. Young men on the pavement, staring. Suddenly all turn and scamper to the nearest shop door as an enraged sergeant screams at the sea of cars surrounding him and looses his pistol in the air. It does no good since no one can move. The absurdity is paramount. Today the tanks lurk discreetly in side streets.

'You must think we are wildly overoptimistic', someone tells me, 'to think we can destroy the Shah, without a party, without organisation or arms'. But I do not, thinking of the arrogant old man who once proclaimed: 'I promise you the Great Civilisation, but the Communists promise you the Great Terror'. Whose is the Terror now? Socialism without a party is a daydream, but the warriors of Teheran can crack the morale of the soldiers, and so prize open the palace.

We are all conspirators. There are no defenders of the regime. He has destroyed the loyalists, tossed them to the crowd as expiation for his crimes; or they have fled with their fortunes to Geneva. Only the wavering bayonets now protect him.

At night the drama begins again. At ten, the wails rise from the city just as all the lights go out. The flash of rifles make a splatter of sound amid the cries, a ritual answer in the great hymn, followed by the chorus, a roar of rage from a multitude of demonstrations. They spring from nowhere, in dozens of different places. The military machine, like a blinded bull, turns and lumbers towards the sound. But the wailers, standing like clumps of trees on the rooftops, always have the last word.

Sunday, December 3

At long last, I manage to bribe a taxi driver to overcome his terror and take me to the bazaar. On the way, the familiar traffic and shooting soldiers. The Majlis stands empty with only soldiers, picking their teeth.

November the 8th has left its careful scars. There was no blind 'rampage'. The demonstrators selected buildings carefully and sacked them (having made sure there was no one within): the largest banks, two Western hotels, the British Embassy, etc. But all the adjoining buildings were untouched.

The shops within the labyrinth of the bazaar are boarded up. Shafts of sunlight through the roof catch the lines of dust thrown up by scooters and bicycles. Within the bazaar it is safe. Dozens of wall newspapers attract a quick crowd, laughing and gasping at their impudence. There is a cartoon of the Shah with donkey's ears, riding a donkey general. And dozens of black flags. The young men smile and joke; they feel the war is theirs. The Shah cannot last long.

In a main government office, I talk to a friendly senior official. Of course, he has spent three days doodling, for the staff only come to the office for an hour each day to swap stories of how the Shah's power is collapsing. The Iran team for the Asian games have all withdrawn in protest. The portraits of the Shah, presented with menaces to every institution by the secret police, remain everywhere as objects of derision, though many of the statues have been torn down.

At night, on schedule, the wail of the dispossessed covers the city with that strange mixture of mourning and defiance. The style is religious, but the spirit is rebellion – a formless spontaneous tide of rebellion, without programme or design, but universal.

It is only the prelude. Next Sunday and Monday, the agony of Muharram reaches its crescendo for the day when Hussein was killed.

The Shah in his palace counts the hours, and watches the generals from the corner of his eye.

Churchill: A Ruling-Class Militant*

So the old man is retired, really, at long last gone. With him goes the world of Stalin, Roosevelt, and even John Foster Dulles; the world of Hitler and Chamberlain, of Lloyd George and even Gladstone: a world that spans history from middle to managerial capitalism.

Churchill's fame is the reward paid to him by a grateful bourgeoisie for services rendered over half a century. Those services were to act as the ruling class's trouble-shooter at any time of crisis, to be a sort of national Pinkerton, ready at any moment for any job that needed merely strength, tenacity and force, rather than tact and sympathy. Modern bourgeoisies do not often require such services – in general, they rather need intelligence, tact, and sympathy for the minute and mutual adjustment of day-to-day claims. But when they do need a toughie, the rewards are very high if he succeeds. Churchill was never a sharp man, and had little intellectual depth: he was always observably an amateur in day-to-day routine, dependent in his career on the manoeuvring of professional politicians to create and sustain his power. He could not build an organisation from scratch, work alone and isolated over a long period towards given ends, nor even offer a new and original platform to defend the *status quo* (as did, for example, Roosevelt). But he did have the ability to make up his mind quickly, and stick to some course of action through all obstacles – even if he was wrong. In time of war, that ability was at a premium, and whatever his weakness for routine or system, Churchill could supply a strong and positive centrepiece to the ideology of national war.

In time of peace and quiet, he had nothing to offer but rather dated rhetoric, but in a crisis, he offered the decision that better men could not. Like Hitler's disposal of the dithering Weimar politicians, Churchill seemed able to impose order and simplicity on bewildering complexity: that imposition was more characterological than based on a genuine ability to comprehend the complex. When the flair seemed to pay off, the man became a god.

Victorian bourgeois society offered little at home of adventure and excitement, and many men consequently sought uninhibited action in less regulated parts of the world – as local colonial autocrats, explorers, adventurers and mercenaries. Too much of an aristocrat for trade, too little talented for academic

---

* From: *International Socialism*, 18, Autumn 1964.

life, Churchill as a youth was a sort of soldier of fortune who revelled in the zest of war. He was in Cuba for the destruction of the guerilla rebels (did he think of it when Castro finished the job?), at Khartoum with Kitchener, on the North-West Frontier with the Pathans, and in the Boer War as fighter and reporter. With these wild oats behind, he became a Tory MP in the Khaki elections of 1900. As could be expected, he was a rebel on defence, and became a Liberal at just the time when it was the Liberals who were being called upon to defend the status quo by some measure of more radical social reform. Under Asquith, he took the Board of Trade, and then as a Lloyd George lieutenant, the Home Office. It was as Home Secretary that he had the job of clearly demarcating the limits of Liberal radicalism – when the Cambrian Combine pits locked out some 12,000 miners (who retaliated), Churchill ordered into South Wales some 800 Metropolitan police and 3,000 troops. The army was also moved in to quell the 1911 dock strike, and also the sympathetic railway strike – two strikers were shot directly, and five others killed when a gelignite railway truck exploded under fire. Overall, some 58,000 troops were deployed for the strikes.

This initial effort, plus his callous treatment of a suffragette who fainted in Downing Street, and the clumsy bullying of two anarchists trapped in Sidney Street (he refused to let the fire be extinguished in the building where the two had taken refuge) earned him the reputation of a thug. The quickness with which he resorted to the use of soldiers against unarmed strikers, his delight in the use of direct power, his total lack of sympathy with any sort of 'underdog' alienated even the liberals.

However, the record meant that Churchill naturally should play an import-ant role in the War organisation, where brutality is legitimised. He went to the Admiralty, the front-line service in view of the naval rivalry with Germany, in 1911, and in the War, again to the key Ministry, that of Munitions – here Churchill's brand of militancy could be put to maximum effect (compare Bea-verbrook who played the same role in the Second World War). From here he also dabbled in an amateur way in overall strategy, and later began pressing for action to kill the Russian Revolution, a campaign more effectively prosecuted after the jingo election of 1918. With the Irish revolution in full spate, Churchill was called to the War Office, both to tackle Ireland, and the serious mutinies over demobilisation – there were riots in Glasgow, Belfast, Luton and Calais, and Churchill ordered out the troops once more to intern some 3,000 demon-strators.

Help to Denikin in Southern Russia was expanded and British officers des-patched (task forces had earlier been landed at Archangel and elsewhere). Bri-tain recognised the puppet government of Omsk. But all this was small stuff against what could be done, and the War Lord was frustrated by the dithering of the politicians at Versailles – he complained to Lloyd George in 1920: 'Since the Armistice my policy would have been "Peace with the German people, war on the Bolshevik tyranny" ... We may well be within measurable distance of universal collapse and anarchy throughout Europe and Asia. Russia has gone into ruin. What is left of her is the power of these deadly snakes'.

He proposed independent British action against Russia – a buccaneering raid on the prostrate country. The approach was one of the earliest signs of that rallying cry for the lunatic Right, in particular, Hitler. Despite the co-operation of the War, it was Churchill who publicly turned the attention of the Western bourgeoisies back to Russia in 1947 at Fulton, Missouri, when he coined the phrase, 'the iron curtain', having sought so consistently for so long to raise just such a curtain round Russia.

His pre-war record, repression in Ireland and Russia, the dirt piled up: and when Churchill went to the polls with his Coalition government, he shared their fate to an exaggerated degree. Hostile crowds shouted down his speeches in Dundee and sang *The Red Flag* in his face. His 1918 majority of 15,000 was cut to defeat by 10,000, and he was out in the wilderness with a Liberal Party already showing signs of severe decay. The year following, the police had to protect his election campaign at West Leicester, but this did not prevent his meetings being wrecked nor his defeat. The causes for which he stood seemed in disintegration, and he called despairingly for the formation of a strong 'middle' party, the old Wartime Coalition, united now not by war on Germany but by the sole issue of war on socialism and Bolshevism. Churchill was no politician and no organiser – without his divisions ordered by others, he had no power and no ability to create it. Despite some Conservative support, he was again defeated in the Abbey division of Westminster when he stood as a mere 'anti-socialist'. The sojourn in the wilderness was brief – unlike Lloyd George who continued through until the end as a Liberal, Churchill swallowed his pride and realistically made his peace with the new, hardened political front of the bourgeoisie – and joined the Conservatives. In the Zinoviev letter election of 1924, the ex-Liberal returned to the Commons to present himself for new duties.

The duties required were as onerous as any Churchill had earlier faced – to lower real wages sufficiently to expand British exports, to restore the pre-war conditions of financial freedom, to enable capital to move as it wished. As Chancellor, Churchill approached the problem directly and accepted the word of his immediate advisers – he lowered taxation on industry, and helped towards protecting industry from foreign competition. Both were to be 'matched' by Chamberlain's social reform measures, the concessions intended to bribe the workers into accepting the help to industry. The attempt to free rentier capital from State control, however, could not be garnished in the same way, and Churchill as a consequence introduced the return to the Gold Standard in one swoop. 'Mr. Churchill's policy', Keynes wrote, 'of improving the exchange by 10 percent was, sooner or later, a policy of reducing everyone's wages by two shillings in the pound. He who wills the end wills the means. What now faces the government is the ticklish task of carrying out their own dangerous and unnecessary decision; the miners', he went on, 'represent in the flesh the "fundamental adjustments" engineered by the Treasury and the Bank of England to satisfy the impatience of the City Fathers'. With considerable care, the government postponed the inevitable General Strike in order to make military and civil preparations to break it. The militants in the Cabinet demanded that when the conflict came, it should be a 'final solution' to the question of the class struggle – the unions must be settled once and for all. 'It is a conflict', Churchill said, 'which if it is fought out to a conclusion, can only end in the overthrow of Parliamentary government or its decisive victory.'

Baldwin restrained his hotheads until the strike actually broke out, when, like all the peacetime men, he became 'a passenger' while stronger men took over. But those stronger men could not include Churchill – the situation was so delicate that he would have been more menace than help; diplomacy was needed to woo the coy members of the General Council, rather than blood and thunder. So he was diverted into editing the British Gazette, making it into the flag of militancy around which the young patriotic bourgeoisie could gather. But even here his militancy was an embarrassment, particularly when he wrote in the 8 May issue: 'All ranks of the armed forces of the Crown are hereby notified that any action which they may find necessary to take in an honest endeavour to aid the Civil Power will receive both now and afterwards the full support of His Majesty's Government'. Even George the Fifth protested.

But times were changing and already leaving the soldier of fortune high and dry. Bureaucratic organisation, State control and some forms of rudimentary planning, the lineaments of State capitalism, had already substantially overtaken the 'freedom' of pre-war days. The War pushed the process forward further than it could ever retract, and despite the efforts in the 1920s to turn the clock back, the great 1929 slump settled the issue conclusively. While it did not in Britain precipitate the explicit managerialism of Roosevelt's New Deal, nor the aggressive *étatisme* of Nazism, it did, however, decisively circumscribe the area of 'free' political and economic activity. Now the bureaucrat, the professional politician, the manager, cautious and moderate, stressing the overall interests of the bourgeoisie rather than those of a particular section (and coldly sacrificing such sections when the need arose – for example, the rentiers), stressing the need for radical reform to defend the *status quo* – these were the ascendant types, not the old soldier of fortune, romantic demagogue, aggress-

ive entrepreneur. In times of peace, in such a world Churchill was redundant – his only appeal was for the decaying remnants of Victorianism, and he
offered in return only symbols of a romantic past. Had it not been for the War,
his break with the Baldwin government over some increased measure of self-
determination for India might have been his permanent retirement; like Lloyd
George, he would have remained an extinct volcano from which only periodic
gusts of smoke suggested continued life.

As it was, his opposition to Baldwin on India led him to a more generalised
opposition, and brought him into association with radical Tories far removed
from opposing the Party's India stand. Despite his earlier concern solely with
Bolshevism, he was able from the Right to attack Baldwin on defence, and
develop a critique of German rearmament (his information on German arms
is said to be based on his sources as a shareholder of *Metallgesellschaft*). Thus
when the time came for War, not only was he one of the most forceful and
war-experienced members of the Commons, but also he was not associated
with the record of the Baldwin-Chamberlain government. Again, relying on a
Conservative revolt, his chance came: the bourgeoisie turned once more to him
for protection. His record in the War, much as might be imagined considering
his earlier record and too well-known to be recounted here, overshadowed all
that had gone before. The terrors of entire classes can only be answered by men
seen as demi-gods, and in the Coalition that governed the War, both political
parties cosily agreed that Churchill was neither a troublemaker nor a nasty
warmonger nor an enemy of the workers, but really a divinity. That war-record,
however, posed very serious problems for the Conservatives; for when the
fighting was done they discovered that, like Sinbad, they were burdened with
a leader who had only heavily dated rhetoric to offer the peacetime electorate.
Churchill for his part did not fancy a return to the complexities of politics – he
made a determined bid to form his old 'middle' party, united only by its hatreds,
and labelled 'National'. Fortunately, the Labour Party Conference ensured the
Labour leadership did not accept the offer, so Churchill was forced back into
being a 'sectional' politician, and leaning heavily on Edwardian notions of
political conflict. His notorious speech comparing Labour to the Gestapo, his
foolishly extravagant attempts to ignite fears long since dead in the bourgeoisie,
his vague imputations against Laski (with a slightly anti-Semitic undertone –
however, the marriage of one of Churchill's daughters to a Rothschild shows he
was not really anti-semitic), all helped to speed the disaster that annihilated
the Tories at the polls. After the election, a salutary lesson to the leadership on
the dangers of trusting Churchill and his immediate followers (Beaverbrook,
Bracken, etc.), the Party revived insofar as Churchill left all practical domestic
issues to his professional aides, Butler, Macmillan, Stanley. They could draw

Party policy into line with the new postwar scene, refashion a welfare image, and leave the Leader to fulminate on foreign affairs (even here, Churchill was slightly overshadowed by Labour's own Churchill, Ernest Bevin). The taste of defeat died, and the old man retired into the grandiose eminence of acting as aide to and extraordinary ambassador of what had now become the front line, the United States. Occasionally he reminded people of his pure anti-Bolshevist consistency: 'I think the day will come', he said in 1949, 'when it will be recognised without doubt, not only on one side of the House but throughout the civilised world, that the strangling of Bolshevism at its birth would have been an untold blessing to the human race'. Bolshevism and all its terrors never dampened Churchill's respect for Stalin.

In 1951, carefully controlled by his lieutenants (who publicly rejected Beaverbrook this time), the tired old man had some semblance of being a politician: 'I have always been a friend of the miners', he protested innocently, 'those who work in these hard and dangerous conditions far from the light of the sun have the right to receive exceptional benefits from the nation which they serve'. The Tories returned to office, more by reason of Labour's failing than any positive policy of their own. Churchill was again shunted (or wisely shunted himself) into foreign affairs, leaving the management of the economy to the professionals. Thus it was possible for Churchill, despite all the bombast, to preside over a government domestically labelled Butskellite, bipartisan, coloured the terrible Labour pink. He was too old to care, and Britain too big to change – and Bolshevism was still there to conjure up his choicest images. For the first time, Churchill became not much more than a passive Chairman – his days of fighting were done. Churchill's politics were undistinguished, conventionally Right-wing. Like others, he would have preferred strong one-party government (whenever defeated, he demanded a new 'middle' party), and, commensurately, always stressed the need for 'unity', 'loyalty', 'obedience', and so on. The War offered him the means and rationale for all this – virtually one-party government with his own personal dictatorship, a reason for absolute loyalty and the masochism of simple hierarchic subordination. Listen to his account of the impact of the First World War, redolent with self-righteous flagellation and the demand to dominate or be dominated in one simple aggressive activity:

We have been living in a sheltered valley for generations. We have been too comfortable and too indulgent ... and the stern hand of fate has scourged us to an elevation where we can see the great everlasting things that matter for a nation – the great peaks we have forgotten of Honour, Duty, Patriotism, and, clad in glittering white, the great pinnacle of Sacrifice.

Instinctively, the ruling-class militant reaches for the key ethics – loyalty to the *status quo*, and willingness to die for it. The only mildly distinctive suggestion made by Churchill was his 1930 advocacy of an Industrial Parliament. This proposal, for a third Parliamentary House in which trade union leaders, employers, professions and Civil Servants would sit, has a long pedigree, and periodically crops up again in the Conservative Party. It demonstrates the continuing need to assimilate trade union leaders fully into the bourgeoisie, and the attempt to use the unions as means to organise workers rather than defend them. It was a central idea in Mussolini's corporatism. Churchill's use of the idea was momentary – he never made any attempt to actually achieve it. He was an orthodox imperialist, vaguely favoured free trade and competition, was not wildly bothered about nationalisation of industry, and, in general, was fairly conventional. In his later years, before retirement, Churchill did little politically except deprive the people of Woodford of representation. Periodic reports showed him basking on an Onassis yacht in the Mediterranean, receiving yet another superfluous medal, or returning periodically to bask in the painful and vulgar adulation of the House of Commons, only too delighted to find an opportunity for bi-partisan cheering. His last illness knocked away the remaining struts that had sustained his genuine courage and vigour. His War record will ensure he is remembered, and the memory of the people on crimes against them will fade even more than it has now. But, perhaps more than most, events made Churchill – the gallery of national gods would be one less without the last War.

Two Notes on a Visit to the United States (January 1976)*

I

Old Mrs. Jackson has given up the two-mile walk to the welfare clinic. She used to go on the subway, but now it is too expensive. Then, despite her 67 years, she walked. But now she says that there are so few staff at the clinic she does not get a hearing anyway, and it is too cold and slippery to walk.

There are thousands of others in New York who are similarly learning to live with the slow destruction of the minimum conditions of city life. The city officials, caught between the voters and the city's creditors, plaintively urge 'self-reliance'; the city dustmen's chief recommends householders to sweep the gutters themselves, 'out of a sense of civic responsibility'.

New York has been the heart of American capitalism for more than 150 years. But now the heart has gone somewhere else, and in the general crisis of profitability in the whole system, New York has become victim instead of victor.

A series of processes have combined to destroy the financial basis of the city. Three of the most important are detailed below.

The Flight of Industry

For nearly half a century, American industry has been moving its activities away from the cities of the northeast of the country. It is now also moving away from the North-Central region (Chicago-Detroit). Business has been pursuing low costs, escaping from the high living, housing and transport cots of the old cities, and more recently, the urban riot. High technology new industry paying the highest wages has moved to the West (California) and the South (Texas).

The workers have chased the jobs. Put crudely, the relatively high income skilled whites have moved westwards and southwards, while the relatively unskilled blacks and immigrants have moved northwards from the south. A relatively declining average income in the northern cities bites deep into municipal revenue unless there is redistribution between the cities of different

---

* From: *International Socialism* (1st series), 85, January 1976.

regions. Most of the big cities in the expanding regions have continued to increase jobs and incomes through the slump, while the cities of the north and northeast have, to a greater or lesser extent, had financial crises.

This only relates to cities. Every southern and western city has its impoverished ghetto of blacks, Mexicans, poor whites and other ethnic groups, just as the northern cities sport the leafy garden suburbs of the rich.

Nevertheless, the flight of industry changes the whole distribution of income in the north, increasing the extremes of income and making it impossible to finance, let alone rehabilitate, the old cities. Only the centralisation of the country's government so that business could not escape paying would overcome this. In more centralised countries, like Britain and Japan, the similar problems of London and Tokyo are concealed by direct government subsidies.

New York's loss of jobs has steadily grown more severe. It is concealed to some extent when the national economy booms, but is starkly exaggerated when there is a slump. Between 1969 and 1974, the city lost 340,000 jobs (or more than had been created in the preceding 15 years). It missed the national boom of 1971–3, which, if the city had expanded as the national economy did, should have brought it a quarter of a million new jobs. In the year of slump up to May 1975, another 93,000 jobs disappeared (or a quarter of a million jobs if we include the surrounding New York – northeast New Jersey area). The decline in jobs prompts people to leave the city altogether – since 1970, the city has been losing about 2.5 percent of its population every year (this is the official figure, and does not include 'illegal immigrants'). As a result of the contraction in the size of the labour force, unemployment rates have been kept down – 11.7 percent in the middle of 1975 (as against a national average of about 8 percent).

The Flight of the Rich

At the same time as industry has been moving nationally, the rich and the middle classes have been trying to escape high city costs by moving beyond the city boundaries. The spread of car ownership is a key factor in this process. The long run census figures show the movement over a long period – the areas of most rapid population growth at different times was as follows: 1900–10, central city areas; 1910–20, a five mile ring around the cities; 1920–50, a five to ten mile ring round the cities; thereafter, beyond the ten mile radius. Indeed, most city growth since the Second World War has been by extending city boundaries, not by increasing the number of people inside the old boundaries. Where cities are allowed – as New York is not – to extend their boundaries, they have come to cover an immense area. Houston in Texas now covers 503 square miles, and its suburbs, over 6,000 square miles.

In the 1960s, the American suburban population increased by 30 percent, the central cities by five percent. The relatively poor continue to move into the central city areas, as the rich leave in even larger numbers. Those left in the cities are those who cannot escape and are politically important only when they riot. The municipal boundary – where it will not be extended – becomes the frontier between the suburban rich and city poor, between whites and blacks or 'immigrants' (the Mexicans, Puerto Ricans and others, regardless of whether they were born in the United States or not). In the case of New York, between 1945 and 1970, about two million richer people ($10,000 or more income per year) left the city, and slightly fewer poor ($6,500 or less) settled there.

The incomes of the city's residents is the base for municipal income, so that if the average falls, the corporation has to raise more taxes to keep the same revenue flowing – or extend the boundaries to recapture the rich. But this last reform is impossible while the rich continue to control the State Assembly which could alone sanction a change in boundaries. As a result, New York becomes a kind of poor house, and the financial crisis is insoluble.

The Predatory Banks

As the tax base has shrunk because of the loss of jobs and the rich, New York municipality has become dependent on increasing taxation (which accelerates the flight of business and richer households from the city) and bank loans. In a boom, when interest rates are high, the city borrows heavily to pay the interest. In the slump, the tax base contracts, the banks become increasingly savage in recovering their loans and most reluctant to offer further advances except under cast iron guarantees. To escape this last problem, the municipality has – like some of the medieval kings did – offered the yield on particular municipal taxes before any other expenditures are considered. The situation is complicated by the sheer corruption of municipal government. The councillors are often there as representatives of local business, out to make a killing in municipal contracts. The web of bank-financed land speculators, large property owners, building and construction contractors, includes municipal officials and councillors. It is said that, while city workers are being sacked to cut costs, the municipality is still leasing office blocks that stand empty because they are not needed; the leases are favours to the banks that finance the land-purchase, the property speculators and building companies.

A different structure secures the voting base. The winning party rewards its followers not only with contracts, but also with lucrative sinecures on the municipal payroll. The leaders of particular ethnic communities get their slice if they supported the winning horse. The trade union bureaucrats get their share of the spoils too, and if they seem to be effective in delivering the vote, in prosperous days, a grateful mayor looks to the conditions of trade union members.

The municipal unions have been able to build up a moderately strong position on wages as a result of this share out of spoils. In addition, successive administrations have tried to extend their political base by financing an extensive system of public welfare – hospitals and clinics, schools and what was until recently a free university (CUNY, with about a quarter of a million students), as well as unemployment relief. In a slump, all these elements tend to increase in cost just as the municipal revenue is contracting.

It is the welfare-education expenditure of the city, as well as its wage bill, which has made the New York crisis of national significance. The city has become a test case, the 'creeping socialist menace' to rally the backwoodsmen of the Right. As in Britain, one section of the ruling class is arguing that the crisis of profitability is so severe because of 'unproductive' public expenditure. Private profits must be salvaged by pruning the public sector.

Felix Rohatyn is a banker, leading proponent of the case against 'the social wage', and was head of the Municipal Assistance Corporation ('Big Mac'), the group of bankers set up by the State government last June at the time of New York's first default crisis, to promote the sale of city bonds. When asked what sum the municipality needed to cut from its expenditure, Rohatyn replied, 'It's not a question of how much. The city has to change its lifestyle'. Thus, the city's 'lifestyle' became the anvil on which American capitalism was to hammer a new strategy of profitability.

The myth of New York's working class wallowing in its feather bed, on a diet of welfare and free milk, was a useful one, particularly in demoralising the working class itself. It turned class anger into attacks on other workers, supposedly living off the fat of taxes. With some of the worst slums in the United States, a much higher level of unemployment, and a dirty ill-kept city, the myth would have been a joke if it had not been so effective.

The myth has been confirmed by the continual concessions made to the banks by the municipal authority and to the municipal authority by the trade union leadership. Mayor Beame spent a year vacillating, veering between the demands of his political base and the bankers, but all the time promising to pay until he was publicly removed from effective control by the State Governor. Yet still he had promised 67,000 redundancies, a sizeable pay cut for municipal employees, a three year wage freeze, severe cuts in welfare, medical and educational expenditure. It was never in doubt that 'changing the lifestyle of the city' meant in practice an assault on the poor. But to keep some credibility, Beame also had to fiddle the books, yet that only increased the hysteria of the banks and the State Governor. It must have been the banks who put around the rumour in August that Beame was about to have a mental breakdown.

The municipality claims to have sacked 35,000 since last December. Some of the cuts were perhaps directed by Beame at the strongest unions (including the police and firemen) in the hope that the banks would relent or that strikes might be provoked which would frighten the banks. The overall pattern of sacking inevitably hit the poorest city workers hardest, particularly black and Puerto Rican employees, and affected the top paid least. As a result, as city services deteriorate, the unemployment relief bill soars.

The Labour Movement

The attack could have been rolled back. But it required a national demonstration of the commitment of New York's workers not to be used to bail out the banks. In July, Rohatyn himself warned of the dangers of a general strike. But he need not have feared, for the trade union leadership bent all their best efforts to prevent any but token action. At the end, the union leaders pathetically offered up their members' pension funds to buy their own survival (by September, the pension funds of the teachers, firemen, policemen and municipal employees were all, to some extent, being used to stave off the bankruptcy of the city). De Loury of the dustmen even offered $1.5 million of his members' funds to buy off redundancies (Beame took the money, and continued with the sackings).

In July, there was a sudden upsurge in popular anger. The dustmen took unofficial strike action for three days; the highway workers occupied their depots, and sacked policemen blocked Brooklyn Bridge. But the teachers' union leader, Shankar, said he would take no initiative until early September when his members' contract came up for renegotiation. The transport workers restricted themselves to a demonstration, and welfare and hospitals did not move. The union leadership scuttled its members back to work. In September, as a result, the teachers were left to fight alone, being finally sold out by Shankar, despite his earlier bold talk (14,000 teachers were not rehired, class sizes increased). Other union leaders grumbled, or like Barry Feinstein of the Teamsters, restricted themselves to empty bluster: 'I'm in favour of a general strike at this time. We have given our blood. The unions are bleeding to death'.

What finally forced President Ford to extend the minimum level of federal aid for very short-term relief, was not a revolt of New York's workers, but the revelation that if the city defaulted, some of the leading banks and large companies (like the giant ConEdison electricity company) might also go bankrupt. In November, it was discovered that 546 national banks were holding New York city bonds equal to 20 percent of their capital, and 41 banks in New York State had municipal holdings equal to 50 percent or more. Furthermore, the downward slide of the city threatened to impose bankruptcy on the State of New York, Ford, asked to give federal assistance last May, had allowed the situation to deteriorate so far that it had come to threaten the whole structure. There was no way of disentangling public and private capital. But the aid granted is on such restrictive terms, it is no more than keeping the city out of default so that it can continue with the cuts.

The New York working class was and still is in the forefront of the attack to save the system, and the municipal employees in the vanguard. The continuing defeat of New York's workers can only produce a general depression of militancy in other cities and unions. Yet at particular moments, a handful of dedicated city workers could have created the rank and file leadership capable of precipitating a general strike that would have compelled federal intervention on very different terms. One general strike with mass pickets on Wall Street would have forced Ford's hands, compelling him to concede much more as a political defence of the system than just the financial saving of the banks. As it is, workers blame some anonymous 'market' for failing to take up the City's bonds.

The Left in New York is larger than most other places. Yet it suffers from the bitter heritage of isolation and irrelevance. The city's crisis has delivered hammer blows at the traditional attitudes of New York workers, but the Left has not been able to relate to it. The Left's isolation brings the same sense of impotence before gigantic blind forces that afflicts the workers. No one is prepared to gamble. Yet audacity is the precondition for a rank and file movement. It is not created by occasional leaflets or attending union meetings in a handful of workplaces. That is also required, but there is no 'building by slow accretion'. A rank and file movement is created by exercising audacious political leadership in conditions of momentary crisis – 'giving a lead' when there is a vacuum of leadership. That situation, with fluctuations, has existed in New York for the past year and will go on existing. It ought to be a top priority for any group with a serious orientation on building a rank and file movement and a mass workers' party.

II

The growth of American capitalism in the 1950s and 1960s sucked in an enormous number of workers from Mexico, Puerto Rico, the rest of Central America and the Caribbean, from the Philippines and East Asia, just as the growth of the Common Market siphoned workers out of the Mediterranean countries to France and West Germany. Simultaneously, in both Europe and the United States, whites have been moving out of the assembly line and metal fabricating industries into better-paid jobs in the service industries. In the United States, this has meant the movement of black workers and 'immigrants' to the old industrial centres of the north and northeast. The long traditions of southern racialism with its foundations in the interests of the slave owners have been passed over to the industrialists and the cities of the north. In the working class, the whites who cannot escape from the cities are particularly vulnerable to absorbing the interests of a white ruling class, as also are those trapped in a particular district that seems about to be absorbed into a black city. The blacks and immigrant groups similarly absorb the same savageries, opening rifts between, for example, southern-born and northern-born, between American blacks and Jamaicans, between blacks and Hispanic peoples, and so on.

The effects of the divisions are not abstract. Between 1965 and 1968 the American blacks unknowingly assumed the natural militant leadership of the entire working class. Their politics created the tone and style of all mass politics that came after them; their cultural legacy dominates the Left. Yet the challenge to the system was destroyed by walling off the black leadership from its mass – and mainly white – audience, by reinvoking the racialist barrier. The leadership was then either murdered, exiled or bought off. In the last case, the reward was often some toehold in small capitalism (boutiques, record shops, Soul-food stores, African clothes trade, etc.) and absorption into the national political leadership: for example, the NAACP leaders, Julian Bond, Marion Bond and Andrew King, now respectively a Georgia Senator, Washington DC City Councillor and member of the House of Representatives. Much of the small capitalism has been swept away by the slump, but the political perks continue; the US Census authorities estimate that between 1970 and 1974 there was an increase in black elective officers in the country; the black population is 11.5 percent of the whole population.

Yet the condition of the mass of black people remains the same as before or has deteriorated. The National Urban League argues that black people have faced 'chronic depression' for 20 years, compounded by the economic catastrophes of recession in 1969–71 and slump in 1974–6. Real family income declined by over 3 percent in 1973, to reach 58 percent of the average white family income (in 1969, it was 61 percent). About a third of all black families are classified as below the poverty line (9 percent of all whites are below the line), and they make up about a third of all the poor. In mid-summer 1975, the black unemployment rate was officially 13.7 percent (the white rate was 7.6 percent), but according to the National Urban League, 25.7 percent (the rate for black youth was estimated by the League to be between 40 and 60 percent; the official rate for black youth at the end of 1975 was 37 percent, and for white youth, 17.8 percent).

The national picture is reflected in the worst areas of all major cities, whether they are generally prosperous or depressed. Take, for example, one of the most famous districts, Watts, with a population of 28,000 in the southwest corner of Los Angeles. Ten years ago the district became famous through its massive revolt that provided the immediate signal for the struggle of black people throughout the country. Yet, despite worsened conditions, there has been no revolt this year. The area is dominated by those on welfare, single mothers and the aged, with an unemployment rate said to be around 50 percent. The median annual family income – including welfare payments – is around $6,000 (the national average for black families is now $7,500). The area is still 'an economic and spiritual desert', with high incidence of alcoholism, hard drug ailments and suicide (it is said that black males under the age of 25 have the highest rate of suicide for any similar group). However, the people of Watts, like those of Compton further south (a 50 percent unemployment rate), have a consolation they were denied a decade ago – the Los Angeles mayor, the California State Lieutenant Governor and School Superintendent are all black.

The destruction of the Black Panthers' leadership and the decay of the Black Power movement into a defensive cultural style (exploited by black business – witness the shop sign, 'Black is Beautiful but Business is Business – don't ask for credit') has done considerable damage to the confidence of the mass of black people. Of course, the unemployed kids continue sporadic guerilla warfare, half revolt and half crime (against a police force much more heavily armed than ten years ago). According to the FBI, serious crime increased 18 percent in 1974, with an increase of 15 percent for boys under 18 and 21 percent for girls (the under-18s accounted for 27 percent of all arrests for serious crimes in 1974). Some proportion of that figure is black revolt.

There is also sporadic communal warfare, seen most sharply in 1975 in the clashes over bussing in Boston and Louisville, the summer warfare over the beach at Boston and demonstrations against the police and harassment in at least three States. The scale of bussing is enormous – 260,000 children are transported in Detroit daily – all to avoid improving schools adequately outside the rich suburban areas. The movement between black and white working-class districts provides a ready-made audience for the extreme Right.

It is a measure, however, of the relative weakness of the old forms of communal revolt that, fortunately, the extreme Right has not had more growth, whether it is the new retooled Ku Klux Klan ('sophisticated, college-educated, media-oriented'), front organisations like Louisville's 'Kentucky Taxpayers' League' or the openly Nazi organisations. Yet there was a temporary working-class audience in both Louisville and Boston; in Louisville, the backbone of the white demonstrations identified themselves as trade unionists.

However, concealed in the relative decline of communal action is the growth in confidence of black workers in the mass production industries. With an effective basis of power on the shop floor, a new leadership is emerging, a leadership which, as a necessary element in its tactics of fighting, is becoming not simply the leadership of black workers but of all workers, including the whites and Spanish-speakers. To some extent, the demoralisation of communal politics is made that much worse by this development, but on the other hand, the future prospects of the emancipation of black people become much brighter. The press, of course, can see only 'race-conflict', so that the development of rank and file factory leadership receives much less attention than the communal riot. Ex-Black Panthers may well be the most important single source of the new factory leadership; their experience of the violence of the State, their political experience and sophistication, makes them the natural link between the communal revolt of the 60s and the working-class revolution of the late 70s.

There are apparently many such small black groups and newspapers, most of them explicitly socialist, boring deep in the major industries, and to a greater or lesser extent, contesting the leadership of all workers in the workplace, not simply black workers. The discipline of the shop floor and their suspicion of the white Left to some extent insulate them against the absurdities that afflict many of the socialists – growing herbs in Arizona is an alternative to overthrowing capitalism. Yet it will also impede the creation of a mass workers' party. At the moment, the lack of any known national alternative makes the Left much weaker than it should be in terms of numbers. The first organisation to achieve national significance is likely thus to inherit all and grow quickly. But there is very little time to waste, given the perspectives for the system. Before the end of the decade, the Left, black and white, could be facing its decisive confrontation.

Rip Van Winkle in China*

What is emerging in China is not Bukharin and NEP. Then the centrally controlled sector of the economy dominated the national economy and foreign trade was a tight monopoly of the centre. This is a Proudhonian economy, a mass of independent enterprises and authorities, curbed by a market.

It is rather cold now, with the first unusual snow scudding unhindered across the north China plains. It carpets the city allotments and adds an odd touch of grace to the LCC-style blocks of flats going up everywhere. The streets are cold and sodden, a solitary jogger puffing through the sharp dawn fog.

Being in China again is weird for me. My last visit was before history began, in early 1965. It was before the Cultural Revolution, before President Johnson's Tonkin resolution that launched the real Vietnam War, almost before the Beatles and the long forgotten Carnaby Street. There were 300 million fewer Chinese then. I feel like Rip Van Winkle, blinking two decades worth of sleep out of my eyes as I peer at this brave new world.

Only the superficial things seem similar now. The torrents of bicycles flowing down the wide streets in the cold twilight, the few remaining old courtyard houses, now mostly awful slums, the dwindling number of Mao suits and caps that still survive on the aged. Now the shops are packed with things, the cash registers jingle all day; then the shops were empty, and there were very few of them. Then there were no pedlars and petty traders, now every street seems to have an open market. Then the only foreign-made goods were ancient, now they are everywhere in the cities; the plugs in the hotel are MK from Britain, the bathroom gear American, the lifts Japanese – and with the goods, go the hoardings and television adverts. Then, blue denims were universal, the girls with short hair and no make-up; now the young wear black leather and shades, scarlet silk with long hair – and the army and police have shed their old chrysalis to emerge like tropical butterflies in gaudy gold, scarlet and khaki. Then there were flocks of toddlers in the cities; now there are very few, each one treasured beyond belief. Then the always predictable lies came through dour guess-your-weight-machine party cadres; now at least people giggle and relax. The nightmare of daily life then seemed as permanent as the

---

* From: *Economic and Political Weekly*, 16 January 1988.

mountains, yet now it is so long ago, people can no longer remember – or imagine how awful it was.

I went to a pop concert in Tianjin. The noise was deafening, with nine sets of flashing lights, silver clothes and periodically great bursts of smoke like Catholic incense. But the songs were demure, and the packed audience contained a lot of middle-aged party cadres, bemused and mildly surprised at the ocean of sound. They have just opened the first Kentucky Fried Chicken restaurant, off Tiananmen Square. And a video of *Rambo* was playing on the hotel TV. The village cottages had washing machines and refrigerators. 1965 was a very long time ago.

The chairman of the village committee had been running the show since 1949. God knows how he acquired the slipperiness to slide through all those tormented angular years. He is tall, well-built and brown, a rock of immovable authority in the face of a creature from outer space.

He has 250 households under his direction. They did not break up the land into tiny household plots as they have done elsewhere. The villagers constituted themselves as quasi-shareholders in a kind of mini conglomerate. They have turned the land over from grain to high value horticultural goods, fruit and livestock. They have rebuilt most of the village housing now, and are very proud of the new school they have built (they pay the teachers too). They have their own motor pool, with four vehicles (including two new cars); the chairman grumbles that they need and could afford to buy four more vehicles but the government has put a temporary ban on vehicle imports from Japan.

The villagers have also, as shareholders, financed the setting up of four factories. One of them produces chemical fertilisers. Another imports wool yarn from another province, dyes it and sells it to a local jersey factory. Why did they start this and how did they get permission to import wool? The chairman gravely replies that they took an enterprise with a known safe market, and a salesman offered to sell them the wool. Was the party or the government involved? No, not at all – they could start whatever they liked.

The village chairman epitomises the new type of economy that is emerging, an economy with uncanny parallels with the Labour Left's local authority socialism, the GLEBs and what have you. Free markets handle the bulk of agricultural output, and a major and growing part of industrial output comes from small rural enterprises. A quarter of the rural labour force now works outside agriculture, and the official aim is to make this 70 percent by the year 2000.

There is very little central direction outside a few strategic sectors (of which, defence must be a key one). Indeed, there has been little central planning for a long time. In 1966, under the impact of the Cultural Revolution, the central planning and statistical services were combined and pruned – to a total staff of 14. It has not been built up commensurately since, although now at least there are some figures. But interest in the national picture is very limited – the ending of the thirteenth party congress roused much less excitement than the triumph of China beating Japan, two-nil, at soccer. The official plan targets become less and less significant – the 1983 gross industrial output value was greater than the sixth plan target for 1985. The centre controls less and less of national investment – it directed 66 percent in 1978, 38 percent in 1984.

The economy is a kind of set of self-regulating cells, of farms and enterprises. Now they have effectively decollectivised the land, ended the quotas for grain production, and allowed peasants to lease land to each other, private agriculture is returning strongly. The cultivators are not limited in how much land they can farm ('to encourage the efficient farmer', as the centre puts it), what they do with their surpluses, how they invest, how much labour they can hire or machinery they can purchase. The effects of this and the radical price increases have been dramatic – the 1984 harvest exceeded the 1978 target for the year 2000. Farm income per head rose from 134 yuan in 1978 to 424 in 1986 (when the income of urban workers went up about 50 percent). The role of the centre seems to be facilitating, especially with overseas trade (now open to a mass of different agencies). On the margin, the centre periodically curbs unruly animal spirits. The *China Daily* reports that too many television sets are being made so the quality is likely to decline – so no one should start any more TV factories for the moment. The same is true for beer.

This is not even Bukharin and NEP. Then the centrally controlled sector of industry dominated the national economy, and foreign trade was a tight monopoly of the centre. This is a Proudhonian economy, a mass of independent enterprises and authorities, curbed by a market. There are four million small rural enterprises, producing half the national industrial output – production has increased 25 times over in a decade (when total industrial output has increased 12 percent per year since 1978).

It has worked astonishingly, with almost continuous boom since 1978. It is as if the country had been waiting for 30 years for the change. The pent up demand for goods has made millionaires out of some peasants; new export opportunities have appeared (in 1978, China exported no textiles, now it is the third largest in the third world); 1.7 million tourists flowed through last year; peasants have been able to specialise; and there has been a once off massive price increase for farm goods. All of these factors will not last equally, but the effects so far have been dramatic.

It is most dramatic for the 121 economic city regions that now control a quarter of the counties, the sinews of the system in which provincial power is greater than the centre. Further out, increasing differences must appear. The official poverty line is 200 yuan per year and between one and two hundred million get incomes below this. One hundred million get a grain ration below 150 kg a year, giving a calorie intake of about 1,500 per day (which is worse than the 1950s). In Ganso in the north west, the 1980 income per head was 155 yuan, and whole communities are said to live in caves. China's degree of inequality – between the richest and poorest districts – is 35:1 which is greater than most comparable countries.

On the land, the party cadres are now also rich peasants and businessmen. Inflation – 9 percent generally (and 17 percent for foodstuffs) – has returned with a vengeance. The irrationalities remain – for example, the wild overproduction of heavy industrial goods, and the appalling neglect of housing, medical and welfare services (though much more is being done here now). And corruption has become spectacular – those splendid lads in Hainan who imported 2.9 million colour television sets, a quarter of a million video recorders, 122,000 motor cycles, and 10,000 cars and mini buses, and flogged them all off at fancy prices, are only the best known case.

The Left did not draw lessons from the Chinese experience and will not draw lessons from the current phase. Tony Benn still thinks the Cultural Revolution has a positive message. China started a kind of Thatcherite trend well before that lady stumbled upon her identity, and certainly well before some bright spark cobbled together Reaganomics. All of these diverse experiences seem, with the benefit of hindsight, to be less initiated by the people concerned, more the common result of a new world economy. Time for Rip Van Winkle to nod off – and forward to the Chinese People's Capitalism of 2009.

CHAPTER 5.8

Apartheid is Dead! Long Live Apartheid!*

The legal scaffolding of apartheid has been abruptly removed after 40 years and more of construction, leaving the underlying pattern of extreme social inequality intact. But few have begun to face up to the costs of real social change.

Who would have thought it would be possible to visit South Africa? But the transformation here is nearly as remarkable as in the Soviet Union or Eastern Europe – and for much the same sort of reasons: the inexorable pressure of a new world economic order on antiquated national fortresses, relics of the high noon of economic nationalism in the 30s. The legal scaffolding of apartheid has been abruptly removed after 40 years and more of construction – leaving the underlying pattern of extreme social inequality intact. White South Africa rejoices that at long last the sojourn in the wilderness is over, they may rejoin polite world society; they are even smug at their own virtue. Few have begun to face the costs of real social change. Still five percent of the population own 88 percent of personal wealth; 61 percent of the black population are below the poverty line.

I

Real social change there must be, for revolution still ferments beneath the surface in the black townships. There, thousands of volunteers and committees, among them the 'civics', campaign, agitate, sustain boycotts of rent and service payments. In 23 townships, services have been cut off to the fury of the inhabitants. It seems very like Brazil just before military rule ended.

The persistence of agitation, the creation of a generation raised upon the alcohol of revolution, partly explains the change of tack by the regime. After the ferocious repression of the late 80s, the government felt obliged to reverse direction – to recognise the ANC, release Mandela and many others, and negotiate. The government's attempt to create black consultative structures through self-governing councils has all but collapsed. The vote for the councillors in the last elections was derisory, and 200 councillors have felt obliged to resign; 100 councils (of 258) have dissolved themselves for lack of a quorum.

---

* From: *Economic and Political Weekly*, 24 August 1991.

However, the machinery of racism continues, even as supposedly non-racial society is being created. The low white birth rate (and changing white migration) has led to many white schools being closed – when there is a desperate shortage of places for black children. The great revolt of the township school students in the 70s led to the sacking of many schools (as well as police stations and liquor shops) – gutted hulks still stand in the townships, silent monuments to fury. They have not been repaired – and 40 percent of black kids leave school with little or no education. In the same style, there are 4,000 vacancies in white colleges, when 78,000 were turned away from black colleges because of a shortage of places. A major new campaign is under way to occupy white schools and reopen them. But the underlying problem will get worse – the white population is aging, but 82 percent of the blacks are under the age of 35.

The revolution continues. Sharpeville, Soweto, Alexandra, Cross Roads are the battle honours in the long civil war. But there is little clear and decisive leadership. The ANC tries to construct and develop local branches while negotiating with the government and formulating coherent policy positions on all questions, but so far without great success, although the recent national convention in Durban marks a considerable step forward. But sometimes the ageing leadership seems bewildered, as if, after pressing against the Berlin wall of apartheid for 40 years, its abrupt collapse leaves them shocked and unable to act amid the clouds of brick dust. Perhaps this is why some people say the Communist Party is growing since it still seems to offer some clear political lead, even though its entire rationale collapsed in the Soviet Union and Eastern Russia (leaving it as a somewhat conservative Social Democratic party).

Without leadership, the dangers grow. Violence in the townships between rival groups, part hoodlums, part political militants, is a different kind of civil war, with the centrepiece of the clash between the ANC and Inkatha. Over 3,000 people have been killed in the last 18 months (770 in the first quarter of this year). Inkatha champions a fictional Zulu identity (no news in India where fictional collective identities are run up at the drop of a hat), and is well organised in the dormitories of single black migrant workers. The dormitories are the worst of the townships, filthy barracks with broken windows and graffiti, families sometimes occupying them with up to 16 people per room, and razor wire surrounding them (to keep us out or them in?). Inkatha does not, despite its claims, represent Zulus, but the tribal dimensions are carefully emphasised in attacks on Xhosa ANC families. Inkatha has the potential for a homegrown fascism.

Inkatha is wonderful for the embattled whites. They have always needed evidence to support their argument that there are no 'blacks', only different tribes (but, of course, there are whites, not Afrikaners, British, Portuguese,

French, Germans, etc.) and tribes in permanent conflict so that the whites are needed to rule impartially. It is surprising to see once again in use a currency so much employed in the British Empire – the invention of political Hindus and Muslims in pre-partition India is a painfully familiar precedent.

There is another chilling parallel, however. In 1929, the Herrenvolk, the businessmen of the Ruhr, began to make collections for an obscure bully boy, Adolf Hitler, not expecting he would come to power or, if he did, expecting he would be entirely controllable. White business in South Africa – and some of the aid agencies – are financing Inkatha as the 'moderates' at the moment. They may also find that they are creating a monster that is not susceptible to control.

The rise of Inkatha as the bully boys to destroy physically the ANC is as remarkable as the emergence of de Klerk and the Nationalist party as holding the middle ground. The government is no longer defensive. With superb effrontery, after the last four decades of Nationalist apartheid, the government now presents itself as the non-racial moderate centre. There is talk of a 'Christian Democratic' centre, supported by the majority of the whites, many coloureds, Indian property owners, and a significant number of blacks, in alliance with Inkatha. It is not nearly as absurd as it sounds. But it hides a nightmare scenario – white finance to help Inkatha destroy the ANC, after which Inkatha takes over from the Nats, to create a black dictatorship, with its own Ton Ton Macoute, in alliance with white business, much as Tshombe tried to do in Katanga.

II

However, in the short-term, it is the economy which adds a touch of hysteria to prognostications. South Africa ought to be a middle income manufactured exporter, based on high growth. But since the mid-70s, it has stagnated. The structure is still an old fashioned corporatist regime, linking a giant state sector with major private monopolies, making cosy profits behind high tariffs. South Africa has followed an import substitution strategy since the 20s, with strong central direction; some derisively call it 'socialism' after its East European (and Indian) parallels. In fact, South Africa never ended its heavy dependence on raw material exports – easy foreign exchange meant there was little drive to complete the import substitution drive, so manufacturing still depends heavily on imports. From the early 70s, profits have been poor – foreign investment flows began to dry up, and South African business increased its assets abroad (by 1983, the largest South African corporation, Anglo-American, had become the largest single foreign company operating in the United States). Sanctions only exaggerated the trends in the market. With net capital outflow rather than inflow and a sagging gold price, it became impossible to sustain annual growth above three percent without a surge of imports. In fact, the economy did much worse than that. In the 80s, output and employment growth were negative. On the index 1970 = 100, by 1988, when South Korea had reached 365 and Singapore 308, South Africa was a derisory 109. They were years of the locusts.

The problems were made much worse by the soaring public expenditure of the 80s – to finance internal security (and the intervention wars in Angola, Namibia, Mozambique), the tricameral parliamentary system and its associated bureaucracies, increased services to the townships. The government began to borrow to finance current spending. Government employment increased 65 percent in the 80s (so that over 40 percent of white employment came to be in the public sector). Thus, while the surface politics suggest an astonishing rehabilitation of the position of the Nats, the state of the economy is disastrous. And the reform programmes all suggest the need to increase white lay-offs, sawing off the branch on which the government sits. White unemployment has increased, and incomes decreased – soup kitchens operate in some of the white slum areas. 60,000 white farmers (controlling 87 percent of the land) are being crippled by low prices and high interest rates. The militants in January occupied Pretoria in protest at their destruction. Drought has compounded the miseries and forced closures. Since the white farmers are now no longer protected against the purchase of their land by black farmers, a further dimension of economic agony is added to the ending of apartheid.

A high growth middle income economy, living by manufactured exports, needs a radical devaluation of the Rand, and the generation of jobs quickly enough to soften the mass of legitimate furies that course through the townships. There are signs of change – in the last six years of the 80s, merchandise exports increased by over 10 percent per year (the share of manufactured exports grew from 18 to 29 percent). But it is not fast enough. One factor may be the high price of white labour, although the government endlessly reiterates that high black wages are a source of the country's economic difficulties. The government's problem is how to push rapid growth and redistribute incomes without pulling the temple down on its head.

Meanwhile, some changes are coming about. Inner city white areas are increasingly black; the process began long before legislation made it legal, so City Councils have long been tolerating the erosion of apartheid. A significant black trading community is emerging. The universities, if not the schools, are increasingly mixed. Bank staff is mainly black. Some cities are even discussing the creation of single metropolitan authorities, incorporating the black townships and making possible inter-subsidisation.

III

We seem to be emerging from a political ice age. The sound of crashing glaciers is all around us. For whole lifetimes, the political order seemed cut in granite – the cold war monoliths of east and west, the fortress states of which South Africa was such a stark example. Now they are all crumbling, but it is quite unclear what will replace them. The old concepts still persist – South Africa and apartheid have been woven into the psyche of a generation of the Left, an exemplary case of oppression (although many of the caste features of South Africa existed elsewhere in less stark forms). But now it is unwinding. Or its legal starkness is fading. But white society is still intact – the neat hedges and high walls (with Rotweilers and small arms); the Mrs Grundies still tut-tut at mild lewdness in the press, and cry out in horror at blasphemy.

And the townships remain. So do the high security lights that mark them. The occasional armoured car is still seen in the townships, frightened young white soldiers peering out. There are black homeless kids sleeping by central heating vents to escape the bitter chill of winter nights on the veldt. Only the tide of rubbish betokens the continuing rebellion, and the slogans ('Viva Saddam' in the Cape Malay quarter, with a hammersickle, followed by Junky Funky kids!). The black population watches warily, not at all ready yet to believe anything of substance has changed.

Korea's New Revolution*

The events in South Korea since the last Review was being prepared are astonishing. In the last issue. I discussed the role of private businessmen in the 'democracy movement' that swept the country with spectacular demonstrations in May and June. I remarked at the time on the remarkable lack of worker involvement in the movement.

The old mole was not asleep. Even before the Review was published, matters were changing. Since mid-July, there has been possibly the most spectacular rebellion of Korean workers in recent times. Disputes have at times been running at 200 new ones per week, with sometimes over 100 strikes and sit-ins. There were 650 strikes in July and August, affecting 1,600 companies. The government estimates the workers won in about half the cases.

Particularly badly affected are the giant conglomerate groups that dominate Korean capitalism – Hyundai, Daewoo, Samsung, Lucky-Gold Star, etc. Chung Ju-yung, the mighty autocrat who created and ran for four decades the Hyundai group, was locked in by his workers at Hyundai Heavy Industries when he locked them out to reject their demand for an independent trade union and pay increases.

Some of the strikes have been very violent. Riots have been regular features of police intervention. Strikes and sit-ins are illegal in Korea. But the political crisis of the spring has meant that, for the moment, the government dare not intervene to implement the law. As a result, the pent up frustrations of the past decades of Korea's frenetic economic growth have broken out with extraordinary force. There has never been a free trade union movement in Korea, but the last seven years, since General Chun seized power, have been especially bad.

In 1979, Park was murdered and there followed a great upsurge in worker and student militancy, symbolised in the seizure of the city of Kwangju by workers and peasants. The Kwangju revolt was repressed with horrifying savagery, so it remains an indictment of the regime to the present. When Chun seized power, the police had their revenge. The labour laws were revised to make it impossible to set up a trade union or strike without explicit employer support.

---

* From: sw Review, Oct. 1987.

Meanwhile, conditions remained appalling. Korea's 16 million workers (including 6.5 million women) have officially the longest working week in the world – in 1986, 57 hours, but it is well-known that in many workplaces, 78 or so hours are routinely worked. Often there are only a couple of days per year holiday allowed. Working conditions are frequently dreadful. Korea has the force for change. Korean workers have the worst record in safety at work – in 1986, 1,660 workers were killed at work, and 14,809 suffered work-related accidents. Dormitory life adds a special control by the employers and allows them to get away with not paying workers for three or four months at a time.

The democracy movement of the spring must have caused a great surge of exaltation among the millions in their workplaces and a determination to push the door wide open. And the government has been obliged to permit some movement – the 29 June concessions conceding elections also included a promise by Chun to permit free trade unions.

It could not last for long. By late August, the Labour Minister was warning of imminent chaos that could not be permitted. The Ministry of Justice which had promised to release most of the political dissidents held, arrested 60 alleged leftists and 70 workers of Hyundai Ulsan were arrested in early September. But it has still been a timid grumbling rather than the full force of the state, waiting to see if the democracy movement can be prised apart from the workers. Strikes after all touch businessmen where it hurts, and democracy is all very well until profits are affected. The Federation of Korean Industry has begun to get a bit nervous, urging workers to restrain themselves lest they damage the export drive. And the two key opposition leaders, Kim Dae-jung and Kim Young-sam have appealed to workers not to give the military the excuse for a new coup.

At the time of writing, matters are in the balance. Many large and medium sized companies say, even if with reluctance, that it is time Korea moved on from a low wage to a high skill economy, and many, perhaps with even greater reluctance, that worker representation in independent unions is a vital part of this transition. Only Samsung's Chairman, Lee Byung Chull, threatens to close down his giant enterprise rather than accept unions. But the mass of petty manufacturers, operating on a shoestring out of damp cellars, must view any concessions as spelling their death.

Furthermore, even this degree of employer acceptance – in principle, if not practice – of increasing wages and independent unions, depends on the workers not raising political demands other than those of the parliamentary opposition. Demands for power would panic the employers into the arms of the military. At that stage, the overall politics of the workers' movement and an organisational capacity to fight for those politics would become decisive. However at the moment the militants – like their brothers and sisters of Polish

Solidarity – are nationalist, anti-imperialist, workerist (with a strong Christian flavour in a Buddhist country). What is seeking to emerge in the objective logic, permanent revolution linking the bourgeois democratic to the proletarian socialist revolution, is inevitably frustrated by the lack of a revolutionary party.

So the best that can be hoped for is that the reforms extracted from the ruling order can be entrenched for the moment, entrenched in a bourgeois democracy. That can happen insofar as the employers depend upon worker support in their fight with the military. But great care will be needed to prevent the bourgeois spring that produced a workers' summer not ending in a bleak winter once more.

Structural Adjustment in Romania[*]

After four years of attrition it is easy to envisage the demoralisation of the Romanians. After the great effort of revolution, things seem to have returned to much of the old order all over again, to the same forces, but without the old ideological framework.

The East European economics are very different and becoming increasingly so. Although they are customarily divided between the Visegrad group (Poland, Hungary, Slovakia and the Czech Republic) where reform is supposedly well advanced and three others where it is not (Romania, Bulgaria and Albania), in fact the differences are much greater – between Hungary, with a long-standing reform programme at one extreme and Albania at the other. Hungary, superficially, seems hardly much different from its neighbour Austria, even though on the absurd official figures, its per capita income is only 15 percent of Austria's. Romania, by contrast, is clearly a developing country.

Romania was the last of the old regimes of Eastern Europe to fall, and what Romanians call 'the revolution' was the most violent. Over one thousand were killed in the days of fighting which culminated in the fall – and subsequent execution – of the hated dictator, Nicolae Ceausescu and his wife, Elena, after 24 years' rule. The wider changes in Eastern Europe and the old Soviet Union gave hope to the mass of Romanians opposed to the regime's particularly brutal brand of Stalinism (in part inspired, it is said, by the equally appalling order of Kim II Sung in North Korea). Ceausescu and his family governed Romania with extreme austerity and an obsessive concern with national autarky, heavy industry, and giganticism (in 1990, factories employing 2,000 or more workers accounted for two-thirds of the workforce).

However, two local peculiarities added particular causes of rebellion. The first was Ceausescu's decision to pay off all foreign debt as quickly as possible, regardless of the social cost. The second was possibly the largest urban development project in the world and one of the greatest follies of twentieth-century megalomania, the building of a new capital in the heart of old Bucharest (it is as if the British cleared a third of historic old Delhi to build New Delhi), with possibly the world's largest building, the People's Palace, in the middle. At its peak,

---

[*] From: *Economic and Political Weekly*, 29 October 1994.

the Bucharest project is said to have taken 10 percent of the gross domestic product. With the debt repayment scheme, virtually a decade's investment in industry and infrastructure was sacrificed, with power cuts endemic, water supplies very poor, radical cuts in social spending, and increased food exports when there were severe food shortages at home. The notorious secret police, the Securitate, kept the exhausted population silent. The result in Bucharest is a set of giant highways and buildings and construction sites of stunning mediocrity, many still unfinished and many of those finished, unoccupied.

However, the last heroic spasms of the ruling family had the two great advantages of relieving the new regime of any burden of debt, and leaving a population so heartily sick of the old order, it was desperately eager for radical market reform, despite all the known pain that this process was likely to cause. Yet the first four years of the 1990s was not a promising time to restructure, given a series of shocks to the economy. The old central planning system collapsed without any alternative system of allocation being in place. The old Soviet block trading system, the CMEA, that sustained much of Romania's heavy industry, disintegrated (leading to a nearly 50 percent decline in external trade, affecting 10 percent of Romania's 1988–9 output). Exports to the European Union which might have offset some of this were affected by recession. The Gulf war drove up the price of Romania's oil imports. thus affecting its role as an oil refiner and an exporter of refined products. The trade embargo on Serbia also damaged external trade (the old Yugoslavia took 3.7 percent of Romania's export and supplied 2.9 percent of its imports). Finally, the disorganisation of agriculture following the seizure of land by the peasantry, the break up of common serviccs, the decline in fertiliser supplies and severe drought cut into agricultural production. It was not a good time to be engaged in fundamental macroeconomic reform, and planners, as elsewhere, severely underestimated the scale of decline in production, employment and incomes.

However, the promise of increased exports was met through much of Eastern Europe before the onset of recession. Between 1989 and 1992, Central and Eastern Europe's exports to the European Union increased 53 percent (79 percent for Hungary, 150 percent of the old Czechoslovakia). But Romania's exports to the Union in the same period *declined* by 37 percent (and imports from the Union increased 218 percent).

However, with Europe in recession, Romania's exports have held up better than the rest of Eastern Europe's, with the composition continuing to change away from heavy industry, and large increases in textiles and clothing (increasing by 55 percent per annum since 1990).

The problems of long-term structural change have everywhere in Eastern Europe been complicated by the economic difficulties of the early 1990s. Take, for example, Hungary. Despite a long period of reform, its experience since the early 1980s has not been, on the official figures, much better than economic stagnation and decline. The average rate of growth of gross domestic product (GDP) between 1893 and 1986 was 1.6 percent, peaking at 4.1 percent in 1987, followed by five years or negative growth (−0.1, −0.2, −3.3, −10.2, and −5.0 percent in 1992). Industrial production declined for five years, with 15 and 11 percent declines in 1991 and 1993. Despite a poor agricultural performance (and a severe drought), the main part of this decline was concentrated in heavy industry – in mining, metallurgy, engineering, fertilisers, pesticides and rubber. Industrial employment, 1.8 million in 1970 and 1.7 million in 1980, was barely 1 million by 1991.

The process was even more exaggerated in Romania. Industrial output has declined by over half since 1989. Real gross domestic product fell by 15.4 percent in 1992 (although increasing by 1 percent in 1993), and industrial output by 23.3 percent. Heavy industry, 54 percent of industrial output in 1989, was down to 40 percent by 1993, with even sharper declines in investment (running at 30 to 35 percent of gross domestic product before 1989, but averaging 14 percent between 1991 and 1993) and construction. Agriculture's share of GDP increased from 14 to 24 percent, services from 26 to 32 percent. About one million workers left industrial employment (a quarter of the industrial workforce) in three years and 350,000 joined agriculture.

In fact, this violent restructuring of the economy was probably less to do with reforms and rather more the loss of markets as the result of the collapse of CMEA. External trade has been liberalised: nominal tariffs are about 14 percent (most of them in the range of 10 to 30 percent), and oil and imported industrial input prices have been freed. Price controls now only govern the output of utilities, some agricultural procurement, urban rents and transport, bread and milk; housing has not been touched. But institutional reform has been very limited.

Outside agriculture, trade and tourism, there has been little privatisation so far. However, by 1993, about a third of the GDP was generated by private units, most of it in agriculture, but also including 55 percent of retail sales (66 percent in Bucharest) 30 percent of foreign trade, and covering possibly 40 percent of the workforce.

Agriculture, sustaining about 45 percent of the population, has experienced the most dramatic change here through the break up in 1990 of the 3,200 giant co-operatives (in effect, state farms), which had controlled 73 percent of arable land. However, in the late 1980s between a half and a third of fruit and vegetable production took place on private plots. The co-operatives were replaced by some 5 million private owners of 20 million plots. The process was largely

spontaneous and chaotic. Assets were seized by whoever could get them; irrigation networks were stripped of pipes, tractors cannibalised for parts, herds
divided haphazardly, barns and silos gutted for their materials. Initially, the
plots were small and fragmented, and there was a severe loss of common services (60 percent of the land was said to be irrigated in the late 1980s; 18 percent in 1993). There was a disastrous decline in output of 20 to 30 percent
between 1990 and 1992 (compared to the late 1970s and early 1980s) – exaggerated by a severe drought. However, the reconstitution of an alternative system
has been surprisingly swift. Leasing and co-operative agreements have created
18,000 'family associations' and 5,000 leasing companies. In 1993, agricultural
output increased 12.4 percent (and wheat output grew from 3.2 to 5.4 million
tonnes, 1992 to 1993). The government has instituted a process of registering
new land titles, but this is a slow process. So a market in land has been slow to
start.

In livestock, formerly the source of about half the value of output, the
position has been much worse. The break-up of the collective herds and the
decline of urban market demand has led to a 40 percent decline in the cattle
herds, and 20 percent in swine, sheep and goats. Meat output declined by
nearly a quarter in 1992 to 1993.

Thus, in terms of consumption, there has been a considerable increase in
non-meat food supplies (with the exception of fresh fruit and vegetables), but a
disastrous decline in meat. Furthermore, despite considerable poverty in parts
of the countryside and an antiquated technology (horses, some bullocks and
human muscles are the key sources of energy), the mass of the peasantry seem
relatively prosperous.

However, even in agriculture, the state remains crucial through its monopoly
in the supply of subsidised inputs (particularly fertilisers) and services, directed
credit, price controls, and the procurement and storage of crops. In arable
farming, Bucharest distributes inputs in return for low-priced procurement
of part of the output. However, even here, private operators are nibbling at
the edge of its activities, some public sector managers have started alternative
private suppliers and buyers, and some farmers are rich enough to manage
without the state.

Privatisation in tourism, trade, hotels and restaurants (covering nearly 70
percent of the sector) has taken the form of the state leasing its physical assets
to private operators. Hitherto the leases have been of quite short duration, so
there is a premium upon the rapid exploitation of assets to maximise without
new investment. There has so far been only slight changes in the quality of
retail distribution – the same giant department stores offer a poor range of low
quality goods.

So far as industry is concerned, the 6,000 giant corporations of 1989, accounting for 92 percent of all economic establishments (with 2,000 of them producing over half the GDP and employing 40 percent of workforce) remain. Under five percent of industry is open to private competition (although the employment is said to be as much as a quarter of a million jobs).

The Romanian government has liberalised foreign investment rules and, as elsewhere, this has produced a flood of advertisements for CocaCola and the rest, but precious little investment. There has been an $800 million inflow in four years (compared to the East European leader, Hungary, with $5 billion), most of it in small amounts and peripheral activities. This has not prevented complaints of a take-over of the food industries, and the accusation that this has led to an increase in food prices which cannot be true. Street stalls in Bucharest parade columns of bottles of imported liquor, including Glen Fiddich, but filled with local brews.

There has been little movement on the reform front over the past year, and perhaps this indicates considerable resistance to change from that 'industrial-military complex' (government, heavy industry, banks, army and police) which constitute the ruling order. There were no experiments in reform in Romania before the fall of the *ancien regime*, no testing of the waters as elsewhere, and no fashioning of an alternative ruling order. The reform regime had to be reconstituted from the old order, symbolised in the person of the president, Ion Iliescu, a key figure of the Ceausescu order in the 1970s, or his current prime minister formerly in the Ceauscscu central planning agency. The nomenklatura is basically intact.

Iliescu emerged as head of the National Salvation Front (now the Social Democratic Party of Romania) in December 1989, but was overwhelmingly elected in May 1990 and re-elected in October 1992, even though many blame him for twice using the miners to terrorise the opposition in Bucharest three weeks after the May election and in September 1991.

Iliescu has appointed three governments. The first, under Petre Roman, with a group of young reformers who enthusiastically designed one of the more radical programmes of reform in Eastern Europe, was sacked after the second miners' incursion into the capital. The second, under Theodor Stolejan, is credited with trying to consolidate the reform programme. The third, under Nicolae Vacariou, formed after the elections out of a coalition with the Socialist Labour Party (the new name of the old Communist Party) and two xenophobic Romanian nationalist parties, has, to the despair of all, drifted.

The drift has protected the 'military industrial complex'. Financially, this has been achieved through the perpetuation of the old alliances, as has occurred in Russia, China, and elsewhere, hiding bankruptcy through the accumulation of intercompany arrears and state debts. By 1993, arrears – through unpaid and unserviced loans from public agencies, unpaid taxes and social security contributions – peaked at some 4,200 billion lei (or $2.5 billion) or more than the state budget. A report for the government by the consultants, McKinsey, suggested 130 enterprises were mainly at fault, and 60 of these accounted for the bulk of the debts. The effect of the arrears is to blunt any incentive to reform state enterprises, particularly those notorious mammoths of heavy industry producing an output for which there are no buyers.

Heavy industry trade unions are part of the political establishment, or at least, its praetorian guard, and the regime has tried to neutralise opposition here by keeping wages high. Heavy industry workers have not suffered the official decline of 44 percent in state sector wages (1993 on 1990), so that differentials in public employment have widened. The decline in pay has hit education, health and social services, and light industry. In August, a group of miners' unions struck in central Romania, occupying a group of mines, 22 trade union leaders went on hunger strike. The public official responsible was sacked, and the demands of the unions met in full (with a 30 percent increase in pay).

In general, the state has a low incentive to undertake reforms which might reduce their power of patronage – and thus the essential cement which holds together the establishment. However, what intellectual conviction or economic priority might fail to achieve, greed may. Public sector managers are increasingly tempted to use their position to exploit private operations. In Hungary and Romania, some public managers have tried to seize corporate assets and sell them to foreign companies for hard currency. Less brutally, public sector managers set up private companies to buy deliberately underpriced goods from the public corporations they run, or sell it overpriced inputs, to their own advantage. Thus, public corporation losses (as shown in the arrears) may well be in part private profits, accruing to the public sector managers. Some observers estimate that a not insignificant part of the new private companies may be of this sort, private shadows of public enterprises, existing only to push up incomes (as Chinese public sector corporations initiate subsidiaries in Hong Kong in order to then re-enter China and gain access to the incentives for foreign investment).

The continuity of the Romanian establishment through the 'revolution' is symbolised by the government's ambiguous commitment to liberalism. Using the miners as a battering ram against the opposition was an example of a ruthlessness more characteristic of the Ceausescu order. The press is still dominated by the government's perceptions – and the state is not above refusing to pay the salaries of the staff of state – owned publications to curb critics. In a similar way, the new Romanian intelligence agency has just issued a report of tortuous logic

on the events of 1989, seeking to exonerate its Ceausescu predecessor, Securitate, of the charge of causing the violence. Some critics of the government argue
that Securitate deliberately fomented violence and bloodshed in 1989 to invent
the idea of a popular revolution as a cover for the old order – minus the ruling
family – re-establishing its hold on power. Securitate's successor now says this is
not so; there was a genuine popular revolution, but the violence was caused by
'disorganisation' in the army and the provocation of Russian spies; there were,
it says, a suspiciously large number of Russian 'tourists' in Bucharest at that
time, and some of them acted to precipitate fighting (even, it is alleged, giving
out drugs to demonstrators to encourage them to foolhardy acts). Subtlety is
not the mark of Romanian spooks.

There is plenty of timber to hand with which to make a good nationalist –
and racist – alliance against change in Romania. The changes in Eastern Europe
have allowed the re-emergence of those ferocious xenophobic responses, particularly anti-semitism, which constitute auto-destruct. Romania, like Hungary, the old Czechoslovakia and much of Yugoslavia, was part of the Austro-
Hungarian empire, and the mixing of peoples within empires is incompatible
with the more extreme nationalisms, as can be seen in the countries of the
old Soviet Union (and in India, for that matter). Communities of Saxons and
Swabians, Croatians, Slovenians, Serbians, Hungarians, Albanians, and so on
are scattered throughout the former imperial lands and cannot be regrouped
without great violence. Some of the German speakers in Romania (especially
in Transylvania) may be descendants of the first thirteenth-century settlers,
brought in by the Magyar gentry to repopulate lands cleared by the Tartars. The
Hungarians claimed as their kingdom for a thousand years both the present
Hungary, Slovakia (where one of Hungary's former capitals, Bratislava, is capital of the Slovak Republic), much of Yugoslavia, and Romania's Transylvania.
The last Hungarian government is said to have flirted with the idea of restoring Greater Hungary by claiming Hungarian settlements in Slovakia, Serbia and
Romania (and there were Romanian rumours that Budapest had agents stirring
the waters in Transylvania).

While many minorities were mercilessly savaged in the Second World War,
only the Jews were 'ethnically cleansed'. There were 600,000 in Romania in
1939, and 80,000 today. The magnificent synagogue in Bucharest, second largest
in the world and now being renovated, is a heroic and melancholy symbol of
the horror. The commemorative stones of the former worshippers stop in 1944
as Eichmann's crowded trains steamed north west to Auschwitz.

Each of the East European regimes has some political leaders willing to
exploit the existence of minorities as anvils on which to forge the unity of their
supporters – as the old Bulgarian Communist Party used the hapless Bulgarian

Turkish minority, Milosevic of Serbia used the Kosovo Albanians, and all use the poor long suffering gypsies. In Romania, Romanian Hungarians are a special target. A new educational bill, the Hungarians say, excessively limits their right to education in the Hungarian medium; the Hungarian national party calls for a boycott of schools and the creation of a Hungarian-medium educational system. President Iliescu then accuses his Hungarian citizens of stirring up ethnic conflict and warns them of dire consequences. It is a depressingly familiar refrain. In Cluj, the mayor insists on excavating what he claims are the remains of ancient Romanian civilisation, but unfortunately they lie beneath the statue of the most famous Hungarian medieval king – and the Hungarians are protesting.

Reform has thus opened up all the old issues of ethnic madness once again – without there existing a terrain of political alternatives which make it unnecessary to seek out and savage scapegoats. However, only in old Yugoslavia so far has the full horror returned, but the potential is everywhere.

Structural adjustment is not just a process of change in the economy (or in government financial organisation), but also the creation of growing sectors of activity outside the statistical networks. This makes it most difficult to say what is really happening. The recorded data cover only the shrinking part of the economy and are disastrous – a 44 percent decline in wages, a halving of employment, etc., a scale of contraction so catastrophic, it is impossible for a society to survive. If in China, we restrict our attention to the debt of the state sector, we would have a similarly inexplicable economy. This is not meant to suggest that there are not severe social hardships in the process of reform, but that if we were to take the official figures seriously, it would be impossible to say why there were not continuous riots and civil war – or famine.

Reform has occurred in Romania when the economy is already in grave crisis, a crisis of the overproduction of unusable heavy industry while there is a desperate scarcity of consumer goods (and a mass of unusable excess income). There are other less quantifiable indices of failure – the industrially derelict areas of heavy industrial junk and extreme pollution of water and air, the beggars and maimed children, the seemingly many disabled men suggesting an industrial economy where there was little concern with safety. In Romania, real incomes in 1989 were already among the lowest in Europe, and they – or at least, those in the state sector – are said to have declined by over 40 percent (the October 1990 index of 100 had drifted down to 54.8 by January 1993). Unemployment was over 11 percent (which gave Romania the doubtful privilege of sharing roughly the same rate as Britain and France), particularly affecting women (with an unemployment rate nearly double that for men).

The ending of subsidies and increasing taxes must further have contracted consumption. The greatest severity here seems to have occurred in the first two years of the 1990s. The Romanian Family Budget Survey (which almost certainly underestimates the severity of decline since it excludes the unemployed, women-headed households and those on social security) estimates average per month per capita income and consumption declined by 17 percent between 1989 and 1992 (and by 30 percent between 1990 and 1992). We have no way of knowing how much of this represents a real decline, how much a redistribution of activity between the statistically recorded and unrecorded sectors. To the eye, the country appears very poor by European standards, especially in the rural areas of the west, but certainly without the scale of poverty familiar in other parts of the world.

However, it should be noted, incidentally, that the two main trade union confederations, CNSLR and Alfa Cartel (covering about half the industrial labour force) strongly urge the case for reform, especially privatisation in the recognition that little is economically viable in the old order.

The statistically unrecorded must include the widespread and vigorous peasant markets as well as the legion of clandestine traders and currency touts. In Timosoara in the west, the frequency of Yugoslav vehicle number plates and heavily jewelled Mafiosi masquerading as tourists suggests one economic activity may be breaking the boycott of Serbia and the arms embargo on Bosnia. One almost expects to see in the hotels a warning sign: 'Patrons are respectfully reminded that it is against hotel rules to allow the sale of tanks or other heavy weapons in the hotel forecourt'.

After four years of attrition, it is easy to envisage the demoralisation of Romanians. After the great effort of revolution, things seem to have returned to much of the old order all over again, to the same faces, but without the old ideological framework. There has been a considerable expansion in the supply of goods – at high prices – but a decline in the security of employment and a great deal of doubt about the future. Crossing the border from bustling and – despite the statistics – prosperous Hungary is a depressing experience, a return to the 1950s. The endless queues of vehicles at the border have disappeared almost everywhere else in Europe. So have the yawning seedy immigration officers whose life is based upon avoiding work and obstructing people. Much of the northern border – with the Ukraine – has been closed since 1945 and remains so, since it was here that the old Soviet Union expropriated a chunk of territory inhabited by Romanians.

We are back in an economy where the power of the state depends upon permanent security – so that the state, which creates and maintains the scarcity, is needed to prevent everyone grabbing what they can. The state shops with half empty shelves, dirty windows and surly or indifferent assistants are here intact. The power cuts and water shortages are taken for granted as part of the natural order of things. The revolutionary government is far from placing much trust in the revolutionary people – soldiers with machine guns can be seen patrolling parts of the cities, and each has its prominent barracks.

As for hundreds of years, the mass of Romanian population exercises that incredible patience which allows the fantasies of governments to survive. They go about their business despite all the obstacles put in their way by the state.

The pessimism of the intellect, as everywhere, afflicts the intelligentsia. The entire economic nationalist project has disintegrated so it might appear normal for there to be some intellectual disorganisation. After all the years of being told to fear and hate foreign capital, suddenly it is welcomed back and given pride of place. The vacuum is symbolised by the consistency with which Romanian modern history museums are closed (as also, one supposes, the teaching of modern history in the schools). When they are open, it is clear why since history has now been stopped in 1945 (in many tourist leaflets, however, the dodgy hits have not yet been revised, and heroic socialist Romania continues to make spectacular conquests for mankind). The empty walls are mute protest at this collapse of events before the fluid abstractions of the market.

Optimism is of the will and not easy to identify to the sceptic. The 'military industrial complex' may stand athwart the country, determined to defend its privileges come what may. Yet the 'market forces' which have been released cannot be held at bay. Once the NEP men are at work, as Lenin knew, they will ultimately transform the world. In China, it can be seen with great vividness, with the non-state sector growing with astonishing speed, and like a guerrilla army, surrounding the beleaguered state. The entrenched conservatism of the Romanian bureaucracy ultimately cannot keep the market at bay – the termites gnaw through it all the time. Popular energies, particularly in agriculture, have already been unleashed, and the growing peasant markets show the emerging reality.

In Hungary, at a town in the northeast, Nyiregyhaza, we came across a gigantic market, selling apparently almost everything used in daily life. The municipality had laid down several fields of tarmac, with services and shops, where thousands of amateur and professional sellers traded. By the vehicle number plates, they came from Hungary, Romania, Ukraine, Slovakia, Poland. It is astonishing how quickly people shed the fantasies of their governments when given half a chance. This part of Hungary is one of the major centres of gypsies, so perhaps – like the Jews before them – they have created this massive international network of petty trading, undermining the power of the states. When the NEP men have beaten Stalinism, there will be time to think new thoughts.

Forms of Compulsion*

Riding the Tiger: The Politics of Economic Reform in Post-Mao China
by Gordon White, London: Macmillan, 1993.

Slaughter of the Innocents: Coercive Birth Control in China
by John S. Aird, Washington, DC: AEI Press, 1990.

Since the late 1970s, economic growth in China has been breathtaking. Indeed, never in the history of the world have so many people been affected by radical economic transformation. Gordon White's book is directed to reconstructing the political process which unleashed and facilitated this remarkable pattern of development. The structure of the book covers some theoretical preoccupations which underlie his account and a historical reconstruction of why the old model of development, associated with Mao Tse-tung, failed. He provides an overview of the reforms, in-depth examinations of the reform package in agriculture and in industry, and then an examination of the implications of these for the ideology of the regime, for the Communist Party, and for the development of Chinese civil society. He concludes with a critical examination of the idea of 'market socialism'.

In general, the book is excellent, well argued and well written, supported by a wealth of documentation and data, in sum an admirable overview of an immensely complex and, in many respects, opaque process. If one has disagreements, they arise over a degree of uncertainty of touch in the historical account, a kind of residual Maoism, which seems to overestimate the capacity of the Chinese leadership – and in particular, those around Mao – to freely make choices about what sorts of economic model to pursue, as opposed to being pushed into reactive behaviour whether of domestic or foreign origin, behaviour which in turn imposed a new logic on the regime and its policies. In fact, as White's argument develops, this is precisely the direction in which he proceeds, excellently showing how, having introduced economic reforms on a limited basis as a reaction to one set of problems, the 'tiger' of the title takes its own direction – and the flimsy rationalisation of 'market socialism' fades into

---

* From: *Economic and Political Weekly*, 17 September 1994.

a 'social market' (and the 'social', like the smile on the Cheshire cat's face, gets
pretty faded in the sweatshops of Guangdong):

> To the extent that the reforms do in fact achieve their economic aims,
> however, they set in train basic social and political changes which under-
> mine the legitimacy and effectiveness of the previous state-socialist
> policy. Thus, economic reforms not only fail to restore the legitimacy of
> Marxist-Leninist socialism; they accelerate its political breakdown.[1]

There is a different kind of problem in detecting how interests relate to the
broad policy options as well as to events. Most accounts of China deal in a
division of 'conservatives' and 'reformers', and while some of the leaders are
apparent here, it is not clear how these positions – with their variations – relate
to the structure of China's establishment and the different kinds of places each
occupies. Mao himself was never one or the other in general, but famous – or
notorious in the old Comintern – for his 'pragmatism' and, in that sense, Deng
Xiaoping is his natural heir. Flexibility of reaction was always a mark of the
Chinese leadership, shifting relative to the omnipresent threats from abroad
and home, but always adhering to the central aim, through conservatism or
reform, of a strong China under their direction. This raises an even stronger
criticism of 'market socialism'. For the reforms subject China's economy to
world markets, rather than simply introducing carefully controlled elements
of domestic competition.

This is relevant to the book's discussion of the demise of planning. In the
old ideology, planning was fundamental as supposedly an instrument of class
power over society, the imposition of 'democratic' decisions upon the economy
so that it could be shaped to achieve the will of the class alliance alias the
Communist Party. Without planning, there is no instrument, so the whole
project of 'socialism' is abandoned. With the opening up of the economy, the
central directions derive from global patterns of specialisation, themselves
determined by the form of accumulation of world capital, not the Chinese
state.

However, this somewhat esoteric preoccupation is perhaps remote from the
preoccupations of the Chinese leadership (White excellently shows the ideological slither taking place, one which suggests that provided China becomes
a strong power, the phraseology can be adjusted as events unfold). However,
White shows that the reform programme radically changes the context facing

---

1 White 1993, p. 12.

the Chinese leaders, creating powerful interests that resist any attempt to reverse the process. Indeed, the country now seems well beyond the point of no return, and Beijing's capacity to impose any new direction upon the country has grown increasingly feeble. Here more discussion would have been welcome on how far the old nexus of power, the complex of central bureaucracy, state industry, banks, military and police any longer constitute a coherent entity, how far has China become, willy-nilly, a *de facto* federation of provincial powers and autonomous national fiefdoms. The discussion of centre-local relationships is relatively slight, even though this determines the capacity of the centre to act. How far do the more powerful provinces regard Beijing with impatience or contempt?

However, these points are the result of the excitement generated by the book, rather than meant as negative comments. We are much in the author's debt.

During the Emergency period of Indira Gandhi's government between 1975 and 1977, the administration sought to follow forcefully the remedies for India's problems which derived from the conventional wisdom of international agencies and some domestic opinion – that is, that the growth of India's population constituted a profound threat to the future of the country, and that the growth of the world's population threatened to destroy humanity. While not condoning the countless careless savageries of Sanjay Gandhi's campaign of sterilisation in Uttar Pradesh, it needs to be said that if the diagnosis is correct, it would be irresponsible not to seek by all possible means to *enforce* birth control by whatever means was most effective or acceptable. To permit scruples concerning human rights to stand in the way of a process which supposedly threatens to destroy us all would clearly be irrational; as in war, extreme measures would be required.

The Chinese leadership has also come to be committed to the same diagnosis, and given the powers attached to a centralised and authoritarian government at national and provincial level it has been able to pursue the resulting policy implications with much greater thoroughness and persistence than was ever possible in India. This is the sombre theme of the study by Aird, formerly the leading China specialist in the US Bureau of the Census. In 89 pages of tight analysis, backed as is absolutely required by 71 pages of detailed references to the Chinese sources, he outlines the historical development of Chinese population policy – through the phases of optimism when the more people China possessed, the more hopeful it should be (in the years up to 1953,[2] or during the

---

2   As in Mao's 1949 position: 'It is a very good thing that China has a big population. Even

Great Leap Forward), those of growing doubts, and those of increasing ferocity of enforcement (in the early 1980s and from 1985). It is, as one would expect, a very careful and exhaustively documented account of what has become the most rigorous – and in effect, compulsory – programme of birth control in the world, directed to achieve a one-child family for all and a limit to the population of China of 1.2 billion by the year 2000.

Aird is particularly concerned to show that this coercive policy is supported by the United Nations and other population agencies, even though all are supposedly obliged to support only voluntary birth control programmes. The UNFPA has given financial assistance to the Chinese government since 1980, and in 1983, the first two UN Population Awards were made to China's ministry in charge of the Family Planning Commission and to prime minister Indira Gandhi.

The forms of compulsion employed are elaborate, change over time and vary between localities – from a case of denying food, drinking water and electricity to non-complaint families in the 1970s to 'mass mobilisation' sessions, special study classes from which pregnant women are not released until they agree to an abortion, heavy fines (monthly fines for unauthorised pregnancies which continue until the woman agrees to a termination), loss of employment for urban families and revocation of land contracts for rural, collective punishment for work units or localities,[3] fines for the illegal removal of IUDs or for refusing to have one inserted (with the ultimate sanction of sterilisation for persistent offenders).

The aims of the campaigns have become increasingly precise – the sterilisation of one partner in every couple with more than one child, abortion for unauthorised pregnancies, enforcement of late marriage and late authorised births, the elimination of illegitimate births. Aird cites a set of Yunnan targets for implementation by the party cadres: 90 percent of child-bearing women with one child to have an IUD insertion; 90 percent of those with two children or more to have tubal litigations; 90 percent of unplanned pregnancies to have abortions. Aird examines the evidence for the rumours that hospital doctors routinely induce abortions without permission of the woman concerned and dispose of those newly born but unauthorised: all in pursuit of the administration meeting its targets.

---

if China's population multiplies many times, she is fully capable of finding a solution; the solution is production … All pessimistic views are utterly groundless' (Mao 1961, pp. 453–4).

3   Aird cites the case of a Chinese woman who, while studying in the US, conceived a child. The woman's work unit appealed to her to end her five-month pregnancy as a matter of urgency or 20,000 employees of her factory would be punished (See Aird 1990, p. 75).

Understandably, the policy is immensely unpopular, and the party acknowledges 'the contradiction between birth policies and the masses' wishes about
having children' (Party Central Committee document 13, May 1986, cited here,
p. 63) in urging the cadres to move the masses away from the 'old ideology'. A
1988 survey showed that 72 percent of sampled couples and 90 percent of rural
ones wanted more than one child. Indeed, the economic reform programme
has exacerbated the problem: the return, in effect, to the family farm under
the household responsibility system has put a premium on increasing the loyal
hands available for cultivation which means sons. Increasing incomes of urban
and rural families outside the state sector has also given the means to pay stiff
fines for non-compliance or bribe party cadres to overlook an unauthorised
birth. Other couples move out of the area to escape party supervision to join
what the Chinese call 'the floating population' (Aird argues that this could be
as large as 50 million), although energetic attempts are made by the party network to track them down and enforce compliance.

The party is severely damaged at a local level. The luckless cadres, as the
press reports, are liable to acts of vengeance, destruction of their crops or property. Those that collude are corrupted by bribes to overlook births and falsify the
local statistical returns. A 1987 national sample survey revealed, to the horror
of the party leaders, that the undercount of births was just under 10 percent.
It is clear by now that the party will not meet its target. A Chinese Academy
of Social Sciences report (Policy Choices of China's Economic Development)
which has just been published accepts that the country's population will not
stabilise in the immediate future: it calculates that the country's population
will increase from 1.17 billion now to 1.3 billion in the year 2000, 1.4 billion in
2010 and 1.6 billion in 2050.

Aird presents the evidence, but does not reflect much on why the Chinese
government – and many others – have become so committed to such an
extraordinary diagnosis, even though he notes that 'the coercion issue prompts
a re-examination of the "population crisis" belief, the relationship between
population growth and human welfare in general'. He recounts the thesis that
poverty, hunger, health problems, housing shortages, transport problems, illiteracy, lack of education, unemployment, overcrowding, resources depletion,
soil erosion and environmental degradation all are supposed to flow from the
single cause of population growth, and all are remedied by ending population
growth (the case is equally popular – and no less implausible – when applied
to urbanisation and the growth of large cities). As he notes, the sheer simplicity of the thesis, linked to a global humanitarianism, gives it great strength,
and it has 'the added virtue of putting the blame for socio-economic problems
on the reproductive habits of the people rather than defective political leader-

ship or misconceived policies'[4] – or, we might add, the gross maldistribution of resources both nationally and internationally.

Yet the population thesis, if taken seriously (as with Indira Gandhi and the Chinese leadership), is one of the crassest and cruelest fantasies to grip the minds of governments, especially because it is usually directed most rigorously at the poorest majority. It is also inherently implausible – as the Chinese population has grown, so the standard of living of the Chinese has made extraordinary advances (reflected in improved infant mortality figures, in the average expectation of life, etc.): the growth of population is the most vivid mark of the *success* of the Chinese government rather than its failures. The argument is unbelievably naïve – that increasing population divides the national product in smaller and smaller portions; not only is maldistribution far more important (the national product is never divided in equal portions), but a growing population can increase the output faster than it grows (and so far seems to have done so, particularly in China).

Yet on the basis of this inherently implausible thesis, governments are prepared to risk immense unpopularity, shown most clearly in the devastating defeat of Indira Gandhi's Congress in UP in 1977. It seems that, contrary to what one assumes, governments do not necessarily pursue popularity, but rather self-destruction.

There is a broader question. Should governments seek to determine the size, composition or distribution of population? Can they know what an optimum size might look like, whether in terms of national interest or human welfare? And if they can decide on an optimum, do they have the power – or political right – to pursue it? With all the power at their disposal, it is clear the Chinese government is going to fail. Should it even have tried? One of the unexpected implications of the policy is now emerging – the premature aging of the urban population, the contraction of the active age groups, and a rapidly growing problem of meeting a much higher dependency rate. The developed countries may be able to cope with ageing, but can a still poor country like China?

The strength of the population thesis also derives, I suspect, from a Puritan ethic, associated with early stages of industrialisation, but of general appeal to authoritarian regimes. The Singapore government also used to have a rigorous family planning programme to limit families (stressing sterilisation as the means to achieve this), although the professional classes were excluded (it was to keep down the rate of growth of the working classes). The feckless, wayward breeding habits of undisciplined women, characteristic of the poor, was

---

4   Aird 1990, p. 7.

to be blamed for the world's problems, and almost inevitably it was women alone who were sterilised. Now the government has come to realise the frightening implications of ageing and the possible drastic decline in the size of the city's population. Policy has shifted no less drastically to urging the better educated to have three or more children. Here, the old eugenics theme is explicit, although the government has not pursued the full logic of the case to the compulsory sterilisation of the insane and deformed – or, in the Nazi version, ethnic minorities (interwar doctors quite often shared the view that sterilisation was a proper way of improving the quality of the population, so there were quite enough non-Jewish German doctors to supply a 'scientific' rationale to Nazi policy,[5] as others today rationalise coercive birth control).

In China, as in Singapore, it is primarily women who are the target of birth control policy, just as they are the subject of male bullying to break the rules. It is surprising that the feminist movement has not been active in protest on the issue. What should be a matter of liberation – the freedom of women to decide their own reproductive behaviour – has been turned into another appalling oppression.

Yet the underlying issue remains. Why, on such flimsy grounds, do governments persist in such unpopular policies? The political function of the doomsday rhetoric serves a clear political function in diverting attention away from the responsibility of government, but this macro observation does not easily translate into the dedicated zealotry of thousands of family planning militants worldwide. Perhaps the means of liberation can only be got to so many women by means of a wrong and reckless diagnosis: is this another wretched irony of history?

_____

5   See Proctor 1988.

Economic Fusion, Political Fission*

Berlin will, despite the pessimists, survive, as will Germany. But the angst is real enough, as it is in Washington and many other places in the rich capitalist world.

BERLIN: It is bizarre. They have abolished the Berlin Wall and torn down some of the more offensive statues, but all the old names remain the same. There is Karl Marx Allee, a vast thoroughfare of hideously intimidating buildings, and Thalmann Platz, Lenin Allee, Rosa Luxemburgstrasse, Clara Zetkinstrasse, Dimitroffstrassse: all the fallen icons are still in place as East Berliners scurry home through the cold windy evening. It is worth scurrying since the horrors of Stalin's architectural answer to Le Corbusier planning are even more alienating. The vast empty junctions and giant highways, the sheer intimidatory character of great public spaces designed to impress, drive everyone to flee to their tiny private space: the little yellow lights in the tower blocks of little apartments. It is not the least of the ironies of such a heavily collectivised world as the old German Democratic Republic (GDR) that it created such an intensely private people; real life was necessarily secret.

Not that there are not plenty of signs of the new – the flashing Coca-Cola signs and that ubiquitous symbol of contemporary self-indulgent sensibility, the corner bottle bank (one each for brown, clear and green). The underground railway is now linked, and it is ridiculously easy to walk through the Brandenburger Tor. The great public buildings of the Germany of the Kaisers, of Weimar and the Nazis, and of the GDR are being reclaimed for the glory of greater Germany. But all the bizarre traces of an unhappy past linger on – between the unhappy gloom of the East and the neurotic glitz of the West, what was formerly a little island in a hostile sea.

It is still an unhappy forced cocktail of a city. But then Germany is unhappy, sharing the generalised *angst* of the developed countries, depressed at the world all unwittingly they have created, global economic integration with Sarajevos, Mogadishus, and neo-Nazis. To an outsider, it seems absurdly self-indulgent that the inhabitants of one of the two great engines of advanced manufacturing in the world (Japan is the other) should be so riven with doubts.

---

*   From: *Economic and Political Weekly*, 1–8 January 1994.

Yet though the old war between East and West may have been cold at the divide, on either side it gave a surprising measure of warmth: the partial verities were rendered absolute, unity dragooned, self-righteousness ruled. Ironically, however, the very processes which broke the Soviet Union and its East European allies, global economic integration simultaneously revealed that the West's old preeminence was doomed. Now the sleep of the richer Europeans is disturbed by phantoms of the manufacturing invasion from East Asia, the new Yellow Peril (embodied in car imports), followed closely by Latin America and even south Asia. When the workers of China and India really come on stream, the world economy will be transformed, and who then will remember the little principalities of the West?

National souls are searched to find new compasses. Chancellor Kohl sees moral turpitude as the source of Germany's future downfall – 'a successful industrial nation cannot allow itself to be organised like a collective leisure park'. The famous German work mania – like that of the Japanese – has supposedly collapsed: 'we allow ourselves the luxury of being a country with ever younger pensioners [average retirement age: 59] and ever older students [average matriculation age: 29] ... with ever shorter working hours, rising wage costs, and ever longer holidays'.

Germans themselves might well rejoice at these dreadful sins, especially at receiving the highest wages in the world. In 1992, the average cost of a manufacturing worker was DM42 per hour, compared to DM28 in France and DM9 in Portugal, without comparing to a wider world where Portugal is a rich country. A major part of the sum is ancillary costs of health, unemployment, sickness and old age benefits, which have risen from 27 percent of gross wages in 1970 to a projected 40 percent for 1994. The burden has grown particularly swiftly in the past three years and has been exaggerated by the arrival of 17 million new potential claimants from the East. By 1993, the total cost of social programmes was equal to a third of the gross domestic product. The benefits have hitherto been relatively lavish (and date from a much more generous time) – the unemployed, for example, are entitled to two-thirds of their last salary for 32 months, and to slightly less indefinitely. Individual firms have topped up these provisions with other benefits.

Slump is the moment of truth, the test of what is to survive. Germany's recession has been deeper and longer than feared. It forces restructuring – the ending of activities, which, in boom, might last, the relocation of manufacturing abroad to escape high local costs. It has also produced 3.3 million unemployed, an increasing proportion of whom have been out of work for one year or longer. The budgetary burden has escalated, and, as in many other developed countries, the government is desperate to find ways of reducing it. Culture has been an easy target – two of Berlin's more famous theatres closed in September (the daily subsidy was said to be the highest in Germany, about DM100 per seat).

But it is social security which has been a key target for reforms. To the growing fears of workers over work has been added the threat of cutting away the support for the unemployed. The trade unions – as in much of Europe – are increasingly irritable at this betrayal, and combative. The giant Metal Workers Union has been increasingly angry, there have been scraps in Volkswagen, 100,000 building workers invaded Bonn recently, and steel workers paraded belligerently in the Ruhr.

However, the immediate issues of recession are interwoven with much longer-run fears about the very survival of Germany. The population is ageing with increasing speed, and the active population declining even faster. The total number of Germans is expected to decline by 15–17 million by the year 2030, a reduction roughly equal to the population of the old GDR. There has long been a secular decline in birth rates and family size, and deaths overtook births in the early 1970s. By the year 2000, deaths are projected to exceed births by 300,000 annually; and by 2030, by 600,000 (a figure equal to the population of Frankfurt lost each year). But this is less severe than the decline in the prime age groups, those expected to pay through their contributions for the increasing number of the aged. In 1993, a fifth of the population was 20 or less, and a fifth, 60 or more; by 2000, this is expected to be a fifth and a quarter; and by 2030, 16 percent and nearly 40 percent.

If nothing else, the problem of paying pensions for those currently at work but retiring early in the next century is prompting alarm and exercising ingenuity. The issue is made worse by the rising standards of care for the aged, and thus the rising real costs. An increasing number of very aged disproportionately expands the hospital services. With the declining number of workers – and as a result, increasing wage pressure – who is to staff the prodigiously labour-intensive caring professions?

However, this discussion concerns only 'Germans'; only they are in decline, not the people who live and work in Germany. Alongside the shrinking 72 million Germans are 8 million non-Germans, those who may have worked in Germany all their lives but cannot claim German descent and therefore qualify for a German passport. Again, the 'Germans' equally may include people who have just arrived from Russia or Eastern Europe, who have been there for many generations, but claim original German descent. In the past three years, there have been 3.2 million newcomers, including refugees, those joining non-German families living in Germany, and 1.4 million 'ethnic aged Germans', mainly from the East. The new arrivals have not fully offset the population decline – Germany will need 1.5 million newcomers annually in the 1990s to do that, and a further 13.8 million between 2001 and 2030 (the longer-term effects would be greater because the newcomers are likely to be young and therefore likely to add to the child population).

Now, naively you might think immigration would be a cause of some rejoicing for those that fear the decline of Germany, some gratitude for the well-attested hard work in dirty and ill-paid jobs that immigrants undertake. But the reverse has occurred – slump, the generalised *angst* and periodic attempts to identify immigration as a major problem (and galvanise the bureaucracy to search out defaulters) have all had the opposite effect. Non-Germans, no matter how culturally integrated (whatever that dubious phrase means; how many Germans are culturally integrated?), have come to be seen by an enraged minority as the symbol of that internationalisation of the German economy which has robbed them of some supposed birthright – whether work, opportunity or security. The developed countries, to a greater or lesser degree, share the syndrome.

Berlin has a disproportionate share of non-Germans, is the first stop for refugees from the East, and has its own share of unlovely neo-Nazis. This is added to the city's particular variation on Germany's troubles. Bonn's heavy subsidies to Berlin, it is said, created a manufacturing sector peculiarly vulnerable to recession. Now the subsidies have virtually ceased, accelerating the process of the dispersal of manufacturing away from cities that has been seen throughout the developed world to the surrounding state of Brandenburg (busy building industrial estates and offering incentives to new firms), to other Eastern states or even beyond where wages are much lower, to Poland and the Czech Republic. For a city hitherto disproportionately dependent on manufacturing this would seem to promise major unemployment, for a relatively low skilled and ageing labour force. Berliners see little chance of much substitute activity – the city cannot rival Frankfurt in finance and air transport, Munich in hi-tech and defence manufacturing, Dusseldorf in printing and publishing, Cologne in vehicles (darkly some Berliners mutter that the Allied Occupying Forces organised this division of labour to ensure Berlin would never again be capable of dominating Europe). The city is the gateway only to the impoverished East. The infrastructure of East Berlin is antiquated and its labour force ill-equipped for modern activities. In West Berlin, because of net emigration from the city to old West Germany up to the 1980s, the population is relatively aged.

All is not gloom, however. The federal government is scheduled to move from Bonn, although it now seems that, under pressure from civil servants, only half the government will relocate. But, according to the Berliner Bank, that will mean 55,000 new jobs. Furthermore, the federal government has lavished funds on research centres in the city. The old centre is to be rebuilt both to house the government but also to accord to the proper notion of Germany's capital – Unter den Linden, Tiergarten, the palaces, museums and churches, Wilhelmstrasse (there is a ticklish discussion as to whether the federal ministry of defence should be housed in the office block built by the Nazis). Culture is, despite the cuts, well developed, with three opera houses and a host of theatres, cinemas, museums, and three universities.

Berlin will, despite the pessimists, survive, as will Germany. But the *angst* is real enough, as it is in Washington and many other places. The fisticuffs at the ending of Uruguay Road, the cliff hanging at the conclusion of the North American Free Trade Agreement or the Maastricht Treaty, all display an irritable national egotism more dangerous than the football lager louts who have become a symbol of Britain. Germans became agitated in defence of the sacred Deutsch Mark, hanging on to an empty symbol of a happier past. It seems economic fusion is producing political fission in the long slow process of unifying the world – and that may be no bad thing if it weakens the state.

Mexico's Tiananmen Square*

The Chiapas events have been an earthquake in the Mexican political landscape. They may force the process of political reform which has so often been the stepchild of the system.

The Mexican intelligentsia has been inventing the revolt that has now taken place in the southern state of Chiapas for more than a decade. After the financial collapse of 1982, the following president (de la Madrid) was forced to undertake increasingly radical 'structural reforms' as the price of financial survival. His successor from 1988 (the present president, Salinas de Gotari) embraced the programme with enthusiasm and has by now succeeded in dismantling most of the nationalist economic project through privatisation, decontrol, external liberalisation, etc. Even land reform and communal farming, close to the heart of Mexico, have come under challenge. The process culminated last November in what was, by the standards of Mexico's nationalist past, a quite shocking outcome: the signing of a free trade agreement with the great former enemy, the United States (the NAFTA). The process – domestic reform and external decontrol – has to a greater or lesser extent been accompanied by warnings and predictions that Mexicans would not, or could not, tolerate this combined betrayal of the nation and removal of any protection for the poor against the ravages of the market.

In fact, Mexicans did tolerate it for much of the time, despite the most appalling statistical evidence of decline. It seemed that the statistics must be wrong, that the national project had a much smaller following than expected, and that the defences of the poor had never defended them much, so their removal did not signify what had been thought.

Now all that has changed. On the day the NAFTA came into operation (1 January), some 2,000 young men, mainly of Indian origin, clad in village cloth and sandals, carrying ancient weapons (including some wooden rifles), under the banners of a hitherto unknown organisation, the Zapatista National Liberation Army, ZNLA (Zapata was possibly the most famous peasant leader of the Mexican revolution, 1910–20), seized the town halls in eight towns of Chiapas,

---

* From: *Economic & Political Weekly,* Mar. 1994.

including the important city of San Cristobal de las Casas. From the balcony of city hall, 'sub-comandante' Marcos denounced the NAFTA as a sentence of death on the Indians, attacked the theft of Indian land by the landowners, the poverty of the indigenous people, the corruption and authoritarianism of the dominant political party, PRI (ruling in Mexico for 65 years). He demanded the resignation of president Salinas and his government and the establishment of democracy. A former governor of the state, retired general Absalom Castellanos, was taken as hostage.

The army reacted as if it were fighting the Vietnam war, nothing learned, nothing forgiven. Ultimately, some 20,000 troops with heavy weapons and tanks, accompanied by aerial bombardment, attacked the villages and drove the rebels into the forested hills. There was much evidence for the journalists who poured into San Cristobal of that old central American syndrome, systematic army killings and dumping corpses in unmarked graves (officially, more than 100 were killed).

However, it is no longer possible for a Mexican army to strangle its victim in the night, liquidating rebellion by the sheer weight of brutality. It had turned out not to be possible on the much more vast canvas of Vietnam. Paradoxically, it is NAFTA which has exposed the whole of Mexico to the critical scrutiny of North American public opinion, increasingly sensitive on the issue of human rights, democracy and corruption, and, in any case, half in doubt about the wisdom of NAFTA for the US. NAFTA can still be unstitched if enough Congress persons want it (and, after all, two-thirds of the Democratic Representatives rejected a Democratic president's recommendation – and bribes – on NAFTA). Foreign investment, vital for Mexico's balance of payments, was likewise affected, and the stock exchange took a dizzy fall.

NAFTA saved the rebels. Twelve days after the outbreak, president Salinas issued a unilateral cease fire and called for national reconciliation. He also wisely sacked his interior minister, Patrocino Gonzalez (who was appointed to the job one year earlier, having been a hard-faced governor of Chiapas). The president also accepted the offer of Manuel Camacho Solis (ex-mayor of Mexico City and well-known as a peacemaker) to go to San Cristobal without pay to negotiate a peaceful settlement.

The plot is thicker than this. Mexico is officially embarked on a presidential election campaign (to be held in August). In the country's bizarre political process, the existing president has the right to nominate the candidate of the ruling party, the PRI, for the presidential election; invariably in the past this has meant nominating the next president, since the PRI always wins. There were two leading candidates this time, Luis Donaldo Colosio (former social minister and in charge of the programme of Solidarity, of which more later) and Camacho. Colosio won, and Camacho, despite his publicly expressed fury, allowed himself to be briefly consoled by accepting the post of foreign minister in the dying regime.

Chiapas gave Camacho a great opportunity to turn the tables, to assume centre stage through his own initiative, and, if successful, win the praise of all except Colosio, a man described by some of his close colleagues as 'never having been caught holding an opinion'. Colosio himself had failed to take the initiative when he could and fly to San Cristobal to talk to the rebels and so make himself the star of the proceedings.

The background to this scheming is much more threatening. The sacrifices demanded by the long years of structural adjustment have still not led to promised rapid growth, and in this election year, the achievements promise to be little better. In 1993, Mexico experienced a 0.4 percent rate of growth (the lowest since 1986), compared to the government's forecast of 1.1 percent (manufacturing −1.5; services 0.9; agriculture 1.9 percent). But even 1.1 percent would have been pathetic alongside the ambitions attached to the reform programme. Per capita income declined, unemployment increased and agricultural prices declined. Even the World Bank, that has lavished praise on Mexico's reform programme as a model, in this year's report, deplored the poor growth rate (and the resulting dependence on foreign capital), calling for new reforms in the legal system, in labour, finance, the environment and public infrastructure.

The shock of the revolt in Mexico has been devastating. Its political significance has been vastly greater than any military importance it might have had. Every schoolchild can identify in those ragged rebels his or her ancestors, the giants of the Mexican revolution, the language of which (suitably sterilised) has rung down the years since 1920 as the authentic voice of Mexico. After all, president Salinas himself has a portrait of Zapata hanging in his office. In practice, it did not mean a lot. For much of the Mexican bourgeoisie, Chiapas is nearly as remote as Bombay, and certainly much farther away than Houston, Los Angeles or New York. For them, the heady slogans of the revolution are no more affecting than, for the French ruling order, the motto on the French coat of arms: Liberty, Equality, Fraternity.

When the world's cameras arrived in San Cristobal to witness the hungry children and thin adults, the dirt floored shacks and lack of piped water, the rundown schools and unpaved roads, few in Mexico city could hide the shame. Andrea Barcena, director of the Mexican Centre for Children's Rights, wrote an open letter to the Zapatistas to thank them for their great contribution to the 'historic causes of Mexico: justice, equality and liberty ... in the midst of misery and fears ... [you] have at last shown Mexico is alive, is still ours and that there are still men with the capacity to defend it and to shout "Enough!"'

The illusion of the big city was punctured. There it seems there is a free press, open discussion, freedom to meet and to demonstrate; there is corruption, but still some measure of the rule of law. Despite the shock statistics through the 1980s, the roads are packed with traffic, the restaurants and hotels always full, the shops crowded. It seems a middle-class society, not that much different from the one north of the border. But now the press has suddenly revealed a different world – of great and hopeless poverty, subject to the robbery and arbitrary power of a mafia of landowners (and their hoodlums), PRI politicians and the police. In the 1980s, it is said, some 16,000 Indian cultivators were driven off their land. The government ignored sporadic protests, or sent in the heavies, so people disappeared or ended up permanently in gaol; sometimes bodies are found. It is part of an ancient history of wrongs visited upon the Indians from time immemorial. In the neighbouring state of Oaxaca, there has been sporadic warfare for more than a century as the landless try yet again to recover the land stolen from them, and the armed squads of the landlords beat them off: this is beyond the perimeter of bourgeois society. Most learn to be silent, to gaze helplessly before their own oppression. Indeed, in Chiapas the old order is firmly intact. Elements of the army are said to deplore the government's conciliatory approach and urge massive retaliation against the rebels before it is too late. Camacho was obliged to secure the explicit promise of self-restraint from the military before seeking talks with the rebels. And the local landlords chafe at their inability to do as they always have done – send in the armed squads to settle the issues directly, kill the rebel leaders and enough of their followers to intimidate them all.

If it was a great shock for the urban intelligentsia, it has been a great liberation for those in the same situation as the Indians of Chiapas. The revolt has led to a great outpouring of peasant discontents, particularly in protest at Salinas's ending of land reform (which never arrived in Chiapas) and Mexico's famous system of communal land ownership ('ejidos'). Other towns have been seized and mayors arrested for corruption and stifling democracy, and there have been demonstrations of support in most of the major cities. In Teopica in Chiapas, they complain that they lack running water, schools, drainage, and the mayor makes off with the municipal funds. In 1992, the town delivered 100 percent of its vote to the PRI. The Zapatistas in their four-day excursus broke the spell of fear, of the invincibility of the PRI and the inexorability of the government's reform programme. In a recent poll, *Este Pais* found that 61 percent of Mexicans sympathised with the Zapatistas.

The press has projected the movement to the far corners of the globe, and have done the same with its photogenic leader, the 'sub-comandante' Marcos. The black balaclava he wears to conceal his identity when he meets the press or the government has swiftly displaced what was left of the Sandinista black beret as the symbol of youthful revolt. In San Cristobal, they have even put balaclavas on the little clay dolls they used to sell to the tourists. Marcos's press communiques, interviews (and a full national television interview) have made him a cult hero – relaxed, ironic, self-deprecating, poetic, lacking all that hideous rhetorical claptrap of the old leftists. When the president offered an amnesty, he was swift to ask if the Indians had been pardoned for not dying of dysentery, cholera and typhoid, for not remaining silent, for rejecting a history of contempt and cruelty: 'Who should ask for a pardon and who should give it?'. He disclaimed any ambition by the Zapatistas to impose a new order by force of arms as the government sought to do; their aim was only to affirm, 'Something is wrong in this country, something has to change'.

The president started very badly. He accused the rebels of being – guess what? – 'foreign-lead' (and that does not, as in India, mean Pakistani!) and fomented by the bishop of San Cristobal. But he shifted in good time as public opinion increasingly favoured the rebels. Now he says they are indeed Mexicans and have grievances. He has stressed also that only under his government have serious efforts been made to tackle poverty and the effects of macroeconomic reform through the Solidarity programme (under the direction of the now presidential candidate, Colosio). Solidarity is the regime's great showpiece. Chiapas, on many measures the poorest state in Mexico, has received the largest share of Solidarity funds. But where did the money go? Not to most of the families of the Indians. Cynics say the programme was simply designed to bribe PRI voters, so to ask how the fifth of Mexicans who are poor were affected is naive. Indeed, the macroeconomic changes may well have swamped the programme's small effects at the base – the richest fifth of Mexicans have increased their share of the national income between 1984 and 1992 from 48 to 54 percent; the poorest fifth have seen a decline from 5 to 4 percent. The president acknowledges that the programme is inadequate (but why did his minister not tell him?). He has rejigged the budget, bringing forward spending programmes and seeking to increase the share of social spending from 33 to 54 percent between 1993 and 1994.

If any of this spending reaches the poor, it possibly will not compensate for the elimination of subsidies in agriculture or the decline in coffee prices (president Salinas has announced a $107 million subsidy to offset low coffee prices). None of this has much to do with NAFTA – free trade in agriculture is yet to start and will be spread over a decade – but as in all countries, foreigners are fair game for any blame, so NAFTA is a soft target. The problem in Chiapas, however, is less low agricultural prices and more landlessness – or, more bluntly, the theft of land. NAFTA has not affected anything here; Chiapas is a problem of ancient and continuing oppressions by the powerful.

The cocktail is fiery. Will Camacho succeed in getting an agreement with the Zapatistas, and one of a kind that will constitute a rebuff for Colosio? It has never happened that a presidential nominee has failed to win, but Mexico is changing – could Camacho displace Colosio or run as an independent? The PRD, the leftist party most likely to gain from the issues raised by the revolt, is led by a very famous leader, Cuauhtemoc Cardenas; he claims to have won the 1988 presidential election but to have been deprived of the victory by vote fraud. Certainly, since then his party, in successive state elections, has been systematically blocked by violence and fraud.

The Zapatista revolt has exposed the PRI as never before to an indictment in terms of corruption and authoritarianism. The government's reactions in the political field have always been timid, perhaps because the leadership recognises that they will not be able to hold the PRI together if it is denied the cement of corruption. Salinas has introduced some reforms – giving the opposition the right to veto nominations for the commissions which supervise elections, to equal air time on the two national television networks, and limiting election spending. But it is too little too late.

The Chiapas events have been an earthquake in the Mexican political landscape. They will force the process of political reform which has so often been the stepchild of the system. But this is an election year when the short-term priorities of winning supersede any longer term preoccupations with reform. The PRI is perilously vulnerable in such circumstances: its instincts in an election year drag it back to the discredited old order, thus engendering more Zapatistas and more opposition.

CHAPTER 5.14

Peru: Emerging from Crisis*

The reform government of Alberto Fujimori has succeeded in radically restoring domestic security and economic growth in Peru. Nevertheless, this has been at the cost of an inert civil society and over-concentration of power in the person of the president.

For up to 10,000 years – roughly as long as anywhere else in the world – cultures of great diversity and sophistication have flourished on the three strips of territory, north to south – coastal desert (with oases), the mountains (the sierra) and the jungle (the selva) – the bulk of which came to form modern Peru. The most famous material employed in the more modern of those cultures was gold, and gold is a symbol of an immense wealth of raw materials in the country. Some have called them 'gifts of the devil' because they have allowed, they say, growth without development, or a development for the mass of the population well below those countries with nothing but intelligence and aptitude as a resource.

The raw materials are impressive – the key mining exports of copper, lead, zinc, and gold (with iron, phosphates, manganese and silver); oil; and immense wealth of sea, farm and forest. The exploitation of these riches supported a 1994 per capita GNP of 2,110 dollars (or 3,610 dollars at PPP). They also supported a manic-depressive cycle of boom and slump, political regimes alternating between expansionist export-led boom liberals and import-substituting economic nationalists, sometimes coinciding with the exchange of military and civil orders. And the growth was characterised by extraordinary levels of income inequality (greater than the notorious cases of Brazil and Mexico), and geographical extremities of wealth, between the coastal oases (particularly Lima with a quarter of the population) and the poor villages of the sierra and the selva.

In the 1990s, the country is turning from two decades of economic nationalism and latterly, civil war, a period of unmitigated disaster for the majority of Peruvians. In 1992, private sector wage earners received incomes 35 percent of the 1981 level or 23 percent of 1973. Real incomes in 1996, after six years of growth, were still below the level of 1960. In Lima's downtown, the handsome mansions of the past are half derelict or boarded up, the pedestrian alleys

---

* From: *Economic & Political Weekly*, Nov. 9–16, 1996.

converted to permanent flea markets, selling cheap clothes and plastic goods. National infrastructure investment declined on average by 6.5 percent annually in the decade to 1992, so the roads are potholed, the ports congested, power stations creaking. The cost of moving goods is said to account for half the costs of exports (and are 50 percent above neighbouring Chile). Perhaps the climax of the long nightmare, the great cholera epidemic of 1991 (ultimately spreading as far north as Mexico), is also attributable to the neglect of infrastructure investment – the resulting losses to tourism and agricultural exports, put at $1 billion, were three times what had been invested in water and sanitation in the 1980s.

Historically, exports were relatively easy. But they were produced by big farmers, financed by foreign banks, or big foreign mining companies, neither of which involved masses of the local workforce. With such a ruling class, the state was required to keep order, not develop the country. The military-civil oligarchy that ran the country up to the 1960s was rarely challenged – the structure of the economy entailed weak social movements, trade unions and middle classes. Abundant exports allowed unlimited imports without local development – by the 1970s, a fifth of the food supply was imported. In the 1990s, it is said that a quarter of Lima's food consumption is imported, implying both a relatively weak relationship between the city and agricultural producers, and a weak stimulation of rural output by urban demand.

I

Like other predominantly raw material exporting countries, Peru's economy has been created by surges of growth in world demand. Growth made immense fortunes and thus the means to create the infrastructure to facilitate exports, leaving much of the rest of the country undeveloped. The guayano boom (1830–81) initiated this pattern of growth, followed by a boom in sugar, copper and silver from the 1890s, in cotton after the turn of the century, in wood and rubber. Between 1898 and 1918, exports increased eight-fold.

The interwar great depression forced the government into protectionism like the rest of Latin America. However, after 1945, the country was opened up again to exports – copper, oil, iron, agricultural produce and fish (by 1970, Peru was second only to China in the volume of fish caught, 18 percent, and produced 40 percent of world fishmeal). It was a military regime that supervised this phase of growth, albeit with a social programme to increase mass education, housing and incomes. Electoral politics returned in 1956, but by the middle of 1967, a major foreign exchange crisis was the prelude to a much more radical military intervention.

In 1968, General Juan Velasco introduced 12 years of the revolutionary government of the armed forces. It was Peru's answer to the innovations of third worldism – of Nasser, Sukarno, Nkrumah and many more in the 1950s and 1960s. Velasco was dedicated to employing the state to rectify the perverse patterns of Peruvian development, to establishing national economic independence, to raising the position of the poor, the Indian (Quechua and Aymara-speaking) of the sierra and the selva. To the eyes of an hysterical Washington, he was a second Castro, and briefly aligned Peru with the Soviet Union. The military government carried out a radical land reform to strip the great landowners of their estates, encouraged co-operatives, nationalised the oil industry (Petroperu), the larger mines, public services, and a number of industries and part of the press. The borders were closed to most imports in favour of local production. In 1973, the great postwar success story, the fishing industry, was expropriated – and immediately began to decline.

When, in 1980, elected governments were restored, they faced – in conditions of world recession – the onset of a debt crisis (Mexico defaulted in 1982), shrunken exports, high rates of inflation, the beginnings of two major campaigns of rural guerilla warfare – the Sendero Luminoso (Shining Path; members were known as Senderistas), supposedly of Maoist persuasion in central Ayacucho, and the Fidelista Tupac Amaru in the north. Between 1983 and 1985, the GDP shrank by 13 percent. Nothing daunted, the electorate voted into office in 1985 Peru's famous Left opposition, Apra, under a new president, Alan Garcia.

Under president Garcia, present disasters joined an impressive record of past errors. Apra's diagnosis of Peru's condition attributed economic decline to weak domestic demand, exacerbated by the strain of debt-servicing. The government increased real salaries and public spending, while unilaterally imposing a limit on the servicing of external debt of 10 percent of export revenue (this led straight to default and the ending of most credit to Peru for seven years, a disaster for export industries). Expanding spending had some initial success in stimulating growth, but by late 1986, the economy had come to a halt and the external and budgetary deficits were becoming insupportable. There was a flight of capital, the reserves shrank rapidly, inflation soared and real wages declined. In 1988, the government tried to freeze public sector prices, the exchange and interest rates. The economy was paralysed – and inflation reached 30 percent per month (and at one point, 6 percent per day). In these chaotic conditions, the guerillas advanced on the one hand, and narcotic traders on the other (Peru produces 60 percent of the raw material for the world's cocaine), but even more swift was the growth of the official repressive machine, the army and police.

The economic performance was catastrophic. Consider the GDP growth rates: –8.3 percent (1988); –11.6 percent (1989); –5.4 percent (1990), with an average of –0.2 percent for the decade of the 1980s. Or mining exports (1986–90): –4.5; –3.0; –15.0; –4.9; and –8.7 percent. Or manufacturing (1988–90): –11.2; –15.7; –5.8 percent. Or real wages and salaries (1988–90): –23.6; –46.7; +4.4 percent. Meanwhile the rate of inflation went from 667 percent in 1988, to 3,399 the following year, 7,482 percent in 1990 and 4,095 in 1991. The Garcia government soldiered on, accelerating towards the precipice. It bravely covered the yawning debts of the parastatals –4.2 billion dollars in 1989–90, or enough, according to former privatisation minister Cordova, to build 14,000 12-classroom schools or 42,000 kilometres of road.

In fact, the official picture is misleading. An increasing part of the economy was slipping out of the statistical recording system. Popular ingenuity withdrew the struggle for survival from official view. It was estimated that 35 percent of employment was 'informal' in 1984, and 44.5 percent in 1993. As a proportion of total employment, micro enterprises increased from 10.4 to 14.3 percent in the same period, and street-sellers, from 11.6 to 41.4 (1990) and 50.4 percent (1993).

If the informal sector was the innocent parallel of the economy, the guerillas were the unofficial version of an increasingly brutalised army. The Senderistas, variously compared to the Khmer Rouge or the Japan Red Army, responded in kind, and both competed in steadily mounting scale of savageries. Abimael Guzman was the main leader. Child of an important family in the southern city of Arequipa, he is credited with germinating the ideas of Senderismo, drawn from the thought of Mao, in the philosophy department of Ayacucho University (the Chinese connection made his *nom de guerre* 'chairman' Gonzalo; instead of the normal Latin American title of president). The Sendero grew steadily through the 1980s, creating a cadre drawn from the universities and the intelligentsia but with roots in the shanty towns, to peak at about 10,000. At its height, it seemed capable of paralysing the country with impunity, shutting of Lima's electricity supply, destroying pipelines and highways. Through the activities of the army and the guerillas, possibly one million people were displaced and 30,000 or so killed.

Lawlessness – including the growth of the narcotics trade and associated gangs – justified the building of a repressive apparatus of considerable size: The army is still in charge of five provinces under emergency rule. The belligerents left a trail of devastation – with possibly 30 billion dollars cumulative losses. There is also a pervasive climate of insecurity. Some Lima houses are still encased in steel cages against the sudden bomb, and factories and barracks have guardhouses high up on the corners of their walls with hooded armed men watching through slit holes. Security guards in flak jackets, police and soldiers are everywhere, loafing or watching.

II

After the experience of the 1980s, political parties in Peru were discredited. Both leading candidates for the presidency in 1990 opposed the party system. To general surprise, a little known university rector, Alberto Fujimori, was chosen over Peru's most famous novelist.

As first priority, the new president gave the armed forces their head to smash the guerillas, and in economic affairs, sharply moved into reverse with a drastic stabilisation programme, major cuts in public expenditure, tight fiscal and monetary controls (with the elimination of subsidies), liberalised prices (in one famous case, the price of gasoline is said to have increased overnight from 17.5 to 21,000 Intis per gallon) and the energetic pursuit of foreign investment and privatisation.

In the case of the repression of the guerillas, the new government was more effective than anyone, in the light of the record of the preceding decade, could have imagined. The campaign culminated in the capture of Guzman in 1992, and in a well publicised trial, his sentence to life imprisonment. Thousands of cadres were captured or faded away into NGOs in the slum or squatter areas; some, it is said, joined the narcotics smugglers. Political killings dropped by four-fifths by 1995, when 520 died, none of them in Lima. There were new incidents in the middle of this year, but of marginal significance outside the remote coca growing areas. Military intelligence, not the most reliable source in the past, estimates the number of cadres surviving at under 10 percent of the 1990 level (or between 500 and 1,000), the majority in remote areas and under the command of Oscar Ramirez who, it is said, does not accept Guzman's tactics. Only the sadly defiant slogans remain, with their bizarre echoes of imperatives translated from the Chinese – in London, 'Move heaven and earth to free chairman Gonzalo', and in Lima, 'Overcome the reverse by developing popular war!'

The turnaround in the economy is only slightly less dramatic. In the three years to 1995, the growth of economy averaged 8.7 percent, the fastest in Latin America. This was partly through increased utilisation of very underutilised capacity. But there was also an investment boom – between 1980 and 1990, gross domestic investment declined by 4.2 percent annually, but expanded by 10.7 percent annually in the first four years of the 1990s (while domestic savings increased from 12.5 percent in 1992 to 17.5 percent in 1995). Part of this was an inflow of foreign funds; the restoration of stability and positive real interest rates (as well as the opportunities provided by the privatisation of public enterprises) led to an increase in foreign investment from 1.36 billion dollars in 1990 to 7.8 billion dollars in 1995 (equal to 6.9 percent of GDP between 1993 and 1995; 48 percent of the inflow being long-term capital). The inflow was partly repatriated funds that had earlier fled, but it covered the external deficit and allowed high imports. Exports were rapidly diversified and grew by 9.9 percent annually (1993–5). The public sector deficit was cut (from 7 to 1.5 percent of GDP, 1989–91), and the annual rate of inflation declined to about 10 percent.

Some four-fifths of the holdings of the state in 1990 have been sold, including telecommunications, mining, electricity generation, fishing, banking and transport, raising some five billion dollars for the public exchequer. The government is continuing in the face of some opposition to privatising the oil industry (the first units of Petroperu were sold in March). Finally, Peru has resumed servicing its external debt, and about half the debt has been rescheduled. The cumulative total is said to be about 30 billion dollars, equal to some 406 percent of the value of exports (compared to Argentina's 345; Brazil's 262; and Mexico's 171 percent). The servicing burden takes about 64 percent of export earnings.

In 1992, the president claimed that the bureaucracy of the state and the old political parties campaigned to dilute or obstruct his reforms. With the support of the army (although one general tried to lead a coup), he suspended the constitution and the assembly. He argued that the line ministries were incapable of offsetting the social effects of the reform programme, and sacked about 45 percent of the workforce. He concentrated the powers in an expanded office of the presidency and a number of parastalal organisations. The new constitution created a new, smaller and single-chamber assembly, banned political parties in elections, and allowed, for the first time, the president to run for a second period in office (in the 1995 presidential elections, Fujimori was again victorious).

Perhaps others had higher ambitions. In the late 1980s, the military are said to have prepared a plan, the so-called 'Green Book', to establish an authoritarian regime in Peru for 15 or 20 years to once-and-for-all supersede the chaos inflicted on the country by elected governments. The person said to have been centrally involved in the preparation of the plan is now a high adviser to the president and in charge of his intelligence services, Vladimiro Montesinos. Montesinos, as an army captain in the 1970s, was charged and jailed for spying for the CIA.

Be that as it may, the president made considerable efforts to develop antipoverty programmes. Spending on social sectors, on official claims, was more than doubled in per capita terms (from 64 to 134 dollars or 10 percent of GDP). Educational expenditure was also expanded, and a programme of building new schools is very evident, covering 88 percent of the relevant age groups. However, there are immense deficits to be made up – there may be shiny new schools, but the pay of teachers is only one-fifth of what it had been a decade earlier, there are few books, equipment or infrastructure (many rural schools lack electricity or drinking water); the drop-out rate in some rural areas is said to be 60 percent. Spending per student is still only a fifth of the 1970 level. There has been a similar drive to extend health clinics, but still there are great maldistributions – in Lima, there are 800 people per doctor, but 12,000 in the poorest provinces; hospital beds range from 1 per 666 people in the capital to 1 per 1,250 elsewhere.

III

The most severe problems of Peru concern the striking level of cumulative poverty and inequality, exacerbated by two decades of economic mismanagement. Inequality has always been an issue – in the 1960s, the poorest 40 percent received 8.8 percent of personal income (compared to 14 percent on average for 43 developing countries). Sustained growth between 1950 and 1966 seemed only to make this worse – when per capita income increased 2.1 percent annually in that period, the 'modem sector' increased 4.9 percent; the urban, 2.0; and rural Peru, 1.3 percent. While the coastal areas took the lion's share, the poorest – non-coastal small peasants – experienced no increase: they were not connected to the central dynamic of the economy.

In the years of military and nationalist rule, the problems worsened. Between 1970 and 1980, the proportion of the urban population in poverty increased from 28 to 45 percent (and those in extreme poverty, from 8 to 16 percent); the rural poor decreased from 68 to 64 percent (and those in extreme poverty stayed the same at 39 percent). There was some reversal in the 1990s, although still around half of the population is officially poor (but the extremely poor did decrease, from 24 to 20 percent). In Lima, poverty declined from just under a half of the population to a third; in the urban sierra, from 47 to 46 percent, and the rural sierra, from 68 to 66 percent (there was no data on the thinly populated selva). The Indian-language speakers fared much worse – 42 percent of the Spanish-speakers nationally are poor (and 13 percent very poor), compared to 60 percent of those who speak Quechua (a third are very poor), and 86 percent of those speaking Aymara (70 percent are very poor). For Indian women in the rural sierra, conditions are the worst. The measures are duplicated in each sector. Over a third of the rural population is illiterate, but 70 percent of rural women.

However, despite the record in income, the figures on the average life expectancy have not deteriorated and now stand at 66 years. Infant mortality is nationally 64 per 1,000 – but in Lima, 26, and in the rural sierra Huancavelica, over 100. In the 1990s, consumption for the poorest fifth of the population improved by 32 percent, a change made possible, it is said, more by the establishment of peace so that farmers can get their output to market than any public social programme.

The severe deprivation of thousands of remote Andean settlements – mainly of Quechua and Ayamara speakers – is a key target for public action. Yet the state is still a major obstacle to effective public action, paralysing and paralytic, combining a bloated and inefficient executive, an irrelevant and fractious legislature, and a painfully slow and corrupt judiciary. Furthermore, the civil apparatus is now overshadowed by the security arm, the army, police and intelligence services, backed by a famously brutal prison system. The army directly controls a major part of the country (which includes those areas where coca is grown), and by reputation, it is more terrifying than the guerillas were – even if the 1995 clash with Ecuador suggests it was more effective against a foreign army.

The state, armed and civil, has come to be centralised on the person of the president. Thus, the reform government that has radically turned the country round in terms of domestic security and economic growth has nonetheless immensely exaggerated the traditional issue of the concentration of power – a ceaselessly active president and an inert civil society. The president is in perpetual daily movement, a Santa Claus delivering presents to the most remote areas, through his whirling helicopter personally holding the country together.

His key political base is the army. He purged the high command before the 1992 coup, and in return, the army gave undivided loyalty to the coup. He has protected the army against the numerous accusations of brutality, murderous injustice and corruption. In June last year, he slipped through the assembly an amnesty law to protect the armed forces. His supporters have restructured the intelligence services and have expanded them to include all agencies, including the army. He has also tried to enhance the popular image of the army by pushing it into rural development projects – organising health services and emergency food supplies. Up to late 1995, the president rejected the evidence of military involvement in the narcotics trade, but he has now supposedly accepted the accusation and ordered the army to end its involvement in counter-narcotic activities. The reprimand seems hardly likely to deter anyone.

So far, the popular loathing for the 1980s has meant the president has been popular, with a 60 to 70 percent approval rating in the polls. The popularity does not extend to his minions – his candidates were defeated in last year's municipal elections, most dramatically in Lima. He won a second term as president, and now his supporters in the assembly have, by means of some neat constitutional footwork, forced through a legal amendment that allows him to run for a third term (2000–5). He does not need a Green Book.

However, it is at this stage that elected political leaders usually overreach themselves and start going into terminal decline. The projected rate of growth for 1996 is down to 2.3 percent (the soothsayers foretell a resumption of 6 percent growth for 1997–9), much below what is needed to get Peru back into its peak prosperity. The external debt situation still remains very threatening. And the narcotics issue will not go away while Washington is concerned – Vladimiro Montesinos, a key security adviser to the president, has just been accused by a top narcotics trader on trial of taking bribes of 50,000 dollars per month to secure army protection to fly his cocaine cargo out of his airstrip. The charge has been denied, but less well-known army chiefs in key localities are almost certain to be involved in the drugs business.

President Fujimori can ride these still small waves, but sooner or later, his triumphs will be forgotten and he will come to be hated for directing a virtual dictatorship. It is the natural justice of populist regimes. At that stage, civil society will come back into its own. There are few traditional institutions left – political parties are lying low; the judiciary is discredited; the trade unions defunct; regional and local authorities severely weakened. Only the NGO sector seems to be flourishing.

The country is rich and has, as it always has had, great opportunities. As so often, the economic promise is constantly frustrated by the fantasy world of government and, despite all the protestations and reams of policy paper, the apparent frequent indifference of politicians to the fate of their citizens.

Vietnam: Back at the Beginning*

It is all too much to understand: why so much blood needed to be spilt, so many young people cut down, to arrive in the end back at the beginning, the chaotic market, the values of the quick deal and the fast buck. It is difficult to fit together the two worlds, Vietnam in 1975 and 1998.

Hanoi is dour at this time of year, Lutheran or Calvinist, with lowering grey skies and drizzle. The people dress in sensible thick clothes, grey trousers and quilted jackets. The great Red River delta is also grey and dismal, flat paddy as far as the eye can see.

At dawn, the streets are empty and dark. It is so unlike Delhi in the winter, with old men hooded in shawls or blankets, stamping their feet and blowing their gnarled knuckles, crouched over the pavement fires, yawning over the first tea of the day. But Hanoi's streets are deserted and unlit, only a plump policeman on his scooter going for the first shift. But there is an early market in the darkness; old peasant women in conical hats, squat legs akimbo before their lettuces and chickens. How can anyone see in the dark to haggle? On the unlit roads, ghostly peasants emerge, peddling on bikes piled high with piglets and cabbages.

It is a far cry from the south. Ho Chi Minh City (still Saigon to most people) is balmy and brilliant in the morning sun, crowded with people and noisy markets; here the boom still seems unending. Crisis or no crisis in southeast Asia, the shops, the buses, the streets, the aircraft, are as packed as always. In the seven years since I was last here, the torrent of bicycles has turned into a floodtide of motorbikes and scooters – maybe in seven years, it will be a hideous pack of stationary cars.

No sensible clothes here. The fair maids on their scooters are in diaphanous flowing white silk, slender as flowers. It is difficult to think that it was their equally slender mothers who dug the labyrinth of tunnels around Saigon to destroy the mighty American war machine, and their no less slender grandmothers who hauled the Chinese artillery pieces across the jungle hills to Dien Bien Phu to smash the mighty French war machine.

---

* From: *Economic and Political Weekly*, 11 April 1998.

It is astonishing how little generals learn. They create mighty field armies, bristling with armour and artillery, with which to face each other, and then once or twice a century, the serried ranks of samurai are destroyed by a rag-tag and bobtail band of irregulars, flitting between the trees. How ironic that one of those bands in Vietnam defeated an army that had been born 200 years before in another band of sharp shooting irregulars that did exactly the same thing to the mighty British war machine, both in the name of national liberation.

The Vietnam war was a generation ago and for the young it is now almost as historic as the American war of independence. It took place in a world now remote, a world governed by the fantasy of benevolent government in command of everything, pioneering in the great world march of progress: red scarves and banners, pink cheeks and shining eyes gazing with supreme confidence into the sunrise. In Hanoi's parks, old men silently gyrate in stately exercises. Do they remember how it was then? The glorious global army marched to utopia. So much was sacrificed to that heroic enterprise. And yet the bodies were hardly cold in the ground before it all came to an end – and markets were all the rage. Or is it all just too much to understand: why so much blood needed to be spilt, so many young people cut down, to arrive in the end back at the beginning, the chaotic market, the values of the quick deal and the fast buck. It is difficult to imagine how the two worlds, Vietnam in 1975 and 1998, can be fitted in one mind.

Meanwhile the markets remanufacture all, vigorous and irresistible, reshaping everything – even though the government sustains the fantasy that it still commands, that this is, in the official formula, 'a market economy under the control of the government'. Like the Viet Cong, the guerrilla traders, the army of the unofficial economy, surround the citadel of the state, burrowing like termites through its great walls. The official statistics record – to change the image – only the surface of the pond.

The figures on poverty are horrendous – half the 77 million population is below the nutritionally defined poverty line. The average per capita income is around US $250, but that sinks to $100 for some of the poorer provinces (in comparison to Saigon's $850). Yet the poverty is not as evident as you might expect, and there are anomalies. The average life expectancy figures are much better, 63 for men and 67 for women. That cannot reflect the quality of public health, since the services are poor, but it suggests consumption is much better than income (everyone seems to eat rice, not the millet grains that are the food of the poor), and that the hidden economy is much bigger than the official one. The government believes the official figures and worries. It is the same with unemployment, assumed to be severe, especially now with restructuring (radically cutting the number of soldiers, government and State-

Owned Enterprise employees), though again what is the reality is less clear. The problem in many countries is not that the poor lack work – they cannot afford to be idle – but they are obliged to work far too hard for a pittance. But the government thinks otherwise and as a result has negotiated to send 20,000 workers abroad to work this year.

The unrecorded economy is as vigorous as any, ranging from the white but unrecorded through the shades of the palest of greys to 'the darker to the black economy' (narcotics, fraud, tax avoidance, gambling, prostitution). The World Bank has made a modest estimate of the volume of goods smuggled into the country – about $500 million annually, or equal to a fifth of official imports.

Old habits die hard. Government officials still cling to the notion that they, not markets, call the shots. In a world awash with talk of popular participation, consultation, open government, local development plans like local statistics are still secret. Without a hint of a twinkle in his eye, the local official, leaning on the thick copy of the local plan, apologises that he has only one copy, it is very long and in Vietnamese so it cannot be consulted. The plan is exclusive to the conspiracy of the state, a secret religious ritual (like the prayers offered up by the Chinese emperors to protect the Middle Kingdom). All that we can be allowed to know is that the target annual rate of economic growth of the locality to the year 2010 is 15 percent; thus god decrees without making available the calculations and assumptions for the divine conclusion. But then this is not the world of scientific planning but of religious incantation (would it have made any difference if it had been 14 percent or 16 percent?).

The reforms in many sectors still lack full conviction. Agriculture (employing 70 percent of the labour force and producing half the exports) was indeed decollectivised and prices freed. It produced a spectacular export success, first in rice, turning the country from famine a decade ago to being by 1994 the third largest rice exporter in the world (after Thailand and the US) – and despite the heavy losses still experienced in flooding, in transporting and storing the crop (rats get a fair slice of the harvest). Rice was followed by coffee and other crops. But the government retained a monopoly of processing, distribution and exporting, and land ownership. So the pace of growth has been less than it might have been, and the farmers have been insulated from the profits of exports – or rather, have been obliged to smuggle rice out (possibly one million tons go to south China). In China, agricultural reform lifted rural incomes and stimulated the astonishing growth of rural industries (the famous Town and Village Enterprises), but that has not happened in Vietnam. The state has stolen the cream.

However, more change has been made than in China in the State-Owned Enterprises. The total number was halved (from 12,500 in 1990 to 6,000) through shutting them down, but only three of what remained have been privatised. The government claims that the proportion of SOEs that make losses has been cut from 50 percent to 8 (in 1994) but this means very little – the 8 percent could be a handful of giants with giant debts. Everyone agrees that the four major banks are awash with bad debts from cumulative lending to the SOEs, a public sector version of the crony capitalism of southeast Asia and equally vulnerable to a crisis of confidence. The government now argues that the SOEs should be reorganised in 14 major groups, the nuclei of giant company groups, national champions, modelled on South Korea's *chaebol* (the Chinese government has adopted a similar scheme). But the *chaebol* are now mired in financial crisis and the whole notion of national champions seems financially defective, a recipe for heroic rent-seeking.

Again, compared to China, Vietnam has been much less effective in debureaucratising. This has been especially damaging for foreign investment, particularly now with a regional financial crisis and general pessimism. A number of proposed major investments have been suspended because, it is said, of hideous delays and red tape. Applications have slowed down drastically. Arranging bank backing has been strongly affected by the government's unwillingness to allow land to be privately owned and thus available as a collateral for borrowing. This has affected the attempt to involve private foreign capital in upgrading Vietnam's disastrous infrastructure, particularly the now permitted BOT schemes.

Poor infrastructure is the major restriction on the country's capacity to grow. The southern complex around Saigon is the most favoured, followed a long way behind by the Hanoi region. And this regional disparity forces new investment to the south or to the north. Da Nang, a coastal city in the middle on the narrow waist of the country (hardly 50 miles from the Laotian border) has acres of unfilled industrial zones. Who would invest there when the markets are in the south and north, connected only by an ancient, single-track railway line and a poor two-lane road that goes through every town? One day, perhaps, Da Nang can extend its influence westwards into Laos and link to the great corridor of the Mekong river and beyond to Thailand, but meanwhile these are geographer's dreams: the city is marooned.

The same may be half true of Haiphong. It is 'the largest port in the north', but with a shallow draught (10,000 tonnes); dredging and major investment will raise it only to 20–30,000. Can it be more than the end of the spoke to the hubs of Singapore and Hong Kong, those mighty concentrations of state-of-the-art port infrastructure? A new deeper water port is proposed with an expatriate-run industrial zone, but this is only on the drawing board – and depends on overcoming all the fears of an economic domino effect from southeast Asia. The Nomura Industrial Zone – all shiny and new, with its own operational power station – is still virtually empty. It was conceived and built by the Japanese financial group when Vietnam was flavour of the year and Japanese manufacturing capacity was spreading out through southeast Asia; it seemed obvious then that Nomura would find it easy to pull some of its clients to Haiphong. But all over the region, the best laid plans have come awry – the Japanese managers in Haiphong are understandably nervous that their industrial zone may be one small twig in Japan's economic pruning.

There is another way to make Haiphong live. The governor of Yunnan province in southwest China visited the port in 1993 and urged its opening up to Yunnan's external trade so that the province could avoid the long haul of its cargo to Hong Kong and the east coast – and, he said, raise Haiphong's throughput from 4 to 40 million tonnes per year. Another delegation from Yunnan was in Hanoi this March. If that link could be developed, Vietnamese-Chinese joint ventures as well as Vietnamese and foreign companies exporting to China might fill up the industrial zones. At the moment, Yunnan is doing something similar to its west over the border into Myanmar to gain a route to Yangon (Rangoon) port, with a boom in Sino-Myanmar border development and the export processing zone there. But for Vietnam, China is an ancient enemy – after all, Beijing invited a visit from President Nixon at the height of the Vietnam war with the US, largely to help Nixon get off the hook of the war (in Hanoi, this was a classic 'stab in the back'); and there was a bloody war largely at China's instigation on Vietnam's northern border; and ugly disputes between the two over the Spratly and Paracel islands in the South China Sea. Current land connections to Yunnan via the border crossing point of Lao Cai are very poor, with an ancient, narrow gauge rail track and a poor road. Hanoi worries that upgrading the route would let in the People's Liberation Army rather than Yunnan's traders. In Yangon there are similar grumbles – that the border bridge that the Chinese have built to Myanmar is big enough for tanks, artillery and a couple of divisions rather than simply freight trucks.

The scheme for a link to Yunnan has not yet died. The government's plan for regional development in the country involves developing three 'triangles' (triangles are currently a fashionable shape in southeast Asian economic geography) – one in the south around Saigon (with 9.4 percent of the population and 25.4 percent of the national output), one in the centre (around Da Nang), and one in the north (with 6.5 percent of the population and 10.5 percent of output), between the points of Hanoi, Haiphong and Lao Cai. If the fears could be overcome and the links developed, it would provide a much vaster – and booming – hinterland for the port than anything in the poor north of Vietnam.

So far, the economic crisis in southeast Asia has not affected Vietnam. A lot of the expatriates have been withdrawn by their companies – the Korean school languishes because so many children have left. And the building boom has gone flat – as throughout the region, the urban landscape is studded with half-finished office blocks and hotels. Foreign investment is drying up, and it seems unlikely in the short-term to reach the government's targets. But this has not yet affected the domestic economy that drastically, and sooner or later growth should be resumed. Then the hotels will be needed to reach the target of 8.7 million tourists by 2010. But the cities also need rehabilitating if the tourists are to see the sights – after years of neglect, old Hanoi is virtually a slum and massively overcrowded. In a secondhand bookshop in Saigon, a copy of the 1929 French colonial statistical outline for the three Indo-China territories that became Vietnam records the population as 17 million – and now it is 77 million. Yet the accompanying old photographs suggest the population then was far more impoverished than it is now.

Markets hollow out regimes as much as they ever did – Marx was right in that respect. The southeast Asian crisis – of the managed state economy and crony capitalism – is not likely to be repeated in Vietnam as of now, but it is a salutary warning. Both China and Vietnam are vulnerable to a crisis of confidence if not this year then on the next swing of the cycle or the one after. The vulnerability is inevitable while both economies are dominated by great clusters of rent-seeking SOEs, mopping up national investment and predetermining national priorities. As happened with the Little Tigers, high growth can hide the issues for a long period, but ultimately the conditions for rapid export-led growth are also those which, in the absence of reforms to shift fully to the market, precipitate crises of confidence with severe real effects. Vietnam still has time, even if it does not yet have the will.

Lebanon: There is Life after Death*

The 1960s were the time of liberation, the Beatles and Carnaby Street – and golden Beirut. But the long dark night that followed turned Lebanon into every country's nightmare. Yet astonishingly, life returns, apparently unmarked. What does the future hold for Lebanon trapped between the samurai to the south and the east, two outside players with troops to back their words, Israel and Syria, and a persisting boom as embodied in the tight labour market?

'That intolerance of social freedom which is natural to absolutism is sure to find a corrective in the national diversities which no other force could so efficiently provide. The coexistence of several nations under the same state is a test as well as the best security of its freedoms' (Lord Acton 1862).

But, Lord Acton, is it true? It was not in the Soviet Union nor in Yugoslavia. And in India? And in tiny Lebanon, with a population scarcely a quarter of that of the Calcutta Metropolitan District or Greater Bombay?

Over 15 years, the centre of Beirut – the old city and history, the central business district and money, the hotel quarter and the 'international playground' – was turned into horror, a nightmare. The heart of darkness was the 'Green Line', the old Damascus road, where the changing cast of militias fought to steal an inch of territory (or to stop losing an inch) or just to terrorise. It was green, incidentally, not from some derisive tribute to the environment, but because the neglected tarmac split and sprouted shrubs and grass; nature, as on Bikini Atoll after its successive atomic devastations, reasserted primacy over the desolation of men.

And despite the current demolitions and reconstructions, it remains desolate, ghoulish, surreal: Berlin in 1945, Sarajevo in 1996. Guttered buildings command the heights, eyeless and roofless, splattered with thousands of bullet holes like smallpox, or great gaping wounds, limbs shorn off. Naked walls stand alone, amid the rubble like crumbling monuments, commemorating a past few now remember (most Lebanese were born too late to have memories of the golden 1960s) – except that there are no signs of real life in archaeological sites. Here, the pretty wallpaper flapping, naked to the air, testifies to someone's cherished sitting room; the inner stairs wave slowly in the wind; half a balcony

---

* From: *Economic and Political Weekly*, 27 September 1997.

hangs, defying gravity. In some empty windows, a dusty curtain or potted plant shows where squatters still try to survive.

The 1960s were the time of liberation, the Beatles and Carnaby Street – and golden Beirut supposedly an island of wealthy hedonism and freedom amid the stern and austere dictatorships of west Asia. Indeed, without the wars that followed 1974, Lebanon by now would be another Singapore to prove that growth and development are not a Confucian monopoly. But the long dark night which followed turned Lebanon into every country's nightmare, a legend to frighten all. The wars had no point and no logical end – as Samir Khalaf, the distinguished Lebanese sociologist puts it:

> the horrors spawned by war are particularly galling in the case of Lebanon because they are not anchored in any recognisable or coherent set of causes nor have they resolved the issues which sparked the initial hostilities. It is in this poignant sense that the war has been wasteful and futile, ugly and unfinished.

Yet, astonishingly, life returns, vigorous and apparently unmarked. The story is proudly told of the wealthy Maronite family which insisted on marrying its child in the ruined roofless basilica in the old city where by tradition the family always wed. The Rolls-Royces and Mercedes parked amid the rubble, a vote of confidence that the slaughter was really ended.

The economy expanded rapidly in the 1990s, and vast programmes of infrastructure construction, reconstruction and rehabilitation are underway – the dust of brick, stone and mortar hangs over the empty spaces of the old city. And in demolition, vast archaeological treasures are being discovered in the depths of the site. The power system, the roads, the telephones, the water supply are largely restored, even if not yet wholly reliable.

The government which imploded in the wars, a bystander at auto-destruct, is back in business. The multiplicity of militias, part proto-governments, part-mafia, and the economy and intractable society that they enforced on all, have been smothered by foreign military occupation. The leaders of many of the main factions, the warlords, have donned suits and become ministers, their 'ronin' absorbed into the army. But the government is directed by a group of outsiders, businessmen not warlords, under the richest of them all, prime minister Rafiq al-Hariri (who made his millions in Saudi construction). The Hariri group, his former business staff, associates and friends as well as some sharp technocrats recruited from international agencies and companies, have sidestepped the entrenched interests of the country to bully into place rapid reconstruction as the basis for economic growth. The symbol of it all was collapsing the rights of the owners of land in the old city into shareholdings in the private development corporation, Solidere (where Hariri is the largest shareholder). The government has embodied its hopes in a plan, Horizon 2007, proposing a public investment programme of $17.7 billion.

In the first years, the government seemed very successful – and real per capita income increased from under $1,000 in 1990 to $2,700 five years later (between 1975 and 1990, per capita income is said to have declined by two-thirds). The currency was managed to ensure a stable Lebanese pound, inflation driven down from hyper to normal levels, and dollarisation of the economy (92 percent in 1987) reduced to about 57 percent. But, the critics say, it was all done through domestic and foreign borrowing (with convertibility, there is little practical difference). The fiscal deficit is running at 18 percent of gross domestic product, and servicing the debt takes nearly a third of government revenue. On the trade account, massive imports are needed to expand the economy, and the trade deficit ($6.4 billion pounds in 1996) is covered by an extraordinary capital inflow some put as high as $8.5 billion (to cover both the trade deficit and the remittance payments of the country's large foreign labour force). However, part of the inflow has been short-term speculative funds rather than long-term investment, and there are worries that the economy is vulnerable to capital flight if the currency becomes unstable – shades of Mexico in late 1994 or Thailand, Malaysia and Indonesia this year.

As a result, 'sound money' has to be a central aim of the government, and this, critics say, is now driving the economy into recession. Hariri could reply that economic strategies are always gambles, and he has gambled on restored infrastructure restoring economic growth, even if in the short-term there is a downturn. And it is true that infrastructure has been restored – the entire country is laced with excellently surfaced roads (but with few road markings, traffic lights or signs – vehicles slide tentatively across junctions). Telephones, especially mobile, are everywhere (but Beirut apparently has no telephone directory). And Lebanon already produces a rich country's garbage with very poor disposal facilities – hence some of the more beautiful mountain ridges are sites for smoking dumps, and the beaches are hideously scarred (a recent voluntary campaign to clean up the seafront had no significant results).

More generally, recession or not, the country seems very prosperous, especially so after the long period of wars. Cars pack the streets and traffic jams are becoming Bangkok class. There has been an heroic and extraordinary national private building boom, and hence the proliferation throughout much of the mountains and coast of half-finished unoccupied Dallas-style mansions, monsters with towers, elaborate balconies, domes and battlements, set in isolated acres. They say many are the result of remittances from Lebanon's worldwide diaspora, but especially from those who fled to West Africa and the Gulf during the wars and made good. In the cities, the shops and markets are full of goods and buyers. Even in the poor south or Beirut's southern suburbs, Lebanon seems to be already a middle income country, and there is little of the concentrated poverty of, say, Egypt or India. The poorest are bedouins from the Syrian desert living in encampments of ragged tents in the west of the country along the Syrian border (the Beka'a valley).

Impressions – and anecdotes – have to fill some of the gaps, because the restoration of Lebanon's statistical services is still far from complete. While the official economy may be drooping, the unofficial may be still expanding vigorously.

The critics fasten on the more gloomy official figures – the growing debt-servicing burden, the declining rate of growth – to argue that Hariri's gamble has failed. The restoration of physical infrastructure has not restored economic growth, and now the rising level of debt threatens bankruptcy. The left adds that the gamble was typical of the old irresponsible free enterprise tradition of the Lebanese establishment, sacrificing social rehabilitation to help the poor with infrastructure to support the profits of the already rich, producing steadily greater income inequality. Some go further, saying Lebanon is another example of 'nomenklatura capitalism' where, by the alchemy of public private collaboration, public losses are converted into private profits. At the heart of the process are the corporations, companies and banks of the Hariri group – indeed, some see Lebanon as now just another private subsidiary of the group – his managers direct the programmes of the public sector, his companies are the main private subcontractors. It is a kind of Venetian oligarchy or, like the Marcos' Philippines, 'croney capitalism'.

It is too early to judge the programme. Even if the graver allegations are true, it is not a zero-sum game – Hariri profits may also lift Lebanon into growth. And if there is growth, official or unofficial, with sustained speed, many of the charges will seem less urgent.

Civil Rights

More substantial are the criticisms of the government's heavy-handed style on civil rights issues. There is a ban on demonstrations and strikes. The government turned out the army when the unions called a general strike in protest at declining living standards and a government plan to purge the number of television (and radio) stations to four – of which three, by chance, were owned by the prime minister, the speaker of the assembly and the deputy prime minister's brother (the fourth was owned by the government). The government supported – indeed, fomented – a split in the trade union federation to create a loyal group. It has postponed the local elections, scheduled for this year (the last local elections were held in 1963). This summer, when a leading Shi'ite cleric campaigned for more development funds for the poor – and Shi'ite – areas of the south, the government banned 'inflammatory' statements.

Of course, the government argues that exceptional security measures are merely prudent while the country is under effective Syrian military supervision; under Israeli military occupation (and that of its client, the South Lebanese Army) in the south; while Israel frequently bombs or rockets targets in the south and in the Beka's valley; and in the melancholy light of the decade and a half of military anarchy and governmental collapse. But it is here that some of the complexities start to unravel.

The orthodox account has it that Lebanon was torn apart by its religious divisions – Maronite Christians (the largest Christian minority), the Shi'ites (the largest Muslim minority), the Sunnis, Greek Orthodox, Greek Catholics, the Druzes, the Armenian Catholics, the Syrian Catholics and, they say, nine other confessional groups. In fact, it was mashed between, in the first instance, Israel and the Palestinians, the PLO, and in the second, Israel and Syria. The centre between the two could not hold and disintegrated into shifting fragments, loosely but not essentially related lo confessional allegiances.

Confessionalism was the formal basis for the operation of political power in what is now Lebanon both during the Ottoman Empire, in the constitution of 1926 and during the French Mandate period which ended in 1941. As always such formal distributions cannot contain the changing proportions of population in each group – so a powerful theme has been the fears of the Maronites that their formal position was being undermined by the growth of the Shi'ites. Those fears have blocked the holding of a proper Census (the last was held in 1932) lest this reveal a disastrous decline in the Christian share of population. They have also prevented elementary justice for the Palestinians (many of whom have been in Lebanon since 1948) and others by admission to Lebanese nationality lest this upset the confessional shares.

Inevitably, Lebanon in war fractured initially along confessional lines. As it fractured, it became impossible for anyone born into one of the confessional groups to survive outside the group. It would be courting death to be born with a Muslim name but claim to be an atheist in a stronghold of the Maronites. Confessional identity, as Khalaf puts it, was both 'emblem and armour'. And the wars, to prove the point, slaughtered 62,000, with 83,000 injured and between 2,000 and 17,500 'disappeared' (out of a population of about three million); 790,000 were forced to flee. The territories were confessionally cleansed – in

1975, 55 percent of the Christians lived in the south, now only 1 percent; 40 percent of Beirut Muslims lived in the east, now 5 percent. Yet broad confessionalism was only one theme – Shi'ite militia fought each other; and one of the most terrible episodes of the war, just before hostilities ceased, was between two armed groups of Maronites.

The potent cocktail of outside manipulation, arms and finance, hungry politicians (linked to old ruling families, striving to protect themselves against social change), greedy mafias, arms and narcotic traders, ambitious and embittered clerics, and real social questions made issues that had been resolvable for most of the years since 1800 completely unresolvable. The domestic factions became completely unwilling to compromise when it seemed that an overwhelming outside force would give them total victory over everyone else (just as the power of London makes the Northern Ireland Protestants unwilling to compromise). Israel, the US, and France were all crucial at different stages in the tactical calculations of different parts of the Maronite leadership; Iran and Syria for the Shi'ites and Druzes; Libya and Saudi Arabia for the Sunnis; and for all, at some stage, Syria.

Israel and Syria

In practice, there have been only two serious outside players, with troops to back their word: Israel and Syria. The two have developed a symbiotic relationship in Lebanon. The Syrian military occupation is almost everywhere and has powerful influence over, if not control of, the Lebanese government. It arms and, it is said, controls Hiz'bollah, the Shi'ite militia that is the only force in Lebanon actively seeking to force Israel and the South Lebanon Army to evacuate the country (Ama, the main Shi'ite militia from which Hiz'bollah originally split off, also maintains some military opposition to Israeli forces). Yet Israeli bombing raids never target Syrian military installations in Lebanon – presumably for fear the Syrians could inflict serious damage on Israel and that might shift Israeli opinion to demand a new approach to a peace settlement. The bombing hits only the poor scapegoats, defenceless Lebanon, innocent peasants and the country's infrastructure. Syria uses Hiz'bollah and Lebanon as proxy for its war aims.

Of course, Israel is the starting point in all this and provided the original pretext for Syrian intervention in Lebanon. Netanyahu, the loose cannon, has bombed out the peace process with the Palestinians through the concessions he has made to keep his tottering coalition together – the gradual ethnic cleansing of east Jerusalem; drilling the holes of new Jewish settlements through the West Bank so it becomes honeycombed and ungovernable; from time to time, making the West Bank a prison for its Arab inhabitants, trying to starve them into submission; and refusing to consider returning the Golan Heights to Syria; along with all the other acts of covert and overt aggression. The process renders the PLA (already demoralised and thus vicious and corrupt) impotent. The bomb throwers and suicide warriors become the sole symbol of hope for Palestine's young (and Washington, supine before Israel's initiatives, like Netanyahu, is preoccupied with the tactics of political survival at home).

So far as Lebanon is concerned, the by-product of these far off events in which it has no role or influence, is the continuation of Israel's use of the south of the country as a free fire zone. Over two decades, scarcely a week has passed in which Israel has not attacked targets in Lebanon. It is an astonishing performance. Official Israel is the arch-terrorist of west Asia, imposing collective guilt and punishment on the Lebanese who are neither responsible nor in control of either the Palestinians or Hiz'bollah. The persistent use of terror as an instrument of policy is far more dire than anything either the Palestinians, Hammas or Hiz'bollah can achieve – as the respective body counts show. The overwhelming majority of the victims are innocent bystanders.

What is perhaps most astonishing is that the Israeli ruling order can rest content with this approach when it is clear, 30 years after the Six-Day War, that terrorising its neighbours and colonising the West Bank not only do not increase Israel's security, they increase its insecurity. Perhaps it is a policy of despair: bombing because no one can think of anything else to do, an example of that endemic disease of governments, doing something because something must be seen to be done. To do anything less counterproductive and more sensible – like trying to secure peace (guarantee Palestinian control of the West Bank and east Jerusalem, evacuate south Lebanon and the Golan Heights, etc.) would pull apart the Israeli population and the coalition. With less ferocious implications, Washington's attitude to Cuba (and earlier to Nicaragua) is similar – the policy is completely futile, but no one has the courage to outface Jesse Helms and his crazy cohorts.

Hariri strategy for Lebanon assumed an effective peace process – a settlement with the Palestinians which would allow an Israeli evacuation of south Lebanon, an end to the bombing attacks, disarming of Hiz'bollah (and Ama). The Lebanese army could then claim to be in control of the country – and the Syrians would have no reason not to evacuate their forces and allow Lebanese sovereignty to be restored. Now the mad axeman, Netanyahu, has decapitated the peace process, and as an accidental by-product, put in jeopardy Hariri's economic strategy for the relaunch of the Lebanese economic miracle.

Overall hangs the brooding presence of Lebanon's eastern neighbour. The Syrians do not accept that they are occupying Lebanon, only supporting the legitimate aspirations of their Lebanese friends and brothers. They indignantly repudiate any question of evacuation, at least until Israel leaves the south. Mysteriously, any prominent Lebanese who raises the question of Syrian withdrawal is assassinated shortly thereafter. When an Arab League team raised the question, Christian Beirut was subject to 36 hours shelling by Syrian artillery (it is a treasured folk custom here always to punish the innocent, never the guilty). The Lebanese prime minister visits the Damascus overlord weekly, and leading ministers make the same pilgrimage before important decisions or appointments. Lebanon is rather like a princely state within the old British Raj, but without the imperial trappings.

More vivid for the ordinary Lebanese are the tank and armoured car depots tucked away in city sidestreets or country fields, the artillery and rocket sites, the endless Syrian army checkpoints outside most settlements and at major junctions. Syria has, it is said, 40,000 troops for Lebanon's three and a half million or so people, one to every 88 people (proportionate to, say, the British population that would mean an army of 700,000, to India's one of over 11 million!). Each Syrian military checkpoint is shadowed, at a distance, by a Lebanese military checkpoint (you know they are different because of the flags), and sometimes, further on, another lot in civilian clothes, a sort of 'tonton macoute'. Indeed, Lebanon seems on the surface heavily militarised, and if the checkpoints ever checked anything there would be chaos. But invariably, the yawning soldier wearily waves cars on.

There are thus in Lebanon few domestic issues: foreign policy and domestic cannot be distinguished. Take, for example, the bizarre case of Jezzine. This is a district in the south, now with under 5,000 Christian inhabitants (before the wars there were 60,000). Part of it has been held by the Israeli client, the South Lebanon Army (SLA) under General Antoine Lahd (the army was recruited from Maronite and Shi'ite villages of the border area, but armed and financed by Israel). Some of Israel's leaders recognise that holding a 'security zone' along the border and sustaining further north the SLA is a liability that increases the insecurity of northern Israel by inciting Hiz'bollah attacks. In the peace process, the issue was to be part of a general settlement that would return the Golan Heights to Syria. Now that process is buried, should Israel unilaterally evacuate south Lebanon? Damascus opposes any such change without a deal that includes the Heights – and employs Hiz'bollah to prod Israel in this direction. The alternative strategy, the so-called Jezzine First or Lebanon First, calls for a step-by-step approach, decoupling Lebanon's claims from Syria's.

In fact, the SLA has just evacuated its position in Jezzine as, supposedly, a 'routine deployment of forces'. The Christian notables of Jezzine, fearing that they in turn will be driven out (they are the target of persistent car bomb attacks) to be replaced by Palestinians have called for the Lebanese army to take over the SLA positions (and protect them from Israeli depredations). But some of the leading figures in the central government, notably the speaker of the assembly, the parliamentary leader of the Shi'ites and of the south, oppose Lebanon reoccupying this area, presumably because of Damascus's paradoxical position that Israel must not be allowed to evacuate Lebanon without a settlement of Syrian claims. Meanwhile, the poor Christians of Jezzine accuse the Muslim prime minister of not protecting out of religious prejudice.

Hiz'bollah, the most famous of the Shi'ite militia, is worth a note here. Although it started as a breakaway from the former unified organisation, Ama, on a militant 'fundamentalist' and pro-Palestinian platform, financed by Teheran, it became a much broader social movement, a kind of Islamic version of social democracy in the areas it controlled. It has built and staffed modern hospitals and clinics, schools and orphanages, foundations for the families of the 'martyrs'. Its construction companies move swiftly into areas bombed by Israel to restore services and rebuild houses. It is active in the southern Beirut suburbs housing and serving the refugees who have fled from the south. Its members have a great reputation for self-discipline, for decentralised authority, for encouraging active participation from the mass of the population. It has also become a political party, no longer calling for a Lebanon under Shariat law, but recognising that the country is inevitably multi-confessional in which the rights of all must be protected. Most recently, it held a conference of 27 opposition parties (but including some government ministers) to try to fashion a common programme of Lebanese nationalism (though many of the Christian parties did not attend).

How far this change of direction is self-evolved, how far a tactic masterminded from Damascus, in collaboration with Teheran, is not clear. But if it persists, it does offer a new kind of departure for Lebanese politics. It is also of great importance in understanding the development of so-called fundamentalist parties elsewhere in the region.

Tight Labour Market

So what does the future hold for Lebanon, trapped between the samurai to the south and east? On the one hand is the brooding military presence, on the other, the swiftly revived, almost defiant, hustling and bustling commerce of the coastal cities. Despite the figures, the boom persists, most visibly embodied in a tight labour market.

Some people say there are a million Syrian workers in the country without work permits, but that must be a wild exaggeration. Still they are the basic agricultural and construction workforce, some cleaners and small businessmen and traders. In 1995, 11,000 work permits were issued to citizens of other Arab countries, including 9,000 to Egyptians (the government has recently signed an agreement with Egypt on supplying labour). Most middle- and upper-class families have a Sri Lankan maid (13,000 work permits issued in 1995), or a Filipina (4,000 work permits). Work permits were offered in that year to 5,000 Indians, and there are an unknown number of Bangladeshis (four were just arrested in Sidon on a murder rap). The cumulative total is not clear but it must constitute a significant proportion of the country's labour force (and generates, as mentioned earlier, one and a half billion dollars remittance outflow) – a new working class.

On the other hand, the period of wars led to at least 300,000 (and probably many more) fleeing the country, in the main the best-educated and most skilled. They joined an historical diaspora over the past 150 years, with groups throughout the Americas, Australia and Europe, West Africa, the Gulf and Saudi Arabia. The association of the emigrants, the World Lebanese Cultural Union, claims 12 million, but this must be an heroic exaggeration. However, the number of people abroad who retain a serious link with the country easily constitute the majority of the world's Lebanese (perhaps two-thirds of the total). If the world's Lebanese produced a Lebanese gross domestic product, it would be vastly larger than that of Lebanon. The overseas people have splendidly supported the country since 1990 with remittances and capital flows, and some have returned. The overseas people constitute a pool of human capital, of the most advanced skills (banking and insurance, trading, software programming, medical, scientific and educational services, etc.), that could be of great importance for the country, the difference between pessimism and optimism. Overseas Taiwanese were attracted back to their homeland from Silicon Valley to create a world class electronic industry; Indians in some cases are returning to India with similar effects. Some schemes have been floated – to create a Technopolis for the highly qualified (it came to nothing); and to set up Transfer of Knowhow Through Expatriate Nationals (TOKTEN). For any exploitation of the resources of emigrants, the country must remain stable, secure and open.

But is this the sort of society the Lebanese want? In the old kind of country, emigration and immigration was supposedly marginal to the national population, as residual as imports and exports were to national output. Yet now, the more advanced a country is, the more it processes imports for exports, using imported capital and immigrant labour. Luxembourg is an extreme case where the majority of the inhabitants are foreign-born.

In a world where national identity is, for many, an important component of personality and is supposedly embedded in a defined territory and its symbols, will the Lebanese know who they are if most of them have gone global? Some worry that a country which provides no more than a social focus for a world diaspora, a retirement home for those who have spent their working lives abroad, a place for holidays, an enclave for savings, all based upon immigrant workers, is no country at all. Then to be Lebanese is to be no one and nowhere.

But, to exist, did the Jews need Israel? In the nineteenth-century world of imperialisms and nationalisms, some of them thought they did, but the majority were never persuaded except under the lash of vicious persecution. However, from the perspective of the present, perhaps the Jews of the turn of the century were among the most modern people, unencumbered by the need to sustain a state and its samurai, armed, egotistical, jealous, arrogant, holding its share of the world's population in permanent thralldom.

The new Lebanon, with a minority of its people at home, with an immigrant labour force, sustained by a global people and a global economy, providing a social and cultural focus for its farflung Phoenician trading fleets, perhaps provides a perspective for the future that everybody else will ultimately come to follow.

Such speculations are no doubt remote from the immediate preoccupations of the government of Lebanon. The long shadows of the country's neighbours lie across the land. And the memories of the decade and a half of wars with their extraordinary cruelties also remain – on 13 April 1989, the anniversary of the outbreak of war, some 10,000 shells and rockets fell upon Beirut's Christian enclave, a number exceeded only by Israel's disastrous 1982 siege of the city. Nothing has been settled and if Israel goes to war again, the fragile stability of Lebanon can be swiftly overturned. Nor is the potential savagery of Damascus to be underestimated.

These issues cannot be settled – nor even influenced – in Beirut. Lebanon must assume the best and make a future for itself amid these imponderables. Given stability, the exploitation of the diaspora and the extraordinary entre-preneurial skills of the Lebanese, with an open economy and a liberal govern-ment, prosperity can be created through an economy based on the provision of skills and services. The by-product of such an extended period of horror ought to be a political science, sociology, psychology and psychiatry among the best in the world – and so, education, research and medical services of a high order. A free society can also provide a home for cultural experiment, music, drama and film, serving an Arab market. The potential for tourism is immense. But all that requires an environment of excellent quality, and here the role of government becomes crucial.

Every strategy of economic growth is a gamble, never more so than now when, as a condition of growth, economies are forced to be open – but openness subjects them to uncontrollable external shocks. But that is no more than the political context that Lebanon faces with its neighbours.

Historically, the Lebanese have had great resources of nimbleness and flexibility, just the characteristics required now to negotiate the rocks of a world economic order and the narrow dangerous channels of the west Asian political order.

Moscow's Migrants[*]

Did you see the story about Moscow having a lower standard of living than the rest of the Soviet Union? The tortuous argument went like this: in order to meet the demand for unskilled manual labour in the city over the past 15 years, 700,000 workers have been brought in from poorer parts of the country. Currently, some 70,000 arrive each year to do the jobs Muscovites will not do. Mostly young people, they arrive on temporary visas and live in dormitories, but after three years of good behaviour, they can get permanent status.

The natives, the beneficiaries of this import of cheap labour, complain bitterly that the city and its services are being swamped by outsiders: they want tighter immigration controls. The city authorities did try to restrict entries more tightly, but on all sides the public employers protested that they could not meet their plan targets unless they had the right to bring in cheap labour.

A few issues ago, this column[1] featured the problems of a growing scarcity of unskilled manual labour in Japan (SWR, November 1986) and in the United States (SWR, December 1986) and it is interesting that similar issues afflict the Soviet Union. The problem in the Soviet Union is less an overall shortage in the country than scarcity in particular places like Moscow. The scarcity is a product of controls – otherwise masses of workers would migrate there, since the wages and conditions are the best.

Siberia is the opposite because of its ferocious climate and poor facilities. Workers will only go there for temporary periods and, by Soviet standards, very high wages. The government has long tried to get workers to move out of some areas – for example, from Central Asia – to Siberia. Big construction projects (for example, the Daykal-Amur railway, the Tyumin oil fields) have great difficulties in recruiting and keeping an adequate labour force.

There is a supply of labour, however, which is fully mobile without high pay: foreign workers. It is not clear how big this labour force is. In the spring of 1982 a Japanese newspaper picked up an article by the Vietnamese Minister of Labour in the Hanoi daily, *Nhan Dan*. The minister said an agreement had been reached with the Soviet Union for 10,000 Vietnamese workers to go to work in the Soviet Union. Commentators speculated that this labour was in part

---

[*] From: *Socialist Worker Review*, May 1987.
[1] [Editorial note: This refers to a column Harris wrote in the *SW Review*.]

repayment for Vietnam's £2 billion debt to Moscow. The workers were to work for five to six years, the minister said, in coal mines, chemical plants, textile and engineering factories and in the south where the climate was warmer. They would be joining 'several thousand' other Vietnamese undergoing training as apprentices in Russian factories.

At about the same time, *Radio Prague* reported that some 14,000 Vietnamese workers were working in Czechoslovakia, and another Hanoi daily, *Hanoi Moi*, carried a report that some 50,000 Vietnamese workers were employed in East Germany, Hungary and Bulgaria. *Izvestiya* gave more details on the Russian picture: 'over 7,000' Vietnamese, between the ages of 17 and 35, were in training in the Soviet Union for one year; *Tass* amplified – one year's training and four years working.

Nayan Chanda, one of the leading journalists on Vietnam, reported from Hanoi sources that the flow of workers to the Soviet Union is not at all new. Since at least 1967, workers have been sent there 'supposedly for vocational training but in fact providing cheap labour for Soviet factories'. The workers, he says, get 'board, lodging, clothing and a small amount of pocket money for the first three years', with full pay after that. Most of the workers are aged between 18 and 25, and none are permitted families. Other sources say the overwhelming majority of Vietnamese workers are sent to Siberia, and the Soviet government retains 60 percent of their pay as part repayment of Vietnam's debt.

From Vietnamese refugees in Canada come stories of letters received from their relatives, working as 'guest workers' in the Soviet Union. They complain of the very long separation from their families, the poor conditions and pay. Some say that between 60,000 and 100,000 Vietnamese workers were officially working overseas. One man, living in a work camp next to a construction site in Siberia, wrote:

> We are given seven roubles a month as allowances, enough to buy ten packs of cigarettes. That is all we get. When I first arrived, they issued me with one pair of winter shoes, a thick jacket, a sweater, a pair of trousers, one cheap shirt and some undershirts and shorts, to be used for the next three years ...
>
> When I left home, I never expected life in this Russian region would be so wretched. Winter is raging right now ...

The issue is not the same as in the United States for the numbers are small alongside the Soviet labour force (37 million employed in industry, 11 million in construction). But the mobility and the cheapness must seem remarkable to Soviet industrial planners, as well as the degree of discipline that must be exercised to survive in Siberia's permafrost – rebel workers cannot run away.

The migration of workers is always a response to the anarchic or accidental location of new employment – the movement of labour 'equilibriates' demand and supply. It is essential to maintain profits, and generally costs governments nothing. Furthermore, the migrant is always a good target on which to heap blame for the failures of the government or employers. The same principle seems to be true in the Soviet Union, even though the country still seems to have big reserves of unskilled labour in the countryside and tightly controlled wages. Any increase in the tempo of growth – the target of the Gorbachev regime – can only exaggerate the localised scarcities, forcing either increased wage differentials or increased immigration.

Indonesia's Year of Anniversaries*

> What can we do? We can do much! We can inject the voice of reason into world affairs. We can mobilise all the spiritual, all the moral, all the political strength of Asia and Africa on the side of peace. Yes, we! We, the peoples of Asia and Africa; 1,400,000,000 strong, far more than half the human population of the world, we can mobilise what I have called the *Moral Violence of Nations* in favour of peace.
>
> PRESIDENT SUKARNO of Indonesia, Opening Address to the Asia-Africa Conference, Bandung (Indonesia), 18 April 1955

It is Sunday. The train is not crowded. It climbs slowly towards Bandung, chugging between the terraces of flooded brown paddy, stepped up to the summit of the hills.

Beyond them and higher lie the tea estates, regimented like formal gardens. Bamboo irrigation pipes funnel brown water down the fields. There are five crops in two years here. A volcano or two smoke evilly above.

A plastic toy rolls across the carriage floor between our ankles. It is a black military jeep, an appropriate plaything for a land overshadowed by military-industrial baronies. The iron fist has a glove of prodigious corruption. The police are mean in khaki and brilliant white helmets.

Republic Proclaimed

Mean or not, the tangible evidence of their power – and the effects of a decade or more of oil revenue – are all around. The villages of West Java are prosperous; mopeds pop down the rural tarmac roads.

There are no ancient thatched huts left, few traditional clothes or bare feet. The soil is very rich for those with access to it.

1985 is the fortieth anniversary of the proclamation of the Indonesian Republic, and the picture of President Suharto, now 'father of the nation', beams down from all the walls.

---

* From: *sw Review*, October 1989.

The proclamation was courtesy of the occupying Japanese, so it was not very real. It took three years of bitter and barbarous war to make the Republic stick. The British – Mountbatten and Churchill – held the door open to let the Dutch back in to recreate the 'Netherlands East Indies', and they scorched the red earth of Java to destroy the independence movement.

Only ten years later, there was yet another illustrious anniversary, in Bandung itself. In the former Dutch Pension Fund Building, a dull 1930s cement thing, the first Asia-Africa conference met. It was the foundation of the 'Third World', although they had not invented the phrase then.

The great names were all there – Sukarno, Nehru, Tito, Nkrumah, Ben Bella, Chou En-lai. And they embodied an idea: there was a third alternative to Washington and Moscow, to capitalism and Stalinism, to the terrors of nuclear Cold War.

It was an heroic moment, but when it rained, the Indonesian Ministers had to mop the floors for, as Nehru proclaimed, 'Bandung is the capital city of Asia-Africa' and there must be no puddles. In April of this year, there was a ceremony of commemoration, but the world has moved on. They don't have puddles now, and the delegates all stayed at the Jakarta Hilton.

That was 40 years and 30 years ago. But hang on, wasn't there another anniversary, 20 years ago? On 30 September 1965, Lieutenant Untung with a group of young officers attempted to murder the senior generals of the army.

The generals escaped, and launched a devastating counter-attack that slaughtered anything up to three quarters of a million people – including almost the entire Communist Party (the PKI, the largest Communist party in the world after China and Russia). Children played football with the heads. The rivers ran scarlet instead of brown.

That's where President Suharto came to power as General Suharto. You would think he would want to remember the time when he overthrew Sukarno. You would think in Bandung they would especially remember. For Sukarno was the most famous graduate from the Institute of Technology Bandung. And the city is the headquarters of the Siliwangi Division, the one that the head of the army, General Nasution, relied upon as one of the few loyal units that could be summoned to Jakarta in early October, two decades ago, to begin the slaughter. It announced the opening of that terrible year of the long knives.

But the kindly avuncular Suharto who gazes down from the walls does not like to remember. Perhaps he is ashamed to recall the abattoir from which he snatched his crown. And the left doesn't care to remember either.

For the destruction of the PKI was not only a terrible defeat, but an even more massive rejection of the politics of class collaboration than that which took place in Chile eight years later, or in Shanghai in 1927.

The strategy of the PKI had been collaboration, on a programme of mild reform. The President, Sukarno, needed the PKI to counter-balance the army – and offered the Communist leaders high state office in return for their loyalty.

Almost certainly the PKI were not involved in Untung's adventure. It was not their style to be so daring. But, so unstable was the structure, the removal of only one brick brought the whole gigantic building to the ground. The PKI were smeared with being pro-China, and thus became the object of all the anti-capitalist feeling of Indonesians (capital was heavily concentrated in the hands of Chinese Indonesians).

Bandung Spirit

Furthermore, under Sukarno the country was plunged into a series of adventures and a scale of economic mismanagement which reduced the mass of the population to extremes of poverty. The PKI raised no protest.

1965 was the end of the 'Bandung Spirit', as well as of Sukarno. But the new military regime kept the windy slogans, the litanies and catechisms – the Five Principles of Peaceful Coexistence.

The *pansilo* is still the official intonation, drilled into yawning civil servants and school kids.

It is all long ago, marked now only in the cyphers on the regimental banners, in the melancholic memories of old men in Beijing, in nightmares of the winners in Jakarta. The old emperors have long retired to the history books and now hardly anyone remembers. Just as 1965 smothered 1955 in blood, so 1985 has buried much of 1965.

The train chugs on, reliable, clean and comfortable in reaching the place, Bandung, but it cannot take you to the idea. The famous 'spirit of Bandung' has joined the world of spirits, downed in many a draught in many a bar. It took more than talk to turn the world round, to end the nuclear blocs.

But the spirit lives on in something Suharto and his cronies would not appreciate. For the years of boom that transformed those villages in West Java, and plumped the children's cheeks and showed how corrupt and bloody dictatorships did so much better than incompetent leftist ones, also spread Jakarta into a giant industrial city. And in the industrial areas, the fever of liberty that distantly excited those gentlemen (there were very few ladies) in Bandung so long ago, that seemed horribly crushed in 1965, is as vigorous as ever.

In the waves of strikes in the early 1980s, the new industrial working class of Indonesia began to flex its muscles. The stirrings are still too small to perturb President Suharto, but he may live to learn.

The First Commonwealth Immigration Act 1962: Fifty Years On*

1. Many thanks for this invitation to address you on this issue – to the SOAS, to the Migrant Rights Network, the Royal Commonwealth Society and the Ramphal Centre.

2. The issue of immigration control occurs at a peculiar conjuncture of macroeconomic trends and micro political questions. Thus it is not accidental that in the midst of a catastrophic world economic downturn, virtually all developed countries have become concerned with immigration, even if it is disguised as a concern with 'integration' or as in the US a concern with irregular migration. Put crudely, the concern with immigration is designed to consolidate State political power against the economic threats generated by the crisis.

3. In some of the great tyrannies of the world, the strengthening of State political domination always took priority over the pursuit of economic growth – for example, in Tsarist Russia, Tokugawa Japan, pre-reform Communist China, with their elaborate controls on domestic movement. By contrast, a trading country like Britain perforce had to maintain both freedom of movement at home and open borders – to trade, capital and migration. Indeed, so indifferent was London to immigration in the nineteenth century that no figures were kept on entries (as no figures were kept on domestic migration), and the city was famous for the shelter afforded foreign rebels.

4. With the benefit of hindsight, we can now see what a major change the 1962 Act was – the Conservative Party recognised the end of empire (and the free movement within it) and thereby the end of Britain's aspiration to being a global great power, one of the Big Four of the war years. Immigration, in the imperial years, of no interest then, became an issue of domestic politics founded now in xenophobia rather than global empire.

5. But what a brief moment it was – those who engineered the 1962 Act and its subsequent Acts (1967, 1971) could not have guessed then there would be such a short time before economic globalisation and entry to the European Union would once again force the open borders that had governed Empire (albeit with different favoured migrants). As with empire, open borders, lib-

---

* From: Talk at SOAS, 2012.

eralised trade and free capital movements were once again to be fundamental to the growth of the British economy – and the livelihood of its inhabitants. Nowhere more so than in the surge of economic growth from 1997, manned now by migration from the new entrants to the EU, Poland, etc.

6. There were two other factors that could not have been envisaged in 1962. First, that the new international division of labour that came with globalisation would simultaneously wipe out much of the UK's manufacturing base (and its immobile workforce) and create an economy dependent on global finance and logistics, tourism, research and higher education, all sectors depending to different degrees on global recruitment. Second, by the 1990s, Britain (like all developed countries) seems to have ceased to be self-sufficient in labour (both in numbers and in the changing composition of skills in the workforce). Henceforth, securing the full employment of the native-born and coping with continuous structural change would depend on recruiting abroad workers complimentary to the skills of the native-born. The mismatch between domestic supply of skills and demand is now illustrated by the simultaneous occurrence of high unemployment and significant unfilled vacancies (in the US, unfilled vacancies were put at 3.7 million in March [DK]). To stop the inflow in the future will be to threaten the possibility of growth at home, force the outmigration of capital to set up where the labour force is available and sustain unemployment of the natives.

7. Furthermore, a prospect is emerging that could transform the picture even more radically. As the high growth countries of east and southeast Asia exhaust their native-born labour force (and the existing composition of skills), they are turning to recruit abroad. This seems currently to be affecting South Korea with what is called there the 'multiculturalisation' of its workforce. China is projected to face a radical decline in the size of its workforce up to 2050, and is already experiencing severe shortages in the maritime provinces (with capital migration to the west and abroad). The government, it is said, has already projected scarcities by sector and the requirements for recruitment abroad. Meanwhile, the developed countries will be recruiting at the same time – the US Association of Medical Colleges projects a shortage of primary care doctors of 45,000 by 2020. This might suggest that the central problem in the near future will not be how to keep people out through immigration controls but how to identify and recruit them before someone else does – or recruit them to higher education and allow them to work after studies are complete. Countries will be obliged to compete for mobile workers in terms of favorable hospitality and conditions.

8. Thus international migration threatens to become a serious issue – that is one which affects the future of the whole economy and the welfare of its

inhabitants. It is not publicly discussed in these terms at present but treated frivolously as about numbers entering the country (as if mere numbers were self-evidently good or bad, a cover for xenophobia) – not what the immigrants do – Filipino care workers for retirement homes, Ukrainian harvest workers, financial stars circulating through London. A major step forward here has been the creation of the Migration Advisory Committee to estimate sectoral labour requirements, but its influence seems to be limited, overwhelmed by what I have called the frivolity of overall numerical targets (and the inexplicable need to reduce them whatever they are). In any case, it is still not at all clear that in an open economy, numbers entering can be controlled whether the fences are high (as with the US and others) or the punishments draconian. It is extraordinary that the Minister should set himself a numerical target for entrants that he cannot fail to miss even while damaging key sectors like the City or the universities.

9. The 1962 Act was thus a crucial turning point in British history, not so much in terms of controlling immigration so much as injecting a new tone of xenophobia into questions of movement, a legacy still to be overcome if the welfare of the people of this country is to be secured. In this context, the record of the Commonwealth before 1962 and the development of its institutions and relationships could offer a model for the management of international migration, the bilateral exchange of workers to the enriched experience of the labour force. As argued earlier, the emerging shape of the world labour market will force all countries to seek to recruit abroad as the condition of economic growth and ensuring the welfare of their populations – that offers the opportunity to the Commonwealth to facilitate the process to the mutual benefit of sending and receiving countries and of the migrants.

Bibliography of Nigel Harris's Writings

Not excluding duplicates

Box 1

Spatial Planning and Economic Development, *Habitat International*, 7/5–6, 1983
The Politics of the National Front, ANL (mimeo), 1978
The Crisis of Development, World University Service, Ibadan University (mimeo), 1972
The Future of Urbanization and the Role of British Aid, DPU (mimeo), 1988
Economic Growth and the Problem of World Settlements, DPU working paper 4 (mimeo), 1976
Economic Growth and Spatial Planning, DPU Occasional Paper 1 (mimeo), 1981
Planning Cities in the 1980s, *Urban India*, 2/2 Jun., 1982
Some Trends in the Revolution of Big Cities, *Studies in the USA and India*, HI 8/1, 1984

Box 2

China: counter revolution and crisis, *Against the Current*, Sept.–Oct., 1989
History begins again, *Sanity*, CND, Feb., 1990
México y las economicas exteriores de la Cuenca del Pacifico, *Cuadernos de Política Internacional* (Mexico) 50, Feb. 1990
Urbanization, economic development and policy in developing countries, HI, 14/4, 1990
Labour's right to move, *Against the current*, Jul–Aug. 1991
Mexico and North American Free Trade, DPR (*Development Policy Review*, ODI), 9/1991
China: Export-led Market Capitalism, EPW (*Economic and Political Weekly*, Mumbai), XXVI/2, May, 1991
Manufactured Exports and Newly Industrializing Countries: Mexican Trade and Mexico-US economic relations, EPW, Mar. 1991
New Towns and Structural Adjustment, World Bank, Cairo (mimeo), Jul. 1992
Wastes, the Environment and the International Economy, *Cities*, Aug. 1992
The Urban Contribution to National Economic Growth: the Case of Nepal, DPU working paper 60, 1992
Vietnam: Old Men Remember, EPW, Sept. 1992
Pure Loving Hearts (China), *New Statesman*[?], 1992

Economia y desarrollo: teoria y practica, CIDE (Mexico City), 1988

The End of the Third World, HI 11/1, 1987

Metropolitan Planning in Developing Countries: Tasks for the 1980s, HI7/3–4, 1983

The Bank's China, EPW XVII/9, Feb. 1982

Box 3

The Scissors Crisis in India and China (mimeo paper), 1966[?]

Some Economic Statistics Relating to Madras, DPU (mimeo), Jul/Nov. 1981

Report to the Ministry of Works and Housing, Government of India (urban economic research), Jan. 1979

Report on Training Workshops for the Madras Metropolitan Development Authority 1981

Report prepared for the MMDA., Oct. 1980.

Box 4

The Pacific Rim, *Journal of Development Studies*, 25/3, Apr. 1989

Finance Capital today, *Society and Change*, Calcutta, 11/3, Apr.–Jun. 1981

Bombay in a Global Economy: Structural Adjustment and the Role of Cities, *Cities*, 12/3, 1995

Can the West survive? *Competition and Change*, I, 1995

Cities in a Global Economy: Structural Change and Policy Reactions, *Urban Studies*, 34/10, 1997

Macro Economic Reform and the Centrally Planned Economies, *Competition and Change*, 1996

The Road from 1910, *Economy and Society*, 11/3, Aug. 1982

The Emerging Global City: Transport, *Cities* 11(5), 1994

Urban England, *Economy and Society*, 3/3, Aug. 1974

Industrialization, the World Bank and Sub Saharan Africa, CDC *Magazine*, Commonwealth Development Bank, 2, 1990

Was Socialism a Mistake? *Society and Change* (Calcutta), viii/i 1992

Free International Movement of Labour, EPW, Jan. 1991

The Pacific Rim and Mexico's External Economic Relationships: a Survey, PRSCO, ITB Bandung 1990

The Agenda of Urban Issues, *Courier* (EU), 131, 1992

On Nationalism, working paper 42, Centre for Urban Studies, University of Hong Kong, 1989

State Capitalism Versus the World Market, *Society and Change* (Calcutta), vi/i, Jun. 1989

Mexico and North American Free Trade, DPR 9, 1991

Apartheid is Dead! Long Live Apartheid, EPW, Aug. 1991

Export Processing in Mexico, *Journal of Development Studies* 27/1, Oct. 1990

New bourgeoisies? *Journal of Development Studies*, 23/2 Jan. 1988

Immigration: the Real Danger, *Diplomat.*, Jul.–Aug. 1996

Endangered Tigers, *Red Pepper*, Jan. 1988

Italy: a Different Style, EPW, May. 1996

China: What Price Culture? IS (*International Socialism*), 1966

Brazil Diary, SW (*Socialist Worker*), Oct. 1981

Metropolitan Development in Newly Industrializing Countries: the Agenda of Issues, Glasgow, June 1990

China's Cities, *Economy and Society*, 1/1 196?

More Recent Stuff (Box 4)

Immigration and State power, EPW, XLV/5, Jan. 30, 2010

Playing the Numbers Game, *Red Pepper*, May 2008

Review, *Journal of South Asian Development*, 3/2, 2008

Letter, *The Guardian*, 3 April, 2008

Globalization is Good for You, *Red Pepper*, Dec.–Jan. 2008

Land-Use in Bombay, EPW Oct. 16, 1993

Privatization in Eastern Europe, EPW Oct. 7, 1995

Structural Adjustment on the Baltic, EPW XXX/48, Dec. 2, 1995

Peru: Emerging from Crisis, EPW, Nov. 9–16, 1996

Review (India), *Contemporary South Asia*, 14/1, Mar. 2005

Integration into what? *Connections* (Commission for Racial Equality), Winter 2004/5

Strangulation of Palestine, EPW, Dec. 2004

New Theories of Regional and Urban Development, EPW XL/7, Feb. 12, 2005

Israel's Familiar Logic (Editorial), EPW, Mar. 30 2002

Sharon's Game (Editorial), EPW, 20 Apr. 2002

Collapse of the Peace Process, EPW, 15 Sept. 2001

Migration, SHS (UNESCO) *Newsletter*, Apr.–Jun. 2004

Role of Revisionism in History, EPW, 1 Jun. 2002

Bombay in Transition, EPW, 24 Jan. 2004

Krishna Raj, *The Guardian*, 17 Feb. 2004

Towards an Economic Strategy for the City of Santiago de Cali, World Bank, 1999

Analisis de los Proyectos para la zona franca de Bogota, DPU/Bogota, 1994

Cities and Structural Adjustment: the Case of Shanghai, DPU?

An Economic Advisory Unit within the Alcadia of Santafe de Bogota, 1992

Myanmar: Poverty, Human Settlements and Economic Development, UNCHS, Nairobi, 1995[?]

Box 5

Interview, *Excelsior*, 22 Apr. 1987

The National Front and the Jews, Anti Nazi League, 1967[?]

Deindustrialization, *IS*, 2/7[?]

World Crisis and the System, International Socialist pamphlet (Canadian IS)[?]

Theories of Unequal Exchange, *Society and Change* (Calcutta), IV/4, Jul.–Sept. 1985

Settlements, People and Jobs, EPW XI/31–3, Special No. Aug. 1976.

The Asian Boom Economies and the 'Impossibility' of Economic Development, IS2/3[?]

Two Notes on a Visit to the United State, *IS*, 1976[?]

China and World Revolution (Norwegian), 1982

Aid – or a Golden 'Fleece', *The Guardian*, 16 Apr. 1970

Effects of Economic Conditions on Human Settlements, United Nations, NY, 1976

Economic Growth and the Problem of World Settlements, DPU WP4, 1976

L'imperialisme aujourd'hui, *Gauche Marxiste* [?]

Development Planning, *Dag Hammerskjold project*, 1975

Box 6

State Capitalism versus the World Market, *Society and Change*, VI/1, Apr.–Jun. 1989

Forces of Compulsion (China), *EPW*, 17 Sept. 1994

Introduction to Cities in the 1990s (Mss)

No Passport to Anywhere, *New Society*, 1987

The Capitalist Revolution, *New Society*, 1987

Aid and Urbanization, *New Society?* [?]

Promoting Urban Economic Development, INLOGOV (mimeo), *Sept. 1989*

Singapore?? Mss.

East Asia, Mss.?

Misc. Mss.

Studies in Indian Economic Development, *The Economic Journal*, Sept. 1987

Ni subtilités, ni empirisme, *Espaces Temps 36*, CNRS/CNL, 1987

The Bank's China, *EPW*, XVII/9, Feb. 1982

Third World Cities, *South African Property Owners Association* (mimeo), Jun. 1991

Key to Korean Development: Economic Nationalism or World Economy, UCLA (mimeo), 1989

Deindustrialization, *International Socialism* [?]

Box 7

Myanmar: Poverty, Human Settlements and Economic Development, DPU/UNCHS, 1996

Structural Adjustment on the Baltic, *EPW*, 2 Dec., 1995

The War-making State and Privatization (with David Lockwood), Budapest, May 1995

Economic Interdependence in the Asia-Pacific, *DPR* [?]

Analisis de los Proyectos de Servicios para la Zona Franca de Bogots (mimeo), Oct. 1994

Global Economy, Flexibility and Urban Development – Emerging City Economy, Shanghai 1994

Preparatory Work for Defining an Escor Research Programme ...

Italian Elections, *EPW, Mss.*

Cities in the Global Economy, Mss. OECD Melbourne, 1994

States and Economic Development, *DPR* [?]

Privatization in East Europe, *EPW*, 7 Oct. 1995

International Financial Centres, *DPR* [?]

Towns: the Mainspring of Economic Development in Third World Countries, (mimeo), Lille 1989

El fin del tecera mundo, Mss [?]

The Urban Contribution to National Economic Growth in Nepal, mimeo, UNDP, Jan. 1991

Strategy for African Mining, Mss., Dec. 1991

Free International Movement of Labour, EPW, 26 Jan. 1991

Urbanisation, Economic Development and Policy in Developing Countries, *HI*, 14/4, 1990

Aid and Operations Maintenance, Mss. Norad, Oslo [?]

misc. mss.reviews

Day in the life of Fred, *New Internationalist* [?]

World Trade, *New* Internationalist, Feb. 1990

Prospects for Paralysis, *Against the Current*, 26, Detroit, May-Jun. 1990

Box 8

(Mainly mss)

Review: UNCHS Urbanizing World, DPR, Jan. 1997

Privatization and the State: Russia, Eastern Europe and East Asia (with David Lockwood), in Jeffrey Henderson (ed.), Industrial Transformation etc. 1998

Preferring the lie, EPW, xxi/34, Aug. 24, 1996

Review – Nolan's China/Russia, DPR [?], 1996 [?]

Macro Economic Reform and the Centrally Planned Economy, DPR [?]

Peru: Emerging Crisis, EPW [?]

The War-making State and Privatization (with David Lockwood), Journal of Development Studies, 1996

The War-making State and Structural Adjustment (with David Lockwood), Budapest,
1995

Review Article: Social Science, History and Options in Transitional Economies, DPR [?]

Cultural Diversity ... Migration, paper for OECD conference, Melbourne [?]

Urbanization in Developing Countries, report for the Urban Foundation, Johannesburg, 1994

Review: Aspe, Mexican Economy, DPR [?], [date?]

Mexico's Tianamen Square, [?]

Cities and a Global Economy, EPW [?], 1992 [?]

Will Women become Redundant as 'Women', Femina, Bombay, 23 Sept. 1993

Bombay in a Global Economy: Structural Adjustment and the Role of Cities [?]

Transport, Urban Age, [date?]

Urban Economic Development in Europe: Five Case Studies, Warsaw, Nov. 1993

Role of New Towns in a Period of Adjustment, World Bank, Jun.–Jul. 1992

Nationalism and Development, [?], [date?]

Box 9

Cities in a Global Economy: Structural Change and Policy, Urban Affairs, 1996

Economic Fusion and Political Fission: Globalization and Regionalism, EFS/EMOT,
Malaga 1997

There is Life after Death: Lebanon, EPW [?], 1997

Review: On the Question of the State (WDR 1978), EPW [?], 1978

Reviews – China, Singapore, DPR, Dec. 1997

Notes on a Possible Marxist Theory of Personality, unpublished, Sept. 1989

Reviews: Hong Kong, DPR [?], [date?]

Crisis in South-east and East Asia, *Red Pepper*, 1997
Cities as Engines of Economic Growth and Development, WB Urban Strategy Workshop, Washington DC, Dec. 1997
Address, 5th Asian Urbanization Conference, SOAS, London, Aug. 1997
Cities, Structural Adjustment and Urban Management, Arab States Region: Urban Management Programme, Agadir, Jun. 1993

Box 10

The Pacific Rim, *Journal of Development Studies*, 25/3, Apr. 1989
New Bourgeoisies, *Journal of Development Studies*, 24/2, Jan. 1988
ODA and Urbanization: an Overview, *Cities*, 6/3, Aug. 1989
A Comment on 'World bank support for institutional and policy reform in metrop areas: Calcutta', *HI*, 13/3, 3, 1989
Urbanisation and British aid, ODA, Feb. 1989
China 1989: State Capitalism versus the World Market, *Enclitic*, 111/3,23, Los Angeles, 1989
Review: Metropolis Era, *HI*, 13/4, 1989

Box 11

The Urban Contribution to National Economic Growth in Nepal, Kathmandu, (mimeo), Jan. 1991
Environmental Issues in the Cities of the Developing World, DPU WP 20, Aug. 1990
Environmental Issues in the Cities of the Developing World: the Case of Mexico City, *Journal of International Development*, 2/4, Oct. 1990
Mexico and North American Free Trade, *DPR*, 9/3, Sept. 1991
The Pacific Rim and Mexico's External Economic Relationships: a Survey, DPUWP21, Sept. 1990
Ibid. (in Spanish), Instituto Matías Romero de Estudios Diplomáticos, Feb. 1990
Was the Development of Korea and the 'Gang of Four' Unique? DPU WP22, Oct. 1990
Urbanization, Economic Development and Policy in Developing Countries, DPU WP 19 Jan. 1990
Ibid., *Habitat International*, 14/4, 1990
Political Economy of Singapore's Industrialization (review), *Journal of Development Studies*, 26/3, Apr. 1990

Box 12

Urban Contribution to National Economic Growth: the Case of Nepal, *DPU WP 60*, 1992

Manufactured Exports and Newly Industrializing countries, Mexican trade, etc, *EPW*, xxvi/11–12, Annual No, Mar. 1991

Dossier: The Urban Crisis: the Agenda of Issues, *The Courier*, 131, Jan–Feb. 1992

Reaching the Poor: New Directions in Urban Development, DPU (mimeo): Cd. Juarez, Jul. 1992

The Urban Environment in Developing Countries, UNDP, New York, Jan. 1992

Ibid., published version, May 1992

The Role of New Towns in a Period of Adjustment (Egypt Urban Sector review), World Bank (mimeo), Cairo, Jul. 1992

Wastes, the Environment and the International Economy, *Cities*, 9/3, Aug. 1992

Slums Policy and Labour Market Study, India (Overseas Development Administration), mimeo, Oct. 1992

Juraez: Urban Issues Survey (William Dillinger et al.), discussion paper, World Bank May, 1992 Ciudad Juarez: Productivity and the Macro Economic Perspective (Mss), 1992

Vietnam: Old Men Forget, Mss. [?]

Box 13

Press interviews, Bombay, Jul. 1993

Single Europe and the Third World, *EPW*, Jan. 1993

Land Use in Bombay, *EPW*, Oct. 1993

Tibet and Empire, *EPW*, Sept. 1993

Fue el socialismo un error? *Estudios Sociales*, CIAD (Hermosillo), Jul.–Dec., 1993

Reaching the Poor: New Directions in Urban Development (ODA workshop), Nov. 1993

Investment Roundtable, Luxembourg, Nov. 1993

Slumdwellers and the Cuttack Labour Market, ODA (mimeo), 1993 [?]

Urban Economic Development in Europe: five case studies (Barcelona, Berlin, Birmingham, Glasgow, Lyons), USAID, Warsaw, Dec. 1993

Box 14

The Economic Future of I-Lan country (Taiwan), *RSP Singapore*, 1994

Urbanization in Developing Countries: a World Overview, *DPU/Urban Foundation Johannesburg*, Jun. 1994

Structural Adjustment and Cities: Three Papers, DPU WP 63, Sept. 1994
Analisis de los proyectos de servicios para zona franca de Bogota, DPU/Ibarra, Oct. 1994
The Emerging Global City: Transport, Cities ll/5, Oct. 1994
Structural Adjustment and Romania, EPW, Oct. 1994
Economic Fusion, Political Fission (Germany), EPW, Jan. 1994
Forms of compulsion (China), EPW, Sept. 1994
Mexico's Tianamin Square, EPW, Mar. 1994

Box 15

Stopping Immigration? (review article), DPR, 13/l, Mar. 1995
Financial Centres (review), DPR 13/3, Sep. 1995
Privatisation in Eastern Europe (review), EPW, Oct. 1995
Mega Cities (review), DPR [?], 1995
Capital Strikes Back: Globalisation and the State, (re)construction, a socialist journal of enquiry and debate, 4, Melbourne, Autumn 1995
Management of Cities during Structural Adjustment (proposal to PR China), DPU, 1995
ESCOR proposal: sustainable cities, DPU, 1995
Ciudades y ajuste estructural: el caso de Quito (proposal), DPU, Jun. 1995
Bombay and the Global Economy, Cities, 12/3, Jun. 1995
Dhaka Structure Plan, World Bank, DPU, 1995

Box 16

Preferring the Lie: China's Rise, Russia's Fall, EPW, Aug. 24 1996
Myanmar: Poverty, Human Settlements and Economic Development, DPU, WP 78, Jul. 1996
Reviews of my books, interviews, etc.
Emerging from Crisis (Peru), EPW, Nov. 19 1996
Why immigration is good for you, Diplomat, Jul/Aug. 1996
Reviews, DPR, JDS various, 1996

Box 17

Cities in a Global Economy: Structural Change and Policy Reactions, Urban Studies, 34/10, 1997

The War-making State and Privatization (with David Lockwood) (Dudley Seers prize), *Journal of Development Studies*, 33/5, Jun. 1997

Macroeconomic Reform and the Centrally Planned Economy, *Competition and Change*, 2, 1997

On the Question of the State, *EPW*, Dec. 13 1997

Over Here, Overworked, Overlooked, *Times Higher Education Suppl.*, Feb. 14 1997

Vietnam: Back at the Beginning, *EPW*, 1998

Economic Fusion and Political Fission: Globalisation and Industrial Transformation in Europe (paper), *EMOT*, Malaga Jan. 1997

There is Life after Death (Lebanon), *EPW*, 27 Sept. 1997

Reviews (New Untouchables), 1997

Hidden World of Narcotics, *EPW*, 4 Jan, 1997

The Economic Future of Ji-long City, *DPU/RSP* (Singapore), Apr. 1997

Cities as Engines of Economic Growth and Development (World Bank Urban Strategy workshop), Washington DC, Dec. 1997

Box 18

Urban England, *Economy and Society*, 3/2, Aug. 1974

Underdeveloped Europe (review), *Guru Nanak Journal of Sociology*, 1/1–2, Apr.–Oct. 1980

Why the World Goes Hungry, *Socialist Worker Party Pamphlet*, Apr. 1987

Finance Capital Today, *Society and Change*, II/3, Apr.-Jun., 1981

On the Petty Bourgeoisie: Marx and the Twentieth Century, *Society and Change*, III/3, Calcutta, Apr-Jun. 1983

The Boat People (review), *Journal of Administration Overseas*, 1983 [?]

In search of MN Roy: the Mexican period, *Society and Change*, V/2–3, 1983 [?]

International Assistance Strategy, *UNCHS*, Nairobi, June 1986

Free International Movement of Labour, *EPW*, Jan. 1991

Manufactured Exports and Newly Industrializing Countries, *EPW*, XXVI/11–12, Mar. 1991

Newly Emergent Bourgeoisies? University of Hong Kong, Nov. 1987

China: Export-led Capitalism, *EPW*, May 1991

Comment: WB Support Programme, Calcutta, *HII*, 3/3, 1989

Export Processing in Mexico (review article), *JoDS*, 27/1, Oct. 1990

Environmental Issues in the Cities of the Developing World: Mexico City, *Journal of International Development*, 2/4, Oct. 1990

Theories of Unequal Exchange, *Society and Change*, IV/4, Jul.–Sept. 1985

Some Trends in the Evolution of Big Cities: US/India, *HI* 8/1, 1984

State Capitalism versus the World Market, *Society and Change*, VI/1, Apr.–Jun. 1989

National Governments and an Integrated World Economy, *Public Administration and Development* 10, 1990

Mexico and North American Free Trade (review), *DPR*, 9, 1991

Economic Development and Urbanisation (inaugural lecture), *HI*, 12/3, 1988

Metropolis Era (review), *HI*, 13/4, 1989

The Pacific Rim (review), *JoDS*, 25/3, Apr. 1989

New Bourgeoisies? (review), *JoDS*, 14/2 Jan. 1988

Economia y desarrollo mundial, *SIDE*, Mexico City Apr. 1988

Indian Urban Development (review), *Economic Journal*, 97/387, Sept. 1987

Stopping Immigration (review), *DPR 13*, 1995

Some Economic Statistics Relating to Madras, *DPU*, Jul. 1981

Towns: the Mainspring of Economic Development in Third World Countries (mimeo), *Lille International Meeting*, Nov. 1989

Box 19

Review, p. 280, *Journal of Latin American Studies*, 26/1, 1994

Structural Adjustment on the Baltic, *EPW*, Dec. 2 1995

Global Economy, Flexibility and the Urban Economy (Mss) [?]

Wastes, the Environment and the International Economy, *Cities*, Aug. 1992

Urban Contribution to National Economic Growth: the Case of Nepal, *DPU WP60*, 1992

Privatization in Eastern Europe (review), *EPW*, Oct. 7, 1995

Bombay in a Global Economy, *Cities*, 12/3, 1995

Can the West Survive? *Competition and Change*, 1, 1995

Single Europe and the Third World (review), *EPW*, Jan. 30 1993

Forms of Compulsion (review, China), 17 Sep., 1994

The Asian Boom Economies and the 'Impossibility' of National Economic Development, *International Socialism*, 3, Winter, 1978/79

The New Untouchable: the International Migration of Labour, *International Socialism*, 8, 1980

MMDA: an Economic Advisory Unit (report), Apr. 1986

The 'Scissors Crisis' in India and China, *DPU*, WP12 [?]

Structural Adjustment and Cities: three papers, *DPU*, WP63, Sept. 1994

Urban Agenda for the 1990s – DPU workshop, Nov. 21–2, 1991

Address to WB Urban Sector review, new towns, Cairo, Jul. 1992

Urbanisation and British Aid, ODA workshop, Feb. 1989

The Road from 1910 (review, Hilferding), *Economy and Society*, 11/3, Aug. 1982

Finance Capital Today (review), *Society and Change*, 11/3, Apr–Jun 1981

Box 20

Review (Lipton), *Journal of Administration Overseas*, XVI/3, Jul. 1977

Underdeveloped Europe (review), *Guru Nanak Journal of Sociology*, 1/1–2, Apr.–Oct. 1980

The Economic Crisis and Planning: Cities and Regions, *Society and Change* (*essays in honor of Sachin Chadhuri*), 1977

Spatial Planning and Economic Development, *HI*, 7/5–6, 1983

The National Front and the Jews, *Anti-Nazi League*, Mar. 1978

Medieval Howrah (review), *EPW*, Sept. 1963

Settlements, People and Jobs, *EPW*, XI/31–3, (annual no.), Aug. 1976

The Bank's China, *EPW*, XVII/9, Feb. 1982

Economic Growth and Spatial Change, *DPU Occasional Paper 1* (Mexico City), Sept. 1981

The End of the 'Third World', *HI*, ll/1, 1987

Economic Development and Urbanization (inaugural lect.), *HI*, 12/3, 1988

Urbanisation: an Economic Overview of some of the Issues, *HI*, 12/3, 1988

Notes on the ODA Workshop (Feb. 1988), *HI*, 12/3, 1988

Urban Decentralization, *HI*, 3/1–2, 1978

Box 20

Madras Diary (Mss), *SW*, 12 Jan. 1980

In the Eye of the Storm: Tehran Diary (Mss), *SW*, 3rd Jan., 1979

The Politics of Famine, *SW*, May 1985

Where is China Going? *SR* (Mss), Jun. 1985

Famine (Mss), [?], [date?]

Mexico Diary, *SR Review*, Apr. 1985

Happiest Days of Your Life (working children, Mss.)

China, *Irish Sunday Tribune*, Sept. 1982

Cataline (novel, Mss)

Box 21

Arab Summit, *EPW*, 18 Jan. 1964

Arabs: Shifting Alignment, *EPW*, 23 Nov. 1963

Portugal (Mss. John Ashdown), [?], [date?]

Student Revolt, *SW*, 12 Dec. 1968

Some Problems in the Formation of an Industrial Labour Force (Mss), *Indian Statistical Institute, Calcutta*, 1964

New York (Mss)

Rumbling in the South-east (Malaysia) (Mss), EPW, 28 Sept. 1963

Malaysia, EPW, 14 Sept. 1963

Malaysia Again, EPW, 14 Mar. 1964

Maphilimbo, EPW, 27 Jun. 1964

Tunku's Victory, EPW, 9 May 1964

Bangkok (John Ashdown, Mss)

Lord of the Thais, EPW, 21 Dec. 1963

Thailand, Mss., 16 Mar. 1973

Thailand (Mss)

Burma (John Ashdown), *The Observer*, London

Burma (Mss), *The Economist*

Sturgeon, John Ashdown (Mss)

Unending Chaos (Burma), EPW, 18 Apr. 1964

Burma: Peace Talks Founder, EPW, 23 Nov. 1963

Changing Cambodian Wind, EPW, 7 Dec. 1963

Living with Indo-China, EPW, 13 Jun. 1964

Laos Flare Up, EPW, 23 May 1964

Abortive Coup in Laos, EPW, 2 May 1964

Laos: Dangerous Drift, EPW, 2 Nov. 1963

Vietnam and the Generals, EPW, 9 Nov. 1963

The Vietnam swamp, EPW, 7 Mar. 1964

Facts about Vietnam, with Supplem., 2nd ed., *York Vietnam Group*, York Jun. 1965

More Facts about Vietnam, 3rd ed., *York Vietnam Group*, Jun. 1965

5th ed. Oct. 1965

Philippines (Mss), SW, 3 Oct. 1972

Report on a Visit to Portugal by N H and B L (mimeo), *IS International Subcommittee*, Jun. 1974

Assorted Undated Mss – New Cold War, Goldwater, Czechoslovakia, Notes on Richard Garretts

Kings and Cabbages (US elections), EPW, 23 May 1964

Civil Rights: the Real Fight (US), EPW, 31 Aug. 1963

Commonwheeling, EPW, 4 Jul. 1964

The King is Dead (Home and Brit. Conservatives), EPW, 26 Oct. 1963

Middle Africa, EPW, 29 Feb. 1964

The African Galaxy, EPW, 18 Jan. 1964

On the Frontier (Tanganyika), EPW, 6 Jun. 1964

Prelude to Independence (Kenya), EPW, 2 Nov. 1963

Unending Chaos (Burma), *EPW*, 18 Apr. 1964
Southern Rhodesia, *EPW*, 9 May 1964
Apartheid in New Guise, *EPW*, 23 Apr. 1965
US Dilemma in S. Vietnam, *EPW*, 7 Sept. 1963
Black Power and the 'Third World' (Mss)
Iraq's Challenge to Nasser, *The Economist*, 23 Feb. 1963
Anti-Nasser Nasserist, *EPW*, 16 May 1964
Cyprus Stalemate, *EPW*, 16 May 1964
Gunboat Diplomats, *EPW*, 29 Feb. 1964
Communalism in Cyprus, *EPR*, 4 Jan. 1964
Ben Bella's Algeria, *EPW*, 5 Oct. 1963
Maghreb Malaise. *EPW*, 26 Oct. 1963
Living with Indo-China, *EPW*, 13 Jun. 1964
Arab Summit, *EPW*, 18 Jan. 1964
Student Revolt, *SW*, 12 Dec. 1968
Rumbling in South East (Indonesia), *EPW*, 28 Sept. 1963
Thailand: Workers' Struggle, *The Battler 7*, 7 Apr. 1975 [?]
Mss. – Thailand, Burma
Burma, *The Observer*, 21 Aug. 1964
Burma, *The Economist*, Aug. 1964
Sturgeon (Burma), John Ashdown (Mss), *Economist Foreign Report?* Aug. 1964

Box 22

Mss (undated), Iran, Muslim revolt?, US/Carter Iran;
Afghanistan & SU invasion; Dhaka (Apr. 1972); Bangladesh, sundry Pakistan (1979)
Mss. The Struggle for Bangladesh (pamphlet)
Turmoil Shakes Pakistan Rulers, *SW*, 27 Mar. 1971
Pakistan, *IS*, 35, Feb. 1969
Ayub Khan's Problems, *EPW*, 21 Sept. 1963
Man on Horseback (Mss) (Pakistan), *The Economist* [?], 1963 [?]
Pakistan (Mss), *SW*, Mar/Apr. 1969
Misc. India Mss, *SW*, *IS*, Chingari
Sri Lanka: Again, Hunting with the Hounds (Mss)
India: a First Approximation (Mss.), *IS*
Emergency in Ceylon, *EPW*, 28 Mar. 1964
As you Were? (Ceylon), *EPW*, 20 Jun. 1964

Box 23

Nazi Publications (NF etc.)
Free International Movement of Labour, *EPW*, 26 Jan. 1991
Chingari copies

Box 24

Forced Labour (review), *New Society*, 5 Feb. 1988
The Capitalist Revolution (review article), *New Society*, 29 May 1987
New Bourgeoisies? (review article), *Journal of Development Studies*, 24/2, Jan. 1988
Mexican Labour Market (review, Mss), *The Economic Journal*, Jun. 1987
Newly Emergent Bourgeoisies?, University of Hong Kong (CUSUP), *WP 28*, Nov. 1987
In Search of MN Roy: the Mexican Period (*Times of India*, but not publ.), 1986
Rip Van Winkle in China, *EPW*, 16 Jan. 1988
Urbanisation in Vietnam (review), *New Society*, 1, 22 Jan. 1988
Chinese Economy (Mss review), *DPR*
Mexico (review), *New Society*, 28 Aug. 1987
No Passport (review), *New Society*, 12 Jun. 1987
Racism (review), *New Society*, 16 Oct. 1987
Commentary, *SW Review*, Sept. 1987
Same (Korea), *SW Review*, Oct. 1987
Same (Tibet), *SWReview*, Nov. 1987
Debt as a Threat, *SW Review*, Apr. 1987
Fraud and Famine, *SW Review*, Feb. 1987
Store Wars, *SW Review*, Mar. 1987
Moscow's Migrants, *SW Review*, May 1987
Mountains of Profit (Famine), *SW Review*, Jan. 1987
A 'Big Bang'? *SW Review*, Apr. 1986
Why Half the World goes Hungry: the Socialist Case, *SWP pamphet*, Apr. 1987
Food (mss.)
The Half-open Door (immigration), *SW Review*, Dec. 1986
Conqueror or Conquered (Japan), *SW Review*, Nov. 1986
Mexican Stand Off (Elections), *SW Review*, Sept. 1986
Thorn in the Crown (MN Roy), *SW Review*, Jul/Aug. 1986
Disturbing the Whale (Nepal), *SW Review*, Jun. 1986
The End of Civilization as we Know It (Oil Prices), *SW Review*, May 1986
Killer from Manila (Marcos), *SW Review*, Dec. 1985
What to do with London: the Strategies of the GLC (Mss), *IS*

BIBLIOGRAPHY OF NIGEL HARRIS'S WRITINGS

The Eastern Sun Rises (China), *sw Review*, Nov. 1985

The Year of Anniversaries (Indonesia), *sw Review*, Oct. 1985

Frontiers of Control (Neo-liberalism), *sw Review*, Sept. 1985

Divide and Rule, *sw Review*, Jul./Aug. 1985

The Mobile Industry (World Car Industry), *sw Review*, Jan. 1986

Heart of Darkness (Khmer Rouge), *sw Review*, Feb. 1986

No Urban Explosion in India, *Times of India*, Sept. 5 1985

Trading Faces, *sw Review*, Oct. 1986

No end in sight (world economy), *SWReview* Jan. 1983

A Bandung Diary, *EPW*, 28 Jan. 1984

Misc. mss. – Nicaragua (1979), India (1980), Singapore (1984?), Japan and China, Nota sobre el desarrollo de un sistema para evaluar y controlar el gasto publico, *SPP Mexico*, Aug. 1979,

The New Untouchables – the International Migration of Labour, *IS*, 2/8, spring 1980

The Mandate of Heaven: Marx and Mao in Modern China, *Quartet*, 1978

Of Bread and Guns: the World Economy in Crisis, Penguin, 1983

Peter Sedgewick, an obituary (unpublished).

Who Will Reform the Chinese Reformers? *Sunday Tribune* (Dublin), 12 Sept. 1982

Will Russian Visitor Shift Power Axis (China), *Sunday Tribune*, 10 Oct. 1982

Tijuana Diary, *EPW*, 15 May. 1982

Sweating the Third World, *Socialist Worker*, 30 Jan. 1982

Global Report on Human Settlements (Review), *HI*, 1987

Box 25

Race and Nation, *IS*, 34, autumn 1968

Urban England, *Economy and Society*, 3/3, [date?]

Economic Crisis and Planning: Cities and Regions, *Society and Change* (*Essays in honor of Sachin Chaudhuri*), 1977

Why Import Controls won't Save Jobs (with Duncan Hallas), *SWP pamphlet*, 1981

Pure Loving Hearts (review), *New Society*, 8 Jun. 1990

Men on Horseback, *The Economic Weekly*, May 23 1964

Urbanisation: an Economic Overview of some of the Issues, *HI*, 12/3, 1988

Stateless Left in Mid-air, *sw Review*, Jun. 1987

Misc. mss:

Madras View

The Tigers of Wrath (Sri Lanka), *sw Review*, Jul. 1987

Businessmen and the State, *sw Review*, Oct. 1987

Korea and Permanent Revolution, *sw Review*, Oct. 1987

Philippines

NH Comments on AC's Review of The End of the Third World

Kaikoku, the Internationalization of Japan

The Nightmare of Colonel Kurtz (Cambodia)

Tibet

The New Helots (migration, review)

(US-Europe trade)

Closed Borders (review)

Charity – in Declining Doses (refugees)

(Moscow and labour shortages)

Immigration

Privatization

Cars (World Industry)

Poems, Sept. 1956

So this is Moscow, *Reynolds News*, Aug. 1957 [?]

Political Eyewash, ibid.

Misc scribbles from 1950s

Short stories, 1956

Spying at Oxford/ articles

Graphic Journalist (review), *Labour Review*

Bernal (review), *Labour Review*, Apr/May 1959

SU–China clash, *Irish Sunday Tribune*, Oct. 1982

Under the Shadow of Uncle Sam (Mexico), SW and EPW, Apr. 1982

Box 26

Debt Trap (review), *Times Higher Education Suppl.* 28 Feb. 1974

Thailand: Workers Struggle Explodes, *The Battler, Sydney*, Apr. 7 1977 [?]

Mss. Food, Development and the Crisis

Mss. Black Power and the 'Third World'

The Boat People (review), *Journal of Administration Overseas?*

Industry, Cities and States, in *Economic development and the Indian States* (edited by T.J. Byres), Cass, 1975

The Black Worker in Britain, IS/*Chingari pamphlet*, [date?]

The Decline of Reformism, IS, *53*, [date?]

The State of the Organisation (with DP), [date?]

China's Cities (review article), *Economy and Society*, 1/1

Reviews of NH Competition

India: the Motor Falters, *Socialist Worker*, 15 Jul. 1972

Competition and the Corporate Society, Methuen, 1972
India-China: Underdevelopment and Revolution, *Carolina Academic Press*, 1974
Mss. The crisis of capitalism, *IS*, 53, Aug. 1972
The Crisis of Development, WUS Symposium, University of Ibadan, Aug. 1972
India: Capitalism and Revolution, *IS*, 52, Jul.–Sept. 1972
The Marxist Left in India, *IS*, 53, Oct./Dec. 1972
Independence for Bengalis Postponed by India victory, *Socialist Worker*, 24. Dec. 1971
Nixon's China Trip, *Socialist Worker*, 24 Jul. 1971

Box 27

List of longer articles in *IS*, 1961–81:
The Decline of Welfare, *IS*, 7, 1961
Tories and Trade Unions, *IS*, 13, 1963
India, a First Approximation, I and II, *IS*, 17 and 18, 1964
Marxisn: Leninism-Stalinism-Maoism, *IS* 26, 1966
China: What Price Culture? *IS*, 28, 1967
Monopoly Capital, *IS*, 30, 1967
China: Let a Hundred Flowers Bloom, *IS* 35, 1968 (republished in *The Revolution is Dead,
    Long Live the Revolution: Readings in the Great Proletarian Cultural Revolution*, '70s
    group, Hong Kong 1976)
Agriculture, Peasants and Accumulation, *IS*, 40, 1969
The Revolutionary Role of the Peasantry, *IS*, 41, 1972
The Anarchist Argument, *IS*, 54, 1973
China since Lin Piao, *IS*, 55, 1973
Economic Growth in India and China, *IS*, 60, 1973
China and World Revolution, *IS*, 78, 1975
Black Power and the 'Third World', *IS*, 79, 1975
Two Notes on a Visit to the United States, *IS*, 85, 1976
Mao and Marx, *IS*, 92, 1976
Mao-Tse-tung and China, *IS*, 92, 1976
World Crisis and the System, *IS*, 100, 1977
The Asian Boom Economies, *IS* (New series), 1978/9
The New Untouchables: the International Migration of Labour, *IS*, 8, 1980
Crisis and the Core of the System, *IS*, 10, 1981
Deindustrialization, *IS*, 7, 1980
(last five republished as *World Crisis and the System*, WP, Toronto 1981)
Aid or a 'Golden Fleece', *The Guardian*, 26 Sept. 1970
The Global Market, *New Society*, 30 Jul. 1976

The Third World, *Times Higher Educational Suppl.* 28 Feb. 1974

Planning Cities in the 1980s (Mss), *Urban India*, Dec [?] 1981

A Nicaragua Diary, *EPW*, 22 Sept. 1979

Why Don't they Eat Cake? (comment on Sweezy), *Problems of Communism*, 11, Summer 1978

The other Korean War, *Socialist Worker*, 17 Nov. 1979

Is there a Muslim Revolt? *Socialist Worker*, 1 Dec. 1979

Bleeding Hearts (Indian Elections), *Socialist Worker*, 1 Mar. 1980

India Today (Elections), *Socialist Worker*, 12 Jan. 1980

The Bullshit Behind the Boardroom Blues, *SW*, 7 Feb. 1981

Gang of 4 Trial Marks the End of the Maoist Era, *Sunday Tribune*, 23 Nov. 1980

Apocalypse Tomorrow, *SW*, 25 Oct. 1980

Car Wars, *SW*, 7 Nov. 1981

The Famine Makers, *SW*, 2 Aug. 1980

Box 28

Reviews of NH books

Migration of Labour: Constructing Transitional Arrangements, *EPW*, xxxvii/42, 18 Oct. 2003

incl. In *Migration of Labour: Global Perspectives*, ICFAI University Press, 2006

Does Britain Need more Immigrants? (debate with David Coleman), *World Economics*, 4/2, Apr/Jun. 2003

Towards New Theories of Regional and Urban Development, *EPW*, xl/7, 12 Feb. 2005

Migration and Development, *EPW*, 22 Oct. 2005

Globalisation and the Management of Indian cities, *EPW*, xxxviii/25, 21 Jun. 2003

Interview, *ISHS/Unesco Bulletin*, Apr/Jun. 2004

3rd Managed Migration, conference, Dublin (GD, Immigr Servs), May 2008

Garment-making and Urbanisation, an Introductory Study of Four Cases, *Urban Partnership*, WP6, *World Bank*, Mar. 2000

Immigration and State Power, *EPW*, xlv/5, 30 Jan. 2010

Urban Development Mission, DPU/Ministry of Overseas Development, Jan. 1979

Economic and Social Implications of Migration (with Papademetriou), *EPC Issue paper No. 2*, Jun. 2003

National Limits to Compassion (review), *Patterns of Prejudice*, 37/1, 2003

The Power of Cities, *Eischborn Dialogue*, GTZ, 2003 [?]

Migrants ... Mumbai, *Times of India*, 7 Jan. 2005

The Urban Contribution to National Economic Growth in Nepal, UNDP/IBRD/NEP, Jan. 1991

Jobs for the Poor: A Cuttack Case Study (with Colin Rosser and Sunil Kumar), 1996
Cities Alliance: Independent Evaluation of the First Three Years, DPU, Sept. 2002
ESRC, Evaluation of the Programme: Cities: Competitiveness and Cohesion, tender May
   2003

Box 29

Catiline, unpubl. novel (Mss), 1956
Short story (Mss), Mist, 1953
Beliefs in Society, proofs and publ., *Watts and Penguin*, 1968
World Crisis: Essays in Revolutionary Socialism (with others), Hutchinson, 1971
Die Ideologien der Gesellscaft, CH Beck, 1970 [?]
The Russian Scene (review), *The Sunday Statesman*, Calcutta 9 Aug. 1964
The Struggle for Bangladesh, Pluto Press, Jul. 1 1971
Misc. early writings,
Belgrade and Bandung, *The Economic Weekly*, 28 Mar. 1964
Splits and Splinters (Sino-Sov disp.), *The Economic Weekly*, 30 May 1964
Misc. writings, 60s
Aid or a Golden 'Fleece'? *The Guardian*, 16 Apr. 1970
China's Cities, *Economy and Society*, 1/1, 1970 [?]
Chile's New President Walks the Tightrope, *SW*, 28 Nov. 1970
Turmoil Shakes Pakistan Rulers, *SW*, 27 Mar. 1971
Lipset (review), *Sociology*, 1969
Lukács (review) [?]
The Socialist Register (review), *New Society*, 1970
Perspective on the Seventies, *Socialist Register* [?]
Prospects for the Seventies, *IS*, 42, Feb/Mar 1970
Perspectives, doc for IS National Committee, Annual Conference Nov. 1969
China and the Russian Offensive, *IS*, 41, Dec./Jan 1969/70
The Revolutionary Role of the Peasantry (with Malcolm Caldwell, ibid. 1969/70)
War Against the Innocents (Laos), *SW*, 9 May 1970
Workers and Peasants Alliance (Pakistan), *SW*, 8 Mar. 1969
Keep off my Patch – Moscow's 'Internationalism', *SW*, 26 Jun. 1969
Problems of IS Organisation (doc.) 1968 [?]
The Far East and Neo-colonialism, *IS*, 34, Autumn 1968
The Loneliness of the Left, *IS* 29, summer 1967
Churchill: Ruling Class Militant, *IS* 18, autumn 1964
Pax Americana, *IS*, 21, summer 1965
Czechoslovakia, *IS*, 27, winter 1966/7

China, *IS*, 26, autumn 1966

Indonesian Coup, *IS*, 24, spring 1966

Turkish Elections, *IS*, 23, winter 1965/6

Politics and Society in India (review), *The Economic Weekly*, 14 Dec. 1963

Men Horseback (review), *EW*, 23 May 1964

Race and Nation, *IS*, 34, autumn 1968

China: Let a Hundred Flowers Bloom, *IS*, 35, winter 1968/9

China: What Price Culture?, *IS*, 28, spring 1967

Siege of Dien Bien Phu (review), *International Affairs*

Social structure … economic development (review), *Sociological Review*, 15/2, Jul. 1967

The Owl of Minerva, *Soviet Studies*, xvii/3, Jan. 1967

Review of Books on Asia, *Political Quarterly*, [date?]

Marxism (review), *Political Quarterly*

Marxism in Modern France (review), *Political Quarterly*, Mar. 1967

Letter from Prague (John Ashdown), *EPW*, Oct. 15 1966

The Burma Scene, *The Statesman*, Calcutta, 14 Sept. 1964

China: 'Consolidation Period', *EW*, 6 Mar. 1965

Indian Political Anatomy (review), *EW*, 14 Dec. 1963

Russia's Vietnam, Mss, *IS*, 34, autumn 1968

Prometheus Bound (review of Deutscher trilogy), [date?]

Medieval Howrah (review), *EW*, 28 Sept. 1963

Month of Decisions (John Ashdown, Mss)

South Asia in Crisis, *IS*, 48, Jun./Jul. 1971

Chinese Policy, Ibid

Unloading Ulster, *EPW*, 8 Apr. 1972

For Whom the Flame Flickers, *EPW*, 26 Feb. 1972

In Lieu of Bread (Pakistan), *EPW*, 22 Jan. 1972

Tears and Rhetoric do not Make a Meal, *EPW*, 19 Feb. 1972

Bengal, *SW*, 12 Jun. 1971

China's Proletarian Problems (John Ashdown), *Far Eastern Economic Review*, 12 Mar. 1969

China's Nursed Grudges, *Far Eastern Economic Review*, 22 Apr. 1965

Congress and the Kamraj Plan, *EW*, 5 Oct. 1963

Tories and Trade Unions, *IS*, 13, summer 1963

Mss – Burma/Cambodia

Box 30

Mss. Slum Dwellers and the Cuttack Labour Market, ODA (*contract report*), 1996 [?]

The Role of Revisionism in History (review), EPR, 1 Jun. 2002

Everybody in? (migration), *Red Pepper*, Aug. 2002

Turning the Indifferent to Anger, EPW, 30 Nov. 2002

The United Nations of Bedlam, *Red Pepper*, Dec. 2002

Reviews (mss): Migration (Jordan and Duvell), DPR

Displaced Persons, *Patterns of Prejudice*, 37/1, 2003 African immigration in SA, DPR?

States and Cities, DPR?

Egyptian reform, DPR?

Ancient India,

Middle Eastern development

Destruction of SU

APEC and China

Yugoslavia

Regionalism

Egypt and Reform

Globalisation (Streeten)

Chinese Labour Market Reform

Regions and Development

War and Underdevelopment, 2 vols.

Can Japan compete (Porter)

History of the world, Harman, EPW, 3 Jun. 2000

Reform in Ghana

On Borders (southern Africa)

Capital and Coercion

Global Social Movements

LA garment industry

Rural labour in Egypt, *Times Higher Educational Suppl.*, 18 Feb. 2000

Mss Duncan Hallas: Death of a Revolutionary, *Journal of Revolutionary History*

The Freedom to Move, in Dale and Cole (eds.), *The European Union and Migrant Labour*, Berg, 1999

EU immigration, *Red Pepper*, 30 Jun. 2002

Palestine, 18 Apr. 2002

After Israel's Worst, What Next?, Editorial, EPR, 9 Feb. 2002

Palestine Editorial, 21 Mar. 2002

Palestine Editorial

Palestine Editorial, 25 Jul. 2001

Globalisation and the Management of Cities, OECD, 10 Apr. 2000

Death of Princess Margaret, 10 Feb. 2002

Bain D'souza, obit, *The Guardian*

Britain and the Euro, 25 Jan. 2002

City Trends, *Mumbai First*, 25 Jan. 2002

China: Globalisation and the New Agenda, *International Socialist Review*, Aug/Sept. 2001

Same: The Old Order Changes, *EPW*, 13 Oct. 2001

Vietnam: One Step Forward, Two Steps Back?, *EPW*, 15 Sept. 2001

Russia: Crashing into the Modern World, *EPW*, 18 Aug. 2001

Migration in Europe

Colombia: Sliding into Civil War, *EPW*, 16 Jun. 2001

Chinese Workers in Israel: a Bizarre Tale, *EPW*, 19 May 2001

Japan: from the Other Side of the Hill, *EPW*, *xxxv/37*, 9 Sept. 2000

State of Britain, 28 Jun. 2001

Cali, Colombia, 8 Jun. 2001

Food and Appetite (UK elections, 2001), Jun. 2001

British Elections, 22 May 2000

West African Kidnapped Children, 17 Apr. 2001

Vietnam, 23 Mar. 1998

The Disappearing Economy

Bahia; Economic Prospects and Proposals (*World Bank, report*), 23 Feb. 2000

Should Europe End Immigration Controls? a Polemic, *European Journal of Development Research*, 12/1, Jun. 2000

Ibid, EADI 9th general conference Sept. 1999

End the Nightmare (refugees), *The Diplomat*, Sept/Oct. 2000

Ken Watts, obit, *The Guardian* 29 Sept. 2000

Racists are so Blind, *The Guardian*, 2 May 2000

Genova Globale citta Cosmopolita, *Il Secolo, XIX*, 21 May 2000

Playing the Numbers Game (immigration), *Red Pepper*, May 2000

Towards New Theories of Regional and Urban Development, EPW xl/7 Feb. 12 2005

The Owl of Minerva, *Soviet Studies*, XVIII/3, Jan. 1967

Review: Export processing Mexico, *JDS*, 27/1 Oct. 1990

Pamphlet: The Struggle for Bangladesh, Pluto Press, 1973 [?]

Pamphlet: Why Half the World goes Hungry, SW pamphlet Apr. 1987

The End of the Third World, Chinese ed. (transl. Li Yu-ling and Je Ye-hong 1989)

Reviews by K.P. Moseley (Theory and Society), Alex Callenicos (IS) 1989

Food, Development and the Crisis, *Contemporary Review*, 226/1310, Mar. 1975

Review (Mexico), *The Economic Journal*, 386/97 Jun. 1987

The Disappearing Economy, Mss

The Role of New Towns in a Period of Adjustment, mss., World Bank 1992

Japan: from the Other Side of the Hill, *EPW*, xxxv/37, 9 Sept. 2000
Russia: Crashing into the Modern World, *EPW*, 18 Aug. 2001

Box 31

Oil and Empire, Zaman, Istanbul Jan 2007
The death of Saddam Hussein, *Zaman*, 7, Istanbul Dec. 2006
World Crisis and Migration, *ISR* (unpupl.), 2008 [?]
Future of the Left, notes for *Red Pepper*, Oct. 2007
Globalization and the Left, [?]
Workers of the World – Welcome, *Red Pepper*, 152 May 2007
Briefing: the Naxalites and the Bangladesh Left, mss. 1973 [?]
Tapes: View of the Century 19, Working, BBC Education [?]
Governance of Cities in Transition, 2000 and Beyond, World Bank Prague [?] 2000
Dilemmas in China Today, KPFK Los Angeles, 1989
Paper: Mexico Conference, UAM Xochimilco [?] 2008
Impact of Globalisation II, TV Choice 2009
Lauri Taylor interview, 1995
Swedish Immigration Film [?]

Box 32

Review of Who needs Migrants (Martin Ruhs and Bridget Anderson), *Journal of Ethnic and Migration Studies*, Jan. 2011
Migration and Recession, Dublin (Goethe-Institut) Feb. 2011
The Trade in Warm Bodies, draft TV program (Atlas), not used Dec. 1982
ESRC, Evaluation of Cities: Economic Competitiveness and Social Cohesion programme (with Peter Townroe), Dec. 2003
University of East Anglia, Report of the External Examiner, 2000/2001
Power Points: The Economic Future of the Yogyakarta Special Province, Jul. 2003
How to Manage Internal Migration, DFID workshop, Jul. 2004
Asylum and the Future of Economic Migration, ASAP Warsaw, Jun. 2007
BBC Radio 4 (Laurie Taylor), Migration in China, Apr. 2007
Managed Migration from an International Perspective, General Directors Immigration Services Conference, Dublin May 2008
Symposium: Structural Change and Development Policies,
UAM (Xochimilco), Mexico DF, May 2008
World Crisis and Migration, *International Socialist Review* (not used), Jan. 2007 [?]

World Economic Crisis and the Management of Cities, Tehran Municipality (conference and journal), Jul. 2009

Tehran – Reply to Comments by Mr Sarrafi and others Jun. 2010

Gresham Lecture, CARA, City of London, Dec. 2009

Asylum and the Future of UK Managed Migration Policies, CARA Jun. 2008

From Global Migration to Managing a Global Labour Market, Ramphal Centre, Warwick consultation, Oct. 2009

Immigration and State Power, Mss [?]

Guest editor: Urban Age, Gambling on the City Economy, spring 1999

Migration and Development, written submission, Parliamentary International Development Ctee Feb. 2004

The Impact of the Reform of International Trade on Urban and Rural Change, draft, Dept for International Development Apr. 2004

New Thinking about Urban and Rural Development

(with Frank Ellis), DFID, Guildford (University of Surrey), Jul. 2004

Research Proposal: Managing the City Economy – comparative studies of Shanghai and Mumbai in the decline of the textile industry (not pursued), Apr. 2000

DFID Research Priorities. DFID, 2004 [?]

Migration and Development (World Federation of Scientists, Erice), Aug. 2005

Poverty, Globalization and the Left, Mss (*Red Pepper* [?]), [date?]

Interview on Immigration, US Socialist Worker, Jun. 2006

Comment, David Goodhart, Too Diverse?, *Prospect*, Feb. 2004

Europe: Migration and Development, CIAD journal, Hermosilla, Mexico May, 2006

Europe and Immigration, Challenge Europe, EPC Brussels [?]

Migration and Developoment, EPW, Oct. 2005

Integration – into what? Connections (Commission for racial equality), winter, 2004/5

'Modern Warfare'? *Il Secolo*, XIX, Genoa [?]

Iraq? *Il Secolo*, XIX, Genoa [?]

Change of US President, *Il Secolo*, XIX [?]

Globalization, *Il Secolo*, XIX, May 2000 [?]

Blair, *Il Secolo* XIX, Nov. 2001

Depleted Uranium, *Il Secolo* XIX, Jan. 2001

Mad Cow Disease, *Il Secolo*, XIX [?]

Global Warming, *Il Secolo*, XIX, Nov. 2000

Slaughter on the borders, *Il Secolo*, XIX, Nov. 2000

Palestinian Civil War, Zaman, Istanbul, Dec. 2006

Should we be Frightened of China and India, Zaman, Dec. 2006

Cosmopolitanism, Zaman [?]

Building a Development Cadre, memo, EPC Brussels, 26 Nov. 2003

Letter, *Financial Times*, 16 Apr. 2004

Should we End Immigration Controls?, lecture, Royal Society of Arts Nov. 2000
Does Britain Need more Immigrants: a debate (with David Coleman), World Economics
   Apr., 2003
Economic Migration and the European labour market, EPC Brussels, May 2003
Immigration Debate (with Anthony Brown), Prospect, Jun. 2002
The Migration of Labour, Encyclopaedia, Jun. 2003
Paper: Durban, Cities as Engines of Economic Growth, Jul. 1998
Bahia Economy, World Bank subnational development study 2,000 [?]
The Literate City? Urban Age rough draft? 2,000?
A Survey of the Technology of Cities (edited), Urban Age Autumn, 1998
Comment on GHK International memo on City Development Strategies Nov. 1999
The Economic Development of Haiphong, World Bank CDS report Jul. 1998
Mss – Urbanization and Economic Development [?]

Published Works on Shelves

Globalisation and the Management of Indian Cities, pp. 1–29, in *Indian Cities in Transition*, ed. Annapurna Shaw, Orient Longman, 2007
The Economics and Politics of the Free Movement of People, pp. 33–50, in *Migration
without Borders: essays on the free movement of people*, ed. Antoine Pecaud and Paul
de Guchteneire, UNESCO 2007
Privatization and the State: Russia, Eastern Europe, east Asia (with David Lockwood),
   pp. 64–99,
in *Industrial Transformation in Eastern Europe in the Light of the East Asian Experience*,
   ed. Jeffrey Henderson, International Political Economy, Macmillan/St Martin's Press,
   1998
Extract from Thinking the Unthinkable, in *Bender's Immigration Bulletin*, 7/19, pp. 1139–
1148, Oct. 2002
The Return of Cosmopolitan Capitalism: Globalization, the State and War, IB Tauris
   2003
Thinking the Unthinkable: the Immigration Myth Exposed, IB Tauris, 2002
Introduction, pp. ix–xi. *Outward from home: a Planner's Odyssey*, by Kenneth Watts,
   Book Guild, 1997
National limits to compassion (review), *Patterns of Prejudice*, 37/1, Mar. 2003
Migration of Labour: constructing transitional arrangements, in Migration of Labor:
   Global Perspectives, edited by Rajarshi Ghosh and Anis Kumar Pain, ICFAI Uni-
   versity Press, Hyderabad (India), 2006
Migration and Development, pp. 7–25, in *Estudios Sociales*, XIV/27, CIDA (Hermosilla),
   Jan-Jun. 2006

The Mandate of Heaven: Marx and Mao in Modern China, Quartet, 1978

Should Europe End Immigration Controls? EADI 9th General Conference, Paris Sept. 1999

republ. Of Development Research, 12/1, Jun. 2000

China: Globalization and the New Agenda, *International Socialist Review*, Aug.–Sept. 2001

Cali, Colombia: Towards a City Development Strategy, World Bank Country Study, World Bank, Washington, DC, 2002

Should We End Immigration Controls? *RSA Journal*, 1/4, 2001

End the Nightmare, The Diplomat, Sept.–Oct. 2000

All Praise War! *International Socialism*, 102, Mar. 2004

Garment-making and Urbanisation: an Introductory Study of Four Cases, Urban Partnership, WP 6, World Bank, Jun. 1999

Migration: a Welcome Opportunity, a New Way Forward, report of the Royal Society of Arts Migration Commission, Nov. 2005

Democracy (interview), Newsletter, SHS, UNESCO Apr-Jun. 2004

Holding Back the Tide, *The Diplomat*, Jan/Feb. 2003

Towards a Global Accord on Migration and Refugees, Challenge Europe 5, EPC, Brussels, Oct. 2001

I Nuovi Intoccabili: perchè abbiamo bisogno degli immigrati, il Saggiatore, Milan, 2000.

The Urban Environment in Developing Countries, UNDP, New York 1992

JDS 37/1 review, Oct. 2000

Las ciudades y el cambio estructural, in *Transiciones* 1, ed. Javier Delgado y Blanca Ramirez, UAM 1999

Overview: Urbanisation in Asia, pp. 6–19, in *Urban growth and development in Asia 1*, (ed. Chapman, Dutt. Bradnock), SOAS, 1999

The Freedom to Move, pp. 265–80, in *The European Union and Migrant Labour*, ed. Gareth Dale and Mike Cole, Berg, 1999

Review, pp. 455–62, *Historical Materialism*, 12/4, 2004

The War-making Machine and Privatisation (with David Lockwood), *Journal of Development Studies*, 33/5 (Dudley Seers Memorial prize), Jun. 1997

Preparing an Economic and Strategic Vision for a City, pp. 53–62, in *The Challenge of Urban Government*, ed. Mila Freire and Richard Stren, World Bank, 2001

Duncan Hallas: death of a Trotskyist, pp. 259–72, *Revolutionary History*, 8/4, 2004

Spatial Development Policies and Territorial Governance in an Era of Globalisation, pp. 33–58, in Towards a New Role for Spatial Planning, OECD, 2001

The Future is Cosmopolitan, in Window over the Mediterranean Sea, 370, ed. Sergio Buonadonna, Il *Secolo*, XIX, il melangolo 2001

Relaciones económicas Mexico-Estados Unidas en el contexto mundiale, in *La modernization de Mexico*, Co-ord Arturo Anguiano, UAM-Xochimilco 1990

The Terrorist (novel), Book Guild, 2007

Why Europe Needs to Open its Doors for Labour Migration, Challenge Europe 13, 2005

Europe, Economic Migration and the Conquest of Poverty, EPC, Revamping development efforts, Issue, paper 36, Jul. 2005

Migration – an Effective Strategy for Development, in *Challenge Europe*, 11, May. 2004

Unlocking the Fortress: Managing Migration in Europe, *Challenge Europe*, 10 Nov. 2003

Beliefs in Society: the Problem of Ideology, Watts/New Thinker's Library (2 copies), 1968 (Penguin ed. 1971)

Die Ideologien in der Gesellschaft: eine untersuchung über entstehung, wesen und wirkung, CH Beck, Munich, 1970

Japanese ed. 1970 [?]

Competition and the Corporate Society: British Conservatives, the State and Industry, 1945–1964, Methuen 1972 (2nd ed., Routledge, 2004)

With John Palmer (eds.): World Crisis: Essays in Revolutionary Socialism, Hutchinson 1971

India-China: Underdevelopment and Revolution, Vikas, Delhi 1974

The 'Scissors Crisis in India and China', in *Urbanization: early development, current trends and Prospects*, 30th Congress of human sciences in Asia and North Africa, ed. Luis Unikel, El Colegio de México 1981

China: Let a Hundred Flowers Bloom, in *The Revolution is Dead: Long Live the Revolution*, Readings, the 70s group, 1976 [?]

The New Untouchables – the international migration of labour, *International Socialism*, 8, 1980

Development Studies: Schools of Thought, in *The Developing World*, readings, ed. Abba Farmar, DESC, Dublin, 1988

Nationalism and Development, in *Market Forces and World Development*, eds. Prendergast and Frances Stewart, St Martin's Press 1994

Of Bread and Guns: the World Economy in Crisis, Penguin, London 1983

The End of the Third World: Newly Industrializing Countries and the Decline of an Ideology, IB Taurus, 1986; Penguin ed. 1987; National Liberation, IB Taurus 1990; Penguin 1990; US ed., University of Nevada Press 1993

Cultural Diversity and Economic Development: Migration, Vol. 1, p. 294, in *Cities and the New Global Economy: Proceedings of a Conference*, OECD/Government of Australia, 1995

Urbanisation and Economic Development, in *Cities, the mainspring of economic development in developing countries*, Proceedings of an International meeting, Cities Unieés, Lille 1990

Contributing editor, *The Family: a social history of the twentieth century*, ed. John Harriss, Oxford 1991

Economic Development, Cities and Planning the Case of Bombay, OUP, Bombay, 1978

The Mandate of Heaven: Marx and Mao in Modern China, Quartet, London, 1978; Korean ed. [?]

Londres, in *São Paulo. planejamento e gestão*, seminario internacional, Emplasa etc. 1990

The Economic Crisis and Planning: Cities and Regions, in *Society and Change: essays in honour of Sachin Chaudhuri*, ed. Krishnaswamy al., Sameeksha Trust/OUP 1977

City, Class and Trade: Social and Economic Change in the Third World, IB Tauris/DPU 1991

with Sergio Puente, Environmental issues in cities of the developing world: the case of Mexico city, *Journal of International Development*, 2/4, Oct. 1990

Jobs for the Poor: a Case Study of Cuttack (with Colin Rosser, Sunil Kumar), Research Press, Delhi 1996

Cities in the 1990s (edited), UCL Press, London, ODA/DPU 1992

Cities and Structural Adjustment (edited with Ida Fabricius), UCL Press, DPU/ODA, 1996

Relaciones económicas Mexico-Estados Unidos en el contexto mundial, in *La Modernizacion de Mexico*, Arturo Anguiano coo-ord., UAM-Xochimilco 1990

Comment on *National Liberation, International Socialism*, 53, winter 1991

Mexican Trade and Mexico-US Economic Relations, in *Mexico: dilemmas of transition*, ed. Neil Harvey, ILAS, 1993

The New Untouchables: Immigration and the New World Worker, IB Taurus, 1995

Bombay in the Global Economy, in Bombay: Metaphor for Modern India, ed. by Sujata Patel and Alice Thorner, OUP Bombay 1995, Penguin, 1995

References

Aird, John S. 1967, 'Population Growth and Distribution in Mainland China', in *An Economic Profile of Mainland China*, Volume 2, Joint Economic Committee, Congress of the United States, Washington, DC: Government print off.

Aird, John S. 1990, *Slaughter of the Innocents: Coercive Birth Control in China*, Washington, DC: AEI Press.

Amin, Samir 1974, *Accumulation on a World Scale: A Critique of the Theory of Underdevelopment*, New York: Monthly Review Press.

Anderson, Stuart 2000, 'Muddled masses', *Reason Magazine*, February, available at: http://www.reason.com/archives/2000/02/01/muddled-masses

Andrews, M.J. 1979, *Crossroads: A Consequence of Ideology or Urbanization*, unpublished dissertation.

Appadurai, Arjun 1996, *Modernity at Large: Cultural Dimensions of Globalization*, Minneapolis, MN: University of Minnesota Press.

Ashton, Trevor Henry and Charles H.E. Philpin (eds.) 1985, *The Brenner Debate: Agrarian Class Structure and Economic Development in Pre-industrial Europe*, Cambridge: Cambridge University Press.

Åslund, Anders and Richard Layard (eds.) 1993, *Changing the Economic System in Russia*, New York: St Martin's Press.

Balcerowicz, Leszek and Alan Gelb, 1994a, 'Macropolicies in Transition to a Market Economy: A Three Year Perspective', paper for World Bank Annual Conference on Development Economics, Washington, DC: World Bank.

Balcerowicz, Leszek 1994b, 'Transition to the Market Economy Poland, 1989–93, in Comparative Perspective', *Economic Policy: A European Forum*, 19: 71–98.

Baran, Paul 1957, *The Political Economy of Growth*, New York: The Monthly Review Press.

Baran, Paul and Paul Sweezy 1966, *Monopoly Capital: An Essay on the American Economic and Social Order*, New York: Monthly Review Press.

Baum, Richard 1975, *Prelude to Revolution: Mao, the Party and the Peasant Question 1962–66*, New York: Columbia University Press.

Benoit, Emile 1973, *Defence and Economic Growth in Developing Countries*, Lexington, MA: Lexington Books.

Berliner, Joseph S. 1988, *Soviet Industry from Stalin to Gorbachev*, New York: Cornell University Press.

Bernstein, Thomas P. 1968, 'Problems of Village Leadership after Land Reform', *The China Quarterly*, 36: 1–22.

Bhagwati, Jagdish 1999, 'A close look at the newest newcomers', *The Wall Street Journal*, 13 October.

Bhagwati, Jagdish and Marvin Kosters (eds.) 1994, *Trade and Wages*, Washington, DC: American Enterprise Institute.

Bhagwati, Jagdish and Vivek Dehejia 1994, 'Freer Trade and Wages of the Unskilled. Is Marx Striking Again?', in *Trade and Wages*, edited by Jagdish Bhagwati and Marvin Kosters, Washington, DC: American Enterprise Institute.

Blackaby, Frank (ed.) 1979, *De-industrialisation*, London: National Institute of Economic and Social Research – Heinemann Educational Books.

Blaho, Andras 1994, 'Russian Transition-Chinese Reforms: A Comparative View', Helsinki: United Nations University-WIDER (Research for Action).

Blum, William 1995, *Killing Hope: United States Military and CIA Interventions since World War II*, Monroe, ME: Common Courage Press.

Böhning, Wolf-Rudiger 1972, *The Migration of Workers in the United Kingdom and the European Community*, London: The Institute of Race Relations, Oxford University Press.

Böhning, Wolf-Rudiger and D. Maillat 1974, *The Effects of the Employment of Foreign Workers*, Paris: OECD Publications.

Boyce, David George and Alan O'Day (eds.) 1996, *The Making of Modern Irish History: Revisionism and the Revisionist Controversy*, London: Routledge.

Boote, Anthony R. and János Somogyi 1991, 'Economic Reform in Hungary since 1968', IMF Occasional Paper 83, Washington, DC: International Monetary Fund.

Borjas, George J. 1999, *Heaven's Door: Immigration Policy and the American Economy*, Princeton, NJ: Princeton University Press.

Bose, A.N. 1978, *Calcutta and Rural Bengal*, Calcutta: Minerva.

Brabant, Josef M. 1994, 'The Hobbled Transition: Mined Privatization Paths in the East', in *Privatization in the Transition Process: Recent Experiences in Eastern Europe*, by UN Conference on Trade and Development (UNCTAD), Kopint-Datorg, Geneva.

Brady, Robert Alexander 1943, *Business as a System of Power*, New York: Columbia University Press.

Brookes, Karen McConnell 1994, 'Decollectivization and the Agricultural Transition in East and Central Europe', Working Paper Series 793, Washington, DC: World Bank.

Brown, Annette N., Barry Williams Ickes and Randi Ryterman 1994, 'The Myth of Monopoly: A New View of Industrial Structure in Russia', Research Working Paper 1331, Washington, DC: World Bank.

Brown, J.J.F. and T.D. Sheriff, 'Deindustrialization in the UK: Background Statistics', in *De-industrialisation*, edited by Frank Blackaby, London: National Institute of Economic and Social Research – Heinemann Educational Books.

Brus, Wlodzimierz 1994, 'General Problems of Privatization in the Process of Transformation of Post-Communist Economies', in UNCTAD 1994.

Bukharin, Nikolaï Ivanovich 1972 [1915], *Imperialism and World Economy*, London: Merlin Press.

Bukharin, Nikolaï Ivanovich 1971 [1921], *The Economics of the Transformation Period*, New York: Bergman.

Bukharin, Nikolaï Ivanovich 1972 [1924], *Imperialism and the Accumulation of Capital*, translated by Rudolf Wichmann, London and New York: Monthly Review Press.

Burtin, Yuri 1994, 'Nomenklaturnaya sobstvernost'vchera icegodnya', *Moskovskie Novesti*, 35, 7 (September).

Carr, Edward Hallett 1950, *A History of Soviet Russia: The Bolshevik Revolution, 1917–23*, Volume 1, London: Macmillan.

Carr, Edward Hallett 1954, *A History of Soviet Russia: The Interregnum 1923–24*, Volume 4, London: Macmillan.

Carr, Edward Hallett and R.W. Davies 1969, *Foundations of a Planned Economy, 1928–29*, London: Macmillan.

Chakravarti, Ranabir (ed.) 2001, *Trade in Early India: Themes in Indian History*, New Delhi: Oxford University Press.

Chang, John K. 1969, *Industrial Development in Pre-Communist China: A Quantitative Analysis*, Chicago, IL: Aldine Publishing Company.

Chen, C.S. (ed.) 1969, *Rural People's Communes in Lien Chiang, Documents Concerning Communes in Lien-Chiang County, Fukien Province, 1962–63*, Stanford, CA: Hoover Institution Press.

Chen, Kuan-I and Jogindar Singh Uppal (eds.) 1971, *Comparative Development of India and China*, New York: Free Press.

Chishti Sumitra and B. Bhattacharya 1976, 'India's Terms of Trade', *Economic and Political Weekly*, 11, 11: 429–35.

Cliff, Tony 1955, *Stalin's Russia: A Marxist Analysis*, London: Mike Kidron.

Cliff, Tony 1963, 'Permanent Revolution', *International Socialism*, 12.

Cliff, Tony 1964–65, 'Marxism and the Collectivisation of Agriculture', *International Socialism*, 19: 4–16.

Cliff, Tony 1967, 'Crisis in China', *International Socialism*, 29: 7–16.

Cohen, Stephen F. 1971, *Bukharin and the Bolshevik Revolution: A Political Biography 1888–1938*, New York: Alfred A. Knopf.

Collins, Susan Margaret and Carol Graham 2006, *Global Labour Markets? Brookings Trade Forum 2006*, Washington, DC: Brookings Institution Press.

Commander, Simon, Fabrizio Coricelli and Karston Staehr 1991, 'Wages and Employment in the Transition to a Market Economy', Working Paper Series 736, Washington, DC: EDI-World Bank.

Commander, Simon, James Kollo and Cecilia Ugaz, 1994, 'Firm Behaviour and the Labour Market in the Hungarian Transition', Working Paper 1373, Budapest: The World Bank (Economic Development Institute) and Institute of Economics.

Commission on Growth and Development 2008, *The Growth Report: Strategies for Sustained and Inclusive Development*, Washington, DC: World Bank.

Constant, Amelie and Douglas Massey 2002 'Return Migration by German Guestworkers: Neoclassical versus New Economic Theory', *International Migration*, 40, 4: 5–39.

Coricelli, Fabrizio and Ana Revenga 1991, 'Wages and Unemployment in Poland: Recent Developments and Policy Issues of 1990', Working Paper 732, Washington, DC: World Bank.

Cornelius, Wayne A. 2001, 'Death at the Border: Efficacy and Unintended Consequences of US Immigration Control Policy', *Population and Development Review*, 27, 4: 661–85.

Currie, John Martin, John A. Murphy and Andrew Schmitz 1971, 'The Concept of Economic Surprise and Its Use in Economic Analysis', *The Economic Journal*, 81, 324: 741–99.

Dabrowski, Marek 1994, 'Ukrainian Way to Hyperinflation', Discussion Paper 94/12, Warsaw: Centre for Social and Economic Research.

Datta-Chaudhuri, Mrinal 1981, 'Industrialisation and Foreign Trade: The Development of South Korea and Philippines', in *Export-led Industrialisation and Development*, edited by Eddy Lee, Geneva: Asia Employment Programme, International Labour Office.

de Ste Croix, Geoffrey Ernest Maurice 1981, *The Class Struggle in the Ancient Greek World from the Archaic Age to the Arab Conquests*, London: Duckworth.

Deane, Phyllis 1975, *The Evolution of Economic Ideas*, Cambridge: Cambridge University Press.

Deleyne, Jan 1973, *The Chinese Economy*, London: Deutsch.

Democratic Staff of the Joint Economic Committee of the Congress of the United States 1986, *The Bi-coastal Economy: Regional Patterns of Economic Growth During the Reagan Administration*, Washington, DC.

Desai, Mihir A., Devesh Kapur and John McHale 2001, 'The Fiscal Impact of the Brain Drain: Indian Emigration to the US', Third Annual NBER-NCAER Conference, Neemrana, India.

Desai, Mihir A. 2003, 'The Fiscal Impact of High-skilled Emigration: Flows of Indians to the US', Working Paper 03–01, Weatherhead Centre for International Affairs, Cambridge, MA: Harvard University.

Deutscher, Isaac 1954, *The Prophet Armed. Trotsky 1879–1921*, London: G. Cumberlege.

Dhanji, Farid and Brando Milanovic 1991, 'Privatization in East and Central Europe: Objectives, Constraints and Models of Divesture', Working Paper Series 770, Washington, DC: The World Bank.

Diaz, Gil 1992, 'Macro Economic Policies, Crisis and Growth in the Long Run: Mexico', unpublished paper.

Dlouhy, Vladimir and Jan Mládek 1994, 'Privatization and Corporate Control in the Czech Republic', *Economic Policy: A European Forum*, 19: 155–70.

Donnithorne, Audrey 1967, *China's Economic System*, New York: Praeger.

Donnithorne, Audrey 1972, 'China's Cellular Economy: Some Economic Trends since the Cultural Revolution', *The China Quarterly*, 52: 605–19.

Dornbusch, Rudiger, Michael Bruno, Guido di Telia and Stanley Fisher (eds.) 1988, *Stopping High Inflation*, Cambridge, MA: MIT Press.

Dornbusch, Rudiger, Paul Krugman and Yung Chul Park 1989, *Meeting World Challenges: United States Manufacturing in the 1990s*, Rochester, NY: Eastman Kodak Company.

Draper, Hal 1968, 'Marx and Bolivar: A Note on Authoritarian Leadership in a National Liberation Movement', *New Politics*, 7, 1: 64–77.

Draper, Theodore 1965, *Castroism: Theory and Practice*, London: Pall Mall.

Easterly, William and Fischer Stanley 1994, 'The Soviet Economic Decline', Policy Research Working Paper 1284, Washington, DC: World Bank.

Eckstein, Alexander, Walter Galenson and Ta-chung Liu (eds.) 1968, *Economic Trends in Communist China*, Chicago, IL: Adeline.

Economic Commission for Latin America 1950, *The Economic Development of Latin America and its Principal Problems*, New York: United Nations.

Economic Commission for Latin America 1951, *Economic Survey of Latin America 1949*, New York: United Nations.

Emmanuel, Arghiri 1972 [1969], *Unequal Exchange: A Study of the Imperialism of Trade*, translated by Brian Pearce, New York and London: Monthly Review Press.

Engels, Friedrich 1972 [1884], *Origin of the Family, Private Property and the State*, New York: Pathfinder Press.

Engels, Friedrich 1978 [1850], 'Two Years of a Revolution; 1848 and 1849', in *The Collected Works of Marx and Engels*, Volume 10, London: Lawrence & Wishart.

Erlich, Alexander 1960, *The Soviet Industrialisation Debate, 1924–28*, Cambridge, MA: Harvard University Press.

Fan, Gang 1994, 'Incremental Changes and Dual-Track Transition: Understanding the Case of China', *Economic Policy: A European Forum*, 19: 99–122.

Fan Gang and Wing Thye Woo 1993, 'Decentralisation, Socialism and Macro-economic Stability: Lessons from China', Working Paper 112, Helsinki: United Nations University-WIDER.

Fanon, Frantz 1965, *The Wretched of the Earth*, London: MacGibbon & Kee.

Field, Robert Michael 1975, 'Civilian Industrial Production in the People's Republic of China, 1949–74', in *China: A Reassessment of the Economy*, Joint Economic Committee, Congress of the United States, Washington, DC: Government print off.

Florence, Sargent 1961, *Ownership, Control and Success of Large Companies*, London: Sweet & Maxwell.

Frank, André Gunder 1979, *Dependent Accumulation and Development*, New York: Monthly Review Press.

Frank, André Gunder 1980, *Crisis in the World Economy*, London: Heinemann.

Fröbel, Folker, Jürgen Heinrichs, and Otto Kreye 1980 [1976], *The New International Division of Labour. Structural Unemployment in Industrialised Countries and Industrialisation in Developing Countries*, translated by Pete Burgess, Cambridge: Cambridge University Press.

Galbraith, John Kenneth 1967, *The New Industrial State*, Boston, MA: Houghton Mifflin Co.

Galuszka, Peter, Patricia Kranz and Stanley Reed 1994, 'Russia's New Capitalisms', *Business Week*, 10: 68–80.

Garnaut, Ross 1994, 'Australia', in *The Political Economy of Policy Reform*, edited by John Williamson, Washington, DC: Institute of International Economics.

Gershenkron, Alexander 1952, 'Economic Backwardness in Historical Perspective', in *The Progress of Underdeveloped Areas*, edited by Bert Hoselitz, Chicago, IL: Chicago University Press.

Ghosh, Bimal (ed.) 2000, *Managing Migration: Time for a New International Regime?*, Oxford: Oxford University Press.

Gily, Adolfo 1965, 'The Guerrilla Movement in Guatemala I', *The Monthly Review*, 17: 9–40.

Glenny, Misha 2008, *McMafia: Crime without Frontiers*, London: Bodley Hill.

Gluckstein, Ygael 1957, *Mao's China, Economic and Political Survey*, London: George Allen & Unwin Ltd.

Goldman, Marshall 1994, *The Last Opportunity: Why Economic Reforms in Russia Have Not Worked*, New York: Norton.

Goncha, Ksenia 1991, 'The Economics of Disarmament: A Difficult Matter', *Problems in Economics*, 33, 9: 76–90.

Government of India 1969, *Economic Survey 1968–69*, New Delhi: Ministry of Finance.

Government of India 1975, *Economic Survey 1974–75*, New Delhi: Ministry of Finance.

Greenwood, Michael, Gary Hunt and Ulrich Kohli 1997 'The Factor Market Consequences of Unskilled Immigration to the US', *Labour Economics*, 4, 1: 1–28.

Halperin, Ernst 1967, *Proletarian Class Parties in Europe and Latin America*, Cambridge, MA: Harvard University Press.

Hamilton, Bob and John Whalley 1984, 'Efficiency and Distributional Implications of Global Restrictions on Labour Mobility: Calculations and Political Implications', *Journal of Development Economics*, 14, 1–2: 61–75.

Hammer, Ellen Joy 1966 [1954], *The Struggle for Indochina, 1940–55*, Stanford, CA: Stanford University Press.

Harris, Nigel 1964, 'India: A First Approximation', *International Socialism*, 18: 19–21.

Harris, Nigel 1968a, *Beliefs in Society: Problem of Ideology*, London: C.A. Watts & Co Ltd.

Harris, Nigel 1968b, 'The Far East and Neo-colonialism', *The Notebook, International Socialism*, 34: 7–8.

Harris, Nigel 1968-9, 'China: Let a Hundred Flowers Bloom, or A Host of Dragons Without a Leader', *International Socialism*, 35: 11–23.

Harris, Nigel 1969, 'Agriculture, Peasants and Accumulation', *International Socialism*, 40: 37–9.

Harris, Nigel 1969-70, 'China and the Russian Offensive', *International Socialism*, 41: 2–4.

Harris, Nigel 1970, 'Prospects for the Seventies – The Third World', *International Socialism*, 42: 20–30.

Harris, Nigel 1971, 'Imperialism Today', in *World Crisis: Essays in Revolutionary Socialism*, edited by Nigel Harris and John Palmer, London: Hutchinson.

Harris, Nigel 1972, *Competition and Corporate Society: British Conservatives, the State and Industry, 1945–64*, London: Routledge.

Harris, Nigel 1973a, 'Economic Growth in India and China', *International Socialism*, 60: 12–6.

Harris, Nigel 1973b, 'The Anarchist Argument', *International Socialism*, 54.

Harris, Nigel 1974, *India-China: Underdevelopment and Revolution*, Delhi: Vikas.

Harris, Nigel 1978, *The Mandate of Heaven: Marx and Mao in Modern China*, London: Quartet.

Harris, Nigel 1983, *Of Bread and Guns: The World Economy in Crisis*, New York: Penguin.

Harris, Nigel 1986, *The End of the Third World: Newly Industrializing Countries and the Decline of an Ideology*, London: Tauris.

Harris, Nigel 1992, *National Liberation*, London: Penguin.

Harris, Nigel 1994, 'Nationalism and Development', in *Market Forces and World Development*, edited by Renee Prendergast and Frances Stewart, London: St Martin's Press.

Harris, Nigel 1995, *The New Untouchables: Immigration and the New World Worker*, London: Tauris.

Harris, Nigel 2003a, 'Economic Migration and the European Labour Market', EPC Issue Paper No. 2 – Part I, Brussels: The European Policy Centre.

Harris, Nigel 2003b, *The Return of Cosmopolitan Capitalism: Globalization, the State and War*, London: Tauris.

Harris, Nigel and Malcom Caldwell 1969-70, 'The Revolutionary Role of the Peasants', *International Socialism*, 41: 18–31.

Havrylyshyn, Oleh and David Tarr 1991, 'Trade Liberalization and the Transition to a Market Economy', Working Paper Series 700, Washington, DC: World Bank.

Havrylyshyn, Oleh 1994a, 'Ukraine', in *The Political Economy of Policy Reform*, edited by John Williamson, Washington, DC: Institute of International Economics.

Havrylyshyn, Oleh 1994b, 'Reviving Trade Among the Newly Independent States', *Economic Policy: A European Forum*, 19: 171–90.

Hewett, Edward A. 1988, *Reforming the Soviet Economy*, Washington, DC: Brookings Institution.

Hilferding, Rudolf 1902–3, *Der Funktionswechsel des Schutzzolles, Die Neue Zeit*, 12, 2: 274–81.

Hilferding, Rudolf 1981 [1910], *Finance Capital: A Study of the Latest Phase of Capitalist Development*, translated by Morris Watnick and Sam Gordon, edited and introduced by Tom Bottomore, New York: Routledge & Kegan Paul.

Hinds, Manuel and Gerhard Pohl 1991, 'Going to Market: Privatization in Central and Eastern Europe', Working Paper Series 768, Washington, DC: World Bank.

Ho, Ping-ti and Tang Tsou (eds.) 1968, *China in Crisis*, Chicago, IL: University of Chicago Press.

Hobsbawm, Eric J. 1959, *Primitive Rebels: Studies in Archaic Forms of Social Movement in the Nineteenth and Twentieth Centuries*, Manchester: Manchester University Press.

Hobson, John Atkinson 1902, *Imperialism: A Study*, New York: James Pott and Co.

Hoffman, Charles 1968, *Work Incentive Practices and Policies in the People's Republic of China, 1953–65*, New York: SUNY Press.

Hoffman, Charles 1974, *The Chinese Worker*, Albany, NY: SUNY Press.

Howe, Christopher 1971, 'The Level and Structure of Employment and the Sources of Labour Supply in Shanghai', in *The City in Communist China*, edited by John Wilson Lewis, Stanford, CA: Stanford University Press.

Howe, Christopher 1973, *Wage Patterns and Wage Policy in Modern China, 1919–72*, Cambridge: Cambridge University Press.

Hsia, Adrin 1972, *The Chinese Cultural Revolution*, London: Orbach G. Chambers.

Hubberd, Michael 1995, 'Bureaucrats and Markets in China: The Rise and Fall of Entrepreneurial Local Government', *Governance*, 8, 3: 335–53.

IMF-World Bank-OECD-EBRD 1990, *The Economy of the USSR*, Washington, DC: World Bank.

International Migration 2002, 'Special Issue: The Migration-Development Nexus', *International Migration*, 40, 5.

Iregui, Ana Maria 2005, 'Efficiency Gains from the Elimination of Global Restrictions on Labour Mobility: An Analysis Using a Multiregional CGE Model', in *Poverty, International Migration and Asylum*, edited by George J. Borjas and Jeff Crisp, Basingstoke: Palgrave Macmillan.

Isaacs, Harold Robert 1961 [1938], *The Tragedy of the Chinese Revolution*, Stanford, CA: Stanford University Press.

Iudin, I. 1989, 'Ekon o micheskie aspekty sokrashchenila vooruzhehhykh sil i konversi voennogo proizvodstia', *Voprosy ekonomiki* 6.

Jalée, Pierre 1969, *The Third World in World Economy*, translated by Mary Klopper, New York: Monthly Review Press.

Jenkins, Clive 1958, *Power at the Top*, London: MacCibbon and Kee.

Johnson, Gordon 1990, 'Government and Nationalism in India, 1880–1920', in *South Asia and World Capitalism*, edited by Sugata Bose, Delhi: Oxford University Press.

Johnston, W.B. 1991, 'Global Workforce 2000: The New World Labor Market', *Harvard Business Review*, March–April: 115–27.

Jones, Charles 1987, *International Business in the Nineteenth Century: The Rise and Fall of a Cosmopolitan Bourgeoisie*, Brighton: Wheatsheaf.

Jones, Leroy P. and Il Sakong 1980, *Government, Business and Entrepreneurship in Economic Development: The Korean Case*, Cambridge, MA: Harvard University Press.

Kagarlitsky, Boris 1990, *The Dialectics of Change*, London: Verso.

Kanter, Rosabeth Moss 1991, 'Transcending Business Boundaries: Twelve Thousand World Managers View Change', *Harvard Business Review*, 69, 3: 151–64.

Kaser, Michael and Christopher Allsop 1992, 'The Assessment: Macroeconomic Transition in Eastern Europe, 1989–91', *Oxford Review of Economic Policy*, 8, 1: 1–13.

Kaufmann, David 1994, 'Diminishing Returns to Administrative Controls and the Emergence of the Unofficial Economy: A Framework of Analysis and Application to the Ukraine', *Economic Policy: A European Forum*, 19: 52–70.

Kayser, Bernard 1971, *Manpower Movements and Labour Markets (Report)*, Paris: OECD Publications.

Kelecki, Michal 1976 [1967], 'Observations on Social and Economic Aspects of Intermediate Regimes', in *Essays on Developing Economies*, Brighton: Harvester.

Keynes, John Maynard 1936, *General Theory of Employment, Interest and Money*, London: Macmillan.

Kidron, Michael 1962, 'Imperialism, Highest Stage of Capitalism but One', *International Socialism*, 9.

Kidron, Michael 1965, *Foreign Investments in India*, London: Oxford University.

Kidron, Michael 1969, 'Pearson on Foreign Investment', unpublished paper.

Kidron, Michael 1970, *Western Capitalism since the War*, Harmondsworth: Penguin.

Kidron, Michael 1974a, 'Black Reformism: The Theory of Unequal Exchange', in *Capitalism and Theory*, London: Pluto Press.

Kidron, Michael 1974b, 'Imperialism, Highest Stage of Capitalism but One', in *Capitalism and Theory*, London: Pluto Press.

Kidron, Michael 1974c, 'International Capitalism', in *Capitalism and Theory*, London: Pluto Press.

Kolpinsky, Nikita Y. (ed.) 1972, *Marx, Engels, Lenin: Anarchism and Anarcho-Syndacalism*, Moscow: Progress Publishers.

Kornai, János 1986, 'The Hungarian Reform Process: Visions, Hopes and Reality', *Journal of Economic Literature*, 24, 4: 1687–737.

Krumm, Kathie, Branko Milanovic and Michael Walton 1994, 'Transfers and the Transition from Socialism', Policy Research Working Paper 1380, Washington, DC: World Bank.

Landau, David 1993, 'The Economic Impact of Military Expenditures', Working Paper Series 1138, Washington, DC: World Bank.

Lange, Oscar 1957, *The Political Economy of Socialism*, Warsaw: State Publishing House.

Lant, Pritchett 2003, *The Future of Migration: Irresistible Forces Meet Immovable Ideas*, Conference on the Future of Globalization: Explorations in the Light of Recent Turbulence, 10 October, Yale University.

Lawrence, Robert Z. 1984, *Can America Compete?*, Washington, DC: Brookings Institution.

Lawrence, Robert Z. 1994, 'The Impact of Trade on OECD Labour Markets', Occasional Paper 45, Washington, DC: Group of Thirty.

Lawrence, Robert Z. and Mathew Slaughter 1993, 'International Trade and American Wages in the 1980s: Giant Sucking Sounds or Small Hiccup?', *Brookings Papers: Macroeconomics*, 2: 161–226.

Learner, Edward 1994, 'Trade, Wages and Revolving Door Ideas', NBER Working Paper No. 4716, Cambridge, MA: National Bureau of Economic Research.

Lenin, Vladimir Ilych 1936a [1917], 'Imperialism, the Highest Stage of Capitalism', in *Selected Works*, Volume V, London: Lawrence and Wishart.

Lenin, Vladimir Ilych 1936b [1912], 'Democracy and Narodism in China', in *Selected Works*, Volume IV, London: Lawrence and Wishart.

Lenin, Vladimir Ilych 1936c [1915], 'Petty Bourgeois and Proletarian Socialism', in *Selected Works*, Volume III, London: Lawrence and Wishart.

Lenin, Vladimir Ilych 1937 [1917], 'The State and Revolution', in *Selected Works*, Volume VII, London: Lawrence and Wishart.

Lewin, Moshe 1968, *Russian Peasants and Soviet Power: A Study of Collectivisation*, London: George Allen and Unwin.

Lieberman, Ira W. and John Nellis (eds.) 1994, *Russia: Creating Private Enterprises and Efficient Markets*, Washington, DC: World Bank.

Leiberman, Ira W. and Suhail Rahuja 1994, 'An Overview of Privatization in Russia', in *Russia: Creating Private Enterprises and Efficient Markets*, edited by Ira W. Lieberman and John Nellis, Washington, DC: World Bank.

Lin, Justin Yifu, Fang Cai and Zhou Li 1994, 'China's Economic Reforms, Pointers for other Economies in Transition', Policy Research Working Papers 1310, Washington, DC: World Bank.

Lipton, Merle 1985, *Capitalism and Apartheid: South Africa 1910–84*, Aldershot: Gower Publishing Company.

Little, Ian Malcom David, Richard N. Cooper, W. Max Corden and Sarath Rajapatirana (eds.) 1993, *Boom, Crisis, and Adjustment: The Macroeconomic Experience of Developing Countries*, Oxford: Oxford University Press.

Long, Millard and Izabela Rutkowska 1995, 'The Role of Commercial Banks in Enterprise Restructuring in Central and Eastern Europe', Policy Research Working Paper 1423, Washington, DC: World Bank.

Lopatin 1990, 'Est'li vykhod iz krizisa', *Voprosy ekonomiki*, 4 April.

Lowe, Philip and Jacqueline Dwyer (eds.) 1995, *International Integration of the Australian Economy*, Conference Proceedings, Sydney: Economic Group, Reserve Bank of Australia.

Lubeck, Paul M. (ed.) 1987, *The African Bourgeoisie: Capitalist Development in Nigeria, Kenya, and the Ivory Coast*, Boulder, CO: Lynne Rienner.

Ludden, David 1990, *Peasant History and South India*, Delhi: Oxford University Press.

Luxemburg, Rosa 1951 [1913], *The Accumulation of Capital*, translated by Agnes Schwarzschild, edited by W. Stark, London: Routledge and Kegan Paul.

Luxemburg, Rosa 1972 [1915], *The Accumulation of Capital: An Anti-Critique*, in *Imperialism and the Accumulation of Capital*, by Nikolai Bukharin and Rosa Luxemburg, New York: Monthly Review Press.

Ma, Jun 1995, 'Macroeconomic Management and Intergovernmental Relations in China', Policy Research Working Paper 1408, Washington, DC: World Bank.

Macmillan, Harold 1938, *The Middle Way: A Study of the Problem of Economic and Social Progress in a Free and Democratic Society*, London: Macmillan.

Maddison, Angus 2001, *The World Economy: A Millennial Perspective*, Paris: Development Centres Studies, OECD.

Magdoff, Harry 1969, *The Age of Imperialism: The Economics of US Foreign Policy*, New York: Mothly Review Press.

Magdoff, Harry 1970, 'Militarism and Imperialism', *Monthly Review*, 21, 9: 1–14.

Mandel, Ernst 1975, *Late Capitalism*, London: Verso.

Mandel, Ernst 1978 [1977], *The Second Slump: A Marxist Analysis of Recession in the Seventies*, translated by Jon Rothschild, London: Verso.

Mann, Michael 1980, 'State and Society: 1130–1815: An Analysis of English State Finances', *Political Power and Social Theory*, 1: 165–208.

Mann, Michael 1988, *States, War and Capitalism*, Oxford: Blackwell.

Mao, Tse-tung 1955, *Selected Works of Mao Tse-tung*, Volume III, New York: International Publishers.

Mao, Tse-tung 1961 [1949], *The Bankruptcy of the Idealist Conception of History*, in *Selected Works of Mao Tse-tung*, Volume I, Peking: Foreign Languages Press.

Mao, Tse-tung 1966 [1955], *On the Question of Agricultural Co-operation*, Peking: Foreign Languages Press.

Markus, György 1981, 'Planning the Crisis', *Praxis International*, 3: 240–57.

Martin, Philip, Lindsay Lowell and Edward Taylor 2000, 'Migration Outcomes of Guest Worker and Free Trade Regimes: The Case of Mexico-US Migration', in *Managing Migration: Time for a New International Regime?*, edited by Ghosh Bimal, Oxford: Oxford University Press.

Marx, Karl 1930 [1867], *Capital*, Volume I, London: J.M. Dent & Sons.

Marx, Karl and Friedrich Engels 1978 [1849–51], *Marx and Engels Collected Works*, Volume 10, London: Lawrence & Wishart.

Marx, Karl 1996, *Marx and Engels Collected Works*, Volume 35, London: Lawrence & Wishart.

Marx, Karl 1969–70a, 'The Eighteenth Brumaire of Louis Napoleon Bonaparte', in *Selected Works in Three Volumes*, Volume 2, Moscow: Progress Publishers.

Marx, Karl 1969–70b, 'Wage Labor and Capital', in *Selected Works in Three Volumes*, Volume 1, Moscow: Progress Publishers.

Marx, Karl 1969–70c, 'Address to the Central Council of the Communist League', in *Selected Works in Three Volumes*, Volume 1, Moscow: Progress Publishers.

Massey, Douglas S., Jorge Durand and Nolan J. Malone, *Beyond Smoke and Mirrors: Mexican Immigration in an Era of Economic Integration*, New York: Russell Sage Foundation.

Maxfield, Sylvia and Ricardo Anzaldua Montoya (eds.) 1987, *Government and Private Sector in Contemporary Mexico*, San Diego, CA: University of California at San Diego.

McAuley, Alasdair 1992, 'The Economic Transition in Eastern Europe: Employment, Income Distribution and the Social Security Net', *Oxford Review of Economic Policy*, 8, 1: 93–105.

McCarthy, Desmond, Chandra Pant, Kangbin Zheng and Giovanni Zanalda 1994, 'External Shocks and Performance Responses during Systematic Transition: The Case of Ukraine', Policy Research Working Paper 1361, Washington, DC: World Bank.

McCarthy, Kevin and Robert Valdez 1986, *Current and Future Effects of Mexican Immigration in California*, Santa Monica, CA: The Rand Corporation.

McCormack, Michael 2001, *Origins of the European Economy: Communications and Commerce, AD300–900*, Cambridge: Cambridge University Press.

McMillan, John and Barry Naughton 1992, 'How to Reform A Planned Economy: Lessons from China', *Oxford Review of Economic Policy*, 8, 1: 130–43.

Meillassoux, Claude 1970, 'A Class Analysis of the Bureaucratic Process in Mali', *Journal of Development Studies*, 6, 2: 97–110.

Meillassoux, Claude 1972, 'From Reproduction to Production', *Economy and Society*, 1: 93–105.

Meisner, Maurice 1967, *Li Ta-chao and the Origins of Chinese Marxism*, Cambridge, MA: Harvard University Press.

Miller, Marcus and William Perraudin 1994, 'Deficits, Inflation and the Political Economy of Ukraine', *Economic Policy: A European Forum*, 19: 354–401.

Mitchell, Brian Redman and Hywel G. Jones 1971, *Second Abstract of British Historical Statistics*, Cambridge: Cambridge University Press.

Mitchell, Brian Redman and Phyllis Deane 1962, *Abstract of British Historical Statistics*, Cambridge: Cambridge University Press.

Morishima, Michio 1982, *Why has Japan 'Succeeded'? Western Technology and the Japanese Ethos*, Cambridge: Cambridge University Press.

Morris, Benny 1987, *The Birth of the Palestinian Refugee Problem, 1947–49*, Cambridge: Cambridge University Press.

Morris, David 1965, *The Emergence of an Industrial Labour Force in India: A Study of the Bombay Cotton Mills, 1854–1947*, Berkeley, CA: University of California Press.

Moses, Johnaton W. and Bjørn Letnes 2004, 'The Economic Costs of International Labor Restrictions: Revisiting the Empirical Discussion', *World Development*, 32, 10: 1609–26.

Nafziger, Wayne E. 1986, *Entrepreneurship, Equity and Economic Development*, Greenwich, CT: JAI Press.

National People's Congress of the People's Republic of China 1955, *Documents of the First Session of the First National People's Congress of the People's Republic of China*, Peking: Foreign Languages Press.

O'Brien, Patrick 1998, 'Inseparable Connexions: Trade Economy, Fiscal State and the Expansion of Empire, 1688–1825', in *The Oxford History of the British Empire: Volume II, the Eighteenth Century*, edited by Peter James Marshall, Oxford: Oxford University Press.

O'Connor, James 1966, 'The Organised Working Class in the Cuban Revolution', *Studies on the Left*, 6, 2: 3–30.

OECD 1993, *Employment Outlook*, Paris: OECD.

OECD 1994, *The OECD Job Study: Facts, Analysis, Strategies*, Paris: OECD.

OECD, Continuous Reporting System on Migration 2003, *Trends in International Migration (SOPEMI) 2002*, Paris: OECD.

Olsen, Mancur 1982, *The Rise and Decline of Nations*, New Haven, CT: Yale University Press.

Okun, Arthur 1970, *The Political Economy of Prosperity*, Washington, DC: Brookings.

Orleans, Leo A. 1975, 'China's Population: Can the Contradictions Be Resolved?', in *China: A Reassessment of the Economy*, Joint Economic Committee, Congress of the United States, Washington, DC: Government print off.

Papademetriou, Demetrios 2003, 'Reflections on Managing Rapid and Deep Change in the Newest Age of Migration', Paper presented at Greek President's conference *Managing Migration for the Benefit of Europe*, Athens.

Pearson, Lester Bowles 1969, *Partners in Development*, Report of the Commission on International Development, New York: Praeger.

Pinto, Brian and Sweder van Wijnbergen 1994, 'Ownership and Corporate Control in Poland: Why State Firms Defied the Odds', Working Paper 1308, Washington, DC: International Finance Corporation.

Polanyi, Karl 1944, *The Great Transformation*, New York: Farrar & Rinehart.

Polk, William Roe 2007, *Violent Politics: A History of Insurgency, Terrorism and Guerrilla Warfare from the American Revolution to Iraq*, New York: Harpercollins.

Preobrazhensky, Evgenii Alekseevich 1965 [1926], *The New Economics*, Oxford: Clarendon Press.

Proctor, Robert 1988, *Racial Hygiene: Medicine under the Nazis*, Boston, MA: Harvard University Press.

Prybyla, Jan S. 1975, 'Hsia-Fang: The Economics and Politics of Rustication in China', *Pacific Affairs*, 48, 2: 153–72.

Prybyla, Jan S. 1990, *Reforms in China and Other Socialist Economies*, Washington, DC: AEI Press.

Rawski, Thomas 1973, 'Recent Trends in the Chinese Economy', *China Quarterly*, 53: 1–33.

Rawski, Thomas 1975, 'China's Industrial System', in *China: A Reassessment of the Economy*, Joint Economic Committee, Congress of the United States, Washington, DC: Government print off.

Regis, Debray 1968, *Revolution in the Revolution? Armed Struggle and Political Struggle in Latin America*, London: Pelican.

Reich, Robert B. 1991, *The Work of Nations: Preparing Ourselves for 21st Century Capitalism*, New York: Vintage Books.

Riskin, Carl 1975, 'Surplus and Stagnation in Modern China', in *China's Modern Economy in Historical Perspective*, edited by Dwight Heald Perkins, Stanford, CA: Stanford University Press.

Robison, Richard 1986, *Indonesia: The Rise of Capital*, Sydney: Allen and Unwin.

Sachs, Jeffrey and Wing Thye Woo 1994, 'Structural Factors in the Economic Reforms of China, Eastern Europe and the Former Soviet Union', *Economic Policy: A European Forum*, 18: 101–46.

Sadowski, Zdzislaw L. 1992, 'Privatisation in Eastern Europe: Goals, Problems and Implications', *Oxford Review of Economic Policy*, 7, 4: 46–56.

Samuelson, Paul Anthony 1948, *Economics*, New York: McGraw-Hill.

Samuelson, Paul Anthony 1949, *Market Mechanisms and Maximization*, Santa Monica, CA: The Rand Corporation.

Schleifer, Andrei and Maxim Boycko 1994, 'Next Steps in Privatization: Six Major Challenges', in *Russia: Creating Private Enterprises and Efficient Markets*, edited by Ira W. Lieberman and John Nellis, Washington, DC: World Bank.

Sender, John and Sheila Smith 1986, *The Development of Capitalism in Africa*, London and New York: Methuen.

Serge, Victor 1963, *Memoirs of a Revolutionary, 1901–41*, translated by Peter Sedgwick, Oxford: Oxford University Press.

Shanin, Teodor 1966, 'The Peasantry as a Political Factor', *Sociological Review*, 5, 14: 5–27.

Shapiro, Judith 1994, 'Socio-Economic Survey 17', Moscow: Macro Economic and Finance Unit.

Shatalov, Sergei 1991, 'Privatization in the Soviet Union: The Beginnings of a Transition', Working Paper Series 805, Washington, DC: World Bank.

Shirley, Mary M. 1984, 'Managing State Owned Enterprises', World Bank Staff Working Papers 577, Washington, DC: World Bank.

Shonfield, Andrew 1965, *Modern Capitalism: The Changing Balance of Public and Private Power*, London: Oxford University Press.

Shrenk, Martin 1991, 'The CMEA System of Trade and Payments: The Legacy and the Aftermath of its Termination', Working Paper Series 753, Washington, DC: World Bank.

Silberstein, Laurence J. 1999, *The Postzionism Debates: Knowledge and Power in Israeli Culture*, London: Routledge.

Smith, [General Sir] Rupert 2005, *The Utility of Force: The Art of War in the Modern World*, London: Allen Lane.

Snow, Edgar 1970, *Red China Today: The Other Side of the River*, London: Penguin Books.

Solimano, Andrés 1991, 'On the Economic Transformation in East-Central Europe: An Historical and International Perspective', Working Paper Series 677, Washington, DC: World Bank.

Solimano, Andrés 1992, 'After Socialism and Dirigisme: Which Way', Policy Research Working Paper 981, Washington, DC: World Bank.

Spiro, Peter John 2008, *Beyond Citizenship: American Identity after Globalization*, Oxford and New York: Oxford University Press.

Strachey, John 1957, *Contemporary Capitalism*, London: Gollancz.

Strachey, John 1959, *The End of Empire*, London: Gollancz.

Straubhaar, Thomas 1992, 'Allocational and Distributional Aspects of Future Immigration to Western Europe', *International Migration Review*, 26, 2: 506–23.

Strong, Anna Louise 1964, *Letters from China, Numbers 11–20*, Peking: New World Press.

Suejnar, Jan and Katherine Terrell 1991, 'Reducing Labour Redundancy in State Owned Enterprises', Policy Working Paper Series 792, Washington, DC: World Bank.

Sunkel, Osvaldo 1969, 'National Development Policy and External Dependence in Latin America', *The Journal of Development Studies*, 6, 1: 23–48.

Sutela, Pekka 1994, 'Insider Privatisation in Russia: Speculations on Systemic Change', *Europe-Asia Studies*, 46, 3: 417–35.

Swamy, Subramanian 1973, 'Economic Growth in China and India, 1952–70: A Comparative Appraisal', *Economic Development and Cultural Change*, 21, 4: 1–84.

Sweezy, Paul 1942, *The Theory of Capitalist Development; Principles of Marxian Political Economy*, New York: Monthly Review Press.

Sweezy, Paul 1968, 'The Proletariat in Today's World', *Tricontinental*, 9.

Tanzer, Michael 1970, *The Political Economy of International Oil and the Underdeveloped Countries*, London: Temple Smith.

Tarifa, Fatos 1995, 'Albania's Road from Communism, Political and Social Change, 1990–1993', *Development and Change*, 26, 1: 133–62.

Thorner, Daniel 1955, 'Long-term Trends in Output in India', in *Economic Growth: Brazil,*

India, Japan, edited by Simon Kuznets, Wilbert Ellis Moore and Joseph John Spengler, Durham, NC: Duke University Press.

Thurow, Lester Carl 1989, 'Must We Manage Trade?', *World Link*, 11, 6: 8–11.

Tibi, Bassam 1981, *Arab Nationalism: A Critical Enquiry*, New York: St Martin's Press.

Tilly, Charles 1975, 'Reflections on the History of European State Making', in *The Formation of Nation-States in Western Europe*, edited by Charles Tilly, Princeton, NJ: Princeton University Press.

Tilly, Charles 1990, *Coercion, Capital, and European States, AD 990–1990*, Cambridge MA: Basil Blackwell.

Tirthankar, Roy 2012, 'Empire, Law and Economic Growth', *Economic and Political Weekly*, 47, 8: 98–104.

Titmuss, Richard Morris 1958, *Essays on 'The Welfare State'*, London: Allen and Unwin.

Trotsky, Leon 1962 [1930], *The Permanent Revolution: Together with Results and Prospects*, London: New Park Publications.

Trotsky, Leon 1971 [1914], *The War and the International*, Colombo: Young Socialist Publication Edition.

ULR 1957, *The Insiders*, London: Universities and Left Review.

UNCTAD 1994, 'Privatization in the Transition Process: Recent Experiences in Eastern Europe', UN Conference on Trade and Development, Kopint-Datorg, December, Geneva.

UN Economic Commission for Europe (UNECE) 1995, *Economic Survey for 1995*, Geneva: UNECE.

UNIDO 1993, *Hungary: Progress Towards a Market Economy*, Vienna: UN Industrial Development Organisation.

United Nations Development Programme (UNDP) 1992, *The Human Development Report 1992*, New York: UNDP.

Vacroux, Alexandra 1994, 'Privatization in the Regions: Primorsky Krai', in *Russia: Creating Private Enterprises and Efficient Markets*, edited by Ira W. Lieberman and John Nellis, Washington, DC: World Bank.

Vasiliev, Sergei 1994, 'Market Forces and Structural Change in the Russian Economy', *Economic Policy: A European Forum*, 19: 124–36.

Veenkamp, Theo, Tom Bentley and Alessandra Buonfino 2003, *People Flow: Managing Migration in a New European Commonwealth*, London: Demos and Open Democracy.

Vernon, Raymond 1963, *The Dilemma of Mexico's Development: The Role of the Private and the Public Sectors*, Cambridge MA: Harvard University Press.

Vorobyov, Alexander Yn 1993, 'Production Aspects of the Russian Transition', Research Paper 105, Helsinki: United Nations University – WIDER.

Walker, Kenneth R. 1966, 'A Tenth Anniversary Appraisal: Collectivisation in Retrospect: The "Socialist High Tide" of Autumn 1955–Spring 1956', *The China Quarterly*, 26: 1–43.

Walmsley, Terrie and Alan Winters 2005, 'Relaxing the Restrictions on the Temporary Movement of Natural Persons: A Simulation Analysis', *Journal of Economic Integration*, 20, 4: 688–726.

Warren, Bill 1980, *Imperialism, Pioneer of Capitalism*, London: NLB and Verso.

Washbrook, David 1990, 'South Asia, the World System, and World Capitalism', *Journal of Asian Studies*, 49: 479–508.

Wheelwright, Edward Lawrence and Bruce McFarlane 1973, *The Chinese Road to Socialism: Economics of the Cultural Revolution*, London: Penguin Books.

White, Gordon 1993, *Riding the Tiger: The Politics of Economic Reform in Post-Mao China*, London: Macmillan.

White, Gordon 1994, 'Urban Government and Market Reform in China', *Public Administration and Development*, 11: 149–70.

Williamson, John 1990, *Latin American Adjustment: How Much has Happened?*, Washington, DC: Institute of International Economics.

Williamson, John 1994 (ed.), *The Political Economy of Policy Reform*, Washington, DC: Institute of International Economics.

Winiecki, Jan and Elisabeth Winiecki 1992, *The Structural Legacy of Soviet-Type Economy. A Collection of Papers*, London: Centre for Reseach on Communist Economies.

Winter, Jay M. (ed.) 1975, *War and Economic Development (Essays in Memory of David Joslin)*, Cambridge: Cambridge University Press.

Wong, Christine 1993, 'Between Plan and Market: The Role of the Local Sector in Post-Mao China', in *China's Economic Reform*, edited by Bruce Reynolds, Boston, MA: Academic Press.

Wood, Adrian 1994, *North-South Trade, Employment and Inequality: Changing Fortunes in a Skill-Driven World*, Oxford: Clarendon Press.

World Bank 1992, *Vietnam: Restructuring Public Finance and Public Enterprise*, Report 10134-VN, Washington, DC: World Bank.

World Bank 1993, *Vietnam: Transition to the Market*, Country Operations Division (East Asia and Pacific Region), Washington, DC: World Bank.

World Bank 1994a, *India: Recent Economic Developments and Prospects*, Report 12940 IN, Washington, DC: World Bank.

World Bank 1994b, *China: Internal Market Development and Regulation*, Country Operations Division (East Asia and Pacific Region), Report 12291-CHA, Washington, DC: World Bank.

World Bank 1994c, *Albania: Building A New Economy*, Report 12342-ALB, Washington, DC: World Bank.

Yevstigneyev, Ruben N. and Arkady M. Voinov 1994, *Economic Reform and Its Interpretations in Russia*, Helsinki, United Nations University – WIDER (Research in Action).

Zarnowitz, Victor (ed.) (1972), *Economic Research Retrospect and Prospect, Fifth Anniversary Colloquium, Vol. 1, The Business Cycle Today*, National Bureau of Economic Research General Series No. 96, New York: Columbia University Press.

Zlotnik, Hania 1991, 'Trends in South to North Migration: The Perspective from the North', *International Migration*, 29, 4: 317–31.

Index

CPSIA information can be obtained
at www.ICGtesting.com
Printed in the USA
LVHW081210031218
598923LV00009B/8/P

9 781608 460106